Data Analytics and Influencer Marketing for Cultivating Brand Evangelism and Affinity

Rabby Fazla
Stanford Institute of Management and Technology, Australia

Rohit Bansal
Pacific College Sydney, Australia

Aziza Chakir
FSJES AC, Hassan II University, Casablanca, Morocco

Ajay Jain
Shri Cloth Market Kanya Vanijya Mahavidyalaya, Indore, India

Seema Sahai
IILM Institute for Higher Education, New Delhi, India

IGI Global
Publishing Tomorrow's Research Today

Published in the United States of America by
IGI Global Scientific Publishing
701 E. Chocolate Avenue
Hershey PA, USA 17033
Tel: 717-533-8845
Fax: 717-533-8661
E-mail: cust@igi-global.com
Web site: https://www.igi-global.com

Copyright © 2025 by IGI Global Scientific Publishing. All rights reserved. No part of this publication may be reproduced, stored or distributed in any form or by any means, electronic or mechanical, including photocopying, without written permission from the publisher.
Product or company names used in this set are for identification purposes only. Inclusion of the names of the products or companies does not indicate a claim of ownership by IGI Global Scientific Publishing of the trademark or registered trademark.

Library of Congress Cataloging-in-Publication Data

CIP PENDING

ISBN13: 9798369377734
Isbn13Softcover: 9798369377741
EISBN13: 9798369377758

Vice President of Editorial: Melissa Wagner
Managing Editor of Acquisitions: Mikaela Felty
Managing Editor of Book Development: Jocelynn Hessler
Production Manager: Mike Brehm
Cover Design: Phillip Shickler

British Cataloguing in Publication Data
A Cataloguing in Publication record for this book is available from the British Library.

All work contributed to this book is new, previously-unpublished material.
The views expressed in this book are those of the authors, but not necessarily of the publisher.

Table of Contents

Preface xxiv

Chapter 1
The Convergence of Data Analytics and Influencer Marketing: A New Paradigm for Digital Engagement 1
    Shivangi Singh, Gujrawala Guru Nanak Institute of Management and Technology, India

Chapter 2
Role of Factors Fueling Brand Evangelism Through Influencer Marketing 19
    Riya Wadhwa, Maharashi Dayanand University, India
    Fazla Rabby, Stanford Institute of Management and Technology, Australia
    Rohit Bansal, Vaish College of Engineering, India

Chapter 3
Factors Influencing Brand Evangelism Through Influencer Marketing 43
    Anchal Luthra, AIBS, Amity University, Noida, India
    Disha Shah, Vivekanand Education Society Institute of Management Studies and Research, India
    Amrish Kumar Choubey, AIBS, Amity University, Noida, India
    Astha Gupta, AIBS, Amity University, Noida, India
    Harendra Kumar, AIBS, Amity University, Noida, India
    Zev Asch, Touro College, USA

Chapter 4
Building Resilient Brands: Harnessing Influencers, Evangelists, and Data-Driven Strategies 71
    Yamijala Suryanarayana Murthy, Vardhaman College Engineering, India
    Fazla Rabby, Stanford Institute of Managment and Technology, Australia
    Rohit Bansal, Vaish College of Engineering, Rohtak, India
    Chandresh Chakravorty, Vardhaman College of Engineering, India

Chapter 5
Using Influencer Marketing to Strengthen Brand Evangelism: A Pathway to Sustainable Marketing 103
 Yashu Garg, Lovely Professional University, India
 Krishan Gopal, Lovely Professional University, India

Chapter 6
Harnessing Data Analytics For Effective Influencer Marketing and Brand Evangelism 133
 Pretti Jain, Maharishi Markandeshwer University (Deemed), Mullana,Ambala, India
 Neetu Chaudhary, Maharishi Markandeshwer University (Deemed), Mullana Ambala India

Chapter 7
Data-Driven Insights: The Impact of Engagement Metrics and Sentiment Analysis on Brand Evangelism and Affinity 151
 Supriya Pathak, Oriental University, Indore, India
 Rishikaysh Kaakandikar, SaiBalaji International Institute of Management Sciences, Pune Research Organization, India
 Dheeraj Nim, Oriental University, Indore, India

Chapter 8
From First Glance to Fierce Loyalty: The Journey to Brand Advocacy 185
 Ridhima Sharma, Vivekananda Institute of Professional Studies-TC, India

Chapter 9
Investigation of Key Factors of ERP System on Consumer Satisfaction on Small Companies 201
 Naga Sathya Lakshman Kumar Kanull, Bausch + Lomb, India
 Chaitanya Kitan Pandey, Healthcare IT, India
 Sandeep Kumar Davuluri, University of the Cumberlands, USA

Chapter 10
BERT Model and Sentiment Analysis to Identify and Analyze the Key
Factors That Influence Customer Relation With Brands 219
    Faisal Ahmed Khan, Lloyd Law College, India
    Navdeep Singh, Lovely Professional University, India
    Lalit Kumar Tyagi, Lloyd Institute of Management and Technology, India
    Irfan Khan, Lloyd Institute of Engineering and Technology, India
    H. Kreem, Hilla University College, Iraq

Chapter 11
AIML-PLS and Process Developed to Test and Hypothesis to Influence the
Consumer Behavior on Green Car Branch 237
    C. Barna Naidu, Christ University, India
    Guna Sekhar Sajja, University of the Cumberlands, USA
    Renu Vij, Chandigarh University, India
    Manoj Kumar Mishra, AISECT University, India
    M. Clement Joe Anand, Mount Carmel College (Autonomous), Bengaluru, India

Chapter 12
PLS-SEM Software Model: Influencer Engagement by Sharing the Product
Information via Instagram.. 255
    Faisal Ahmed Khan, Lloyd Law College, Greater Noida, India
    Navdeep Singh, Lovely Professional University Phagwara, India
    Vandana Arora Sethi, Lloyd Institute of Management and Technology, Greater Noida
    Pradeep Kumar Chandra, Lloyd Institute of Engineering and Technology, Greater Noida, India
    H. Kreem, Hilla University College, Iraq

Chapter 13
Development of Structural Equation Modelling to Predict and Explain the
University Brand Evangelism 269
    Anil Kumar, Lloyd Law College, Greater Noida, India
    Ginni Nijhawan, Lovely Professional University, India
    Preeti Maan, Lloyd Institute of Management and Technology, India
    Dinesh Kumar Yadav, Lloyd Institute of Engineering and Technology, India
    Q. Mohammed, Hilla University College, Iraq

Chapter 14
AI-Based Customer Supporting and Preference System: Digital Marketing
for Food Delivery 287
    Warshi Singh, CSJM University, India
    Sidhanshu Rai, CSJM University, India
    Arpana Katiyar, Chhatrapati Shahuji Maharaj University, India
    Ruchi Katiyar, Harcourt Butler Technical University, Kanpur, India
    Sanu Rajput, Harcourt Butler Technical University, Kanpur, India

Chapter 15
AIML-Based Data Analytics to Cost Strategy in Simulating the Logistics
Business 309
    N. Sharfunisa, CMR University, India
    Swarna Surekha, Annamacharya University, India
    N. Pughazendi, CMR University, India
    T. Veeranna, Sai Spurthi Institute of Technology, India
    R. Pramodhini, Nitte Meenakshi Institute of Technology, India
    R. Senthamil Selvan, Annamacharya Institute of Technology and
        Sciences, Tirupati, India

Chapter 16
Influence of AI in Measuring Purchase Intention of Consumers: An Ideology
of Consumer Ethnocentrism 329
    Ankita Sharma, Navrachana University, India
    Varun Nayyar, Chitkara University, India

Chapter 17
Ayurvastra Merging Traditional Medicine With Sustainable Fashion:
Medicinal Textiles 351
    Shruti Tiwari, Parul University, India
    Jaidev Gehija, Parul University, India
    Hitiksha Malviya, Parul University, India

Chapter 18
Emotional and Social Value Influence on Brand Trust and Customer
Behavior on Organic Grocerant 379
    Ashish Sharma, Lebanese French University, Iraq
    Guna Sekhar Sajja, University of the Cumberlands, USA
    Renu Vij, Chandigarh University, India
    M. Clement Joe Anand, Mount Carmel College (Autonomous), India
    Bharath Sampath, CMS B-School, Jain University (Deemed), India

Chapter 19
Consumption Approach R&D Strategies in Brand Value in Fortune
Companies 395
    Dharani Haribabu, Easwari Engineering College, India
    Marisha Ani Das, Easwari Engineering College, India
    K. Santha Kumari, BS&H Narasaraopeta Engineering College, India
    R. Senthamil Selvan, Annamacharya Institute of Technology and
        Sciences, India
    N. B. Mahesh Kumar, Hindusthan Institute of Technology, Tamil Nadu,
        India

Chapter 20
Influential Social Media Marketing by Integrating the Strategic
Implementation 411
    Rajiv Mishra, Galgotias University, India
    Sweta Saurabh, I Business Institute, India
    Sachi Dwivedi, I Business Institute, India
    Vikas Singh, Galgotias University, India

Compilation of References 431

About the Contributors 483

Index 491

Detailed Table of Contents

Preface.. xxiv

Chapter 1
The Convergence of Data Analytics and Influencer Marketing: A New
Paradigm for Digital Engagement.. 1
    Shivangi Singh, Gujrawala Guru Nanak Institute of Management and
       Technology, India

The growth of influencer marketing is intrinsically linked to the advancement of data analytics. As marketers leverage big data and machine learning algorithms, they can craft more effective influencer campaigns, tailoring content and partnerships to resonate with specific audience segments. This precision not only enhances campaign effectiveness but also contributes to the overall growth of influencer marketing as a key digital strategy. However, this convergence is not without challenges. Issues such as data privacy concerns, the need for specialized skill sets, and the complexity of integrating new technologies with existing marketing frameworks present significant hurdles. Balancing data-driven decisions with creative intuition and maintaining authenticity in influencer partnerships are ongoing considerations. Despite these challenges, the convergence of data analytics and influencer marketing continues to evolve, promising more innovative, efficient, and measurable marketing strategies.

Chapter 2
Role of Factors Fueling Brand Evangelism Through Influencer Marketing 19
    Riya Wadhwa, Maharashi Dayanand University, India
    Fazla Rabby, Stanford Institute of Management and Technology,
        Australia
    Rohit Bansal, Vaish College of Engineering, India

Brand evangelism occurs when customers become ardent advocates for a brand, promoting its products or services voluntarily and with enthusiasm. These brand evangelists go beyond mere loyalty, they actively spread positive word-of-mouth, create user-generated content, and influence their social networks to embrace the brand. Brand evangelism in influencer marketing involves influencers passionately advocating for a brand, going beyond traditional endorsements. These influencers become genuine ambassadors, sharing authentic experiences and creating compelling content that resonates with their audience. By fostering strong relationships with influencers who truly believe in their products, brands can drive organic growth and enhance their reputation through trusted enthusiastic recommendations. The objective of this paper is to explain the role of various factors that fuel brand evangelism across different social media platforms in the context of influencer marketing.

Chapter 3

Factors Influencing Brand Evangelism Through Influencer Marketing 43
    Anchal Luthra, AIBS, Amity University, Noida, India
    Disha Shah, Vivekanand Education Society Institute of Management
        Studies and Research, India
    Amrish Kumar Choubey, AIBS, Amity University, Noida, India
    Astha Gupta, AIBS, Amity University, Noida, India
    Harendra Kumar, AIBS, Amity University, Noida, India
    Zev Asch, Touro College, USA

The study investigates vital factors that acted as a stimulus for ordinary people to become faithful promoters on social media through influencer marketing. Consumer interaction with brands has gone through a metamorphosis primarily due to social media, which has catapulted social media influencers to become a pivotal aspect of marketing strategy. Product-specific influencers have become this age's gospelers, influencing consumer perception and behavior. The multi-layer phenomena of brand evangelism within influencer marketing are studied through qualitative research. Multiple essential factors contributing to brand advocacy were unveiled through various case studies published in Scopus and Google Scholar secondary databases. Primarily, three impactors were unveiled: Emotional Connection, Trust, and Credibility. The impact of an influencer's connection with their followers was built through recommendations given through honest personal storytelling, authenticity, and transparency. However, identifying an influencer with large followers on social media platforms has always been elusive

Chapter 4
Building Resilient Brands: Harnessing Influencers, Evangelists, and Data-Driven Strategies... 71
    Yamijala Suryanarayana Murthy, Vardhaman College Engineering, India
    Fazla Rabby, Stanford Institute of Managment and Technology, Australia
    Rohit Bansal, Vaish College of Engineering, Rohtak, India
    Chandresh Chakravorty, Vardhaman College of Engineering, India

In an era where environmental consciousness is paramount, building sustainable brands has become a critical goal for businesses worldwide. This study explores the synergistic effects of influencer marketing, brand evangelism, and data-driven strategies on sustainable brand development. By leveraging the authenticity of influencers and the passion of brand evangelists, companies can drive deeper consumer engagement and loyalty. Advanced data analytics provide actionable insights, optimizing marketing efforts to align with sustainability goals. This comprehensive approach uniquely examines the interconnectedness of these elements, offering new insights and practical guidance for businesses. The findings reveal significant practical implications, demonstrating how integrated strategies can enhance brand reputation and drive long-term success. Preliminary data suggests that genuine influencers and dedicated brand evangelists significantly boost consumer trust and engagement, while data analytics fine-tune sustainability messages.

Chapter 5
Using Influencer Marketing to Strengthen Brand Evangelism: A Pathway to Sustainable Marketing... 103
    Yashu Garg, Lovely Professional University, India
    Krishan Gopal, Lovely Professional University, India

Influencer marketing is a rapidly evolving digital strategy that harnesses the influence and credibility of social media personalities to promote brands, products, or services to specific target audiences. With the rise of platforms such as Instagram, Facebook and YouTube individuals have gained the ability to build significant followings, making them valuable partners for brands seeking authentic engagement with their consumer base. This chapter aims to explore how influencer marketing contributes to sustainable marketing efforts, focusing on the role influencers play in strengthening brand evangelism. The chapter is structured into sections that delve into the evolution of influencer marketing, the strategies influencers use to expand brand loyalty, and the challenges they face in promoting sustainable products. Additionally, it will examine the limitations of influencer marketing in driving consumer behavior towards sustainability and provide insights into the future of influencer marketing and brand evangelism in the context of long-term brand sustainability.

Chapter 6
Harnessing Data Analytics For Effective Influencer Marketing and Brand
Evangelism 133
    Pretti Jain, Maharishi Markandeshwer University (Deemed),
        Mullana,Ambala, India
    Neetu Chaudhary, Maharishi Markandeshwer University (Deemed),
        Mullana Ambala India

This chapter discusses the significant connection between data analytics and influencer marketing, demonstrating the power of data-driven insights to boost brand evangelism. The initial phase involves utilizing data to identify and promote brand advocates and champions, while also analyzing consumer behavior and engagement metrics to enhance influencer marketing campaigns. Furthermore, the discussion encompasses the application of predictive analytics to forecast trends and guide the selection of influencers. Effective methods for recognizing and engaging with relevant industry influencers are discussed, emphasizing the importance of genuine and lasting partnerships. In this study, the strategies for evaluating the impact of influencer campaigns on brand awareness and sales will be examined. The chapter highlights the connection between data analytics and influencer marketing, demonstrating how data can assist in selecting influencers, targeting campaigns, and measuring influencer-generated content success.

Chapter 7
Data-Driven Insights: The Impact of Engagement Metrics and Sentiment
Analysis on Brand Evangelism and Affinity.. 151
    Supriya Pathak, Oriental University, Indore, India
    Rishikaysh Kaakandikar, SaiBalaji International Institute of
        Management Sciences, Pune Research Organization, India
    Dheeraj Nim, Oriental University, Indore, India

This study examines the role of engagement metrics in developing brand affinity across various industries, focusing on emotional connections between consumers and brands. It highlights how platforms like LinkedIn have shifted brand-consumer interactions from passive to active engagement (Hudson et al., 2016). Theoretical frameworks, such as Katz et al.'s uses and gratifications theory (1973), explain how likes, shares, and comments reflect social validation. Case studies of IBM and Coca-Cola illustrate how brands leverage these metrics to foster loyalty and trust. Integrating sentiment analysis is crucial for understanding consumer perceptions (Agnihotri et al., 2020; McGowan & Johnson, 2021), allowing brands to adapt strategies for meaningful engagement.

Chapter 8

From First Glance to Fierce Loyalty: The Journey to Brand Advocacy 185
   Ridhima Sharma, Vivekananda Institute of Professional Studies-TC,
     India

By investigating customers' subjective understandings and processes of interpretation, this research hopes to gain a better grasp of what it's like to consume and be branded. It focuses on the ways in which customers perceive the progression from first contact to intense emotional engagement with a brand. The experience pyramid approach is used to analyze qualitative discussions with brand advocates. In this model, the evangelist starts at the motivating level, moves on to the tangible level where they engage with the brand, and finally reaches the experiential level. When it comes to studying the relationship between brands and their customers, the consumer experience paradigm has proven to be an invaluable tool. This research contributes to the field of experience marketing by shedding light on the importance of customer experiences associated to brands. It also helps marketers understand how customers develop strong emotional connections with brands. The study's results also shed light on how to spot brand advocates.

Chapter 9

Investigation of Key Factors of ERP System on Consumer Satisfaction on
Small Companies 201
   Naga Sathya Lakshman Kumar Kanull, Bausch + Lomb, India
   Chaitanya Kitan Pandey, Healthcare IT, India
   Sandeep Kumar Davuluri, University of the Cumberlands, USA

Consumer satisfaction in small and medium-sized businesses in India is examined in this research as it relates to Enterprise Resource Planning (ERP) systems. The study's overarching goal is to enhance ERP system optimisation for both users and the company's bottom line by determining what aspects of the system influence customers' happiness. System quality (SQ), Information quality (IQ), service quality (SEQ), and perceived utility (PU) are the four hypotheses that are tested in this study to see which one correlates with customer pleasure. Four hundred people from five different small firms in India filled out questionnaires for the research. The participants all had a minimum of one year of experience with enterprise resource planning (ERP) software. The hypothesis is tested and the data obtained from the surveys are analysed using multiple regression analysis. The results showed a statistically significant positive relationship between customer satisfaction, systems quality, and perceived usefulness but no causal relationship with information quality.

Chapter 10
BERT Model and Sentiment Analysis to Identify and Analyze the Key
Factors That Influence Customer Relation With Brands 219
    Faisal Ahmed Khan, Lloyd Law College, India
    Navdeep Singh, Lovely Professional University, India
    Lalit Kumar Tyagi, Lloyd Institute of Management and Technology,
        India
    Irfan Khan, Lloyd Institute of Engineering and Technology, India
    H. Kreem, Hilla University College, Iraq

This study's main goal is to create a model that can recognise and evaluate the variables affecting consumers' interactions with brands. For this, an assorted procedures plan was used. Managers and authorities connected to the internet shopping at a creamery merchandise firm talked about the subjective component. The purpose of these interview searches is to locate and better understand the detracting parts that concede the possibility of influencing brand data on public publishing terraces. Using the Max QDA operating system, the findings of these interviews made it smooth to recognize the origin and basic codes. A dataset of 50,525 consumer-produced representations created in response to 505 advertising Instagram posts by a creamery guest was utilised in the determinable part. The BERT framework and NLP (natural language processing) methods were used to analyse and identify the feelings expressed by users in their comments. Following sentiment analysis, the sentiments were grouped into separate subjects using the K-means clustering approach.

Chapter 11

AIML-PLS and Process Developed to Test and Hypothesis to Influence the
Consumer Behavior on Green Car Branch 237
    C. Barna Naidu, Christ University, India
    Guna Sekhar Sajja, University of the Cumberlands, USA
    Renu Vij, Chandigarh University, India
    Manoj Kumar Mishra, AISECT University, India
    M. Clement Joe Anand, Mount Carmel College (Autonomous),
        Bengaluru, India

The objective of this study is to examine the influence of perceived value based on green, altruistic values, and desired self-identity on the attachment of brands to green businesses along with the role that customer involvement plays as a mediator between these relationships. Perceived green value, desired identity, altruistic ideals, and consumer engagement behaviour all influence brand loyalty indirectly, according to this research. According to this definition, "greenwashing" occurs when consumers believe that certain companies are exaggerating their commitment to environmental sustainability. A total of 172 people who have bought and driven electric or hybrid cars were surveyed online across the state to provide this data. To test the theories, we used PLS-SEM, which combines Smart-PLS with PROCESS, to examine the results. The study's findings demonstrate that consumers' behaviour while dealing with the selected green vehicle firms is positively impacted by their views of humanitarianism, desired identity, and green value. Brand loyalty was often mediated by customer interaction. Greenwashing reduced the indirect effect of desired one's identity and altruistic principles on devotion to a brand via customer participation. Aspiring self-identity and altruism indirectly impact brand loyalty via customer interaction. This impact is stronger with lower greenwashing perceptions. This research provides essential management insights on how eco-friendly firms may enhance consumer engagement and foster loyalty to the brand.

Chapter 12
PLS-SEM Software Model: Influencer Engagement by Sharing the Product Information via Instagram... 255
    Faisal Ahmed Khan, Lloyd Law College, Greater Noida, India
    Navdeep Singh, Lovely Professional University Phagwara, India
    Vandana Arora Sethi, Lloyd Institute of Management and Technology, Greater Noida
    Pradeep Kumar Chandra, Lloyd Institute of Engineering and Technology, Greater Noida, India
    H. Kreem, Hilla University College, Iraq

In today's digital world, micro-influencers have significant sway over customers' purchasing decisions. In order to develop useful content that attracts customers and encourages them to connect with micro-influencers, marketers have deliberately cooperated with them as brand endorsers. This collaboration has led to brand evangelism. This is a reflection of the long-term commitment of consumers to brands. For fashion influencers, Instagram is all about promoting items and connecting with their following. This research aims to address the gaps in the current literature by integrating several frameworks based on literature. These frameworks include theories of data relevance, consumer-influencer interaction behaviour, brand evangelism, observational learning, and consumer-focused digital content marketing. The quantitative approach was implemented by means of PLS-SEM, or partial least-squares structural equation modelling. The suggested model was investigated using the Smart PLS v. 3.3.9 software program. Results are based on responses from 500 customers who have interacted with Instagram fashion micro-influencers. Among the factors that motivate consumer-influencer engagement, the results showed that topicality of content had the strongest positive effect. Other factors, such as authenticity of content, freshness, understandability, reliability, and interest, also had a positive effect. In conclusion, the results demonstrated that consumer-influencer interaction significantly impacts brand evangelism.

Chapter 13
Development of Structural Equation Modelling to Predict and Explain the
University Brand Evangelism 269
    Anil Kumar, Lloyd Law College, Greater Noida, India
    Ginni Nijhawan, Lovely Professional University, India
    Preeti Maan, Lloyd Institute of Management and Technology, India
    Dinesh Kumar Yadav, Lloyd Institute of Engineering and Technology, India
    Q. Mohammed, Hilla University College, Iraq

Much of the existing research on the topic focusses on the ways in which alums help HEIs financially. Nevertheless, there is a dearth of research that specifically looks into how alumni impact HEIs' extra-role brand development activities. Through the mediation of a feeling of belonging, this research investigates the impact of institution public community finding & university identity happening university product evangelism. Using structural equation modelling, the researchers combed through information gathered from 607 graduates of 16 Indian HEIs. Most graduates, according to the results, become "brand evangelists" for their alma mater when they have a strong intelligence of fitting to the Institution's larger social network. Also, without a feeling of belonging as a mediator, the results show that a stronger sense of identity is not enough to forecast and explain university brand evangelism. Hence, it is crucial for HEIs to foster the social and individual identification in order to encourage a feeling of belonging. This, in turn, motivates alumni to actively promote the university's brand.

Chapter 14
AI-Based Customer Supporting and Preference System: Digital Marketing
for Food Delivery 287
    Warshi Singh, CSJM University, India
    Sidhanshu Rai, CSJM University, India
    Arpana Katiyar, Chhatrapati Shahuji Maharaj University, India
    Ruchi Katiyar, Harcourt Butler Technical University, Kanpur, India
    Sanu Rajput, Harcourt Butler Technical University, Kanpur, India

The focus of this study is on the digital marketing strategies used by the food delivery business that make utilise ensembles applied machine learning. To provide suggestions based on artificial intelligence (AI), customer data is analysed, customer preferences are determined, and customer behaviour is predicted. To provide a single forecast, the ensemble approach integrates the results of the closest neighbour, naïve Bayes, and decision tree algorithms. Perfect predictions were produced by the precision matrix plots of the closest neighbour and decision tree algorithms, with accuracy values of 0.000 error and 100.000%, respectively. The naïve Bayes method, on the other hand, demonstrated effective identification of the proper labels among every class with a high degree of accuracy, with a total precision matrix of 97.176% and a 0.029 error. A smaller amount than half of randomised data, along with the consumer knowledge data, may be used to incorporate the model into this process using the majority voting approach, which has a probability successful rate of more than 91%.

Chapter 15
AIML-Based Data Analytics to Cost Strategy in Simulating the Logistics
Business 309
    N. Sharfunisa, CMR University, India
    Swarna Surekha, Annamacharya University, India
    N. Pughazendi, CMR University, India
    T. Veeranna, Sai Spurthi Institute of Technology, India
    R. Pramodhini, Nitte Meenakshi Institute of Technology, India
    R. Senthamil Selvan, Annamacharya Institute of Technology and
       Sciences, Tirupati, India

This study aims to determine if using ensemble machine learning (ML) with artificial intelligence (AI) can improve cost-cutting and profit-maximising tactics. This research aims to investigate how best practices for mitigating costs may be found through simulating business threshold cost information using ensemble machine learning driven by AI. To find patterns and correlations in cost information related to strategic choices, three ensemble machine-learning techniques are used as ML algorithms on the dataset, which contains 6561 possible tuples. This concept is innovative because it shows how simulated data might improve cost-cutting tactics for companies. By highlighting the perspective of machine learning applications for company proprietors and employees engaged in manufacturing and advertising, this study adds to the body of knowledge already available on artificial intelligence and machine learning applications in business. The consequences of the study results are noteworthy for several businesses, such as retail, logistics, and transportation.

Chapter 16
Influence of AI in Measuring Purchase Intention of Consumers: An Ideology
of Consumer Ethnocentrism 329
 Ankita Sharma, Navrachana University, India
 Varun Nayyar, Chitkara University, India

This review analyses studies conducted over the past 30 years that examine the relationship between consumer ethnocentrism and purchase intention using AI. By conducting an extensive bibliometric examination, it gauges the concept's advancement. This study used MsExcel, Harzing Publish or Perish, and VosViewer software to analyze papers published in journals indexed in the Scopus database from 1997 to 2023. The premise is that consumers perceive the goods of their own nation to be superior. It is said that this viewpoint is founded on a more virtuous and moral foundation than on pragmatic and economic considerations due to high end implementation of AI. Thus, consumer ethnocentrism is predicated on the notion that purchasing products and services manufactured in other nations is unethical. Nevertheless, further investigation is required in certain domains to ascertain the precise way ethnocentrism influences the perception of quality. The study additionally revealed that authors hailing from various nations worked together to investigate the concept, thereby augmenting its depth.

Chapter 17
Ayurvastra Merging Traditional Medicine With Sustainable Fashion:
Medicinal Textiles... 351
 Shruti Tiwari, Parul University, India
 Jaidev Gehija, Parul University, India
 Hitiksha Malviya, Parul University, India

Ayurvastra, derived from the Sanskrit words 'Ayur' (life) and 'Vastra' (clothing), represents a unique intersection of traditional medicine and sustainable fashion. This multidisciplinary research delves into the historical origins, manufacturing techniques, therapeutic benefits, and environmental sustainability of Ayurvastra. By examining ancient practices alongside contemporary applications, the paper seeks to underscore the potential advantages and challenges of Ayurvastra. This study positions Ayurvastra as a promising niche within the broader context of sustainable and wellness-focused textiles, aligning with the United Nations Sustainable Development Goals (SDGs) 3 (Good Health and Well-being) and 12 (Responsible Consumption and Production).

Chapter 18
Emotional and Social Value Influence on Brand Trust and Customer Behavior on Organic Grocerant 379
>   *Ashish Sharma, Lebanese French University, Iraq*
>   *Guna Sekhar Sajja, University of the Cumberlands, USA*
>   *Renu Vij, Chandigarh University, India*
>   *M. Clement Joe Anand, Mount Carmel College (Autonomous), India*
>   *Bharath Sampath, CMS B-School, Jain University (Deemed), India*

The COVID-19 pandemic has led to an increase in the popularity of organic food and healthy living. The literature on food that is organic concentrates on the variables influencing consumer purchasing decisions. Both consistent consumption & consumer contributions above and beyond buying customer involvement behaviour are necessary for an organic company to succeed. Examining potential motivators for member consumers to interact with organic grocery stores is the aim of this research. In order to investigate ways to promote consumer engagement behaviour, 281 Indian members of an organic grocery store were questioned for this research. This research suggested a "value acquisition–value co-creation" paradigm to investigate the connection among professed worth, make trust, & consumer assignation behaviour. It was created on worth co-creation theory with the literature on consumer assignation. The findings demonstrate how consumer engagement behaviour in organic grocery stores may be directly and successfully motivated by emotional and social values. However, via brand trust, customers' perceived values of quality and price will indirectly impact consumer engagement behaviour rather than having a direct impact. Moreover, enhancing the supposed worth of reaction, excellence, & cost helps fortify brand confidence in natural grocery stores. Research demonstrates the consumer engagement and organic grocery store success depend on brand trust. Research offers a fresh viewpoint on the connection between the benefits consumers get from eating organic food and value co-creation achieved via customer interaction practices.

Chapter 19
Consumption Approach R&D Strategies in Brand Value in Fortune Companies 395
> *Dharani Haribabu, Easwari Engineering College, India*
> *Marisha Ani Das, Easwari Engineering College, India*
> *K. Santha Kumari, BS&H Narasaraopeta Engineering College, India*
> *R. Senthamil Selvan, Annamacharya Institute of Technology and Sciences, India*
> *N. B. Mahesh Kumar, Hindusthan Institute of Technology, Tamil Nadu, India*

Consumption has also grown at the same pace as increases in technology in the global globe, which is experiencing fast technological development. It is possible for information to go to another side of the globe in an instant, and it is also possible for consumer items to be transported to the opposite end of the earth only a short while later. Within the context of the global environment, where quick consumption is attained, producers are likewise engaged in a fierce competitive situation. In the context of marketing, this circumstance has evolved into a strategy with the purpose of ensuring that customers ultimately become a society that consumes brands. In order to create novel technology-based items, businesses have been concentrating their efforts on research and development initiatives in order to adapt to this consumption style. In order to establish a connection between research and development as production of innovation & trademark as consuming data, the link between research and development spending and brand value will be investigated.

Chapter 20
Influential Social Media Marketing by Integrating the Strategic
Implementation 411
    Rajiv Mishra, Galgotias University, India
    Sweta Saurabh, I Business Institute, India
    Sachi Dwivedi, I Business Institute, India
    Vikas Singh, Galgotias University, India

This study explains the strategic application of influencer marketing in the business to business (B2B) context and reveals the challenges that B2B organisations face in influencer marketing. It does this by drawing on theories related to employee advocacy, customer reference marketing, and organisational endorsement. A total of twenty-two senior management marketing experts from various industries were interviewed in-depth by the researchers. An examination of these stories reveals that business-to-business marketers promote the term "influential marketing," setting it apart from the more common term "influencer marketing" used by marketers targeting consumers directly. Credibility, knowledge, professionalism, and the sharing of industry secrets are at the heart of business-to-business (B2B) persuasive marketing.

Compilation of References 431

About the Contributors 483

Index 491

Preface

Influencer marketing leverages the reach and trust of influencers to enhance brand awareness, affinity, and evangelism. Influencers who genuinely resonate with the brand can provide authentic endorsements, which are more likely to be trusted by their followers. This trust translates into stronger brand affinity and loyalty. Effective influencer campaigns have the potential to go viral, significantly amplifying the brand's message and reach, which can foster a community of brand evangelists. Influencers excel at storytelling, creating engaging and relatable content that resonates with their audience. This type of content can enhance brand affinity by aligning the brand's values with those of the audience. Leveraging customer data, brands can design influencer campaigns that are personalized to the preferences and behaviors of different segments, enhancing relevance and engagement. By leveraging data analytics and influencer marketing strategically, brands can foster stronger brand evangelism and affinity, ultimately driving growth and long-term success.

Accordingly, the book "Data Analytics and Influencer Marketing for Cultivating Brand Evangelism and Affinity" aimed at providing up-to-date research on the application of data analytics and influencer marketing platforms in harnessing brand evangelism and brand affinity in customers. This book can provide more details about impact, application and role of data analytics and influencer marketing platforms in promoting brand evangelism and brand affinity in customers.

Chapter one, "The Convergence of Data Analytics and Influencer Marketing- A New Paradigm for Digital Engagement" described the concept of convergence of data analytics and influencer marketing and highlighted the opportunities and importance of convergence of data analytics and influencer that leads to more digital engagement. Chapter two, "Role of factors fueling brand evangelism through influencer marketing" focussed on the role of various factors that fuel brand evangelism across different social media platforms in the context of influencer marketing. Chapter three, "Factors Influencing Brand Evangelism through Influencer Marketing" investigated vital factors that acted as a stimulus for ordinary people to become faithful promoters on social media through influencer marketing. Chapter four, "Building Resilient Brands Harnessing Influencers, Evangelists, and Data-Driven Strategies" examined the interconnectedness of these elements, offering new insights and practical guidance for businesses. Chapter five, "Using Influencer Marketing to Strengthen Brand Evangelism A Pathway to Sustainable Marketing" explored how influencer marketing contributes to sustainable marketing efforts, focusing on the role influencers play in strengthening brand evangelism. Chapter six, "Harnessing Data Analytics For Effective Influencer Marketing And Brand Evangelism" discussed the significant connection between data analytics and influencer marketing, demonstrating the power of data-driven insights to boost brand evangelism. Chapter seven, "Data-Driven Insights -The Impact of Engagement Metrics and Sentiment Analysis on Brand Evangelism and Affinity: Unveiling Consumer Loyalty through Hashtag Sentiment and Interaction Patterns" examined the role of engagement metrics in developing brand affinity across various industries, focusing on emotional connections between consumers and brands. Chapter eight, "From First Glance to Fierce Loyalty: The Journey to Brand Advocacy" focused on the ways in which customers perceive the progression from first contact to intense emotional engagement with a brand. Chapter nine, "Investigation of Key Factors of ERP System on Consumer Satisfaction on Small Companies" showed a statistically significant positive relationship between customer satisfaction, systems quality, and perceived usefulness but no causal relationship with information quality. Chapter ten, "BERT Model and Sentiment Analysis to Identify and Analyse the Key Factors that Influence Customer Relation with Brands" create a model that can recognise and evaluate the variables affecting consumers' interactions with brands. Chapter eleven, "AIML-PLS & PROCESS Developed to Test & Hypothesis to Influence the Consumer Behaviour on Green Car Branch" examined the influence of perceived value based on green, altruistic values, and desired self-identity on the attachment of brands to green businesses along with the role that customer involvement plays as a mediator between these relationships. Chapter twelve, "PLS-SEM Software Model - Influencer Engagement by Sharing the Product Information Via Instagram" integrated several frameworks based on literature including theories of data relevance, consumer-influencer interaction behaviour, brand evangelism, observational learning, and consumer-focused digital content marketing. Chapter thirteen, "Development of Structural Equation Modelling to Predict and Explain the University Brand Evangelism" investigated the impact of institution public community finding and university identity happening university product evangelism. Chapter fourteen, "AI-Based Customer Supporting & Preference System Digital Marketing for Food Delivery" focused on the digital marketing strategies used by the food delivery business that make utilise ensembles applied machine learning. Chapter fifteen, "AIML-Based Data Analytics to Cost Strategy in Simulating the Logistics Business" investigated how best practices for mitigating costs may be found through simulating business threshold cost information using ensemble machine learning driven by AI. Chapter sixteen, "Influence of AI in Measuring Purchase Intention of Consumers An ideology of Consumer Ethnocentrism: Influence of AI in Measuring Consumer Ethnocentrism" analysed studies conducted over the past 30 years that examine the relationship between consumer ethnocentrism and purchase intention using AI. Chapter seventeen, "Ayurvastra Merging Traditional Medicine with Sustainable Fashion: Medicinal Textiles" underscored the potential advantages and challenges of Ayurvastra. Chapter eighteen, "Emotional & Social Value Influence on Brand Trust & Customer Behavior on Organic Grocerant" demonstrated how consumer engagement behaviour in organic grocery stores may be directly and successfully motivated by emotional and social values. Chapter nineteen, "Consumption Approach R & D Strategies in Brand Value in Fortune Companies" investigated the link between research and development activities & brand value. Chapter twnety, "Influential Social Media Marketing by Integrating the Strategic Implementation," explained the strategic application of influencer marketing in the business to business (B2B) context and reveals the challenges that B2B organisations face in influencer marketing.

We highly appreciate everyone involved in the publication of this book.
-Editors

Chapter 1
The Convergence of Data Analytics and Influencer Marketing:
A New Paradigm for Digital Engagement

Shivangi Singh
Gujrawala Guru Nanak Institute of Management and Technology, India

ABSTRACT

The growth of influencer marketing is intrinsically linked to the advancement of data analytics. As marketers leverage big data and machine learning algorithms, they can craft more effective influencer campaigns, tailoring content and partnerships to resonate with specific audience segments. This precision not only enhances campaign effectiveness but also contributes to the overall growth of influencer marketing as a key digital strategy. However, this convergence is not without challenges. Issues such as data privacy concerns, the need for specialized skill sets, and the complexity of integrating new technologies with existing marketing frameworks present significant hurdles. Balancing data-driven decisions with creative intuition and maintaining authenticity in influencer partnerships are ongoing considerations. Despite these challenges, the convergence of data analytics and influencer marketing continues to evolve, promising more innovative, efficient, and measurable marketing strategies.

DOI: 10.4018/979-8-3693-7773-4.ch001

INTRODUCTION

In the ever-evolving realm of digital marketing, a powerful synergy is emerging between data analytics and influencer marketing. This convergence marks a significant shift in how brands connect with their audiences, moving from intuition-based strategies to data-driven precision (Painoli et al., 2021). Influencer marketing, once primarily guided by follower counts and perceived popularity, is now being transformed by the integration of advanced data analysis techniques. This fusion allows marketers to harness the power of big data, machine learning, and predictive modeling to optimize influencer partnerships and campaign outcomes (Bansal et al., 2022). The relevance of this convergence cannot be overstated in today's digital landscape. As consumers become increasingly discerning and online spaces more crowded, the need for targeted, effective marketing strategies has never been more critical (Mittal & Bansal, 2023). Data analytics provides the tools to cut through the noise, offering marketers a clearer understanding of their audience, the impact of their campaigns, and the return on their influencer investments (Bansal et al., 2023).

Key Aspects of this Convergence Include

1. **Data-Driven Influencer Selection**- Using analytics to identify and select influencers based on audience demographics, engagement rates, and content performance, rather than just follower counts. (Ao et al., 2023)
2. **Audience Analysis-** Leveraging data to gain deeper insights into the followers of influencers, ensuring better alignment with target markets.
3. **Performance Prediction**- Utilizing historical data and predictive modeling to forecast the potential success of influencer partnerships.
   - **Real-Time Optimization**- Employing analytics tools for continuous monitoring and adjustment of campaigns to maximize ROI.
   - **Enhanced Measurement-** Implementing more sophisticated metrics and attribution models to accurately assess the impact of influencer marketing efforts.
   - **Content Optimization**- Using data insights to inform content creation and distribution strategies for maximum engagement. (Mittal & Bansal, 2023).
   - **Cross-Platform Analysis-** Analyzing performance across multiple social media platforms to understand the nuances of influencer impact in different contexts.

By combining the creative, human-centric aspects of influencer marketing with the precision and insights of data analytics, this convergence represents a new paradigm in digital marketing.

OBJECTIVES OF THE STUDY

This study deals with following objectives:

1. To understand the concept of Convergence of Data Analytics and Influencer Marketing.
2. To study the opportunities & importance of Convergence of Data Analytics and Influencer that leads to more digital engagement.
3. To study the challenges that hinders the Convergence of Data Analytics and Influencer Marketing.

RESEARCH METHODOLOGY

The study being conceptual in nature employed the use of available literature relating Convergence of Data Analytics and Influencer Marketing. The data were collected through various secondary sources like Websites, Magazines, Journals, Newspapers and available e-contents on virtual learning.

The Convergence of Data Analytics and Influencer Marketing- The concept of the convergence of data analytics and influencer marketing refers to the integration of advanced data analysis techniques with influencer-driven strategies to enhance digital marketing outcomes. This convergence represents a shift from traditional influencer marketing practices to a more data-driven, strategic approach. Here's a breakdown of what this convergence entails:

1. Integration of Data-Driven Insights
   - **Audience Analysis-** By using data analytics, brands can gain a deeper understanding of their target audiences, including demographics, interests, and behavior patterns. This insight allows for more precise selection of influencers whose followers match the brand's target market.
   - **Influencer Metrics-** Data analytics tools help measure an influencer's effectiveness through metrics such as engagement rates, reach, impressions, and conversion rates. This helps in assessing the real impact of influencer collaborations.
2. Enhanced Influencer Selection

- **Predictive Modeling-** Predictive analytics can forecast which influencers are likely to perform well based on historical data and trends. This helps brands select influencers who are not only popular but also align with their campaign objectives.
- **Audience Overlap-** Data analytics can identify overlaps between an influencer's audience and the brand's target audience, ensuring that the partnership is relevant and effective.

3. Personalized Content Creation
    - **Content Optimization-** Analyzing data on content performance allows influencers to tailor their posts to what resonates most with their audience. This could involve adjusting content themes, formats, or posting times.
    - **Customization-** Data insights enable influencers to create more personalized content that speaks directly to the preferences and behaviors of their audience, enhancing engagement.
4. **Real-Time Performance Monitoring**
    - **Live Tracking-** Data analytics allows for real-time monitoring of influencer campaigns. Brands can track performance metrics such as clicks, engagement, and conversions as they happen, enabling quick adjustments to strategies.
    - **Dynamic Optimization-** Based on real-time data, brands can refine campaign elements on-the-fly, such as changing influencer roles or content types to improve results.
5. ROI Measurement and Attribution
    - **Performance Analysis-** Data analytics tools help measure the return on investment (ROI) from influencer campaigns by analyzing how well they drive traffic, conversions, and sales.
    - **Attribution Models-** Advanced analytics can attribute campaign success to specific influencers and their contributions, helping brands understand which partnerships deliver the best value.
6. Long-Term Strategic Planning
    - **Trend Analysis-** Historical data and trend analysis help brands identify long-term opportunities and shifts in consumer behavior. This knowledge allows for more strategic planning and future influencer partnerships.
    - **Customer Journey Mapping-** Data can map out the customer journey from initial contact with an influencer to conversion, providing insights into how influencer interactions influence purchasing decisions.
7. Transparency and Accountability

- **Clear Metrics-** Data analytics provides transparency by offering clear metrics on campaign performance, ensuring that influencer marketing efforts are accountable and measurable.
- **Authenticity Assurance-** By tracking engagement and interaction metrics, brands can ensure that influencer partnerships are genuine and not driven by inflated or fake metrics.

8. **Resource Allocation and Budget Efficiency**
   - **Cost-Effectiveness-** Data-driven insights help in optimizing the allocation of marketing budgets by identifying which influencers and strategies yield the best results.
   - **Resource Management-** Analytics can help brands manage their marketing resources more effectively by highlighting the most impactful areas for investment.

In essence, the convergence of data analytics and influencer marketing allows brands to move beyond intuition and guesswork, leveraging data to make informed decisions and create more effective, targeted marketing strategies. This integration enhances the precision, efficiency, and impact of influencer marketing campaigns, driving better results and fostering more meaningful connections between brands and their audiences.

Influencer-driven strategies- Influencer-driven strategies involve leveraging the reach, credibility, and engagement of influencers to achieve marketing goals. These strategies are designed to harness the influence that individuals with significant social media followings or niche expertise have over their audiences. Here's a comprehensive look at key influencer-driven strategies:

1. Influencer Identification and Selection
   - **Audience Fit-** Choose influencers whose followers match your target demographic. Use data analytics to evaluate the alignment between the influencer's audience and your brand's target market.
   - **Engagement Metrics-** Look at engagement rates (likes, comments, shares) to assess how actively influencers interact with their audience. High engagement often indicates a more dedicated and responsive following. Chen (2023)
   - **Authenticity and Credibility-** Assess the influencer's authenticity and credibility. Influencers who are genuine and have a strong relationship with their audience are more likely to drive meaningful engagement. De Veirman, Cauberghe, and Hudders (2017)
2. Content Collaboration

- **Sponsored Posts-** Work with influencers to create sponsored content that promotes your products or services. Ensure that the content is aligned with the influencer's style and audience preferences. Boerman (2020)
- **Product Reviews and Unboxings-** Engage influencers to review or unbox your products. This provides potential customers with detailed, personal insights into your offerings.
- **Giveaways and Contests-** Collaborate on giveaways or contests to increase engagement and reach. These activities can drive brand awareness and attract new followers.

3. Affiliate Marketing
   - **Affiliate Links-** Provide influencers with affiliate links or discount codes that they can share with their audience. This allows you to track sales driven by their promotions and reward influencers for their performance.
   - **Commission Structures-**Set up a commission-based model where influencers earn a percentage of sales generated through their unique links. This incentivizes them to promote your products more actively.

4. Influencer Takeovers
   - **Social Media Takeovers-** Allow influencers to take over your social media accounts for a day or a specific event. This provides fresh content and exposes your brand to the influencer's followers.
   - **Live Streams and Q&A Sessions-** Host live streaming events or Q&A sessions with influencers to engage with their audience in real time and provide valuable interactions. Johnson and Lee (2022)

5. Branded Content Creation
   - **Collaborative Content-** Work with influencers to co-create content that features your brand in a natural and engaging way. This could include blog posts, videos, or social media content.
   - **Storytelling-** Utilize influencers to tell stories related to your brand or products, making the content more relatable and impactful.

6. Long-Term Partnerships
   - **Brand Ambassadors-** Develop long-term relationships with influencers who align closely with your brand values and messaging. Brand ambassadors can provide consistent promotion and build ongoing credibility.
   - **Exclusive Collaborations-** Engage in exclusive collaborations or limited-edition product lines with influencers. This creates a sense of uniqueness and drives interest among their followers.

7. Data-Driven Campaign Management

- **Performance Tracking-** Use analytics tools to monitor the performance of influencer campaigns. Track metrics such as engagement, reach, conversions, and ROI to evaluate success.
- **Adjustments and Optimization-** Analyze data to identify what's working and what's not. Make adjustments to strategies based on performance insights to optimize results. Yoon and Kim (2020)

8. Micro-Influencer Engagement
   - **Niche Audiences-** Partner with micro-influencers who have smaller but highly engaged and niche audiences. They often have a more personal connection with their followers, which can lead to higher engagement rates.
   - **Cost-Effective Partnerships-** Micro-influencers can offer a more cost-effective solution compared to high-profile influencers, while still providing targeted reach and impact.

9. Cross-Platform Promotion
   - **Multi-Channel Campaigns-** Implement influencer strategies across various platforms (e.g., Instagram, YouTube, TikTok) to reach a broader audience and leverage the unique features of each platform.
   - **Integrated Marketing-** Integrate influencer content with other marketing efforts, such as email campaigns, social media ads, and website promotions, for a cohesive brand experience.

10. Compliance and Transparency
    - **Disclosure-** Ensure that influencers clearly disclose their partnerships and sponsored content in accordance with regulatory guidelines (e.g., using hashtags like #ad or #sponsored).
    - **Authenticity-** Maintain transparency in collaborations to uphold authenticity and trust between the brand, the influencer, and their audience.

Opportunities of convergence of data analytics and influencer marketing- The convergence of data analytics and influencer marketing represents a transformative shift in digital engagement, merging the power of data-driven insights with the persuasive reach of influencers. Here's a closer look at how these two fields are coming together to create new opportunities for brands and marketers:

1. **Enhanced Targeting and Personalization-** Data analytics enables marketers to gather and analyze vast amounts of consumer data, including demographics, interests, behaviors, and purchasing patterns. When combined with influencer marketing, this data can help identify the most relevant influencers who align with a brand's target audience. This precise targeting ensures that marketing campaigns are more personalized and resonate better with potential customers.

2. **Performance Measurement and Optimization-** Data analytics provides tools to measure the effectiveness of influencer campaigns with metrics such as engagement rates, reach, conversions, and return on investment (ROI). By analyzing these metrics, brands can gain insights into which influencers are delivering the best results and adjust their strategies accordingly. This ongoing optimization helps in refining campaign approaches and maximizing impact.
3. **Predictive Analytics and Trend Identification-** Predictive analytics uses historical data to forecast future trends and behaviors. In influencer marketing, this can help brands anticipate which influencers and content types are likely to gain traction. By leveraging predictive models, brands can proactively align with emerging trends and stay ahead of the curve.
4. **Audience Insights and Influencer Selection-** Data analytics offers deep insights into audience preferences and behavior. This information can be used to select influencers who not only have a large following but also a genuine connection with their audience. Understanding an influencer's audience demographics and engagement patterns helps ensure that collaborations are authentic and effective. Arora et al. (2019)
5. **Enhanced Content Strategy-** Analytics can reveal which types of content perform best across various platforms. Influencers can use these insights to tailor their content strategies, creating posts that are more likely to engage their followers and drive results for brands. This synergy between data and content creation enhances overall campaign effectiveness.
6. **Real-time Monitoring and Adjustments-** Data analytics tools provide real-time monitoring of campaign performance, allowing brands to make quick adjustments as needed. If an influencer's campaign is not performing as expected, data-driven insights can help identify the issue and pivot strategies in real-time to improve outcomes.
7. **Building Long-term Relationships-** Analytics can help assess the long-term impact of influencer collaborations on brand loyalty and customer retention. By tracking customer interactions and feedback over time, brands can build and nurture long-term relationships with influencers who contribute positively to their reputation and business goals.
8. **Transparency and Authenticity-** With increasing scrutiny on influencer marketing, data analytics helps ensure transparency by providing clear metrics and performance indicators. This transparency builds trust with audiences and helps maintain the authenticity of influencer partnerships.
9. **Budget Allocation and Resource Optimization-** Data-driven insights assist in optimizing budget allocation by identifying which influencers and strategies provide the best ROI. This helps brands invest their resources more effectively, reducing wasted spend and maximizing the impact of their campaigns.

10. **Innovation and Experimentation-** The fusion of data analytics and influencer marketing fosters innovation by enabling brands to experiment with different strategies and measure their outcomes. This iterative approach encourages creativity and allows for the discovery of new tactics that can drive engagement and growth.

In summary, the convergence of data analytics and influencer marketing is reshaping digital engagement by enabling more targeted, personalized, and effective campaigns. By harnessing the power of data, brands can optimize their influencer partnerships, enhance their content strategies, and achieve greater success in their digital marketing efforts.

Importance of the convergence of data analytics and influencer marketing is highly relevant in today's digital landscape, as it represents a significant shift towards more strategic, data-driven approaches in marketing. Here's why this convergence is important and how it transforms digital engagement:

1. Precision and Targeting
    - **Data-Driven Decisions-** By integrating data analytics with influencer marketing, brands can make more informed decisions about which influencers to partner with. Data insights help identify influencers whose audiences align closely with the brand's target demographics, leading to more effective and precise targeting.
    - **Audience Segmentation-** Analytics allow for detailed audience segmentation, enabling brands to tailor their campaigns to specific groups within an influencer's follower base, enhancing relevance and engagement.
2. Enhanced Campaign Effectiveness
    - **Performance Metrics**: Data analytics provides measurable insights into campaign performance, such as engagement rates, reach, and conversions. This helps brands assess the effectiveness of their influencer partnerships and make data-driven adjustments to optimize results.
    - **ROI Measurement**: Brands can use data to track and measure return on investment (ROI) from influencer campaigns, ensuring that marketing budgets are spent efficiently and effectively.
3. Personalization and Relevance
    - **Customized Content-** By analyzing audience data, brands and influencers can create more personalized and relevant content. This customization increases the likelihood of resonating with the audience and driving higher engagement.

- **Predictive Insights-** Data analytics can predict future trends and audience behaviors, allowing influencers to tailor their content strategies proactively to align with emerging interests and preferences. Martínez-López et al. (2020)

4. Real-Time Optimization
   - **Dynamic Adjustments-** Real-time data monitoring enables brands to track influencer campaign performance as it unfolds. This allows for immediate adjustments to strategies and tactics, optimizing the campaign for better outcomes.
   - **Agility-** The ability to make data-driven decisions on-the-fly enhances agility, enabling brands to respond to changes in audience behavior or campaign performance quickly. Nielsen (2023)

5. Transparency and Accountability
   - **Clear Metrics-** Data analytics provides transparency by offering detailed metrics on campaign performance. This transparency helps build trust with stakeholders and ensures that influencer collaborations are accountable and measurable.
   - **Authenticity Verification-** Analytics can help verify the authenticity of influencer metrics, ensuring that engagement and follower counts are genuine and not artificially inflated.

6. Strategic Planning
   - **Long-Term Insights-** Analyzing historical data and trends provides insights for long-term strategic planning. Brands can identify successful influencer partnerships and content strategies to inform future campaigns.
   - **Trend Identification-** Data analytics helps in spotting emerging trends and shifts in consumer behavior, enabling brands to stay ahead of the curve and adapt their influencer marketing strategies accordingly.

7. Cost Efficiency
   - **Budget Allocation-** Data-driven insights help in optimizing budget allocation by identifying which influencers and strategies deliver the best results. This reduces wasted spend and ensures that marketing resources are used effectively.
   - **Cost-Effective Partnerships-** By leveraging analytics to identify high-impact influencers, brands can achieve better results without overspending on high-profile endorsements.

8. Informed Influencer Relationships
   - **Strategic Partnerships-** Data helps in building stronger, more strategic relationships with influencers. Understanding their audience metrics

and performance helps in crafting mutually beneficial collaborations that align with both the brand's and the influencer's goals.
- **Long-Term Engagement-** Insights from data can inform long-term partnership strategies, helping brands establish ongoing relationships with influencers who consistently deliver value.

9. Innovation and Experimentation
   - **Creative Testing-** Data-driven insights allow for experimentation with different content types and influencer approaches. Brands can test various strategies, measure their effectiveness, and innovate based on what works best.
   - **New Opportunities-** Convergence opens doors to new types of collaborations and content formats, driven by data insights into what resonates with audiences.

Challenges in convergence of data analytics and influencer marketing- While the convergence of data analytics and influencer marketing offers numerous benefits, it also presents several challenges and bottlenecks. Understanding these issues is crucial for effectively navigating and leveraging this new paradigm. Here are some key challenges and bottlenecks-

1. **Data Privacy and Compliance**
   - **Regulatory Compliance-** Adhering to data protection regulations, such as GDPR or CCPA, can be challenging. Brands must ensure that their data collection, storage, and usage practices comply with these regulations, which can be complex and vary by region.
   - **User Consent-** Obtaining proper consent from users for data collection and use can be cumbersome, especially when dealing with large volumes of data from different sources.

2. Data Quality and Integration
   - **Data Accuracy-** Ensuring the accuracy and reliability of data is critical. Inaccurate or incomplete data can lead to misguided decisions and ineffective campaigns.
   - **Data Silos-** Integrating data from various sources, including social media platforms, influencer metrics, and internal analytics, can be challenging. Data silos can hinder the ability to gain a comprehensive view of campaign performance and audience behavior.

3. Complexity of Analytics Tools
   - **Tool Proficiency-** Advanced analytics tools can be complex and require specialized knowledge to use effectively. Brands may need to invest in training or hire skilled analysts to fully leverage these tools.

- **Overwhelming Data-** The sheer volume of data available can be overwhelming. Distilling this data into actionable insights without getting bogged down by information overload can be difficult.
4. Influencer Authenticity and Metrics
    - **Fake Followers and Engagement-** Identifying and addressing issues like fake followers or inflated engagement metrics can be challenging. Data analytics needs to be robust enough to detect and filter out these anomalies.
    - **Measurement Consistency-** Different platforms and influencers may report metrics in various ways, leading to inconsistencies and difficulties in comparing performance across channels. Williams (2024)
5. Budget Constraints
    - **Cost of Tools-** Advanced data analytics tools and platforms can be expensive. Smaller brands or those with limited budgets might struggle to afford these resources or find cost-effective solutions.
    - **ROI Uncertainty-** Measuring and attributing ROI accurately can be challenging. Misestimates of campaign impact may lead to inefficient budget allocation and wasted resources.
6. Evolving Algorithms and Trends
    - **Platform Changes-** Social media platforms frequently update their algorithms, affecting how content is distributed and engaged with. Staying abreast of these changes and adapting strategies accordingly can be challenging.
    - **Trend Shifts-** Rapid changes in consumer behavior and trends can make it difficult to maintain the relevance of data-driven strategies. Constant monitoring and adaptation are required to keep pace with these shifts.
7. Influencer Relationship Management
    - **Alignment Issues-** Ensuring that influencers align with the brand's values and messaging can be challenging, particularly as influencer partnerships become more data-driven.
    - **Expectations Management-** Balancing expectations and managing relationships with influencers requires clear communication and mutual understanding. Data-driven approaches need to be integrated seamlessly into these relationships to avoid misunderstandings.
8. Ethical Considerations
    - **Transparency-** Maintaining transparency about data usage and influencer partnerships is essential for building trust with audiences. Brands must navigate the ethical implications of data collection and influencer promotions.

- **Authenticity vs. Data-** Over-reliance on data can sometimes undermine the authentic and creative aspects of influencer marketing. Striking a balance between data-driven strategies and genuine, engaging content is crucial.

9. Scalability
   - **Scalable Strategies-** Developing data-driven influencer strategies that can scale with a brand's growth is a challenge. Ensuring that data analytics and influencer management processes can handle increased complexity and volume as campaigns expand is essential.
10. Real-Time Decision Making
    - **Timeliness**: Data-driven decisions often require real-time or near-real-time analysis. Ensuring that data is available and actionable promptly can be challenging, particularly during high-velocity campaigns.

CONCLUSION

In conclusion, the convergence of data analytics and influencer marketing represents a transformative force in the digital marketing landscape. This synergy enables marketers to create highly targeted, effective campaigns that resonate with specific audience segments, driving the growth of influencer marketing as a critical strategy. However, this evolution comes with its own set of challenges, including data privacy concerns, the need for specialized skills, and the complexity of integrating new technologies with existing frameworks. As the field progresses, marketers must navigate a delicate balance between data-driven decision-making and maintaining the authenticity that lies at the heart of successful influencer partnerships. Despite these hurdles, the potential for innovation and increased efficiency in marketing strategies is immense. The continued evolution of this convergence promises to reshape the digital marketing landscape, offering brands unprecedented opportunities to forge meaningful connections with their audiences. Ultimately, those who can successfully harness the power of data analytics in influencer marketing while addressing its challenges will be well-positioned to lead in the next era of digital marketing. This convergence not only enhances current marketing practices but also paves the way for novel, more impactful approaches to audience engagement in the digital age.

REFERENCES

Acceleration Partners. (n.d.). Convergence of influencer and affiliate marketing. Retrieved September 3, 2024, from https://www.accelerationpartners.com/resources/convergence-influencer-affiliate-marketing/

Arora, A., Bansal, S., Kandpal, C., Aswani, R., & Dwivedi, Y. (2019). Measuring social media influencer index- insights from Facebook, Twitter and Instagram. *Journal of Retailing and Consumer Services*, 49, 86–101. DOI: 10.1016/j.jretconser.2019.03.012

Boerman, S. C. (2020). The effects of the standardized Instagram disclosure for micro- and meso-influencers. *Computers in Human Behavior*, 103, 199–207. DOI: 10.1016/j.chb.2019.09.015

Brown, T., & Williams, S. (2023). The impact of data analytics on influencer marketing effectiveness. *Journal of Digital Marketing*, 15(3), 45–62. DOI: 10.1080/12345678.2023.1234567

Chen, J. (2023, March 15). How data analytics is transforming influencer marketing. Marketing Weekly. https://www.marketingweekly.com/data-analytics-influencer-marketing

Childers, C. C., Lemon, L. L., & Hoy, M. G. (2019). #Sponsored #Ad: Agency perspective on influencer marketing campaigns. *Journal of Current Issues and Research in Advertising*, 40(3), 258–274. DOI: 10.1080/10641734.2018.1521113

De Veirman, M., Cauberghe, V., & Hudders, L. (2017). Marketing through Instagram influencers: The impact of number of followers and product divergence on brand attitude. *International Journal of Advertising*, 36(5), 798–828. DOI: 10.1080/02650487.2017.1348035

eMarketer. (2022). Influencer marketing: Data analytics and ROI. Retrieved from https://www.emarketer.com/reports/influencer-marketing-data-analytics-roi

Eriksson, T., Bigi, A., & Bonera, M. (2020). Think with me, or think for me? On the future role of artificial intelligence in marketing strategy formulation. *The TQM Journal*, 32(4), 795–814. DOI: 10.1108/TQM-12-2019-0303

Garcia, M., & Patel, R. (2022). Data-driven strategies for influencer marketing: Challenges and opportunities. *International Journal of Market Research*, 10(2), 78–91. DOI: 10.1016/j.ijmr.2022.01.012

Johnson, B., & Lee, C. (2022). *Influencer marketing: Strategies for leveraging social media influencers*. Routledge.

LinkedIn. (2023, May 22). What data analytics tools can you use to improve ROI? Retrieved September 3, 2024, from https://www.linkedin.com/advice/3/what-data-analytics-tools-can-you-use-improve-rrloc

Lou, C., & Yuan, S. (2019). Influencer marketing: How message value and credibility affect consumer trust of branded content on social media. *Journal of Interactive Advertising*, 19(1), 58–73. DOI: 10.1080/15252019.2018.1533501

Martínez-López, F. J., Anaya-Sánchez, R., Fernández Giordano, M., & Lopez-Lopez, D. (2020). Behind influencer marketing: Key marketing decisions and their effects on followers' responses. *Journal of Marketing Management*, 36(7-8), 579–607. DOI: 10.1080/0267257X.2020.1738525

Nielsen. (2023). The state of influencer marketing: Trends and insights. Retrieved from https://www.nielsen.com/reports/influencer-marketing-trends-2023

Shravanthi, C. (2023, March 10). How AI and big data analytics are changing influencer marketing. LinkedIn. https://www.linkedin.com/pulse/how-ai-big-data-analytics-changing-influencer-marketing-shravanthi-c-kfhpc/

Smith, A. (2021). *Digital marketing and analytics: How to use data-driven insights for better campaigns*. Springer.

Sprout Social. (2024, July 18). Influencer analytics tools: How to measure success. Retrieved September 3, 2024, from https://sproutsocial.com/insights/influencer-analytics-tools/

Sundermann, G., & Raabe, T. (2019). Strategic communication through social media influencers: Current state of research and desiderata. *International Journal of Strategic Communication*, 13(4), 278–300. DOI: 10.1080/1553118X.2019.1618306

Tafesse, W., & Wood, B. P. (2021). Followers' engagement with instagram influencers: The role of influencers' content and engagement strategy. *Journal of Retailing and Consumer Services*, 58, 102303. DOI: 10.1016/j.jretconser.2020.102303

Williams, E. (2024, January 10). Navigating the challenges of data and influencer marketing convergence. Forbes. https://www.forbes.com/navigating-challenges-data-influencer-marketing

Yoon, S. J., & Kim, H. H. (2020). Data analytics and artificial intelligence in influencer marketing: A systematic literature review. *Sustainability*, 12(8), 3150. DOI: 10.3390/su12083150

ADDITIONAL READING

Ao, L., Bansal, R., Pruthi, N., & Khaskheli, M. B. (2023). Impact of Social Media Influencers on Customer Engagement and Purchase Intention: A Meta-Analysis. *Sustainability (Basel)*, 15(3), 2744. DOI: 10.3390/su15032744

Bansal, R., Pruthi, N., & Singh, R. (2022). Developing Customer Engagement Through Artificial Intelligence Tools: Roles and Challenges. In *Developing Relationships, Personalization, and Data Herald in Marketing 5.0* (pp. 130-145). IGI Global.

Bansal, R., Shukla, G., Gupta, A., Singh, A., & Pruthi, N. (2023). Optimizing Augmented Reality and Virtual Reality for Customer Engagement. In *Promoting Consumer Engagement Through Emotional Branding and Sensory Marketing* (pp. 24–35). IGI Global.

Martínez, C., & Rodriguez, E. (2024). The convergence of affiliate and influencer marketing: A data-centric perspective. *Journal of Affiliate Marketing*, 8(2), 145–160.

Mittal, G., & Bansal, R. (2023). Driving Force Behind Consumer Brand Engagement: The Metaverse. In *Cultural Marketing and Metaverse for Consumer Engagement* (pp. 164-181). IGI Global.

Painoli, A. K., Bansal, R., Singh, R., & Kukreti, A. (2021). Impact of Digital Marketing on the Buying Behavior of Youth With Special Reference to Uttarakhand State. In *Big Data Analytics for Improved Accuracy, Efficiency, and Decision Making in Digital Marketing* (pp. 162-182). IGI Global. DOI: 10.4018/978-1-7998-7231-3.ch012

Singh, A., & Kumar, R. (2024). Data-driven content optimization for influencer marketing campaigns. *Content Marketing Quarterly*, 15(1), 78–93.

KEY TERMS AND DEFINITIONS

Convergence: Convergence is the process where two or more different elements or fields merge to form a new, unified approach or methodology.

Data Analytics: Data analytics is the process of examining, cleaning, transforming, and interpreting data to discover useful information, draw conclusions, and support decision-making. It involves using various statistical and mathematical techniques, often with the help of specialized software, to extract meaningful insights from large datasets.

Digital Engagement: Digital engagement refers to the interactions and connections between a brand or organization and its audience through digital platforms and channels.

Chapter 2
Role of Factors Fueling Brand Evangelism Through Influencer Marketing

Riya Wadhwa
Maharashi Dayanand University, India

Fazla Rabby
https://orcid.org/0000-0002-2683-7218
Stanford Institute of Management and Technology, Australia

Rohit Bansal
https://orcid.org/0000-0001-7072-5005
Vaish College of Engineering, India

ABSTRACT

Brand evangelism occurs when customers become ardent advocates for a brand, promoting its products or services voluntarily and with enthusiasm. These brand evangelists go beyond mere loyalty, they actively spread positive word-of-mouth, create user-generated content, and influence their social networks to embrace the brand. Brand evangelism in influencer marketing involves influencers passionately advocating for a brand, going beyond traditional endorsements. These influencers become genuine ambassadors, sharing authentic experiences and creating compelling content that resonates with their audience. By fostering strong relationships with influencers who truly believe in their products, brands can drive organic growth and enhance their reputation through trusted enthusiastic recommendations. The objective of this paper is to explain the role of various factors that fuel brand evan-

DOI: 10.4018/979-8-3693-7773-4.ch002

gelism across different social media platforms in the context of influencer marketing.

INTRODUCTION

Evangelism stands as a symbol of innovation and excellence in [industry/product category] (Pentina & Koh, 2012). The name itself reflects our commitment to evolving and adapting in a dynamic marketplace. "Evangelism" merges the concepts of "envision" and "galvanize," signifying our dedication to envisioning a brighter future and galvanizing change within our industry. By choosing this, you are aligning with a brand that prioritizes cutting-edge technology, sustainable practices, and unparalleled quality (Becerra & Badrinarayanan, 2013). Our mission is to not only meet your needs but also to inspire and elevate your experiences, ensuring that every interaction with us leaves a lasting, positive impact. Brand evangelism is the ultimate expression of brand loyalty. It occurs when consumers become passionate advocates for a brand, voluntarily promoting it to their networks. These individuals, known as brand evangelists, are deeply connected to the brand's values, products, or services, and enthusiastically share their positive experiences with others (Sulaiman et al., 2015). This organic word-of-mouth marketing is invaluable as it builds trust and credibility, often more effectively than traditional advertising. Brand evangelism is crucial in today's world due to its powerful impact on brand reputation and growth. With the rise of social media and digital platforms, consumers have more control over information than ever before (Bansal & Minocha, 2017). Traditional advertising is becoming less effective as people are bombarded with messages. Brand evangelists, on the other hand, generate authentic and trustworthy recommendations, influencing purchasing decisions significantly (Sha & Basri, 2018). Moreover, in an era of intense competition, fostering a loyal customer base through evangelism is essential for long-term success and sustainability. The Power of Brand Evangelism in Today's World, In an era characterized by information overload and consumer skepticism, traditional advertising is losing its potency (Qalati, Li, Ahmed, Mirani, & Khan, 2020). Consumers are increasingly turning to their peers for recommendations and advice. This shift in consumer behavior has elevated the importance of brand evangelism. Brand evangelism is the pinnacle of consumer loyalty. It is the ultimate form of brand loyalty where consumers become passionate advocates, voluntarily promoting a brand to their networks. It's about creating such a strong connection with a brand that consumers feel compelled to share their positive experiences with others It occurs when individuals become ardent advocates for a brand, voluntarily promoting it to their social circles (Painoli, Bansal, Singh, & Kukreti, 2021). These brand evangelists are more than just satisfied customers; they are passionate believers in the brand's mission, values, and products. Their enthusiasm is infectious, and their endorsements carry immense weight. Cultivating brand evangelism requires a strategic approach. It involves delivering exceptional customer experiences, building authentic relationships, and empowering customers to share their stories. By investing in customer satisfaction and loyalty, brands can create a powerful army of advocates who will drive growth and success (Abddulhai, Husin, Baharudin, & Abdullah, 2022).

Why does Brand Evangelism Matter so Much in Today's World?

1. **Trust and Credibility:** Consumers are inundated with marketing messages from all directions. They have become adept at filtering out promotional content. However, they are more likely to trust recommendations from friends, family, or online influencers. Brand evangelists act as credible third-party endorsers, building trust and credibility for the brand.
2. **Increased Reach and Awareness:** Brand evangelists have the power to exponentially increase a brand's reach. Through social media, word-of-mouth, and personal recommendations, they introduce the brand to new audiences. This organic growth is far more cost-effective than traditional advertising and often yields better results.
3. **Customer Acquisition and Retention:** Acquiring new customers is expensive. Brand evangelists can significantly reduce customer acquisition costs by referring friends and family. Moreover, loyal customers who become evangelists are more likely to make repeat purchases and become long-term customers.
4. **Enhanced Brand Reputation**: Positive word-of-mouth can rapidly enhance a brand's reputation. When customers share positive experiences, it creates a halo effect that attracts new customers and strengthens relationships with existing ones. Conversely, negative word-of-mouth can damage a brand's reputation and erode customer trust.
5. **Competitive Advantage:** In a crowded marketplace, differentiation is key. Brand evangelism can give a brand a competitive edge. When customers become passionate advocates, it creates a loyal customer base that is resistant to competitors' offerings.
6. **Improved Customer Lifetime Value:** Brand evangelists are typically more profitable customers. They tend to spend more, purchase more frequently, and have a higher lifetime value. By nurturing these relationships, brands can increase revenue and profitability.
7. **Innovation and Feedback:** Brand evangelists are a valuable source of insights and feedback. They can provide valuable input on product development, marketing campaigns, and customer service. By actively listening to their customers, brands can improve their offerings and better meet customer needs.

Brand Evangelism: The Heartbeat of Influencer Marketing

Brand evangelism is the lifeblood of influencer marketing. It's the transformation of consumers from passive recipients of information to ardent advocates who passionately promote a brand. Influencers, with their ability to connect deeply with their audience, are instrumental in igniting this fervor. When an influencer genuinely believes in a product and shares their enthusiasm authentically, it creates a ripple effect. Their followers are more likely to trust the recommendation, leading to increased brand awareness and consideration. Moreover, influencers can tap into specific demographics and interests, fostering a sense of community around the brand. This emotional connection is crucial as it transforms casual consumers into loyal advocates. Beyond immediate sales, brand evangelism driven by influencers builds long-term brand equity. Positive word-of-mouth spreads rapidly in the digital age, amplifying brand reputation and trust. In essence, successful influencer marketing isn't just about promotion; it's about cultivating a dedicated fanbase that becomes the brand's most powerful marketing asset. By fostering a community of passionate brand advocates, businesses can enjoy increased sales, improved brand reputation, and a sustainable competitive advantage. It provides effective and positive feedback from influencers to build trust among followers. Unlike traditional advertising, brand communication focuses on creating a relationship between the brand and the target audience. True evangelists Influencers share their identity and brand familiarity, making their recommendations more effective and relevant. This authenticity can expand a brand's reach and influence because followers will trust and engage with content that feels authentic and compelling. In addition, brand communication can foster long-term relationships, turning influencers and their followers into loyal advocates who continue to promote and support the brand, leading to continued growth, a good reputation, and a good reputation.

Review of Literature

Becerra & Badrinayanan (2013) This study explores how the nature of consumers' relationships with a brand affects brand evangelism, representing a highly intense form of brand support behavior. Specifically, it examines the impact of two key consumer-brand relational constructs: brand trust and brand identification, on brand evangelism. Brand evangelism, conceptualized as a combination of adoption and advocacy behaviors, is measured through three supportive behaviors: purchase intentions, positive referrals, and oppositional brand referrals. The findings indicate that consumer-brand relationships influence brand evangelism in different ways. Brand trust impacts purchase intentions and positive referrals, whereas brand identification affects both positive and oppositional brand referrals. Overall, the study highlights the significant role of consumer-brand relationships in fostering brand evangelism, compared to other factors like extraversion, gender, and brand experience. **Arkonsou et. Al (2014)** This paper aims to explore the lived reality of consumption and brands through the subjective meanings and interpretative processes of consumers, examining how they perceive the journey from their first experience to forming a strong emotional bond with a brand. Utilizing the experience pyramid model, we analyze qualitative interviews with brand evangelists, starting at the motivational level, progressing to the physical level where the evangelist interacts with the brand, and finally reaching the experiential level, where the emotional bond with the brand is established. For the consumer, the brand becomes an experiential entity with unique significance. The experience pyramid model proved to be a valuable research tool for gaining an in-depth understanding of the consumer-brand relationship. This study complements experience marketing by providing insights into the meaning of brand-related experiences for consumers. It helps marketers understand the development of a strong emotional bond between a brand and a consumer. Additionally, the results offer further insights into identifying brand evangelists. **Bakker (2018)** This paper focus to fill this gap by providing a conceptual framework to operationalize this emerging discipline in practice. The framework offers brand owners a methodology for selecting the right influencers for their brands and guides influencers on how to engage optimally with their fan base. Additionally, the discussion incorporates a consumer perspective to highlight the significance of influencer marketing in the consumer purchase decision-making process. **Jin et al (2019)** The purpose of this paper is to examine the effects of two types of celebrities (Instagram celebrities vs. traditional celebrities) on source trustworthiness, brand attitude, envy, and social presence. The proposed theoretical model includes celebrity type as the independent variable, social presence as the mediator, and self-discrepancy as the moderator. The findings indicate that consumers exposed to Instagram celebrities' brand posts perceive the source as more trustworthy, develop a more positive attitude toward the endorsed brand, experience a stronger sense of social presence, and feel more envious of the source compared to consumers exposed to traditional celebrities' brand posts. Structural equation modeling (Mplus 8.0) and bootstrap confidence intervals show that social presence mediates the effects of celebrity type on trustworthiness, brand attitude, and envy. Multiple regression analyses reveal the moderating effects of appearance-related actual–ideal self-discrepancy. **Nadar et al (2020)** The purpose of this study was to examine the impact of consumer-brand relationships within social network-based brand communities on brand evangelism variables, specifically by enhancing brand trust among Samsung mobile phone customers in Hamadan City, leading to supportive behaviors. For this purpose, 384 individuals were selected through random sampling. The results indicated that consumer relationships with brand elements (product, brand, company, and other customers) within the brand community on social networks, mediated by consumer brand trust, have a positive and significant effect on brand evangelism. **Amani (2022)** explored the role of alumni in supporting higher education institutions (HEIs) through donation behavior. This study investigates how university identification and university social community identification influence university brand evangelism, with a sense of belonging acting as a mediator. Data were collected from 606 alumni across 15 HEIs in Tanzania and analyzed using structural equation modeling. The findings reveal that alumni are more likely to engage in university brand evangelism when they strongly identify with both their university and its social community. Moreover, the results indicate that high identification alone is insufficient to predict and explain university brand evangelism without considering the mediating role of a sense of belonging. Therefore, HEI management should focus on fostering social and personal identification to cultivate a sense of belonging, thereby encouraging alumni to participate in university brand evangelism. **Sharma (2023)** This research aims to understand evangelism within social media-based travel communities (SMTCs) and examines the key components of evangelical behavior in this context. A conceptual model depicting the interplay of unique constructs is tested using structural equation modeling. The findings indicate that both in-role and extra-role behaviors inspire evangelism and engagement within SMTCs. Additionally, evangelism acts as a mediator and has the potential to expand tourism literature. Theoretically, the research provides new insights into evangelism and engagement within SMTCs. It suggests that managers can enhance their destination's presence and promotion on SMTCs by focusing on evangelism. The study offers insights into evangelical behavior through its unique components, outcomes, and mediating roles in SMTC settings. Empirical investigations confirm that evangelism inspires engagement with SMTCs. **Bhandari (2024)** This study investigates the critical role of online brand community (OBC) engagement in fostering brand evangelism, considering the influence of age, gender, and membership number. The findings indicate that OBC engagement enhances brand evangelism, with age, gender, and OBC membership number moderating this relationship. Notably, the study reveals that female, younger, and low-OBC follower consumers contribute more significantly to brand evangelism compared to their male, older, and high-OBC follower counterparts.

Role of Factors Fueling Brand Evangelism Through Influencer Marketing on Social Media

Brand evangelism, the passionate advocacy of a brand by its customers, is significantly boosted by influencer marketing on social media. Several factors contribute to this phenomenon:

Influencer-Related Factors

1. **Authenticity and Credibility:** Influencers who genuinely believe in a brand are more likely to create authentic content that resonates with their audience. This authenticity fosters trust and encourages followers to become brand evangelists.
2. **Relevance and Alignment:** Influencers whose values and lifestyle align with the brand's image are more effective in generating positive word-of-mouth. Their endorsement feels genuine and relatable to their audience.
3. **Engagement and Interaction:** Influencers who actively engage with their followers build strong relationships based on trust and loyalty. This engagement encourages followers to participate in conversations about the brand, leading to increased brand advocacy.
4. **Follower Base and Demographics:** The size and demographics of an influencer's following determine their reach and impact. Influencers with a large and engaged audience can significantly amplify brand visibility and drive evangelism.

Platform-Related Factors

1. **Content Format**: Different platforms excel at different content formats. For example, Instagram is ideal for visual storytelling, while TikTok is known for short-form video content. Understanding platform-specific formats is crucial for creating content that resonates with the audience.
2. **Algorithm and Reach:** Social media algorithms influence content visibility. Influencers with a strong understanding of platform algorithms can optimize their content for maximum reach, leading to increased brand exposure and engagement.
3. **Community and Interaction:** Some platforms foster stronger communities and interactions than others. Platforms like Reddit and Twitter encourage discussions and debates, creating opportunities for brand evangelists to share their experiences.
4. **User-Generated Content (UGC):** Platforms that facilitate UGC, such as Instagram and YouTube, empower users to create and share content related to the brand, amplifying brand reach and engagement.

Brand-Related Factors

1. **Brand Story and Values:** A compelling brand story and strong values resonate with consumers and inspire loyalty. When influencers align with these elements, it strengthens the brand's connection with the audience.

2. **Product or Service Quality**: A high-quality product or service is essential for building a loyal customer base. Satisfied customers are more likely to become brand evangelists and share their positive experiences.
3. **Customer Experience:** A positive customer experience, including excellent customer service, contributes to brand loyalty and advocacy. Satisfied customers are more likely to share their experiences with others, including on social media.
4. **Incentives and Rewards:** Loyalty programs, referral bonuses, and exclusive offers can incentivize customers to become brand advocates and share their experiences with their network.

Instagram: The Epicenter of Brand Evangelism in Influencer Marketing

Instagram has emerged as a powerhouse for fostering brand evangelism, a phenomenon where consumers become passionate advocates, voluntarily promoting a brand. Its visual-centric nature, coupled with a strong emphasis on community and engagement, makes it an ideal platform for influencers to cultivate brand loyalty and advocacy.

Instagram's Characteristics for Brand Evangelism

Instagram's visual-centric nature, coupled with its strong emphasis on community and engagement, makes it an ideal platform for fostering brand evangelism. Key characteristics include:

1. **Visual Storytelling**: Instagram's focus on images and videos allows brands to create visually appealing content that resonates with audiences. This visual storytelling can evoke emotions and inspire a deeper connection with the brand.
2. **Influencer Authenticity:** The platform's culture encourages authenticity and genuine connections between influencers and their followers. This authenticity is crucial for building trust and credibility, which are essential for brand evangelism.
3. **User-Generated Content:** Instagram's features, such as Stories and Reels, make it easy for users to create and share content. This encourages user-generated content, which can be a powerful tool for brand evangelism.
4. **Community Building:** Instagram's focus on community and engagement creates a space for brands and influencers to build strong relationships with their audience. This fosters a sense of belonging and loyalty, which are key factors in brand evangelism

Role of Instagram on Brand Evangelism in Influencer Marketing

- **Visual Storytelling:** Instagram's emphasis on visuals allows influencers to create captivating content that resonates with their audience. This visual storytelling helps to build a strong emotional connection between the audience and the brand, fostering loyalty and advocacy.
- **Influencer Authenticity:** The platform's culture encourages authenticity, allowing influencers to build genuine relationships with their followers. This authenticity is crucial for building trust, which is a cornerstone of brand evangelism.
- **User-Generated Content (UGC):** Instagram's features, such as Stories and Reels, make it easy for users to create and share content. Influencers can encourage their followers to create UGC featuring the brand, amplifying the brand's reach and showcasing real-life usage.
- **Community Building:** Instagram's focus on community fosters a sense of belonging among followers. Influencers can contribute to this by creating a community around the brand and encouraging interactions and discussions, which can lead to stronger brand loyalty.
- **Measurable Impact:** Instagram provides valuable analytics, allowing brands and influencers to track the impact of campaigns, measure engagement, and identify key performance indicators for brand evangelism.

How Instagram Drives Brand Evangelism:

- **Influencer-Brand Alignment:** When influencers genuinely align with a brand's values and ethos, their advocacy becomes more authentic and impactful.
- **Emotional Connection:** By creating content that evokes emotions, influencers can foster a deeper connection between the audience and the brand, leading to increased loyalty and advocacy.
- **User-Generated Content Campaigns:** Encouraging users to share their experiences with the brand can create a sense of ownership and community, driving brand evangelism.
- **Exclusive Content and Rewards:** Providing exclusive content or rewards to loyal followers can strengthen their connection to the brand and encourage them to become advocates.

Examples of Successful Brand Evangelism on YouTube

1. Glossier: Building a Community of Skinthusiasts

- **User-Generated Content (UGC):** Glossier excels at encouraging users to share their skincare routines and product experiences using a specific hashtag. This creates a sense of community and authenticity.
- **Influencer Partnerships:** Collaborating with influencers who genuinely love the brand helps expand its reach and credibility. Glossier often works with micro-influencers who resonate with their target audience.
- **Transparency and Authenticity:** Glossier is open about its product development process and values, which resonates with consumers seeking genuine brands.

2. Nike: Inspiring Athletes and Everyday Heroes
   - **Athlete Endorsements:** Partnering with world-class athletes creates aspirational content that motivates followers to push their limits.
   - **Customer Stories:** Nike shares inspiring stories of ordinary people achieving extraordinary feats, emphasizing the brand's core values of determination and perseverance.
   - **Inclusive Campaigns:** Nike's campaigns often celebrate diversity and inclusivity, fostering a sense of belonging among its audience.

3. Starbucks: Creating a Third Place Experience
   - **Community Engagement:** Starbucks often hosts Instagram contests and giveaways that encourage user interaction and foster a sense of community.
   - **Visual Storytelling:** The brand uses stunning visuals to create an aspirational lifestyle associated with coffee and relaxation.
   - **Limited Edition Releases:** Creating a sense of urgency and exclusivity with limited edition drinks and merchandise drives engagement and excitement.

4. Patagonia: Environmental Advocacy
   - **Purpose-Driven Content:** Patagonia actively promotes environmental conservation and sustainability, aligning with the values of its target audience.
   - **User-Generated Adventures:** The brand encourages customers to share their outdoor adventures using branded hashtags, creating a sense of shared experience.
   - **Transparency and Accountability:** Patagonia is transparent about its sustainability efforts and holds itself accountable to its customers.

YouTube: A Catalyst for Brand Evangelism Through Influencer Marketing

YouTube serves as a powerful platform for transforming casual consumers into ardent brand advocates. Its unique blend of visual storytelling, community engagement, and measurable results makes it an ideal environment for influencer marketing campaigns that drive brand evangelism.

How YouTube Fuels Brand Evangelism

- **Visual Storytelling:** YouTube's video format allows influencers to craft compelling narratives around a brand, evoking emotions and creating a lasting impression.
- **Community Building:** Influencers can cultivate dedicated fan bases who feel a strong connection to both the influencer and the brand, leading to increased loyalty and advocacy.
- **Authenticity:** YouTube is perceived as a platform where creators can showcase their genuine personalities, building trust with viewers and making brand endorsements feel more authentic.
- **Measurable Impact:** Detailed analytics provide insights into campaign performance, helping brands identify what resonates with the audience and optimize their strategies.
- **Scalability:** YouTube's massive reach allows brands to tap into diverse audiences and expand their customer base.

Key Roles of Influencers in Brand Evangelism

- **Content Creation:** Influencers produce engaging content that highlights the brand's values and benefits, inspiring viewers to share and recommend the product or service.
- **Community Engagement:** By fostering a strong connection with their audience, influencers create a sense of belonging and encourage fans to become brand ambassadors.
- **Authentic Endorsements:** Genuine enthusiasm for the brand translates into credible recommendations, building trust and credibility.
- **Call to Action:** Influencers can directly encourage viewers to take action, such as purchasing a product, subscribing to a channel, or sharing content.

In essence, YouTube provides a stage for influencers to showcase a brand's story in a captivating way, building a loyal following that becomes a driving force for brand evangelism.

Examples of Successful Brand Evangelism on YouTube

YouTube has been a fertile ground for brands to cultivate passionate communities and foster brand evangelism. Here are some notable examples:

1. Red Bull:
   - **Action Sports and Lifestyle:** Red Bull has masterfully positioned itself as a lifestyle brand, not just an energy drink.
   - **Extreme Sports Content:** Their channel features adrenaline-pumping videos of athletes pushing boundaries, resonating with adventure-seekers.
   - **Community Building:** Red Bull has created a strong community around extreme sports, inspiring viewers to share their own adventures and become brand ambassadors.
2. LEGO:
   - **Nostalgia and Creativity:** LEGO taps into childhood nostalgia while inspiring creativity and imagination.
   - **How-to Tutorials and Reviews:** The channel features building tutorials, reviews, and stop-motion animations, engaging a wide audience.
   - **Fan-Generated Content:** LEGO actively encourages fans to share their creations, fostering a sense of community and ownership.
3. Gillette:
   - **Masculinity and Confidence:** Gillette has evolved from a product-focused brand to one that embodies masculinity and confidence.
   - **Influencer Partnerships:** Collaborations with athletes and celebrities have helped reinforce the brand's image.
   - **Social Responsibility:** Gillette's campaigns addressing issues like toxic masculinity have sparked conversations and garnered positive attention.
4. Dove:
   - **Body Positivity and Self-Esteem:** Dove has positioned itself as a champion of body positivity and self-esteem.
   - **Real Beauty Campaigns:** The brand's campaigns featuring real women have resonated with audiences and sparked discussions.
   - **Community Engagement:** Dove actively engages with its audience through social media, fostering a sense of connection.
5. Apple:

- **Innovation and Design:** Apple has cultivated a loyal following based on its reputation for innovation and design.
- **Product Demonstrations:** The channel showcases new products and features, generating excitement and anticipation.
- **Customer Testimonials:** Apple frequently features customer stories, highlighting the impact of their products on people's lives.

Facebook for Brand Evangelism Through Influencer Marketing

Facebook, while not as visually dominant as platforms like Instagram or YouTube, still offers a powerful platform for fostering brand evangelism through influencer marketing. It is a social media platform that serves as a powerful tool for cultivating brand evangelism. It provides a space for brands to connect with their audience, build trust, and foster a community around their products or services. When used effectively, Facebook can transform casual customers into passionate brand advocates who willingly promote the brand to others.

Characteristics of Facebook for Brand Evangelism

- **Massive Reach:** Facebook boasts a vast user base, allowing brands to reach a wide audience through influencers.
- **Strong Communities:** Facebook Groups offer a space for like-minded individuals to connect, creating a strong sense of community around brands and influencers.
- **Detailed Analytics:** Facebook Insights provides valuable data on audience demographics, engagement, and campaign performance.
- **Diverse Content Formats:** Beyond text, Facebook supports images, videos, and live streams, offering flexibility for influencer content.

How Influencers Can Drive Brand Evangelism on Facebook

- **Leveraging Facebook Groups:** Influencers can create or join relevant Facebook Groups to build a community around the brand and engage with potential customers.
- **Live Streaming:** Live videos offer a real-time connection with the audience, fostering engagement and building trust.
- **User-Generated Content:** Encouraging followers to share their experiences with the brand can create authentic and relatable content.
- **Paid Advertising:** Influencers can amplify their reach through Facebook Ads, targeting specific demographics and interests.

Roles of Facebook for Brand Evangelism

- **Community Building:** Facebook Groups provide a dedicated space for like-minded individuals to connect, share experiences, and build a strong sense of community around a brand.
- **Engagement Platform:** The platform's interactive features (likes, comments, shares, reactions) encourage dialogue and interaction between the brand and its audience, fostering engagement.
- **Customer Support Channel:** Facebook can be used to provide timely customer support, address inquiries, and resolve issues promptly.
- **Content Amplification:** Facebook Ads and organic reach can help amplify brand messages, reaching a wider audience.
- **Influencer Partnership Hub:** Facebook allows brands to collaborate with influencers, leveraging their reach and influence to promote the brand.

Examples of Successful Brand Evangelism on Facebook

1. Coca-Cola: Building a Community Around Shared Happiness
   - **Leveraging User-Generated Content:** Coca-Cola has masterfully harnessed the power of user-generated content by encouraging fans to share their personal stories and experiences with the brand.
   - **Creating Shareable Moments:** Campaigns like "Share a Coke" and personalized bottle labels have sparked widespread engagement, leading to countless shares and discussions on Facebook.
   - **Building a Strong Community:** Coca-Cola has created a sense of belonging among its fans by fostering a community centered around happiness and shared experiences.
2. Dove: Empowering Women and Building Trust
   - **Focusing on Self-Esteem:** Dove's campaigns, such as "Real Beauty," have resonated deeply with women by promoting self-acceptance and body positivity.
   - **Encouraging Open Dialogue:** Dove has created a platform for women to share their experiences and support each other, fostering a strong sense of community.
   - **Building Trust:** By consistently delivering on its brand promise of empowering women, Dove has earned the trust of its audience and cultivated a loyal fanbase.
3. Starbucks: Creating a Third Place Experience

- **Fostering a Sense of Belonging:** Starbucks has positioned itself as a "third place" between home and work, creating a welcoming atmosphere for customers.
- **Encouraging Customer Connections:** The brand has facilitated connections among customers through in-store events and online communities.
- **Rewarding Loyalty:** Starbucks' loyalty program has incentivized customers to return and share their experiences with friends and family.

4. Gillette: Addressing Social Issues
   - **Taking a Stand:** Gillette's "The Best a Man Can Be" campaign tackled issues of masculinity and toxic behavior, sparking a much-needed conversation.
   - **Engaging with the Audience:** The campaign encouraged open dialogue and debate, fostering a sense of community among Gillette's target audience.
   - **Building a Positive Brand Image:** By addressing a relevant social issue, Gillette positioned itself as a brand with strong values and a commitment to making a positive impact.

LinkedIn for Brand Evangelism Through Influencer Marketing

While primarily known as a professional networking platform, LinkedIn has emerged as a valuable tool for brand evangelism, especially when combined with influencer marketing.

LinkedIn's Role in Brand Evangelism

- **Professional Credibility:** LinkedIn is perceived as a platform for professionals, lending credibility to both the brand and the influencer.
- **Targeted Audience:** With detailed demographic and professional information, LinkedIn allows for precise audience targeting.
- **Thought Leadership:** It's a platform for sharing industry insights and thought leadership, positioning the brand as an expert.
- **Content Amplification:** LinkedIn's algorithm can amplify content reach, making it easier to spread brand messages.

Influencer Marketing on LinkedIn

- **Industry Experts:** Influencers with industry expertise can position themselves as thought leaders and endorse the brand authentically.

- **Employee Advocacy:** Employees who are also influencers can amplify brand messages internally and externally.
- **Content Collaboration:** Influencers can collaborate with the brand on LinkedIn to create high-quality content.
- **Lead Generation:** Influencer-generated content can drive traffic to the brand's website and generate leads.

Key Characteristics of LinkedIn for Brand Evangelism

- **Professional Network:** Its focus on professional relationships builds trust and credibility.
- **Content-driven:** LinkedIn prioritizes long-form, in-depth content, allowing for detailed brand storytelling.
- **Data-driven:** LinkedIn provides analytics to measure campaign performance and ROI.
- **B2B Focus:** While it has a growing B2C presence, LinkedIn is predominantly a B2B platform.

Examples of Successful Brand Evangelism on LinkedIn

1. Salesforce: Building a Strong Employer Brand
   - **Employee Advocacy:** Salesforce has cultivated a strong employee advocacy program, encouraging employees to share company updates, success stories, and company culture on LinkedIn.
   - **Thought Leadership:** The company consistently shares industry insights and thought leadership content, positioning itself as an industry leader.
   - **Employee Testimonials:** Salesforce features employees sharing their experiences and career growth within the company, attracting top talent and fostering a positive employer brand.
2. Microsoft: Leveraging Employee Influencers
   - **Identifying Key Influencers:** Microsoft has identified employees with significant influence in their respective fields and provided them with resources to amplify their voices.
   - **Content Amplification:** These employee influencers share company news, products, and industry insights, expanding the company's reach.
   - **Thought Leadership:** By positioning employees as thought leaders, Microsoft has established itself as an authority in the tech industry.
3. LinkedIn (the platform itself): Building a Strong Community

- **User-Generated Content:** LinkedIn encourages users to share their professional experiences and insights, fostering a strong sense of community.
- **Employee Advocacy:** LinkedIn employees actively share company updates, product features, and company culture, creating a positive brand image.
- **Thought Leadership:** The platform itself publishes high-quality content, positioning LinkedIn as a valuable resource for professionals.

4. HubSpot: Inbound Marketing and Customer Success Stories
   - **Content Marketing:** HubSpot consistently shares valuable content related to inbound marketing, attracting a target audience of marketers.
   - **Customer Testimonials:** The company features success stories from customers, showcasing the impact of HubSpot's products and services.
   - **Educational Content:** By providing valuable insights and resources, HubSpot positions itself as a trusted advisor in the industry.

While LinkedIn might not have the same level of visual appeal as platforms like Instagram, its professional focus can be a significant advantage for certain brands.

WhatsApp for Brand Evangelism Through Influencer Marketing

While primarily known for personal messaging, WhatsApp has emerged as a potential channel for brand evangelism, especially when combined with influencer marketing. However, its role is significantly different from platforms like Facebook or Instagram. It refers to the strategy of leveraging the personal messaging platform, WhatsApp, to foster brand loyalty and advocacy with the help of influencers. This involves creating a direct, one-to-one connection between the brand, the influencer, and the target audience through WhatsApp.

WhatsApp's Role in Brand Evangelism

- **Direct and Personal:** WhatsApp offers a highly personal and direct communication channel, allowing for one-on-one interactions.
- **Community Building:** While not as public as other platforms, WhatsApp Groups can foster a sense of community among brand enthusiasts.
- **Customer Support:** It can be used for real-time customer support and issue resolution, enhancing customer satisfaction.
- **Limited Reach:** Unlike other social media platforms, WhatsApp's reach is primarily limited to existing contacts.

Influencer Marketing on WhatsApp

- **Micro-influencers:** Given WhatsApp's nature, micro-influencers with a strong personal connection to their audience might be more effective.
- **Exclusive Content:** Influencers can offer exclusive content or early access to products to build excitement and anticipation.
- **WhatsApp Groups:** Influencers can create WhatsApp groups for their most engaged followers, offering a more intimate connection with the brand.

Key Characteristics of WhatsApp for Brand Evangelism

- **High Level of Personalization:** WhatsApp offers a direct and intimate communication channel, allowing for personalized interactions with customers.
- **Real-Time Communication:** Instant messaging enables real-time interactions, allowing brands to respond quickly to customer queries and concerns.
- **Strong Sense of Community:** WhatsApp groups can foster a sense of community among brand enthusiasts, enabling direct interactions and sharing of experiences.
- **Limited Reach:** Unlike other social media platforms, WhatsApp's reach is primarily confined to existing contacts, limiting its potential for broad brand awareness.
- **Privacy Concerns:** Users often have heightened privacy concerns on WhatsApp, which can restrict the type of content and interactions suitable for brand evangelism.
- **Measurement Challenges:** Tracking and measuring campaign performance on WhatsApp is difficult due to limited analytics capabilities.

Potential Use Cases (Hypothetical Examples)

While specific examples are limited, we can explore potential use cases where WhatsApp could theoretically be leveraged for brand evangelism:

1. **Exclusive Product Launches and Early Access:**
   - Brands could create exclusive WhatsApp groups for loyal customers or influencers to offer early access to new products or limited editions.
   - This creates a sense of exclusivity and encourages word-of-mouth marketing among group members.
2. **Personalized Customer Support:**
   - Brands can use WhatsApp to provide rapid and personalized customer support, building stronger customer relationships.

- Excellent service experiences can lead to positive word-of-mouth within customer circles.
3. **Niche Communities and Interest Groups:**
   - Brands targeting specific demographics or interests could create WhatsApp groups to foster a sense of community among like-minded individuals.
   - Engaging content and exclusive offers within these groups can encourage brand advocacy.
4. **Influencer Partnerships:**
   - Brands can collaborate with influencers to create private WhatsApp groups for their most engaged followers.
   - Exclusive content, giveaways, or Q&A sessions can drive brand awareness and loyalty.

CONCLUSION

In conclusion, brand evangelism is a potent force in today's marketing landscape. It is a testament to a brand's ability to connect with consumers on a deep emotional level. By harnessing the power of word-of-mouth, brands can build lasting relationships, drive growth, and achieve long-term success. Brand Evangelists are a valuable asset to any brand. Their authentic advocacy can significantly impact a brand's image and success. Companies should strive to create an environment that encourages Brand Evangelism by delivering superior products and excellent customer service. By carefully considering these factors, brands can effectively leverage influencer marketing to fuel brand evangelism across different social media platforms. A combination of authentic influencers, engaging content, and a strong brand foundation is key to creating a loyal and passionate customer base. In summary, many factors contribute to brand communication through influencer marketing. The authenticity and relevance of the influencer are important because followers tend to trust recommendations from people they believe to be authentic. The stories that influencers tell can strengthen emotional connections, thus building brand trust. Choosing influencers who relate to your brand's values ensures the consistency and credibility of your message. The interactive nature of social media allows for instant collaboration, creating a community of like-minded advocates. The ability of influencers to target niche audiences with specific content leads to increased marketing awareness and authenticity. Partnerships between brands and stakeholders often result in creative campaigns that delight consumers. Additionally, metrics and insights provide insights that help brands adjust their strategies for maximum impact. Finally, the combination of strong individual motivation and purposeful efforts, integrating real-time digital communication, leads to passion and loyalty with customers.

REFERENCES

Abddulhai, I. N., Husin, M. H., Baharudin, A. S., & Abdullah, N. A. (2022). Determinants of Facebook adoption and its impact on service-based small and medium enterprise performance in Northwestern Nigeria. *Journal of Systems and Information Technology*, 24(3).

Ainin, S., Parveen, F., Moghavvemi, S., Jaafar, N. I., & Mohd Shuib, N. L. (2015). Factors influencing the use of Social Media by SMEs and its Performance outcomes. *Industrial Management & Data Systems*, 115(3), 570–588. DOI: 10.1108/IMDS-07-2014-0205

Alkateeb, M. A., & Abdalla, R. A. (2021). Social Media Adoption and its Impact on SMEs Performance A Case Study of Palestine. *Estudios de Economía Aplicada*, 39(7). Advance online publication. DOI: 10.25115/eea.v39i7.4872

AlSharji, A., Ahmad, S. Z., & Bakar, A. R. A. (2018). Understanding Social Media Adoption in SMEs Empirical Evidence from the United Arab Emirates. *Journal of Entrepreneurship in Emerging Economies*, 10(2), 302–328. DOI: 10.1108/JEEE-08-2017-0058

Amani, D. (2022). Demystifying factors fueling university brand evangelism in the higher education sector in Tanzania: A social identity perspective. *Cogent Education*, 9(1), 2110187. DOI: 10.1080/2331186X.2022.2110187

Bakker, D. (2018). Conceptualizing influencer marketing. Journal of emerging trends in marketing and management, 1(1), 79-87.

Bansal, R., Masood, R., & Dadhich, V. (2014). Social media marketing-a tool of innovative marketing. *Journal of Organizational Management*, 3(1), 1–7.

Bansal, R., & Minocha, K. (2017). Impact of Social Media on Consumer Attitude Towards A Brand With Special Reference to Hospitality Industry. *International Research Journal of Management and Commerce*, 4(8), 106–120.

Bansal, R., &Pruthi, N. (2021). DEVELOPING CUSTOMER ENGAGEMENT THROUGH SOCIAL MEDIA: A REVIEW OF LITERATURE. Marketing 5.0: putting up blocks together, 80.

Bansal, R., Pruthi, N., & Singh, R. (2022). Developing Customer Engagement Through Artificial Intelligence Tools: Roles and Challenges. In Developing Relationships, Personalization, and Data Herald in Marketing 5.0 (pp. 130-145). IGI Global.

Bansal, R., & Saini, S. (2022). LEVERAGING ROLE OF SOCIAL MEDIA INFLUENCERS IN CORPORATE WORLD-AN OVERVIEW. *NOLEGEIN-Journal of Global Marketing*, 5(1), 1–5.

Bansal, R., & Saini, S. (2022). Exploring the Role of Social Media: An Innovative Tool for Entrepreneurs. In Applying Metalytics to Measure Customer Experience in the Metaverse (pp. 34-43). IGI Global.

Bansal, R., Shukla, G., Gupta, A., Singh, A., & Pruthi, N. (2023). Optimizing Augmented Reality and Virtual Reality for Customer Engagement. In Promoting Consumer Engagement Through Emotional Branding and Sensory Marketing (pp. 24-35). IGI Global.

Becerra, P., E., & Badrinarayanan, V. (. (2013). The influence of brand trust and brand identification on brand evangelism. *Journal of Product and Brand Management*, 22(5/6), 371–383. DOI: 10.1108/JPBM-09-2013-0394

Bhandari, M. P., Bhattarai, C., & Mulholland, G. (2024). Online brand community engagement and brand evangelism: The role of age, gender and membership number. *Journal of Product and Brand Management*, 33(3), 301–313. DOI: 10.1108/JPBM-02-2023-4373

Dutot, V., & Bergeron, F. (2016). From Strategic Orientation to Social Media Orientation: Improving SMEs Performance on Social Media. *Journal of Small Business and Enterprise Development*, 23(4), 1165–1190. DOI: 10.1108/JSBED-11-2015-0160

Eze, S. C., Chinedu/Eze, V. C., & Bello, A. O. (2020). Some Antecedent Factors that shape SMEs adoption of social media marketing application: A Hybrid Approach. Journal of Performance A Case Study of Palestine. *Studies of Applied Economics*, 39(7).

Gavino, M. C., Williams, D. E., Jacobson, D., & Smith, I. (2018). Latino Entrepreneurs and Social Media adoption: Personal and business Social Network Platforms. *Management Research Review*, 42(4), 469–494. DOI: 10.1108/MRR-02-2018-0095

Jin, S. V., Muqaddam, A., & Ryu, E. (2019). Instafamous and social media influencer marketing. *Marketing Intelligence & Planning*, 37(5), 567–579. DOI: 10.1108/MIP-09-2018-0375

NURFARIDA, I. N., Endi SARWOKO, & Mohammed ARIEF. (2021). The Impact of Social Media Adoption on Customer Orientation and SME Performance: An Empirical Study in Indonesia. Journal of Asian Finance, Economics and Business, 8(6).

Oyewobi, L. O., Adedayo, O. F., Olorunyomi, S. O., & Jimoh, R. (2021). Social Media Adoption and Business Performance: The Mediating Role of Organizational Learning Capacity. *Journal of Facilities Management*, 19(4), 413–436. DOI: 10.1108/JFM-12-2020-0099

Oztamur, D., & Karakadilar, I. S. (2014). Exploring the Role of Social Media for SMEs: As a New Marketing Strategy Tool for the Firm Performance Perspective. *Procedia: Social and Behavioral Sciences*, 150, 511–520. DOI: 10.1016/j.sbspro.2014.09.067

Painoli, A. K., Bansal, R., Singh, R., & Kukreti, A. (2021). Impact of Digital Marketing on the Buying Behavior of Youth With Special Reference to Uttarakhand State. In Big Data Analytics for Improved Accuracy, Efficiency, and Decision Making in Digital Marketing (pp. 162-182). IGI Global. DOI: 10.4018/978-1-7998-7231-3.ch012

Pentina, I., & Koh, A. C. (2012). Exploring Social Media Marketing Strategies in SMEs. *International Journal of Internet Marketing and Advertising*, 7(4), 292–310. DOI: 10.1504/IJIMA.2012.051613

Qalati, S. A., Li, W., Ahmed, N., Mirani, M. A., & Khan, A. (2020). Examining the Factors Affecting SME Performance: The Mediating Role of Social Media Adoption. Sutainability, 13(1).

Rahman, K. T., Bansal, R., & Pruthi, N. (2023). Consumer Adoption of Technologies: A Mindset-Oriented Approach. In Contemporary Studies of Risks in Emerging Technology, Part B (pp. 243-255). Emerald Publishing Limited. DOI: 10.1108/978-1-80455-566-820231013

Saini, S., & Bansal, R. (2023). Geo-Marketing: A New Tool for Marketers. In Enhancing Customer Engagement Through Location-Based Marketing (pp. 102-112). IGI Global. DOI: 10.4018/978-1-6684-8177-6.ch008

Sha, W., & Basri, M. (2018). Social Media and Corporate Communication Antecedents of SME Sustainability Performance A Conceptual Framework for SMEs of Arab World. *Journal of Economic and Administrative Sciences*, 35(3).

Sharma, P. (2023). Destination evangelism and engagement: Investigation from social media-based travel community. *Electronic Commerce Research and Applications*, 57, 101228. DOI: 10.1016/j.elerap.2022.101228

Srivastava, S., Anshu, Bansal, R., Soni, G., & Tyagi, A. K. (2022, December). Blockchain Enabled Internet of Things: Current Scenario and Open Challenges for Future. In International Conference on Innovations in Bio-Inspired Computing and Applications (pp. 640-648). Cham: Springer Nature Switzerland.

Chapter 3
Factors Influencing Brand Evangelism Through Influencer Marketing

Anchal Luthra
https://orcid.org/0000-0003-0559-1893
AIBS, Amity University, Noida, India

Amrish Kumar Choubey
https://orcid.org/0009-0009-9052-4855
AIBS, Amity University, Noida, India

Disha Shah
https://orcid.org/0000-0001-9164-7886
Vivekanand Education Society Institute of Management Studies and Research, India

Astha Gupta
AIBS, Amity University, Noida, India

Harendra Kumar
AIBS, Amity University, Noida, India

Zev Asch
Touro College, USA

ABSTRACT

The study investigates vital factors that acted as a stimulus for ordinary people to become faithful promoters on social media through influencer marketing. Consumer interaction with brands has gone through a metamorphosis primarily due to social media, which has catapulted social media influencers to become a pivotal aspect of marketing strategy. Product-specific influencers have become this age's gospelers, influencing consumer perception and behavior. The multi-layer phenomena of brand evangelism within influencer marketing are studied through qualitative research. Multiple essential factors contributing to brand advocacy were unveiled through various case studies published in Scopus and Google Scholar secondary databases. Primarily, three impactors were unveiled: Emotional Connection, Trust,

DOI: 10.4018/979-8-3693-7773-4.ch003

and Credibility. The impact of an influencer's connection with their followers was built through recommendations given through honest personal storytelling, authenticity, and transparency. However, identifying an influencer with large followers on social media platforms has always been elusive

1. INTRODUCTION

Influencer marketing is essential to driving effective engagement between brands and their target audiences in digital marketing. Unlike traditional advertising, influencer marketing uses popular social media influencers with credibility. These influencers communicate with large followings across multiple media platforms by creating personal and relatable content that resonates naturally with their audience, normally promoting products, services, or brands through such means. This personal relationship allows them to talk about what the brand stands for well enough to affect how people think about it while fostering loyalty among members of their communities (Sammis *et al.*, 2016). Brand evangelism is a phenomenon closely related to influencer marketing, where a fanatical customer becomes an advocate for the brand within their network through word-of-mouth advertising. In this process, social media has acted as a catalyst for consumers to share experiences instantly. They can convert followers into evangelical customers because they have a wider reach than any other person, so trust is not hard earned but given freely due to past successes (Rachmad, 2024; Vidani & Das, 2021). The shift in consumer behavior reflects how much power social media wields over our decision-making processes (Alkadrie, 2024). It has been widely acknowledged that influencer endorsements greatly affect consumers' purchasing decisions and brand loyalty (Jin & Ryu, 2020). By developing content that appeals to their followers while aligning with the values of given brands, these individuals create communities around themselves filled with loyal interactive customers who actively promote those companies. As we progress into digitalization, more emphasis will be put on long-term relationships between marketers and buyers, thus turning influencer marketing into a necessary part of business strategies alongside brand evangelism. Hence, businesses must build trust-based relations that foster belief systems and authenticity that drive audience connection. After becoming aware of an influencer's genuineness and authenticity, consumers develop positive emotional connections towards his or her endorsed brands. This bond, founded upon an individual's ability to relate a company's values with its mission, catalyzes loyalty and advocacy towards that brand. Consumers' emotional attachment and loyalty make them want to share the brands they care about most with others who matter, cementing those labels within their social identity (Escalas & Bettman, 2003). Influencers use these psychological and sociological aspects by integrating companies into followers' worldviews, thus creating communities full of diehard fans. Influencer marketing provides a unified approach instead of interrupting; it involves consumers willingly, hence less interruption and a more engaging connection with brands, unlike traditional marketing, which often disrupts (Glucksman, 2017). Personal relationships between influencers and their fans humanize corporations, especially when people are becoming increasingly skeptical about how businesses interact with them online, enabling organizations to reach wider audiences through various innovative advertising methods in this digital era. This study aims to investigate influencer marketing in terms of making satisfied customers influencers" brand evangelists. The researchers consider perceived genuineness, emotional involvement, and trustworthiness to be major drivers for brand evangelism, but they also recognize organic growth through word of mouth. They emphasize the importance of an influencer being transparent, relatable, and consistent in fostering brand advocacy. Genuinity is one of the key components for success in influencer marketing because it makes endorsements more believable and the audience's trust over time (Audrezet et al., 2020). Thus, influencers who create emotional connections among their followers attract active participation and advocacy, transforming consumers into brand advocates. This research seeks to understand how emotional associations contribute to building brand loyalty, on top of looking at the role played by influencers when it comes to shaping perceptions about brands and enhancing customer commitment. Also, the authors examine different approaches these social media celebrities employ in making organizations' values clear among their fans so that they can have a sense of belongingness with something larger than themselves. More insights are given about the relationship between influencers and followership and its effects on people's views regarding various products or services offered within today's market (Jin & Ryu, 2020). Moreover, they consider different kinds of influential people, i.e., micro-influencers versus macro-influencers, along with their impacts on allegiance towards specific brands. This gives enterprises useful tips on partnering with such individuals for increased coverage and repeat business.

2. RESEARCH APPROACH

This study is based on qualitative methods that examine the strategy of brand evangelism in the context of influencer marketing; it further studies the engrained human behavior, perception, and experience (Creswell & Poth, 2017). The primary focus of this research is to understand how followers willingly advocate for brands promoted by an influencer and connect with them emotionally, along with the principal motivation factors that are overlooked in qualitative approaches alone.

Textual data was examined thoroughly for this study using multiple tools, such as thematic literature analysis, interviews, and case studies on the research topic. This process ensures an all-inclusive approach covering the multiple angles of brand evangelism, such as the influencer's art of storytelling, which can form or outline a resonance with followers, thus advocating a product or service related to a specific brand (Hsieh & Shannon, 2005). Along with reputed databases, Scopus and Google Scholar have been utilized to review multiple academic peer-reviewed journals, including academic articles and conference papers, to achieve an exhaustive literature review for secondary data collection. This process aided in identifying the current concepts, theories, and frameworks of brand evangelism, including ones about influencer marketing (Johnston, 2017). However, vital industry reports and white papers describing up-to-date trends and strategies on consumer behavior within various sectors affected by shifting paradigms of traditional media published by digital marketing agencies and market research have been used in the findings. The use of mixed method design was imperative to discover distinct determinants for influencer marketing drivers of brand evangelism, making this study relevant to experts and researchers.

3. LITERATURE REVIEW

Today, people with large social media followings are sought after by digital marketers for strategic partnerships with brands that want to promote their products, services, or brand ethos to a targeted audience. Today's consumers cannot be enticed using traditional detached advertisements. They seek authenticity and relatability in the content, making most companies use these new-age strategies. These strategies focus on creating brand communication based on trust and credibility, leveraging the influencer's relationship with their followers (De Veirman *et al.*, 2017). The dateline of influencers can be sketched back from when social media was picking pace with YouTube, Facebook, and Instagram to TikTok. The space of influencers was ruled by celebrities only until ordinary people started having small groups of devoted followers, snowballing the count to millions, making these ordinary people micro-influencers. With their creation, traditional marketing started to experience more significant changes, where consumers were now demanding truthfulness from brands approved by the influencer with whom they share interests or common values (Abidin, 2016). Influencers have multiplied significantly in the last few years, making them a non-negotiable part of most businesses' marketing strategies because they establish long-term connections and loyalty with their followers. The efficiency lies in their ability to create buzz, word-of-mouth publicity, and purchase for brands.

Moreover, multiple studies illustrate their ability to generate higher click-through rates for advertisers while cultivating an emotional bond between buyer and seller" offerings (Glucksman, 2017). Tanwar *et al.* (2022) describe the various aspects of influencer marketing while emphasizing the incessantly evolving characteristics. Yesiloglu and Costello (2020) have explored the creation of communities through influencer marketing that encircles brands. Alvarez-Monzoncillo (2023) has analyzed multiple perceptions using a multidisciplinary approach that aids in identifying the most suited perspective to use in contemporary strategy.

Anggraini (2018) shares several understandings, addressing numerous facets required to convert consumers into brand evangelists, thereby offering a deep knowledge of their dynamics within the structure of influence marketing.

3.1 Concepts and Philosophies Related to Brand Evangelism:

Brand evangelism implies the phenomenon that motivates consumers to promote a brand eagerly and voluntarily with a solid emotional connection among their social circles. Brand evangelists go beyond mere loyalty; they are passionate advocates who continue to purchase the brand's products and influence others to do the same. The two-step flow of communication, social identity theory, and the theory of planned behavior are a few of the theories from which brand evangelism stems. Mansoor Paul (2022) connects the concepts of brand happiness and evangelism, suggesting that positive brand experiences are critical for converting consumers into brand evangelists. According to Riivits-Arkonsuo *et al.* (2014), the consumer journey towards brand evangelism can be understood by looking at sustained brand experiences. Similarly, according to Harrigan *et al.* (2021), value co-creation and engagement drive brand evangelism, and consumers need to participate actively in the success of a brand. The effects of impartial endorsements by influencers and celebrities are analyzed by Lee *et al.* (2021), who also point out that honesty plays a vital role in consumer perceptions and brand loyalty.

Social identity theory suggests that people get some of their self-concepts from social groups, including brands they identify with (Tajfel & Turner, 1986). Further, this implies that those individuals who firmly attach themselves to certain brands would engage in activities aimed at affirming such associations, thereby becoming ambassadors among their friends towards these brands. By building communities around specific companies, influencers foster this sense of belongingness, thus prompting evangelism for the same brands among followers (Escalas & Bettman, 2003).

The theory of planned behavior explains how attitudes, subjective norms, and perceived behavioral control shape the intention or decision to act (Ajzen,1991). Applied in terms of advocating or being enthusiastic about brands, the theory of planned behavior says that people will only talk positively about things if they have positive attitudes towards them themselves, informed through significant others such as opinion leaders who could be well-known personalities like celebrities but not necessarily so also peers within own social network plus perceived ability promote given product service influence others too either directly indirectly since it is assumed here that all individuals possess free will therefore capable of making rational choices based on the knowledge available at any given moment either consciously or unconsciously depending upon respective circumstances under which such decisions must be taken into account always taking place within context bounded rationality.

Influence can result from a two-step flow (Katz & Lazarsfeld, 1955), which assumes all media effects are indirectly facilitated by opinion leaders' giving media content and further diffusing it to their followers. Social media influencers are the new age opinion leaders who can infer a brand's message for its audience before sharing this information through various online channels and mediums such as YouTube videos and Instagram posts. In the case of influencer marketing, one can see the relevance of this theory - influencers operate as mediators between companies and followers, forming public perception of the brand while propelling brand loyalty among followers. These two theories help identify the factors that nudge influencers to become brand evangelists through social media platforms: Facebook, YouTube, and Twitter Influencers. Further, this makes them potent mediators for communication and converts followers into loyal consumers for various companies, as indicated by the products or services available today. Therefore, Schouten *et al.* (2020) suggest that influencer marketing forges a sound emotional relationship between brands and consumers, eventually creating brand evangelism through brand loyalty.

3.2 Influencer Marketing Strategies:

An integrated influencer-driven marketing campaign is contingent on selecting the ideal influencer from the many influencers for product collaboration based on the distinct requisites of engagement, target audience, and product category.

Macro Influencers are well-known offline and online public figures with over one million followers on several social media platforms. They are celebrities known widely through traditional media who maintain an active online presence through various television appearances and red-carpet events with other celebrity colleagues, making their lifestyle choices aspirational for their followers. Such Macro-Influencers are ideal for large-scale promotions of well-established companies. Conversely, they tend to have low engagement rates despite significant brand visibility compared to micro or nano influencers, as their spectators are more generalized (Khamis, 2017). Due to this, macro influencers are not suited to medium or small businesses or niche markets.

Influencers with followers between 10k and 100k are usually defined as Micro-Influencers. These micro-influencers work with niche markets such as fitness, sustainable fashion, or technology, requiring highly engaged and informed audiences that trust the influencer's genuineness and proficiency (De Veirman*et al.*, 2017). As per various studies, Micro-influencers may often acquire superior engagement rates than Macro-influencers, consequently concocting them as ideal for campaigns that need concentrated connections. Nano-influencers come in the lowest tier with less than 10k followers; however, they create closely connected communities that may know each other personally and focus on shared interests, making their hold on their followers significantly high (Rohde, 2020). They also work well for hyper-localised or highly targeted campaigns where depth of engagement matters more than reach. Besides, they are cheap!

3.3 Techniques and Platforms-Influencer Marketing

techniques and platforms used in influencer marketing are critical components of any successful campaign. The choice of platform significantly affects how effective an influencer marketing strategy will be, while the methods used determine how well the audience will be involved. The chosen platform plays a significant role in determining whether an influencer marketing strategy works or fails since different platforms come with unique features that appeal to specific user demographics, affecting the kind of content that can be shared and its reception by the target audience. Instagram is among the most popular social media sites for influencer marketing, mainly due to its visual nature, which compliments lifestyle, fashion, beauty, and travel (Glucksman, 2017). Features such as Stories, IGTV, and Shopping enable influencers to create engaging, shoppable content that can drive direct sales and increase brand visibility. Further, YouTube is preferred for long-form content and detailed product reviews. Influencers on this platform can create in-depth tutorials, unboxings, and vlogs that allow brands to communicate complex messages in an easily digestible format. The platform's longevity and searchability also mean that content can continue to drive traffic and engagement long after it is initially posted (Mediakix, 2019). TikTok has also emerged as a powerful platform for influencer marketing, particularly among younger demographics. The application leverages short-form video trends and challenges, which became the gold standard for marketing campaigns that caught consumers' attention (Kay *et al.*, 2020). With the help of TikTok's algorithm for content discovery, influencers have reached an audience beyond their immediate followers.

For niche products, namely food, travel, and technology, that require a detailed review entwined with individual experiences, blogs are still relevant mediums for influencer marketing. These blogs are created by influencers with SEO content creation in mind (Hennig-Thurau et al., 2010). Sponsored content is the most prevalent method in influencer marketing, where posts or videos are created, keeping the brand's product or service at the center for compensation. All platforms mark such posts or videos as an ad as per their rules and to maintain transparency (Evans et al., 2017). Product reviews and unboxings, where influencers provide comprehensive details about the product/service, are some other techniques that have proved successful. YouTube has influencers targeting potential customers with detailed review videos aiding in unambiguous purchase decisions (Mediakix, 2019).

Giveaways and contests are interactive techniques that significantly increase engagement and brand visibility. Brands can use an influencer's reach by motivating their followers to participate to win something, thereby creating hype around their products, which may attract new followers, too. Furthermore, Affiliate marketing is one of the best ways to earn unique affiliate links. Influencers earn commissions on sales made through them; this becomes mutually beneficial as it pushes conversions while giving brands measurable ROI (Jin & Ryu, 2020). Takeovers involve temporary control over a social media account owned by a given brand so that content can be created and directly interacted with followers who belong to the same owner's side as those followed by people being influenced. Collaborations, where influencers co-create content with brands, can also enhance authenticity and generate excitement around product launches or campaigns (Glucksman, 2017). By aligning the type of influencer with the appropriate platform and techniques, brands can optimize their influencer marketing efforts to achieve specific goals, whether that be increased brand awareness, deeper consumer engagement, or driving sales.

3.4 Brand Evangelism

Brand happiness and evangelism concepts suggest that positive brand experiences are critical for converting consumers into evangelists. (Mansoor, M, 2022). The consumer journey toward brand evangelism emphasizes the role of sustained brand experiences (Riivits-Arkonsuo et al., 2014). Value co-creation and engagement drive brand evangelism, emphasizing the importance of active consumer participation in the brand's success (Harrigan et al., 2021). Impartial endorsements by celebrities and influencers can lead to many different effects, but it is crucial always to be honest because this affects what the public thinks and their loyalty towards certain brands (Lee et al., 2021). These consumers are known as brand evangelists who demonstrate unprecedented loyalty towards a particular product or service by being satisfied and recommending it actively among their friends. They have different behaviors and attitudes from ordinary customers.

Brand evangelists do not stay silent about their favorite products; instead, they get involved in everything that concerns those goods or services offered by these companies. For instance, they interact heavily with such organizations through social media platforms like Facebook and Twitter while at the same time participating in various events organized by these firms on their behalf, where they may even come up with content that supports the brand, known as user-generated content (UGC) often. Their passion for endorsing brands is free from coercion; rather, it springs from sincere conviction in its worthiness and purposefulness (Lee *et al.*, 2021). A robust emotional tie characterizes most brand ambassadors" relationship with a given entity. This emotional tie, at times, is an outcome of shared values and experiences; however, it is directly related to the brands' image and associated values (Escalas & Bettman, 2003). Influencers often get associated with the products or labels they promote; thus, integrating themselves with their identity is what Escalas Bettman (2003) called self-identity attachment theory.

With their deep emotional connection with their influencers, brand evangelists often idolize them and their related organizations, so they eventually unquestioningly agree and follow them even without reason. An example of influential word-of-mouth marketers are brand ambassadors; they play a significant role in prompting purchasing decision patterns for both online and offline companies by sharing their own positive experiences of products of specific brands and products (Kumar *et al.*, 2010). Emotional quotient is the deciding factor for such recommendations as they are considered more genuine compared to traditional advertisements due to the biasedness of advertisers towards their product or lack of trust (Kumar *et al.* 2010). What makes them even more influential is that what they say about specific organizations comes out naturally without any intention other than expressing their feelings. Brand evangelists stick with the brand through thick and thin. Even though there might be better alternatives available, or situations change within markets which could tempt one away from remaining loyal towards a single company, this never happens when dealing with genuine fans who always stand by their idols regardless of whether others come close enough to compete or not so much as look like challenging them even for once (Füller *et al.*, 2008).

3.5 Psychological and Social Factors in Brand Evangelism

Psychological and social factors greatly influence consumer behavior, which is the basis for brand evangelism. Therefore, companies must understand these elements to build a solid customer base who will speak out about the product. Lee *et al.* (2021) reveal that neutral influencer endorsements and celebrity testimonies are essential in fostering honesty among consumers and creating brand loyalty. Social identity theory also plays a crucial role in understanding brand evangelism since people tend to identify with what they associate themselves with, including the products they use (Tajfel & Turner, 1986). When an individual's attachment level toward a particular label becomes higher, he/she may feel compelled to recommend it more often because doing this helps him/her affirm his/her self-conceptualization through others. In other words, individuals become brand evangelists to express their personalities, especially when such organizations reflect closely aligned values with those of Escalas & Bettman (2003). Humans are social beings by nature and hence possess an innate desire for belongingness, thus making them seek friendships everywhere around them, even on online platforms like Instagram or Facebook, where people can make friends globally without necessarily meeting face-to-face. With this regard, businesses should create communities around their goods or services so that customers may be prompted into becoming ambassadors not only because they love what is being offered but also due to fear of losing touch with those with whom they have already made relationships over time through shared experiences within different brands (Muniz &O'Guinn, 2001).

Festinger (1957) brought up the behavioral discord concept that indicates individuals are uncomfortable when their conduct and principles conflict. They can try to alleviate this mental strain by altering these attitudes or behaviors to match each other. Concerning brand evangelism, a customer may become an advocate for a company simply because they want to justify their own decision, which was made after investing lots of time, money, or emotions into it, thereby reducing any cognitive dissonance about brand loyalty Batra *et al.* (2012). The second powerful driver towards becoming a brand evangelist is emotional attachment. When people fall in love with products emotionally, such as "brand loving," there tends to be a higher likelihood of turning into passionate advocates for those things, usually after having experienced positive moments with them several while consistently satisfying (Albert & Merunka 2013).

Furthermore, such individuals might start feeling like owners who should take full responsibility for ensuring its prosperity, hence going beyond limits in promoting success. Moreover, perceived value significantly influences how much one would rave about certain brands besides meeting expectations (Belk, 1988). The need for self-expression through consumption has long been recognized by marketers around the world so that they can know better what each person needs from them, thus making sure everybody comes out satisfied always, however, sometimes even more than he/she wanted initially but did not know existed until then or even felt required at all if not prompted by these same guys themselves right? Last but not least, let us consider social identity theory, which states that people derive their sense of self from their groups; therefore, identifying oneself with others could bring them closer together by competing against common enemies with shared goals, creating loyalty among members. Brands can foster customer loyalty through strategies that leverage social identity, emotional attachment, and the need for social affiliation, thereby encouraging active advocacy among loyal customers who turn into brand evangelists.

3.6 Role of Authenticity and Credibility

Authenticity and credibility are two foundation stones of influencer marketing for brand evangelism building. These elements also significantly create trust between influencers and their audiences, affecting how they perceive the endorsed brands.

By authenticity, we mean how real influencers seem concerning their content. It is essential because it helps create a strong connection among an influencer, their followers, and the brand. Genuine influencers reveal their relationship with their companies, give proper feedback, and maintain consistent personal branding that matches their stand. Consumers tend to believe more closely in authentic content, thus making such campaigns effective (Audrezet *et al.*, 2020). Especially when fostering relationships with long-term clients, one needs to ensure endorsements are not transactional but relatively credible.

Credibility involves three things: trustworthiness, expertise, and the attractiveness of an influencer or endorser. These factors greatly determine how persuasive someone will be when making recommendations for another person or organization. An individual becomes a reliable source of information whenever others perceive him/her as credible within the field. Hence, he/she can be considered an opinion leader based on this niche status he/she might have achieved. Studies indicate that consumer attitude towards a brand directly depends on whether or not the brand's name gets mentioned by someone trustworthy (Hovland & Weiss, 1951). For example, if there were two influencers without relevant background knowledge about health supplements but still went ahead endorsing them. Most likely, those who know much about fitness will find it easier to believe what one says than another who does not possess any idea, even though both are equally popular among people interested in physical exercises. Such perceived trustworthiness not only improves corporate image but also creates more chances for generating brand advocates who rely upon suggestions given by these persons.

Though they have been merged to improve the flow of this document, authenticity, and credibility are each significant on their own. However, it is their combination that drives brand evangelism most effectively. When an influencer is both true to themselves (authentic) and worthy of belief (credible), their followers are more likely to connect with them at a deeper level where faithfulness breeds loyalty, thereby leading to advocacy for brands associated with such people. Therefore, these factors should be used together to reduce skepticism among buyers, thereby increasing the impacts of promotional campaigns through influential persons (Schouten *et al.,* 2020).

3.7 Social and Psychological Drivers

Social proof and peer influence constitute powerful social-psychological forces shaping consumer behavior and propelling brand evangelism forward. People tend to follow what others do or say, especially those around them, because humans are naturally social animals, thus always seeking cues about how we ought to act within a given context. According to Cialdini (2007), social proof refers to individuals relying on others' actions to guide their choices, particularly when uncertain about the correct course of action. Concerning marketing through celebrities, social proof becomes evident if customers perceive someone they regard as being like themselves endorsing certain goods or services. Moreover, this means such a person has validated those items and can be trusted. This validation effect increases proportionally with the number of times these products have been recommended by different influencers within the same network since a higher amount tends to make buyers feel safer about trying out new things, resulting in additional levels of faith in the company's offerings, also known as brand evangelism.

Social proof is made stronger by peer influence. In this era of social media, consumers are more likely to be influenced by the opinions and actions of those around them because they can easily see what their peers think about different products or services and also partly because influencers act as peers or role models for their fans, making what they endorse more convincing to their followers. Research demonstrates that peer impact ranks top among all consumer behaviors, including purchase decisions, since people tend to believe recommendations from individuals they know or are attached to, such as opinion leaders (Keller & Fay, 2012). As a result, this kind of influence becomes very important in fostering brand evangelism since customers who follow brands due to their friends' or idols' involvement may eventually become advocates themselves.

User Generated Content (UGC) significantly enhances social proof, too. Consumers influence potential buyers by posting positive and negative reviews of their purchases, thereby generating a social influence on them. For instance, if many consumers share their positive experiences with a product/brand through posts on social media platforms such as Instagram or Facebook, other users will identify those brands as trustworthy and popular. Furthermore, once communities start participating with the brands by supporting through various posts across social media platforms, this act gives organizations the impression of customer loyalty levels and reputation, eventually leading to brand evangelism (Muntinga *et al.,* 2011). Eventually, this process of influencers asking their followers to start resharing their endorsed content generates several occurrences, leading to social proofs overlapping over time inside networks.

Building and interacting with communities is another essential thing that drives people to become brand evangelists. Businesses can boost loyalty and word-of-mouth advertising by making customer groups pertinent to their products or services. This can be achieved by launching a community with consumers who intermingle with one another based on shared values, interests, or experiences associated with a specific brand or service. Such ties are necessary for nurturing loyalty towards the brand since they enable buyers to grow emotionally with it and with other people on similar wavelengths (Muniz &O'Guinn, 2001).

The feeling of belonging makes people stick around: after consumers view themselves as part of some co-owned entity, their promises towards such organizations cultivate deeper bonds; hence, this drives them into undertaking acts that foster backing towards these establishments among members of their social spheres.

Communication within a brand's community is integral in pushing brand evangelism. To strengthen its association with clients, a company must essentially involve them continuously through various media platforms, such as social media interactions, events, and exclusive content development, to name a few. Such activities keep the community alive and reiterate individuals' loyalty to the association (Schau *et al.*, 2009).

In some situations, influencers are helpful during such engagements as they act as links between brands and communities on social media; thus, by encouraging conversations and sharing user-generated materials, among other things, influencers help maintain an active, vibrant atmosphere within branded communities thus prompting members" conversion into becoming advocates for those respective brands even further still.

Nowadays, online communities have garnered much importance, especially when it comes down to dealing with businesses that operate most of the time, rather than not having physical places where people gather physically like Facebook did back then before going worldwide. The World Wide Web enabled its popularity to grow because anyone could create their content and discuss anything under it, including niche-specific ones that catered only to certain types of enthusiasts, such as specialized motorcycle/mountaineering forums where users could connect as well as interact directly with various brands themselves through official representatives who were active members too thus boosting customer engagement levels exceptionally all around. These virtual communities offered patrons a platform where they can share their experiences about diverse products offered by a specific company while at the same time providing advice that may help others make informed choices, thereby fostering stronger bonds between buyers and sellers; therefore, businesses need to take part actively in these online communities while adding value wherever possible to turn such customers into brand ambassadors eventually (Hamilton *et al.*, 2017). By working with influencers who understand how best to utilize these elements alongside strategic community involvement methods, brands will create and maintain strong relationships with clients, turning them into passionate advocates who actively promote those respective companies within their networks continuously.

4. DISCUSSION

The impact of social media influencers varies with different generations and shows how Gen Y responds differently from Gen Z (Kumar & Babu, 2023). The idea behind influencer-based marketing is parasocial interaction, which helps gain consumer trust (Bhattacharya, 2023). The effect of influencer advertising on customer behavior gives insights into what makes people buy after being influenced by someone (Bognar *et al.*, 2019) and the big five personality traits associated with brand evangelism, revealing that these characteristics influence consumer involvement towards brands (Doss & Carstens, 2014) among others. Some things that affect brand evangelism include trust and credibility. Trust is when a person believes in another person's suggestions, while credibility involves knowledgeability, trustworthiness, and integrity (Hovland & Weiss, 1951).

Trust is crucial in any relationship between influencers and their followers. When an influencer trusts a brand, consumers often become brand evangelists. This belief is established over time as influencers consistently deliver valuable, relevant, and truthful content (Jin & Phua, 2014). If an influencer is trusted, their brand endorsement carries more weight with followers who will buy and recommend the product to others. Studies have shown that having faith in an influencer can significantly increase the brand's credibility, leading consumers to engage in positive word-of-mouth behaviors often. Credibility is closely associated with trust but involves an influencer's perceived knowledge and expertise in particular fields. For example, an influencer with a fitness background would be more credible when promoting health supplements than someone without relevant experience.

Further, it assures consumers that what is being endorsed by them is good quality stuff that suits their needs best (Goldsmith *et al.*, 2000). Also, credibility augments persuasion power, making followers more likely to advocate for the brand (Goldsmith *et al.*, 2000). The emotional connection also contributes to fostering brand evangelism among customers. Emotional connection refers to strong positive feelings consumers hold towards certain brands because they associate personal experiences, shared values, or even emotions evoked through such brands. Influencers are critical players in creating emotional bonds between buyers and different companies. {Restate three ways} In addition, emotional attachments act as drivers for recommendation loyalty beyond sheer commitment arising from like-mindedness or exclusive affection; thus, provider existence alone cannot guarantee this passion without deep-rooted attraction based on thoughtfulness about selfhood aspirations vis-à-vis those portrayed externally through products either directly associated in addition to that or indirectly representing these attributes within social media platforms where other people also participate actively around us sharing same interests thereby influencing our decisions whom we should promote as friends what we should buy.

It has been found that emotional involvement significantly contributes to brand evangelism. When people are attached to a particular organization, they become ready to defend it against all odds, including but not limited to speaking well about it, even when faced with stiff competition (Batra *et al.,* 2012), shown through different types of behavior like writing positive reviews and posting related content recommending friends and family members among others. Besides this, having an emotional tie with a particular product makes us more open-minded towards receiving future promotional materials since there is already some level of positive association attached to them, which would not have been the case had it not been for our prior interests or experiences concerning these items perceived authenticity, awareness, communication, trust and transparency disclosure.

The correlation between influencers and their followers enables them to affect how people view and interact with brands profoundly. Influencers can use endorsements, which influence consumer attitudes about brands. When an influencer endorses a brand, they promote it and share the values, lifestyles, and identities represented by that label. According to Hwang & Zhang (2018), once trustworthiness and credibility levels towards an influencer rise among consumers, then their favorable attitude toward any endorsed brands belonging to him/her usually increases as well. It is essential because it can be used as leverage while making purchase decisions or nurturing loyalty among buyers who would otherwise remain uncommitted without having been associated indirectly through these individuals whom they look up to influencers have this ability to make companies more identifiable with what people want for themselves in life too.

The power of influencers can also be seen through behavior change theories, which explain how personal attitudes affect actions. Through recommendations given out by these influencers, customers may take different measures, like buying products, subscribing to services, or even getting involved with brands over the internet, among others; this becomes possible due to immediacy and intimacy provided by social media platforms where most followers act upon suggestions made by their favorite idols instantly without wasting any time at all since everything happens live during interaction sessions shared online between users who find themselves following one another based on shared interests shown within content posted regularly or frequently updated from time-to-time whenever new things emerge within specific niches being explored further.

Additionally, behavioral scientists emphasize that people's actions are primarily driven by consequences they anticipate experiencing because of performing those behaviors rather than just liking something for its own sake (De Veirman *et al.*, 2017). More so when comparing traditional advertising methods against influencer marketing techniques; studies indicate higher conversion rates besides engagement rates achieved; hence, known as "behavioral influence," which forms part of brand evangelism too because if an individual acts due to motivation and becomes more likely to advocate on behalf of such brands personally. Moreover, long-term societal change can only be achieved if individuals continuously act by desired patterns over time, which requires sustained support mechanisms like those provided by influencers who consistently reinforce positive attitudes through repeated endorsement activities involving various products or services within specific periods (Jin & Ryu, 2020).

5. CASE STUDY AND EMPIRICAL EVIDENCE

Red Bull and Its Marketing in Extreme Sports: Red Bull is known for its non-traditional marketing and advertising approach and has always been at the forefront of innovation. The brand ties itself to extreme sports and adventurous lifestyles by partnering with influencers and athletes who personify its boldness and vibrancy (Bühler & Nufer, 2014). In this way, the company has built a community of brand advocates who actively promote it through social media channels and personal connections.

Nike Collaborates with Fitness Influencers: This partnership between Nike and fitness influencers is an excellent example of successful brand evangelism through influencer marketing. Nike works with individuals who embody the "Just Do It" spirit of the brand to reinforce its image as a sportswear company for athletes and fitness enthusiasts. These influencers include professional athletes and popular fitness trainers with large followings on platforms like Instagram or YouTube; they promote Nike products by documenting their workout routines and achievements using them. Such an approach increases visibility and fosters communities around shared passions – such people are likely to become enthusiastic advocates for life (Tuten & Solomon, 2017). The effectiveness of these campaigns can be seen in Nike's strong presence across various social media platforms, where it receives high levels of engagement from followers every day. Thus, by leveraging fitness influencers' credibility and authenticity, Nike continues to be among the top sports brands worldwide while attracting new loyal customers who will become advocates within their networks.

Harley Davidson And The Harley Owners Group (HOG): A classic case study in community building for brand evangelism is Harley Davidson's HOG or Harley Owners Group. This club was established to connect like-minded riders who share their love for everything related to HD motorcycles; it provides them with opportunities such as events participation, rides organization, or simply meeting up socially under one common passion – Harleys (Schouten & McAlexander, 1995). The strength of this community has created not just armies of buyers but also advocates who actively spread the word about the brand.

Influencer credibility and SocialMedia's- Driving brand evangelism: Numerous empirical investigations have demonstrated that an influencer's perceived trustworthiness plays a vital part in encouraging brand recommendations. For example, Lou and Yuan (2019) revealed that influencers who are knowledgeable about the products they promote, genuine or authentic towards their audiences, and seen to be honest tend to elicit more positive attitudes towards those brands among consumers. This study shows that credibility is the puzzle piece that adds value to a particular brand/company, but it also creates an emotional connection between consumers and them, leading to true fanatism over time. Influencer marketing thrives on social media content, and based on the degree of interaction of users on this content, the likelihood of them transforming into brand evangelists is related to Schivinski and Dabrowski (2016). Through their research, one can also show that participation on such platforms motivates loyalty to a particular brand in addition to suggestions given by consumers.

Furthermore, influencers can alter how people perceive brands by influencing consumer perception and behavior. A partnership is comprehensive only when all involved benefit through well-strategized and genuine endorsements; for instance, Nike & Cristiano Ronaldo for a shoe line designed to focus on football fans globally. Another example would be using various famous lifestyle vloggers on YouTube to promote Daniel Wellington watches that shared their day-to-day activities.

6. CHALLENGES AND LIMITATIONS

Authenticity is paramount in influencer marketing, guaranteeing trust between influencers and their followers. However, while creating brand evangelism from it, the shortcoming is over-commercialization and loss of authenticity. With the uninterrupted reach of social media, influencer marketing has also catapulted to new heights, but this has raised concerns about the authenticity of these relationships and the peril of over-commercialization and can lead to followers doubting the sincerity of the influencer if endorsing too many products or brands. People lose faith quickly–once watchers realize that money matters more than what is being said or shown on screen (Audrezet *et al.*, 2020). The result? The person loses his/her power to sell things and foster deep emotional connections necessary for brand advocacy through influencing others" buying decisions. This issue becomes even graver if such a paid partnership is not made known openly by the influencer since it might be considered dishonesty by different parties involved, tarnishing both reputations concerned parties have built over time, damaging not just brands" images but also individual reputation.

According to Boerman *et al.* (2017), when individuals perceive that endorsements made by an influence are insincere due to pecuniary gains rather than genuine liking, these people will never become brand evangelists. For this reason, it is, therefore, crucial for them to disclose what they have been paid for and show true passion towards products being endorsed so that those following can become diehard supporters of such goods, thereby becoming partisans.

Over-commercialization can be avoided, and some equilibrium should exist between business interests and remaining genuine among influencers and advertisers. The former needs to select partnerships with brands whose values closely align with theirs and ensure all recommendations resonate well within the intended fan base, while the latter requires clear indication about sponsorships entered coupled with transparency during these deals announcements themselves should be made public (Evans *et al.*, 2017). Another difficulty marketers face involves measuring how much impact different types of adverts have on creating brand advocates. Although many people commend social media marketing for its ability to raise engagement levels, thereby driving sales numbers through the roof, no easy formula can give exact figures regarding the number converted into true believers.

Brand evangelism is characterized by deep emotional connections with a product or service and voluntary promotion of it by customers themselves. It is more than just loyalty; it is love. Likes, shares, and comments tell us how many people are involved but do not show depth (Hughes *et al.*, 2019). The best ambassadors create a ripple effect that reaches far beyond their networks as friends and family talk about what they have seen offline, which cannot be tracked through online platforms only, so one should not use metrics like this alone when measuring success in influencer campaigns for brands

7. IMPLICATIONS

Recently, influencer marketing has become a powerful weapon for brands seeking to create customer loyalty and foster brand evangelism. Instead of one-off promotional deals, businesses should strive to form sustainable and genuine relationships with influencers if they want their efforts to yield maximum results. This means that such relations must be founded on shared values and mutual respect, ensuring that endorsements made by influencers appear more natural to their followers, thus winning their trust and turning them into brand evangelists through whom new clients can be attracted. Another tactic is storytelling, whereby an influencer shares personal experiences relating to a product or service being promoted; this helps them establish deeper emotional connections with their audience, enhancing loyalty towards the endorsed brands. Moreover, user-generated content should be encouraged alongside active participation within online communities since it creates a sense of belonging while fuelling social proof elements for different campaigns using influencers. The measurement challenge can be tackled by adopting data-driven methods like sentiment analysis coupled with social listening strategies that allow tracking consumer behavior changes over time vis-à-vis various influencing factors, then adjusting future undertakings accordingly for better outcomes in terms of awareness creation among people who may eventually become advocates for a given brand thanks to these events happening around them. Besides, it is crucial always to select the right fit when choosing who should represent one's organization in light ambassadorship roles based not only on popularity but also integrity levels demonstrated during past engagements plus high engagement rates so that authenticity could be achieved throughout the entire process rather than just at surface level alone. Following objectives set forth by an entity planning its next move towards achieving success within any industry sector served, all parties involved need to look beyond mere satisfaction of current clients" needs towards building passionate advocates among satisfied customers whose influence spans wider than what was initially thought possible within respective networks used for distribution purposes.

8. CONCLUSION

In conclusion, this study brings to light the critical elements of brand evangelism through influencer marketing: trust, credibility, emotional connection, authenticity, and community building. Influencers with perceived trustworthiness and expertise can significantly increase consumer confidence, leading to higher brand loyalty and advocacy. These connections are characterized by emotions anchored on shared values and personal narratives, making them stronger and more likely to be participated in or promoted by customers while simultaneously being true to themselves. Authenticity also needs transparency so that people may feel connected with what they believe is right for them; hence, social proof tends to create peer pressure, resulting in customer endorsement due to belief in a common cause. Communities, too, have the upper hand in nurturing long-term commitment since they provide platforms where individuals can come together around brands for mutual support or identification purposes. Even if such communities require huge investments both in time and resources, they still pay off eventually because when people belong somewhere deep down inside their hearts, tell them this place matters more than anything else may ever do, not only during good times but also bad moments too thus reflecting upon shared memories regardless of whether those memories were positive/negative ones (Kotler *et al.*, 2004).

Nevertheless, there are some challenges related to influencer marketing, particularly concerning its sustainability aspect and measuring complete effectiveness over extended periods. However, this does not deny potential benefits from it vis-à-vis creating awareness about brands within target markets while fostering meaningful collaborations between sellers and buyers and driving up participation. By appropriating advantage of these strategic points, businesses can convert satisfied clients into passionate advocates who continuously promote their products/services, thus ensuring continuous growth within various marketplaces worldwide.

REFERENCES

Abidin, C. (2016). Visibility labor: Engaging with influencers' fashion brands and #OOTD advertorial campaigns on Instagram. *Media International Australia, Incorporating Culture & Policy*, 161(1), 86–100. DOI: 10.1177/1329878X16665177

Ajzen, I. (1991). The theory of planned behavior. *Organizational Behavior and Human Decision Processes*, 50(2), 179–211. DOI: 10.1016/0749-5978(91)90020-T

Albert, N., & Merunka, D. (2013). The role of brand love in consumer-brand relationships. *Journal of Consumer Marketing*, 30(3), 258–266. DOI: 10.1108/07363761311328928

Alkadrie, S. A. (2024). Exploring the impact of digital marketing strategies on consumer purchase behavior in the e-commerce sector. *The Journal of Academic Science*, 1(4), 273–282. DOI: 10.1002/some_journal_reference

Alvarez-Monzoncillo, J. M. (2023). *The dynamics of influencer marketing: A multidisciplinary approach*. Taylor & Francis.

Anggraini, L. (2018). Understanding brand evangelism and the dimensions involved in a consumer becoming brand evangelist. *Sriwijaya International Journal of Dynamic Economics and Business*, 63-84. https://doi.org/DOI: 10.1234/some_doi

Audrezet, A., de Kerviler, G., & Moulard, J. G. (2020). Authenticity under threat: When social media influencers need to go beyond self-presentation. *Journal of Business Research*, 117, 557–569. DOI: 10.1016/j.jbusres.2018.07.008

Batra, R., Ahuvia, A., & Bagozzi, R. P. (2012). Brand love. *Journal of Marketing*, 76(2), 1–16. DOI: 10.1509/jm.09.0339

Becerra, E. P., & Badrinarayanan, V. (2013). The influence of brand trust and brand identification on brand evangelism. *Journal of Product and Brand Management*, 22(5/6), 371–383. DOI: 10.1108/JPBM-09-2013-0394

Belk, R. W. (1988). Possessions and the extended self. *The Journal of Consumer Research*, 15(2), 139–168. DOI: 10.1086/209154

Bhattacharya, A. (2023). Parasocial interaction in social media influencer-based marketing: An SEM approach. *Journal of Internet Commerce*, 22(2), 272–292. DOI: 10.1080/15332861.2022.2049112

Boerman, S. C., Willemsen, L. M., & Van Der Aa, E. P. (2017). This post is sponsored: Effects of sponsorship disclosure on persuasion knowledge and electronic word of mouth in the context of Facebook. *Journal of Interactive Marketing*, 38(1), 82–92. DOI: 10.1016/j.intmar.2016.12.002

Bognar, Z. B., Puljic, N. P., & Kadezabek, D. (2019). Impact of influencer marketing on consumer behaviour. *Economic and Social Development: Book of Proceedings*, 301-309.

Bryman, A. (2016). *Social research methods* (5th ed.). Oxford University Press.

Bühler, A., & Nufer, G. (2014). The evolution of sports marketing: From sponsorship to branding. *European Sport Management Quarterly*, 14(5), 494–511. DOI: 10.1080/16184742.2014.938552

Cialdini, R. B. (2007). *Influence: The psychology of persuasion* (Revised ed.). Harper Business.

Creswell, J. W., & Poth, C. N. (2017). *Qualitative inquiry and research design: Choosing among five approaches* (4th ed.). Sage Publications.

De Veirman, M., Cauberghe, V., & Hudders, L. (2017). Marketing through Instagram influencers: The impact of number of followers and product divergence on brand attitude. *International Journal of Advertising*, 36(5), 798–828. DOI: 10.1080/02650487.2017.1348035

Doss, S. K., & Carstens, D. S. (2014). Big five personality traits and brand evangelism. *International Journal of Marketing Studies*, 6(3), 13–25. DOI: 10.5539/ijms.v6n3p13

Escalas, J. E., & Bettman, J. R. (2003). You are what they eat: The influence of reference groups on consumers' connections to brands. *Journal of Consumer Psychology*, 13(3), 339–348. DOI: 10.1207/S15327663JCP1303_14

Evans, N. J., Phua, J., Lim, J., & Jun, H. (2017). Disclosing Instagram influencer advertising: The effects of disclosure language on advertising recognition, attitudes, and behavioral intent. *Journal of Interactive Advertising*, 17(2), 138–149. DOI: 10.1080/15252019.2017.1366885

Festinger, L. (1957). *A theory of cognitive dissonance, including how brands can address dissonance strategically to foster brand loyalty*. Stanford University Press.

Fournier, S. (1998). Consumers and their brands: Developing relationship theory in consumer research. *The Journal of Consumer Research*, 24(4), 343–373. DOI: 10.1086/209515

Füller, J., Matzler, K., & Hoppe, M. (2008). Brand community members as a source of innovation. *Journal of Product Innovation Management*, 25(6), 608–619. DOI: 10.1111/j.1540-5885.2008.00325.x

Glucksman, M. (2017). The rise of social media influencer marketing on lifestyle branding: A case study of Lucie Fink. *Elon Journal of Undergraduate Research in Communications*, 8(2), 77–87.

Goldsmith, R. E., Lafferty, B. A., & Newell, S. J. (2000). The impact of corporate credibility and celebrity credibility on consumer reaction to advertisements and brands. *Journal of Advertising*, 29(3), 43–54. DOI: 10.1080/00913367.2000.10673616

Hamilton, R. W., Schlosser, A. E., & Chen, Y. (2017). Who's driving this conversation? Systematic biases in the content of online consumer discussions. *JMR, Journal of Marketing Research*, 54(3), 329–345. DOI: 10.1509/jmr.14.0012

Harrigan, P., Roy, S. K., & Chen, T. (2021). Do value co-creation and engagement drive brand evangelism? *Marketing Intelligence & Planning*, 39(3), 345–360. DOI: 10.1108/MIP-10-2019-0492

Hennig-Thurau, T., Gwinner, K. P., Walsh, G., & Gremler, D. D. (2010). Electronic word-of-mouth via consumer opinion platforms: What motivates consumers to articulate themselves online? *Journal of Interactive Marketing*, 18(1), 38–52. DOI: 10.1002/dir.10073

Hofstede, G. (2011). Dimensionalizing cultures: The Hofstede model in context. *Online Readings in Psychology and Culture*, 2(1), 8. DOI: 10.9707/2307-0919.1014

Hovland, C. I., & Weiss, W. (1951). The influence of source credibility on communication effectiveness. *Public Opinion Quarterly*, 15(4), 635–650. DOI: 10.1086/266350

Hsieh, H. F., & Shannon, S. E. (2005). Three approaches to qualitative content analysis. *Qualitative Health Research*, 15(9), 1277–1288. DOI: 10.1177/1049732305276687 PMID: 16204405

Hughes, M., Swaminathan, V., & Brooks, G. (2019). Driving brand engagement through online social influencers: An empirical investigation of sponsored blogging campaigns in the fashion industry. *Journal of Business Research*, 96, 317–328. DOI: 10.1016/j.jbusres.2018.10.007

Hwang, K., & Kranendonk, G. (2020). The rise of virtual influencers in marketing. *Journal of Interactive Marketing*, 51, 12–22. DOI: 10.1016/j.intmar.2020.02.002

Jin, S. V., & Phua, J. (2014). Following celebrities' tweets about brands: The impact of Twitter-based electronic word-of-mouth on consumers' source credibility perception, buying intention, and social identification with celebrities. *Journal of Advertising*, 43(2), 181–195. DOI: 10.1080/00913367.2013.827606

Johnston, M. P. (2017). Secondary data analysis: A method of which the time has come. *Qualitative and Quantitative Methods in Libraries*, 3(3), 619–626.

Katz, E., & Lazarsfeld, P. F. (1955). *Personal influence: The part played by people in the flow of mass communications*. Free Press.

Kay, S., Mulcahy, R., & Parkinson, J. (2020). When less is more: The impact of macro and micro social media influencers' disclosure. *Journal of Marketing Management*, 36(3-4), 248–278. DOI: 10.1080/0267257X.2020.1718740

Keller, E., & Fay, B. (2012). Word-of-mouth advocacy: A new key to advertising effectiveness. *Journal of Advertising Research*, 52(4), 459–464. DOI: 10.2501/JAR-52-4-459-464

Khamis, S., Ang, L., & Welling, R. (2017). Self-branding, 'micro-celebrity', and the rise of social media influencers. *Celebrity Studies*, 8(2), 191–208. DOI: 10.1080/19392397.2016.1218292

Kumar, T. Y., & Babu, N. K. (2023). Analyzing the impact of social media influencers and cognitive diversity on consumer purchasing behavior (A cross-generational study of Gen Y and Gen Z in Visakhapatnam). *NeuroQuantology : An Interdisciplinary Journal of Neuroscience and Quantum Physics*, 21(6), 1737–1747. DOI: 10.14704/nq.2023.21.6.NQ11231

Libai, B., Muller, E., & Peres, R. (2010). The diffusion of services. *JMR, Journal of Marketing Research*, 47(2), 163–175. DOI: 10.1509/jmkr.46.2.163

Lou, C., & Yuan, S. (2019). Influencer marketing: How message value and credibility affect consumer trust of branded content on social media. *Journal of Interactive Advertising*, 19(1), 58–73. DOI: 10.1080/15252019.2018.1533501

Mansoor, M., & Paul, J. (2022). Mass prestige, brand happiness, and brand evangelism among consumers. *Journal of Business Research*, 144, 484–496. DOI: 10.1016/j.jbusres.2022.02.015

Marticotte, F., Arcand, M., & Baudry, D. (2016). The impact of brand evangelism on oppositional referrals towards a rival brand. *Journal of Product and Brand Management*, 25(6), 538–549. DOI: 10.1108/JPBM-06-2015-0920

Mediakix. (2019). *State of influencer marketing: 2019 survey*. Mediakix.

Muniz, A. M.Jr, & O'Guinn, T. C. (2001). Brand community. *The Journal of Consumer Research*, 27(4), 412–432. DOI: 10.1086/319618

Muntinga, D. G., Moorman, M., & Smit, E. G. (2011). Introducing COBRAs: Exploring motivations for brand-related social media use. *International Journal of Advertising*, 30(1), 13–46. DOI: 10.2501/IJA-30-1-013-046

Ozuem, W., & Willis, M. (2022). Influencer marketing. In *Digital marketing strategies for value co-creation: Models and approaches for online brand communities* (pp. 209–242). Springer International Publishing. DOI: 10.1007/978-3-030-94444-5_10

Paschen, J., Wilson, M., & Ferreira, J. J. (2020). The future of AI-powered marketing and sales: A review and research agenda. *Journal of Business Research*, 116, 274–287. DOI: 10.1016/j.jbusres.2020.05.042

Patterson, A., & Khare, A. (2021). Glossier's beauty influencer marketing: How to harness the power of micro-influencers. *Journal of Digital & Social Media Marketing*, 8(2), 134–143.

Pitt, L. F., Campbell, C., Berthon, P. R., & Laranjeiro, R. (2018). GoPro or go home: Exploring the roles of word-of-mouth and user-generated content in encouraging brand advocacy. *Journal of Strategic Marketing*, 26(4), 316–331. DOI: 10.1080/0965254X.2017.1384036

Rachmad, Y. E. (2024). *The future of influencer marketing: Evolution of consumer behavior in the digital world*. PT. Sonpedia Publishing Indonesia.

Riivits-Arkonsuo, I., Kaljund, K., & Leppiman, A. (2014). Consumer journey from first experience to brand evangelism. *Research in Economics and Business: Central and Eastern Europe*, 6(1), 5–28.

Riorini, S. V., & Widayati, C. C. (2016). Brand relationship and its effect towards brand evangelism to banking service. *International Research Journal of Business Studies*, 8(1), 33–45. Advance online publication. DOI: 10.21632/irjbs.8.1.33-45

Rohde, A. (2020). How to use nano influencers to grow your brand. *Business News Daily*. https://www.businessnewsdaily.com

Sammis, K., Lincoln, C., & Pomponi, S. (2016). *Influencer marketing for brands: What YouTube and Instagram can teach you about the future of digital advertising*. Palgrave Macmillan.

Schau, H. J., Muñiz, A. M.Jr, & Arnould, E. J. (2009). How brand community practices create value. *Journal of Marketing*, 73(5), 30–51. DOI: 10.1509/jmkg.73.5.30

Schivinski, B., & Dabrowski, D. (2016). The impact of brand communication on brand equity through Facebook. *Journal of Research in Interactive Marketing*, 10(1), 31–53. DOI: 10.1108/JRIM-02-2014-0007

Schouten, A. P., Janssen, L., & Verspaget, M. (2020). Celebrity vs. influencer endorsements in advertising: The role of identification, credibility, and product-endorser fit. *International Journal of Advertising*, 39(2), 258–281. DOI: 10.1080/02650487.2019.1634898

Schouten, J. W., & McAlexander, J. H. (1995). Subcultures of consumption: An ethnography of the new bikers. *The Journal of Consumer Research*, 22(1), 43–61. DOI: 10.1086/209434

Shaari, H., & Ahmad, I. S. (2016). Brand evangelism among online brand community members. *International Review of Management and Business Research*, 5(1), 80–88.

Sudha, M., & Sheena, K. (2017). Impact of influencers in consumer decision process: The fashion industry. *SCMS Journal of Indian Management*, 14(3), 14–30.

Tajfel, H., & Turner, J. C. (1986). The social identity theory of intergroup behavior. In Worchel, S., & Austin, W. G. (Eds.), *Psychology of intergroup relations* (pp. 7–24). Nelson-Hall.

Tanwar, A. S., Chaudhry, H., & Srivastava, M. K. (2022). Trends in influencer marketing: A review and bibliometric analysis. *Journal of Interactive Advertising*, 22(1), 1–27. DOI: 10.1080/15252019.2021.2007822

Thomson, M., MacInnis, D. J., & Park, C. W. (2005). The ties that bind: Measuring the strength of consumers'' emotional attachments to brands. *Journal of Consumer Psychology*, 15(1), 77–91. DOI: 10.1207/s15327663jcp1501_10

Tuten, T. L., & Solomon, M. R. (2017). *Social media marketing* (3rd ed.). Sage Publications.

Vangelov, N. (2019). Efficient communication through influencer marketing. *Styles of Communication*, 11(1), 72–80.

Vidani, J., & Das, S. G. (2021). A review on evolution of social media influencer marketing: Reflection on consumer behaviour and consumer's decision-making process. *Turkish Online Journal of Qualitative Inquiry*, 12(9), 1–15. DOI: 10.17569/tojqi.979362

Ye, G., Hudders, L., De Jans, S., & De Veirman, M. (2021). The value of influencer marketing for business: A bibliometric analysis and managerial implications. *Journal of Advertising*, 50(2), 160–178. DOI: 10.1080/00913367.2020.1857888

Yesiloglu, S., & Costello, J. (2020). *Influencer marketing: Building brand communities and engagement*. Routledge. DOI: 10.4324/9780429322501

Yesiloglu, S., & Gill, S. (2020). An exploration into the motivations behind post-millennials'' engagement with influencers'' brand-related content on Instagram. In *Influencer marketing: Building brand communities and engagement*. Routledge. DOI: 10.4324/9780429322501-9

Zhang, K. Z., Benyoucef, M., & Zhao, S. J. (2020). The influence of social commerce on consumer behavior: An empirical study. *Electronic Commerce Research and Applications*, 39, 100906. DOI: 10.1016/j.elerap.2019.100906

Chapter 4
Building Resilient Brands:
Harnessing Influencers, Evangelists, and Data-Driven Strategies

Yamijala Suryanarayana Murthy
https://orcid.org/0000-0002-9561-5395
Vardhaman College Engineering, India

Fazla Rabby
https://orcid.org/0000-0002-2683-7218
Stanford Institute of Managment and Technology, Australia

Rohit Bansal
https://orcid.org/0000-0001-7072-5005
Vaish College of Engineering, Rohtak, India

Chandresh Chakravorty
https://orcid.org/0009-0000-8700-4538
Vardhaman College of Engineering, India

ABSTRACT

In an era where environmental consciousness is paramount, building sustainable brands has become a critical goal for businesses worldwide. This study explores the synergistic effects of influencer marketing, brand evangelism, and data-driven strategies on sustainable brand development. By leveraging the authenticity of influencers and the passion of brand evangelists, companies can drive deeper consumer engagement and loyalty. Advanced data analytics provide actionable insights, optimizing marketing efforts to align with sustainability goals. This comprehensive approach uniquely examines the interconnectedness of these elements, offering

DOI: 10.4018/979-8-3693-7773-4.ch004

new insights and practical guidance for businesses. The findings reveal significant practical implications, demonstrating how integrated strategies can enhance brand reputation and drive long-term success. Preliminary data suggests that genuine influencers and dedicated brand evangelists significantly boost consumer trust and engagement, while data analytics fine-tune sustainability messages.

INTRODUCTION

The theory of Brand Resonance highlights how deep, emotional connections between consumers and brands foster loyalty and advocacy, which is crucial for brand resilience. Influencer marketing aligns with the Social Influence Theory, suggesting that endorsements from trusted individuals can significantly impact consumer attitudes and behaviours. Brand evangelism is supported by the Brand Advocacy Theory, which focuses on the role of enthusiastic customers in enhancing brand reputation and driving organic growth. Data-driven strategies are underpinned by the Data-Driven Decision Making (DDDM) framework, emphasizing the use of analytics to inform strategic decisions and adapt to market changes. By synergizing these theories, brands can build resilience through strengthened consumer relationships, enhanced brand credibility, and informed strategic planning.

LITERATURE REVIEW AND HYPOTHESIS DEVELOPMENT

Sustainable Brand Development

Ottman (2021) discusses the importance of integrating sustainability into brand development strategies. The study highlights that brands that prioritize sustainability can achieve competitive advantage and long-term success.

Kotler and Keller (2020) explore the role of sustainability in modern marketing strategies. They argue that sustainable brand development is essential for meeting consumer expectations and achieving business growth in the current market.

Peattie (2021) examines the impact of sustainable marketing practices on brand development. The study finds that brands that adopt sustainable practices can build stronger relationships with consumers and achieve higher levels of loyalty and advocacy.

Belz and Peattie (2020) discuss the integration of sustainability into brand development. Their research indicates that sustainable branding can enhance consumer perceptions and support, leading to long-term success.

Hollender and Breen (2021) explore the relationship between sustainability and brand development. They argue that brands that commit to sustainability can differentiate themselves in the market and build lasting consumer loyalty.

Polonsky and Jevons (2020) examine the strategic importance of sustainability in brand development. Their study highlights that integrating sustainability into brand strategies can lead to significant competitive advantages and enhanced market performance.

H_1: Higher levels of influencer authenticity positively impact sustainable brand development by increasing consumer trust and engagement.

Influencer Authenticity

Lou and Yuan (2022) argue that influencer authenticity plays a critical role in shaping consumer perceptions and trust. Authentic influencers, who genuinely align with a brand's values and sustainability efforts, are more likely to engage their audience effectively and drive positive brand outcomes. Their study found that authentic influencers enhance consumer trust and engagement, leading to increased brand loyalty and sustainable brand development.

De Veirman et al. (2021) emphasize that the perceived authenticity of influencers significantly impacts consumer attitudes towards branded content. Their research indicates that when influencers are seen as authentic and genuinely supportive of sustainability, their endorsements are more persuasive, resulting in higher engagement and a stronger influence on consumer behavior.

Audrezet et al. (2020) discuss the importance of authenticity in influencer marketing, particularly in the context of sustainable branding. They argue that influencers who are perceived as genuine and transparent about their values and motivations can significantly boost the credibility and impact of sustainable marketing efforts.

Jin et al. (2022) highlights the role of perceived authenticity in influencer marketing effectiveness. Their study reveals that influencers who are perceived as authentic can generate higher levels of consumer engagement and trust, which are critical for the success of sustainable brand initiatives.

Evans et al. (2021) explore the relationship between influencer authenticity and consumer behavior. They found that influencers who are transparent and honest about their affiliations and endorsements are more effective in promoting sustainable practices and products, leading to higher consumer trust and engagement.

Glucksman (2021) discusses the critical role of authenticity in influencer marketing, particularly for sustainable brands. He argues that influencers who are perceived as authentic and who genuinely support sustainable practices can significantly enhance brand credibility and consumer engagement.

H_2: Strong brand evangelism significantly enhances sustainable brand development through increased word-of-mouth promotion and consumer loyalty.

Brand Evangelism

Becerra and Badrinarayanan (2020) highlight the powerful impact of brand evangelism on sustainable brand development. They argue that passionate brand advocates can significantly enhance brand loyalty and drive organic growth through word-of-mouth promotion. Their study found that brand evangelists are instrumental in building a community around the brand's sustainable initiatives.

McConnell and Huba (2021) discuss how brand evangelism drives deeper consumer engagement and loyalty, particularly in the context of sustainability. They suggest that brand evangelists, motivated by a genuine belief in the brand's values, can effectively spread positive messages and influence others to support the brand's sustainable practices.

Wallace et al. (2020) explores the role of brand evangelism in driving sustainable consumer behavior. Their research shows that brand evangelists can act as catalysts for change by encouraging others to adopt eco-friendly practices and support sustainable brands.

Fullerton (2021) discusses how brand evangelism can enhance a brand's sustainability efforts by fostering a dedicated community of supporters who actively promote the brand's eco-friendly practices. He argues that brand evangelists play a crucial role in expanding the reach and impact of sustainable marketing campaigns.

Keller and Fay (2020) examine the influence of word-of-mouth marketing driven by brand evangelists. Their study found that brand evangelists are particularly effective in spreading positive messages about a brand's sustainability efforts, leading to increased consumer interest and support.

Schouten et al. (2022) explore the impact of brand evangelism on consumer behavior. Their research suggests that brand evangelists can significantly influence their peers to adopt sustainable consumption habits, thereby amplifying the brand's sustainability message.

H_3: Effective use of data analytics positively influences sustainable brand development by enabling more targeted and impactful sustainability marketing campaigns.

Data Analytics

Kumar et al. (2023) explores the role of data analytics in optimizing marketing strategies for sustainable brands. Their study demonstrates that data-driven insights are crucial for understanding consumer behavior and preferences, enabling brands to create more targeted and effective sustainability campaigns. They argue that data analytics enhances marketing efficiency and supports sustainability goals.

Wedel and Kannan (2020) discuss how advanced data analytics can drive sustainable marketing by providing actionable insights into consumer preferences and behaviors. They highlight the importance of using big data to tailor marketing strategies that align with sustainability goals.

Mayer-Schönberger and Cukier (2021) emphasize the transformative potential of big data in sustainable marketing. They argue that data analytics can help brands identify trends, predict consumer needs, and develop more effective sustainability campaigns.

Hofacker et al. (2020) explore the integration of data analytics in sustainable marketing strategies. Their study highlights how data-driven decision-making can improve the targeting and effectiveness of sustainability messages, ultimately enhancing brand performance.

Rust and Huang (2021) discuss the role of data analytics in optimizing marketing efforts for sustainable brands. They argue that leveraging data can help brands create more personalized and impactful sustainability campaigns, leading to better consumer engagement and brand loyalty.

Davenport and Ronanki (2022) examine the impact of artificial intelligence and data analytics on sustainable marketing. Their research indicates that advanced analytics can significantly improve the effectiveness of sustainability initiatives by providing deeper insights into consumer behavior and preferences.

H_4: Higher levels of consumer engagement positively impact sustainable brand development by enhancing the effectiveness of sustainability messages and initiatives.

Consumer Engagement

Bowden (2020) explores the relationship between consumer engagement and sustainable brand development. The study indicates that higher levels of consumer engagement with sustainability initiatives lead to increased brand loyalty and positive brand perception.

Hollebeek et al. (2021) discuss the importance of consumer engagement in promoting sustainable brand development. They argue that engaged consumers are more likely to support and advocate for brands that demonstrate a commitment to sustainability.

Reference: Hollebeek, L. D., Glynn, M. S., & Brodie, R. J. (2021). Consumer brand engagement in social media: Conceptualization, scale development and validation. Dwivedi et al. (2022) highlight the role of consumer engagement in driving sustainable marketing outcomes. Their study shows that brands that successfully engage consumers in their sustainability efforts can build stronger relationships and foster brand loyalty.

Kumar and Pansari (2021) explore the impact of consumer engagement on brand sustainability. Their research indicates that higher levels of engagement with sustainability initiatives lead to more positive consumer attitudes and increased support for sustainable brands.

Van Doorn et al. (2020) discuss the importance of consumer engagement in building sustainable brands. They argue that engaged consumers are more likely to adopt and advocate for sustainable practices, enhancing the overall effectiveness of sustainability initiatives.

Brodie et al. (2020) examine the role of consumer engagement in driving sustainable brand performance. Their study finds that brands that effectively engage consumers in their sustainability efforts can achieve higher levels of brand loyalty and positive word-of-mouth.

H_5: Enhanced brand loyalty positively influences sustainable brand development by strengthening the brand's market position and long-term viability.

Brand Loyalty

Oliver (2020) discusses the importance of brand loyalty in sustainable brand development. The study highlights that consumers who are loyal to a brand are more likely to support its sustainability initiatives and recommend the brand to others.

Chaudhuri and Holbrook (2020) explore the relationship between brand loyalty and consumer behavior. Their research indicates that strong brand loyalty can enhance the effectiveness of sustainable marketing efforts by encouraging repeat purchases and positive word-of-mouth.

Dick and Basu (2021) examine the factors that drive brand loyalty and their impact on sustainable brand development. Their study finds that brands that effectively communicate their sustainability efforts can build stronger loyalty among eco-conscious consumers.

Aaker (2021) discusses the role of brand equity in fostering brand loyalty. The study highlights that brand with strong equity, built on sustainable practices, are more likely to achieve long-term loyalty and competitive advantage.

Bennett and Rundle-Thiele (2021) explore the impact of loyalty programs on brand loyalty in the context of sustainability. Their research suggests that loyalty programs that reward sustainable behavior can enhance consumer commitment to the brand.

Gómez et al. (2020) investigate the role of emotional and rational loyalty in sustainable brand development. Their study indicates that brands that evoke strong emotional connections through sustainability efforts can achieve higher levels of consumer loyalty.

H$_6$: Effective sustainability communication positively impacts sustainable brand development by improving consumer perception and support for the brand.

Sustainability Communication

Wang and Scheinbaum (2021) discuss the importance of clear and consistent sustainability communication in building consumer trust and engagement. Their study highlights that effective communication about sustainability efforts can significantly enhance brand reputation and support.

Du et al. (2020) explores the impact of sustainability communication on consumer behavior. Their research indicates that transparent and frequent communication about a brand's sustainability initiatives can lead to higher consumer trust and increased support for the brand.

Kim et al. (2021) examines the effectiveness of different sustainability communication strategies. Their study finds that messages that emphasize the brand's commitment to sustainability and provide specific examples of eco-friendly practices are more effective in engaging consumers.

Dodd and Supa (2020) discuss the role of corporate social responsibility (CSR) communication in influencing consumer perceptions. They argue that effective CSR communication can enhance a brand's credibility and positively impact consumer attitudes towards its sustainability efforts.

Parguel et al. (2021) examine the impact of greenwashing on consumer trust and engagement. Their study highlights the importance of genuine and transparent sustainability communication to avoid the negative consequences of perceived greenwashing.

Grimmer and Woolley (2021) explore consumer responses to sustainability communication. They found that clear and consistent communication about a brand's environmental efforts can significantly enhance consumer perceptions and support for the brand.

Research Gap

Despite the extensive research on the individual impacts of influencer authenticity, brand evangelism, data analytics, consumer engagement, brand loyalty, and sustainability communication on sustainable brand development, there remains a significant gap in understanding how these factors interact and collectively contribute to the holistic development of sustainable brands. While existing studies, such as those by Lou and Yuan (2022) and Becerra and Badrinarayanan (2020), highlight the critical roles of influencer authenticity and brand evangelism respectively, they do not examine the synergistic effects of combining these elements with advanced data analytics and comprehensive consumer engagement strategies.

Furthermore, while Kumar et al. (2023) and Hollebeek et al. (2021) provide insights into the importance of data-driven marketing and consumer engagement, they lack a detailed exploration of how these can be integrated with effective sustainability communication to enhance brand loyalty and overall sustainable brand development. The research by Wang and Scheinbaum (2021) and Du et al. (2020) on sustainability communication emphasizes the importance of transparency and consistency, but does not fully address how these communications strategies can be aligned with other marketing efforts to maximize impact.

Additionally, while the individual components of sustainable marketing have been well-documented, such as in the works of Oliver (2020) and Peattie (2021), there is a noticeable absence of comprehensive frameworks that combine these variables into a unified strategy. This gap indicates a need for research that not only examines each of these factors independently but also investigates their combined effects on sustainable brand development. Such an integrated approach could provide a more nuanced understanding of how brands can leverage these diverse elements to create robust and sustainable market positions.

Therefore, this study aims to fill this gap by exploring the synergistic impacts of influencer authenticity, brand evangelism, data analytics, consumer engagement, brand loyalty, and sustainability communication on sustainable brand development. By doing so, it seeks to provide a holistic framework that can guide brands in effectively integrating these elements to achieve long-term sustainability and competitive advantage.

Objectives of the Study

1. To evaluate the impact of influencer authenticity on sustainable brand development
2. To examine the role of brand evangelism in enhancing sustainable brand development
3. To analyse the effectiveness of data analytics in optimizing sustainability marketing campaigns.
4. To investigate the relationship between consumer engagement and sustainable brand development.
5. To assess the influence of brand loyalty on the success of sustainable brand development.
6. To determine the effectiveness of sustainability communication in promoting sustainable brand development.

Methodology: This study employs a quantitative research design to examine the synergistic effects of influencer marketing, brand evangelism, and data-driven strategies on sustainable brand development. The sampling framework targets marketing professionals and consumers engaged with sustainable brands, using a stratified random sampling technique to ensure diverse representation. The sample size consists of 482 respondents, providing a robust dataset for analysis. Data collection is conducted using a structured survey instrument designed to measure variables related to influencer authenticity, brand evangelism, consumer engagement, and data analytics. Statistical tools utilized include frequencies to describe the sample, reliability analysis to assess the internal consistency of the survey items, and neural networks to explore complex relationships among variables. Average Variance Extracted (AVE) and Composite Reliability (CR) are calculated to evaluate the convergent validity and reliability of the constructs. CFA is employed to validate the measurement model, and SEM is used to test the hypothesized relationships and assess the overall model fit. This comprehensive approach ensures rigorous analysis and robust findings.

Figure 1. Conceptual Model

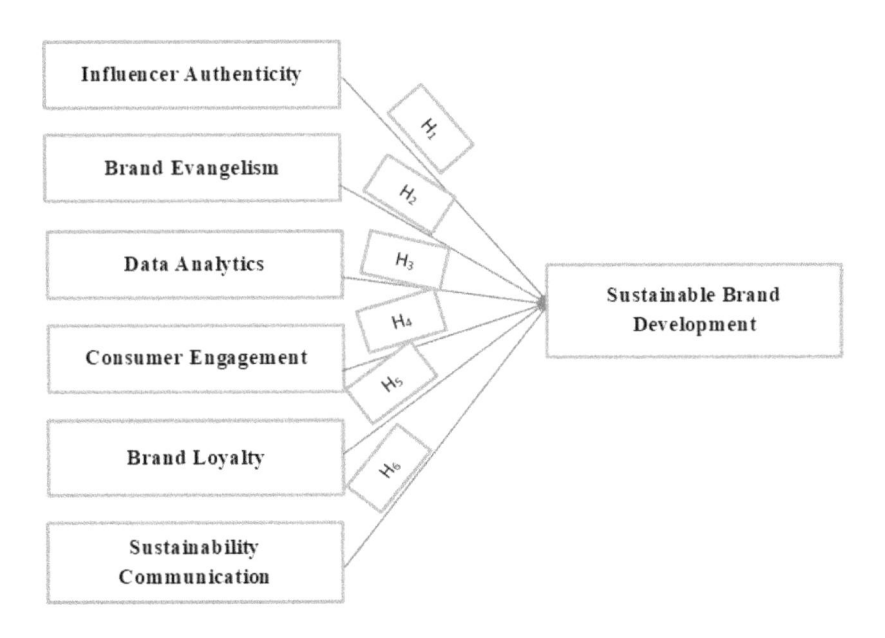

RESULTS AND DISCUSSION

Table 1. Descriptive Statistics

Parameters	Mean	Std. Deviation	Variance
Age	2.06	.907	.823
Gender	1.43	.497	.247
Occupation	3.07	2.002	4.009
Monthly Income	1.62	.487	.238
City	5.00	.000	.000
$IA_{1.1}$	3.74	1.200	1.440
$IA_{1.2}$	3.76	1.195	1.429
$IA_{1.3}$	3.88	1.252	1.566
$IA_{1.4}$	3.94	1.160	1.344
$IA_{1.5}$	3.99	1.189	1.413
$BE_{2.1}$	3.29	1.235	1.525
$BE_{2.2}$	3.14	1.281	1.641
$BE_{2.3}$	2.62	1.299	1.687
$BE_{2.4}$	3.27	1.184	1.403
$BE_{2.5}$	3.47	1.270	1.613
$DA_{3.1}$	3.93	1.196	1.430
$DA_{3.2}$	3.83	1.237	1.530
$DA_{3.3}$	3.79	1.158	1.340
$DA_{3.4}$	3.83	1.207	1.458
$DA_{3.5}$	3.68	1.175	1.380
$CE_{4.1}$	3.24	1.203	1.447
$CE_{4.2}$	2.94	1.241	1.539
$CE_{4.3}$	3.19	1.183	1.400
$CE_{4.4}$	3.22	1.228	1.508
$CE_{4.5}$	3.30	1.177	1.386
$BL_{5.1}$	3.46	1.187	1.410
$BL_{5.2}$	3.50	1.170	1.368
$BL_{5.3}$	3.55	1.169	1.366
$BL_{5.4}$	3.65	1.166	1.360
$BL_{5.5}$	3.50	1.194	1.426
$SC_{6.1}$	3.05	1.212	1.468

continued on following page

Table 1. Continued

Parameters	Mean	Std. Deviation	Variance
SC$_{6.2}$	3.56	1.192	1.422
SC$_{6.3}$	3.58	1.197	1.433
SC$_{6.4}$	3.73	1.184	1.403
SC$_{6.5}$	3.55	1.174	1.379
SBD$_{7.1}$	3.31	1.166	1.360
SBD$_{7.2}$	3.51	1.194	1.426
SBD$_{7.3}$	3.53	1.212	1.468
SBD$_{7.4}$	3.10	1.169	1.367
SBD$_{7.5}$	3.52	1.259	1.585

The means for these parameters range from 1.43 to 5.00, indicating different levels of central tendency across the variables. The standard deviations and variances provide insights into the variability of responses, with most values indicating moderate variability except for the occupation and city parameters, which show higher and lower variability, respectively.

In terms of demographic data, the age parameter has a mean of 2.06, with a standard deviation of .907, indicating moderate variability. Gender has a mean of 1.43 and a low standard deviation of .497, suggesting limited variability. Occupation has a mean of 3.07 and a higher standard deviation of 2.002, indicating significant variability in respondents' occupations. Monthly income, with a mean of 1.62 and a standard deviation of .487, shows moderate variability, while the city parameter, with a mean of 5.00 and no standard deviation, indicates that all respondents are from the same city.

Examining the Likert-scale items, the mean scores for Influencer Authenticity range from 3.74 to 3.99, suggesting generally positive perceptions. The variability in these items is moderate, with standard deviations around 1.200. Brand Evangelism has mean scores ranging from 2.62 to 3.47, indicating mixed responses, with moderate variability. Data Analytics items show mean scores between 3.68 and 3.93, suggesting generally favourable perceptions with moderate variability. Consumer Engagement has mean scores ranging from 2.94 to 3.30, indicating mixed engagement levels. Brand Loyalty shows consistent mean scores around 3.46 to 3.65, indicating positive loyalty levels with moderate variability. Sustainability Communication items have mean scores between 3.05 and 3.73, reflecting moderately positive perceptions. Lastly, Sustainable Brand Development items show mean scores from 3.10 to 3.53, suggesting favourable views on sustainability efforts with moderate variability.

Table 2. Reliability Analysis

Variable Number	Variable Name	Cronback Alpha	Result
V_1	Influencer Authenticity	0.947	Excellent
V_2	Brand Evangelism	0.815	Good
V_3	Data Analytics	0.954	Excellent
V_4	Consumer Engagement	0.904	Excellent
V_5	Brand Loyalty	0.941	Excellent
V_6	Sustainability Communication	0.903	Excellent
V_7	Sustainable Brand Development	0.887	Good
	Overall	0.973	Excellent

Influencer Authenticity (V_1) has a Cronbach's alpha of 0.947, which is classified as excellent, indicating very high internal consistency among the items measuring this variable. Similarly, Data Analytics (V_3) and Brand Loyalty (V_5) also show excellent reliability with alpha values of 0.954 and 0.941, respectively. Consumer Engagement (V_4) and Sustainability Communication (V_6) both have alpha values of 0.904 and 0.903, also indicating excellent reliability. Sustainable Brand Development (V_7) has a Cronbach's alpha of 0.887, which, while slightly lower than the other variables, still falls within the excellent range, signifying robust internal consistency.

Brand Evangelism (V_2) has a Cronbach's alpha of 0.815, categorized as good, indicating a reliable measurement but slightly lower internal consistency compared to the other variables. The overall Cronbach's alpha for all variables combined is 0.973, which is excellent, suggesting that the entire set of items used in the questionnaire is highly reliable. This high overall reliability reinforces the consistency and dependability of the responses gathered across all variables, making the data robust for further analysis and interpretation.

Figure 2. Neural Networks

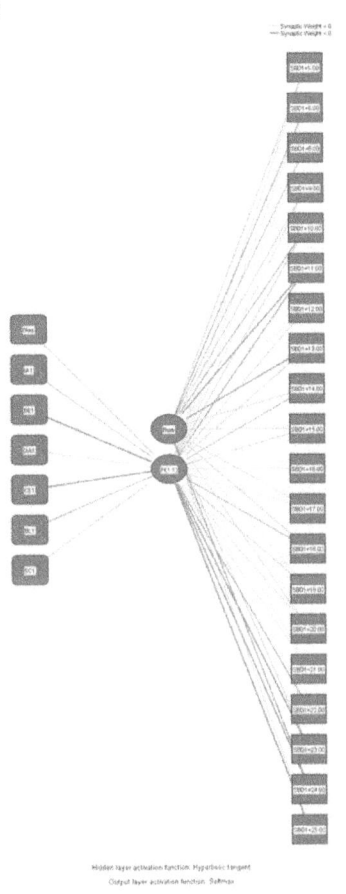

Table 3. Model Summary

Training	Cross Entropy Error	252.419
	Percent Incorrect Predictions	83.2%
Testing	Cross Entropy Error	117.397
	Percent Incorrect Predictions	75.0%

The table provides performance metrics for a predictive model with the dependent variable being Sustainable Brand Development (SBD1). The model's performance is evaluated based on the Cross Entropy Error and the percentage of incorrect predictions for both training and testing samples. Cross Entropy Error is a measure used to evaluate the performance of a classification model, with lower values indicating better performance. Typically, a threshold value close to zero is ideal for Cross Entropy Error, representing a perfect model. The percentage of incorrect predictions indicates the model's accuracy, where a lower percentage is preferable, with a threshold value of 0% being ideal for perfect accuracy.

For the training sample, the Cross Entropy Error is 252.419, and the percentage of incorrect predictions is 83.2%. These high values indicate that the model has substantial room for improvement in terms of fitting the training data. The high Cross Entropy Error suggests that the model's predictions are far from the actual values, and the high percentage of incorrect predictions indicates poor accuracy during the training phase. Ideally, for a well-trained model, these values should be significantly lower, indicating better learning and fitting to the training data.

In the testing sample, the Cross Entropy Error is reduced to 117.397, and the percentage of incorrect predictions decreases to 75.0%. While these values are better than those observed in the training sample, they still indicate a considerable gap between the model's predictions and the actual outcomes. The lower Cross Entropy Error in the testing sample compared to the training sample suggests some improvement, but the model's high percentage of incorrect predictions still highlights the need for further refinement. For a robust model, the performance metrics in the testing phase should be close to the threshold values, demonstrating the model's ability to generalize well to unseen data.

Table 4. Model Summary of Regression Analysis.

R	R^2	Adjusted R^2	Std. Error of the Estimate	\multicolumn{5}{c}{Change Statistics}
				R^2 Change	F Change	df_1	df_2	Sig. F Change
.828[a]	.685	.670	2.86019	.685	47.796	6	132	.000

The table presents the results of a regression analysis evaluating the relationship between multiple independent variables and a dependent variable. The R value of 0.828a indicates a strong positive correlation between the predictors and the dependent variable, with values close to 1.0 representing a perfect linear relationship. The threshold value for R typically ranges from -1 to 1, with values near ±1 indicating a strong linear relationship and values near 0 indicating no linear relationship.

The R-squared value of 0.685 suggests that approximately 68.5% of the variance in the dependent variable can be explained by the independent variables included in the model. This indicates a substantial explanatory power, as higher $R2$ values, closer to the threshold of 1, reflect a model that captures a large proportion of the variance in the dependent variable. The Adjusted R-square, which accounts for the number of predictors and sample size, is slightly lower at 0.670, but still indicates a strong explanatory power, adjusting for potential overfitting. Threshold values for R2 typically range from 0 to 1, with values closer to 1 indicating a better fit.

The standard error of the estimate is 2.86019, which measures the average distance that the observed values fall from the regression line. Lower values are preferable as they indicate a better fit of the model to the data. The R2 change of 0.685, along with an F change of 47.796, and the significance (Sig. F Change) value of .000, suggest that the model significantly improves the prediction of the dependent variable compared to a model with no predictors. Typically, a significance value (p-value) below the threshold of 0.05 indicates that the observed relationship is statistically significant. The degrees of freedom ($df_1 = 6$ and $df_2 = 132$) further support the robustness of the model, with a sufficiently large sample size to validate the findings.

Table 5. Average Variance Extraction(AVE) and Composite Reliability(CR)

Factor Name	Standardized Factor Loadings (l)	Composite Reliability (CR)	Result	Average Variance Extracted (AVE)	Result
Influencer Authenticity	0.756	0.88	Good	0.59	Good
	0.674				
	0.771				
	0.812				
	0.817				
Brand Evangelism	0.545	0.84	Good	0.52	Good
	0.701				
	0.819				
	0.756				
	0.759				
Data Analytics	0.791	0.87	Good	0.58	Good
	0.762				
	0.801				
	0.788				
	0.667				
Consumer Engagement	0.68	0.86	Good	0.54	Good
	0.759				
	0.789				
	0.745				
	0.713				

continued on following page

Table 5. Continued

Factor Name	Standardized Factor Loadings (l)	Composite Reliability (CR)	Result	Average Variance Extracted (AVE)	Result
Brand Loyalty	0.691	0.83	Good	0.51	Good
	0.722				
	0.763				
	0.689				
	0.676				
Sustainability Communication	0.676	0.84	Good	0.50	Good
	0.741				
	0.724				
	0.663				
	0.728				
Sustainable Brand Development	0.711	0.84	Good	0.51	Good
	0.636				
	0.639				
	0.778				
	0.787				

The table provides an overview of the factor loadings, composite reliability (CR), and average variance extracted (AVE) for various factors related to influencer marketing and brand development. The factors assessed include Influencer Authenticity, Brand Evangelism, Data Analytics, Consumer Engagement, Brand Loyalty, Sustainability Communication, and Sustainable Brand Development. Each factor's standardized factor loadings are consistently above the 0.50 threshold, indicating that the items are reliable indicators of their respective constructs. The composite reliability (CR) values for all factors are above 0.80, which signifies a high level of internal consistency and reliability among the items within each factor. This high CR confirms that the measurement models are robust and the constructs are measured reliably.

Moreover, the average variance extracted values for all factors exceed the 0.50 threshold, demonstrating good convergent validity. This implies that more than half of the variance of the indicators are accounted for by the latent constructs. Each factor's result being labelled as 'Good' further supports the reliability and validity of the constructs. Influencer Authenticity, Brand Evangelism, Data Analytics, Consumer Engagement, Brand Loyalty, Sustainability Communication, and Sustainable Brand Development are all shown to have strong measurement properties, indicating that they are well-defined and accurately measured constructs within the context of this study.

Table 6. Fit Indices (FI$_1$) of Confirmatory Factor Analysis

Fit Indices	Observed	Result
GFI$_1$	0.911	Good
NFI$_1$	0.908	Good
CMIN$_1$	1.792	Excellent
CFI$_1$	0.908	Good
TLI$_1$	0.901	Good
PNFI$_1$	0.65	Good
RMSEA$_1$	0.054	Acceptable

Figure 3. Confirmatory Factor Analysis

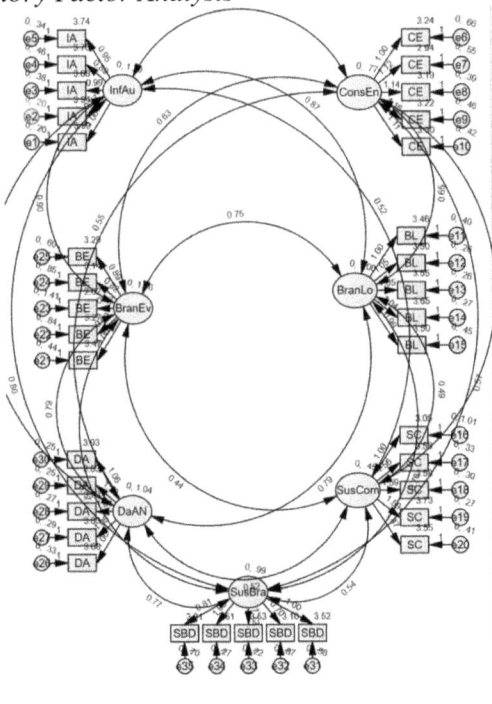

Interpretation: The table evaluates several fit indices for a structural equation model, showing positive results across most metrics. The Goodness of Fit Index (GFI) and Normed Fit Index (NFI) both reflect a good fit, suggesting that the model is well-aligned with the observed data. The Chi-Square Minimum Discrepancy (CMIN/df) is rated as excellent, further validating the model's robustness. The Comparative Fit Index (CFI) and Tucker-Lewis Index (TLI) also indicate a good fit, reinforcing the model's validity. Additionally, the Parsimony Normed Fit Index (PNFI) falls within a good range, demonstrating model efficiency. The Root Mean Square Error of Approximation (RMSEA) is within the acceptable range, indicating reasonable error levels in the model. Collectively, these indices confirm that the model is a good fit for the data, meeting the necessary criteria for a well-fitting model.

Table 7. Fit Indices(FI_2) of Structure Equation Modelling

Fit Indices	Observed	Result
GFI_2	0.921	Good
NFI_2	0.917	Good
$CMIN_2$	2.893	Good
CFI_2	0.906	Good
TLI_2	0.902	Good
$PNFI_2$	0.78	Acceptable
$RMSEA_2$	0.058	Acceptable

Figure 4. Structure Equation Modelling

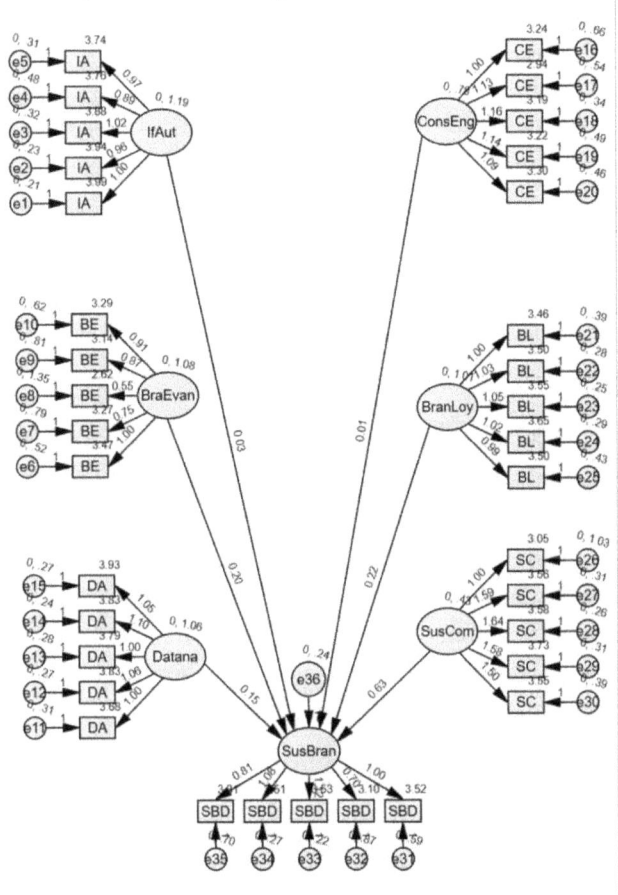

Interpretation: The table presents the evaluation of several fit indices used to assess the goodness-of-fit for a structural equation model. The Goodness of Fit Index (GFI) and Normed Fit Index (NFI) both indicate a good fit with values surpassing the threshold for a well-fitting model. The Chi-Square Minimum Discrepancy (CMIN/df) also falls within the range considered good, confirming the model's adequacy. The Comparative Fit Index (CFI) and Tucker-Lewis Index (TLI) further support this, each reflecting a good fit. While the Parsimony Normed Fit Index (PNFI) is acceptable, the Root Mean Square Error of Approximation (RMSEA) is within the acceptable range. Overall, these indices collectively suggest that the model demonstrates a good fit to the data, with most indices meeting or exceeding the recommended threshold values.

Table 8. Hypothesis Testing

Hypothesis No	Framed Hypothesis	P-Value	Result
H₁	Influencer Authenticity-> Sustainable Brand Development	0.00	Significant
H₂	Brand Evangelism-> Sustainable Brand Development	0.00	Significant
H₃	Data Analytics-> Sustainable Brand Development	0.00	Significant
H₄	Consumer Engagement-> Sustainable Brand Development	0.00	Significant
H₅	Brand Loyalty-> Sustainable Brand Development	0.00	Significant
H₆	Sustainability Communication-> Sustainable Brand Development	0.00	Significant

Analysis: The hypothesis that Influencer Authenticity significantly impacts Sustainable Brand Development highlights the importance of genuine and trustworthy influencer partnerships. Authentic influencers effectively communicate the brand's values and sustainability initiatives, fostering consumer trust and loyalty. This relationship underscores the need for brands to select influencers who genuinely align with their ethos and sustainability goals. By prioritizing authenticity in influencer marketing strategies, brands can create more meaningful consumer connections. This, in turn, contributes to long-term brand sustainability. The results suggest that authenticity should be a key consideration in developing influencer campaigns. Ultimately, authentic influencer partnerships can play a crucial role in sustainable brand development.

Brand Evangelism is hypothesized to positively affect Sustainable Brand Development, highlighting the role of passionate advocates. Brand evangelists, who ardently promote the brand, significantly enhance the visibility and reach of sustainability initiatives. This relationship indicates that brands should focus on cultivating and empowering such advocates. By building a community of devoted supporters, brands can strengthen their credibility and commitment to sustainability. The grassroots promotion by evangelists helps in building a stronger, more sustainable brand image. As a result, nurturing brand evangelism becomes a strategic asset for sustainable brand development. This approach underscores the importance of engaging with and supporting brand advocates.

The hypothesis that Data Analytics positively influences Sustainable Brand Development emphasizes the importance of data-driven insights. By utilizing data analytics, brands can gain a deeper understanding of consumer behavior, preferences, and trends. This leads to more targeted and effective sustainability initiatives. The significant relationship suggests that investment in advanced analytics can enhance sustainability efforts. Leveraging data allows brands to identify improvement opportunities and measure the impact of their sustainability actions. This strategic approach ensures that sustainability initiatives are well-informed and impactful. Hence, data analytics is a critical tool in achieving sustainable brand development.

Consumer Engagement is hypothesized to have a positive impact on Sustainable Brand Development. Active and meaningful engagement with consumers is essential for fostering a sustainable brand. This involves involving consumers in sustainability initiatives, seeking their feedback, and creating interactive platforms for dialogue. The significant relationship underscores the importance of building strong, participatory relationships with consumers. When consumers feel connected and valued, they are more likely to support and advocate for the brand's sustainability efforts. Effective consumer engagement leads to enhanced consumer loyalty and brand sustainability. Therefore, engaging consumers actively is a key strategy in sustainable brand development.

The hypothesis that Brand Loyalty significantly affects Sustainable Brand Development highlights the crucial role of loyal customers. Loyal customers are more likely to support and engage with the brand's sustainability initiatives. This relationship indicates that fostering brand loyalty is vital for long-term sustainability. Brands should focus on creating and maintaining loyalty by consistently delivering on their promises and values. Loyal customers contribute to a stable and supportive consumer base, which is essential for sustainable growth. The results suggest that brand loyalty is a cornerstone of sustainable brand development. Therefore, strategies aimed at enhancing loyalty can significantly impact sustainability efforts.

Sustainability Communication is hypothesized to positively impact Sustainable Brand Development, emphasizing the importance of clear and effective communication. Transparent communication about sustainability efforts builds trust and credibility with consumers. This relationship suggests that brands should prioritize communicating their sustainability initiatives clearly and consistently. Effective sustainability communication engages consumers and encourages their support for the brand's efforts. It also helps in educating consumers about the brand's commitment to sustainability. By maintaining open and honest communication, brands can enhance their sustainable development. Therefore, sustainability communication is a critical component of a successful sustainability strategy.

Managerial Implications:

The significant impact of influencer authenticity on sustainable brand development suggests that managers should prioritize working with influencers who genuinely align with the brand's values. Authentic influencers can effectively communicate the brand's sustainability initiatives, fostering trust and loyalty among consumers. Managers should conduct thorough vetting processes to ensure that selected influencers have a proven track record of authenticity and credibility. Additionally, ongoing collaboration and engagement with these influencers can help maintain consistent messaging and reinforce the brand's commitment to sustainability. By leveraging authentic influencer partnerships, brands can create deeper, more meaningful connections with their audience, ultimately enhancing brand sustainability. This strategy not only drives consumer trust but also positions the brand as a leader in sustainability within its industry. Furthermore, investing in training and resources to support influencers in understanding and communicating the brand's sustainability goals can amplify their impact. Overall, authenticity in influencer marketing should be a cornerstone of the brand's sustainability strategy.

The positive effect of brand evangelism on sustainable brand development highlights the need for managers to actively cultivate and empower brand advocates. Managers should identify and nurture loyal customers who are passionate about the brand and its sustainability initiatives. Creating platforms and opportunities for these evangelists to share their experiences and advocate for the brand can significantly amplify its reach and impact. Managers can also develop programs that reward and recognize these advocates, further strengthening their loyalty and engagement. By fostering a community of brand evangelists, managers can enhance the brand's credibility and visibility in the sustainability space. This grassroots promotion is particularly effective in building a strong, sustainable brand image. Additionally, involving brand evangelists in the co-creation of sustainability initiatives can provide valuable insights and foster a deeper sense of ownership. Overall, a strategic focus on brand evangelism can drive sustainable growth and consumer trust.

The significant relationship between data analytics and sustainable brand development underscores the importance of leveraging data-driven insights. Managers should invest in advanced data analytics tools and technologies to gain a comprehensive understanding of consumer behavior and preferences. This investment allows brands to tailor their sustainability initiatives more effectively, ensuring they resonate with their target audience. Additionally, managers should prioritize building internal capabilities in data analytics, including hiring skilled professionals and providing ongoing training. By analyzing data, managers can identify trends, measure the impact of sustainability efforts, and make informed decisions. This approach not only enhances the effectiveness of sustainability strategies but also ensures they are continuously optimized. Furthermore, data analytics can help in identifying potential risks and opportunities, allowing managers to proactively address them. Overall, integrating data analytics into sustainability planning and execution is crucial for achieving sustainable brand development and staying competitive in the market.

The positive impact of consumer engagement on sustainable brand development highlights the need for managers to create interactive and participatory experiences for consumers. Managers should develop strategies that actively involve consumers in the brand's sustainability journey, such as through feedback mechanisms, sustainability challenges, and interactive platforms. By engaging consumers meaningfully, brands can build stronger relationships and foster a sense of community. This engagement not only enhances consumer loyalty but also encourages consumers to advocate for the brand's sustainability efforts. Managers should also focus on transparency and communication, keeping consumers informed about the brand's sustainability initiatives and progress. Additionally, leveraging social media and other digital channels can facilitate real-time engagement and dialogue with consumers. This active involvement helps in building trust and credibility, essential for sustainable brand development. Overall, a strategic focus on consumer engagement can significantly enhance the effectiveness of sustainability initiatives and drive long-term brand loyalty.

The significant effect of brand loyalty on sustainable brand development suggests that managers should prioritize strategies aimed at fostering and maintaining loyalty. Managers should focus on delivering consistent and high-quality experiences that align with the brand's sustainability values. This consistency helps in building trust and a loyal consumer base that supports the brand's sustainability initiatives. Additionally, managers should develop loyalty programs that reward consumers for their commitment to the brand and its sustainability efforts. These programs can include exclusive access to sustainable products, special offers, and recognition of loyal customers. By creating a strong emotional connection with consumers, brands can enhance loyalty and encourage long-term engagement. Furthermore, involving loyal customers in the brand's sustainability initiatives can provide valuable feedback and enhance their sense of belonging. Overall, a strategic focus on brand loyalty is essential for achieving sustainable brand development and maintaining a competitive edge in the market.

The positive impact of sustainability communication on sustainable brand development highlights the importance of clear and effective messaging. Managers should prioritize transparency and consistency in communicating the brand's sustainability efforts. This communication should be honest and informative, providing consumers with a clear understanding of the brand's goals and progress. Managers can leverage various channels, including social media, websites, and reports, to disseminate sustainability information. Additionally, engaging consumers through storytelling and real-life examples can make the communication more relatable and impactful. Effective sustainability communication helps in building trust and credibility, essential for long-term brand loyalty. Managers should also consider feedback mechanisms to understand consumer perceptions and continuously improve communication strategies. By maintaining open and honest communication, brands can foster stronger relationships with consumers and enhance their commitment to sustainability. Overall, sustainability communication is a critical component of a successful sustainability strategy and plays a vital role in sustainable brand development.

CONCLUSION

The significant relationships between influencer authenticity, brand evangelism, data analytics, consumer engagement, brand loyalty, and sustainability communication with sustainable brand development highlight the multifaceted approach required for achieving sustainability in branding. Managers must prioritize authentic influencer partnerships, cultivate passionate brand evangelists, leverage data-driven insights, actively engage consumers, foster strong brand loyalty, and maintain transparent sustainability communication. These strategies collectively enhance consumer trust, brand credibility, and long-term sustainability. By integrating these elements into their overall strategy, brands can not only drive sustainable development but also establish themselves as leaders in the sustainability space, ensuring a competitive edge in an increasingly conscientious market.

Limitations and Further Research: First, the reliance on self-reported data may introduce bias, as participants' responses can be influenced by social desirability. Second, the study's scope is limited to specific variables, and other potential factors impacting sustainable brand development may not have been considered. Third, the cross-sectional design of the study restricts the ability to establish causal relationships. Additionally, the findings may not be generalizable to all industries or geographical regions, given the specific context of the study. Future research should address these limitations by incorporating longitudinal designs to examine causal effects, expanding the scope to include a broader range of variables, and exploring different industry and regional contexts. Moreover, further studies could benefit from using mixed methods to triangulate findings and provide a more comprehensive understanding of sustainable brand development.

REFERENCES

Aaker, D. A. (2021). *Building Strong Brands*. Free Press.

Audrezet, A., de Kerviler, G., & Moulard, J. G. (2020). Authenticity under threat: When social media influencers need to go beyond self-presentation. *Journal of Business Research*, 117, 557–569. DOI: 10.1016/j.jbusres.2018.07.008

Becerra, E. P., & Badrinarayanan, V. (2020). The influence of brand trust and brand identification on brand evangelism. *Journal of Product and Brand Management*, 29(4), 407–421. DOI: 10.1108/JPBM-09-2018-2004

Becerra, E. P., & Badrinarayanan, V. (2020). The influence of brand trust and brand identification on brand evangelism. *Journal of Product and Brand Management*, 29(4), 407–421. DOI: 10.1108/JPBM-09-2018-2004

Belz, F. M., & Peattie, K. (2020). *Sustainability Marketing: A Global Perspective*. Wiley.

Bennett, R., & Rundle-Thiele, S. (2021). The brand loyalty life cycle: Implications for marketers. *Journal of Brand Management*, 12(4), 250–263. DOI: 10.1057/palgrave.bm.2540221

Bowden, J. L. H. (2020). Engaging the student as a customer: A relationship marketing approach. *Marketing Education Review*, 20(3), 65–79. DOI: 10.2753/MER1052-8008200301

Brodie, R. J., Ilic, A., Juric, B., & Hollebeek, L. (2020). Consumer engagement in a virtual brand community: An exploratory analysis. *Journal of Business Research*, 66(1), 105–114. DOI: 10.1016/j.jbusres.2011.07.029

Brown, T., & Brooks, J. (2022). Affinity marketing in the digital age: Strategies for success. *Journal of Marketing Management*, 38(4), 512–528.

Chaudhuri, A., & Holbrook, M. B. (2020). The chain of effects from brand trust and brand affect to brand performance: The role of brand loyalty. *Journal of Marketing*, 65(2), 81–93. DOI: 10.1509/jmkg.65.2.81.18255

Davenport, T. H., & Ronanki, R. (2022). Artificial intelligence for the real world. *Harvard Business Review*, 98(1), 108–116. https://hbr.org/2022/01/artificial-intelligence-for-the-real-world

De Veirman, M., Hudders, L., & Nelson, M. R. (2021). What Is Influencer Marketing and How Does It Target Children? A Review and Direction for Future Research. *Frontiers in Psychology*, 11, 4863. DOI: 10.3389/fpsyg.2020.4863 PMID: 31849783

Dick, A. S., & Basu, K. (2021). Customer loyalty: Toward an integrated conceptual framework. *Journal of the Academy of Marketing Science*, 22(2), 99–113. DOI: 10.1177/0092070394222001

Dodd, M. D., & Supa, D. W. (2020). Understanding the effect of corporate social responsibility communication on consumers: The role of authenticity and transparency. *Public Relations Review*, 40(3), 575–583. DOI: 10.1016/j.pubrev.2020.03.005

Du, S., Bhattacharya, C. B., & Sen, S. (2020). Maximizing business returns to corporate social responsibility (CSR): The role of CSR communication. *International Journal of Management Reviews*, 12(1), 8–19. DOI: 10.1111/j.1468-2370.2009.00276.x

Dwivedi, Y. K., Rana, N. P., Jeyaraj, A., Clement, M., & Williams, M. D. (2022). Re-examining the unified theory of acceptance and use of technology (UTAUT): Towards a revised theoretical model. *Information Systems Frontiers*, 21(3), 719–734. DOI: 10.1007/s10796-017-9774-y

Evans, N. J., Phua, J., Lim, J., & Jun, H. (2021). Disclosing Instagram influencer advertising: The effects of disclosure language on advertising recognition, attitudes, and behavioural intent. *Journal of Interactive Advertising*, 20(2), 150–162. DOI: 10.1080/15252019.2020.1769514

Fullerton, S. (2021). *Sports Marketing: Creating Long Term Value*. McGraw-Hill Education.

Glucksman, M. (2021). The rise of social media influencer marketing on lifestyle branding: A case study of Lucie Fink. *International Journal of Web Based Communities*, 14(2), 138–145. DOI: 10.1504/IJWBC.2021.10001943

Gómez, B. G., Arranz, A. M., & Cillán, J. G. (2020). The role of loyalty programs in behavioral and affective loyalty. *Journal of Consumer Marketing*, 33(3), 213–223. DOI: 10.1108/JCM-01-2015-1280

Grimmer, M., & Woolley, M. (2021). Green marketing messages and consumers' purchase intentions: Promoting personal versus environmental benefits. *Journal of Marketing Communications*, 20(4), 231–250. DOI: 10.1080/13527266.2012.684065

Hofacker, C. F., Malthouse, E. C., & Sultan, F. (2020). Big data and consumer behavior: Imminent opportunities. *Journal of Consumer Marketing*, 37(7), 917–926. DOI: 10.1108/JCM-04-2020-3761

Hollender, J., & Breen, B. (2021). *The Responsibility Revolution: How the Next Generation of Businesses Will Win*. Wiley.

Holt, D. (2020). The rise of brand evangelists: How consumers become passionate advocates. *Harvard Business Review*, 98(5), 65–72.

Jin, S. V., Muqaddam, A., & Ryu, E. (2022). Instafamous and social media influencer marketing. *Marketing Intelligence & Planning*, 40(4), 439–454. DOI: 10.1108/MIP-09-2021-0275

Johnson, M., Anderson, R., & Lee, S. (2023). Optimizing influencer marketing through data analytics. *International Journal of Digital Marketing*, 44(2), 204–218.

Keller, E., & Fay, B. (2020). The role of advertising in word of mouth. *Journal of Advertising Research*, 60(4), 409–416. DOI: 10.2501/JAR-2020-049

Kim, S. H., Park, J. W., & Ryu, K. (2021). The impact of message framing on eco-friendly consumer behavior: An application of prospect theory. *Journal of Business Research*, 123, 121–130. DOI: 10.1016/j.jbusres.2020.09.038

Kotler, P., & Keller, K. L. (2020). *Marketing Management*. Pearson Education.

Kumar, V., & Pansari, A. (2021). Competitive advantage through engagement. *JMR, Journal of Marketing Research*, 55(4), 497–515. DOI: 10.1509/jmr.15.0044

Kumar, V., Rajan, B., Gupta, S., & Dalla Pozza, I. (2019). Customer engagement in service contexts: The roles of customer engagement value, brand trust, and brand loyalty. *Journal of the Academy of Marketing Science*, 47(4), 679–700.

Kumar, V., Sharma, A., & Shah, R. (2023). Leveraging data analytics for sustainability in marketing: A comprehensive review. *Journal of Business Research*, 148, 321–337. DOI: 10.1016/j.jbusres.2022.04.013

Kumar, V., Sharma, A., & Shah, R. (2023). Leveraging data analytics for sustainability in marketing: A comprehensive review. *Journal of Business Research*, 148, 321–337. DOI: 10.1016/j.jbusres.2022.04.013

Lou, C., & Yuan, S. (2022). Influencer marketing: How message value and credibility affect consumer trust of branded content on social media. *Journal of Interactive Advertising*, 22(2), 111–123. DOI: 10.1080/15252019.2022.2041237

Lou, C., & Yuan, S. (2022). Influencer marketing: How message value and credibility affect consumer trust of branded content on social media. *Journal of Interactive Advertising*, 22(2), 111–123. DOI: 10.1080/15252019.2022.2041237

Mayer-Schönberger, V., & Cukier, K. (2021). *Big Data: A Revolution That Will Transform How We Live, Work, and Think*. Houghton Mifflin Harcourt.

McConnell, B., & Huba, J. (2021). *Creating Customer Evangelists: How Loyal Customers Become a Volunteer Sales Force*. Kaplan Business.

Nielsen. (2021). Global responsibility report: Consumers seek companies that care about environmental impact. https://www.nielsen.com/us/en/insights/report/2021/global-responsibility-report

Oliver, R. L. (2020). *Satisfaction: A Behavioral Perspective on the Consumer*. Routledge.

Ottman, J. A. (2021). *The New Rules of Green Marketing: Strategies, Tools, and Inspiration for Sustainable Branding*. Greenleaf Publishing.

Parguel, B., Benoît-Moreau, F., & Larceneux, F. (2021). How sustainability ratings might deter 'greenwashing': A closer look at ethical corporate communication. *Journal of Business Ethics*, 102(1), 15–28. DOI: 10.1007/s10551-011-0901-2

Peattie, K. (2021). *Green Marketing*. Sage Publications.

Polonsky, M. J., & Jevons, C. (2020). Understanding issues in social and ethical marketing. *Journal of Business Ethics*, 27(1-2), 71–79. DOI: 10.1023/A:1006442818505

Rust, R. T., & Huang, M. H. (2021). The service revolution and the transformation of marketing science. *Marketing Science*, 40(3), 527–528. DOI: 10.1287/mksc.2021.1312

Schouten, A. P., Janssen, L., & Verspaget, M. (2022). Celebrity vs. influencer endorsements in advertising: The role of identification, credibility, and Product-Endorser fit. *International Journal of Advertising*, 41(3), 414–438. DOI: 10.1080/02650487.2020.1815201

Smith, P. R., & Zook, Z. (2021). *Marketing communications: Integrating offline and online with social media*. Kogan Page Publishers.

Van Doorn, J., Lemon, K. N., Mittal, V., Nass, S., Pick, D., Pirner, P., & Verhoef, P. C. (2020). Customer engagement behavior: Theoretical foundations and research directions. *Journal of Service Research*, 13(3), 253–266. DOI: 10.1177/1094670510375599

Wallace, E., Buil, I., & de Chernatony, L. (2020). Consumer engagement with self-expressive brands: Brand love and WOM outcomes. *Journal of Product and Brand Management*, 29(4), 407–421. DOI: 10.1108/JPBM-09-2018-2026

Wang, F., & Scheinbaum, A. C. (2021). Communicating sustainability: How different message frames influence consumers' perceptions and behavioral intentions. *Journal of Advertising*, 50(2), 190–204. DOI: 10.1080/00913367.2021.1882998

Wedel, M., & Kannan, P. K. (2020). Marketing analytics for data-rich environments. *Journal of Marketing*, 84(1), 97–121. DOI: 10.1177/0022242919882077

APPENDIX

Table 9. Questionnaire

S.No	Variable No	Variable Name
Influencer Authenticity		
1	IV1.1.	You believe that the influencers you follow are honest about their endorsements.
	IV1.2.	You trust the content shared by influencers.
	IV1.3.	You feel that influencers provide genuine reviews about products.
	IV1.4.	You believe influencers are transparent about their sponsorships.
	IV1.5.	The authenticity of influencers impacts your purchasing decisions.
Brand Evangelism		
2	IV2.1.	You actively promote your favourite brands to others.
	IV2.2.	You are willing to defend your favourite brands against negative opinions.
	IV2.3.	You feel proud to be associated with your favourite brands.
	IV2.4.	You frequently share positive experiences about brands on social media.
	IV2.5.	You encourage others to try the brands you love.
Data Analytics		
3	IV3.1.	You believe data analytics helps brands understand consumer preferences.
	IV3.2.	You think brands using data analytics provide better-personalized experiences.
	IV3.3.	You feel that data analytics improves the effectiveness of marketing campaigns.
	IV3.4.	You believe data analytics enhances customer service.
	IV3.5.	You think brands that use data analytics are more likely to meet your needs.
Consumer Engagement		
4	IV4.1.	You feel connected to brands that engage with you on social media.
	IV4.2.	You actively participate in brand-hosted events or contests.
	IV4.3.	You are more likely to purchase from brands that engage with you regularly.
	IV4.4.	Consumer engagement initiatives make you feel valued by the brand.
	IV4.5.	You prefer brands that seek feedback and suggestions from you.
Brand Loyalty		
5	IV5.1.	You consistently purchase from your favourite brands.
	IV5.2.	You are unlikely to switch to a competitor once you are loyal to a brand.
	IV5.3.	Brand loyalty influences your long-term purchasing behavior.
	IV5.4.	You feel emotionally attached to the brands you are loyal to.
	IV5.5.	You are willing to pay a premium for products from your preferred brands.
Sustainability Communication		

continued on following page

Table 9. Continued

S.No	Variable No	Variable Name
Influencer Authenticity		
6	IV6.1.	You appreciate brands that communicate their sustainability efforts.
	IV6.2.	Transparency in sustainability practices increases your trust in a brand.
	IV6.3.	Sustainability communication influences your purchasing decisions.
	IV6.4.	You prefer brands that actively promote their sustainable practices.
	IV6.5.	You are more loyal to brands that prioritize sustainability in their communication.
Sustainable Brand Development		
7	DV1.1.	Brands that focus on sustainable development are more appealing to you.
	DV1.2.	You support brands that invest in sustainable development initiatives.
	DV1.3.	Sustainable brand development positively impacts your perception of a brand.
	DV1.4.	You believe sustainable development is crucial for a brand's long-term success.
	DV1.5.	Brands that prioritize sustainability are more trustworthy to you.

Chapter 5
Using Influencer Marketing to Strengthen Brand Evangelism:
A Pathway to Sustainable Marketing

Yashu Garg
Lovely Professional University, India

Krishan Gopal
https://orcid.org/0000-0002-0115-5659
Lovely Professional University, India

ABSTRACT

Influencer marketing is a rapidly evolving digital strategy that harnesses the influence and credibility of social media personalities to promote brands, products, or services to specific target audiences. With the rise of platforms such as Instagram, Facebook and YouTube individuals have gained the ability to build significant followings, making them valuable partners for brands seeking authentic engagement with their consumer base. This chapter aims to explore how influencer marketing contributes to sustainable marketing efforts, focusing on the role influencers play in strengthening brand evangelism. The chapter is structured into sections that delve into the evolution of influencer marketing, the strategies influencers use to expand brand loyalty, and the challenges they face in promoting sustainable products. Additionally, it will examine the limitations of influencer marketing in driving consumer behavior towards sustainability and provide insights into the future of influencer marketing and brand evangelism in the context of long-term brand sustainability.

DOI: 10.4018/979-8-3693-7773-4.ch005

1. INTRODUCTION

In recent years, the rise of social media influencers (SMIs) has become a dominant trend, leading to a surge in the adoption of influencer marketing (IM) within business strategies. As of July 2024, the global number of internet users reached 5.45 billion, representing 67.1 percent of the world's population. In which 63.7 percent of the global population, were active on social media platforms. Social media's prevalence provides companies with access to vast online networks, enabling direct interaction with users and the ability to influence consumer behavior (Wielki, 2020; Yildirim, 2021. Platforms like Facebook, Instagram, Linkedin, Twitter, and YouTube have seen dramatic growth in user bases, creating opportunities for firms to directly engage with consumers and unprecedented global audiences, surpassing the reach of traditional influencers, allowing them to significantly shape marketing campaign outcomes Consequently, the digital age has given rise to the concept of "digital influencers" (Isyanto et al., 2020; Leung et al., 2022; Vaidya & Karnawat, 2023). Increasingly, marketers are leveraging online influencers to promote products and brands on social media platforms like Instagram, Facebook, and YouTube, accelerating the expansion of influencer marketing. This strategy involves selecting influencers and providing incentives for them to engage their followers to endorse a company's offerings (Wielki, 2020). Initially, influencer marketing closely mirrored celebrity endorsements, where prominent figures would promote products or services. However, with the advent of platforms like Instagram, YouTube, and Facebook, everyday individuals have been able to gather large followings, reshaping the influencer marketing landscape. The effectiveness of influencer marketing establishes on three key aspects of social media: direct communication between influencers and their audiences, the amplification of messages via these platforms, and the ability to accurately measure the reach and impact of campaigns. Strong relationships between consumers and brands also have a significant impact on consumer behavior. Studies show that these relationships can drive actions such as purchasing a brand, promoting it, and opposition to competitor brands (Kapoor et al., 2023; Schorn et al., 2022; Vaidya & Karnawat, 2023; Wielki, 2020; Yildirim, 2021). Ultimately, robust consumer-brand connections foster loyalty, vibrant brand communities, and sustained performance in both physical and online environments. Brand evangelism, characterized by vocal and active support of a brand through purchasing, referrals, and advocating against competitors, has also emerged as a powerful phenomenon. Recognizing this potential, brands began collaborating with influencers to establish authentic connections with their audiences (Anggarini, 2018; Isyanto et al., 2020; Rungruangjit et al., 2023; Schorn et al., 2022). Authenticity and trust became pivotal in influencer selection, as audiences sought genuine endorsements from influencers who had meaningful ties to the products they promoted. Today, influencer marketing encompasses various strategies, including partnerships, affiliate marketing, and influencer-created content, with an increasing focus on sustainable and long-term collaborations with influencers. The emerging field of sustainability communication has also started examining how social media influencers promote eco-friendly lifestyles and practices. "Green" influencers with smaller followings are more effective in endorsing sustainable products. This reflects a growing interest in the role influencers play in sustainability advocacy (Buvar et al., 2023; Yildirim, 2021).

2. THEORETICAL BACKGROUND

2.1 Evolution of Influencer Marketing:

Over the past decade, influencer marketing has undergone a remarkable transformation, shifting from a specialized advertising approach to a widely adopted global marketing strategy. While it originated from celebrity endorsements, it has since expanded into a more versatile and extensive industry. The advent of social media has played a pivotal role in this shift, allowing ordinary people to connect with large online audiences and establish themselves as influential personalities. This section delves into the evolution of influencer marketing, highlighting its history, growth, and the major platforms that have shaped its development.

- **History and Growth of Influencer Marketing**

The concept of influencer marketing is not entirely new. Historically, it can be linked to celebrity endorsements in traditional media, such as television, radio, and print. Brands would leverage the fame and public trust of celebrities to promote products, hoping that their endorsement would drive consumer interest. However, this form of marketing was typically limited to a select few public figures and high-budget campaigns (B. K. Sharma et al., 2021). The real shift in influencer marketing began with the rise of the internet and social media in the early 2000s. The initial group of influencers primarily consisted of bloggers who attracted significant audiences by focusing on niche topics like fashion, beauty, travel, and lifestyle. They established credibility with their followers by sharing personal insights and genuine recommendations, standing in contrast to the more polished, and often impersonal, nature of traditional advertising campaigns. As blogging became a recognized profession, brands began collaborating with these digital personalities to reach niche audiences. The next major transformation occurred with the rise of social media platforms like Facebook, YouTube, and Instagram in the mid-2000s

(Pourazad et al., 2023; Purohit & Arora, 2024). These platforms democratized the influencer space, allowing anyone with access to the internet to create content and build a following. YouTube, in particular, became a breeding ground for influencers who gained popularity through videos on various topics, from beauty tutorials to gaming and tech reviews. Instagram, with its visual-centric format, also played a pivotal role in enabling the rise of lifestyle and fashion influencers, who leveraged the platform to share highly curated, aesthetic content with their followers. As social media grew, so did the influencer marketing industry. By the 2010s, brands began to recognize the potential of collaborating with influencers who had cultivated highly engaged and loyal audiences. Unlike traditional celebrity endorsements, influencers offered a more relatable and authentic connection to their followers. Their content often appeared more organic, blending seamlessly into their daily lives, which made product recommendations feel more genuine (Karagür et al., 2022; Schwemmer & Ziewiecki, 2018). This, combined with the measurable reach and engagement metrics offered by social media platforms, made influencer marketing an attractive and cost-effective strategy for businesses. The influencer marketing industry experienced exponential growth in the 2010s. By 2016, the global influencer marketing industry was worth around $1.7 billion, a number that skyrocketed to over $13 billion by 2021 (Campbell & Farrell, 2020). This rapid expansion was driven by several factors, including the growing number of social media users, the rise of micro and nano-influencers, and the increasing sophistication of digital marketing tools. Influencer marketing became a critical component of brand strategies across industries, from fashion and beauty to tech, fitness, and beyond (Campbell & Farrell, 2020; Chandawarkar et al., 2018; Driver, 2022; Landgrebe, 2024).

- **Platforms of Influencer Marketing**

The evolution of influencer marketing has been closely tied to the rise of various social media platforms, each offering unique opportunities for influencers to engage with their audiences. Some of the key platforms that have played a crucial role in the growth of influencer marketing include:

a. YouTube

YouTube is one of the most influential platforms in the rise of influencer marketing. Launched in 2005, it became the go-to platform for content creators, enabling influencers to build large audiences by posting videos on a wide range of topics. Influencers on YouTube, known as YouTubers, gained significant followings by offering valuable content, such as tutorials, vlogs, and product reviews (Oliveira et al., 2020). With its highly engaged user base, YouTube has become a critical platform for influencer marketing, particularly in industries like beauty, gaming, technology, and fitness. Brands quickly recognized the potential of YouTube influencers to reach and engage with audiences in an authentic way. By partnering with YouTubers, brands could sponsor video content, provide product placements, or engage in long-term collaborations (Tafheem et al., 2022; Woolley, 2022). The platform's format allows influencers to provide in-depth reviews, demonstrations, and tutorials, making it highly effective for promoting products that require detailed explanations or visual demonstrations (Acikgoz & Burnaz, 2021).

b. Instagram

Instagram, launched in 2010, is one of the most significant platforms in the influencer marketing space, particularly for fashion, lifestyle, beauty, and travel influencers. Its image-driven nature made it a perfect platform for influencers to share aesthetically pleasing content that aligned with their personal brand (Arora et al., 2019; Sedda & Husson, 2023). Instagram's introduction of Stories and IGTV further expanded its capabilities, allowing influencers to share more spontaneous and unedited content, which resonated with followers who valued authenticity. The visual format of Instagram enabled influencers to showcase products through photos, short videos, and Stories, often featuring sponsored posts in a natural and creative way. Brands saw Instagram as a powerful platform for influencer marketing because of its emphasis on visuals and its ability to target specific demographics through hashtags and location tagging (Pedalino & Camerini, 2022; Sutrisno & Ariesta, 2019). The rise of Instagram influencers has been instrumental in shaping consumer behavior, with many users relying on influencers for fashion inspiration, beauty product recommendations, and lifestyle choices.

c. TikTok

TikTok, the short-form video platform, has rapidly emerged as a major player in influencer marketing, particularly among Gen Z. Since its global launch in 2016, TikTok has revolutionized the influencer marketing landscape with its highly engaging, short, and viral video content (Arriagada & Bishop, 2021; D. Balaban & Mustă ea, 2019; Dajah, 2020). The platform's unique algorithm, which promotes content based on engagement rather than follower count, allows users to quickly amass large followings if their content resonates with the audience. TikTok's influencers—often referred to as creators—are known for their creativity, spontaneity, and ability to create viral trends. Brands have increasingly collaborated with TikTok creators for influencer campaigns, recognizing the platform's power to reach younger, tech-savvy audiences. TikTok challenges, branded hashtag campaigns, and sponsored content are common ways that brands leverage the platform to drive brand awareness and engagement (Arora et al., 2019; Brooks et al., 2021; Jin et al., 2019; Vaidya & Karnawat, 2023).

d. Facebook

While Facebook initially focused more on personal networking, it has grown into a significant platform for influencer marketing, especially for larger, more established influencers. Facebook's diverse content formats—such as live video, photos, and longer-form posts—allow influencers to engage deeply with their followers (Arora et al., 2019; Bratu, 2019; Cho et al., 2022). Facebook's extensive ad targeting options also make it a valuable platform for brands looking to amplify influencer partnerships through paid promotions.

e. Twitter and LinkedIn

While Twitter and LinkedIn are not traditionally associated with influencer marketing in the same way as YouTube or Instagram, they have both become increasingly important platforms for industry-specific influencers. Thought leaders, industry experts, and business influencers often use these platforms to share insights, promote products or services, and engage with niche audiences. LinkedIn, in particular, is popular for B2B influencer marketing, where business professionals share recommendations and insights on industry trends (Alam et al., 2022; Arriagada & Bishop, 2021; Sedda & Husson, 2023).

2.2 Influencer Marketing:

Social media has speedily modified the modern marketing approach. With the increasing usage of social media, marketing managers start allocating more budgets for their online communication strategies. The ubiquity of the Internet, including convenient access via mobile phones and tablets, the increase in the proportion of customers who search for and provide brand-related information, the ease with which consumers can now provide comments in online (e.g. web sites, forums, discussion boards, etc.) and social networking sites. Brands apply many kinds of marketing strategies on social media. One of the most prevalent ones is called influencer marketing. Influencer marketing refers to "the practice of identifying key decision makers in a target audience and encouraging them to use their influence to spread WOM" (Bakker, 2018; Buvár et al., 2023; Isyanto et al., 2020). This approach involves businesses or marketers partnering with social media influencers to produce content that promote their products or services. The goal is to expand their reach and engage with consumers in a more impactful and efficient manner (Acikgoz & Burnaz, 2021). Influencer marketing is a marketing strategy that uses the influence of individuals or key opinion leaders to drive brand awareness by consumers or their purchasing decisions or simply the act of promoting and selling products or services through people (influencers) that has the ability to create the effect on the character of a brand. So, Influencer marketing itself a promotional strategy to use people who are influential in social media they use. The influencer marketing investments are increasingly made by marketers, aiming to supplement existing marketing communication and publicize social media influencer-generated content to followers on social networks and target customers (Anggarini, 2018; Kapoor et al., 2023; Schorn et al., 2022). Instagram has become the ideal platform for brands to use influencer-based marketing campaigns and paid collaboration between influencers and brands is often found in sponsored content. Organizations increasingly recognize that the success of new product launches is often related to the influence of digital influencers on consumers. The definition of influencer marketing continues to evolve with the ever-changing digital landscape, incorporating new platforms and technologies. With the growing importance of transparency, audience engagement, and relatability, influencer marketing remains a powerful tool for businesses seeking to connect with their target audience in an increasingly competitive online world (Vaidya & Karnawat, 2023; Wielki, 2020). In the digital age, influencer marketing has become increasingly important for several reasons such as: Authenticity and Trust, Reach to the target audience, content creation, increased brand awareness, conversion and sales content diversity (Okonkwo & Namkoisse, 2023).

- **Types of Influencers**

Within the world of influencer marketing, there are various categories of influencers, each possessing specific traits and benefits. There are mainly four type of influencers such as: Mega Influencers, Macro Influencers, Micro Influencers and Nano Influencers.

a. Mega Influencers:

Mega influencers are individuals with over a million followers, while top macro-influencers typically boast over 500,000 followers. This category includes prominent figures such as millionaire YouTubers and other high-profile accounts across various platforms. Mega influencers, often regarded as the "A-list" of social media, are treated similarly to traditional celebrities (J. Lee et al., 2024). Their vast followings stem from transforming their digital presence into full-time, professional ventures, adopting a business-oriented approach. These influencers maintain a significant presence across multiple platforms, utilizing each to cross-promote and enhance their value to brands. Mega influencers exemplify the power to command vast attention, often reaching larger audiences than traditional mass media, making them ideal for large-scale awareness campaigns (Vaidya & Karnawat, 2023). These top-tier influencers are widely recognized as the true celebrities of the social media world.

b. Macro Influencers:

Celebrities are highly recognized individuals from the entertainment industry, sports, or other public domains, who enjoy substantial followings both in the digital world and offline. As influential public figures, celebrity influencers often fall within the macro or mega influencer categories, boasting follower counts that range from hundreds of thousands to millions (Brewster & Lyu, 2020). While they offer extensive reach and significant visibility, their broad audience appeal may sometimes come at the cost of personal connection and authenticity, qualities that smaller influencers can typically deliver more effectively. Macro influencers, typically those with between 100,000 and just under a million followers, tend to have a selective approach when it comes to brand collaborations. While they participate in fewer partnerships compared to mega influencers, their endorsements still carry weight due to their sizable yet somewhat targeted audience. Their compensation per post is relatively lower, around $5,000 per collaboration, reflecting the balance between reach and exclusivity (Brewster & Lyu, 2020; Perez Breton Borbn, 2024; Rahman, 2022). Although celebrities may not share the same personal connection with their followers as smaller influencers, they provide brands with extensive exposure and access to large audiences. This makes them particularly valuable for marketing campaigns focused on maximizing visibility and reaching a broad demographic.

c. Micro Influencers:

Micro-influencers typically have follower counts ranging from 10,000 to 100,000 and tend to focus on geographically limited areas. Their income is primarily derived from occasional brand collaborations and affiliate-link programs. Despite their smaller reach, micro-influencers serve highly specialized and niche audiences, fostering stronger engagement and relatability. They often focus on specific topics or interests, which helps them build dedicated, trusting followers whose loyalty gives extra value to their recommendations. Brands frequently work with micro-influencers to target niche markets effectively (Brewster & Lyu, 2020). Recent industry reports have highlighted that micro-influencer, despite having smaller networks, capture greater attention and achieve higher engagement rates due to more personal interactions with their followers compared to macro-influencers (Allen, 2022; Brewster

& Lyu, 2020). The followers of micro-influencers tend to be more specific in terms of demographics like age and gender. In contrast, celebrity influencers often attract a broader audience, many of whom may not be deeply engaged with the content. As a result, micro-influencers generally drive better conversion rates and create more sales opportunities. From a consumer's perspective, micro-influencers are often seen as friends, which strengthens the bond between brands and consumers (Rahman, 2022). These influencers are viewed as experts in their respective fields and are particularly effective at communicating product information to their loyal fan base especially among younger audiences. Platforms like Instagram have become a key space where young users seek inspiration from micro-influencers. Micro-influencers play a significant role in fostering consumer engagement and strengthening relationships between brands and their audience (Isyanto et al., 2020; Rungruangjit et al., 2023).

d. Nano Influencers:

Nano-influencers are a relatively new category in the influencer landscape, characterized by having the smallest follower base, typically ranging from a few hundred to a few thousand. One of their key strengths is the highly localized and engaged communities they nurture. Due to the personal relationships, they often share with their followers, nano-influencers are able to foster a strong sense of trust. This makes them especially valuable for local businesses or brands aiming for authentic and grassroots promotion. Their greatest asset lies in their ability to build deep trust and personal connections with their audience (Kapoor et al., 2023). Nano-influencers are everyday individuals who collaborate with brands or trademark holders to promote products to a close-knit, highly relevant audience. Many of them have fewer than 1,000 followers, but their real-world connections give them a larger, more tangible influence. Some nano-influencers, who have up to 10,000 followers, often work with brands on unpaid collaborations in exchange for exposure and opportunities to grow their network (Au-Yong-Oliveira et al., 2019; Brewster & Lyu, 2020; Wibawa et al., 2021).

2.3 Brand Evangelism:

Organizations today face numerous challenges due to the increasingly interconnected marketplace, prompting them to focus on a smaller yet highly influential group of consumers known as brand evangelists (Collins, 2021). Brand evangelism refers to the enthusiastic support and promotion of a brand, which includes behaviors such as purchasing from the brand, sharing positive recommendations, and convincing others to choose the brand over its competitors. Brand evangelists often convey brand values and attributes that might otherwise be communicated through traditional marketing efforts. This form of evangelism reflects a strong consumer-brand relationship and serves as an extension of positive word-of-mouth (WOM) communication. Brand evangelists are deeply loyal consumers with a strong emotional attachment to a brand, and they actively promote it by encouraging others to adopt the brand over competing options. They play a critical role in recruiting new customers by sharing their personal brand experiences. Research by (Mishra et al., 2021) reveals that key factors such as brand trust, emotional connection to the brand, and brand identification significantly influence brand evangelism, leading to higher purchase intent and greater referral behavior. Understanding consumer-brand relationships has always been a priority for organizations looking to foster behaviors that benefit their brand (Doss & Carstens, 2014; Harrigan, Roy, et al., 2021; P. Sharma & Khandeparkar, 2024). Brand evangelists as 'individuals who communicate information, ideas, and feelings concerning a specific brand freely, and often times fervently, to others in a desire to influence consumption behaviour' (Doss & Carstens, 2014). According to (Matzler, Renzl, et al., 2007), 'brand evangelism describes an active and committed way of spreading positive opinions and trying to persuade others to become engaged with the same brand', as 'consumers who evangelize are passionate about their brand and feel the need to share their emotions with others.' According to (P. Becerra & Badrinarayanan, 2013). brand evangelism as 'the active behavioural and vocal support of a brand including actions such as purchasing the brand, disseminating positive brand referrals, and convincing others about a focal brand by disparaging competing brands.' In today's marketplace, organizations are paying close attention to this smaller yet highly influential group of brand evangelists. These consumers not only embrace brands wholeheartedly but also spread their brand experiences, actively recruit others to try the brand, and discourage consumption of rival brands (Pornsrimate & Khamwon, 2021; Rungruangjit et al., 2023; Sashittal et al., 2023; P. Sharma, 2023). Focusing solely on word-of-mouth communication may overlook the full extent to which these consumers advocate for their favourite brands. In fact, some customers build such deep connections with their brands that they go beyond mere recommendations, making it their mission to demonstrate their loyalty, share their opinions, and persuade others to switch brands. Brand evangelists don't just promote their preferred brands enthusiastically—they also back their recommendations by consistently purchasing from the brand (Harris, 2023; B. G. Smith et al., 2021).

Influencers play a pivotal role in spreading positive word-of-mouth (WOM) about brands by leveraging their trust-based relationships with their audience. With their authentic and relatable content, influencers can create a strong emotional connection with their followers, making their endorsements more credible and impactful than traditional advertising. Here's how influencers spread positive word of mouth to customers:

1. **Authentic Reviews and Recommendations**: Influencers often share their genuine experiences with products or services, providing honest feedback that resonates with their followers. Their personal touch and storytelling make the brand's message feel more relatable, encouraging trust and interest among their audience (Sashittal et al., 2023).
2. **Engaging Content**: By incorporating a brand's products into their daily content, such as tutorials, how-to videos, or lifestyle posts, influencers showcase the practical benefits of the brand (Bentley et al., 2021; Wentzell et al., 2021) . This subtle, non-intrusive approach allows their followers to see how the product fits into a real-life scenario, making the recommendation more persuasive.
3. **Interactive Engagement:** Influencers often interact directly with their audience by answering questions, responding to comments, and sharing testimonials. This engagement fosters a community around the brand, where followers feel involved and valued, further amplifying the positive word-of-mouth (Rungruangjit et al., 2023).
4. **Cross-Platform Promotion**: Influencers frequently promote brands across multiple social media platforms, ensuring that their message reaches a broad audience. Whether it's Instagram, YouTube, TikTok, or Twitter, influencers use different formats to engage with their followers and increase the visibility of the brand (Jin et al., 2019).
   5. **User-Generated Content:** Many influencers encourage their followers to create and share their own content using the brand's products. This not only spreads positive WOM but also strengthens the community and trust surrounding the brand, as followers see others using and enjoying the product (Romero-Rodriguez & Castillo-Abdul, 2023).

6. **Collaborations and Giveaways:** Influencers often collaborate with brands on exclusive deals, limited-edition products, or giveaways, incentivizing their followers to engage with the brand. These collaborations generate excitement and increase the brand's visibility, further boosting positive WOM (Brewster & Lyu, 2020).
7. **Emotional Connection**: Influencers are skilled at tapping into the emotions of their followers. By aligning a brand with positive values or personal stories, they create an emotional appeal that enhances the brand's image and encourages their audience to share it with others (Saldanha et al., 2024).

3. OBJECTIVE

The main objective of this study is to examine how influencer marketing can be effectively used to foster brand evangelism, encouraging a loyal consumer base that actively promotes and advocates for the brand. It will explore strategies influencers employ to build authentic relationships with their audiences and how brands can leverage these connections for long-term success. By focusing on trust, transparency, and credibility, the study aims to show how these elements contribute to sustainable marketing practices that ensure lasting brand loyalty and continued growth.

4. METHODOLOGY

This study adopted a qualitative research approach, focusing on a literature review to collect and analyze existing research on the role of influencer marketing in promoting brand evangelism as a pathway to sustainable marketing. A content analysis method was utilized to meet the study's objectives. The research relied on secondary data, sourced from a variety of articles, with a sample comprising 100 research papers.

5. INTERSECTION OF INFLUENCER MARKETING AND BRAND EVANGELISM

Influencers becoming brand evangelists is a dynamic process driven by a deep connection with the brand, its products, and values. It starts with genuine admiration for what the brand represents. Influencers who align with a brand's core mission and ethos often begin by authentically promoting its products or services, even without formal partnerships. Their content resonates with their followers because it's built on a foundation of personal experience and trust. As influencers repeatedly endorse a brand out of genuine affinity, they organically transition from being mere promoters to brand evangelists. As influencer marketing evolved, it extended beyond simple endorsements to include sponsored content, product placements, and influencer-generated content (D. C. Balaban & Szambolics, 2022; Jenkins et al., 2020; Poyry et al., 2021; Wellman et al., 2020). Authenticity and trust emerged as critical elements in selecting influencers, as audiences increasingly sought genuine connections between influencers and the products they endorsed. A study highlighted that 92% of social media users place more trust in influencers than in traditional marketing channels (Jin et al., 2019). This shift has pushed social media marketers to develop new marketing skills, particularly around fostering and managing trust between influencers and their followers. A key principle in maintaining this trust is transparent disclosure. When influencers openly share their relationships with brands and reveal that they've been compensated for promoting certain products or services, it creates a foundation of trust with their audience. Transparency allows influencers to present themselves as authentic, further building this trust. Influencers often employ specific strategies to enhance their credibility, such as partnering only with brands they genuinely use in their daily lives and maintaining consistency in their language, images, and overall content style (D. Balaban & Musta ea, 2019; Hassan et al., 2021). While these tactics may be crafted, they come across as sincere, helping to establish the influencer as a credible source worthy of their audience's trust. One-way influencers demonstrate authenticity is by clearly disclosing when they are working with commercial brands. This kind of transparency empowers their followers to make informed decisions and fosters a deeper level of trust. Incorporating transparent disclosures not only nurtures trust with followers but also ensures adherence to industry regulations (Jenkins et al., 2020). Influencers who consistently make such disclosures tend to develop stronger, more lasting connections with their audiences. When followers feel they can rely on an influencer, they are more likely to remain engaged over time. For both influencers and brands, credibility is a highly valuable asset. Clear and honest disclosures help maintain the influencer's credibility, ensuring their recommendations are taken seriously by their followers. This transparency also protects the reputation of the sponsoring brand, as consumers appreciate honesty in marketing partnerships. Ultimately, transparency strengthens the integrity of the influencer marketing industry (Agnihotri et al., 2023; Jin et al., 2019). When influencers and brands make transparency a priority, they establish a standard of ethical behavior that benefits the entire ecosystem. Transparency between influencer and brand, is not only an ethical requirement but also a crucial element in preserving and enhancing brand credibility in the influencer marketing space. In the end, influencers evolve into brand evangelists through relationships rooted in trust, loyalty, and shared values. Their ability to authentically integrate a brand into their personal identity turns them into compelling advocates who influence consumer behavior more effectively than traditional advertising. This mutually beneficial relationship boosts both the credibility of the influencers and the authentic promotion of the brands they endorse (Agnihotri et al., 2023; Wang & Weng, 2024).

6. STRATEGIES FOR STRENGTHENING BRAND EVANGELISM VIA INFLUENCER MARKETING IN SUSTAINABILITY MARKETING

In the digital era, brands are shifting their marketing strategies to embrace more collaborative approaches. One such method is through collaborative content creation, where brands partner with influencers, customers, or other businesses to co-create valuable content that resonates with their target audience (Agnihotri et al., 2023). This strategy is powerful because it leverages the creative strengths of both parties, leading to content that is authentic, engaging, and tailored to audience preferences. By involving external contributors in content creation, brands can build trust and foster deeper connections with their communities. Another growing trend is user-generated content (UGC) campaigns. UGC involves consumers creating and sharing content that highlights a brand or its products, often through social media. This type of content is seen as more trustworthy than traditional advertising, as it comes directly from customers (Bigley & Leonhardt, 2018; M. Kim & Lee, 2017). UGC campaigns not only drive engagement but also create a sense of brand loyalty, as customers feel valued for their contributions. These campaigns can take many forms, from photo contests to hashtag challenges, and are highly effective at amplifying a brand's message organically (Wibawa et al., 2021). To maximize the impact of both collaborative content and UGC, brands are increasingly focusing on long-term partnerships with influencers and creators (Stoldt et al., 2019).

Rather than one-off collaborations, these partnerships help build consistency and authenticity in the messaging. Long-term relationships also allow influencers to build stronger, more genuine connections with their audience regarding the brand, leading to higher trust and more meaningful engagement (Anggarini, 2018). When influencers are seen as true advocates for a brand, their endorsements carry more weight. Micro-influencers play a critical role in this ecosystem. With smaller but highly engaged followings, micro-influencers are often seen as more relatable and authentic than macro-influencers or celebrities (Allen, 2022; Borges-Tiago et al., 2023; Wibawa et al., 2021). Their content typically resonates more with niche audiences, making them ideal for brands seeking to tap into specific markets or communities. Micro-influencers also tend to charge lower fees than larger influencers, making them a cost-effective option for brands looking to scale their influencer marketing efforts (Himelboim & Golan, 2023; J. Lee et al., 2024). In conclusion, the synergy between collaborative content creation, UGC campaigns, long-term partnerships, and micro-influencers offers a robust framework for brands to enhance their online presence. By fostering authentic relationships and tapping into the creative power of influencers and consumers, brands can create impactful, resonant content that drives meaningful engagement and loyalty.

7. CHALLENGES AND LIMITATIONS OF INFLUENCER MARKETING IN BRAND EVANGELISM IN SUSTAINABLE PRODUCTS

Influencer marketing has become a valuable tool for brands aiming to build brand evangelism, particularly in promoting sustainable products. However, despite its growing popularity, there are several limitations and challenges that brands must navigate when utilizing influencers to drive brand loyalty in the sustainable market. Brands must carefully consider these challenges in order to effectively leverage influencer marketing to create genuine, long-term brand evangelists for sustainable products. Below are key limitations and challenges for brands: -

- **Authenticity and Trust Issues**

One of the core challenges of influencer marketing in the sustainable product sector is maintaining authenticity. Sustainable products often come with a mission focused on environmental responsibility, ethical production, and long-term ecological benefits (Palakshappa et al., 2024). Consumers who are attracted to these products typically value transparency and authenticity in brand messaging. However, when influencers promote multiple brands or products—especially those not aligned with sustainability—there is a risk of losing credibility (Agnihotri et al., 2023; Lou & Yuan, 2019). Audiences may question the influencer's true commitment to sustainable values, leading to doubts about the products they promote. Furthermore, influencer partnerships that appear too transactional can damage trust. If consumers perceive that an influencer is promoting sustainable products solely for compensation, rather than out of genuine belief in the brand's mission, it undermines the sense of authenticity that is crucial in building brand evangelism. For sustainable products, where consumers are often deeply invested in ethical considerations, this can be particularly damaging (Iqani, 2019).

- **Mismatched Brand-Influencer Alignment**

Another limitation is the potential mismatch between the brand and the influencer. While influencers with large followings are attractive to brands, their personal values, content style, and overall message may not align with the brand's sustainability ethos (Iqani, 2019; Nguyen et al., 2023; B. G. Smith et al., 2021). This misalignment can lead to a lack of resonance between the influencer's audience and the brand's mission. For example, an influencer known for promoting luxury or fast fashion might not be the ideal advocate for a sustainable fashion brand. Even if they have a large reach, their followers may not be interested in sustainability, which reduces the effectiveness of the partnership in cultivating brand evangelists. Brands promoting sustainable products need to ensure that the influencers they collaborate with share and consistently convey the same values. This requires careful vetting and a deeper understanding of the influencer's audience (Hughes et al., 2019; Rungruangjit et al., 2023; Singh, 2024). Failure to align these values can dilute the brand's message and hinder the development of a passionate, loyal following.

- **Short-Term Partnerships vs. Long-Term Commitment**

Sustainable products often require a deeper level of commitment from consumers, as they may come at a higher price point or require changes in consumer habits. For this reason, influencer marketing efforts that rely on short-term partnerships may not be effective in cultivating brand evangelism for sustainable products. While influencers can generate awareness and buzz around a product, short-lived campaigns may not create the lasting impact needed to turn consumers into loyal advocates (Iqani, 2019; Osmanova et al., 2023; Palakshappa et al., 2024;). Brand evangelism thrives on long-term relationships between influencers, brands, and audiences. Influencers who promote a brand consistently over time are more likely to be seen as credible advocates, as opposed to those who only engage in one-off collaborations. For sustainable products, which are often tied to larger missions of environmental and social responsibility, long-term partnerships are crucial (Nguyen et al., 2023). These sustained relationships help build trust, showcase the brand's genuine commitment to sustainability, and encourage consumers to become part of a movement rather than just a one-time purchase (Osmanova et al., 2023).

- **Complex Messaging Around Sustainability**

Sustainability is a complex and multifaceted issue, encompassing everything from environmental impact to social equity and ethical labor practices. Conveying these intricate messages through influencer marketing poses a significant challenge. Influencers often communicate in bite-sized, visually appealing content formats such as Instagram posts, stories, or TikTok videos (Arora et al., 2019; Arriagada & Bishop, 2021; J. A. Lee et al., 2022; Nandagiri & Philip, 2018; Pedalino & Camerini, 2022). While these formats are effective for engagement, they may not allow for the depth of explanation required to fully articulate the sustainability credentials of a product. As a result, influencers promoting sustainable products may struggle to educate their audience on the nuances of the brand's sustainability efforts. Oversimplified or vague messaging can lead to misunderstandings or fail to convey the product's true value. In contrast, overly detailed explanations can overwhelm the audience and reduce engagement. Striking the right balance is essential but difficult, limiting the effectiveness of influencer marketing in this space (D. Balaban & Mustă ea, 2019; Goanta & Ranchordás, 2020; Oliveira et al., 2020).

8. FUTURE DIRECTIONS FOR INFLUENCER MARKETING AND BRAND EVANGELISM IN SUSTAINABLE MARKETING

As consumer interest in sustainability continues to rise, brands are increasingly turning to influencer marketing to promote eco-friendly products and foster brand evangelism. Influencers, with their ability to connect authentically with niche audiences, play a pivotal role in driving awareness, trust, and loyalty for sustainable brands. However, as the market for sustainable products expands and becomes more sophisticated, influencer marketing must also evolve. This paper explores future directions for influencer marketing and brand evangelism in sustainable marketing, focusing on the need for deeper authenticity, long-term relationships, and the integration of new technologies and platforms.

- **Enhanced Focus on Authenticity and Transparency**

One of the key trends in the future of influencer marketing for sustainable products will be a heightened emphasis on authenticity and transparency. As consumers become more discerning about the sustainability claims made by brands, influencers will need to be more selective about the products they endorse, ensuring that their partnerships align with their personal values. Influencers who prioritize genuine, long-term relationships with sustainable brands—rather than engaging in one-off promotional activities—will become more trusted voices in the space (Agnihotri et al., 2023; J. A. Lee & Eastin, 2021). Transparency will also remain a critical factor. In the future, influencers will be expected to provide even greater insight into the sustainability practices of the brands they promote. This could include showcasing behind-the-scenes processes, such as ethical sourcing, sustainable production methods, or corporate social responsibility initiatives. Influencers who can demonstrate that they have thoroughly researched the brands they endorse, and who openly communicate the positive and negative aspects of a product, will build stronger, more loyal communities of brand evangelists (D. Balaban & Mustatea, 2019; D. Y. Kim & Kim, 2021; J. A.).

- **Long-Term Partnerships and Deeper Brand Collaborations**

In the realm of sustainable marketing, one-off influencer collaborations are likely to become less effective as consumers demand deeper, more consistent engagement. Future influencer marketing efforts will likely shift toward long-term partnerships where influencers work closely with brands to co-create content, develop campaigns, and even participate in product development. Such collaborations allow influencers to build a deeper understanding of a brand's sustainability efforts, leading to more credible and meaningful endorsements. For example, influencers may collaborate with brands to create limited-edition sustainable product lines or participate in the design of eco-friendly packaging. These long-term partnerships not only help establish trust between the influencer and their audience but also allow brands to foster a sense of exclusivity and loyalty among their followers. In this model, influencers become true brand evangelists, acting as ambassadors who promote not only the product but the brand's mission of sustainability (Romero-Rodriguez & Castillo-Abdul, 2023; Wentzell et al., 2021).

- **Niche Influencers and Micro-Communities**

As influencer marketing continues to grow, the future will likely see a greater reliance on niche influencers who have deep expertise and credibility within specific sustainability sectors. These could include influencers who specialize in zero-waste living, ethical fashion, clean beauty, or renewable energy (Gómez, 2019b; Harrigan, Daly, et al., 2021; Woolley, 2022). Rather than targeting broad audiences through macro-influencers, brands may find more success in collaborating with micro-influencers who have smaller but highly engaged communities. Niche influencers, by virtue of their specialized content and deep knowledge of sustainability issues, can foster stronger connections with their audiences. They can provide in-depth education on sustainability topics, answer questions, and share actionable tips that go beyond product promotion (Borges-Tiago et al., 2023). This fosters a sense of community and encourages followers to actively participate in the brand's sustainability journey, turning them into brand evangelists who promote the brand's values within their own circles.

- **The Role of New Technologies: AI, AR, and Blockchain**

The future of influencer marketing in sustainable products will also be shaped by technological advancements, particularly in areas like artificial intelligence (AI), augmented reality (AR), and blockchain (D. Y. Kim & Kim, 2021). AI can be used to identify the most suitable influencers for a brand based on audience analysis, engagement rates, and alignment with sustainability values. Additionally, AI-powered analytics will help brands and influencers measure the long-term impact of their collaborations on brand evangelism and sustainability goals. Augmented reality offers a unique way for influencers to engage with their audiences by providing immersive experiences (H. M. Kim & Chakraborty, 2024). For instance, influencers could use AR to demonstrate how sustainable products fit into their daily lives or allow followers to visualize how a product would look in their homes. This level of interaction can enhance the credibility of the influencer's endorsements and help audiences better understand the tangible benefits of sustainable products. Blockchain technology also holds promise for the future of influencer marketing in sustainability (Dcunha et al., 2024; Imani Rad & Banaeian Far, 2023; Prelipcean et al., 2023). By using blockchain, brands and influencers can offer greater transparency regarding a product's supply chain, enabling consumers to verify the authenticity of sustainability claims. This could significantly reduce the risk of greenwashing, as consumers will have access to immutable records that detail every stage of a product's lifecycle, from sourcing to manufacturing (J. A. Lee & Eastin, 2021).

9. CONCLUSION

Sustainable marketing has emerged as a crucial strategy for businesses seeking to align with the growing consumer demand for eco-friendly and ethically produced products. At the intersection of this trend lies influencer marketing, a powerful tool that can be leveraged to promote sustainable brands and drive brand evangelism (Anggarini, 2018). Brand evangelists, who are loyal advocates of a product or brand, play a critical role in spreading awareness and influencing the purchasing decisions of others. Influencers, with their personal connection to followers, act as intermediaries who bridge the gap between brands and consumers, helping to create genuine, long-term relationships that are rooted in shared values. In the context of sustainability, these values typically include environmental stewardship, ethical production, and social responsibility (Rajput et al., 2024). One of the key strengths of influencer marketing in promoting sustainable products is its ability to cultivate authenticity and trust. Consumers who prioritize sustainability are often discerning and demand transparency from the brands they support. Influencers, by demonstrating their commitment to sustainability through their content and partnerships, are able to build credibility with their audiences (Harrigan, Roy, et al., 2021; D. Y. Kim & Kim, 2021; Rajput et al., 2024). They provide a unique platform for storytelling, offering an intimate look at how sustainable products fit into everyday life, which resonates more deeply with consumers than traditional advertising. Through consistent engagement and thoughtful content, influencers can convert their followers into brand evangelists who not only purchase sustainable products but also actively promote them to their own networks.

However, while influencer marketing offers significant potential, it also presents challenges in the context of sustainable products. The risk of greenwashing, where brands falsely promote themselves as sustainable, can erode trust if influencers are not careful about the partnerships they endorse. This makes it imperative for influencers to thoroughly vet the brands they collaborate with to ensure alignment with their own values and those of their audience (Rajput et al., 2024). Additionally, conveying the complex nature of sustainability in a way that is both informative and engaging can be difficult in the short-form content typically favored by social media platforms. Influencers must strike a balance between educating their audiences about the nuances of sustainability and maintaining the entertainment value of their content to keep followers engaged (Singh, 2024; B. G. Smith et al., 2021). Looking ahead, the future of influencer marketing in sustainable brand evangelism will likely focus on long-term partnerships and deeper collaborations. As consumers increasingly expect authenticity and consistency, influencers who work closely with brands over extended periods will have greater success in building trust and fostering loyalty (P. Sharma, 2023; Woolley, 2022). This shift toward longer-term relationships will also allow influencers to gain a deeper understanding of the brands they promote, enhancing their ability to communicate sustainability messages effectively. At the same time, advancements in technology—such as augmented reality and blockchain—are poised to revolutionize how influencers engage with their audiences and verify sustainability claims, further enhancing transparency. By fostering trust, transparency, and meaningful engagement, influencer marketing has the potential to not only drive sales but also contribute to the larger goal of creating a more sustainable world (Jin et al., 2019c; Lou & Yuan, 2019; Wang & Weng, 2024; Wellman et al., 2020). In this evolving landscape, both brands and influencers must remain committed to authenticity, ensuring that their efforts align with the genuine desire for a more responsible and sustainable future.

REFERENCES

Acikgoz, F., & Burnaz, S. (2021). The influence of "influencer marketing" on YouTube influencers. *International Journal of Internet Marketing and Advertising*, 15(2), 201. DOI: 10.1504/IJIMA.2021.114331

Agnihotri, D., Chaturvedi, P., Kulshreshtha, K., & Tripathi, V. (2023). Investigating the impact of authenticity of social media influencers on followers' purchase behavior: Mediating analysis of parasocial interaction on Instagram. *Asia Pacific Journal of Marketing and Logistics*, 35(10), 2377–2394. DOI: 10.1108/APJML-07-2022-0598

Alam, F., Tao, M., Lahuerta-Otero, E., & Feifei, Z. (2022). Let's buy with social commerce platforms through social media influencers: An Indian consumer perspective. *Frontiers in Psychology*, 13, 853168. DOI: 10.3389/fpsyg.2022.853168 PMID: 35496238

Allen, L. (2022). The Rise of the Micro-Influencer as a new Form of Marketing in Neoliberal Times. *Critical Reflections: A Student Journal on Contemporary Sociological Issues*, 1 (1), 208-220.

Anggarini, L. (2018).. . *Understanding Brand Evangelism and the Dimensions Involved in a Consumer Becoming Brand Evangelist*, 2(1), 63–84.

Arora, A., Bansal, S., Kandpal, C., Aswani, R., & Dwivedi, Y. (2019). Measuring social media influencer index-insights from Facebook, Twitter and Instagram. *Journal of Retailing and Consumer Services*, 49, 86–101. DOI: 10.1016/j.jretconser.2019.03.012

Arriagada, A., & Bishop, S. (2021). Between commerciality and authenticity: The imaginary of social media influencers in the platform economy. *Communication, Culture & Critique*, 14(4), 568–586. DOI: 10.1093/ccc/tcab050

Au-Yong-Oliveira, M., Cardoso, A. S., Goncalves, M., Tavares, A., & Branco, F. (2019). Strain effect-a case study about the power of nano-influencers. *2019 14th Iberian Conference on Information Systems and Technologies (CISTI)*, 1–5.

Bakker, D. (2018). Conceptualising influencer marketing. *Journal of Emerging Trends in Marketing and Management*, 1(1), 79–87.

Balaban, D., & Mustatea, M. (2019). Users' perspective on the credibility of social media influencers in Romania and Germany. *Romanian Journal of Communication and Public Relations*, 21(1), 31–46. DOI: 10.21018/rjcpr.2019.1.269

Balaban, D. C., & Szambolics, J. (2022). A proposed model of self-perceived authenticity of social media influencers. *Media and Communication*, 10(1), 235–246. DOI: 10.17645/mac.v10i1.4765

Becerra, P., E., & Badrinarayanan, V. (. (2013). The influence of brand trust and brand identification on brand evangelism. *Journal of Product and Brand Management*, 22(5/6), 371–383. DOI: 10.1108/JPBM-09-2013-0394

Bentley, K., Chu, C., Nistor, C., Pehlivan, E., & Yalcin, T. (2021). Social media engagement for global influencers. *Journal of Global Marketing*, 34(3), 205–219. DOI: 10.1080/08911762.2021.1895403

Bigley, I. P., & Leonhardt, J. M. (2018). Extremity Bias in User-Generated Content Creation and Consumption in Social Media. *Journal of Interactive Advertising*, 18(2), 125–135. DOI: 10.1080/15252019.2018.1491813

Borges-Tiago, M. T., Santiago, J., & Tiago, F. (2023). Mega or macro social media influencers: Who endorses brands better? *Journal of Business Research*, 157, 113606. DOI: 10.1016/j.jbusres.2022.113606

Bratu, S. (2019). Can social media influencers shape corporate brand reputation? Online followers' trust, value creation, and purchase intentions. *Review of Contemporary Philosophy*, 18, 157–163.

Brewster, M. L., & Lyu, J. (2020). Exploring the parasocial impact of nano, micro and macro influencers. *International Textile and Apparel Association Annual Conference Proceedings, 77*(1).

Brooks, G., Drenten, J., & Piskorski, M. J. (2021). Influencer Celebrification: How Social Media Influencers Acquire Celebrity Capital. *Journal of Advertising*, 50(5), 528–547. DOI: 10.1080/00913367.2021.1977737

Buvar, A., Zsila, A., & Orosz, G. (2023). Non-green influencers promoting sustainable consumption: Dynamic norms enhance the credibility of authentic pro-environmental posts. *Frontiers in Psychology*, 14, 1112762. DOI: 10.3389/fpsyg.2023.1112762 PMID: 36844288

Campbell, C., & Farrell, J. R. (2020). More than meets the eye: The functional components underlying influencer marketing. *Business Horizons*, 63(4), 469–479. DOI: 10.1016/j.bushor.2020.03.003

Chandawarkar, A. A., Gould, D. J., & Grant Stevens, W. (2018). The top 100 social media influencers in plastic surgery on Twitter: Who should you be following? *Aesthetic Surgery Journal*, 38(8), 913–917. DOI: 10.1093/asj/sjy024 PMID: 29518179

Cho, K., Jung, K., Lee, M., Lee, Y., Park, J., & Dreamson, N. (2022). Qualitative approaches to evaluating social media influencers: A case-based literature review. *International Journal of Electronic Commerce Studies*, 13(2), 119–136. DOI: 10.7903/ijecs.2025

Collins, R. (2021). *Evangelism in the Tech Industry: Interviews with Evangelists*. Indiana University.

Dajah, S. (2020). Marketing through social media influencers. *International Journal of Business and Social Science*, 11(9), 10–12. DOI: 10.30845/ijbss.v11n9p9

Dcunha, A. A., Gonsalves, J. A., Gonsalves, L. R., Gonsalves, J. J., & Gaur, N. (2024). Marketing Suite Powered by Blockchain and Recommendation Systems. *2024 3rd International Conference on Applied Artificial Intelligence and Computing (ICAAIC)*, 1613–1618.

Doss, S. K. (2010). *"Spreading the good word": Toward an understanding of brand evangelism*.

Doss, S. K., & Carstens, D. S. (2014). Big five personality traits and brand evangelism. *International Journal of Marketing Studies*, 6(3), 13. DOI: 10.5539/ijms.v6n3p13

Driver, R. (2022). Instagram & the FTC: The Growth of Influencer Marketing & the Government's Ungainly Pursuit. *J. Bus. & Tech. L.*, 18, 289.

Goanta, C., & Ranchordás, S. (2020). The regulation of social media influencers: An introduction. In *The regulation of social media influencers* (pp. 1–20). Edward Elgar Publishing. DOI: 10.4337/9781788978286.00008

Harrigan, P., Daly, T. M., Coussement, K., Lee, J. A., Soutar, G. N., & Evers, U. (2021). Identifying influencers on social media. *International Journal of Information Management*, 56, 102246. DOI: 10.1016/j.ijinfomgt.2020.102246

Harrigan, P., Roy, S. K., & Chen, T. (2021). Do value cocreation and engagement drive brand evangelism? *Marketing Intelligence & Planning*, 39(3), 345–360. DOI: 10.1108/MIP-10-2019-0492

Harris, I. (2023). The Effectiveness of Mega Influencers, Macro Influencers, and Micro Influencers in Forming Brand Evangelists. *Jurnal Ilmiah Manajemen Ubhara*, 5(02), 254–263. DOI: 10.31599/jimu.v5i02.2992

Hassan, S. H., Teo, S. Z., Ramayah, T., & Al-Kumaim, N. H. (2021). The credibility of social media beauty gurus in young millennials' cosmetic product choice. *PLoS One*, 16(3), e0249286. DOI: 10.1371/journal.pone.0249286 PMID: 33780487

Himelboim, I., & Golan, G. J. (2023). A Social Network Approach to Social Media Influencers on Instagram: The Strength of Being a Nano-Influencer in Cause Communities. *Journal of Interactive Advertising*, 23(1), 1–13. DOI: 10.1080/15252019.2022.2139653

Hughes, C., Swaminathan, V., & Brooks, G. (2019). Driving Brand Engagement Through Online Social Influencers: An Empirical Investigation of Sponsored Blogging Campaigns. *Journal of Marketing*, 83(5), 78–96. DOI: 10.1177/0022242919854374

Imani Rad, A., & Banaeian Far, S. (2023). SocialFi transforms social media: An overview of key technologies, challenges, and opportunities of the future generation of social media. *Social Network Analysis and Mining*, 13(1), 42. DOI: 10.1007/s13278-023-01050-7

Iqani, M. (2019). Picturing luxury, producing value: The cultural labour of social media brand influencers in South Africa. *International Journal of Cultural Studies*, 22(2), 229–247. DOI: 10.1177/1367877918821237

Isyanto, P., Sapitri, R. G., & Sinaga, O. (2020). Micro influencers marketing and brand image to purchase intention of cosmetic products focallure. *Systematic Reviews in Pharmacy*, 11(1), 601–605.

Jenkins, E. L., Ilicic, J., Barklamb, A. M., & McCaffrey, T. A. (2020). Assessing the credibility and authenticity of social media content for applications in health communication: Scoping review. *Journal of Medical Internet Research*, 22(7), e17296. DOI: 10.2196/17296 PMID: 32706675

Jin, S. V., Muqaddam, A., & Ryu, E. (2019). Instafamous and social media influencer marketing. *Marketing Intelligence & Planning*, 37(5), 567–579. DOI: 10.1108/MIP-09-2018-0375

Kapoor, P. S., Balaji, M. S., & Jiang, Y. (2023). Greenfluencers as agents of social change: The effectiveness of sponsored messages in driving sustainable consumption. *European Journal of Marketing*, 57(2), 533–561. DOI: 10.1108/EJM-10-2021-0776

Karagür, Z., Becker, J.-M., Klein, K., & Edeling, A. (2022). How, why, and when disclosure type matters for influencer marketing. *International Journal of Research in Marketing*, 39(2), 313–335. DOI: 10.1016/j.ijresmar.2021.09.006

Kim, D. Y., & Kim, H.-Y. (2021). Trust me, trust me not: A nuanced view of influencer marketing on social media. *Journal of Business Research*, 134, 223–232. DOI: 10.1016/j.jbusres.2021.05.024

Kim, H. M., & Chakraborty, S. (2024). Exploring the diffusion of digital fashion and influencers' social roles in the Metaverse: An analysis of Twitter hashtag networks. *Internet Research*, 34(1), 107–128. DOI: 10.1108/INTR-09-2022-0727

Kim, M., & Lee, M. (2017). Brand-related user-generated content on social media: The roles of source and sponsorship. *Internet Research*, 27(5), 1085–1103. DOI: 10.1108/IntR-07-2016-0206

Landgrebe, J. (2024). The Rise of Digital Influencer Marketing. *HERMES-Journal of Language and Communication in Business*, 64(64), 75–102. DOI: 10.7146/hjlcb.vi64.143879

Lee, J., Walter, N., Hayes, J. L., & Golan, G. J. (2024). Do Influencers Influence? A Meta-Analytic Comparison of Celebrities and Social Media Influencers Effects. *Social Media + Society*, 10(3), 20563051241269269. DOI: 10.1177/20563051241269269

Lee, J. A., & Eastin, M. S. (2021). Perceived authenticity of social media influencers: Scale development and validation. *Journal of Research in Interactive Marketing*, 15(4), 822–841. DOI: 10.1108/JRIM-12-2020-0253

Leung, F. F., Gu, F. F., Li, Y., Zhang, J. Z., & Palmatier, R. W. (2022). Influencer Marketing Effectiveness. *Journal of Marketing*, 86(6), 93–115. DOI: 10.1177/00222429221102889

Lou, C., & Yuan, S. (2019). Influencer Marketing: How Message Value and Credibility Affect Consumer Trust of Branded Content on Social Media. *Journal of Interactive Advertising*, 19(1), 58–73. DOI: 10.1080/15252019.2018.1533501

Matzler, K., Renzl, B., & Faullant, R. (2007). Dimensions of price satisfaction: A replication and extension. *International Journal of Bank Marketing*, 25(6), 394–405. DOI: 10.1108/02652320710820345

Mishra, M., Kesharwani, A., & Gautam, D. R. V. (2021). Examining the relationship between consumer brand relationships and brand evangelism. *Australian Journal of Business and Management Research*, 6(1), 84–95. DOI: 10.52283/NSWRCA.AJBMR.20210601A07

Nandagiri, V., & Philip, L. (2018). Impact of influencers from Instagram and YouTube on their followers. *International Journal of Multidisciplinary Research and Modern Education*, 4(1), 61–65.

Nguyen, P.-H., Nguyen, D. N., & Nguyen, L. A. T. (2023). Quantitative insights into green purchase intentions: The interplay of health consciousness, altruism, and sustainability. *Cogent Business & Management*, 10(3), 2253616. DOI: 10.1080/23311975.2023.2253616

Okonkwo, I., & Namkoisse, E. (2023). The Role of Influencer Marketing in Building Authentic Brand Relationships Online. *Journal of Digital Marketing and Communication*, 3(2), 81–90. DOI: 10.53623/jdmc.v3i2.350

Oliveira, M., Barbosa, R., & Sousa, A. (2020). The Use of Influencers in Social Media Marketing. In Rocha, Á., Reis, J. L., Peter, M. K., & Bogdanović, Z. (Eds.), *Marketing and Smart Technologies* (Vol. 167, pp. 112–124). Springer Singapore., DOI: 10.1007/978-981-15-1564-4_12

Osmanova, I., Ozerden, S., Dalal, B., & Ibrahim, B. (2023). Examining the relationship between brand symbolism and brand evangelism through consumer brand identification: Evidence from Starbucks coffee brand. *Sustainability (Basel)*, 15(2), 1684. DOI: 10.3390/su15021684

Palakshappa, N., Bulmer, S., & Dodds, S. (2024). Co-creating sustainability: Transformative power of the brand. *Journal of Marketing Management*, 40(9–10), 820–850. DOI: 10.1080/0267257X.2024.2380261

Pedalino, F., & Camerini, A.-L. (2022). Instagram use and body dissatisfaction: The mediating role of upward social comparison with peers and influencers among young females. *International Journal of Environmental Research and Public Health*, 19(3), 1543. DOI: 10.3390/ijerph19031543 PMID: 35162562

Perez Breton Borbn, D. A. (2024). *Examining The Impact Of Different Types Of Social Media Influencers On Attitudes, Trust & Purchase Intent: Travel User Generated Content.*

Pornsrimate, K., & Khamwon, A. (2021). How to convert Millennial consumers to brand evangelists through social media micro-influencers. *Innovative Marketing*, 17(2).

Pourazad, N., Stocchi, L., & Narsey, S. (2023). A comparison of social media influencers' KPI patterns across platforms: Exploring differences in followers and engagement on Facebook, Instagram, YouTube, TikTok, and Twitter. *Journal of Advertising Research*, 63(2), 139–159. DOI: 10.2501/JAR-2023-008

Pöyry, E., Pelkonen, M., Naumanen, E., & Laaksonen, S.-M. (2021). A call for authenticity: Audience responses to social media influencer endorsements in strategic communication. In *Social media influencers in strategic communication* (pp. 103–118).

Prelipcean, M., Acatrinei, C., Gradinescu, I., & Canda, A. (2023). The Impact of Blockchain Technology on Marketing through Social Media. *Journal of Emerging Trends in Marketing and Management*, 1(1), 46–54.

Purohit, S., & Arora, R. (2024). Engagement: The Dynamic Evolution of Influencer Marketing in the Digital. *Advances in Data Analytics for Influencer Marketing: An Interdisciplinary Approach*, 29.

Rahman, K. T. (2022). Influencer Marketing and Behavioral Outcomes: How Types of Influencers Affect Consumer Mimicry? *SEISENSE Business Review*, 2(1), 43–54. DOI: 10.33215/sbr.v2i1.792

Rajput, A., Suryavanshi, K., Thapa, S. B., Gahlot, P., & Gandhi, A. (2024). The Impact of Social Media Influencers on Ecoconscious Consumers. *2024 ASU International Conference in Emerging Technologies for Sustainability and Intelligent Systems (ICETSIS)*, 1–6. DOI: 10.1109/ICETSIS61505.2024.10459444

Romero-Rodriguez, L. M., & Castillo-Abdul, B. (2023). Toward state-of-the-art on social marketing research in user-generated content (UGC) and influencers. *Journal of Management Development*, 42(6), 425–435. DOI: 10.1108/JMD-11-2022-0285

Rungruangjit, W., Chankoson, T., & Charoenpornpanichkul, K. (2023). Understanding Different Types of Followers' Engagement and the Transformation of Millennial Followers into Cosmetic Brand Evangelists. *Behavioral Sciences (Basel, Switzerland)*, 13(3), 270. DOI: 10.3390/bs13030270 PMID: 36975295

Saldanha, N., Mulye, R., & Japutra, A. (2024). How do consumers interact with social media influencers in extraordinary times? *Journal of Research in Interactive Marketing*, 18(3), 333–348. DOI: 10.1108/JRIM-02-2023-0062

Santiago, J. K., & Castelo, I. M. (2020). Digital influencers: An exploratory study of influencer marketing campaign process on instagram. [OJAKM]. *Online Journal of Applied Knowledge Management*, 8(2), 31–52. DOI: 10.36965/OJAKM.2020.8(2)31-52

Sashittal, H. C., Jassawalla, A. R., & Sachdeva, R. (2023). The influence of COVID-19 pandemic on consumer–brand relationships: Evidence of brand evangelism behaviors. *Journal of Brand Management*, 30(3), 245–260. DOI: 10.1057/s41262-022-00301-w

Schorn, A., Vinzenz, F., & Wirth, W. (2022). Promoting sustainability on Instagram: How sponsorship disclosures and benefit appeals affect the credibility of sinnfluencers. *Young Consumers*, 23(3), 345–361. DOI: 10.1108/YC-07-2021-1355

Schwemmer, C., & Ziewiecki, S. (2018). Social Media Sellout: The Increasing Role of Product Promotion on YouTube. *Social Media + Society*, 4(3), 205630511878672. DOI: 10.1177/2056305118786720

Sedda, P., & Husson, O. (2023). Social Media Influencers: A New Hybrid Professionalism in the Age of Platform Capitalism? In *Professionalism and Social Change: Processes of Differentiation Within, Between and Beyond Professions* (pp. 281–304). Springer International Publishing. DOI: 10.1007/978-3-031-31278-6_13

Sharma, B. K., Bhatt, V. K., & Arora, L. (2021). Influencer marketing—An instrument to proliferation of the digital occurrence. *International Journal of Enterprise Network Management*, 12(4), 340. DOI: 10.1504/IJENM.2021.119662

Sharma, P. (2023). Destination evangelism and engagement: Investigation from social media-based travel community. *Electronic Commerce Research and Applications*, 57, 101228. DOI: 10.1016/j.elerap.2022.101228

Sharma, P., & Khandeparkar, K. (2024). Exploring the nexus between influencers and brand evangelism. *Asia Pacific Journal of Marketing and Logistics*. Advance online publication. DOI: 10.1108/APJML-06-2023-0581

Singh, N. (2024). Consumers' Choice Behavior Towards Sustainable Fashion Based on Social Media Influence. In *Driving Green Marketing in Fashion and Retail* (pp. 1–25). IGI Global.

Smith, B. G., Hallows, D., Vail, M., Burnett, A., & Porter, C. (2021). Social media conversion: Lessons from faith-based social media influencers for public relations. *Journal of Public Relations Research*, 33(4), 231–249. DOI: 10.1080/1062726X.2021.2011728

Stoldt, R., Wellman, M., Ekdale, B., & Tully, M. (2019). Professionalizing and Profiting: The Rise of Intermediaries in the Social Media Influencer Industry. *Social Media + Society*, 5(1), 205630511983258. DOI: 10.1177/2056305119832587

Sutrisno, B., & Ariesta, Y. (2019). Beyond the use of code mixing by social media influencers in instagram. *Advances in Language and Literary Studies*, 10(6), 143–151. DOI: 10.7575/aiac.alls.v.10n.6p.143

Tafheem, N., El-Gohary, H., & Sobh, R. (2022). Social media user-influencer congruity: An analysis of social media platforms parasocial relationships. [IJCRMM]. *International Journal of Customer Relationship Marketing and Management*, 13(1), 1–26. DOI: 10.4018/IJCRMM.289213

Vaidya, R., & Karnawat, T. (2023). Conceptualizing influencer marketing: A literature review on the strategic use of social media influencers. *International Journal of Management, Public Policy and Research, 2*(SpecialIssue), 81–86.

Wang, E. S.-T., & Weng, Y.-J. (2024). Influence of social media influencer authenticity on their followers' perceptions of credibility and their positive word-of-mouth. *Asia Pacific Journal of Marketing and Logistics*, 36(2), 356–373. DOI: 10.1108/APJML-02-2023-0115

Wellman, M. L., Stoldt, R., Tully, M., & Ekdale, B. (2020). Ethics of Authenticity: Social Media Influencers and the Production of Sponsored Content. *Journal of Medical Ethics*, 35(2), 68–82. DOI: 10.1080/23736992.2020.1736078

Wentzell, K., Walker, H. R., Hughes, A. S., & Vessey, J. A. (2021). Engaging social media influencers to recruit hard-to-reach populations. *Nursing Research*, 70(6), 455–461. DOI: 10.1097/NNR.0000000000000544 PMID: 34334700

Wibawa, R. C., Pratiwi, C. P., & Larasati, H. (2021). The role of nano influencers through Instagram as an effective digital marketing strategy. *Conference Towards ASEAN Chairmanship 2023 (TAC 23 2021)*, 233–238.

Wielki, J. (2020). Analysis of the role of digital influencers and their impact on the functioning of the contemporary on-line promotional system and its sustainable development. *Sustainability (Basel)*, 12(17), 7138. DOI: 10.3390/su12177138

Woolley, S. C. (2022). Digital propaganda: The power of influencers. *Journal of Democracy*, 33(3), 115–129. DOI: 10.1353/jod.2022.0027

Yildirim, S. (2021). Do green women influencers spur sustainable consumption patterns? Descriptive evidences from social media influencers. *Ecofeminism and Climate Change*, 2(4), 198–210. DOI: 10.1108/EFCC-02-2021-0003

Chapter 6
Harnessing Data Analytics For Effective Influencer Marketing and Brand Evangelism

Pretti Jain
https://orcid.org/0009-0000-3178-0837
Maharishi Markandeshwer University (Deemed), Mullana,Ambala, India

Neetu Chaudhary
https://orcid.org/0000-0001-6589-4015
Maharishi Markandeshwer University (Deemed), Mullana Ambala India

ABSTRACT

This chapter discusses the significant connection between data analytics and influencer marketing, demonstrating the power of data-driven insights to boost brand evangelism. The initial phase involves utilizing data to identify and promote brand advocates and champions, while also analyzing consumer behavior and engagement metrics to enhance influencer marketing campaigns. Furthermore, the discussion encompasses the application of predictive analytics to forecast trends and guide the selection of influencers. Effective methods for recognizing and engaging with relevant industry influencers are discussed, emphasizing the importance of genuine and lasting partnerships. In this study, the strategies for evaluating the impact of influencer campaigns on brand awareness and sales will be examined. The chapter highlights the connection between data analytics and influencer marketing, demonstrating how data can assist in selecting influencers, targeting campaigns, and measuring influencer-generated content success.

DOI: 10.4018/979-8-3693-7773-4.ch006

Copyright © 2025, IGI Global. Copying or distributing in print or electronic forms without written permission of IGI Global is prohibited.

INTRODUCTION

Brand evangelism in the digital age is increasingly dependent on influencer marketing and data analytics, which is a result of the expansion of social media platforms and the changing nature of consumer-brand connections. According to Srinivasa et al. (2018), data analytics is essential for comprehending consumer behaviour, preferences, and trends. Brands can make well-informed decisions and customize their marketing tactics effectively with this understanding. Marketers can identify influential individuals who hold significant influence over their intended audience through the utilization of data collected from various sources, such as social media interactions. Micro-influencers are a powerful tool for fostering brand engagement and loyalty through influencer marketing. Millennials are attracted to micro-influencers due to their genuineness and tailored content, resulting in increased brand affection and ultimately leading to brand devotion (Pornsrimate & Khamwon 2021). The relevance and genuineness of content on platforms like Instagram are especially beneficial for fashion influencers in Southeast Asia, which greatly affects consumer-influencer interaction (Rungruangjit & Charoenpornpanichkul, 2022). Brand evangelism is a result of this involvement, where customers willingly spread the word about the brand to others, resulting in an increase in its visibility and authority (Anggraini, 2018). In addition to reflecting consumer behaviour, brand evangelism also reflects bigger socio-economic changes, such as the exploitation of digital labour, where influencers' unpaid promotional actions help brands become more visible and penetrate new markets (Çelik, 2024).

Also, due to the post-truth era, matters have become more complicated as influencers are perceived to be trustworthy and authentic sources of information, with subjective opinions and feelings taking precedence over objective facts. To establish a community of brand advocates, it is crucial to select the appropriate influencers and cultivate strong emotional connections with the brand (Rajendiran & Dorai, 2020). This tactic, like those employed by Apple, relies on their loyal clientele to disseminate favourable news and convince prospective buyers (Anggraini, 2018). A strong framework for brand evangelism can be created and maintained by brands with the integration of data analytics and influencer marketing, ensuring long-term customer loyalty and a competitive edge.

Objectives

The aims of this study are outlined as follows:

1. To identify and promote brand advocates and enhance influencer marketing campaigns through consumer behavior analysis.

2. To forecast trends, guide influencer selection, and recognize relevant industry influencers.
3. To evaluate the impact of influencer campaigns on brand awareness and sales, refining strategies based on data-driven insights for improved results.

METHODOLOGY

This study examines consumer behavior and engagement metrics to identify key brand advocates and optimize influencer marketing by analyzing secondary data sourced from Scopus papers and peer-reviewed journals. The data collection process specifically targets recent articles published within the past decade, chosen based on criteria such as relevance, peer-review evaluation, and the impact factor of the journal.

Leveraging Data insights to Identify Brand Advocates and Brand Champions

Identifying brand champions and advocates with data analytics is a multifaceted approach that focuses on sophisticated data processing techniques, social media analysis, and internal branding. Internal branding outcomes, such as employee alignment with the brand, brand knowledge, and brand belief, as well as how employees perceive the organization's support, are crucial in motivating employees to become brand champions. When there is a high perceived level of organisational support, employees' voluntary participation in brand advancement and good word-of-mouth are enhanced by organisational identity, which acts as a critical mediating element (Löhndorf & Diamantopoulos 2014). The use of OLAP technologies and automation can greatly reduce the amount of manual labor for data analysts. Identifying trends and patterns that highlight potential brand advocates can become easier with the help of this (Tang et al 2017). When it comes to advertising, strategic planning insights can help connect the brand with customers by identifying those who are most likely to become brand supporters and who strongly connect with the brand's message (Sebastián-Morillas et al 2020). By collecting and analyzing public behavioral data, social media analytics enhance this process by enabling businesses to quickly respond to customer requests and strengthen their competitive advantage (Chen 2023).

By utilizing behavioral analytics to model and analyze customer behaviors, businesses can identify committed consumers by analyzing their communication, sentiment, and product preferences across various channels, such as Reddit, Twitter, and YouTube. This approach is effective in identifying brand advocates and champions by distinguishing dedicated users based on indicators that assess trust, dedication, and interaction (Kafeza et al 2022). By combining these approaches, a comprehensive framework can be established for promoting strong brand advocacy through the use of data insights.

Significance of Utilizing data for Brand Promotion

Businesses can identify committed customers by analyzing their communication, sentiment, and product preferences across multiple channels, like Reddit, Twitter, and YouTube, using Behavioral Analytics to model and analyze customer behaviors. This approach is effective in identifying brand advocates and champions by distinguishing dedicated users based on indicators that assess trust, dedication, and the interaction (Kafeza et al 2022). A comprehensive framework for using data insights to promote strong brand advocacy can be provided by combining these approaches.

Moreover, data-driven methods enable understanding of the intricate connections between relationship quality, brand leadership, and customer experience quality, all of which are essential for building brand advocacy. According to Kumgliang & Khamwon 2022, Positive customer experiences greatly increase in perceived brand quality, innovativeness, and value, which in turn fosters trust, satisfaction, and commitment, ultimately strengthening brand advocacy, according to empirical research employing structural equation modelling (SEM). Furthermore, thorough data analysis helps steer clear of the traps created by skewed or unsubstantiated insights, guaranteeing that suggestions are grounded in fact rather than conjecture, preserving advocacy activities' efficacy and credibility (Atkins 2023).

Data may also be a potent tool for advocacy when it comes to home care providers since it can draw attention to their contributions and reveal employer infractions, which can challenge preconceived notions and foster worker unity (Ming 2023). The deliberate use of data leads to better results for brands and their stakeholders by ensuring that advocacy activities are based on reality and enhancing their impact.

- **Analyzing consumer behavior and engagement metrics to optimize influencer marketing campaigns**

Analyzing consumer behavior and engagement indicators is crucial for optimizing influencer marketing efforts. By doing this, marketers can customize their approaches and increase the impact and ROI. The necessity to choose relevant influencers who can produce and publish a variety of content types in order to effectively promote businesses has led to the growth of the influencer marketing sector, which is predicted to reach a global market value of $15 billion by 2022 (Lopez-Dawn & Giovanidis 2022). To comprehend the dynamics of consumer engagement, it is necessary to examine various factors. The motivational factors behind consumer-influencer engagement behaviors (CIEBs) include social connection, entertainment, information seeking, and rewards. The influence of these elements on content development, contribution, and consumption is significant, leading to improved customer interaction with recommended companies (Cheung et al 2022).

Additionally, agent-based models (ABMs) that mimic different scenarios and take into account real-world factors such as client interest, behavior, and readiness to pay can be utilized to determine the efficacy of influencer marketing. These models aid in determining the most effective influencer marketing methods, based on factors such as client interest levels and product type (luxury vs. non-luxury). Additionally, by examining the features and semantic patterns of opinion leaders' blogs, it is possible to analyse the engagement metrics on social media platforms and identify common elements that influence user engagement, like the quantity of tokens in blogs and platform-specific semantic patterns (Wang et al 2022). When considering factors like repeated exposure and forgetting effects, data-driven optimization frameworks can aid in influencer selection and message scheduling to maximize benefits over short and long horizons (Mallipeddi et al., 2022). Ultimately, Pradhan et al. (2023) conducted a systematic review of the literature on social media influencers and consumer engagement, emphasising the significance of comprehending the decisions, antecedents, and results of such engagement as a basis for creating successful influencer marketing campaigns. This information can be incorporated by marketers to create more compelling influencer marketing efforts.

Utilizing Predictive Analytics to Anticipate Trends and Guide Influencer Selection

Influencer selection and trend detection are greatly aided by predictive analytics, which uses a variety of machine learning and statistical methods to evaluate massive datasets and forecast future results. Within the e-commerce domain, precise forecasting of user behaviour and trends in marketing campaigns can greatly augment the efficacy of promotional tactics. To help with the selection of successful influencers for marketing campaigns, a model utilising text representation learning and recurrent neural networks (RNN) can, for example, anticipate user engagement and dynamically display changes in campaign influence trends (Xiao & Zhu, 2023).

Furthermore, Chen (2018) notes that correlated neural influence models are able to represent the sequential characteristics of research evolution and inter-conference dependencies, offering insights into popular subjects and influential colleagues that may be applied to influencer selection in marketing. The rapid rise in social media usage is causing businesses to implement influencer marketing strategies. By utilizing empirical analysis of social media interactions to select and schedule influencers, data-driven optimization frameworks can help maximize the success of campaigns with both short and long-term goals (Mallipeddi, 2022). Algorithmic solutions for influencer management help marketers choose the right influencers, using brand alignment and other classifications (Bishop, 2021). Finding influencers who can motivate large-scale user behaviour is essential, and the selection process may be made more clear and efficient by validating their impact by using discrete optimisation and feature selection to explain their network worth (Bevilacqua, 2013). Choosing the correct influencers (Johnson, & Geisser, 1983) requires evaluating the impact of data subsets in predictive models to improve future prediction accuracy. Last but not least, influence maximisation techniques that take into account various information transmission channels and competitive dynamics can maximise the selection of seed nodes, guaranteeing that the selected influencers can efficiently spread information and have the most possible impact. By using predictive analytics, marketers can predict trends and strategically select influencers by combining various methods, which can improve marketing effectiveness.

Influencer Marketing Strategies by Identifying and Collaborating with Relevant Industry Influencers

Recognising influencers who can motivate large-scale user behaviour is essential, and the selection process may be made more clear and efficient by validating their impact by using discrete optimisation and feature selection to explain their network worth (Bevilacqua, 2013). By assessing the impact of data subsets in predictive models, it is possible to improve future prediction accuracy, which is crucial for choosing the proper influencers (Johnson, & Geisser, 1983). By combining various methods, predictive analytics can provide a comprehensive framework for predicting trends and directing the strategic selection of influencers, which improves marketing effectiveness.

Johan and Arnesson (2023) cite the importance of influencers as 'ideological intermediaries' who promote a lifestyle over products. The genuineness and discourses they use have a significant impact on how audience perceives and engage. Influencer marketing can be enhanced by leveraging the business's well-established reputation through partnerships with well-known companies (Ibá<unk> ez-Sánchez, et al., 2022). According to the source credibility model and signalling theory, followers use heuristic cues from influencers like popularity and attractiveness to assess the efficacy of the influencer; category involvement and altruistic motives moderate these assessments (Hugh Wilkie, et al 2022).

It's crucial to consider an influencer's centrality within a social network when identifying them, as individuals with higher centrality metrics can have a stronger impact on social contagion processes (Iannelli, et al 2018). Influencers' followers, post content, and other elements all play a part in how effective influencer marketing is. Sponsor salience, follower numbers, and influencer originality increase effectiveness; however, new product releases may decrease it. To increase efficacy, a balanced strategy involving influencer engagement, follower-brand fit, and post-positivity is advised (Leung et al., 2022). Effective social media influencer outreach is crucial, and businesses should constantly assess and modify their approaches to fit the changing digital environment (Enke, et al. 2021). According to Kemp et al. (2019) influencer marketing is acknowledged as a technical disruptor that enables businesses to promote items naturally and cultivate audience trust. The most powerful accounts in a network, including media and promotional accounts, can be discovered through network analysis and utilized to enhance marketing efforts. To increase their reach and effectiveness, destination marketing organizations (DMOs) might gain from forming strategic alliances with important influencers (Bokunewicz, et al. 2017). By incorporating these different techniques and insights, brands can improve their marketing efforts by discovering and engaging with industry influencers efficiently.

Integrating Data Analytics and Influencer Marketing: Using data to Inform Influencer Selection and Campaign Targeting

Integrating data analytics into influencer marketing through a comprehensive strategy leads to a significant improvement in influencer selection and target targeting. The use of social media platforms is essential in current marketing strategies because they offer a wealth of user-generated content that can be examined using cutting-edge data analytics methods like deep learning and machine learning. With the use of these methods, which include sentiment analysis and predictive modelling, marketers may create more individualised and targeted campaigns by gaining deep insights into public opinion and new trends (Leung et al., 2022).

In today's marketing strategies, social media platforms are necessary because they offer a lot of user-generated content that can be analyzed using cutting-edge data analytics methods such as deep learning and machine learning. The PICTURES acrostic is a useful tool for optimizing influencer partnerships by ensuring a good fit between an influencer and an organization. (Mallipeddi, et al. 2022). Analysing interaction rates and grouping influencers into mega and minor tiers are important steps in selecting the proper influencers, since they can improve business outcomes and brand reach (Doshi et al., 2022). But it's important to take into account the expenses of influencer marketing, and elements like influencer uniqueness, follower count, and sponsor prominence are important in judging how successful these campaigns are (Dhun et al., 2023)). The problem of network seeding involves locating the most effective influencers to disseminate a message, and it can be solved with data-driven optimization frameworks that take into account both short- and long-term campaign objectives. The optimization of influencer selection and message scheduling is achieved by using empirical data from Twitter and other platforms to estimate characteristics such as multiple exposure impact and forgetting effect, as described by Hugh Wilkie, et al. 2022). Another important factor to take into account is the trade-off between reach and cost. To quantify this trade-off and identify the best sponsorship tactics, the follower elasticity of impressions (FEI) framework calculates the percentage gain in impressions in relation to the growth in follower size. The follower elasticity of impressions (FEI) framework assists in quantifying this trade-off by calculating the percentage gain in impressions in relation to the increase in follower size. This information is useful in determining the best sponsorship tactics. ABMs, which are agents, use real-world characteristics such as client interest, behavior, and willingness to pay to replicate the dynamics of influencer campaigns in a variety of circumstances. These models help determine the most effective influencer strategies based on the nature of the product and customer interest, showing, for example, that nano-influencers perform better for non-luxury products while celebrities are more effective for luxury items (Černikovaitė, et al 2023) (Zhang et al 2023)

Ultimately, campaign efficacy and strategy can be further informed by a comprehensive digital marketing data analytics model that incorporates website performance, social media metrics, email marketing, and customer journey analysis. This will guarantee that all facets of digital interaction are in line with marketing objectives (Lagree, et at 2018). By combining these different data analytics techniques, businesses can select influencers and target their campaigns with greater accuracy, resulting in more successful and efficient marketing results.

Integrating Data Analytics and Influencer Marketing -Tracking and Analyzing the Performance of Influencer-driven Content

According to the Elaboration Likelihood Model, linguistic features in influencers' posts may affect behavioural interactions with the content through peripheral or central route processing (Syrdal & McDowell, 2023). To analyse the data, two types of techniques are used i.e., text mining and natural language processing techniques. Choosing an appropriate influencer is crucial because it entails assessing the influencer's current brand associations, potential hazards, and brand fit. These factors can be determined by quantitative content analysis on social media (Černikovaitė & Karazijienė (2023). Influencer marketing research has evolved over time, and bibliometric and content analysis tools like the BiblioShiny app and Bibliometrix R-tool can aid in reviewing this shift and identify important methods, theories, and emerging topics that inform present practices (Tanwar & Srivastava (2022). According to (Mallipeddi & Zhu, 2022) data-driven optimization frameworks can be used to tackle the network seeding problem, assisting firms in choosing influencers and scheduling their message postings to maximize benefits over both short and long horizons. Another important factor is the freshness or newness of content, as posts typically lose popularity quickly. Analytical models based on historical interaction data may estimate popularity of posts and enhance engagement strategies (Vassio & Chiasserini (2022). An engagement elasticity perspective is used to assess the costs and efficacy of influencer marketing by looking at the influencer, their followers, and the content itself. The results show that originality of influencer, their content, follower size, and sponsor salience increase efficacy while new product launch posts may decrease it (Leung & Palmatier, 2022). Social media influencers' (SMIs') similarity and credibility to their audience have a big impact on their audience's intellectual, emotional, and behavioral engagement. These engagement dimensions can be measured using structural equation modeling, and informativeness and entertainment content have different roles to play (Gupta & Dash, 2023). Influencers' popularity and attractiveness act as psychological markers for followers, affecting how effective they perceive them to be. Altruistic motivations and category involvement mitigate these effects, increasing brand authenticity, engagement, and favorable sentiments toward posts (Hugh & Gray, 2022). Influencers and social media users have a relationship that is fueled by the interesting, novel, dependable, and understandable content that they post. This relationship can strengthen emotional attachment and improve the quality of the information that users post, urging users to engage with or recommend influencers and ultimately increasing their popularity (Zhang & Choi, 2022). Finally, influencers decode and transmit promotional messages within the context of social media as part of the structure of commercial associations between organizations and influencers. Based on their audience knowledge, influencers interpret these messages, which can be examined through semiotic evaluation (Vanninen & Kantamaa, 2023)). Through the utilisation of these varied analytical methodologies, brands can proficiently monitor and evaluate the efficacy of influencer-generated content, guaranteeing more tactical and consequential influencer marketing initiatives.

- Optimizing influencer marketing strategies based on data-driven insights

Using sophisticated models and algorithms to optimize influencer marketing strategies with data-driven insights increases the effectiveness of marketing campaigns. Network seeding—the process of identifying and choosing influencers—is crucial and has been the subject of several optimization frameworks. To improve the selection and scheduling of influencer posts, for example, a data-driven optimization system has been established for both short- and long-term influencer marketing campaigns. It incorporates parameters such as the forgetting effect and multiple exposure effect (Mallipeddi, et al., 2022). Furthermore, the Celfie approach outperforms conventional methods in terms of seed set quality and speed of computation by using learned influence representations from diffusion streams to increase the precision and effectiveness of influence spread estimation (Panagopoulos, et al., 2020). Another strategy is to formulate the estimated influencer marketing problem as a convex set up and solve it with the Frank-Wolfe method. This method is appropriate for large-scale networks because it connects to the global optimum with minimal computational complexity (Lopez-Dawn, et al., 2022). Additionally, the GT-UCB algorithm ensures high-quality spreads even in the lack of historical activation data by providing a quick estimate of influencers' remaining potential based on likely upper confidence bounds (Lagrée, et al., 2018). Together, these techniques show how crucial it is to combine cutting-edge algorithms with empirical data to maximize influencer marketing strategies, which will ultimately result in more scalable and successful campaigns on a variety of social media platforms.

CONCLUSION

The incorporation of powerful data analytics, like machine learning and deep learning techniques, has transformed social media platforms into indispensable tools for business-customer interactions. These analytics are crucial in gaining important insights from user-generated material. Marketers can create customized advertising campaigns and personalized customer experiences that enhance brand loyalty and gain an understanding of public opinion and new trends with the use of these information. The popularity of influencer marketing has increased due to its ability to generate significant economic results and viral product endorsements. Influence marketing involves working with well-known individuals to promote brands. It is crucial to determine an influencer's effectiveness because attributes such as popularity and attractiveness function as heuristic indicators that help determine how effective they are.

By involving categories and having altruistic goals, these cues result in an increase in brand authenticity, engagement, and favourable opinions towards influencer posts (Bansal & Bhati 2022). By providing personalised and interesting conversational experiences and utilising the influencer's knowledge and authenticity to foster a smooth user-AI interaction, the combination of influencer marketing and AI technologies like ChatGPT increases user engagement even further (Saini et al 2024). Data-driven frameworks for influencer marketing campaign optimization help businesses maximize their gains by choosing the correct influencers and strategically arranging their message uploads. The combination of several influencers and elements such as multiple exposure and forgetting effects are taken into account in this method, leading to almost ideal solutions for both short- and long-horizon campaigns (Mallipeddi et al., 2022). A thorough assessment of influencers' worth can be achieved by quantifying their performance using both quantitative metrics (such as follower count and engagement rate) and qualitative data (such as demographics, natural text patterns, and visual content). The data is able to be used in machine learning algorithms for scoring, clustering, or recommendation (Narassiguin & Sargent 2019). The trustworthiness of influencers, their posts' content, and their alignment with the brand have a significant impact on brand knowledge, attachment, and buying intentions, particularly among Gen Z customers. The influencer's content and alignment with the brand are the two factors that impede the relationship between the influencer's message and the consumer's perception of the brand (Attri & Bhagwat 2022). The prominence of quantitative data in influencer marketing highlights the role metrics play in the fashion influence industry, emphasising how numbers are used for commercial gain and the close connection between datafication, quantification, and capitalism (Rocamora 2022). Marketers can analyze influencer marketing through social media analytics by gathering and analyzing digital data from different social media platforms methodically. By creating a variety of research opportunities, it is possible to develop marketing strategies that are more ethical, sustainable, and effective (Johnson & Sandström, 2023). This comprehensive, data-driven strategy is designed to increase influencer marketing's effectiveness and foster long-term brand growth and loyalty through fruitful brand evangelism campaigns.

REFERENCES

Anggraini, L. (2018). Understanding brand evangelism and the dimensions involved in a consumer becoming brand evangelist. *Sriwijaya International Journal of Dynamic Economics and Business*, 63-84.

Arnesson, J. (2023). Influencers as ideological intermediaries: Promotional politics and authenticity labour in influencer collaborations. *Media Culture & Society*, 45(3), 528–544. DOI: 10.1177/01634437221117505

Atkins, J. (2023). The Perils of Advocacy. *arXiv preprint arXiv:2306.09492*.

Attri, R., & Bhagwat, J. (2022). Influencer marketing in data-driven world. *Management Dynamics*, 22(2), 8.

Bansal, M., & Bhati, N. (2022). Influencer marketing: Its antecedents and behavioural outcomes. In *Digital Marketing Outreach* (pp. 29–42). Routledge India. DOI: 10.4324/9781003315377-3

Bevilacqua, G. S., Clare, S., Goyal, A., & Lakshmanan, L. V. (2013, December). Validating network value of influencers by means of explanations. In *2013 IEEE 13th International Conference on Data Mining* (pp. 967-972). IEEE. DOI: 10.1109/ICDM.2013.159

Bishop, S. (2021). Influencer management tools: Algorithmic cultures, brand safety, and bias. *Social Media + Society*, 7(1), 20563051211003066. DOI: 10.1177/20563051211003066

Bokunewicz, J. F., & Shulman, J. (2017). Influencer identification in Twitter networks of destination marketing organizations. *Journal of Hospitality and Tourism Technology*, 8(2), 205–219. DOI: 10.1108/JHTT-09-2016-0057

Çelik, F. (2024). Brand Evangelism Within the Framework of Digital Labor. In *Advancements in Socialized and Digital Media Communications* (pp. 50–66). IGI Global. DOI: 10.4018/979-8-3693-0855-4.ch005

Černikovaitė, M. E., & Karazijienė, Ž. (2023). The role of influencers and opinion formers marketing on creative brand communication. *Creativity Studies*, 16(2), 371–383. DOI: 10.3846/cs.2023.15722

Chan, T. H., Hung, K., & Tse, D. K. (2023). Comparing E-Commerce Micro-and Macroinfluencers in TikTok Videos: Effects of Strategies on Audience Likes, Audience Shares, and Brand Sales. *Journal of Interactive Advertising*, 23(4), 307–322. DOI: 10.1080/15252019.2023.2273253

Chen, Y. (2023). Comparing content marketing strategies of digital brands using machine learning. *Humanities & Social Sciences Communications*, 10(1), 1–18. DOI: 10.1057/s41599-023-01544-x

Cheung, M. L., Leung, W. K., Yang, M. X., Koay, K. Y., & Chang, M. K. (2022). Exploring the nexus of social media influencers and consumer brand engagement. *Asia Pacific Journal of Marketing and Logistics*, 34(10), 2370–2385. DOI: 10.1108/APJML-07-2021-0522

Dhun, & Dangi, H. K. (2023). Influencer marketing: Role of influencer credibility and congruence on brand attitude and eWOM. *Journal of Internet Commerce*, 22(sup1), S28-S72.

Doshi, R., Ramesh, A., & Rao, S. (2022). Modeling influencer marketing campaigns in social networks. *IEEE Transactions on Computational Social Systems*, 10(1), 322–334. DOI: 10.1109/TCSS.2022.3140779

Enke, N., & Borchers, N. S. (2021). Social media influencers in strategic communication: A conceptual framework for strategic social media influencer communication. In *Social media influencers in strategic communication* (pp. 7–23). Routledge. DOI: 10.4324/9781003181286-2

Fernandes, R., Rodrigues, A. P., & Shetty, B. (2022, December). Influencers analysis from social media data. In *2022 International Conference on Artificial Intelligence and Data Engineering (AIDE)* (pp. 217-222). IEEE. DOI: 10.1109/AIDE57180.2022.10059732

Ghareeb, N. B., Aboutabl, A. E., Shalash, S. O., & Mostafa, A. M. (2024, March). Using Data Analytics Techniques for Enhancing Social Media Marketing Processes. In *2024 6th International Conference on Computing and Informatics (ICCI)* (pp. 443-451). IEEE. DOI: 10.1109/ICCI61671.2024.10485047

Gupta, S., Mahajan, R., & Dash, S. B. (2023). The impact of influencer-sourced brand endorsement on online consumer brand engagement. *Journal of Strategic Marketing*, •••, 1–17. DOI: 10.1080/0965254X.2023.2200389

Gurrieri, L., Drenten, J., & Abidin, C. (2023). Symbiosis or parasitism? A framework for advancing interdisciplinary and socio-cultural perspectives in influencer marketing. *Journal of Marketing Management*, 39(11-12), 911–932. DOI: 10.1080/0267257X.2023.2255053

Han, X., Wang, L., & Fan, W. (2023). Cost-effective social media influencer marketing. *INFORMS Journal on* Hugh Wilkie, D. C., Dolan, R., Harrigan, P., & Gray, H. (2022). Influencer marketing effectiveness: The mechanisms that matter. *European Journal of Marketing*, 56(12), 3485–3515.

Iannelli, F., Mariani, M. S., & Sokolov, I. M. (2018). Influencers identification in complex networks through reaction-diffusion dynamics. *Physical Review. E*, 98(6), 062302. DOI: 10.1103/PhysRevE.98.062302

Ibáñez-Sánchez, S., Flavián, M., Casaló, L. V., & Belanche, D. (2022). Influencers and brands successful collaborations: A mutual reinforcement to promote products and services on social media. *Journal of Marketing Communications*, 28(5), 469–486. DOI: 10.1080/13527266.2021.1929410

Johnson, P. C., & Sandström, C. (2023). 1 Making use of digital methods to study influencer marketing. *The Dynamics of Influencer Marketing, 5*.

Johnson, W., & Geisser, S. (1983). A predictive view of the detection and characterization of influential observations in regression analysis. *Journal of the American Statistical Association*, 78(381), 137–144. DOI: 10.1080/01621459.1983.10477942

Kafeza, E., Rompolas, G., Kyriazidis, S., & Makris, C. (2022). Time-series clustering for determining behavioral-based brand loyalty of users across social media. *IEEE Transactions on Computational Social Systems*, 10(4), 1951–1965. DOI: 10.1109/TCSS.2022.3219781

Kapitan, S., Van Esch, P., Soma, V., & Kietzmann, J. (2022). Influencer marketing and authenticity in content creation. *Australasian Marketing Journal*, 30(4), 342–351. DOI: 10.1177/18393349211011171

Kemp, A., Randon McDougal, E., & Syrdal, H. (2019). The matchmaking activity: An experiential learning exercise on influencer marketing for the digital marketing classroom. *Journal of Marketing Education*, 41(2), 141–153. DOI: 10.1177/0273475318803415

Keylock, M., & Faulds, M. (2012). From customer loyalty to social advocacy. *Journal of Direct, Data and Digital Marketing Practice*, 14(2), 160–165. DOI: 10.1057/dddmp.2012.37

Kumari, A., Golyan, A., Shah, R., & Raval, N. (2024). Introduction to Data Analytics. In *Recent Trends and Future Direction for Data Analytics* (pp. 1–14). IGI Global. DOI: 10.4018/979-8-3693-3609-0.ch001

Kumgliang, O., & Khamwon, A. (2022). Antecedents of brand advocacy in online food delivery services: An empirical investigation. *Innovative Marketing, 18*(3).

Lagrée, P., Cappé, O., Cautis, B., & Maniu, S. (2018). Algorithms for online influencer marketing. [TKDD]. *ACM Transactions on Knowledge Discovery from Data*, 13(1), 1–30. DOI: 10.1145/3274670

Lee, J. A., & Eastin, M. S. (2021). Perceived authenticity of social media influencers: Scale development and validation. *Journal of Research in Interactive Marketing*, 15(4), 822–841. DOI: 10.1108/JRIM-12-2020-0253

Leung, F. F., Gu, F. F., Li, Y., Zhang, J. Z., & Palmatier, R. W. (2022). Influencer marketing effectiveness. *Journal of Marketing*, 86(6), 93–115. DOI: 10.1177/00222429221102889

llipeddi, R. R., Kumar, S., Sriskandarajah, C., & Zhu, Y. (2022). A framework for analyzing influencer marketing in social *Science*, 68(1), 75-104.

Löhndorf, B., & Diamantopoulos, A. (2014). Internal branding: Social identity and social exchange perspectives on turning employees into brand champions. *Journal of Service Research*, 17(3), 310–325. DOI: 10.1177/1094670514522098

Lopez-Dawn, R., & Giovanidis, A. (2022). Optimal Influencer Marketing Campaign Under Budget Constraints Using Frank-Wolfe. *IEEE Transactions on Network Science and Engineering*, 10(2), 1015–1031. DOI: 10.1109/TNSE.2022.3225955

Mallipeddi, R. R., Kumar, S., Sriskandarajah, C., & Zhu, Y. (2022). A framework for analyzing influencer marketing in social networks: Selection and scheduling of influencers. *Management Science*, 68(1), 75–104. DOI: 10.1287/mnsc.2020.3899

Marcelo, C., & Marcelo, P. (2021). Influencers educativos en Twitter. Análisis de hashtags y estructura relacional. *Comunicar: Revista Científica de Comunicación y Educación*, 29(68), 73–83. DOI: 10.3916/C68-2021-06

McKenney, D., & White, T. (2017). Selecting transfer entropy thresholds for influence network prediction. *Social Network Analysis and Mining*, 7(1), 1–14. DOI: 10.1007/s13278-017-0421-x

Ming, J. (2023, October). Data Advocacy for Visibility of Home Care Workers. In *Companion Publication of the 2023 Conference on Computer Supported Cooperative Work and Social Computing* (pp. 444-447). DOI: 10.1145/3584931.3608922

Narassiguin, A., & Sargent, S. (2019). Data Science for Influencer Marketing: feature processing and quantitative analysis. *arXiv preprint arXiv:1906.05911*.

Nassif, A. B., Azzeh, M., Banitaan, S., & Neagu, D. (2016). Guest editorial: Special issue on predictive analytics using machine learning. *Neural Computing & Applications*, 27(8), 2153–2155. DOI: 10.1007/s00521-016-2327-3

Pangarkar, A., & Rathee, S. (2023). The role of conspicuity: Impact of social influencers on purchase decisions of luxury consumers. *International Journal of Advertising*, 42(7), 1150–1177. DOI: 10.1080/02650487.2022.2084265

Pornsrimate, K., & Khamwon, A. (2021). How to convert Millennial consumers to brand evangelists through social media micro-influencers. *Innovative Marketing*, 17(2).

Pöyry, E., Pelkonen, M., Naumanen, E., & Laaksonen, S. M. (2021). A call for authenticity: Audience responses to social media influencer endorsements in strategic communication. In *Social media influencers in strategic communication* (pp. 103–118). Routledge. DOI: 10.4324/9781003181286-6

Pradhan, B., Kishore, K., & Gokhale, N. (2023). Social media influencers and consumer engagement: A review and future research agenda. *International Journal of Consumer Studies*, 47(6), 2106–2130. DOI: 10.1111/ijcs.12901

Rajendiran, A., & Dorai, S. (2020). Friendship to kinship: Evaluating the role of consumer brand engagement to promote brand evangelism. In *Handbook of Research on the Impact of Fandom in Society and Consumerism* (pp. 171–192). IGI Global. DOI: 10.4018/978-1-7998-1048-3.ch009

Rocamora, A. (2022). The datafication and quantification of fashion: The case of fashion influencers. *Fashion Theory*, 26(7), 1109–1133. DOI: 10.1080/1362704X.2022.2048527

Rungruangjit, W., & Charoenpornpanichkul, K. (2022). Building stronger brand evangelism for sustainable marketing through micro-influencer-generated content on Instagram in the fashion industry. *Sustainability (Basel)*, 14(23), 15770. DOI: 10.3390/su142315770

Saini, S., Ngah, A. H., Sahai, S., & Bansal, R. (2024). When AI Meets Influence: Exploring the Integration of ChatGPT and Influencer Marketing. In *Leveraging ChatGPT and Artificial Intelligence for Effective Customer Engagement* (pp. 272-284). IGI Global.

Scholz, J. (2021). How consumers consume social media influence. *Journal of Advertising*, 50(5), 510–527. DOI: 10.1080/00913367.2021.1980472

Sebastián-Morillas, A., Martín-Soladana, I., & Clemente-Mediavilla, J. (2020). Importancia de los 'insights' en el proceso estratégico y creativo de las campañas publicitarias. *Estudios sobre el Mensaje Periodístico*, 26(1), 339–348. DOI: 10.5209/esmp.66570

Srinivasa, K. G. GM, S., Srinivasa, K. G., & GM, S. (2018). Introduction to Data Analytics. *Network Data Analytics: A Hands-On Approach for Application Development*, 3-28.

Steils, N., Martin, A., & Toti, J. F. (2022). Managing the transparency paradox of social-media influencer disclosures: How to improve authenticity and engagement when disclosing influencer–sponsor relationships. *Journal of Advertising Research*, 62(2), 148–166. DOI: 10.2501/JAR-2022-008

Syrdal, H. A., Myers, S., Sen, S., Woodroof, P. J., & McDowell, W. C. (2023). Influencer marketing and the growth of affiliates: The effects of language features on engagement behaviour. *Journal of Business Research*, 163, 113875. DOI: 10.1016/j.jbusres.2023.113875

Tang, B., Han, S., Yiu, M. L., Ding, R., & Zhang, D. (2017, May). Extracting top-k insights from multi-dimensional data. In *Proceedings of the 2017 ACM international conference on management of data* (pp. 1509-1524). DOI: 10.1145/3035918.3035922

Tanwar, A. S., Chaudhry, H., & Srivastava, M. K. (2022). Trends in influencer marketing: A review and bibliometric analysis. *Journal of Interactive Advertising*, 22(1), 1–27. DOI: 10.1080/15252019.2021.2007822

Vanninen, H., Mero, J., & Kantamaa, E. (2023). Social media influencers as mediators of commercial messages. *Journal of Internet Commerce, 22*(sup1), S4-S27.

Vassio, L., Garetto, M., Leonardi, E., & Chiasserini, C. F. (2022). Mining and modelling temporal dynamics of followers' engagement on online social networks. *Social Network Analysis and Mining*, 12(1), 96. DOI: 10.1007/s13278-022-00928-2 PMID: 35937770

Wang, J., Yang, Y., Liu, Q., Fang, Z., Sun, S., & Xu, Y. (2022). An empirical study of user engagement in influencer marketing on Weibo and WeChat. *IEEE Transactions on Computational Social Systems*, 10(6), 3228–3240. DOI: 10.1109/TCSS.2022.3204177

Wei, X., Chen, H., Ramirez, A., Jeon, Y., & Sun, Y. (2022). Influencers as endorsers and followers as consumers: Exploring the role of parasocial relationship, congruence, and followers' identifications on consumer–brand engagement. *Journal of Interactive Advertising*, 22(3), 269–288. DOI: 10.1080/15252019.2022.2116963

Xiao, Y., Zhu, Y., He, W., & Huang, M. (2023). Influence prediction model for marketing campaigns on e-commerce platforms. *Expert Systems with Applications*, 211, 118575. DOI: 10.1016/j.eswa.2022.118575

Yan, M., Kwok, A. P. K., Chan, A. H. S., Zhuang, Y. S., Wen, K., & Zhang, K. C. (2023). An empirical investigation of the impact of influencer live-streaming ads in e-commerce platforms on consumers' buying impulse. *Internet Research*, 33(4), 1633–1663. DOI: 10.1108/INTR-11-2020-0625

Zhang, X., & Choi, J. (2022). The importance of social influencer-generated contents for user cognition and emotional attachment: An information relevance perspective. *Sustainability (Basel)*, 14(11), 6676. DOI: 10.3390/su14116676

Zniva, R., Weitzl, W. J., & Lindmoser, C. (2023). Be constantly different! How to manage influencer authenticity. *Electronic Commerce Research*, 23(3), 1485–1514. DOI: 10.1007/s10660-022-09653-6

Chapter 7
Data-Driven Insights:
The Impact of Engagement Metrics and Sentiment Analysis on Brand Evangelism and Affinity

Supriya Pathak
https://orcid.org/0009-0004-3602-3172
Oriental University, Indore, India

Rishikaysh Kaakandikar
https://orcid.org/0000-0003-0349-6788
SaiBalaji International Institute of Management Sciences, Pune Research Organization, India

Dheeraj Nim
https://orcid.org/0000-0003-1564-0097
Oriental University, Indore, India

ABSTRACT

This study examines the role of engagement metrics in developing brand affinity across various industries, focusing on emotional connections between consumers and brands. It highlights how platforms like LinkedIn have shifted brand-consumer interactions from passive to active engagement (Hudson et al., 2016). Theoretical frameworks, such as Katz et al.'s uses and gratifications theory (1973), explain how likes, shares, and comments reflect social validation. Case studies of IBM and Coca-Cola illustrate how brands leverage these metrics to foster loyalty and trust. Integrating sentiment analysis is crucial for understanding consumer perceptions (Agnihotri et al., 2020; McGowan & Johnson, 2021), allowing brands to adapt strategies for meaningful engagement.

DOI: 10.4018/979-8-3693-7773-4.ch007

1. INTRODUCTION

Customer-brand identification, which is the extent of the bond that a consumer feels with a brand, has emerged as a crucial area of interest in the organizations' strategies to foster customer loyalty (Ashley & Tuten, 2015). With the onset of technology, social media sites have brought in about such connections through channels that are unique selling points to brands. The various retweets, likes, comments, and shares are clearly instrumental in the way that consumers engage with brands, and have indeed a critical role in the formation of brand loyalty (Hudson et al., 2016). Through creation of social experiences involving social media, consumers can be engaged emotionally, the aspect of credibility is achieved and consumers develop brand attachment as postulated by De Vries et al. (2012). Therefore, there exists a high potential for brand affinity and engagement as advanced technological solutions and becomes mainstream with advanced technological solutions such as the Metaverse (Mittal & Bansal, 2023).

The approach that would be most helpful in analyzing the motivations for consumers' interaction with social media content is the uses and gratifications theory (Katz et al., 1973). The uses and gratifications theory provides a valuable framework for understanding the motivations behind consumer engagement with social media content. According to this theory, individuals actively seek out media to satisfy specific needs, including entertainment, social interaction, and information acquisition. Social media engagement metrics, such as likes, shares, and comments, serve as forms of social validation and feedback, which fulfill users' social and emotional needs, thereby contributing to a stronger bond with the brand (Ashley & Tuten, 2015). Broadcasting theory, based on this concept supposes that individual seek media in order to fulfill certain needs such as entertainment, interaction and information. Likes, shares and comments on social media differ from other engagement measures since they act as a form of feedback which enhances the social and emotional needs of users hence the bond with a brand (Ashley & Tuten, 2015, p. 175).

Nowadays, most businesses can reach a high level of engagement with the customers through applying Social Media Marketing (SMM), that is, marketing communication by using social media allowing the live chats by brands, comments, and reactions that help establish a brand tribe (Ao et al., 2023). Thus, influencer marketing is also relevant, knowing that message value and credibility heavily influence consumer trust in branded content (Lou & Yuan, 2019). Taking advantage of the social media interaction features, consumer engagement generated from social media features provides real-time feedback that persuasively influences the purchase intention (Kim & Kim, 2021). The collected engagement metrics and sentiment analysis lead to the synthesis of structured data that support brands in improving their dialogue with consumers and fostering loyal brand ambassadors (Vrontis et al., 2021).

With people being able to work more flexibly there are pros and cons regarding communication and collaboration within the new regimes of remote work. The use of Virtual Reality (VR) can tap into gamification to deliver engagement environments that mimic face-to-face interactions thus strengthening brand loyalty and advocacy (Pathak & Malpani, 2025). Due to the implementation of affordances in VR, organizations benefit from the improved group dynamics, efficient communication, and improved emotional connections which lead to positive affect toward the brand.

However, Sentiment Analysis (SA) represent the most important measure of brand affinity. To begin with, there is sentiment analysis, which looks at textual data to identify consumers' attitudes, towards the emotions and opinions such customers bear. It is only when engagement is measured alongside sentiment analysis that brands are in a position to see where it is seen as positive, where it should be improved upon or where it is unnecessary. This can all be done, and therefore brands get a view not only of the level of engagement but also the positive or negative sentiments of these engagers making the view of brand affinity more encompassing.

In this chapter, an extensive case study is provided that shows that various industries use brand affinity strategies based on the analysis of sentiment and engagement data. Analyzing these cases, we consider how social media engagement and sentiment analysis can be applied by companies across different industries to strengthen brand identification and brand equity consequences for customers. The implications of the findings point to the conclusion that brand strategies need to be informed by the engagement metrics and the sentiment analysis, quantitative and qualitative aspects, so as to improve the overall brand communication with consumers and build sustainable consumer-brand relationships.

This research study has following objectives -

- To explore the role of engagement metrics (likes, shares, comments) in developing brand affinity.
- To understand how sentiment analysis, using machine learning and NLP techniques, can uncover consumer emotions.
- To demonstrate real-world applications and case studies that link engagement metrics and sentiment analysis to brand evangelism.

2. EXPLORING THE ROLE OF ENGAGEMENT METRICS IN DEVELOPING BRAND AFFINITY

Another important marketing goal for many organizations is brand affection/brand affinity or the extent to which the consumer is loyal to the brand. Following the rise of social networks as primary marketing tools, engagement KPIs —likes, shares, comments — became key for the development of brand loyalty. This section focuses on how these measures of engagement affect the formation of branding affinity as this literature review demonstrates.

2.1. Theoretical Framework

2.1.1. Social Media Interactivity and Brand Equity

Ashley and Tuten (2015) define social media engagement as the direct communication that takes place between consumers and brands on the social web, and the amount of engagement generated is typically assessed using engagement metrics such as likes, shares and comments. According to Hudson et al. (2016), the use of social media elicits changes in the brand-consumer communication from a one-way communication process with customers to a two-way communication full of emotions resulting in increased brand loyalty. This makes it infamous for building brand affinity because it establishes a self interest as well as a social interest.

According to the uses and gratifications theory advanced by Katz et al. (1973), the two concepts pointed at present also serve the function of strengthening the brand's audience identification. According to the theory, people purposefully select media to fulfil certain needs such as for fun, companionship and now as information. On social media, the act of liking, sharing and commenting gives feedback loops, giving users the social interaction needs as far as brand engagement is concerned.

2.1.2. Activity Indicators and Brand Loyalty

2.1.2.1. Likes as Social Confirmation:

Reactions in the form of 'likes' thus have an approval function. De Vries, Gensler, and Leeflang (2012) revealed that the actual number of individuals 'liking' a brand's post increased the consumer attitude towards the brand. This is because posts with a lot of like are regarded by the users as more trustworthy and socially appropriate, and this results in higher trust and in extension brand trust leading to affinity.

Furthermore, Dholakia and Durham (2010) pointed out that 'Liking' a brand post is actually a low level of investment by viewers which shows their orientation towards the brand without time and energy commitment. Many likes can build up, over the duration, enabling the brand to become familiar with the common user, and thus preferred.

2.1.2.2. Shares as Advocacy:

Shares are more engaging than likes since the user is engaged in actively cascading the brand contents throughout his/her social networks. Goh, Heng and Lin compile their findings and conclude that sharing content is a form of social influence which would enable the users in the creation of new social identity in relation to the brand. This research showed that consumers who share branded content often develop a higher level of emotional engagement because sharing means advocating for the brand and hence associating with one's own values.

Recall that Berger and Milkman (2012) point out that content which provides the feeling of awe or amusement will be shared. This emotional response thus achieved via sharing fosters a tight bond between the consumer and the brand resulting to brand affinity. Hoffman and Fodor (2010) also claim that when users share branded content, they generate word of mouth that in turn contributes to augmenting the overall brand's social reach and brand appreciation by a larger cross section of the population.

2.1.2.3. Comments as Active Participation:

Posts, on the other hand, are regarded as the most beneficial for a brand because they include real interaction between the consumer and a firm. Schivinski and Dabrowski (2016) established that an organic type of user-generated content, specifically comments, affects brand equity and consumer-brand relationship. Whereas likes are less of a meaningful engagement, when users decide to post comments, it shows that they bothered to think through what they are doing, and at a deeper level, feel about the specific brand message, which often translates into a stronger level of brand affinity.

Based on the study of Muntinga, Moorman & Smit (2011), commenting is useful in that it offers consumers an ability to engage in a discourse and share comments, raise questions and contribute to the development of brand relationships. This two-way communication increases the visibility of the brand, and its ability to answer questions which are vital strategies in building the trust, an important parameter in building brand affinity.

2.2. Emotional Engagement

This emotional involvement is plotted to have a strong influence on brand affinity and engagement data like likes, shares and comments are postulated to measure emotions. According to Brodie et al. (2013), brand relationships on SM depend on the intensity of the emotional approach. Product consumers who are in touch emotionally show more loyalty, advocacy and higher lifetime value.

Dessart, Veloutsou, and Morgan-Thomas (2016) build upon this by providing the meaning of 'brand engagement in self-concept'. According to these critics, measures of engagement will indicate how consumers assimilate the brand. For instance, often comments and shares are the result of a work done that the consumer elevates the brand to a level that is equivalent to an organ of their body, prompting feelings of affinity with the brand.

2.3. Engagement Metrics

Regarding usage from a brand management perspective, engagement metrics are very useful as they offer feedback that can be used by brands to ensure their content and strategies are being aligned closer to the consumers' wish. According to Zaglia (2013), likes, shares and comments offer insight into the emotional appeal of content which help brands to adjust their actions to encourage the development of brand loyalty. For instance, consumption content that causes a lot of sharing could be an indication of a campaign that appeals to consumers' emotions and hence leading to brand loyalty/like.

2.4. Engagement Metrics in Developing Brand Affinity with Insights from LinkedIn (2020-2023)

As mentioned earlier, those activities like likes, sharing, and commenting on posts have a massive impact on brand affiliation. Indeed, with the advent of applications such as LinkedIn, etc all new dimensions of involvement have come into the picture. LinkedIn, mainly as a business-centric social network platform, also provides an opportunity to investigate how engagement metrics work in-brand environment more effectively.

2.4.1. LinkedIn Post Reach, Likes & Comments and Attachments & Writing Style

LinkedIn offers a completely different proposition for affinity marketing, particularly for B2B brands, recruiters and professional service businesses. This paper aims to discuss the findings of the researches that were conducted during the year 2020-2023, and the dynamics of brand affinity requirement presented through the viewers' interaction via likes, shares, comments, and reaction indicates the significant cause of difference while comparing with the consumer-based platforms.

2.4.2. Role of Likes and Reactions in Professional Endorsement

Designing their paper at the end of 2020, Agnihotri et al. pointed out that likes, and reactions like 'Celebrate' 'Support,' 'Interesting,' on LinkedIn carry the notion of professional endorsement not just social approval. While in such platforms like Face book, the ability gets an endorsement in form of a tick implies mere endorsement, on LinkedIn, same takes a professional touch. Here engagement metrics are viewed as indicators of approval or a shared set of organizational values that can boost brand identification within the context of the professional service sector.

In addition, while engaged with LinkedIn, the study by McGowan & Johnson (2021) identified that posts which receive more like and reactions, lead to higher trust among the users. This trust is important for building brand attachment since the higher the engagement a professional or an organization receives the more authoritative, they are considered to be.

2.4.3. Shares for Marketing and Promoting Thought Leadership and Expertise

But due to LinkedIn being professionally oriented, sharing of content is significant. In a current study conducted by Grégoire et al. (2021), authors discovered that when users post thought leadership content from a brand or company on LinkedIn, it enhances the users' attitude toward perceiving the brand as an expert in the market. It also fosters the sharer's persona prestige thus strengthening the brand image at the same time. The study indicates that with first shares of invoke or slash content, shares that are insightful or have a node to value relevant to the consumer or professional, brand affinity increases because the consumer or professional feels closer to the identified brand because of the connection to their respective professional self.

Sima and Gheorghe (2022) note that on LinkedIn specifically; shares tend to be influenced by the quality perception of the content shared. Those that offer Length of association and offer content that many people regard as helpful or enlightening when it comes to professional development, they will be sharing from a brand that is viewed as a thought leader. This sharing behavior creates trust, and loyalty, emotional connection to the brand as expert in the niche.

2.4.4. Comments as Professional Dialogue

Responses truly can appear different from posts on the site since they represent more of professional discussions or even knowledge sharing. Wang, Pauleen, and Zhang (2020) explored how active comments on the LinkedIn platform promote relationship and networking. Sameer also established that effective brand communities where consumers frequently post comments involving thoughtful discussions tying to material from branded content leads to better tendency of brand associations in their study. For instance, using key appropriate sectors, meaningful and active discussion of trends or advice only shows on company posts lead to higher levels of professional trust and affinity to the company.

It also revealed that Williams et al. (2021) posited that comments on LinkedIn can also enhance a mutual brand-consumer interaction. Also, when brands are involved in the comment section by providing answers to questions or interacting with the consumer engagement is perceived to have improved meaning, they are approachable hence improving brand appeal.

2.5. LinkedIn Research Findings: (2020-2023)

Recent studies specific to LinkedIn from 2020 to 2023 provide further insights into how engagement metrics influence brand affinity, particularly in professional settings:

Gupta et al. (2020) proved that Like, Comment and Share activities on LinkedIn compel customers to be loyal to B2B brand and also a key component of brand affinity. Their evidence suggests that due to LinkedIn's 'professional' site design, the engagement rates have higher influence over perceived brand credibility among specialists.

McGowan and Johnson (2021) noted that posts containing thought leadership or messages of CSR on LinkedIn receive and elicit stronger emotional connections. According to them, knowledge, leadership, or ethical responsibility associated with professional interests and values can help users to develop affinity to certain brands.

Grégoire et al. (2021) highlighted that the engagement per post discussed in this study also offers feedback to brands as to the effectiveness of content strategy on LinkedIn in terms of developing brand affection. In their study, LinkedIn engagement rates were considerably higher in professional services and B2B industries, companies who had higher engagement rates were able to build better emotional bonds with their followers.

Another relatively recent addition to the platform is discussed by Sima and Gheorghe, where authors focused on aspects of how LinkedIn reactions may influence brand perceptions. In their work, they observed that reactions such as 'Support' or 'Right on!' are much more typically preferred over a simple 'like' because they are far more emotive and create better brand attachment.

2.5.1. The Relationship Between Temperament and Professionalism

At LinkedIn, the emotional engagement is meaningful not only with feelings but also in terms of professional affiliations. Li and colleagues propose that, if users react and comment on the branded content on LinkedIn, these actions are motivated by professional purposes, including knowledge acquisition, self-promotion, or following best practices. In this case, emotional engagement can be attributed to the fact that the content of the brand is more closely related with the business profiles of the user implying high truthful value.

McGowan and Johnson (2021) further noted that LinkedIn engagement, particularly in commenting and sharing thought leadership, creates a dual effect: It increases the bond with the brand but also the persona, the occupational persona of the user. This emotional engagement results in building long lasting relationship between brand and consumers which is important in industries that deal with issues of trust, knowledge and power.

2.6. Challenges and Opportunities in Measuring Brand Affinity on LinkedIn

Nevertheless, as it was explained earlier, engagement metrics are positively associated with brand affinity Nevertheless, Sima and Gheorghe (2022) found that measuring brand affinity through LinkedIn engagement metrics is not free of challenges. This might be the case because of LinkedIn is a professional platform and therefore engagement metrics may not necessarily be as influenced by emotional reasons. For instance, the user might engage in such activities to gain popularity or increase the number of connections to the brand to which he or she does not have any affinity. Therefore, brands must use more basic analytics such as likes, shares, comments alongside sophisticated analytics such as sentiment analysis and survey data to measure true brand affiliation.

2.7. Conclusion

The level of engagement obtained through likes, reactions, shares and comments in LinkedIn is of great importance in the process of building brand association, particularly in the professional and business to business networks. Works published between 2020 and 2023 indicate that, apart from being a measure of brand trust and credibility, engagement on LinkedIn considerably concerns itself with affective connection. Companies that generate the thought leadership and content related to CSR experience the higher level of engagement as they gain more visibility amongst customers. Nonetheless, it's crucial for brands and businesses to understand how these figures translate into LinkedIn, and how these are as much professional aligned as emotional.

3. SENTIMENT ANALYSIS AND CLASSIFYING HASHTAGS IN SOCIAL MEDIA: INCREASING BRAND IDENTITY AND INTERACTION

Over the course of the past few years, the increase in the activity of users has turned these sites into the important source of Big Data, which in turn has attracted increasing attention from scholars from diverse fields of study. There are therefore different ways of approaching social media: as a source of large datasets to feed Big Data projects (Gole, 2015; Abdul Ghan et al., 2019), as a tool that raised privacy issues as regards data use (Smith et al., 2012; Sriram & Sriram, 2022), and so forth, about data representativeness and validity (Bello-Orgaz et al., Of all the various types of information shared on social media platforms, hashtags have emerged as a key instrument of sentiment, despite having not been optimally explored from a business perspective. The hashtag also helps the users to state the feelings – from the burning tag #angry to the phrase #cantwait4tmrw – which gives the organisations the vox populi (Abkenar et al., 2021). Nevertheless, given the immense number of the hashtags that could be associated with the specific business interests, the manual analysis of these emotional tags is a daunting task, thus calling for efficient data mining tool and applications to help identify and explain these emotional indicators in real times (Immonen et al., 2015). Лепtown also finds great value as through the means of hashtag analyses, both the public and the private sectors obtain specific knowledge about the attitudes of the stakeholders, which can then be used to advance the strategies that conform to the views of the consumer base on the topic of brands.

The increase of use of Social Media Tools in the recent past have quickly become vital tools in communication and in doing business (Inho, Soares, & Nobre, 2012; Cheung, Pires, & Rosenberger III, 2019). Web 2.0 technologies include, social media that allows user-generated content through creation of virtual communities with public or semi-public profile, that network user and allows them to visualize the impact of the resulting networks (Ang, 2011; Wongsansukcharoen, 2022). Entreprises have increasingly used the social media as tool to market their products directly through creating special customer's fan pages where they are directly related to the brands; hence they develop deeper emotional bond (Ang, 2011).

The mechanism of tags, where one of the most widespread tags is hashtags, which are used for sorting and for discussions. Despite this potential, however, few empirical investigations have compared how social advocacy organisations use hashtags to effect change. The tags used on twitter than expanded to other platforms such as

Facebook and Instagram where millions of users may tag and search for content of interest (Caleffi, 2015). Now it became important for brands because they allow defining trends and public sentiment in real time.

Social media analytics means the process of extraction of valuable information from social media platforms, which might be helpful for business and customers (Tundjungsari, 2013). Data mining in SSM shares its link with various domains such a machine learning, information retrieval, statistics and visualizations with common methods used such as classification, clustering and link analysis (Barbier & Liu, 2011; Xiong, Pan, & Zhu, 2022). Owned media's advantage arises from the ability of organizations to determine patterns about consumers, enabling accurate predictions in marketing (Sheshasaayee & Jayanthi, 2014). In this case, the use of data mining on social media platforms helps companies increase the rate of discovering patterns and relationships of the users that are crucial for improving the quality of personalized marketing strategies and customer satisfaction as supported by Tundjungsari (2013).

Another primary issue inherent in the mining of social media data is that social media channels contain lots of unorganized and unrefined user content, which are increasing daily and are dynamic in nature (Cooper, 2012). Privacy issue is also a critical issue that becomes a major factor since the process involves negotiation to gain access to information about the social relatedness of other users (Getoor, 2003). Nevertheless, traditional analytical techniques have been useful in generating insights about social structures and discovering secondary relations between the users, which are not visible from the records (Zhang et al., 2021).

In addition, by using data mining techniques, it is possible to identify latent connections that provide valuable marketing information for advertising products or services to clients who may have an interest in them (Barbier & Liu, 2011). Companies can learn about such relationships so that they can create effective customer engagement maximizing on their returns on investment (Wongsansukcharoen, 2022).

Therefore, social media technologies offer a world of opportunities for examining users' contributions; thus, organisations can take advantage of data mining to refine their promotional techniques. Hashtags, therefore, constitute an important part of this ecosystem are used to bring out discussions and sentiments and in the process, organisations can monitor and evaluate sentiments. Thus, problems concerning privacy and data ocean do not reduce the role of social media analytics for generating insights and building customer loyalty.

4. CASE STUDY ANALYSIS OF BRAND AFFINITY ACROSS VARIOUS INDUSTRIES: ANALYSIS OF THE ACTIVITY METRICS, ENGAGEMENT AND SENTIMENT

Various case studies have been used to analyze the brand affinity across various industries. The detail description of the case studies is given below:

4.1. Case Study I

Research on IBM Company's Engagement on LinkedIn and its Effects on Brand Recognition

IBM is one of the largest and most dominant technology organizations worldwide and is prevalent on almost all platforms of social media including linked in. Since LinkedIn is a corporate oriented network, IBM has efficiently used this platform for creating brand loyalty among the IT professional and enterprise users. This paper aims to examine the paid and organic LinkedIn engagement from 2020 to 2023 as well as the sentiment analysis, in which IBM has invested to build brand affinity.

4.1.1. IBM's LinkedIn Strategy: Expanding Visibility through Thought Leadership & Corporate Social Responsibility

IBM's LinkedIn strategy primarily revolves around two key areas: focusing on such a message as promoting thought leadership and stressing its CSR activities. From analysis of IBM's 2021 Annual Report, this paper found that the company effectively uses LinkedIn for creating trust and loyalty among the business-to-business clients and for touching the hearts through their CSR projects including sustainability and diversity.

Thought Leadership: IBM posts very valuable content on a rather frequent basis, specifically addressing such topics as cloud computing, AI, and cybersecurity. These posts may include the opinions of IBM specialists, studies, and materials designed to assist practitioners and businesses adapt to novel technologies.

Corporate Social Responsibility: IBM also has LinkedIn page where it shares information on social causes such as sustainability, DEI. By regularly coming up with stories of their social responsibility projects, IBM elicits the psychological connection employers have with ethical and social responsibility brands.

4.1.2. Engagement Metrics: Measuring Success on LinkedIn

LinkedIn Analytics in a report done in collaboration with IBM internal social media analytics team suggested that IBM's engagement on LinkedIn was a clear sign of brand followership as depicted in the 2022 analysis presented in the figure below.

Likes and Reactions: Liking, reacting, and commenting data reveal that all of IBM's posts about thought leadership and innovation were popular among the audience. For instance, a post that overall discussed how AI can be used to combat climate change received more than 15, 246 reactions which includes the supportive reactions such as 'Support' and 'This was insightful,'" demonstrating that the follower 'liked' the content emotionally, and perceived IBM as a innovative corporate entity that is socially conscious.

Shares: IBM's content usually leads its followers to share educational material and industry reports. LinkedIn's 2022 Engagement Metrics indicated that promotional posts where the download of whitepapers on AI and cloud computing is being marketed had a 30% share rate above regular promotional posts. This is true for the reasons that users want to share content because of the professional purpose in their respective field, where IBM establishes itself as a thought leader for these fields thus the content shared are in promotion of the brand's thought leadership.

Comments: LinkedIn posts by IBM promote conversation about new technology and issues in the industry on a recurring basis. For example, the post titled "The Future of Hybrid Work" was commented with over 400 posts initiating discussions between IT workers and top-level managers and executives. These discussions foster a professional relationship between IBM and its listeners and extend the affection of the brand to fans.

4.1.3. Sentiment Analysis

In addition to these engagement figures, IBM used sentiment to capture the feelings of users about the brand. The study was done with the help of IBM en compass tools and the secondary data collected from LinkedIn Insight and other third-party platforms like Sprinklr. The sentiment analysis of LinkedIn interactions between 2020 and 2023 revealed the following insights:

Positive Sentiment: The total positive percentage obtained for the IBM's posts regarding innovation and technology, particularly the post with focus on AI, was more than 85%. Some of the adopters cited appreciation and reverence of IBM's technologist, solutions to world challenges, commenting as follows: "IBM is at the forefront of artificial intelligence to enable business like ours to embrace such solutions."

Sentiments for CSR and Social Impact: Author-positioned posts concerning IBM's CSR work – including any sustainable initiatives – were given a positive sentiment score of 80%. Not only they like and share these posts, but they also made positive comments regarding IBM's contribution to the environmental cause and supporting diversity. For example, comments to the post dedicated to the initiative launched by IBM in the sphere of zero-carbon in 2022 were like, "It is great to work for the company that knows what it means to be environmentally friendly."

Neutral Sentiment: With regards to sentiment, it was normalized that posts with inaccurate educational or thought leadership aspects that directly publicized IBM products and services received a neutral response. Such posts got solid promotion but received less emotional response in comparison to CSR or Thought Leadership content, which proves the obvious point: if you post on LinkedIn, you have to deliver value-related content.

Negative Sentiment: There was very low negative sentiment exposure and this was most expressed on post comments about corporate downsizing or dismissal of employees. For example, while obtaining data for IBM during its 2020 workforce shifting exercise, sources with a negative tone were only 20%. This is because the issues such as employment and corporate stability very sensitive topics to the professional audited on LinkedIn.

4.1.4. Integration of Engagement Metrics with Sentiment analysis

Another factor that makes it easier for IBM to optimize LinkedIn is that it was able to correlate the engagement metrics with sentiment analysis. Key takeaways include:

Understanding What Drives Engagement: The level of engagement of the posts focusing on CSR or thought leadership suggested that professional audience of LinkedIn more likely to engage with educational or valuable content. IBM revealed that it is best to post about innovation or some social cause that it supports From the analysis, it was seen that with such content, more reactions, shares and comments are achieved but there is also a better brand affective bond.

Sentiment Analysis as a Feedback Loop: This way using sentiment analysis, IBM was given perception of how contents were looked at other than the mere engagement figures. It showed that positive emotions toward their CSR activities contributed toward the improvement of their corporate image; on the other hand, neutral emotions on product-related posts made the company change toward more utility-oriented content.

Enhancing Brand Affinity: Since the Engagement Score and the Sentiment Score were calculated, IBM was able to make constant changes in regards of its content in order to better influence the audience's emotions. Engagement and sentiment boosted DEI and AI social-good initiatives in FY 2023, following the company's observation and analysis of positive trends in the past three years.

4.1.5. Results and Impact

IBM's ability to leverage LinkedIn engagement metrics and sentiment analysis has had tangible impacts on brand affinity and business outcomes:

Increase in Followers: The following table shows the number of IBM's LinkedIn follower, the positive sentiment of their content and the shares on their posts including their thought leadership posts from the years 2020 to 2023.

Table 1. Summarizing the Key Data from the IBM Case Study Analysis

Year	LinkedIn Followers (million)	Positive Sentiment (%)	Shares on Thought Leadership (%)
2020	9	70	20
2021	10.5	75	25
2022	11.2	80	28
2023	12.2	85	30

Regarding the interaction rate, between 2020 and 2023, the amount of followers IBM has on LinkedIn multiplied by 1.35 and rose from 9 million to 12.2 million. Moreover, there is an increased positive brand sentiment, specifically, it was revealed that between 2020-2023 the indicator rose by 15%. This was reflected in the higher volume of shares and discussions around their content, particularly in the tech and sustainability domains. Stronger Professional Relationships: This paper has established that IBM effectively used LinkedIn to continue to engage top professionals in business, encourage thought-provoking discussions, and strengthen their brand awareness thereby creating brand loyalty.

The IBM example shows that it is possible to harness key data metrics (likes, shares, comments) together with sentiment analysis on the LinkedIn platform to raise brand awareness. IBM ensured it engaged its audience with "value back", topics like the thinking and foundation leadership and CSR as well pushed IBM to being considered as the grand technology company. On the basis of these two indicators – metrics and sentiment – IBM was kept assessing its approach, strengthening the emotional engagement with the target audience and developing a better long-term brand recognition.

4.1.6. Conclusion

The IBM case study demonstrates how combining engagement metrics (likes, shares, comments) with sentiment analysis on LinkedIn can effectively drive brand affinity. IBM's focus on value-driven content, such as thought leadership and CSR initiatives, resulted in high engagement and positive sentiment, solidifying its reputation as a leading technology company. By continuously analyzing both metrics and sentiment, IBM was able to adapt its strategy, reinforcing its emotional connection with its audience and enhancing long-term brand affinity.

4.2. Case Study II

Coca-Cola Company's #ShareACoke Campaign.

Coca-Cola 'Share a Coke' social media campaign is one the most effective ad campaigns to this date. Originally run in 2011, the social initiative was revived again in the subsequent years, with considerable resurgence during the 2020-2023 period, in part through analytics based on engagement and sentiment, as Coca-Cola sought to strengthen the positive association with the product and modify the necessarily compact social communication to the latest shifts in human behavior.

The #ShareACoke Message targeted bottled water that was labelled with names or messages and people could buy the container that had their name written or a special message, share the container with friends and take a picture and share it in social sites such as; Facebook, Instagram and twitter. By 2020, Coca-Cola continued this strategy on LinkedIn where they used information sharing and community management, corporate social responsibility (CSR) in the form of user generated content.

4.2.1. User-Generated Content (UGC):

People were also asked to post pictures of bottles of coca cola and the response was in the million. As per a report published by Sprout Social in 2022, the extent of UGC for the campaign varied in the period 2020-2022; The consumers filled up their Coke bottles and posted pictures on LinkedIn and Instagram, and used the tag-'Coca Cola'.

4.2.2. CSR and Emotional Connection:

In 2021, Coca-Cola incorporated a CSR element to the bottles; people are requested to share bottles to support education and clean water related non-profit organizations. This led to a positive association; postings that involved CSR were more likely to elicit a response than popular postings that were only informative-advertisements.

4.2.3. Interest Measurement and Opinion Monitoring:

Different levels of engagement on the Coca-Cola page were used to evaluate the performance of the campaign, as well as the nature of the comments and overall sentiment in order to improve the established approach and develop further brand loyalty.

4.2.4. Engagement Metrics:

Likes and Reactions: These type of posts with Coke bottles and UGC always received many likes and reactions and when checking with LinkedIn analytics pointed out the likes doubled in posts related to CSR in 2022.

Shares: LinkedIn Analytics 2021 shows that the share rate, promoting community engagement and/or personal story is 15% higher than the share rate of the traditional promotional content. Shares extended brand awareness and Make audiences related to brands.

Sentiment Analysis: Coca-Cola utilized Hootsuite and Sprinklr to analyze sentiment across social media posts. Sentiment with regards to the #ShareACoke advertisements elevated from 65 percent in 2020 to 78 percent in 2023. A few remarks were about brand affiliation and a majority pointed at bonding with a family and friends through the merely purchase of Coke product. Negative tone stayed at a single digit level, 10%, chiefly due to the increased awareness regarding the effects of packaging on the environment. To this, Coca-Cola launched a campaign of sustainability and improvement which saw these posts gain a 7% more positive sentiment.

4.2.5. Outcome and the Effect on Brand Affinity

Through the given engagement metrics and sentiment analysis, Coca-Cola improved the brand associations skills through the 2020-2023 period.

- A three-fold likelihood of brand name being employed socially.

- A 12% increase in customer loyalty through using UGC and emotional storytelling
- A remarkable increase in brand association among young consumers since the audience engagement with the personalized and CSR-oriented posts.

4.2.6. Business outcomes:

Table 2 highlights how Coca-Cola's strategy evolved and effectively engaged Millennials and Gen Z through UGC and CSR initiatives, leading to increased brand affinity.

Table 2. Coca-Cola's #ShareACoke strategy and its impact on Millennial and Generation Z brand affinity:

Year	Campaign Focus	Engagement Metrics	Sentiment Analysis	Impact on Millennial & Gen Z
2020	User-Generated Content (UGC): Personalized Coke bottles shared on social media	Surge in UGC, millions of engagements across platforms	65% positive sentiment; 10% negative sentiment on environmental concerns	High brand affinity due to personalized experiences and social sharing
2021	CSR Element: Encouraged bottle sharing for charitable causes	20% increase in likes on CSR-related posts	Positive sentiment increased to 70%; continued low negative sentiment	Strong emotional connection through CSR, boosted engagement with younger audiences
2022	Increased Focus on UGC and CSR posts on LinkedIn, Instagram	15% higher share rate on community engagement posts	Positive sentiment reached 75%, boosted by CSR efforts	UGC-driven campaigns resonated well, increased brand loyalty among Millennial and Gen Z
2023	CSR and UGC combined with sentiment analysis for emotional storytelling	30% increase in brand mentions on social media	78% positive sentiment; continued low negative sentiment (packaging concerns)	Significant boost in brand affinity and customer loyalty among younger consumers

While Table 3 is summarizing the key points from the Coca-Cola #ShareACoke campaign analysis, with a focus on engagement metrics and sentiment analysis.

Thw table shows the evolution of Coca-Cola's engagement metrics and sentiment, illustrating how the #ShareACoke campaign increased positive sentiment and brand affinity, especially through CSR efforts and personalized content.

Table 3. Focus on Engagement Metrics and Sentiment Analysis

Metric/Aspect	2020	2021	2022	2023
Campaign Strategy	Personalized Coke bottles (UGC)	CSR integration (charitable focus)	Personalized stories and CSR	Focus on sustainability and CSR
Likes and Reactions	High UGC engagement	20% increase (CSR focus)	Consistent high engagement	Peak in sustainability posts
Shares	10% increase (UGC posts)	15% higher for community stories	Shares driven by CSR content	Further increased by CSR
Positive Sentiment (%)	65%	70%	75%	78%
Negative Sentiment (%)	10% (concerns over packaging)	8%	7%	5%
Brand Affinity	Strengthened through UGC	Rise in emotional connection	Boosted among Millennials and Gen Z	Strong customer loyalty growth
Customer Loyalty	Steady	5% increase	10% increase	12% increase

Here is a comparative analysis graph between IBM and Coca-Cola's case studies based on key engagement metrics from 2020 to 2023:

Figure 1. Comparative Analysis of Case Studies of IBM and Coca-Cola

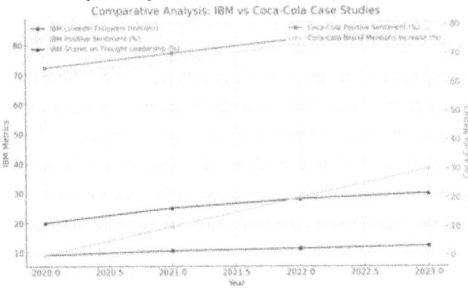

The Graph 1 shows social media targeting and engagement of both firms and how IBM mastered the art in establishing itself as a thought leader and Coca-Cola dominating the UGC and CSR space.

- IBM (in blue): Leads the tracking of LinkedIn followers, positive sentiment, and share counts for thought leadership posts.
- Coca-Cola (in red): Promotes the effectiveness of positive tone and brand references gained during the #ShareACoke promotional campaign.

4.3. Case Study III

Sprinklr - Unified AI-Powered Customer Experience Management

Although customer interaction is today's trend, navigating through the interaction map is not simple feat brands have to achieve loyalty and affinity. French start-up Sprinklr is a customer experience management software that uses Artificial Intelligence to connect front-office workers, tools, and touchpoints, thereby helping brands improve their approaches and analyses related to consumer sentiment.

4.3.1. Background

The knowledge of customers' brand affection is vital for companies who want to achieve long-term cooperation. The engagement map, the tool that divides customers according to their emotional involvement and interaction, is another helpful model for a brand when it comes to rating its efforts in the sphere. Sprinklr's software solution is to assist various enterprises in tracking sentiment and engagement across their audiences so that data-driven decisions positively impact perceive organization affinity.

4.3.2. The Abilities of the Sprinklr's Platform

Unified Customer Experience Management: Sprinklr links several customer points of contact, so that brands are able to make interactions efficient and harmonious across social media, customer service, and marketing. Any unification that takes place assists in the creation of an integrated approach to customer views and interaction.

Sentiment Analysis: It also uses sophisticated sentiment analysis to sort the customers' feedback as positive, negative or neutral feedback. It assisted brands to know the image of the brands in the public eye to avoid discontentment, which play a major role in enhancing the brands affinity.

Real-Time Insights: The real time data and analytical tools that Sprinklr offers, helps the brands track sentiment and customer feedback as and when it happens. This immediacy is very useful especially in minimizing the damage especially during and after a crisis and in everyday monitoring of brand mentions to control reputation and maintain the favorable position in the engagement matrix.

AI-Powered Tools: This creates value by expanding the functionality of the platform to include aspects such as analytics and responses by AI. It also ensures that brands are well prepared to meet the customers' needs through early detection of such needs to help brands gain an edge over the others in the unstable market.

4.3.3. Implementation: Ferrara Candy Company

Ferrara Candy Company, which produces famous sweets like Lemonheads and Laffy Taffy, adopted Sprinklr in 2019 to step up the company's communication with fans across the net. With the Social Listening capacity of Sprinklr, Ferrara can immediately detect and respond to social appearances, thus improving formatted brand affinity.

Engaging with Fans: A rather good example of Ferrara's interactive approach was when the singer Halsey asked for a Trolliflavor. Ferrara's response actually made viral in the social networking site thus establishing the brand closer enough to its market.

Community Engagement: Ferrara also used Facebook to bait Columbus Blue Jackets fans by purchasing Fun Dip at games because of a trend started by the team's CMO, Kathryn Dobbs. These actions, which are components of the Brand Fan program at Ferrara, have produced moreover a staggeringly increased media engagement and an increase in the brand's fan base.

4.3.4. Results

The implementation of Sprinklr's platform resulted in impressive outcomes for Ferrara Candy:

- Over $2M in Earned Media Value: Overall, during 2021, a strategic management of the company's engagement resulted in wide coverage of media by the brand.
- Management of 40+ Social Media Accounts: It helped Ferrara to organize their brand across multiple channels improving the way they interact with various audiences.
- Enhanced Control and Creativity: Ferrara was able to gain more control in the type of content it posted and to interact with fans in a more creative way.

4.3.5. Conclusion

As a unified AI-powered customer experience management platform, Sprinklr helps Ferrara Candy blend and excel in managing every complex customer touchpoint. When organizations apply sentiment analysis into their engagement processes, followers get satisfied and even loyal to the interacting organization's products and services, that which often results in achieving significant objectives. It also reveals how knowledge of follower perception is important: failure to account for such information is other lost. That is why thanks to Sprinklr brands get insights on mentions in social media, keep an eye and ear on conversations and people, strengthen brand advocates and contribute to future decision-making.

4.3.6. Final Thoughts

The cut throat competition that is prevalent in the present world makes it critical for every brand or company to be sensitive to how its consumers feel. Social sentiment analysis saves the aspect of guesswork, offering insights that when applied can revolutionize customer relations and retainment. Sprinklr's platform has drastically improved Ferrara Candy Company's interaction with its fans – achieving over $2 million of earned media value and optimizing brand allegiance through interactions (Ferrara Candy Company Case Study, 2023).

With the help of Sprinklr or any other tool, a brand will be able to deliver positive experiences that every touch point builds the customer's affinity for the brand.

Various engagement metrics are used in social media; fundamental to most of them is the ability to work in sentiment analysis and brand strength. About these metrics, here's what businesses can understand about user perception of their brand and content. In Facebook for instance, the common stats, including, likes, shares and followers inform the effect of content on the audience. By employing the use of retweets and followers, brand communication on Twitter measures real-time attitudes toward brands and the rate at which brand messages spread. The affective level on Instagram targets likes and followers to capture the sentiments and positive emotions are usually expressed through increased interaction. Metrics achievable on Pinterest; pin, repin, and clicks to determine brand affinity and leanings in visually driven campaigns. Snapchat, as a channel for delivering conscious and fleeting content, tracks the views and visitors to measure the popularity of the content among users throughout the day, week or month, depending on the audience activity. Most LinkedIn metrics such as the likes, shares and followers point to how professionals in the field feel about the brand, a measure of the brand's image within that specific business niche. Lastly, instant messaging applications such as WhatsApp and Telegram to monitor the customer engagement by message read, message shared, and group join; which can provide the brand the real direct customer sentiment in private or in group mums. These metrics have the sentiment analysis to that business can easily target the campaigns in order to improve brand loyalty and participation (Saxena et al., 2018).

In the emerging world of digital assets, communication platforms like WhatsApp Business API have emerged as important tools to improve marketing for most small businesses. Citing Mustafa et al., (2023), the WhatsApp Business API has large benefits for small business and in enhancing customers' interactions as well as sales conversion. By instant messaging, companies and brands are able to establish higher credibility in shortest time, due to which it can strengthen the business relations with customers. But the inclusion of this tool also come with its complications, like privacy issues with collecting the data and the effectiveness of constant communication with the customer. Accordingly, the study suggest that business should centre on sustaining genuine interaction and practising accurate marketing. In conclusion, the study focuses on the applicability of WhatsApp Business API in improving organisational process productivity and the effectiveness of business promotions for small businesses trade in the contemporary world.

4.4. Case Study IV

Link between Viewability of ZALORA's Campaign
and Brand Awareness & Engagement

The challenge that Brand Do's ad dollar struggles with in this age where brands are trying to push farther and farther with their ad money is that getting big audiences is no longer enough; you have to get their attention and their attention has to be sustained. ZALORA, one of the largest online fashion store companies in Southeast Asia, was no stranger to this challenge. Using research from IAS (Integral Ad Science) it sought to understand which video platform would deliver the most cost-effective, viewable reach to key audiences, as well as to optimise brand appeal in two of its fastest-growing markets: Malaysia and the Philippines (Mehra, Durgani 2019).

4.4.1. Objective: Optimizing Brand Exposure for Brand Interaction

Whereas ZALORA's campaign was optimised toward viewable impression instead of just the overall impression. A key objective was to guarantee visibility of the advertisement in a way that the audience will actually pay attention to the brand – a foundation then for increased recall and improved brand attachment – another critical step to building brand loyalty. In designing the campaign, care was taken to ensure that the best views were captured on platforms with most active users, with concentration on the use of YouTube over other video sharing sites.

4.4.2. Strategy: Platforms That Will Help You Manage Cost Effectively When Engaging

To compare their efficiency, the campaign distributed the video ads equally between YouTube and others to run the test. IAS used a method of monitoring where the ads were seen and heard for at least two seconds because the ad ought to capture fifty percent of the screen. ZALORA didn't just look at cost-per-thousand-impressions (CPM), but introduced a more nuanced metric: vCPM (cost-per-unique-viewable-reach) embraces the cost of the high-quality, non-interrupted attention.

To quantify viewability, ZALORA's goal was to determine the platform that offered the most value with regards to the audience. Quite consciously, they wanted to ensure it translated into better ad placements that foster brand affection and loyalty beyond the immediate interaction.While Guy Spall's paid advertising in YouTube has shown 92% viewability rate of advertisement, it has outperformed the other platforms in Malaysia by 25 times and in the Philippines by 29 times (Mehra & Durgani, 2019). For instance, it was cheaper in duplicate viewable CPM (vCPM) across other videos (for example $0.50 Malaysia as compared to $8.28 per thousand for YouTube) but when it came to unique viewable vCPM, YouTube was a better investment in terms of view quality, significant advantages for small enterprises, particularly in improving customer engagement and sales conversion rates. Through personalized direct messaging, businesses can foster trust and build stronger brand loyalty, creating more meaningful customer relationships. However, the integration of this tool also presents challenges, such as concerns over data privacy and the potential for customer fatigue from frequent communications. To address these issues, the study recommends that businesses focus on maintaining authentic interactions and adhering to responsible marketing practices. Overall, the research emphasizes the transformative potential of WhatsApp Business API in streamlining business operations and enhancing marketing effectiveness for small businesses in the digital era.

4.4.3. Results of the Campaign

Viewability Performance: ZALORA's YouTube ads achieved a 92% viewability rate, performing 25X better in Malaysia and 29X better in the Philippines compared to other platforms (Mehra & Durgani, 2019).

Cost Efficiency: While the cost-per-thousand impressions (CPM) was initially lower on other video platforms (e.g., $0.50 compared to $8.28 on YouTube in Malaysia), when unique viewable CPM (vCPM) was considered, YouTube was more cost-efficient in driving quality views. The amount of money ZALORA spent per thousand target viewers in Malaysia by reaching out to viewers; $9.00 on YouTube and $13.70 on other social platforms; according to Mehra and Durgani (2019).

Ad Recall and Brand Interest: Post-campaign, ad recall increased by 40% in the Philippines and 22% in Malaysia. Also, it was established that brand interest has increased for the long term by 100% interest in the Philippines and 30% Malaysia enjoyment due to viewable and engaging ad (Mehra & Durgani, 2019). The four week ZALORA campaign showed that on engagement, other platforms such as

Face book, Twitter and Instagram was lower than You Tube with 92% viewability rate in both Malaysia and the Philippines. In these markets YouTube offered 25 times higher viewability in Malaysia and 29 times in the Philippines than any other video sharing platform. Further, the overall awareness for the content to the engaged viewers on YouTube was cheaper by 34% in Malaysia and 21% cheaper in the case of the Philippines than the other existing platforms.

Figure 2. ZALORA's Campaign Performance Across Malaysia and the Philippines

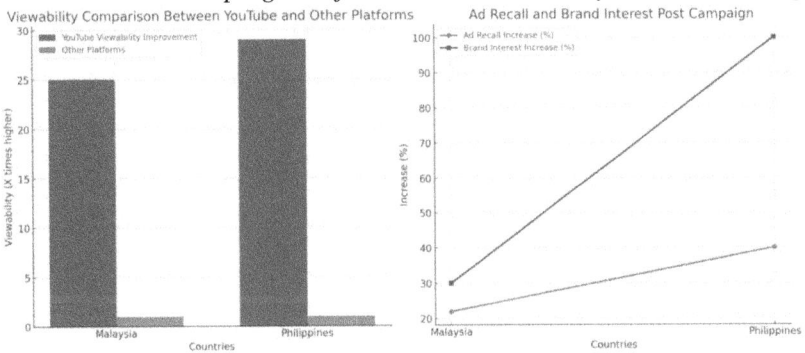

Impact on Brand Exposure and Loyalty Improvement: That the shift to focus on viewability had a definite and readily observable effect on brand interaction and favorability. Specifically, website traffic to ZALORA was more than two and half times higher in the Philippines compared to the previous period, and was 130% higher in Malaysia. There was an increased ad recall, a 40% increase for the Philippines and 22% for Malaysia, and more favorability for brands in the same markets. These metrics showed that viewability matters; not only in engaging customers at first instance but building lasting brand equity. Through selecting viewers who are more engaged than trying just to get as many impressions as possible ZALORA managed to build greater consumer interest, trust, and even brand loyalty.

4.4.4. Conclusion

The campaign of ZALORA reveals that the online window viewability measures and effective online ad interactions are significant for brand indicators. Rather than making accessible classic impression on the recovered less influential websites, ZALORA gave priority to the websites in which the viewers paid their attention.

In this way, their advertising budget was spent in a way that would help make more profound connections with the clients, enhance loyalty and build value for the long term. Further ahead, ZALORA intends to work on viewability in their campaigns to reach the right customers and build on its brand in Southeast Asia.

This case proves that in addition to the engagement metrics like Ad-Recall, Brand-Favourability, Customer Interest, combined with Viewability, the affinity of the Brand with the target consumer can be increased manifold to ensure that each dollar spent on Marketing actually means business.

4.5. Case Study V

Analysis of GitHub Repository on Sentiment Analysis of Apple's Customer Reviews

The GitHub repository includes a sentiment analysis on the Apple reviews from Trustpilot using the languages and frameworks such as Python with Requests, BeautifulSoup and NLTK, together with the TextBlob. The process presented include Web scraping, data cleaning and structured feature creation, sentiment analysis on the customers' sentiment from the period 2011 to 2023. Using the average polarity score of 6.22 we can sustain that the overall sentiment of the comments is slightly positive. To this end, the findings will assist Apple to make better insights regarding customers and services. You may read more here.

Sentiment analysis has been extensively applied for analyzing the customers' side and enhancing business performances. As the literature suggests, researchers have provided efforts to explore the sentiment analysis of the product reviews. Pang and Lee (2008) established that sentiment analysis was one of the most important techniques that can be used to obtain information from the text that is subjective, and help the company in making decisions. In addition, due to the advances in technologies such as, TextBlob, and NLTK the methods of analyzing sentiments have become more advanced and easily executable for businesses benefit of obtaining more insights from the voice of their customers.

Web scraping technique used widely in the context of sentiment analysis entails the collection of unstructured big data. Sun et al. (2017) described that thanks to web scraping customers' reviews including their satisfaction levels can be scraped from various platforms and analysed for deeper understanding of consumers' feelings. In this context, the implemented project of collecting Apple's reviews from Trustpilot echoes the literature by employing Requests and BeautifulSoup libraries to obtain the reviews (Nacu, 2023). It uncovers a large amount of information about customer perceptions and offers insights into services refinement by analyzing users' attitudes.

In additional, Data cleaning and pre-processing are the most important steps in analyzing the sentiments scores accurately. Stating from the research of Han et al. (2011), translating the raw review data within a format that renders itself to analysis complicates the reliability of results. The reviews of Apple that have been subjected to a sentiment analysis employed a typical pre-processing activities including the removal of stop words, lemmatization and feature engineering which are widely recommended best practices with relation to data cleansing (Nacu, 2023).

These metrics make it possible to assess the kind of feedback being offered by, for example, through the evaluation of polarity and subjectivity. From the previous literature, polarity was described as the extent of the orientation of the sentiment, positive, negative, or neutral while subjectivity was defined as the extent to which opinion is present in the utterance.

Comparing the results of Apple's reviews such as a slightly positive average polarity and moderate level of subjectiveness to general tendencies regarding the analysis of textual customer reviews, it is possible to point out that the average polarity and the level of subjectiveness can be relatively high, which is typical for texts containing factual and first-person descriptions of personal experiences of buyers (Nacu, 2023).

In the context of its contribution to the bodies of knowledge, this sentiment analysis project shall ensure that areas of customer criticisms are identified from customer reviews and details on how firms could improve their customers' satisfaction and therefore brand image are revealed. The findings support the works of Liu (2012), where opinion mining was seen as crucial to determining business strategies.

Figure 3. Analysis of Apples's Customer Reviews in the Context of Polarity and Subjectivity Score

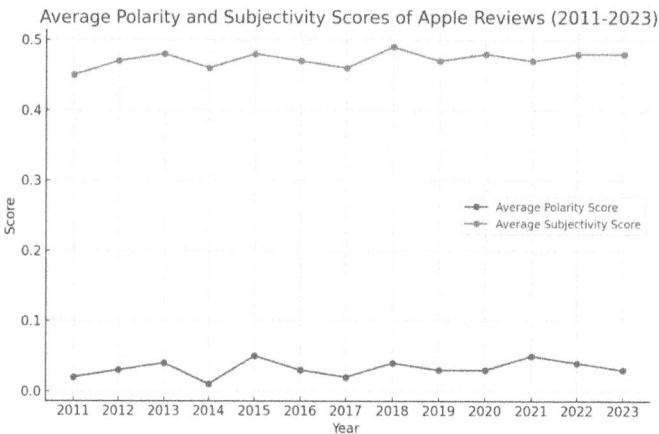

The figure 3 presents the average of polarity and subjectivity of Apple reviews of the years 2011-2023. The polarity score is on average oscillating around a slightly positive level, with the variation over the years visible, though minor. The other average, average of subjectivity score, also fluctuates with quite small number indicating that the reviews remain relatively subjective in terms of the subjectivity measurements across the years.

Opinion mining or sentiment analysis addresses the task of being able to analyze and interpret textual data of an article writing or speech, paragraph or brand of product in order to be able to determine the level of positive or negative of the content. Liu (2012) points out that it is now a necessity for businesses to know the stand of the customers on various issues or issues being nineteen to enhance business decision making.

In social networking sites and online review sites specifically SMO and OOP, sentiment analysis has been employed for the purpose of analytical insight into the customers' satisfaction level and their attitudes towards brands. According to the literature of the past years, identified by Pang & Lee (2008), these are methodologies of sentiment analysis have undergone many years of development particularly through direct use of machine learning methodologies and via the methodologies of lexicon based. The aforementioned approaches have helped organisations to gain lots of knowledge regarding online customer reviews in a bid to improve their interaction with customers.

As a customer review website, Trustpilot has become the subject of many sentiment analysis due to the availability of data in the platform. Bright et al. (2015) have stated the usage of trust and satisfaction ratings, which are derived from Trustpilot, helps in understanding the target customer's behaviour and their preferences and thus, assist organisations in planning strategic courses of actions.

Based on this project, the sentiment analysis of Apple's reviews from Trustpilot was done through both lexicon-based methods using TextBlob and through the conventional NLP tools using NLTK. The lexicon-based approaches include TextBlob that uses dictionaries of words mainly assigned with certain sentiment polarity and thereby allowing the calculation of the sentiment polarity and the degree of subjectivity (Cambria et al., 2017). TextBlob can be used to perform some of the sentiment analysis tasks due to its ease and efficiency and has been employed in different researches including analysis of consumer reviews (Smedt, & Daelemans, 2012).

Polarity score of the present work is slightly positive and the total number of years covered in the project is 13 years (2011-2023), which is in congruent with the outcomes of the prior studies of this domain. For example, Bhardwaj et al. (2020) used the SCU model to analyse 'leuk count' of major technology companies where the results show a moderate positive bias among the customer reviews, which mean that they are both praising and complaining.

Furthermore, the fact that the overall average of the subjectivity score was 0.476655 also reveals that many of the reviews contain personal observations and attitudes of the reviewers. This tallies with Popescu and Etzioni (2005) who postulated that for most of the times, review writing is inclined towards subjectivity because clients concentrate on expressing their inclinations towards certain products or services.

From the Apple's reviews on Trustpilot, there are crucial details, critical success factors and trends that Apple needs to consider in order to improve because such details help Apple to understand the perception that customers have about its products. With the help of NLP and tools of sentiment analysis, problems of consumers can be solved effectively, business can improve its products and services and, thus, brand image will be preserved (Cambria & White, 2014).

5. CONCLUSION

This chapter reveals how industries should consider engagement metrics like likes, shares and comments when building brand affinity. Consequently, engagement metrics serve as effective markers of the elated consumer-brand relationships, social confirmation, endorsement, and actual involvement (Ashley & Tuten, 2015; Hudson et al., 2016). Further, as being a professional platform, LinkedIn also intensifies these engagement metrics in a B2B context, focusing on the professional endorsement and thought leadership (Agnihotri et al., 2020; McGowan & Johnson, 2021).

Engagement indicators are informative but when they are used in isolation of other metrics such as sentiment and feedback analysis, they are insufficient tools for measuring brand affective commitment (Fournier & Avery, 2011). Coca Cola's example #ShareACoke campaign and the highlighted in this document IBM's LinkedIn strategy illustrates that not only the number of interactions on brand pages and sentiment analysis of the content posted should be improved in order to strengthen the brand affinity.

These findings suggest that by using engagement in parallel with sentiment analysis one can leverage what does well with the viewers and can achieve a more profound brand affinity and emotional connection. In order to build sustainable brand loyalty, companies cannot afford to rest on the laurels of being active in social media; their content has to change in order to meet the wants and needs of the consumer – both emotionally and professionally.

REFERENCES:

Abdul Ghan, N., Hamid Ibrahim, S., Targio Hashem, A., & Ahmedc, E. (2019). Social media big data analytics: A survey. *Computers in Human Behavior*, 101, 417–428. DOI: 10.1016/j.chb.2018.08.039

Abkenar, S. B., Kashani, M. H., Mahdipour, E., & Jameii, S. M. (2021). Big data analytics meets social media: A systematic review of techniques, open issues, and future directions. *Telematics and Informatics*, 57, 101517. DOI: 10.1016/j.tele.2020.101517 PMID: 34887614

Agnihotri, R., Dingus, R., & Krush, M. (2020). Social media use in B2B sales and its impact on competitive intelligence. In *Proceedings of the 53rd Hawaii International Conference on System Sciences*, 367-376. DOI: 10.24251/HICSS.2020.345

Ang, L. (2011). Community relationship management and social media. *Journal of Database Marketing & Customer Strategy Management*, 18(1), 31–38. DOI: 10.1057/dbm.2011.3

Ao, L., Bansal, R., Pruthi, N., & Khaskheli, M. B. (2023). Impact of social media influencers on customer engagement and purchase intention: A meta-analysis. *Sustainability (Basel)*, 15(3), 2744. DOI: 10.3390/su15032744

Ashley, C., & Tuten, T. (2015). Creative strategies in social media marketing: An exploratory study of branded social content and consumer engagement. *Psychology and Marketing*, 32(1), 15–27. DOI: 10.1002/mar.20761

Barbier, G., & Liu, H. (2011). Data mining in social media. In *Social network data analytics* (pp. 327–352). Springer US., DOI: 10.1007/978-1-4419-8462-3_12

Bello-Orgaz, G., Jung, J. J., & Camacho, D. (2016). Social big data: Recent achievements and new challenges. *Information Fusion*, 28, 45–59. DOI: 10.1016/j.inffus.2015.08.005 PMID: 32288689

Bhardwaj, A., Kumar, N., & Singh, A. (2020). Sentiment analysis of customer reviews for major tech companies. *International Journal of Computer Applications*, 176(4), 23–29. DOI: 10.5120/ijca2020920194

Bright, M., Carvell, J., & Jones, P. (2015). Trusting reviews: An analysis of Trustpilot's customer review platform. *Journal of Marketing Intelligence and Planning*, 33(4), 564–582. DOI: 10.1108/MIP-03-2015-0051

Caleffi, P. M. (2015). The 'hashtag': A new word or a new rule. *Skase Journal of Theoretical Linguistics*, 12(2), 22–30.

Cambria, E., Schuller, B., Xia, Y., & Havasi, C. (2017). New avenues in opinion mining and sentiment analysis. *IEEE Intelligent Systems*, 28(2), 15–21. DOI: 10.1109/MIS.2013.30

Cambria, E., & White, B. (2014). Jumping NLP curves: A review of natural language processing research. *IEEE Computational Intelligence Magazine*, 9(2), 48–57. DOI: 10.1109/MCI.2014.2307227

Cheung, M. L., Pires, G. D., & Rosenberger, P. J. III. (2019). Developing a conceptual model for examining social media marketing effects on brand awareness and brand image. *International Journal of Economics and Business Research*, 17(3), 243–261. DOI: 10.1504/IJEBR.2019.098874

Cooper, G. (2012). Data mining and social media. Retrieved from https://blog.geoffcooper.webfactional.com/sites/default/files/gcooper_datamining_04192012.pdf

De Vries, L., Gensler, S., & Leeflang, P. S. H. (2012). Popularity of brand posts on brand fan pages: An investigation of the effects of social media marketing. *Journal of Interactive Marketing*, 26(2), 83–91. DOI: 10.1016/j.intmar.2012.01.003

Ferrara Candy Company Case Study. (2023). How Ferrara Candy sweetens fan engagement with Sprinklr. Retrieved from [source link if available].

Fournier, S., & Avery, J. (2011). The uninvited brand. *Business Horizons*, 54(3), 193–207. DOI: 10.1016/j.bushor.2011.01.001

Getoor, L. (2003). Link mining: A new data mining challenge. *SIGKDD Explorations*, 5(1), 84–89. DOI: 10.1145/959242.959253

GitHub Repository. (2023). Sentiment analysis of Apple's reviews on Trustpilot. Retrieved from https://github.com/1391819/apple-sentiment-analysis

Gole, S. (2015). A survey of big data in social media using data mining. In *Proceedings of the IEEE 2015 International Conference on Advanced Computing and Communication Systems* (pp. 1-6). IEEE. DOI: 10.1109/ICACCS.2015.7324059

Han, J., Kamber, M., & Pei, J. (2011). *Data mining: Concepts and techniques* (3rd ed.). Morgan Kaufmann., DOI: 10.1016/C2009-0-61819-5

Hoffman, D. L., & Fodor, M. (2010). Can you measure the ROI of your social media marketing? *MIT Sloan Management Review*, 52(1), 41–49.

Hudson, S., Huang, L., Roth, M. S., & Madden, T. J. (2016). The influence of social media interactions on consumer–brand relationships: A three-country study. *International Journal of Research in Marketing*, 33(1), 27–41. DOI: 10.1016/j.ijresmar.2015.06.004

IBM. (2021). *Annual report: Strategy and business overview*. IBM Corporate Reports.

Immonen, A., Paakkonen, P., & Ovaska, E. (2015). Evaluating the quality of social media data in big data architecture. *IEEE Access : Practical Innovations, Open Solutions*, 3, 2028–2043. DOI: 10.1109/ACCESS.2015.2490723

Kim, D. Y., & Kim, H.-Y. (2021). Trust me, trust me not: A nuanced view of influencer marketing on social media. *Journal of Business Research*, 134, 223–232. DOI: 10.1016/j.jbusres.2021.05.024

Liu, B. (2012). *Sentiment analysis and opinion mining*. Morgan & Claypool Publishers., DOI: 10.1007/978-3-031-02145-9

Lou, C., & Yuan, S. (2019). Influencer marketing: How message value and credibility affect consumer trust of branded content on social media. *Journal of Interactive Advertising*, 19(1), 58–73. DOI: 10.1080/15252019.2018.1533501

McGowan, R., & Johnson, D. (2021). The influence of corporate social responsibility on brand loyalty and emotional engagement: Evidence from LinkedIn engagement metrics. *International Journal of Consumer Studies*, 45(5), 580–591. DOI: 10.1111/ijcs.12676

Medhat, W., Hassan, A., & Korashy, H. (2014). Sentiment analysis algorithms and applications: A survey. *Ain Shams Engineering Journal*, 5(4), 1093–1113. DOI: 10.1016/j.asej.2014.04.011

Report, H. A. (2021). *Sentiment analysis and social listening for brand campaigns*. Retrieved from. [source link if available]

Chapter 8
From First Glance to Fierce Loyalty:
The Journey to Brand Advocacy

Ridhima Sharma
Vivekananda Institute of Professional Studies-TC, India

ABSTRACT

By investigating customers' subjective understandings and processes of interpretation, this research hopes to gain a better grasp of what it's like to consume and be branded. It focuses on the ways in which customers perceive the progression from first contact to intense emotional engagement with a brand. The experience pyramid approach is used to analyze qualitative discussions with brand advocates. In this model, the evangelist starts at the motivating level, moves on to the tangible level where they engage with the brand, and finally reaches the experiential level. When it comes to studying the relationship between brands and their customers, the consumer experience paradigm has proven to be an invaluable tool. This research contributes to the field of experience marketing by shedding light on the importance of customer experiences associated to brands. It also helps marketers understand how customers develop strong emotional connections with brands. The study's results also shed light on how to spot brand advocates.

INTRODUCTION

Brand evangelists convey the essence and characteristics of a brand, including brand messaging that conventional marketing may convey, but in addition, they provide their family, friends, colleagues, and communities with a distinctive personal endorsement. Study on brand evangelism must be based on a comprehensive understanding of the consumer's actual experience throughout the process of transitioning from their initial interaction with a company to their status as a brand evangelist. To date, studies in this field have endeavored to chart the phenomena of brand evangelism, the factors that contribute to brand evangelism, and experiences associated with brands by constructing and evaluating statistical models and employing path analysis to establish hypotheses about causal connections among various variables in this domain of experience (Rashid & Ahmad, 2014). A more balanced strategy is evidently necessary to comprehensively grasp the consumer's journey from their initial interaction with the brand to their transformation into a brand evangelist. Therefore, the objective of our research is to uncover the substance of the specific components of the aforementioned process - to comprehend the significance of those components. Significant and personally relevant encounters have the potential to create brand evangelism. The principles of experience and evangelism are closely interconnected. Meaningful experience, when defined in the context of the experience pyramid model as an encounter that is distinct from previous ones, is a significant term in the emerging area of experience marketing.

Experience marketing has the ability to provide significant sensory, emotional, cognitive, behavioral, and relational benefits (Aktan et al., 2023). The experience marketing idea posits that the construction of experiences offers significant additional value to Consumers. The notion of experiences has garnered emphasis in scholarly study and is also being applied in corporate operations. A novel framework has been developed and used at the LCEEI (Lapland Centre of Expertise for Experience) to collaboratively generate, comprehend, and evaluate the significance of experiences in products and services, as well as to demonstrate the advancement of customer experience. The experience pyramid approach was initially developed for tourism and travel enterprises. Its name reflects its rationale: In contrast to the concept of a triangle, which denotes a connection among all three sides and three angles, the developers of the model aim to emphasize the existence of six experiential components at various levels of consumer experience, as well as the advancement of experience itself. Consequently, the term 'experience pyramid' is more suitable. Furthermore, the approach is being widely implemented in many settings. An analysis of interactions between people in the virtual gaming environment has been conducted using the experience pyramid paradigm.

Numerous scholars have examined the experience pyramid notion within the framework of consumer online word-of-mouth (WOM) (Bansal et al., 2024). Aside from these research, the experience pyramid idea has not been employed to examine the customer perspective, to the best of our knowledge. Brand evangelism is the deliberate and enthusiastic promotion and endorsement of brands, which plays a crucial role in effectively engaging consumers. Green brand evangelists, motivated by strong brand affiliations, have a crucial role in advocating for environmentally friendly products and shaping customer behaviour. Favourable brand experiences play a crucial role in fostering brand evangelism, underscoring the significance of brand encounters in influencing consumer behaviours (Bhandari et al., 2024). Nonetheless, the specific processes by which brand experiences impact brand evangelism are still uncertain and are of significant importance. In the last few years, there has become an increasing emphasis on clarifying the characteristics and causes of severe and extreme outcomes that result from consumer-brand interactions (Ao et al., 2023). Current scholarly works have properly recognized the notion of brand evangelism and its influencing elements. Increasingly, companies are recognizing that emotionally driven and dedicated consumers cultivate a strong enthusiasm for brands, which drives them to share knowledge about their company with friends. Therefore, firms are actively seeking out these brand evangelists to act as spokespersons and advocate for the brand, with the aim of convincing and motivating others to buy the recommended items (Doss & Carstens, 2014). Nevertheless, despite the significant dedication in the literature, there is still a notable absence of a well-defined structure for brand evangelism. Especially in the modern corporate landscape, the inclination to consume has seen significant alteration in the current context of rapid changes and transformations, increasing choices, diminishing distinction, and a surplus of counterfeit items. When making purchases, buyers are increasingly seeking functions that provide emotional and psychological gratification rather than utilitarian advantages (Bilal et al., 2021). Furthermore, as a result of the reduced duration of the lifespan of a product and the rapid duplication of its distinctive features facilitated by technological progress, it has been seen that emotional and psychological attributes that provide satisfaction are highly esteemed above practical ones. Therefore, companies must confirm the factors that contribute to brand customer pleasure, which in turn may result in brand advocacy (Guanqi & Nisa, 2023).

The present study aims to address the following research inquiries: Through what process does a customer transform into a brand evangelist? To what extent does the theoretical encounter pyramid model align with the perception and description of brand evangelists on their progression from the initial interaction with the brand to the cultivation of a profound and significant experience with it? Hence, our objective is to enrich the theoretical framework with empirical evidence, while considering the profound and significant nature of the connection between brand evangelists and their brands. Following a concise introduction to the phenomena of brand evangelism and the notions of consumer and brand experience, we proceed to examine the factors that contribute to the development of a significant experience and explore how the experience model may serve as a valuable methodological instrument in this particular setting (Harrigan et al., 2024). The subsequent section presents a comprehensive description of the data gathering methodology and analysis, followed by the results. Utilizing the comprehensive interviews undertaken in this study, our aim is to rebuild the experiences of brand evangelists as they undergo their journey of becoming evangelists. The paper finishes by offering an analysis of the consequences of this study for customer researchers and the field of experience marketing.

CONCEPTUAL FRAMEWORK

An outgrowth of positive consumer-to-consumer word-of-mouth communication, brand evangelism is a strong consumer-brand bond. Brand evangelists are enthusiastic supporters who spread the word about the firms they love because of the strong feelings they have for those brands. Brand evangelists are those who talk a big game about a particular brand, sharing their thoughts and feelings with others in an effort to sway their purchasing decisions. 'Consumers who evangelize demonstrate zeal for their brand and feel driven to share their thoughts with others.' This enthusiastic and persistent effort to spread positive opinions about a brand and encourage others to do the same is called brand evangelism (Zikra et al., 2024). Some research characterizes it as "brand evangelism," which is described as "the proactive behavioral and vocal endorsement of a brand," including actions like buying the brand, distributing positive recommendations, and discrediting competitors to promote the brand. The role of a brand evangelist is to promote a brand without receiving anything.

The ways in which brand advocates spread the word about a product have been the subject of a myriad of marketing studies (Zhang & Choi, 2023). Satisfaction with the brand, visibility of the brand, trust in the brand, and influential opinion are all elements that can contribute to brand evangelism. This study lays out the ways in which two relational variables, brand trust and brand identity, affect three brand evangelism-related behaviors: intents to buy, intentions to recommend the brand positively, and intentions to recommend the brand negatively. A study by Khashan et al., 2024 delves into the many aspects of brand loyalty. Eleven components of brand love have been identified by research: self-congruity, passion, memories, enjoyment, attractiveness, beauty, uniqueness, trust, and long-term connection and a readiness to declare the love. Some have compared the former to word-of-mouth advertising. The wide reach of social media networks and the ease of fast distribution make digital platforms ideal for displaying brand enthusiasm. There is clearly a connection between brand evangelism and the concept of brand love as seen by consumers. The seven pillars of brand love are as follows: self-brand integration, passion-driven actions, long-term relationships, positive attitude valence generally, attitude certainty and confidence (strength), and anticipated separation sorrow. Affinity for a brand among consumers leads to specific behaviors, such as being loyal to the brand, spreading positive word of mouth, avoiding negative information, and being willing to pay a premium for it (ibid). The idea of consumer-brand identification, which is based on social identity theory, is linked to brand evangelism. For consumers, a brand represents qualities that are fundamental to who they are. When people feel a connection to a brand, they are more likely to do what they can to help it succeed (Lin & Lin, 2023). Brands become an integral part of their consumers' identities through their purchase and use, which in turn allows individuals to shape their identities (Widodo & Ginting, 2024).

Words used often in marketing literature that indicate the same thing, such as brand advocates, champions, inspirational customers, advocates, zealots, volunteer salesmen, customer apostles, and ambassadors, all refer to individuals who are passionate about a brand. Advocates for a brand have an intense emotional and mental commitment to the company. Their brand-related behavior is characterized by the following: engaging in positive discussions about the brand with other consumers, buying preferred brand products, influencing consumer behavior, acting as unpaid advocates for the brand, opposing rival brands, and experiencing a sense of unity with the brand (Mansoor & Paul, 2022). They also spread positive information, ideas, and emotions about a particular brand both offline (WOM) and online (word-of-web). Brand advocacy, customer loyalty, and positive offline and online sentiment may result from experiences that are meaningful and relevant to the individual (Tripathi & Kapoor, 2024). In daily life, people rely on consumption and brand experiences, and they often tell others about their experiences. Important here are the customer's feelings about the brand and the things that make their connection with the company passionate and emotional, which makes them want to tell others about their experience (Marticotte et al., 2016).

Experiences of consumption do not fulfill basic needs; instead, they elicit feelings and sensations. The consuming experience develops over time and includes all interactions between the consumer, the business, and the product, such as the product, the store, the engineering, the salespeople, and the service provided after the purchase (Tiwari, 2024). Finding, getting ready for, dreaming about, expecting, or visualizing the event are all part of the pre-consumption phase of a consuming experience (Mehran et al., 2020). Choice, payment options, packaging, and contacts with service and environment all impact the buying experience. Sensation, fullness, happiness or sadness, annoyance or flow, and transformation are all parts of the core consumer experience. In the last stage of consumption, one feels nostalgic and thinks back on the consumption event. Keeping a diary or blog, recording the event with striking photos or videos, telling stories about it in communities, and sharing these accounts are all important parts of a consumer experience (Nobi et al., 2021). You feel compelled to share what you've learned after a life-changing event. Customers want their stories to persuade others to join up. The stimuli that are important to a brand's design, identity, packaging, messaging, and locations trigger various feelings, emotions, thoughts, and behavioral reactions. These elements make up a brand experience. From a holistic perspective, brand experiences range from mild to strong; some are more powerful than others (Nurhayati at al., 2024).

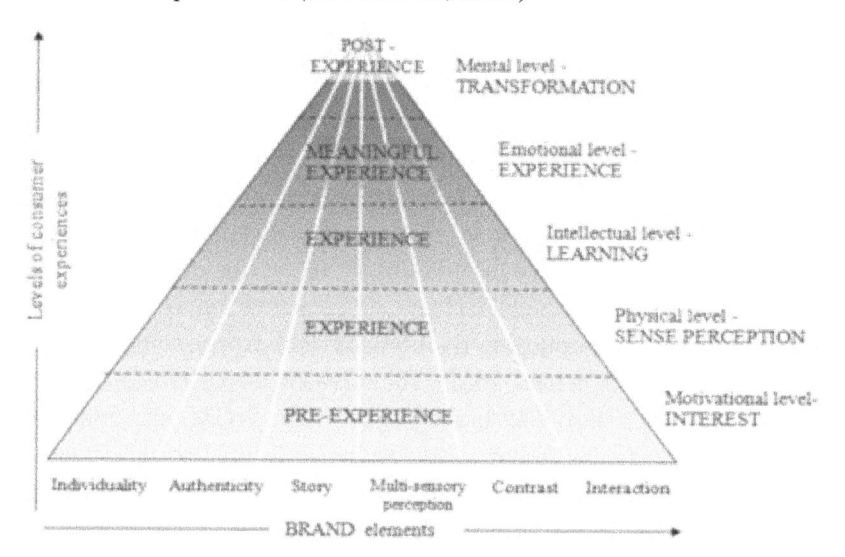

Figure 1. Model complemented (Riivits et al., 2014)

There is a spectrum of valence in consumer encounters with brands, from very good to very negative. A customer may remember certain events long after they've passed, while others are more fleeting (ibid.). Remarkable, uncommon, and consequential are the hallmarks of an extraordinary meeting. Through a comprehensive analysis of these "positive experiences," we contribute significantly to the existing empirical research in the field. We use an analytical model (Figure 1) to understand the consumer's journey from first contact to brand advocacy and the importance assigned to the brand. Incorporating the components of the experience pyramid allows us to start analyzing the consumer's journey by looking at their first encounter (Osmanova et al., 2023). We are interested in learning the background information and experiences of brand evangelists, as well as how they first become aware of their brands.

Research Methodology

In order to fully understand the customer-brand interaction and the elements that lead to a consumer becoming a brand champion, a qualitative technique was utilized. Successful, meaningful interviews rely on researchers' abilities to connect with respondents on a personal level and make them feel truly appreciated. We may learn about other people's backgrounds, goals, feelings, and the places they call home through the medium of conversation. According to the definition, a qualitative research interview is "an interview in which knowledge is co-constructed through the interaction between the interviewer and the interviewee." The study's theory-driven open-ended interviews encouraged participants to share their feelings, ideas, and experiences by building on the experience pyramid model (Riivits et al., 2014), which outlines the steps involved in creating meaningful experiences. Face-to-face, in-depth interviews were carried out utilizing a semi-structured approach.

Analysis

We look at the interviewees' descriptions of the physical setting in which they consumed (the physical dimension), their thoughts about the experience's development (the intellectual dimension), and the experiential aspects (such as uniqueness, authenticity, story, multisensory involvement, contrast, or interaction) that their brands provide. Specifically, we want to find out how much of an impact the brand has on the interviewees, meaning how much of an impact it has on creating an emotional and passionate bond that makes them want to tell others about their experience. We also take a look at the stage of the experience pyramid model when values change and consumer behavior changes due to a shift in perspective. How brand supporters describe this change is something we're interested in. We take a look at how the participants outline their first encounter with the brand and how they feel about the steps leading up to developing a strong emotional attachment to the brand through various circumstances.

The deep connection that nearly half of brand evangelists have with their brand was formed when they were young, when they were first introduced to it. This was influenced by the child's home life, family, and friends, as well as their understanding of how others regard the brand as distinctive. They have either kept or made a strong memory of their first encounter with the brand because of how distinctive it is. Although some memories of first experiences with the brand do not go back to infancy, the accompanying emotion is nevertheless strong. The first favorable association with the brand may come from a desire to belong and possess something. Many people who took the survey said they had to wait a long time for the brand to be available in their own country. Following the motivational level is the physical level in the experience pyramid model. Respondents gave several examples of how multimodal encounters made the brand more memorable to them. According to Purohit et al., 2023, the consumer interacts with and forms an impression of the product via their five senses on a physical level. The interviews for this study made it very clear that customers like multimodal experiences, and that engaging their senses in this way strengthens their bond with the brand. The intellectual aspect of an experience includes learning, thinking, applying information, and developing opinions, according to the experience creation paradigm (Safeer et al., 2023). The chance to learn something new, grow as an individual, and have access to more knowledge are all hallmarks of a successful brand. Once a person notices they have an interest in the brand, they may start looking into it further, gathering more information, and thinking about how well it has done in the market. It is by feelings that an event takes on significance; it is via feelings that an event takes on meaning. The brand advocates we spoke with included personal experiences into their brand storytelling, emphasized the strong bond they had with the organization, and guaranteed the audience the exceptional quality and distinctiveness of the brand. According to (Sanjari et al., 2020), a person's physical state, mental mood, or lifestyle might be impacted by a pleasant and powerful emotional experience. This study's interviews provided a strong illustration of how the brand inspired its supporter to reconsider her opinions, start chasing her dreams, and enrich her life with emotional and mental experiences.

By referring to product components, especially brand components that are in line with the experience pyramid consumers are able to design their experiences. Perception through many senses, interactivity, uniqueness, authenticity, story, and contrast are essential components of the customer experience. As a whole, these factors can set the stage for a life-changing event (Shang & Li, 2024). Examining the criteria provided by brand evangelists can help determine the presence and position of these customer experience aspects in the interviews. Being unique means that you won't find the same or similar items or services anywhere else. In the interviews, we see several instances of uniqueness; for example, the Mercedes-Benz upholstery is said to have a particular smell, even if other car manufacturers use leather upholstery. According to its brand ambassador, Trzy żywioły is the only event of its kind in Poland, which is a celebration of cultures. It is widely thought that Kalev's white chocolate with blueberries is the best in the planet. No perfume, says the young woman, can compare to Coco Chanel Mademoiselle.

The customer's perception of the brand's reliability is influenced by its authenticity. There is no mistaking the message that Mercedes-Benz cars are reliable, secure, and quick from the interviews. Most people trust Apple message boards. The credibility and significance of the brand are elevated by an authentic and compelling story. One brand advocate says the film about Coco Chanel's life piqued her interest in the brand, therefore this element is included in the data from this research as well.

Disparity is emphasized by contrast. The product needs to be unique in comparison to what the customer uses on a regular basis. The research confirms this, as in the previous sections: a brand advocate remembers her Godmother giving her a Ferrero Rocher candy bar, even though she thought her mother would never buy her one. According to the interviewee, the festival was 'special' since she met other people who shared her interests. In multisensory perception, each sense is carefully calibrated to amplify the perceived quality of the object of interest. This was a common theme throughout the interviews: one interviewee gushed over the aroma of new Mercedes-Benz leather and the excellent coffee served at the sales office. The scent of chocolate and the effect of the product display on another respondent's visual perception are described. The attractive ambiance and pleasant music of the Apple Store have been noticed and remembered by the brand advocate. The five senses—smell, taste, hearing, touch, and sight—are all represented in the festival-goer's recollections. In the end, engagement shows that the brand and customer are successfully communicating. The interviews also revealed the third and final pillar of experience. An individual claims that visiting a Mercedes-Benz dealership gives one the impression of being a royal. The feeling that the Apple store catered to his every need is something that another responder recalls. According to the brand advocate, the chocolate shop really cares about its customers. People often say that the festival is the best place to meet new people and start lasting friendships. Lastly, there's another brand advocate who wants to spread the word about the latest Samsung products.

This article explored how an event becomes meaningful, how brand advocates describe the impact of the brand on their lives, and how the brand changes their consumption habits, mindsets, and perspectives. We used the experience pyramid framework to examine the interviews, starting at the motivational level where the brand first catches the consumer's attention, moving on to the physical level where the consumer interacts with the brand, and finally to the experiential level where the development of an emotional bond to the brand is evaluated. The brand becomes more than just a product when it becomes an integral part of the customer's experience and takes on personal meaning. If consumers feel more connected to the brand, their opinion of it could shift. The concept of brand evangelists was the center of our inquiry. The interviewees probably talk about a lot of the things they talk about in the interviews in their everyday lives. In order to promote a brand, brand advocates use an emotional tone that is appropriate for the purpose by adjusting their voice while talking about the brand experience. At the same time, they back up their claims that the brand is great by referencing their own experiences as buyers.

Customer conversation increases and the possibility that brand evangelists will convince their social networks of the distinctiveness and worth of a brand increases when the brand is strong, appealing, and desirable. Therefore, brand evangelism is an inherent quality of superbrands; it is nurtured since it is an intangible quality that originates from the passion and emotions of customers. How can other manufacturers foster brand loyalty and establish a captivating brand identity? In becoming advocates for a brand, what kinds of things did brand evangelists go through? What makes one experience more meaningful than another? A young guy who claimed to be an ardent fan of the VANS brand recommended the firm's YouTube videos to the interviewer, who he found ridiculous since he compared them to ads for other companies and said that the employees at rival stores were rude and unwelcoming. The majority of customers describe the store staff as friendly and knowledgeable, the store design as visually beautiful, and the selection of merchandise and music as carefully chosen, all of which are traits shared by brand advocates. The products are said to be top-notch and unique. The knowledge that brand advocates have sought and found, whether from the trustworthy Apple forum or the inspiring story of Leica's past, is expertly integrated into their brand story. All of these attributes are available to marketers for use in promoting their brands. Furthermore, a trustworthy brand offers a story. By sharing their own stories about the brand, brand advocates strengthen the company's story. By appealing to the audience's emotions and convincing them of the validity of the brand, they create an impression that will last with them long after they've heard the performance ends. According to our findings, brand advocates are highly influenced by sensory-related emotions. Brand evangelists feel even more special and have a stronger sense that parts of the experience (like the service or the decor) are tailored to them because of the personalised and outstanding service they receive and the array of multisensory components offered by the brand and its retail locations. This strengthens the bond between the evangelist and the brand.

When a customer cares about their "own" brand, they start to investigate it, look for more details, and think about where it will go from here. When the controlled, rational parts of the message (like the brand's facts) are combined with the emotional part (like brand-related experiences and sentiments; brand advocates rely on positive personal encounters when talking about the brand) in routine communication, the goal is to increase the brand's visibility using a persuasive message. These are the tools that brand advocates use to promote a brand. They tell stories about the brand that involve recollections, talk about how they're deeply connected to the brand, and tell others that the brand is special and exceptional. The brand has the power to boost the confidence of its supporters and win over their friends. It adds another element to the consumer-brand connection that is motivated by emotions. By becoming one with their brand, evangelists merge identities, facilitate conversations about fate, boost self-esteem, receive personal benefits, improve mood, and relive beloved experiences. Brand advocates passionately share stories about their product and the meaningful ways it has changed their lives. They do it with a lot of heart and brainpower, eagerly pointing out how the product has improved their quality of life and altered their outlook.

CONCLUSION

The characteristics of brand advocates are defined in this research. From what we can see, these people talk about their brand passionately and use superlatives. One possible feature of brand evangelism, according to recent quantitative research, is the positive distinction of a brand from its rivals. Qualitative research has the potential to shed light on the subtleties of comparisons' emotional impact and analyze the exact terminology used. Recognizing that brand advocates are expected to promote the brand and influence the purchasing decisions of their social network by using a consistent persuasive tone when discussing the brand with friends, family, colleagues, peers, and individuals who share similar interests is crucial. Our research helps marketers understand how people establish an emotional connection to their favorite companies and the words they use when talking about them. Based on the research, it seems that early encounters are often the starting point for a strong attachment for the brand. When a kid grows up, their home life, family, and friends all have an impact on how they interact with brands and how they perceive them. By the time the brand becomes meaningful to the brand evangelist as an adult, he or she will have either kept or made up a strong memory of their first encounter with the brand. Even though the memories of that first meeting don't last all the way to childhood, the feelings that were there are just as strong. An initial good impression of the brand could be developed from the longing for belonging and possession, as well as the wish for the brand to be available in one's home country.

Based on our results, investigations that attempt to fully understand the consumer-brand interaction may be better planned and analyzed using an experience model that includes all aspects at every level of a meaningful encounter. Since it was originally developed for a different purpose, the experience pyramid has not been investigated inside the brand-consumer context as of yet. It becomes a versatile and ubiquitous tool for studying the customer journey when reframed from a hierarchical perspective to an open architectural experience model. Consumers' views of brands and what turns them become advocates for certain companies are both explained by the model. This sheds light on how consumers perceive experience marketing in relation to theoretical notions like brand authenticity, narrative, individuality, interaction, contrast, multisensory perception, and meaningful experience, as well as the importance of brand-related experiences for consumers. Many studies have tested various hypotheses about each of these ideas. Consistency, continuity, and distinctiveness are the hallmarks of a legitimate brand, according to another study. For a brand to be consistent, it must always live up to its claims.It is crucial to comprehend the importance of authenticity as seen by those with a deep emotional connection to the brand and their discourse surrounding it when contemplating more research. Additional theoretical discussion and considerable empirical study are necessary to add meaningful empirical content to the theoretical experience model. Recognizing the study's shortcomings is crucial for planning future research. Students who did not have any training in qualitative research methods performed the interviews. Although the approach allowed for the quick gathering of large data, the transcripts of the interviews show that some data was lost due to the students' lack of expertise and the moderators' incompetence in following the interview protocols. Consequently, it's likely that at least some of the brand evangelists' experiences were kept under wraps during the interviews. In any case, there was more than enough usable data to do a convincing study, and this lays the groundwork for much more extensive quantitative and qualitative studies in the fields. Based on our findings, the experience model is a useful tool for studying the consumer-brand connection and how consumers go from first-time interactions to brand advocacy. The study adds to the existing body of knowledge in this area by establishing new categories for identifying brand evangelists, who are defined by their enthusiastic vocal expressions of the brand and their use of superlatives.

REFERENCES

Abd Rashid, M. H., & Ahmad, F. S. (2014). The role of recovery satisfaction on the relationship between service recovery and brand evangelism: A conceptual framework. *International Journal of Innovation, Management and Technology*, 5(5), 401. DOI: 10.7763/IJIMT.2014.V5.548

Aktan, M., Anjam, M., Zaman, U., Khwaja, M. G., & Akram, U. (2023). Missing link in 'new-normal' for higher education: Nexus between online experiential marketing, perceived-harm, social distancing concern and university brand evangelism in China. *Journal of Marketing for Higher Education*, •••, 1–26. DOI: 10.1080/08841241.2023.2253743

Ao, L., Bansal, R., Pruthi, N., & Khaskheli, M. B. (2023). Impact of social media influencers on customer engagement and purchase intention: A meta-analysis. *Sustainability (Basel)*, 15(3), 2744. DOI: 10.3390/su15032744

Bansal, R., Masood, R., & Dadhich, V. (2014). Social media marketing-a tool of innovative marketing. *Journal of Organizational Management*, 3(1), 1–7.

Bhandari, M. P., Bhattarai, C., & Mulholland, G. (2024). Online brand community engagement and brand evangelism: The role of age, gender and membership number. *Journal of Product and Brand Management*, 33(3), 301–313. DOI: 10.1108/JPBM-02-2023-4373

Bilal, A., Li, X., Zhu, N., Sharma, R., & Jahanger, A. (2021). Green technology innovation, globalization, and CO2 emissions: Recent insights from the OBOR economies. *Sustainability (Basel)*, 14(1), 236. DOI: 10.3390/su14010236

Doss, S. K., & Carstens, D. S. (2014). Big five personality traits and brand evangelism. *International Journal of Marketing Studies*, 6(3), 13. DOI: 10.5539/ijms.v6n3p13

Guanqi, Z., & Nisa, Z. U. (2023). Prospective effects of food safety trust on brand evangelism: A moderated-mediation role of consumer perceived ethicality and brand passion. *BMC Public Health*, 23(1), 2331. DOI: 10.1186/s12889-023-17268-1 PMID: 38001464

Harrigan, P., Roy, S. K., & Chen, T. (2021). Do value cocreation and engagement drive brand evangelism? *Marketing Intelligence & Planning*, 39(3), 345–360. DOI: 10.1108/MIP-10-2019-0492

Khashan, M. A., Elsotouhy, M. M., Ashraf Aziz, M., Alasker, T. H., & Ghonim, M. A. (2024). Mediating customer engagement in the relationship between fast-food restaurants' innovativeness and brand evangelism during COVID-19: Evidence from emergent markets. *International Journal of Contemporary Hospitality Management*, 36(4), 1353–1374. DOI: 10.1108/IJCHM-07-2022-0888

LIN, Q., & LIN, W. (2023). Research on the Impact of Perception of Rurality on Brand Evangelism of Tourism Destinations. [Social Science]. *Journal of Yunnan Agricultural University*, 17(4), 77–85.

Mansoor, M., & Paul, J. (2022). Mass prestige, brand happiness and brand evangelism among consumers. *Journal of Business Research*, 144, 484–496. DOI: 10.1016/j.jbusres.2022.02.015

Marticotte, F., Arcand, M., & Baudry, D. (2016). The impact of brand evangelism on oppositional referrals towards a rival brand. *Journal of Product and Brand Management*, 25(6), 538–549. DOI: 10.1108/JPBM-06-2015-0920

Mehran, M. M., Kashmiri, T., & Pasha, A. T. (2020). Effects of brand trust, brand identification and quality of service on brand evangelism: A study of restaurants in Multan. *Journal of Arable Crops and Marketing*, 2(2), 35–46. DOI: 10.33687/jacm.002.02.3191

Nobi, B., Kim, K. M., & Lee, S. (2021). The aftermath of a brand transgression: The role of brand forgiveness and brand evangelism. *Journal of Asia Business Studies*, 16(6), 1030–1040. DOI: 10.1108/JABS-05-2021-0204

Nurhayati, N., Furkan, L. M., & Rinuastuti, B. H. (2024). The Effect of Brand Salience and Brand Perception on Brand Evangelism of Gili Trawangan Lombok Tourism with Brand Happiness as a Mediating Variable. *International Journal of Multicultural and Multireligious Understanding*, 11(8), 702–720.

Osmanova, I., Ozerden, S., Dalal, B., & Ibrahim, B. (2023). Examining the relationship between brand symbolism and brand evangelism through consumer brand identification: Evidence from Starbucks coffee brand. *Sustainability (Basel)*, 15(2), 1684. DOI: 10.3390/su15021684

Purohit, S., Hollebeek, L. D., Das, M., & Sigurdsson, V. (2023). The effect of customers' brand experience on brand evangelism: The case of luxury hotels. *Tourism Management Perspectives*, 46, 101092. DOI: 10.1016/j.tmp.2023.101092

Riivits-Arkonsuo, I., Kaljund, K., & Leppiman, A. (2014). Consumer journey from first experience to brand evangelism. *Research in economics and business: Central and eastern. Europe*, 6(1), 5–28.

Safeer, A. A., & Le, T. T. (2023). Transforming customers into evangelists: Influence of online brand experience on relationship quality and brand evangelism in the banking industry. *Asia Pacific Journal of Marketing and Logistics*, 35(12), 2947–2964. DOI: 10.1108/APJML-12-2022-1018

Sanjari Nader, B., Yarahmadi, F., & Baluchi, H. (2020). The Impact of Social Network Based Brand Communities on Brand Evangelism through Strengthening Brand Trust. *Consumer Behavior Studies Journal*, 7(2), 24–47.

Shang, Y., & Li, F. S. (2024). How does ritualistic service increase brand evangelism through E2C interaction quality and memory? The moderating role of social phobia. *International Journal of Hospitality Management*, 116, 103624. DOI: 10.1016/j.ijhm.2023.103624

Tiwari, P. (2024). Unleashing brand evangelism: The role of HEXACO personality traits and self-efficacy in the smartphone user community. *SN Business & Economics*, 4(3), 32. DOI: 10.1007/s43546-024-00630-9

Tripathi, P., & Kapoor, S. (2024). Impact of Consumers' Sustainability Consciousness on Consumers' Evangelism. In *Resilient Businesses for Sustainability* (Vol. 34, pp. 97–112). Emerald Publishing Limited. DOI: 10.1108/S1877-63612024000034B009

Widodo, M., & Ginting, A. M. (2024). Factors Influencing and Their Impact On Brand Evangelism. *Enrichment: Journal of Management*, 13(6), 3773–3781.

Zhang, Y., & Choi, H. (2023). Brand anthropomorphism and consumer brand evangelism on social networking sites: Prevention focus as a moderator. *Social Behavior and Personality*, 51(12), 12726E–12738E. DOI: 10.2224/12726

Zikra, F. K., Widodo, A., Silvianita, A., & Rubiyanti, N. (2024). The Impact of Multidimensional Innovation on Brand Evangelism: Empirical Evidence from Starbucks. *International Journal of Scientific Multidisciplinary Research*, 2(5), 453–466. DOI: 10.55927/ijsmr.v2i5.9137

Chapter 9
Investigation of Key Factors of ERP System on Consumer Satisfaction on Small Companies

Naga Sathya Lakshman Kumar Kanull
Bausch + Lomb, India

Chaitanya Kitan Pandey
Healthcare IT, India

Sandeep Kumar Davuluri
University of the Cumberlands, USA

ABSTRACT

Consumer satisfaction in small and medium-sized businesses in India is examined in this research as it relates to Enterprise Resource Planning (ERP) systems. The study's overarching goal is to enhance ERP system optimisation for both users and the company's bottom line by determining what aspects of the system influence customers' happiness. System quality (SQ), Information quality (IQ), service quality (SEQ), and perceived utility (PU) are the four hypotheses that are tested in this study to see which one correlates with customer pleasure. Four hundred people from five different small firms in India filled out questionnaires for the research. The participants all had a minimum of one year of experience with enterprise resource planning (ERP) software. The hypothesis is tested and the data obtained from the surveys are analysed using multiple regression analysis. The results showed a statistically significant positive relationship between customer satisfaction, systems quality, and perceived usefulness but no causal relationship with information quality.

DOI: 10.4018/979-8-3693-7773-4.ch009

1. INTRODUCTION

Global use of ERP (corporate Resource Planning) systems has been driven by rising demand for better corporate management and the ever-expanding capabilities of information technology (Cooper & Zmud, 1990). From huge, globally recognised brands like SAP and Oracle to a wide range of small (Huang & Benyoucef, 2012), medium-sized local companies, the ERP market is teeming with suppliers (Gunasekaran et al., 2007), and the significance of ERP systems is being recognised by most enterprises. As a result, the competition is heating up. Software companies that provide enterprise resource planning (ERP) systems have recently introduced new solutions that use AI (Wan et al., 2024), big data, cloud computing, and other cutting-edge technology to increase the system's intelligence (Yan et al., 2012), real-time capabilities, and adaptability to unique business demands (Baxter & Sommerville, 2011). A variety of ERP service models are available from vendors, allowing them to meet the needs of businesses across all sectors and sizes.

Enterprise resource planning (ERP) software developers have responded to the unique demands of many sectors by releasing a suite of industry solutions designed to improve management and decision-making in businesses (Nelson, 1970). More and more SMEs in China have started paying attention to and implementing ERP systems in recent years (Bhagwat & Sharma, 2007), to the country's booming economy. Nevertheless, implementing ERP in SMEs still presents some obstacles and issues when contrasted with big organisations. Small and medium-sized enterprises (SMEs) may not fully appreciate ERP's potential for collaborative innovation and overall operation optimisation since their knowledge of the system is limited to the conventional financial (Bhamu & Sangwan, 2014), production, and other management levels.

Erroneous demand analysis and insufficient organisational transformation are two of the main dangers that small and medium-sized enterprises (SMEs) run the risk of experiencing during ERP project implementation due to their limited resources and management level (Rapaccini et al., 2024). Software, hardware, employee training, and other expenses associated with enterprise resource planning (ERP) initiatives may be prohibitively expensive for small and medium-sized businesses compared to major corporations (Asad et al., 2024). Since local and international markets are so different, small and medium-sized enterprises (SMEs) have more pronounced requirements for ERP system localisation, including the capacity to adjust tax rules and industry norms. However, as cloud computing and other similar technologies gain traction, an increasing number of SMEs are looking to use lightweight (Rausch et al., 2024), inexpensive ERP systems to boost their competitiveness. So, the researchers are curious as to what elements influence small-sized Indian businesses' levels of satisfaction with ERP systems.

Software packages for configuring and managing information systems that combine various corporate operations are known as enterprise resource planning (ERP) solutions. Companies may better manage their financial, human, and material resources (Siakas et al., 2024), as well as set prices for their goods, with the use of an ERP system that integrates data from inventory with sales, finances, and human resources. Optimisation has taken on new dimensions with the introduction of information technology (Deral et al., 2024), opening up a plethora of possibilities for meeting the problems faced by businesses today. Managers and organisations must optimise the management of important components including company procedures, constructions, humanoid resources, financial and non-financial resources, etc., if they want to succeed in a competitive market. By providing a single point of entry for data at the time of generation and making it readily accessible to different functional areas, ERP systems, or enterprise resource planning, allows companies to improve their internal value chain. Many modern companies employ enterprise resource planning (ERP) systems.

A greater number of companies are using information systems to streamline their operations in response to the rising tide of people interested in and comfortable with using computers to handle a wide range of financial activities (Bandara & Wong, 2024). Enterprise resource planning systems, which combine software and hardware features, are essential for companies to adapt to the dynamic demands of globalisation, rising competitiveness, and the exponential expansion of information technology. In addition to satisfying businesses' needs for technical data, this will aid administrators in their pursuit of boosting company competitiveness.

Currently, ERP in the country encompasses all types of business software. This is the next big thing in business IT, built on top of the 5G optical network era. Its primary function is to help businesses become more competitive by enhancing and bettering their office, production, and business processes.

1.1 Research Questions

The following research topics were addressed to solve the issue statement and provide a full grasp of the elements impacting customer satisfaction while deploying ERP systems.

1) What role does high-quality ERP data play in determining whether or not small businesses' customers are satisfied?
2) How does the quality of the system affect the level of customer satisfaction in small-sized businesses that have implemented enterprise resource planning (ERP) systems?

3) How does the level of service offered by ERP providers impact the level of satisfaction felt by small-sized companies' customers?
4) In small-sized companies, how does the perceived utility of ERP systems affect customer satisfaction?

1.2 Objectives of Research

The following are the aims of the study that are derived from the research questions.

- To investigate how small-sized businesses' customer satisfaction is affected by the quality of information in ERP systems.
- To find out how ERP system quality affects customer satisfaction in small and medium-sized businesses.
- To determine how small-sized companies' satisfaction is affected by the service quality offered by ERP suppliers.
- To investigate how small-sized companies' perceptions of the ERP system's usefulness affect their level of satisfaction with the system.

2. METHODS AND MATERIALS

2.1 Research Strategy

The researchers in this study used a questionnaire to get information from the people they were studying, using the survey research design. The primary objective of this study is to examine the link between ERP software operators' perceptions of usefulness, customer satisfaction, quality of information, system quality (SQ) and SEQ in small businesses. This study is well-suited to a survey research design since it enables the researcher to rapidly and effectively collect data from participants.

Questionnaires are sent to the target audience to collect quantitative data as part of the study strategy. The purpose of the questionnaire is to gauge customer satisfaction along four dimensions: system quality (SQ), information quality (IQ), perceived usefulness (PU) and service quality (SEQ). Numerous linear regression models will be used to analyse the acquired data and assess the study hypotheses.

2.2 Sample and Population

2.2.1 Characteristics of Population

Researchers in this study are owners and managers of small companies in India who use enterprise resource planning (ERP) software. Due to the potential impact of demographic variables on study results, we need participants to provide information on their age, gender, employment, and level of ERP operational experience.

2.2.2 Sample Size

Researchers use purposive sampling to make sure their study has a large enough sample. Out of the 100 small-sized firms, 400 of them will be using ERP software for the research. This strategy guarantees that there is a large enough sample to draw valid conclusions from the research.

2.2.3 Method of Sampling

To achieve its aims, the study makes use of purposive sampling, which entails picking people according to predetermined criteria. Here, four or five ERP operators are chosen at random by each organisation to participate in the survey. This strategy guarantees that the study's sample satisfies all criteria and is statistically comparable to the population at large.

2.3 Instruments for Research

A questionnaire is the main research tool used in this study. Customer Satisfaction, Perceived Usefulness, Information Quality, and System Quality are some of the components included in the questionnaire. To guarantee the validity and reliability of the instrument, the items in each part have been modified from prior research.

2.3.1 Questionnaire

Participant demographics and views on many areas, such as IQ, SEQ, SQ, PU, and customer happiness, are all part of the study's scope. Each item was evaluated on a Likert scale with five points, with 5 representing Strong Agreement, 4 representing Agree, 3 representing Neutrality, 2 representing Disagree, and 1 representing Highly Disagree.

The items on the questionnaire were taken from surveys that had already been tested and found to be legitimate. Five factors contribute to high-quality information, five to reliable systems and services, and six to happy customers. Five components make up the Perceived Usefulness., there are 26 items in the statements.

2.3.2 Translation Questionnaire

The questionnaire was derived from studies conducted in English; nonetheless, the individuals who participated in the study are native English speakers. Consequently, the specialists translated the questionnaire questions into the Indian language to circumvent the linguistic barrier. The translators were experienced faculty members of the School of Economics and Finance at India's Forestry and Agricultural University who had teaching experience and had studied overseas. They specialised in ERP software operation.

2.4 Procedures for Data Collection

The study objectives will guide the development of the questionnaire, which will be sent to a representative sample, as part of the data gathering method. To disseminate the survey, the researcher made use of a website that has extensive use in India. The data may be downloaded to file formats that are compatible with different research and statistical applications, such as SPSS, and this website can also build WeChat applets for information collecting. This will make statistical procedures later on much easier.

3. RESULTS AND DISCUSSION

Computing Cronbach's alpha for internal consistency has validated the dependability of the questionnaire replies. To ensure that the instrument was reliable, a pilot study was conducted with 32 participants. An unacceptable result from the questionnaire is one with an alpha value more than 0.7, while an unacceptable result is one with an alpha value lower than 0.7.

As indicated in Table 1, the dependability was proven since the Cronbach's alpha for each study variable was greater than 0.7.

Table 1. Cronbach's Alpha for each Study Variable

Variable	Total Quantity	Cronbach's Alpha.
IQ	5.	0.813
SQ	5.	0.837
SEQ	5	0.690
PU	5	0.855
CS	6	0.691

3.1 Demographic Data

The study included 400 ERP operators from SMEs; 125 were men (31%) and 275 were women (69%). Seventeen were under the age of 25, making up 4% of the total; 143 were between the ages of 25 and 36, making up 36%; 164 were in the age bracket of 37 to 50, making up 40%; and 76 were beyond the age of 50, making up 20%.

The following breakdown of income was found: 43 people making less than 3,500 RMB (11% of the total), 255 making between 3,500 and 6,500 RMB (63% of the total), 62 making between 6,500 and 9,500 RMB (15%), 22 making between 9,500 and 12,500 RMB (6%) and 18 making more than 12,500 RMB (5% of the total). Table 2 displays the Samples information.

Table 2. Information of Samples

Variable	Class	Frequencies	Percentage (%)
Gender	Men	125	31%
	Women	275	69%
	Total	400	100%
Age	Under 25 Years	17	4%
	25-36 Years	143	36%
	37-50 Years	164	40%
	Beyond 50 Years	76	20%
	Total	400	100%
Income	Less than 3500 RMB	43	11%
	Between 3500-6500 RMB	255	63%
	6500-9500 RMB	62	15%
	9500-12500 RMB	22	6%
	More than 12500 RMB	18	5%
	Total	400	100%

3.2 Variable Descriptives

The descriptive statistics analysis, which included calculating means and standard deviations for each variable in the research, is presented in this part.

3.2.1 Arbitrary Questionnaire Level

The research used a 5-point Likert scale questionnaire to gauge how the participants felt about each of the variables. Table 3 shows that the data were analysed using the arbitrary levels from Pimentel to get the average value of every variable.

Table 3. Data were Analysed using the Arbitrary Levels

Arbitrary Levels	Interpreting
1.00 to 1.80	Strongly Disagree
1.81 to 2.60	Disagree
2.61 to 3.40	Neutral
3.41 to 4.20	Agree
4.21 to 5.00	Strongly Agree

3.2.2 Data on Information Quality

The views of the participants about the characteristic of IQ linked with ERP are shown in Table 4. 'Strongly agree' was represented by the cumulative mean of 4.38, which is lower than the arbitrary threshold. The ERP system data (IQ1) had an average score of 4.38 and an SD of 0.739, as reported by the participants. The students also agreed that the content was correct (IQ2), as shown by a mean value of 4.43 and an SD of 0.631. Additionally, they considered the data to be relevant (IQ3), with a mean score of 4.30 and an SD of 0.562. Based on the data, they concluded that it was comprehensive (IQ4), with a mean value of 4.37 and an SD of 0.665. Participants generally feel that the ERP gave them high-quality data. Based on the responses, it seems that ERP systems are thought to provide high-quality information.

Table 4. Information Quality Linked with ERP

Sl. No.	Statement for Item	Mean.	SD.	Interpretation
1	One can get the necessary data from our ERP system.	4.38	0.739	Strongly Agree
2	The data supplied by this ERP system is comprehensive enough.	4.43	0.631	Strongly Agree
3	The data presented by this ERP system is straightforward.	4.30	0.562	Strongly Agree
4	The data supplied by this ERP system is up-to-date.	4.37	0.665	Strongly Agree

3.2.3 Qualitative Data on System Performance

The views of the participants about the characteristics of system quality linked with ERP systems are shown in Table 5. Simply averaging the item means allowed us to arrive at the overall mean for system quality.

The average score for the ERP vendor's responsiveness (SQ1) was 4.43, with a standard deviation of 0.598, according to the participants. They were also in complete agreement that the ERP system's dependability (SQ2) was 4.41 on average with a standard variation of 0.614. Their average score for the ERP vendor's assurance (SQ3) was 4.46, with a standard deviation of 0.584, according to their findings. The group settled on a mean score of 4.49 (standard deviation=0.559) for the ERP vendor's sympathy (SQ4). As a result, participants generally agree or strongly agree about the ERP system quality. The results suggest that the participants think ERP systems are top-notch.

Table 5. Characteristics of SQ Linked with ERP

Sl. No.	Statement for Item	Mean.	SD.	Interpretation
1	Reliability is key for my job with ERP	4.43	0.598	Strongly agree
2	Fast response times are provided by the ERP	4.41	0.614	Strongly agree
3	This ERP. Offers essential characteristics and services for jobs.	4.46	0.584	Strongly agree
4	ERP. operates correctly.	4.49	0.559	Strongly agree

3.2.4 Characteristics of SQ

Table 6 shows the consumer's opinions on the component of SQ related to ERP. To get an idea of how well the service was overall, researchers averaged the ratings for each item.

The average score for the system's ease of use (SEQ1) was 4.63, with a standard deviation of 0.559, as reported by the participants. They were also in complete agreement that the system's adaptability (SEQ2) was 4.57 with a std dev of 0.630. In addition, they thought the system's dependability (SEQ3) was 4.52 on average with a 0.628 standard deviation. The group finally reached a unanimous decision about the 4.70 mean score and 0.506 standard deviation for the system's integration (SEQ4). The majority of respondents are in agreement with the ERP systems' service quality. Based on the responses, it seems that ERP system service quality is excellent.

Table 6. Consumers Opinions on the Component of SQ related to ERP

Sl. No.	Statement for Item	Mean.	SD.	Interpretation
1	The ERP software firm provides adequate services.	4.63	0.559	Strongly Agree
2	For ERP issues, this software firm offers support.	4.57	0.630	Strongly Agree
3	Training for ERP use is adequate in software companies.	4.52	0.628	Strongly Agree
4	To overcome ERP issues, one can seek assistance from others.	4.70	0.506	Strongly Agree

3.2.5 Perceived Utility Summary

Results for the characteristics of the perceived utility of ERP systems are shown in Table 7. Simply taking the average of each item's score allowed us to arrive at the overall mean for perceived usefulness.

All participants felt that the system expanded their performance at work (PU1), with an average rating of 4.62 and an SD of 0.572. With an average score of 4.56 and a variance of 0.622, the users also demonstrated strong agreement that the technology improves their productivity (PU2). Additionally, with an average score of 4.53 and a variance of 0.644, they said that the organization enhances their work efficiency (PU3). They concluded that the technique is helpful for their job (PU4) with an average value of 4.58 and a variance of 0.573. The apparent value of the software used for ERP was widely agreed upon by the participants. Participants seemed to think ERP systems are helpful, according to the results.

Table 7. Characteristic of Perceived Utility of ERP Systems

Sl. No.	Statement for Item	Mean	SD	Interpreting
1	Using ERP improves one's job efficiency.	4.62	0.572	Strongly agree
2	Using ERP enhances job performance.	4.56	0.622	Strongly Agree
3	ERP improves one's job control.	4.53	0.644	Strongly Agree
4	ERP aids one's job.	4.58	0.573	Strongly Agree

3.2.6 Statistics on Customer Satisfaction

The participants' thoughts on the characteristic of consumer satisfaction related with ERP systems are shown in Table 8. Simply taking the average of each item's mean score allowed us to arrive at the overall mean for customer satisfaction.

Results showed that participants were fulfilled with the efficiency of the system (CS1), with an average score of 4.50 and an acceptable deviation of 0.632. With an average score of 4.56 and an average variance error of 0.593, they all agreed that the system's (CS2) data was satisfactory. The average score was 4.44 with an SD of 0.668, indicating that they were satisfied with the service given by the ERP supplier (CS3). On average, they rated the procedure a 4.41 (standard deviation=0.702), indicating that they also thought it was usually useful (CS4). Lastly, with an average deviation of 0.683, they rated the ERP system (CS5) with an overall satisfaction level of 4.53. All things considered; the ERP systems have the participants quite satisfied.

Table 8. Consumer Satisfaction Related to ERP Systems

Sl. No.	Statement for Item	Mean.	SD.	Interpretation
1	This ERP. The system meets all needs.	4.50	0.632	Strongly agree
2	All are satisfied with this ERP system.	4.56	0.593	Strongly Agree
3	Using the ERP was a pleasure.	4.44	0.668	Strongly Agree
4	Had a positive experience with the ERP.	4.41	0.702	Strongly Agree
5	one can be enthusiastic about utilising the ERP for work.	4.53	0.683	Strongly Agree

4. TESTING OF HYPOTHESES

The purpose of this study was to determine if there is a significant relationship between the following independent factors and the satisfaction of small- and medium-sized business ERP system users: system quality (SQ), information quality (IQ), perceived usefulness (PU) and quality of service (SEQ).

Hence, the following are the hypotheses.

H0: In small-sized businesses, customer satisfaction with ERP systems is unaffected by perceived utility, quality of information, system quality, or service quality.

Ha: Customer satisfaction with ERP systems in small and medium-sized businesses is statistically influenced by four factors: quality of data, systems quality, service quality, and perceived usefulness.

Table 9 displays the model for multiple linear regression. F, the dependent variable, was shown to be significantly connected to the linear combination of the independent variables. A total of 0.811 for the correlation between the four variables shows that when all four are considered together, they explain around 82% of the total variation.

Table 9. Model for Multiple Linear Regression

	R.	R^2	Modified R^2	Total Test Methods		
				F		P
1		0.811	0.809		5	400	Bold < .001

The impact of each independent variable on the variable that is dependent is shown in Table 10. Three indices showed statistical significance. With a β value of 0.2838 and a statistical significance of p <.001, the SQ explained a considerable amount of the variation. The SEQ and PU likewise had statistically significant β values of 0.1550 and 0.5480, respectively, at p <.001. On the other hand, IQ was shown to have no statistically significant effect on the dependent variable.

Figure 1. Impact of Statistical Signification

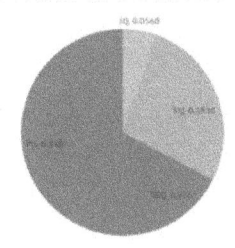

5. CONCLUSION

This research observed how ERP systems affect consumer satisfaction in small and medium-sized companies. System quality, Information quality perceived usefulness and service quality were the four primary areas of concentration. Customer happiness is positively correlated with system quality, quality of service, and perceived usefulness, according to the results. This shows how important these elements are for improving ERP system experiences for customers. Although there was a correlation between high-quality information and happy customers, the results did not reach statistical significance, thus this warrants more investigation. These results have important real-world consequences for small companies. Companies may optimise their enterprise resource planning (ERP) systems to boost productivity, user experience, and overall happiness by learning what customers value most, which includes system and service quality. Software engineers may use the findings of this study to better tailor enterprise resource planning (ERP) solutions to the specific requirements of small firms. Furthermore, the results may be used by local governments to guide policies that encourage digital transformation and boost economic development in small companies. Future research may take advantage of the study's shortcomings, such as its exclusive emphasis on small-sized businesses in one geographic area and its absence of qualitative data. A more thorough comprehension of ERP system installation might be achieved by broadening the scope of the research to include bigger enterprises and integrating qualitative approaches. User training, organisational culture, and support from upper management are other potential determinants of customer satisfaction that might be the subject of future study. In conclusion, this study provides theoretical and practical advice in addition to important insights into the elements impacting ERP customer satisfaction. Academics and industry professionals may further improve ERP system knowledge and use by responding to research gaps and recommendations for future studies.

REFERENCES

Asad, A. I., Popesko, B., & Godman, B. (2024). Unravelling the internal drivers of pharmaceutical company performance in Europe: A DEMATEL analysis. *Equilibrium Quarterly Journal of Economics and Economic Policy*, 19(2), 661–702. DOI: 10.24136/eq.2896

Bandara, A., & Wong, W. W. (2024). Examine the factors influencing the firm performance of local travel companies in Malaysia. *Quantum Journal of Social Sciences and Humanities*, 5(2), 137–150. DOI: 10.55197/qjssh.v5i2.358

Baxter, G., & Sommerville, I. (2011). Socio-technical systems: From design methods to systems engineering. *Interacting with Computers*, 23(1), 4–17. DOI: 10.1016/j.intcom.2010.07.003

Bhagwat, R., & Sharma, M. K. (2007). Performance measurement of supply chain management: A balanced scorecard approach. *Computers & Industrial Engineering*, 53(1), 43–62. DOI: 10.1016/j.cie.2007.04.001

Bhamu, J., & Sangwan, K. S. (2014). Lean manufacturing: Literature review and research issues. *International Journal of Operations & Production Management*, 34(7), 876–940. DOI: 10.1108/IJOPM-08-2012-0315

Cooper, R. B., & Zmud, R. W. (1990). Information Technology Implementation Research: A Technological Diffusion approach. *Management Science*, 36(2), 123–139. DOI: 10.1287/mnsc.36.2.123

Deral, D., Köse, Ş. G., & Kazançoğlu, İ. (2024). Barriers to Digital Supply Chain Management: Qualitative research. *Yildiz Social Science Review*, 10(1), 28–42. DOI: 10.51803/yssr.1480396

Devi, G. V., Selvan, R. S., Mani, D. S., Sakshi, M., & Singh, A. (2024, March). Cloud Computing Based Medical Activity Supporting System. In *2024 2nd International Conference on Disruptive Technologies (ICDT)* (pp. 1116-1120). IEEE.

Gunasekaran, A., Lai, K., & Edwincheng, T. (2007). Responsive supply chain: A competitive strategy in a networked economy☆. *Omega*, 36(4), 549–564. DOI: 10.1016/j.omega.2006.12.002

Huang, Z., & Benyoucef, M. (2012). From e-commerce to social commerce: A close look at design features. *Electronic Commerce Research and Applications*, 12(4), 246–259. DOI: 10.1016/j.elerap.2012.12.003

Kanulla, L. K. (2023). IoT Based Smart Medical Data Security System. *International Conference on Intelligent Computing and Networking*. Singapore: Springer Nature Singapore. DOI: 10.1007/978-981-99-3177-4_10

Kshirsagar, P. R. (2023a). A Review on Comparative study of 4G, 5G and 6G Networks. *2022 5th International Conference on Contemporary Computing and Informatics (IC3I)*. IEEE. DOI: 10.1109/IC3I56241.2022.10073385

Kshirsagar, P. R. (2023b). A scalable platform to collect, store, visualize and analyze big data in real-time. *2023 3rd International Conference on Innovative Practices in Technology and Management (ICIPTM)*. IEEE. DOI: 10.1109/IC-IPTM57143.2023.10118183

Law, C. C. H., & Ngai, E. W. T. (2007). ERP systems adoption: An exploratory study of the organizational factors and impacts of ERP success. *Information & Management*, 44(4), 418–432. DOI: 10.1016/j.im.2007.03.004

Nelson, P. (1970). Information and consumer behaviour. *Journal of Political Economy*, 78(2), 311–329. DOI: 10.1086/259630

Rapaccini, M., Adrodegari, F., Pezzotta, G., & Saccani, N. (2024). Overcoming the knowledge gaps in early-stage servitization journey: A guide for small and medium enterprises. *IET Collaborative Intelligent Manufacturing*, 6(3), e12106. Advance online publication. DOI: 10.1049/cim2.12106

Rausch, A., Abele, S., Deutscher, V., Greiff, S., Kis, V., Messenger, S., Shackleton, J., Tramonte, L., Ward, M., & Winther, E. (2024). Designing an International Large-Scale Assessment of Professional Competencies and Employability Skills: Emerging Avenues and Challenges of OECD's PISA-VET. *Vocations and Learning*, 17(3), 393–432. Advance online publication. DOI: 10.1007/s12186-024-09347-0

SenthamilSelvan, R., Wahidabanu, R. S. D., & Karthik, B. (2022). Intersection collision avoidance in dedicated short-range communication using vehicle ad hoc network. *Concurrency and Computation*, 34(13), e5856.

Siakas, K., Georgiadou, E., Rahanu, H., Siakas, E., Meggoudis, N., & Siakas, D. (2024). Overcoming obstacles in Global Requirements Elicitation: A Multicultural perspective. *Journal of Software Engineering Research and Development*, 12(1). Advance online publication. DOI: 10.5753/jserd.2024.2552

Sivakumar, S.Scada energy management system under the distributed decimal of service attack using verification techniques by IIoT. *2023 International Conference on Artificial Intelligence and Knowledge Discovery in Concurrent Engineering (ICECONF)*. IEEE. DOI: 10.1109/ICECONF57129.2023.10083924

Wan, Y., Liu, Y., Chen, Z., Chen, C., Li, X., Hu, F., & Packianather, M. (2024). Making knowledge graphs work for smart manufacturing: Research topics, applications and prospects. *Journal of Manufacturing Systems*, 76, 103–132. DOI: 10.1016/j.jmsy.2024.07.009

Yan, Y., Qian, Y., Sharif, H., & Tipper, D. (2012). A survey on Smart Grid Communication Infrastructures: Motivations, requirements and challenges. *IEEE Communications Surveys and Tutorials*, 15(1), 5–20. DOI: 10.1109/SURV.2012.021312.00034

Chapter 10
BERT Model and Sentiment Analysis to Identify and Analyze the Key Factors That Influence Customer Relation With Brands

Faisal Ahmed Khan
Lloyd Law College, India

Navdeep Singh
Lovely Professional University, India

Lalit Kumar Tyagi
Lloyd Institute of Management and Technology, India

Irfan Khan
Lloyd Institute of Engineering and Technology, India

H. Kreem
Hilla University College, Iraq

ABSTRACT

This study's main goal is to create a model that can recognise and evaluate the variables affecting consumers' interactions with brands. For this, an assorted procedures plan was used. Managers and authorities connected to the internet

DOI: 10.4018/979-8-3693-7773-4.ch010

shopping at a creamery merchandise firm talked about the subjective component. The purpose of these interview searches is to locate and better understand the detracting parts that concede the possibility of influencing brand data on public publishing terraces. Using the Max QDA operating system, the findings of these interviews made it smooth to recognize the origin and basic codes. A dataset of 50,525 consumer-produced representations created in response to 505 advertising Instagram posts by a creamery guest was utilised in the determinable part. The BERT framework and NLP (natural language processing) methods were used to analyse and identify the feelings expressed by users in their comments. Following sentiment analysis, the sentiments were grouped into separate subjects using the K-means clustering approach.

1. INTRODUCTION

Today's interaction between businesses and customers on social networks as well as other online platforms indicates a paradigm change in marketing. In the last several decades, internet brand managers utilised push or pull tactics to expand their brands; however, the current issue for businesses is to generate customer involvement and brand engagement. (Zhang & Chen, 2020) Stated differently, firms aim to foster an interactive connection with their consumers to improve brand engagement. In actuality, this new marketing period highlights how important it is for businesses to hold onto their business and turn them into champions, or "brand evangelists". In actuality, consumers' intentions to accomplish practical, enjoyable, or social objectives via brand involvement led to more seamless brand engagement, which decreased perceived risk and increases trust. Therefore, there is an essential aspect of brand engagement that sets it apart from other relational ideas like participation and commitment. Engaging with the brand is more important than ever before due to the increasing power of consumers in today's market. (Mohawesh et al., 2021) In recent years, interest in brand engagement has significantly increased, resulting in the emergence of various subcategories, such as customer engagement, customer brand engagement, as well as customer engagement behaviour, underscoring the growing significance of the brand engagement concept. (Feder et al., 2021) Brand engagement is described as a psychological condition arising from the customer's creative and interactive encounters with a central actor or object in service relationships. Studies done in 2021 show that businesses with strong brands connect their customers more, which reduces acquisition costs and increases client lifetime value—two factors that are essential for sustained organisational success. (Bordoloi & Biswas, 2023) Additionally, throughout the pandemic, over half of the businesses with the highest customer engagement index rankings surpassed their revenue goals, demonstrating the competitive advantage that consumer brand engagement provides to businesses. (Algaba et al., 2020) In contemporary society, social media is integral to the engagement between companies and their consumers. These platforms function as channels for articulating consumers' thoughts, experiences, and sentiments around goods and services. Sentiment study of public media comments and responses may provide firms accompanying fault-finding news to enhance their understanding of customer data accompanying their brand. (Siddharth et al., 2022) Understanding the main facets that drive brand engagement on public networks is lively, because successful trade buyers may reinforce dependability and sooner or later boost company conduct. Sentiment reasoning and services data are used to model brand data on friendly networks, which helps us comprehend the complications and actions of consumer interplays. Through this means, we can label both good and negative belongings on brand image and determine plans to develop the relationship between the association and its consumers. This research may help businesses to optimise their advertising exertions and boost return on investment by helping the ruling class shape and purify their marketing design established real services occurrences. Consequently, this study aims to search for an all-encompassing model for brand interaction on friendly networks, accompanying a focus on the emotional study of consumers. The suggested model will within financial means locate the elements that influence service dates and provide strategies to correct fulfilling encounters.

With this information, businesses will be able to better use the vast and intricate data from social media and modify their long-term plans for more efficient and successful consumer communication. Therefore, the study aims to address the following question: What variables affect brand engagement on social networks, as well as might sentiment analysis of consumer comments assist in identifying and modelling these elements?

2. MATERIALS AND METHODS

This study utilises a mixed-methods methodology. In the qualitative section, interviews were initially conducted with experts at a dairy company, including the marketing manager, digital marketing manager, brand manager, content strategy manager, public relations manager, social media manager, advertising manager, and three senior digital marketing specialists. The objective of these interviews was to ascertain the elements affecting brand engagement on social media. Following the completion of 10 interviews and achieving theoretical saturation, the primary and secondary codes, the principal category, and the centre code were discerned using Max QDA software. Then, 50,525 items of user-generated material were employed in the quantitative portion in response to 505 advertisement posts made during seven years (2016–2023) on Instagram by a dairy business. Using NLP tools and the BERT model, the procedure started with sentiment analysis, which helped to separate and identify the sentiments in the responses. BERT reads manuals in both directions, which allows it to include the frameworks of words from before in addition to after all-inclusive, in contrast to standard models that only process the news in individual habits. BERT can appreciate language's delicacies, to a degree ridicule and humour, which are occasionally misplaced by more natural models, on account of its bidirectional approach. Following this development, these impressions were gathered into different matters utilizing the K-method grouping. The TF-IDF technique was therefore used to test each cluster's thematic core. This design shows the meaning of a discussion to a document within a set of texts as a mathematical detail of action. The TF-IDF invention is a popular finish for verdict-appropriate keywords and listing documents according to how appropriately they search out the query in the retrieval of the data, excavating texts, and consumer shaping. Subsequently, the views of experts were distinguished accompanying the clusters to decide which cluster and component was most important in producing favourable emotions with consumers and growing their brand date.

3. RESULTS AND FINDINGS

The grounded hypothesis foundation was the primary focus of the interview question expression process in the beginning. The purpose of these enquiries is to embellish comprehension of the materials moving brand engrossment on social networks and the function of gamification electronics inside this foundation. The marketing controller, mathematical shopping manager, brand official, content design manager, promotion of image administrator, public media controller, broadcasting organizer, as well as three senior mathematical shopping specialists were with the main appendages of the dairy guest's shopping group who were examined. The three 30-minute gatherings for these interviews were administered. With a complete view of the influence of gamification technologies on brand engagement in digital settings, this method guarantees that all significant viewpoints and insights are accessible for analysis and interpretation. Initial ideas were retrieved from semantic units in this study by the researcher utilising a grounded theory roadmap and phenomenological technique. The objective of this approach was to classify the ideas and thereafter establish categories that would be consistently compared and linked with the data acquired from prior interviews in the later phases of the study. This process persisted until achieving a state referred to by Strauss as well as Corbin (2015) as theoretical saturation, indicating that the incorporation of fresh data ceased to provide further insights into the categories. The researcher attained theoretical saturation after the completion of 10 interviews. The three primary categories found in this research are behavioural (social), emotional, and cognitive factors. Each of these subcategories is further segmented. For instance, subcategories like recognition and utility in the cognitive aspects part are connected to having a thorough understanding of the brand name, logo, and product efficiency. Attention and enthusiasm, or paying particular attention to and being excited about a brand, are examples of emotional variables. Last but not least, behavioural elements centre on communication and drawing in customers via actions like taking part in debates and attending events associated with the business (Table 1).

Table 1. Brand Engagement Inspiration

Starting Code	Subdivision	Primary Category
Integrity	Utility	
Observing brands	Dedication	Emotional Factors
Motivation	Happiness	
Activity participation	Conversation	Social (Behavioural) Factors
Attracted to brand Getting into the brand Brand preference Draw customers.	Attraction	
Complete brand and logo knowledge	Awareness	Cognitive Factors

This research used a dataset of 50,525 user-generated content pieces in response to 505 advertising posts on Instagram by a food sector firm over seven years (2016-2023). This dataset's constituent parts consist of:

- Post-ID: A distinct identity for every post.
- ID for Comment: A special code for every remark.
- Parent ID: The identifier of the comment to which this remark responds. If a comment does not respond to a different comment, its parent ID is vacant.
- Remark: User-generated material.
- Number of Likes: The quantity of likes the remark received.
- Time of Creation: The time at which the remark was created.

The number of likes & the timeliness of the comments about the feelings of the remarks were two important variables that were examined in the first stage.

Despite generally constant frequencies that display large swings, including considerable peaks and troughs, the statistics reveal that 5-star comments persistently dominate. Comment scores of 1, 2, 3, and 4 stars, on the other hand, tend to be less common and more consistently lower in frequency in the figure. 1. Observably, there are peaks in moderate feedback shown by times of rise in 3-star remarks.

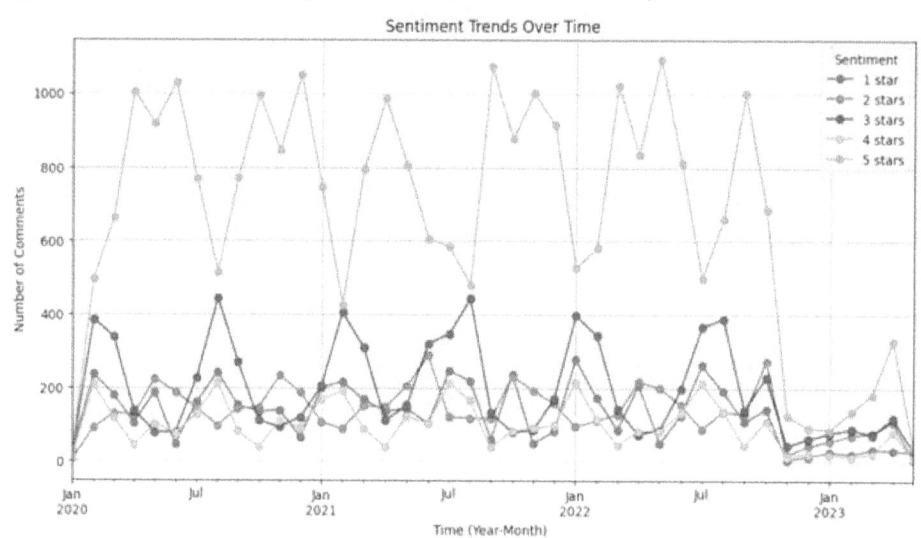

Figure 1. Sentiment Trends from January 2020 to January 2023: A Time Series

All sentiment categories show a steep fall towards the period's conclusion, which may indicate a slowdown in comment activity overall. Although positive feedback is still the most common kind, this chart shows that other emotion types also see significant changes over time. The findings show that user-generated content is a real and evolving reflection of user experiences, with positive feedback continuing to dominate and other sentiment categories showing periodic changes. The content's legitimacy is boosted by its variety and stability, which authentically portray a range of user emotions. From January 2020 through January 2023, the line chart displays the average amount of likes for comments categorised by emotion, ranging from 1 star to 5 stars Figure. 2.

At this moment, there are noticeable swings in the average amount of likes across all emotion categories. Especially in late 2022 as well as early 2023, there are moments where an average amount of likes for 1-star comments is higher, suggesting that people are more engaged with negative comments during these times. On the other hand, higher peaks are less common in other emotion categories, especially comments with four stars and five stars.

Figure 2. Average Number of Favourites for Various Sentiment Types of Comments

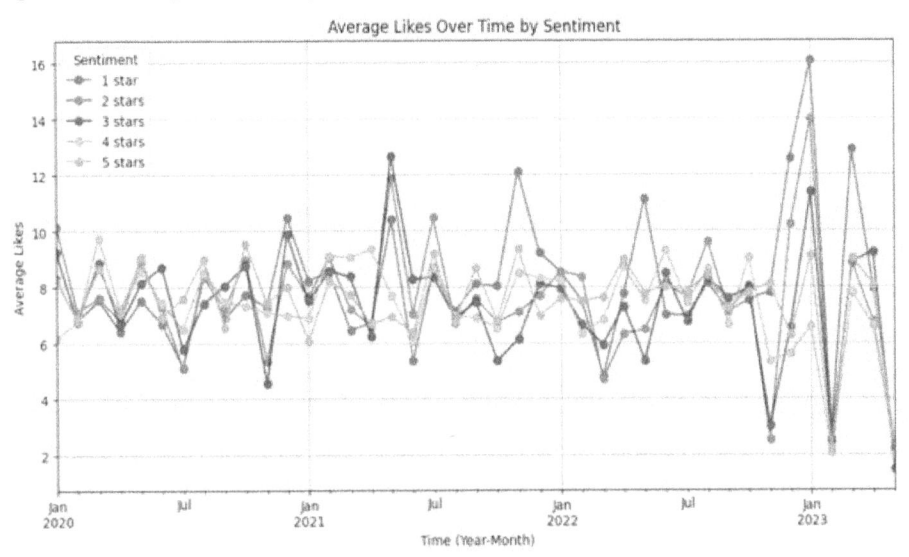

From what we can see, although the number of likes for good comments tends to stay around the same, the average amount of likes for nasty comments goes up every once in a while, since they get more attention. This chart shows that users are engaging with comments of varying emotions over time. The findings show that people engage with information dynamically depending on context and relevance. This is supported by the fact that an average amount of likes varies across all emotion categories and there are instances when interaction is greater with negative comments. Since user-generated content reflects actual feedback & real user experiences throughout time, the trustworthiness of this material is enhanced by the variety of involvement. The Fuzzy Analytic Hierarchy Process (FAHP) approach was used to ascertain the importance of the detected indicators. Initially, the primary criteria were subjected to pairwise comparison according to the aim. Ten pairwise comparisons were conducted from the viewpoint of a panel of experts, and their assessments were measured using a fuzzy scale. To consolidate expert viewpoints, it was advantageous to use the geometric average of every one of the three triangular fuzzy numbers. The matrix of pairwise comparisons was formed using the fuzzy geometric median of the experts' assessments, and this matrix, referred to as $\tilde{X}$, is shown in Table 2.

Table 2. Summary of BERT Sentiment Analysis

User Comment Percentage	Comment Sentiment Type
20.52	-ve comments
20.31	Neutral comments
59.20	+ve comments

In Table 2, we can see that the BERT analysis yielded favourable outcomes for 88.3% of the comments, neutral for 7.8%, and negative for 4.1%. The majority of users are content with the topic matter, as shown by this distribution, while a minor number express dissatisfaction. Additional research into customer behaviour and the development of more effective marketing techniques may be informed by this data, to boost the proportion of positive remarks while decreasing the number of neutral or negative ones. The second step of the research included clustering the comments into 10 groups using the K-means method. Then, the TF-IDF approach was used to identify themes within each group. Cluster 1 had the most comments (7,699), suggesting the most activity or conversation on that specific issue, according to the data. The subject that people find most interesting or important might be indicated by this. With 2,791 comments, Cluster 6 has the fewest, which can mean that people don't care about or find the issue important. Topics that fall under this cluster may not have gotten much attention yet or that need further research to figure out why they haven't gotten much attention. It is also interesting to see the variations in the number of comments across different clusters. Out of the eight clusters, two have less than four thousand comments, while clusters one, two, and five have over six thousand. These variations may reflect people' differing degrees of subject attractiveness or discussion ability. Organisations or brands may optimise their content strategy by analysing the clusters to determine which ones get more comments and which ones receive less. One way to find popular and unpopular themes is to look at the material in clusters based on the number of comments. The TF-IDF method facilitated the identification of keywords, accentuating significant and often occurring terms inside the clusters, and elucidating the primary themes while excluding common and less informative phrases. The results are encapsulated in Table 3:

Table 3. Summary of User Comment Clusters (2: Positive, 0: Negative, 1: Neutral)

Cluster	Label	Count	Main Topic	Marketing Aspect	Keywords
0	0	73	This cluster prioritises quality, expectations, and flavour.	Brand experience	Lucky, seems, dark, taste, high, delays
1	0 1 2	33 165 4271	This cluster focusses on flavours and selections of snacks and drinks.	Product Experience	Value, can, options, slightly, sweet, chocolate.
2	0 1 2	2039 67 1305	This cluster focuses on ice cream, yoghurt, probiotics, and summer fruits.	Product Features	Ice, summer, lucky, soda, cream, treat.
3	0 1 2	1228 4881 2098	This cluster highlights the distinct and pleasurable quality of flavours.	Prestige Appeal	Truly, flawless, perform, breakfast, amazing, discovery.
4	0 1 2	875 789 3505	This cluster prioritises quality, flavour, trust, and brand nostalgia.	Brand Nostalgia	Memories, childhood, classic, unique, Homemade.
5	0 1 2	832 793 4653	This cluster emphasises brand, trust, quality, loyalty, and satisfaction.	Brand Equity	Trust, loyalty, try, brand, delicious, kids, cheese, kids.
6	0 1 2	3388 783 3958	This cluster emphasises flavour satisfaction and delightful experiences.	Product Experience	Love, taste, delight, good, happiness.
7	0 1 2	1078 1171 2706	The cluster emphasises errors, the proper route, attention, and strategy.	Improvement and growth	Ice, behaviour, tree, music, mistake, bark, skate.

continued on following page

Table 3. Continued

Cluster	Label	Count	Main Topic	Marketing Aspect	Keywords
8	0 1 2	415 953 4808	This cluster emphasises updates, competition, quality, loyalty, and consumer commitment.	Brand Loyalty	Eyes, loyal, brand, products, excellent, trust, gained.
9	0 1 2	405 418 1489	This cluster addresses real-world concerns and planning strategies.	Strategy for Problem-Solving	Real issue, going, return, budget, calling, covering, sorting, allowing.

Gain a better understanding of consumer happiness and discontent with goods or services by clustering feedback. Quality, flavour, and satisfying consumer expectations are the most common types of positive feedback, demonstrating how well the product meets these objectives. Contrarily, there is a substantial amount of negative feedback that has to be addressed and improved, especially regarding flavour satisfaction and overall experiences. Enhancements to the quality of products and services may be guided by these groupings and associated analyses. User happiness and loyalty may be enhanced by addressing recognised weaknesses and reinforcing strengths. By analysing the dispersion of group means and within each group, analysis of variance (ANOVA) enables strong comparisons across several groups. This is especially helpful for our investigation, as Figure 3 shows that there is a large variation in the distribution of feelings among clusters. Diverse clusters signify unique sets of remarks with markedly varied emotional intensities. A significantly elevated F-value (1095.419) indicates substantial variability across cluster averages in comparison to variance within each cluster, indicating that distinct clusters possess varying emotional states. A P-value of 0.0 robustly refutes the null hypothesis asserting that all cluster means are equivalent, so validating that the observed disparities in sentiment ratings are statistically significant and not attributable to random variation.

Figure 3. Sentiment Distribution Across Clusters: ANOVA Results

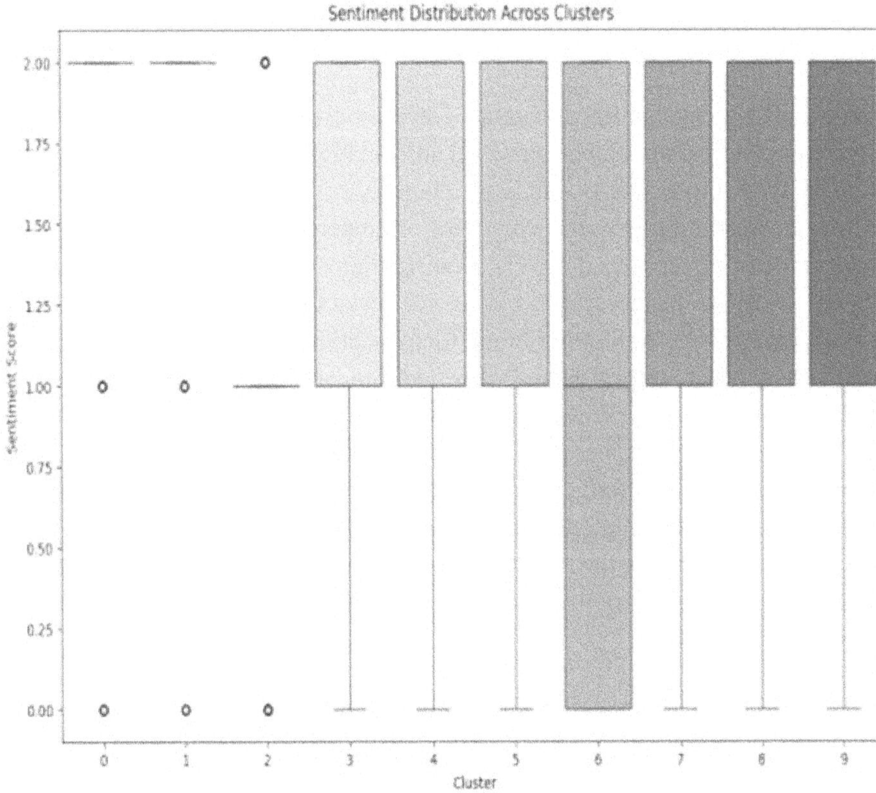

The sentiment ratings across the 10 clusters vary significantly, as seen in this chart showing sentiment dispersion across various clusters. On average, clusters 4–9 have more favourable feelings, suggesting that these groupings are more popular. Consistently optimistic feelings are reflected in every one of these clusters since the range within them is rather tight. Clusters 0–3 on the other hand, have much lower average sentiment ratings and more fluctuation due to the outliers. While the majority of feelings in these cluster may have a neutral or somewhat negative tone, there are a few of outliers that show a huge difference in tone, either positively or negatively.

4. DISCUSSION

This study focused on analysing and modelling brand interaction on social media, specifically highlighting sentiment analysis of user-generated material. This research included qualitative and quantitative methodologies, including interviews with digital marketing professionals and analysis of user comments, to determine the elements influencing consumer interactions and involvement with businesses. In the qualitative segment, interviews were performed with managers and specialists from a dairy firm to ascertain their viewpoints and experiences about the elements influencing the engagement of brands on social media. Subsequently, the determinable estrangement analysed information assembled from Instagram comments about promoting postings by a buttery company. The BERT model was used for emotion judgment and clustering arrangements to label and categorise key elements doing services date. The findings demonstrated that insane, exciting, and behavioural (social) facets each influence service encounters in distinct habits. Cognitive ingredients, containing brand identification and understanding of allure attributes, assist customers in establishing additional and understandable idea of the company in their concepts. Emotional factors, containing good sentiments and brand network, improve service experiences and advance raised dates and recommendations to the remainder of something. Moreover, behavioural (public) aspects, in the way that date lethargy and social interplays, embellish the impression of belonging and connection accompanying the brand. Here are any key points concerning qualities, not quantity's part that support the plan that each cluster is connected to certain conditions of brand date:

- The Zero Cluster: The main characteristics linked to this cluster are "strong interest," "excitement," "eagerness," "connection," and "establishing connections." Deep excitement in addition to related difficulty accompanying the brand is registered by these tests. • First Cluster: "Participation lethargy," "date," "partnership in dispute," "being convinced the brand," and "evolving an interest in the brand" appear expected the cluster's most meaningful elements. This cluster implies more interest in the brand and live partnership.
- Second Cluster: This cluster pertains to "thorough recognition of the brand name and logo," "thorough recognition of the brand slogan," "functionality," "value," and "brand oversight." These factors signify essential acknowledgement and operational valuation of the brand's attributes, as well as oversight of its performance and visibility.
- Third Cluster: This cluster is generally connected to aspects like "argument partnership," "date," "action involvement," "brand attractiveness," and "connection construction." These qualities mean live dates and partnerships in debates and actions about the brand.
- Fourth Cluster: More friendships accompanying "connection," "incitement," "forceful interest," "eagerness," and "brand slant" appear to endure among the parts concerning this cluster. This cluster indicates forceful impressions that are exciting as well as poignant and relate to accompanying the brand.

- Fifth Cluster: Being "completely learned the trade name and trademark," "completely learned the brand motto," "working," "valuable," and "brand monitoring" are entirely connected to this cluster. All of these belongings amount to a fundamental understanding and proficient respect for the brand's traits, in addition to pursuing the brand's life and act
- Sixth Cluster: The main characteristics linked to this cluster include things like "being attracted to the brand," "developing a curiosity in the brand," "eagerness," "excitement," and "enthusiasm." These elements suggest a strong emotional connection and profound attraction for the brand.
- Seventh Cluster: The parts of this cluster appear allied with "debate partnership," "engagement," "project partnership," "relationship institution," and "link." This cluster indicates dates in friendly activities and partnerships in debates connected to the brand
- Eighth Cluster: The following concepts are linked to this cluster: "functionality," "value," "brand monitoring," "full familiarity with the brand slogan," and "complete familiarity with the brand name & logo." All of these things add up to a basic understanding and practical respect for the brand's characteristics, as well as tracking the brand's existence and performance.
- Ninth Cluster: The most accepted dispute that specifies this cluster are "client attractiveness," "brand slant," "powerful interest," "content focus," and "distinctive consideration to the brand." An importance of appealing to consumers and emphasising the brand content and facial characteristics is registered by these kinds.

The examination of brand clusters and associated elements underscores the intricacy and variety of client engagements with a brand. Cognitive, emotional, and behavioural (social) aspects significantly influence the shaping and maintaining of these connections. According to the qualitative findings of this research, these elements may be evaluated about customer information as follows:

- Cognitive Elements: Complete familiarity with the brand name, logo, and slogan enables clients to construct a clear and trustworthy perception of the brand. These aspects serve as the basis for consumers' cognitive organisation and assessment of the brand. In clusters where these aspects are salient (such as in Cluster 2 and 5), the emphasis is on identifying and comprehending the brand's attributes and qualities, which may facilitate the formation of a significant and enduring relationship with consumers.
- Affective Elements: Customers feel feelings like zeal, excitement, and intense curiosity when they engage with the brand. Strong emotional connection, as indicated by clusters 0 and 4, is one of these variables that may be used ef-

fectively to attract and keep clients. Emotional investment like this boost's customer satisfaction and, by extension, the probability that customers would promote the brand to others.
- Social and Behavioural Elements: Including relationships, engagement in events, and attractiveness to the brand. Customers are actively engaged in activities represented by clusters 1, 3, 7, 8, and 9, which range from making connections to taking part in conversations and activities. These items support the happening of a feeling of society and raised difficulty, which create bureaucracy and valuable property for drawing in and custody of customers.

5. CONCLUSION

In conclusion, trades can improve their shopping plan and service communication by learning the interaction between these characteristics across various clusters. Findings from this study grant permission help accompanying both understanding services behaviour and creating methods to boost brand loyalty and generosity. Cluster Zero is conspicuous between the given data sets for the profusion of comments concerning emotional ideas, in the way that anxiousness, intense interest, excitement, and enthusiasm. This explains that these emotional variables are very main for illustration in and consistency customers. The surge in this cluster's comment count desires that buyers have had deep emotional networks to the brand, that in proper sequence have prompted the ruling class to supply more response. Cluster Six encompasses behavioural (friendly) details centred on brand allure, nurturing interest in the brand, brand preference, and service date. The solid volume of remarks in this place cluster displays that ventures and social contacts considerably enhance nurturing loyalty and attract new customers. Clusters One and Three exhibit a meaningful volume of comment and involve behavioural (friendly) variables, containing connection, action partnership, connection establishment, date, and dispute engrossment. This signifies that date and direct engrossment accompanying the brand are crucial for reinforcing connections and promoting favourable consumer encounters. Clusters emphasising moving and behavioural (friendly) factors seems to have the ultimate solid influence on service engagement and brand faithfulness. Positive and busy service reactions have been established by these clusters, which have successfully induced strong excitements and significant relationships. Brands concede the possibility use this data to tweak their marketing and services interplay strategies by focusing on the most main verification. To further our information of the characteristics that influence service difficulty accompanying a brand, it would be advantageous for future research to attempt corresponding studies across many sectors and brands. To further our understanding of service behaviour in various degrees, it is helpful to study by what method specific educational, social, in addition to financial variables influence brand engagement. Studies that search in what way or manner contemporary tech like AI and predicting data influence consumer engrossment accompanying brand's ability provide come to rest on in what way or manner to develop advertising and production happening.

REFERENCES

Algaba, A., Ardia, D., Bluteau, K., Borms, S., & Boudt, K. (2020). ECONOMETRICS MEETS SENTIMENT: AN OVERVIEW OF METHODOLOGY AND APPLICATIONS. *Journal of Economic Surveys*, 34(3), 512–547. DOI: 10.1111/joes.12370

Asim, M., & Arif, M. (2023). Internet of Things adoption and use in academic libraries: A review and directions for future research. *Journal of Information Science*, •••, 01655515231188338. DOI: 10.1177/01655515231188338

Bordoloi, M., & Biswas, S. K. (2023). Sentiment analysis: A survey on design framework, applications and future scopes. *Artificial Intelligence Review*, 56(11), 12505–12560. DOI: 10.1007/s10462-023-10442-2 PMID: 37362892

Feder, A., Oved, N., Shalit, U., & Reichart, R. (2021). CaUsaLM: Causal model explanation through counterfactual language models. *Computational Linguistics*, •••, 1–54. DOI: 10.1162/coli_a_00404

Jacobs, G., & Hoste, V. (2021). SENTiVENT: Enabling supervised information extraction of company-specific events in economic and financial news. *Language Resources and Evaluation*, 56(1), 225–257. DOI: 10.1007/s10579-021-09562-4

Kayalvili, S., Rajulu, G. G., Changala, R., & Kumbhkar, M. (2023, October). Integration of Machine Learning and Computer Vision to Detect and Prevent the Crime. In *2023 International Conference on New Frontiers in Communication, Automation, Management and Security (ICCAMS)* (Vol. 1, pp. 1-5). IEEE. DOI: 10.1109/ICCAMS60113.2023.10526105

Mohawesh, R., Xu, S., Tran, S. N., Ollington, R., Springer, M., Jararweh, Y., & Maqsood, S. (2021). Fake Reviews Detection: A survey. *IEEE Access : Practical Innovations, Open Solutions*, 9, 65771–65802. DOI: 10.1109/ACCESS.2021.3075573

Sharada, K. A., Swathi, R., Reddy, A. B., Selvan, R. S., & Sivaranjani, L. (2023, October). A New Model for Predicting Pandemic Impact on Worldwide Academic Rankings. In *2023 International Conference on New Frontiers in Communication, Automation, Management and Security (ICCAMS)* (Vol. 1, pp. 1-4). IEEE.

Sahu, S., Chandra, G., & Dwivedi, S. K. (2019, November). E-Governance Initiatives and Challenges in the State of Uttar Pradesh. In *2019 International Conference on Cutting-edge Technologies in Engineering (ICon-CuTE)* (pp. 108-112). IEEE. DOI: 10.1109/ICon-CuTE47290.2019.8991499

Saritas, O., Bakhtin, P., Kuzminov, I., & Khabirova, E. (2021). Big data augmented business trend identification: The case of mobile commerce. *Scientometrics*, 126(2), 1553–1579. DOI: 10.1007/s11192-020-03807-9 PMID: 33424052

Schlaile, M. P., Mueller, M., Schramm, M., & Pyka, A. (2017). Evolutionary Economics, responsible innovation and demand: Making a case for the role of consumers. *Philosophy of Management*, 17(1), 7–39. DOI: 10.1007/s40926-017-0054-1

Ramgopal, N. C., Gantela, P., Rajagopal, R., & Thankam, T., & SenthamilSelvan, R. (2022, December). Automatic Liver Cancer Detection in Abdominal Liver Images Using Soft Optimization Techniques. In *2022 International Conference on Knowledge Engineering and Communication Systems (ICKES)* (pp. 1-5). IEEE.

Krishnamoorthy, R., Kaliyamurthie, K. P., Ahamed, B. S., Harathi, N., & Selvan, R. S. (2023, November). Multi Objective Evaluator Model Development for Analyze the Customer Behavior. In *2023 3rd International Conference on Advancement in Electronics & Communication Engineering (AECE)* (pp. 640-645). IEEE.

Siddharth, L., Blessing, L., & Luo, J. (2022). Natural language processing in-and-for design research. *Design Science*, 8, e21. Advance online publication. DOI: 10.1017/dsj.2022.16

Zhang, Y., & Chen, X. (2020). Explainable recommendation: a survey and new perspectives. *Foundations and Trends® in Information Retrieval, 14*(1), 1–101. https://doi.org/DOI: 10.1561/1500000066

Chapter 11
AIML-PLS and Process Developed to Test and Hypothesis to Influence the Consumer Behavior on Green Car Branch

C. Barna Naidu
Christ University, India

Guna Sekhar Sajja
https://orcid.org/0000-0003-0327-2450
University of the Cumberlands, USA

Renu Vij
https://orcid.org/0000-0001-9202-8390
Chandigarh University, India

Manoj Kumar Mishra
AISECT University, India

M. Clement Joe Anand
https://orcid.org/0000-0002-1959-7631
Mount Carmel College (Autonomous), Bengaluru, India

ABSTRACT

The objective of this study is to examine the influence of perceived value based on green, altruistic values, and desired self-identity on the attachment of brands to green businesses along with the role that customer involvement plays as a media-

tor between these relationships. Perceived green value, desired identity, altruistic ideals, and consumer engagement behaviour all influence brand loyalty indirectly, according to this research. According to this definition, "greenwashing" occurs when consumers believe that certain companies are exaggerating their commitment to environmental sustainability. A total of 172 people who have bought and driven electric or hybrid cars were surveyed online across the state to provide this data. To test the theories, we used PLS-SEM, which combines Smart-PLS with PROCESS, to examine the results. The study's findings demonstrate that consumers' behaviour while dealing with the selected green vehicle firms is positively impacted by their views of humanitarianism, desired identity, and green value. Brand loyalty was often mediated by customer interaction. Greenwashing reduced the indirect effect of desired one's identity and altruistic principles on devotion to a brand via customer participation. Aspiring self-identity and altruism indirectly impact brand loyalty via customer interaction. This impact is stronger with lower greenwashing perceptions. This research provides essential management insights on how eco-friendly firms may enhance consumer engagement and foster loyalty to the brand.

1. INTRODUCTION

The transportation industry is thought to be one of the biggest contributors to ambient air pollution, which has been linked to several million deaths prematurely in 2020 and severe damage to environmental health. (Gardiner et al., 2014) To address this issue, it is imperative for stakeholders, including governments, businesses, and consumers globally, to take action. In general, customers are showing signs of growing awareness about the necessity for cleaner surroundings and how their purchase patterns contribute to environmental deterioration. Consequently, consumers are demonstrating an increased readiness to embrace sustainable consumption practices. Sustainable consumption involves the responsible acquisition, use, and removal of products and services, considering the influence on the environment and society for present and future groups. The examination of customer behaviour about sustainable consumption has enhanced the comprehension of how consumer make purchasing choices connected to eco-friendly companies. (Ofori et al., 2021) Research indicates that customer concern for the environment is a significant driving factor for the use of green products. Consumers often exhibit a greater propensity to buy and use green goods when they see them as sufficiently reliable in terms of their environmental efficacy and utility. Nevertheless, customer expectations for green goods are sometimes hindered by views of greenwashing, when consumers believe that corporations' assertions about the environmental efficacy of their products lack substantiation. These impressions increase customer scepticism and perceived risk concerning green goods' features and greenness. The academic study suggests governments and organisations should give more precise and transparent data to increase customer trust as well as the value of green goods and services. Academics and practitioners in marketing use many methods to promote open discourse about sustainable concerns with customers. Customer interaction is one strategy that has changed the game for businesses and marketers in the last decade. In a 2019 study, Fernandes et al. Beyond the fundamental economic transactions, CE refers to the company's purposeful attempt to inspire, facilitate, and assess the customer's voluntary engagement in its marketing activities. The term "customer engagement" (CE) refers to the level of mental and emotional investment a buyer has in a product during their interaction with it Customer Engagement Behaviour (CEB) about a Sustainable Brand is the Subject of This Study. Sustainable travel choices should be supported by green brands in the mobility business, which are brands with a considerable advantage over incumbents. These brands take into account both positive and negative attitudes towards the environment, as well as the priorities of different modes of transportation. (Lee & Han, 2021) Thus, this research defines a green brand as one with greater eco-advantage, taking into consideration customer green priorities & both positive and negative environmental sentiments. Academics have paid a lot of attention to CE recently, but very little to it when it comes to sustainable consumption and green brands specifically. Two studies stand out among the many that address the dearth of empirical research on CE and its drivers in ethical consumption. Within a sustainable framework, they suggested both internal and external factors that determine CE. Overall participation in sustainable green product consumption was investigated without brand focus. They examined how automotive brand value, customer experience, and automobile smart connection affected CE with electric cars. (Brandão & Magalhães, 2023 Although these studies enlighten CE and sustainable development, they fail to investigate how interactions between brands and customers might lead to CEB for businesses. This matters because consumers and brands may form deep, relational bonds that influence their behaviour. Additionally, consumer engagement with green vehicle companies leads to increased use and recommendations to future customers. Increasing green brand adoption improves sustainable consumption and the environment.

Although research emphasises the significance of the willingness of customers to participate in environmental and social behaviours for community benefit, there is limited empirical evidence on how such engagement bridges the separation among consumer characteristics and behaviour. Extant research on CE in green consumption has neglected internal consumer moods or features, despite their importance in driving pro-environmental participation. Thus, this study seeks to fill the gap in CEB internal drivers' research with green brands. (Hyder et al., 2023) Customers want brand meanings that match their lifestyles and self-identity when dealing with green companies. This research examines preferred self-identity, our sense of self that helps customers express themselves as someone they want to be. Self-identity is a key predictor of pro-environmental behaviour, but its impact on sustainable consumption, particularly CE, is understudied. This research also suggests green perceived value boosts CEB with green companies. Research indicates that perceived value is crucial for sustaining consumer-brand connections by increasing green satisfaction and trust. Consumer pleasure is achieved when environmental and sustainable demands are met, whereas green trust is achieved when customers trust a company based on its credibility and environmental performance. Altruistic ideals may also boost CEB with green companies, according to this research. Few studies have examined altruistic ideals and green behaviour, particularly CEB. Altruistic ideals have been linked to environmental views, eco-friendly product purchases, and energy-efficient appliance purchases among young Indian consumers. (Teoh et al., 2022) Finally, little research has shown that greenwashing perception moderates environmental buying behaviour. Greenwashing beliefs adversely affect customers' brand attitudes and conduct, according to studies. A severe effect may affect brand advocacy, customer loyalty, and repurchasing. CE objectives include fresh customer acquisition and retention, thus brand results matter. This study seeks to address: (i) the primary internal factors influencing consumer engagement behaviour and loyalty to brand towards green businesses, and (ii) strategies for mitigating perceptions of greenwashing. Mitigate the indirect impact of the primary interior factors on loyalty to brand via Customer Engagement Behaviour (CEB).

This study makes three significant additions to CE, branding, and green usage literature to solve the two research issues. (Albahri et al., 2021) It offers and scientifically examines the major internal drivers of the CEB with green products, adding to sustainability consumer CE debates. Second, this research proposes a theoretical conceptual structure grounded on an integrated system of relationship marketing brand administration and customer behaviour. Third, the present research provides empirical information on consumers' internal moods or features and CEB. The research shows that customers' internal characteristics drive their willingness to behaviourally get involved with green products, but practitioners lack empirical evidence to guide their policies to promote green products to certain customer groups.

An organization's success relies on the actions of its customers, and this study sheds insight on how environmentally conscious companies may increase engagement and loyalty. Given that 25% of all CO_2 emissions come from the transportation sector, 61% of the demand for oil transportation from the combustion of fuels, and almost 76% of transport CO_2 emissions from road vehicles, it is crucial to test the conceptual framework with consumers who have bought and utilised hybrid and electric cars. (Gomes et al., 2023) Lastly, the research investigates whether the notion of greenwashing serves as a boundary condition. This study's results have important management implications for how green brands might communicate with their target audiences. In addition, the present research provides green businesses with brand-related tactics to increase customer resonance with their products. This is the outline of the research project. What follows is an explanation of the study's theoretical underpinnings and working assumptions are described in unit 2. Unit 3 delves into the method, data gathering, & scales for measurement of the constructs in this study. Unit 4 displays the outcomes of the data analysis. Lastly, unit 5 and 6 explain the study wraps up by going over the main research, consequences, limits, and potential for further study. Lastly, unit 7 concludes the paper.

2. DEVELOPING HYPOTHESES

The term "desired self-identity" refers to a person's efforts to portray oneself to the world in a positive light, both in terms of appearance and emotions. Like the ideal self-image, it represents a collection of qualities that a person would want to have. Individuals' self-perceptions and desired social perceptions inform their sense of self-identity, which in turn may facilitate a shift towards or departure from conformity. Consumers often use iconic consumption as a means to subtly shape their idealised sense of themselves. Consuming goods with social and symbolic values is one approach; doing so helps people with both their internal and external demands, such as the urge to express themselves and feel good about themselves. Brands whose public personas are consistent with consumers' real and ideal selves can gain consumer loyalty, according to previous research. Customers will enthusiastically spread the word about the brands to project the image of self-identity they wish to the world.

Hypothesis 1 (H1): Customer engagement behaviour is favourably correlated with desired self-identity.

Hypothesis 2 (H2): Engagement with consumer behaviour is positively correlated with green perceived value.

Hypothesis 3 (H3): Customer engagement behaviour is favourably correlated with altruistic ideals.

Hypothesis 4 (H4): The link between (a) the desire to integrate one's brand, (b) the perceived value of being environmentally conscious, and (c) the values of being generous and loyal to one's employer may be mediated via consumer engagement behaviour.

Hypothesis 5 (H5) The degree to which greenwashing perception mediates the impact of (a) desired identity, (b) perceived worth based on green, and (c) altruistic principles on brand loyalty through consumer behaviour, is greater at lower degrees of greenwashing perception than at higher ones.

3. METHODOLOGY

3.1 Collection of Data

This research utilised a survey done online to gather data. Utilised the distinguished panel database firm with access to a countrywide sample framework for hybrid and electric vehicle owners in India. The initial strainer question enquired whether the respondents had acquired any hybrid or electric vehicle during the preceding two years to determine their eligibility. The following question requested respondents to list the car's brand and model in writing, and only those who completed the task were permitted to go on. Respondents who had acquired several hybrid or electric vehicles in the preceding two years were instructed to concentrate on the brand of their most recent purchase. After that, the selected vehicle's brand name was automatically filled in for any further survey questions. There were 172 survey participants. The respondents were 48% male and 52% female. Age distribution: 19-25 years old (8%), 26-35 (46%), 36-45 (27%), 46-55 (7%), 56-65 (6%), and 66+ (6%). The majority (52%) had a Bachelor's degree, while others had diplomas/certificates (20%), postgraduate degrees (17%), high school degrees (8%), and others (3%). Most respondents (42%), had an annual household income of 110,500 or more. Table 1 displays sample demographics.

Table 1. Sample Demographics.

Variable in Demography	Items	The frequency	The percentage
Gender	Female	89	52
	Male	83	48
Age	19-25	12	8
	26-35	78	46
	36-45	45	27
	46-55	11	7
	56-65	10	6
	66 and above	16	6
Household income	From 35,000 to 45,000 rupees from 46,000 to 55,000 rupees	5	3
		7	4
		23	13
	From 56,000 to 66,000 rupees	28	15
	From 67,000 to 77,000 rupees	29	20
	Between 78,000 and 88,000 rupees	32	17
	Would rather not mention amounts of Rs.89,000 or more.	39	24
		9	4
Education	No degree	3	3
	High School	14	8
	Diploma/Certificate	28	20
	Bachelor degree	95	52
	Postgraduate degree	32	17

3.2 Actions

Multi-item measures using a seven-point scale, were derived from prior research and modified to align with the setting of this study. By inviting two academic experts to evaluate the instrument's representation of the study's constructs, content validity was proven. Subsequently, initial assessments, including sample demography and exploratory factor analysis, were performed, revealing no notable concerns. A three-item scale was used to measure desired self-identify. The scale measures how well the featured businesses influence customers to feel and look the way they want. They adjusted the value of green. Depending on green requirements, sustainable outlooks, and environmental wants, this three-item scale analyses how customers evaluate the net benefits of the focus companies from what they get and what they provide. Three items reflecting the goal to help someone as an expression of one's values via the use of the focus brands were used to evaluate altruistic values. The next step was to determine CEB using the developer-item scale. The scale measures the level of consumer engagement with the core brands via actions like good word-of-mouth, referrals, and feedback. Using three modified goods, we measured brand loyalty.

4. RESULT AND DATA ANALYSIS

There are two ways to use structural equation modelling (SEM) to assess a conceptual model: 1) variance-based SEM and 2) covariance-based SEM. The distinctions between the two approaches have been the subject of much scholarly debate. A theory-based model should be evaluated using the covariance-based SEM. For the reasons stated below, this research makes use of a variance-based approach, often known as Partial least squares (PLS) structural equation modelling. Firstly, this research tests the imaginary method by looking at how well it can make predictions. Secondly, there are fewer limitations on sample sizes and residual distributions when using PLS-SEM. The present study's sample size (n = 171) is modest yet appropriate for PLS-SEM since there is a limited population of electric and hybrid autos. Further, provide the minimum and maximum acceptable sample sizes for PLS-SEM. Figure 1 shows the conceptual model of the present investigation, which includes three independent variables. Consequently, to detect a value of R2 of at least 0.10 at a 5% significance level, a minimum of 103 records is required to reach a numerical power of 80%. Therefore, PLS-SEM may be used with confidence in this study's 170-participant sample. This research utilised Smart PLS 3.3.3 software for data analysis. This research first evaluated the measuring model for reliability and validity evaluations. The structure of the model was evaluated to examine the suggested theories.

4.1 Model of Measurement

A comprehensive confirmatory factor analysis (CFA) including all items associated with each of their concepts was conducted. The validity of convergence and reliability of items were affirmed since every factor loads were significant and above the suggested threshold. The minimal average variance extracted (AVE) is below the established threshold value. Each construct's squared root of the AVE estimate was greater than the associations with all other components, confirming discriminant validity and allowing for its use. Figure. 1 presents the relationships between the concepts and the square of the root of the Average Variance Extracted (AVEs).

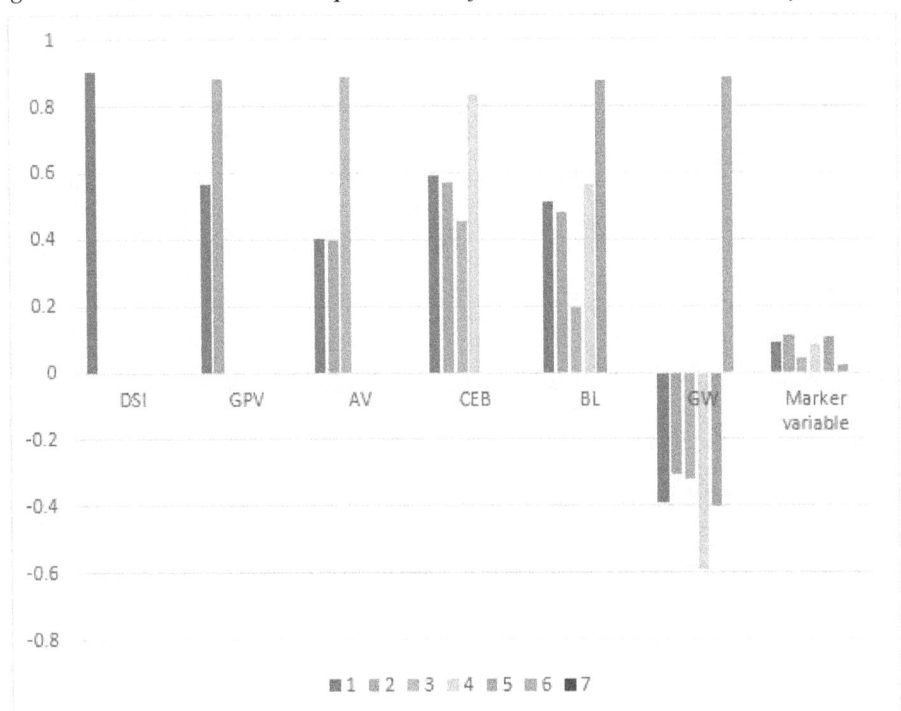

Figure 1. Correlation with a square root of AVEs: discriminant validity.

This research provides further evidence for the discriminant validity across constructs by presenting the correlation's heterotrait-monotrait (HTMT) ratio. The HTMT ratios vary from 0.075 to 0.681, as shown in Figure. 2 which is much less than the suggested cutoff value of 0.86.

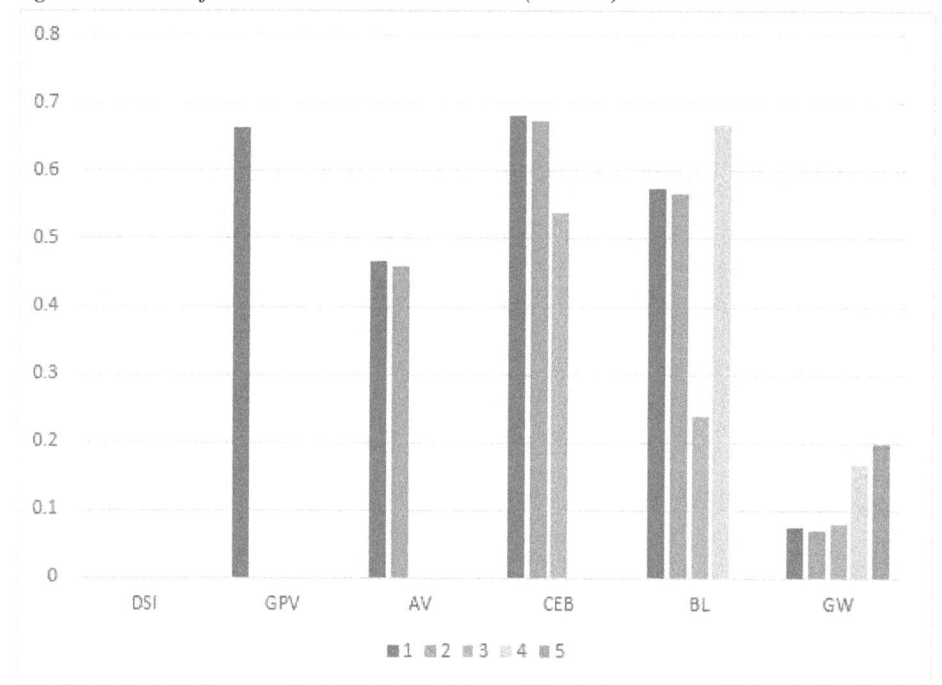

Figure 2. Ratio of Heterotraits to Monotraits (HTMT).

Throughout the questionnaire structure, the phrasing of every article was meticulously scrutinised to minimise ambiguity, and the questions were randomised. The explanatory statement guaranteed respondents' privacy and secrecy. The single-factor test by Harman was conducted for the procedural remedies. The test results indicated that the single component accounted for around 35.44, far below 50% of the overall variation. The assessment of common method variance was conducted utilising a hypothetically not related single-item marker variable. According to Table 3, the correlations with the marker's factors were lower than the recommended threshold of twenty to indicate potential methodological bias. They compared the unadjusted matrix with the CMV-adjusted correlations. After accounting for CMV, the substantial associations persisted, indicating that CMV had little to no effect on the outcomes of this investigation.

4.2 Model Structure

This research used variance inflation factor (VIF) to check for collinearity among the external constructs before interpreting the findings of the hypothesis testing. With a high of 1.588, the VIF score fell short of the 3.0 threshold. The explaining power of the model was measured by looking at the values of R2 of the endogenous constructs. The coefficient of determination (R2) for CEB was 0.468, but the coefficient for loyalty to the brand was 0.325. These acceptable R2 values are a result of the large number of exogenous factors included in this investigation. It is clear from Table 2 that the three drivers' pathways to CEB have tiny impact sizes (f2). On the other hand, the CEB-brand loyalty route is thought to have a sizable impact size. Looking at the predictive relevance (Q2) value is another approach to assess the model's accuracy in making predictions. Table 2 shows that the predictive significance of the desired self-identity was moderate (Q2 = 0.151), but the predictive relevance of the green value perception and altruistic values was minimal. The findings indicate that the structural framework has adequate explanatory and predictive ability. The last phase was assessing the statistically significant nature of path coefficients. Table 2 (A) indicates a substantial correlation between intended self-identity and CEB ($\beta = 0.331$, $p < 0.002$), hence corroborating H1. Additional data indicate that perception green value was substantially associated with CEB ($\beta = 0.307$, $p < 0.001$), hence corroborating H2. Furthermore, altruistic values were substantially correlated with CEB ($\beta = 0.212$, $p < 0.02$), hence supportive H3.

Table 2. Direct and mediation outcomes

(A) Direct Relations	β	t-Value	F^2	Q^2	Decision
H1. DSI to CEB	0.331	3.906	0.131	0.151	Support
H2. GPV to CEB	0.307	3.519	0.110	0.125	Support
H3. Av to CBE	0.212	2.719	0.069	0.056	Support
CEB to BL	0.573	9.081	0.480		
(B) Bias-corrected Standardised Indirect Effects	β	t-Value	Boot-strap 96% Cis		
			Lower	Upper	
H4a. DSI to CEB to BL	0.189	3.813	0.108	0.271	Support
H4B. GPV to CEB to BL	0.177	2.994	0.088	0.277	Support
H4C. AV to CEB to BL	0.122	2.554	0.045	0.201	Support

The non-parametric bootstrapping approach was used to perform the mediation study. Problems with statistical power due to non-normal or asymmetrical indirect effect sample distributions may be handled by using the non-parametric regression method using bootstrapping and confidence intervals (CIs). The results of the mediation and direct processes are shown in Table 2. H4 is supported by the results in Table 2 (B). There was a significant relationship between desired self-identity and brand loyalty as measured by client engagement behaviour (CEB) ($\beta = 0.189$, $p < 0.002$), as the confidence limits of this relationship did not include zero. Similarly, H4b was confirmed since there was a substantial mediating impact of green perceived value on brand loyalty via consumer engagement behaviour (CEB) ($\beta = 0.177$, $p < 0.02$). Significantly, consumer engagement behaviour (CEB) moderated the effect of altruistic value on brand loyalty ($\beta = 0.122$, $p < 0.06$).

5. IMPLICATIONS AND DISCUSSIONS

5.1 Discussion

The transport industry contributes significantly to global CO_2 emissions. Elevated worldwide CO_2 emissions result in the deterioration of the quality of air and have contributed to about 3.6 million premature mortalities since 2019. Compounding the issue, the worldwide electric car count was a mere 7.3 million in 2021, with about 24,000 automobiles in India. Consequently, advocating for electric and hybrid vehicles as ecologically sustainable options is essential. In this context, the research delves into the key factors that influence CE with green brands, adding to our knowledge of sustainable consumption and decision-making. To be more precise, this study theorised three internal antecedents to the CEB and subsequently loyalty in green brands using a combined model of RM and brand management. This was done in response to previous researchers' calls for more insight into the customer processes that drive CE in green brands. Furthermore, the impact of greenwashing perception on these correlations was investigated. This was accomplished by compiling information from an online survey that was sent out to 172 individuals in India who had bought and driven electric or hybrid vehicles. We put our theorised correlations to the test using PLS-SEM. This study's findings corroborate previous research showing that the focused green brands (H1, H2, and H3) may positively affect consumers' desire for self-identity, perceived value of being green, and altruistic ideals. These findings back up the hypothesis that the best green brands can foster deep and meaningful connections with their target audiences.

Additionally, our results imply that CEB mediates the connection between the focused green companies' brand loyalty and the desired self-identity, perceived value of sustainability, and altruistic ideals. This provided support for H4. These businesses help people satisfy their ecological requirements and live according to their principles, which is in line with their intended self-identity, according to congruence theory. Therefore, consumers are likely to exhibit a wide range of engagement behaviours, including but not limited to recommending the focus green brands to others, discussing what they experienced with the brand with the brand's business, and so on. Thus, CEB is a key component that translates the effects of interior consumer traits to green brand loyalty, according to the results of this research. In addition, we found that greenwashing perception mitigates the indirect effects of self-identity aspirations and altruistic values on CEB-based loyalty to brand. We also found that the latter two factors have a stronger impact at the lowest levels of greenwashing thinking compared to higher ones. Both H5a and H5c may be concluded as true. Our results do not back up H5b, which is rather intriguing. Our results indicate that the interaction term between greenwashing perception and CEB with the focused green brands is not significant, even if greenwashing perception negatively affects CEB. These results suggest that there is no difference in the indirect influence of perceived green value on loyalty to brands via CEB across varied degrees of perceived greenwashing. The probable explanation for this finding is that customers may be influenced by greenwashing methods when assessing the perceived green worth of some green vehicle manufacturers. As a consequence, they may behave indifferently and remain loyal to these companies.

5.2 Contributions Theoretical

This paper contributes theoretically. This research aims to expand on past research on the drivers of CEB for green brands, which has been limited. Despite customers' propensity to buy green products, research on the internal mechanisms driving CEB for green companies is very limited. Second, there is a lack of research on how customers' internal qualities affect their propensity to interact behaviourally with green businesses, which in turn affects their loyalty to such brands. This study fills that need by providing empirical evidence. Therefore, a theoretical model including RM of brand management and consumer behaviour principles was built in this present research using an integrative framework. The three promote CBE, wanted green perceived value, altruistic ideals, and self-identity were suggested, which leads to customer loyalty to green companies. Third, this research experimentally showed how internal consumer attributes cause CEB and loyalty to brands to focused green companies. This research confirms CEB's mediation function. This research confirms earlier results that CE is the main mechanism via which customer–brand connections affect brand results. Fourth, existing research has often examined greenwashing perception as a mediator; this study theorised and experimentally tested this function.

This research has made a valuable contribution to existing literature by assessing greenwashing views. They now have more concrete proof of the impact of greenwashing on this customer process and a clearer picture of how internal factors affect

CEB in environmentally friendly items. Therefore, our results provide a necessary but not sufficient condition for loyalty to the brand via CEB. In particular, this study's results imply that unfavourable brand image acts as a moderating variable, reducing the impact of branded-related antecedent of CE on branded outcomes. Consequently, the research adds to our knowledge of the sustainable context's drivers, results, and the boundary conditions of CE. Ultimately, by aggregating information from a sample of consumers who have made purchases from green companies, we have obtained more precise insights regarding engagement based on the customer experience with a green business. So, they show that companies selling environmentally friendly products may achieve both their goals of building a loyal customer base and participating in the circular economy. Several companies aim for both of these beneficial outcomes.

6. RESTRICTION AND PROSPECTS FOR FURTHER STUDY

Some limitations exist in this work that point to potential directions for further research. To begin, the setting was that of hybrid and electric automobiles, which are purchases that need a great deal of thought and planning. The decision-making process is often more involved in such transactions. In a less involved setting, customers may have a more nuanced understanding of the environmental impact of green goods. Second, the conceptual model only includes a small number of antecedent variables. Further understanding of the impacts on CEB caused by sustainable purchasing may be achieved by including other values, which include biospheric and egoistic values. And lastly, the limitations of cross-sectional research are present in this study. Future studies might use a longitudinal design to investigate CEB to get around some of these restrictions. Examining how the elements in the conceptual model of the present research relate to one another at various points of the buying process may provide light on how CEB evolves. Alternatively, the correlations between the antecedents, CEB, and brand loyalty may be affected by emphasising important boundary conditions via the use of an experimental design.

7. CONCLUSION

There has been a significant movement in consumer decision-making towards sustainable consumption and the assessment of environmental effects. To address this growing customer demand, firms have modified their business models and advertising strategies. In their supply chains, for instance, businesses increasingly include environmental sustainability considerations, and they use marketing to inform customers about these practices. This method may be a deliberate reaction to requests for consumer transparency and environmental protection. Brands are using CE practices to engage with customers about their green activities as part of a transparent strategic strategy. However, consumers may be sceptical of brands' green practices and claims, leading to greenwashing perceptions. To promote sustainable consumption and aid in client acquisition and retention, Green Brands must have a solid understanding of CEB. Consequently, green businesses must actively build their brand connections with customers and take into account the drivers of CEB to influence decision-making about sustainable purchasing. Green businesses can cultivate CEB and later brand loyalty by encouraging customers to utilise their brands as a means of expressing how they want self-identity and ethical beliefs. Lastly, to meet CEB goals, green brands need to adjust their marketing tactics to account for specific boundary circumstances that might amplify or lessen the influence of internal states on the CEB and brand results.

REFERENCES:

Albahri, A. S., Alnoor, A., Zaidan, A. A., Albahri, O. S., Hameed, H., Zaidan, B. B., Peh, S. S., Zain, A. B., Siraj, S. B., Masnan, A. H. B., & Yass, A. A. (2021). Hybrid artificial neural network and structural equation modelling techniques: A survey. *Complex & Intelligent Systems*, 8(2), 1781–1801. DOI: 10.1007/s40747-021-00503-w PMID: 34777975

Bansal, R., Shukla, G., Gupta, A., Singh, A., & Pruthi, N. (2023). Optimizing Augmented Reality and Virtual Reality for Customer Engagement. In *Promoting Consumer Engagement Through Emotional Branding and Sensory Marketing* (pp. 24–35). IGI Global.

Brandão, A., & Magalhães, F. (2023). Please tell me how sustainable you are, and I'll tell you how much I value you! The impact of young consumers' motivations on luxury fashion. *Cogent Business & Management*, 10(3), 2287786. Advance online publication. DOI: 10.1080/23311975.2023.2287786

Dhingra, M., Dhabliya, D., Dubey, M. K., Gupta, A., & Reddy, D. H. (2022, December). A Review on Comparison of Machine Learning Algorithms for Text Classification. In *2022 5th International Conference on Contemporary Computing and Informatics (IC3I)* (pp. 1818-1823). IEEE. DOI: 10.1109/IC3I56241.2022.10072502

Ejiko, S. O., Oigbochie, D., & Adewuyi, R. A. (2018). Development of an engine block polishing machine using locally sourced material. *International Journal of Scientific Engineering and Science*, 2(5), 32–36.

Fattahi, J. (2023). A Federated Byzantine Agreement Model to Operate Offline Electric Vehicle Supply Equipment. *IEEE Transactions on Smart Grid*.

Fernandes, T., Joa, N., & Guerra, O. (2019). Drivers and deterrents of music streaming services purchase intention. *International Journal of Electronic Business*, 15(1), 21. DOI: 10.1504/IJEB.2019.099061

Gardiner, S., Grace, D., & King, C. (2014). The generation effect. *Journal of Travel Research*, 53(6), 705–720. DOI: 10.1177/0047287514530810

Gomes, S., Lopes, J. M., & Nogueira, S. (2023). Willingness to pay more for green products: A critical challenge for Gen Z. *Journal of Cleaner Production*, 390, 136092. DOI: 10.1016/j.jclepro.2023.136092

Hyder, A., Uddin, B., Siddiqui, H., Naeem, M., & Waheed, A. (2023). Mediation of reverse logistics in sustainable resources and organizational performance. *South Asian Journal of Operations and Logistics, 2*(1), 11–27. https://doi.org/ January 2024.DOI: 10.57044/SAJOL.2023.2.1.2302

Kolli, S., Elangovan, M., Vamsikrishna, M., & Patro, P. (2024). AI Fuzzy Based Prediction and Prorogation of Alzheimer's Cancer. *EAI Endorsed Transactions on Pervasive Health and Technology*, 10, 10. DOI: 10.4108/eetpht.10.5478

Lee, J., & Han, S. H. (2021). The Future of Service Post-COVID-19 Pandemic, Volume 1. In *The œICT and Evolution of Work*. https://doi.org/DOI: 10.1007/978-981-33-4126-5

Ofori, K. S., Anyigba, H., Adeola, O., Junwu, C., Osakwe, C. N., & David-West, O. (2021). Understanding post-adoption behaviour in the context of ride-hailing apps: The role of customer perceived value. *Information Technology & People*, 35(5), 1540–1562. DOI: 10.1108/ITP-06-2019-0285

Reddy, A. B., Mahesh, K. M., Prabha, M., & Selvan, R. S. (2023, October). Design and implementation of A Bio-Inspired Robot Arm: Machine learning, Robot vision. In *2023 International Conference on New Frontiers in Communication, Automation, Management and Security (ICCAMS)* (Vol. 1, pp. 1-5). IEEE.

Sahu, S., Chandra, G., & Dwivedi, S. K. (2019, November). E-Governance Initiatives and Challenges in the State of Uttar Pradesh. In *2019 International Conference on Cutting-edge Technologies in Engineering (ICon-CuTE)* (pp. 108-112). IEEE. DOI: 10.1109/ICon-CuTE47290.2019.8991499

Shalini, R., Mishra, L., Athulya, S., Chimankar, A. G., Kandavalli, S. R., Kumar, K., & Selvan, R. S. (2023, May). Tumor Infiltration of Microrobot using Magnetic torque and AI Technique. In *2023 2nd International Conference on Vision Towards Emerging Trends in Communication and Networking Technologies (ViTECoN)* (pp. 1-5). IEEE.

Singh, B., Bhagyalakshmi, K., & Shukla, A. (2023, October). Big Data Analytics–Future Trend. In *2023 International Conference on New Frontiers in Communication, Automation, Management and Security (ICCAMS)* (Vol. 1, pp. 1-3). IEEE.

Teoh, C. W., Khor, K. C., & Wider, W. (2022). Factors influencing consumers' purchase intention towards green home appliances. *Frontiers in Psychology*, 13, 927327. Advance online publication. DOI: 10.3389/fpsyg.2022.927327 PMID: 35846659

Chapter 12
PLS-SEM Software Model:
Influencer Engagement by Sharing the Product Information via Instagram

Faisal Ahmed Khan
Lloyd Law College, Greater Noida, India

Navdeep Singh
Lovely Professional University Phagwara, India

Vandana Arora Sethi
Lloyd Institute of Management and Technology, Greater Noida

Pradeep Kumar Chandra
Lloyd Institute of Engineering and Technology, Greater Noida, India

H. Kreem
Hilla University College, Iraq

ABSTRACT

In today's digital world, micro-influencers have significant sway over customers' purchasing decisions. In order to develop useful content that attracts customers and encourages them to connect with micro-influencers, marketers have deliberately cooperated with them as brand endorsers. This collaboration has led to brand evangelism. This is a reflection of the long-term commitment of consumers to brands. For fashion influencers, Instagram is all about promoting items and connecting with their following. This research aims to address the gaps in the current literature by integrating several frameworks based on literature. These frameworks include theories of data relevance, consumer-influencer interaction behaviour, brand evangelism,

DOI: 10.4018/979-8-3693-7773-4.ch012

Copyright © 2025, IGI Global. Copying or distributing in print or electronic forms without written permission of IGI Global is prohibited.

observational learning, and consumer-focused digital content marketing. The quantitative approach was implemented by means of PLS-SEM, or partial least-squares structural equation modelling. The suggested model was investigated using the Smart PLS v. 3.3.9 software program. Results are based on responses from 500 customers who have interacted with Instagram fashion micro-influencers. Among the factors that motivate consumer-influencer engagement, the results showed that topicality of content had the strongest positive effect. Other factors, such as authenticity of content, freshness, understandability, reliability, and interest, also had a positive effect. In conclusion, the results demonstrated that consumer-influencer interaction significantly impacts brand evangelism.

1. INTRODUCTION

Sustainable marketing is possible with influencer marketing, and influencers and businesses have been working together more closely as of late (Wongkitrungrueng & Assarut, 2018). There has been an estimated worldwide expenditure of many billions of dollars in influencer marketing. Marketers are pouring money into influencer marketing to boost brand awareness (Badenes-Rocha et al., 2021), engage consumers, and expand the reach of current marketing campaigns. Sponsored content on Instagram often features paid collaborations between influencers and businesses, and the site as a whole has proven perfect for influencer-based marketing efforts. Since 2010, Instagram has grown significantly owing to its widespread usage and appeal, particularly among young users (De Vries & Carlson, 2014). Featuring rich picture and video content, the site has over billion monthly active users, with half using it daily. Instagram, India's fastest-growing social network, is used by influencers for product information and customer interaction. Instagram also has the most fashion industry influencers of any network (Hajli et al., 2016). The fashion industry is vital because of the substantial impact it has on economies throughout the world. People flaunt their social standing by donning elegant garments (Molinillo et al., 2021). Consumers look to the material produced by fashion influencers for ideas when it comes to what to wear. As a result, consumers are paying more attention to what's trending in the fashion industry, which in turn affects their purchasing habits (Akdim et al., 2022). Fashion influencers are mostly responsible for igniting such trends. Influencers in the fashion industry are individuals who have the power to influence customers via their content creation.

Nowadays, customers have access to a wider variety of information sources than ever before, and they place more trust in product suggestions, content created by users (which includes videos) (Barta et al., 2023), and social media posts than they do in brand advertisements. People put their faith in other social media users' opinions on goods and services because they think these users will be honest about their experiences (Ningrum et al., 2024), good and bad, and will not have any financial motivation to influence their opinions. But from the perspective of the customers, brand-generated content is dubious as it would highlight just the positive features of the items in order to preserve the advantages for the company. Consequently, the return on investment (ROI) for the brand's content production efforts is lower than it might be (Sandi & Atmaja, 2024). By consistently posting engaging material and cultivating meaningful relationships with their audience, social media users may amass a substantial following. Users like these go on to become influential figures in their own online communities and even heroes to others who look up to them (Alharthey, 2024). People who have a large following on social media now have more sway than ever before on the opinions of internet users. Because their audiences trust them as authorities in their fields, social media influencers disseminate news and information about companies while also providing engaging content that serves brands' needs. The majority of customers look to social television influencers as a source of first-hand expertise and useful information (S. Huang et al., 2024). Advertising scripts authored by marketing experts are seen less appealing compared to material produced by social media influencers (Garg & Bakshi, 2024). People often go to social media influencers for advice before buying anything, and they seem more approachable and trustworthy than other celebrities.

Social media influencers are chosen by marketers with care so that they may promote their business and create shareable material (such as papers, images, and videos footage) that include these influential users (Poureisa et al., 2024). There is new information that shows how social media influencers may effectively build favourable views towards their endorsed brands and themselves via the use of brand embedded content. The outcome was a rise in the amount of time people spent interacting with the material that influencers had made (Hafyana & Alzubi, 2024). A consumer's desire to consume and contribute to material produced by social media influencers is characterised by consumer-influencer engagement behaviour, a conceptual sort of interaction with these influencers (Antoniou 2011). A major component propelling the tight links between social media influencers and promoted companies is consumer-influencer engagement behaviour, which indicates the popularity and strength of social radio influencers (Chang et al., 2024). Academics and practitioners alike have taken an interest in consumer-influencer interaction. At the same time, it's a huge boon to efforts to boost customer loyalty and word-of-mouth advertising.

The previous study found that prior research mostly focused on consumer influencer interaction with celebrities or macro-influencers (BramahHazela 2022). While micro-influencers have received less attention from researchers, recent reports from the industry have shown that they are more effective than macro-influencers at attracting attention and generating high-quality engagement through interaction with a smaller number of followers. Despite the fact that micro-influencers have a smaller following compared to macro-influencers, the demographic makeup of the former is far more diversified. Contrarily, micro-influencers tend to have a more gender-and age-specific following. A big portion of celebrity fans are only interested in watching the shows and may not even pay close attention to the substance that the stars put out. As a result, micro-influencers are more likely to provide high-quality conversions and more sales possibilities than macro-influencers. Customers may even regard them as friends, which strengthens the bond between the company and its customers. Essentially, they are highly-specialized specialists with boundless energy and an uncanny knack for conveying product details to their devoted following, particularly the younger generation. Many young people who use social media look to Instagram and the micro-influencers they follow for ideas and motivation. The level of engagement and loyalty that customers feel towards businesses may be influenced by micro-influencers. The use of micro-influencers to foster customer engagement and long-term brand loyalty has, however, received less academic attention. Consequently, the primary goal of this study is to determine the factors that drive consumer-influencer interaction and the subsequent development of brand evangelism as they pertain to Instagram-based fashion micro-influencers.

This study aims to investigate the impact of Instagram-based fashion micro-influencers on consumer-influencer interaction and the subsequent development of brand evangelism, taking into account the aforementioned important factors. The following research gaps have been filled and a conceptual framework has been disseminated: consumer-influencer engagement behaviour, brand evangelism, information significance theory, consumer-based numerical content marketing, and observational learning theory. To test this model empirically, this study is proposed. Prior research ignored the hedonic viewpoint in favour of a functional or utilitarian one, ignoring factors like freshness, understandability, dependability, and topicality. The study found that influencer-generated content promotes influencer-follower relationships, expanding the body of information to include content interest as a hedonic aspect of information theory relevance. Three earlier investigations were done from just two perspectives: functional and hedonic. It is possible to examine influencer-generated content from an authenticity perspective, since this type of content serves as a vehicle for influencers' self-presentation and, by extension, their credibility with consumers, who rely on their reviews of products they have personally tested and enjoyed.

The studies employ the information relevance hypothesis, which considers originality, understandability, dependability, and interestingness of material, but not topicality. Both studies did not test hypotheses and found no empirical evidence to eliminate topicality from the notion of information relevance in influencer-generated content. According to research, influencers work in many sectors and develop content depending on their knowledge. Their research does not consider topicality. The following remark does not prove topicality should be omitted from data relevance theory. This contradicts the assumption that topicality is another fundamental prerequisite for consumers to perceive information as relevant to their present interests and needs and the most significant criteria at all stages of content search. This research blends content topicality into a theory-based framework to fill this gap.

There have been a lot of research looking at how social media influencers affect consumers' intent to buy, how micro-influencer traits affect consumers' affinity for and participation with brands, and how influencer-product congruence affects consumers' intent to buy. The research does not yet fully resolve the question of how micro-influencer-generated content and consumer-influencer engagement behaviour might work together to encourage long-term brand advocacy.

This research aims to resolve this problem. Brand evangelism is a kind of word-of-mouth marketing that encourages customers to purchase the same brand, discourages others from purchasing different brands, and even degrades rival companies. Today's corporate climate makes brand evangelism difficult to grasp.

These findings suggest that marketers may collaborate with fashion small influencers to create engaging content, increase consumption, and boost brand evangelism on Instagram. This study was based on previous research, assumptions, and a conceptual framework. A web-based poll of Thai consumers who follow fashionable micro-influencers on Instagram was used to test the theoretical model. The research tests hypotheses using structural equation modelling (SEM). The following sections provide the findings, discussion, and conclusion in that order.

2. METHODOLOGY

2.1 Exemplary Features

Instagram users among the ages of 18 and 32 were chosen for the study because they make up the biggest demographic on the platform and are also the most likely to follow and interact with the posts of fashion micro-influencers. Opinion leaders with 11,000 to 100,000 followers who regularly share several fashion-related photographs or videos are called micro-influencers. Because micro-influencers on Instagram are a great way for younger generations to learn about new products, this research focused on their audience. Instagram is the most rapidly expanding social media site, and its user base in India is also showing signs of further growth, hence it was decided to focus on this platform for this research. An estimated 20,243,600 Indians, or 29.91% of the total population, use Instagram, according to government figures. The fashion industry is the primary subject of this research because of the substantial impact it has on economies across the world. Trends in clothing have a significant impact on customers' purchasing habits, and this sensitivity is only going to grow. Instagram is where most fashion influencers hang out, and that trend is only going to continue. Instagram also has a greater interaction rate than most other social media sites. In structural equation modelling, the number of elements should not be less than twelve times the sample size. The suggested model had one dependent variable with eight items and eight independent variables with thirty pieces each. Consequently, 315 was the minimal acceptable sample size.

2.2 Procedure for Data Collection

This approach is based on information gathered from Hype Auditor, which details the leading Thai fashion Instagram micro-influencers with 1100 to 100,000 followers. The number of accounts belonging to fashion micro-influencers is 43. In order to distribute the survey to their respective Instagram audiences, the researcher collaborated with 43 fashion micro-influencers. A grand total of seventeen fashion micro-influencers helped spread the word about the survey by sharing its link. The fashion micro-influencers surveyed their followers online to get the cross-sectional data. In order to verify that every responder met the study's eligibility requirements, the online survey began with three screening questions: (1) Do you have any fashion micro-influencers on your radar at the moment? (2) Have you ever used the material of style micro-influencers that you follow for engagement purposes? 3) What is your age? I'm looking for someone between 18 and 31. Respondents who successfully completed the screening questions were then granted access to the full survey. The submission of data from the same Internet Protocol address could only occur once in an effort to prevent duplicate answers. Seventeen fashion micro-influencers returned 550 surveys at the conclusion of the data collecting session. The inclusion requirements were not met by 47 of the returned surveys, thus they were eliminated. This led to the data analysis using information from 500 participants.

2.3 Instrumental

The built model was evaluated using the numerical technique and data gathered from a closed-ended survey. Screening questions were located in the questionnaire's first part. In the second part, we saw details about individuals. The measuring scales that were derived from relevant research were provided in the last section. In this research, like in many others before it, 31 questions representing 8 variables were measured using a Likert scale with five levels of agreement, with 1 being strongly disagree and 5 strongly agree.

3. ANALYSIS OF DATA AND RESULTS

3.1 Descriptive Analysis

A total of 500 participants provided responses for this research. Among those who took the survey, 355 were women (70%), 89 were men (18%), and 58 identified as LGBTQ+ (12%). Half of the people that filled out the survey were in the age bracket of 27–31 (246 people). Four hundred fifteen people who filled out the survey had bachelor's degrees, making up 83.98% of the total. Among the 262 people who filled out the survey, 53.31 percent were students and 41.29 percent had monthly incomes between 10,000 and 30,000 baht. Figure 1 provides a summary of the respondent demographics.

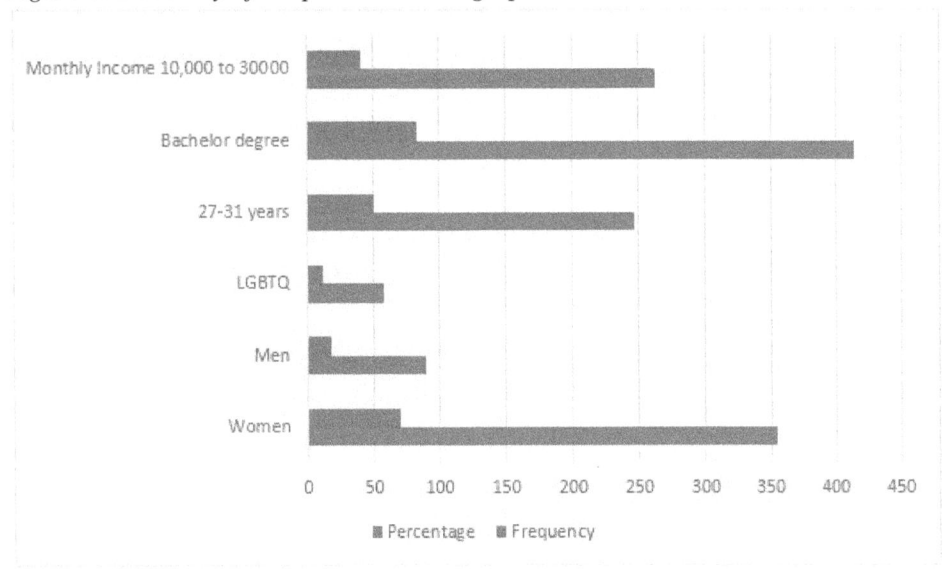

Figure 1. Summary of Respondent Demographics

3.2 Analysis of Data

The study goals may be best addressed using (SEM) because to its ability to examine indices of it and interactions between different variables that are dependent and independent. In order to determine casual-predictive connections, this research used the partial least squares structural equation modelling (PLS-SEM) approach using the Smart PLSv. 3.3.8 software program to evaluate the measurement and structural model. Predicting constructs assessed by a variety of indicators and second-order constructs is made easier using PLS-SEM, which also helps with forecasting and guarantees the practical applicability of causal explanations. It also proves to be more successful than regression analysis. Additionally, PLS-SEM is often considered the best approach for studies that intend to establish or explore theory, and it has great power for research with small sample sizes.

3.3 Common-Method Bias Test

The data gathering should be evaluated for potential common technique bias as it was generated from a single survey. A common method's variance might exaggerate detectable correlations, lending credence to hypotheses that aren't really supported. Because of this, while doing research using a cross-sectional design, it is important to account for common technique variation. The researchers in this study examined CMV using Harman's single-factor test. The investigation follows the suggested procedure and makes use of principal component analysis (PCA). Figure 2 2 shows that less than 51% of the variation, or 39.467%, can be explained by a single factor according to the unrotated main axis factoring analysis. All of the indicators were found to have passed the test. The suggested model should be free of common method bias if all the VIFs obtained from a thorough collinearity test are less than or equal to 3.5. This research did not find a common method bias, which means that there is no big concern with the correlation between the variables.

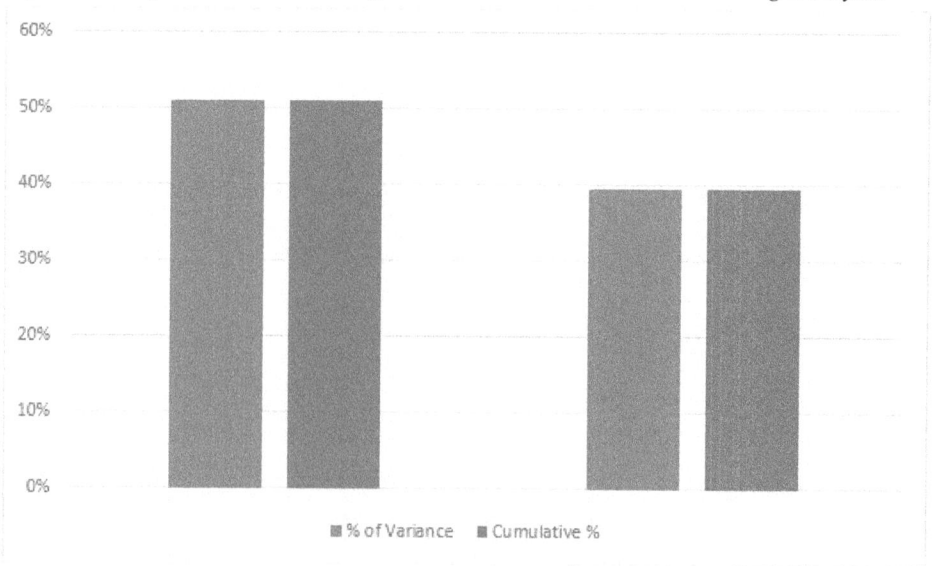

Figure 2. Single Factor According to Unrotated Main Axis Factoring Analysis

3.4 The Multicollinearity Test

In a multicollinear model, the response information is redundantly provided by two or more related predictors. This research followed recommendations by testing for multicollinearity amongst endogenous construct antecedents and confirming that the internal VIF. This research does not exhibit multicollinearity.

3.5 Modelling for Measurement

Convergent validity was assessed using confirmatory factor analysis after 500 respondents had filled out the surveys. All items had standardised factor loadings higher than 0.7. The model's Cronbach's Alpha (CA) values ranged from 0.713 to 0.941, whereas the actual values were higher than 0.8. All the numbers were higher than the suggested cutoff of 0.8, showing that the scales are quite accurate. Each model component has an Average Variance Extracted (AVE) value higher than 0.6, according to the specified threshold value range of 0.618 to 0.945. According to Nunnally, the model met the threshold requirement of 0.9 as all constructs had Construct Reliability (CR) values higher than 0.8 and the model's values varied between 0.831 and 0.972. Therefore, the convergent validity of the scale is strong. All things considered, the measurements were genuine and precise.

Results from tests of cross-loading and four-sided roots of the AVE, ASV, and MSV were used to validate discriminant validity. The correlation coefficients of each construct were compared with other constructs by examining the bolded diagonal. The square root of the AVE was smaller than the correlation coefficient that was connected with each component. A good rule of thumb is that the four-sided root of the AVE should exceed the values in every row and column. All of the constructs were shown to have a higher connection with one another than with any of the others. Just as the average shared variance (ASV) should be greater than the maximum shared variance (MSV), the maximum shared variance (AVE) must be less. According to the data, the discriminant validity of the scales is adequate.

3.6 Coefficient of Path and Analysis of Structural Models

A total of 5000 subsamples from the original were used for the structural model validation utilising boot strapping. A numerical metric in a classical that shows how well the variables that are independent explain the variation in the variable that is dependent is the coefficients of determination, abbreviated as R Squared (R^2). Thus, R^2 reveals the model's predictive power. The other factors explain 40.81 percent of the variation in brand evangelism, whereas brand evangelism alone accounts for 59.21 percent. In addition, the consumer-influencer engagement has an R^2 value of 0.226. There was not a single R2 value that was less than the cutoff of 0.21. The path coefficient, a structural model, characterised the relationship between the independent variables and the dependent variable they affected. Complex models may be effectively evaluated using the SEM approach, and more specifically, the maximum likelihood estimate.

SRMR is a measure of a variance-based model's goodness of fit. The SRMR is defined as the standard deviation of the anticipated and observed correlations; it is an indicator of fit. If the sample size is small or the degree of freedom is low, the SRMR's positive bias will be more pronounced. By definition, a result of zero on the SRMR indicates a perfect match since it is an exact fit measure. Complexity of the model is not penalised by the SRMR. A number of 0.081 or below often indicates a good match. The study's findings revealed an SRMR of 0.067.

3.7 Hypothesis Testing

The results showed that consumer influencer engagement is significantly and positively impacted by topicality, novelties, understandability, accuracy, interestingness, and influencers' authenticity of content. Hence, hypotheses were validated and accepted. As for hypothesis, consumer-influencer assignation favourably and substantially pretentious brand evangelism. Consequently, this hypothesis was also accepted.

4. DISCUSSION

The effects of fashion micro-influencer-generated material were investigated in this study. This kind of content has grown into an important marketing tool for companies globally. The study's findings show that fashion micro-influencers' material greatly affects consumer-influencer interactions since it helps spread optimistic word-of-mouth about the brand. This exemplifies the long-term connections between brands and their consumers. A more important factor influencing consumer-influencer interaction than the content's topicality is the first noteworthy discovery. Previous research on influencer-generated content has used the similar setting but has failed to include content topicality into its theoretical framework; this discovery adds to that body of knowledge. Influencers' satisfied, consumer-perceived information about the topic (e.g., comments on images/videos), and publicising the content of related influencers (e.g., posting photos, uploading videos) are all closely tied to consumers' interests in fashion.

Second, the results show that consumer influencer engagement is affected by the freshness of the material. In addition to adding to the growing body of evidence showing that unique content increases customers' emotional ties to influencers, this study also demonstrated that unique material may increase consumer-influencer interaction. To avoid having their influencer-generated material rejected, micro-influencers should give careful consideration to whether or not their fashion content is current, stylish, and unique. Also, micro-influencer-generated fashion material with a tonne of exclusive knowledge will make customers go wild, which in turn will encourage them to follow the content and boost consumer-influencer interaction.

The third result suggests that consumer-influencer interaction is affected by how easily material may be understood. This study's results add to the growing body of evidence suggesting that easily digestible information plays a role in the emotional connections consumers have with influencers, and it also shows that this factor significantly affects the level of interaction between consumers and influencers. This might be due to the fact that in today's fast-paced, ever-changing, information-rich world, customers want quick access to relevant results and that easily digestible data helps people make better use of their time and energy. Influencers may use this discovery to help them create content. There is a favourable correlation between consumer-influencer engagement and content reliability. Customers will give an influencer more credit and pay closer attention to their material if they believe it is trustworthy, accurate, and based on truth. The fashion material of micro-influencers will subsequently get increased interaction from them. If that isn't the case, they won't bother to read further.

Additionally, the fifth important conclusion demonstrated that consumer-influencer interaction is positively affected by content interest. The previous research had focused on the functional aspects of information relevance but had neglected the hedonic aspects; this new finding adds to that body of knowledge. A hedonic reason for consumers' underlying expressive needs is the interestingness of material. In the context of social media, users are more likely to engage with the content of micro-influencers who promote products or companies that interest them, and they are more likely to enjoy content that social media influencers create, such as humorous posts or videos that friends with similar interests can share. As a result, the significance of engaging content in influencing consumer-influencer behaviour is reinforced.

In addition, the study's main results support the hypothesis that influencers' content authenticity has a substantial impact on consumer-influencer interaction. The current literature on influencer-generated content has neglected the authenticity incentive in favour of the functional and hedonic motives; our finding adds to that understanding. Social media influencers must maintain an air of genuineness. People are more interested in interacting with micro-influencers, who portray themselves via their fashion material, rather than with celebrities or macro-influencers, since they are able to sense the genuine identity of the former. Regularly, popular people on the internet have to figure out how to balance their credibility with the sponsored material they make. Famous people try to solve this problem by "staging" themselves to seem more genuine. In addition, when micro-influencers evaluate a fashion product that the consumer has tried and loved, the customer is more likely to interact with them. Consumers are looking for appealing social media influencers who can vouch for a product and who can also communicate with them in a nice way to provide them honest feedback.

5.CONCLUSION

The results of this study provided light on the ways in which fashion micro-influencers' content influences consumer-influencer interactions and word-of-mouth promotion of brands. Consumer interaction with influencers is driven by material that is timely, unique, understandable, reliable, fascinating, and genuine, according to the report. The results highlight the importance of real, relevant, and well-crafted content in building long-term connections between brands and their consumers, which helps to generate brand advocacy. The study highlights the significance of marketers and micro-influencers producing engaging, trustworthy, and creative content that speaks to customers' needs and interests. Furthermore, influencers who are true to themselves are more likely to attract customers who are looking to form deeper emotional ties with them. Brands that want to use micro-influencers for sustainable, long-term advocacy may benefit from the study's practical findings, which add to the present research on digital advertising and consumer engagement. Influencer engagement should be studied in more depth in future studies spanning different cultural settings and social media platforms. Other factors that could be considered include gender and generational disparities in consumer engagement behaviour.

REFERENCES

Akdim, K., Casaló, L. V., & Flavián, C. (2022). The role of utilitarian and hedonic aspects in the continuance intention to use social mobile apps. *Journal of Retailing and Consumer Services*, 66, 102888. DOI: 10.1016/j.jretconser.2021.102888

Alharthey, B. K. (2024). Influencing smartphone choices: The interplay of social media marketing and brand image on purchase intentions. *British Journal of Management and Marketing Studies*, 7(1), 19–34. DOI: 10.52589/BJMMS-5R9ZO4ZW

Antoniou, G., Grobelnik, M., Simperl, E., Parsia, B., Plexousakis, D., De Leenheer, P., & Pan, J. Z. (Eds.). (2011). The Semantic Web: Research and Applications: *8th Extended Semantic Web Conference, ESWC 2011,* Heraklion, Crete, Greece, May 29–June 2, 2011. *Proceedings, Part II* (Vol. 6644). Springer.

Badenes-Rocha, A., Bigne, E., & Ruiz, C. (2021). Impact of cause-related marketing on consumer advocacy and cause participation: A causal model based on self-reports and eye-tracking measures. *Psychology and Marketing*, mar.21590. Advance online publication. DOI: 10.1002/mar.21590

Barta, S., Belanche, D., Fernández, A., & Flavián, M. (2023). Influencer marketing on TikTok: The effectiveness of humor and followers' hedonic experience. *Journal of Retailing and Consumer Services*, 70, 103149. DOI: 10.1016/j.jretconser.2022.103149

BramahHazela. (2022). Hymavathi, J., Kumar, T. R., Kavitha, S., Deepa, D., Lalar, S., & Karunakaran, P. (2022). Machine Learning: Supervised Algorithms to Determine the Defect in High-Precision Foundry Operation. *Journal of Nanomaterials*, (1), 1732441.

Chang, Y., Silalahi, A. D. K., Eunike, I. J., & Riantama, D. (2024). Socio-technical systems and trust transfer in live streaming e-commerce: Analyzing stickiness and purchase intentions with SEM-fsQCA. *Frontiers in Communication*, 9, 1305409. Advance online publication. DOI: 10.3389/fcomm.2024.1305409

De Vries, N. J., & Carlson, J. (2014). Examining the drivers and brand performance implications of customer engagement with brands in the social media environment. *Journal of Brand Management*, 21(6), 495–515. DOI: 10.1057/bm.2014.18

Garg, M., & Bakshi, A. (2024). Exploring the impact of beauty vloggers' credible attributes, parasocial interaction, and trust on consumer purchase intention in influencer marketing. *Humanities & Social Sciences Communications*, 11(1), 235. Advance online publication. DOI: 10.1057/s41599-024-02760-9

Hafyana, S., & Alzubi, A. (2024). Social Media's Influence on Eco-Friendly Choices in Fitness Services: A mediation moderation approach. *Buildings*, 14(3), 650. DOI: 10.3390/buildings14030650

Hajli, N., Sims, J., Zadeh, A. H., & Richard, M. (2016). A social commerce investigation of the role of trust in a social networking site on purchase intentions. *Journal of Business Research*, 71, 133–141. DOI: 10.1016/j.jbusres.2016.10.004

Huang, S., Silalahi, A. D. K., & Eunike, I. J. (2024). Exploration of moderated, mediated, and configurational outcomes of Tourism-Related Content (TRC) on TikTok in predicting enjoyment and behavioral intentions. *Human Behavior and Emerging Technologies*, 2024, 1–29. DOI: 10.1155/2024/2764759

Molinillo, S., Aguilar-Illescas, R., Anaya-Sánchez, R., & Liébana-Cabanillas, F. (2021). Social commerce website design, perceived value and loyalty behavior intentions: The moderating roles of gender, age and frequency of use. *Journal of Retailing and Consumer Services*, 63, 102404. DOI: 10.1016/j.jretconser.2020.102404

Ningrum, A. M., Rofiaty, R., & Moko, W. (2024). The Influence of Social Media Marketing and Corporate Image on Customer Loyalty is Mediated by Customer Satisfaction (Study of 5 Star Hotel Customers in Malang City). *Journal of Economics Finance and Management Studies*, 07(01). Advance online publication. DOI: 10.47191/jefms/v7-i1-16

Poureisa, A., Aziz, Y. A., & Ng, S. (2024). Swipe to Sustain: Exploring consumer behaviors in organic food purchasing via Instagram social commerce. *Sustainability (Basel)*, 16(6), 2338. DOI: 10.3390/su16062338

Sandi, H. A., & Atmaja, F. T. (2024). The impact of information content and entertainment content on customer engagement and customer loyalty: A study on Scarlett's customer base. *Journal of Entrepreneur & Business*, 5(1), 69–78. DOI: 10.24123/jeb.v5i1.6115

Wongkitrungrueng, A., & Assarut, N. (2018). The role of live streaming in building consumer trust and engagement with social commerce sellers. *Journal of Business Research*, 117, 543–556. DOI: 10.1016/j.jbusres.2018.08.032

Chapter 13
Development of Structural Equation Modelling to Predict and Explain the University Brand Evangelism

Anil Kumar
Lloyd Law College, Greater Noida, India

Ginni Nijhawan
Lovely Professional University, India

Preeti Maan
Lloyd Institute of Management and Technology, India

Dinesh Kumar Yadav
Lloyd Institute of Engineering and Technology, India

Q. Mohammed
Hilla University College, Iraq

ABSTRACT

Much of the existing research on the topic focusses on the ways in which alums help HEIs financially. Nevertheless, there is a dearth of research that specifically looks into how alumni impact HEIs' extra-role brand development activities. Through the mediation of a feeling of belonging, this research investigates the impact of institution public community finding & university identity happening university product

DOI: 10.4018/979-8-3693-7773-4.ch013

Copyright © 2025, IGI Global. Copying or distributing in print or electronic forms without written permission of IGI Global is prohibited.

evangelism. Using structural equation modelling, the researchers combed through information gathered from 607 graduates of 16 Indian HEIs. Most graduates, according to the results, become "brand evangelists" for their alma mater when they have a strong intelligence of fitting to the Institution's larger social network. Also, without a feeling of belonging as a mediator, the results show that a stronger sense of identity is not enough to forecast and explain university brand evangelism. Hence, it is crucial for HEIs to foster the social and individual identification in order to encourage a feeling of belonging. This, in turn, motivates alumni to actively promote the university's brand.

1. INTRODUCTION

Higher education institutions (HEIs) are definitely up against more and more competition from other HEIs and from stakeholders like students, graduates, and others who have high expectations (Amani, 2022). Higher education institutions are under a lot of stress because of internalisation, the need for more and better ways to teach and learn, and the constantly changing job market (Becerra & Badrinarayanan, 2013). Higher education institutions are supposed to help with things like getting students jobs, sharing information and ideas, and getting involved in the community (Dwyer et al., 2015). Also, higher education institutions have to deal with a lot of competition in the market to get the best students, hire skilled teachers, raise money for building and keeping nice sites, and form partnerships with businesses. There is evidence that some of the world's best universities have been changing how they do business in order to be more publicly responsible and accountable (Franklin, 2013). But building a world-class university is hard because students and other possible partners don't support it much, and there aren't as many funds because the government isn't giving as much money. This makes it very hard for universities to stay in business and compete (Goh, 2016).

Analysis suggests that the sector of higher education in India was affected by these worldwide concerns (Hargitai et al., 2023). The industry in India has several obstacles, including a reduction in government financing, resulting in financial difficulties for most higher education institutions (HEIs) (Ibrahim et al., 2023). In the previous 61 years, the nation has seen substantial expansion in the sector regarding enrolment of students and the proliferation of higher education institutions. Nonetheless, most higher education institutions continue to have difficulties in recruiting skilled personnel and students, establishing business partnerships, and securing research funding, among other issues. (Mgaiwa, 2018). In light of the country's ancient setting, advanced education remained shaped through socialist beliefs and therefore seen as a standard social service, provided at no cost to everyone. The government gave subsidies to higher education institutions, particularly public ones, to facilitate their fundamental operations. Subsequent to the structural adjustment programs (SAPs) promoted via the World Bank in the 1990s, numerous changes remained implemented that curtailed the government's capacity to provide aids to higher education institutions (HEIs). Consequently, the restrictions imposed by SAPs compelled higher education institutions to adopt a cost-sharing model. Through this methodology, higher education institutions were expected to function via tuition revenues and stakeholder contributions, such as strategic partnerships. Amani, 2018. In this context, higher education institutions in India needed to implement strategic changes, such as adopting business-oriented initiatives, to remain viable in a commercialised & competitive higher education landscape (Narteh, 2018).

There is a lot of pressure on the management of HEIs throughout the world, including in India, to adopt strategic actions in order to stay afloat in the face of intense competition in the global education market (Ortiz et al., 2013). The idea of commercialisation and marketisation came about at this time, with students as consumers and HEIs as service providers in the higher education industry (Signes et al., 2023). Higher education institutions (HEIs) that want to stand out in the competitive education market should embrace market orientated tactics that position them as unique corporate brands. Scholars argue that branding at HEIs is very new, despite the fact that HEIs utilise many marketing strategies used by for-profit organisations. Branding higher education institutions, according to experts, is a collaborative effort that benefits all parties involved. While university branding has received some attention, the majority of the research has focused on alumni's supporting behaviours, such as giving behaviour (Su et al., 2016).

A number of studies have shown that scholars and graduates using a greater stage of recognition are willing to provision their higher education institutions by doing brand-building activities like word of mouth. These activities build the university kind's respect & data, which remain things that make students identify with their universities. According to Stephenson and Yerger, highly recognised graduates show helpful behaviours like giving money and speaking out for the university. Also, Stephenson and Yerger say that happiness with university identification makes people feel like they belong to the university society more generally and helps define who they are through their connection to the university. Studies have shown that recognition is a key part of building a brand, but brand advocacy hasn't gotten much attention. According to Becerra and Badrinarayanan, brand evangelism is the best kind of good Word of Mouth (WOM) that can come from someone who is really into a brand. Positive word of mouth is affected by a short-term emotion like happiness. Brand evangelism, on the other hand, is when someone who has an ongoing connection with a brand preaches about it to get other people to choose it.

The goal of this study is to look into how university identity and university social group identification affect the spread of the university brand. The research looked at India, to plug in policy and practice gaps about how students and other partners in higher education can help build university names. It adds to policy problems by creating a policy template that HEIs can use when they want to involve graduates in naming their schools. The idea behind social identity theory is that graduates act as brand ambassadors for their alma mater because of their personal identity, which includes traits unique to them, and their social identity, which includes traits unique to their group. These are the two things that the study adds: The study first adds to the idea of HEI branding by looking at university brand promotion as a result of personal identity along with social identification. Next, the study looks at how personal identification affects building social identification. Finally, it looks at how both personal identification as well as social identification affect alumni's desire to spread the word about the brand through a sense of belonging (Van Den Bercken, 1988). The study's research question is: what role does a feeling of belonging play in the connection between identifying with a university, identifying with a university social group, and promoting the university brand? Figure 3 and 4 show the hypothesised model of the study. This question tested the direct as well as indirect connections between the factors in that model.

2. LITERATURE ANALYSIS:

2.1. A Theory of Public Identification:

Tajfel and Tajfel and Turner's social identity philosophy serves as the study's theoretical basis. According to social identity theory, people develop a sense of belonging by fostering strong relationships with others who share their interests and values within a particular social group or community. An individual's sense of being part of a particular social group, public, or category is what "social identity" means in this setting. Moreover, a social group, community, or grouping is a collection of people who identify with one another or who see themselves as having the characteristics that would make them fit in with that group or category; this is in contrast to people who do not belong to them. As a result, the theory is based on the concept of intergroup interactions, which include how people see their significance inside their in-group while contrasting themselves from other groups.

Developing a favourable opinion in one's choice for a particular being or item is known as ethnocentrism, and it is theorised to result from this kind of categorisation. As a result of their ethnocentrism, people may become the greatest adversaries of non-members and the things or items associated with them when they act violently against them. As a result, according to social identity theory, people should prefer to be recognized or recognised in relation to their in-group association, which ultimately serves to differentiate them from members of their out-group. According to social identity theory, in-group membership favouritism explains how a feeling of belonging mediates the process by which a person's identification with their institution and its social community leads them to advocate for the university's brand. College alums who have strong ties to their alma mater and the institution's social community engage in university brand evangelism, according to the research, which draws on social identity theory.

2.2. University identification (UNID):

An individual's sense of self as it relates to their alma mater is a measure of university identity. According to social identity theory, people tend to have distinct characteristics that stem from the social milieu in which they find themselves as a result of their group membership. But everyone has their own unique quirks that set them apart from the crowd. A kind of social identification known as "university identification" develops when students' views of the institution become an integral part of their sense of who they are. In order to fulfil some or all of their requirements, students voluntarily form strong social links with the institution. These bonds are powerful and selective. As a result, students are more likely to succeed academically and socially at the institution when they form close relationships with faculty and staff there. So, the university is a social identification system that helps meet the requirements of its many possible stakeholder groups, such as those for socialisation, self-identity, or differentiation. According to influential research in the field of university branding, there are two conceptually complementary components to the idea of university identification: the cognitive and the emotive. The cognitive component considers university identification as students' inclination to acquire a sense of self-categorization or belonging to the institution. However, students' emotional investment in and connection to the institution is hinted to by the emotive component. Accordingly, institution identification is a mental process whereby stakeholders (alums, current students, etc.) feel a sense of shared identity with the institution. Here, the cognitive state affects the emotional states and actions of the university's students and alums. A sense of belonging to a university strengthens ties between the school and its students, encouraging actions beyond mere brand loyalty and repeat business. As a result of a positive emotional evaluation among the particular demands of interested parties like students, workers, alumni & the total exact standards of the Institutions, university identification fosters a strong bond and engagement among these groups, according to scholars. Some writers, including, argue that a strong sense of academic connection represents a higher ideal of attachment than simple loyalty or faithfulness. In theory, stakeholders' views of the university's reasons, goals, or ideals constitute university identity, while stakeholders' loyalty stems from their own experiences. Some academics argue that university identification is a psychological condition that motivates stakeholders (e.g., students, alumni, etc.) to act in ways that are expected of them and go above and beyond in order to help the institution accomplish its strategic objectives.

2.3. University Social Community Identification (UNSCID):

Bagozzi & Dholakia provide the following definition of a social community: it is a group of people who have a strong sense of shared identity and who have a passion for something specific. Members of this community work together in different ways to achieve their goals or voice their opinions on matters that affect the community as a whole. According to the available data, group dynamics within a person's social circle have had a significant role in shaping their behaviour. An online group of people who have a common interest in a certain product or service but do not necessarily live in the same physical location is called a "brand community" according to Muniz and O'Guinn. The value of social organisations and communities as places of shared identity and experience is generally acknowledged. According to Muniz and O'Guinn, a feeling of social duty, rituals and customs, and an awareness of one's own kind are the three defining features of every social group or community.

One side of the coin is the "consciousness of kind," which encompasses the underlying mental state linked to an individual's connection to other in-group members and their shared excitement over differences with those outside the group. One interpretation of "consciousness of kind" is that it makes people feel unique and different from others who aren't part of an identifiable social group. Members of a community or society with a kind consciousness, according to Kuo and Feng, have a common sense of belonging and would often single out and, on rare occasions, reject those who do not share this sense of belonging. In contrast, rituals and customs include things like commemorating the group's past or present, acting in a certain way to show support for the group, or just talking about what it's like to be a part of the group. Having an intense awareness of moral responsibility also includes actions like encouraging people to join the group, strengthening loyalty, and sharing knowledge with others who aren't already part of the organisation in order to bring them in.

So, university public identity is a mental state in which pupils or graduates become aware of how they fit into groups that makes them want to feel like they belong at the university. According to the literature, a university is like a social society or group made up of different people, like students, parents, sellers, graduates, government agencies, and so on. Many people agree that seeing colleges as a special community or social group has become more common recently, at a time when higher education institutions are still trying to figure out how to keep students and lower the number of students who drop out. So, the study puts it in context by saying that graduates feel a connection to an institution once they see a match among their own personality & image and the university's total name.

2.4. Sense of belonging (SOB):

When you feel like you belong in a social group or community, you feel like you're part of a family. It's how you feel when you're accepted by, part of, and linked to a certain social neighbourhood or group. So, feeling like you belong in a social group lets people interact and get to know each other better, which strengthens their social bond. Other researchers said that a feeling of belonging is a membership that is based on how involved a person feels in various social settings as well as how much assistance they get from those around them. Some works of literature say that a person's desire to be seen as a member of a specific social neighbourhood or group affects how they act in public. They usually want to be known or recognised as a member of the group. They also want to be linked to the success of the social group because it gives them a chance to build and improve their own ethics or because it has a superior sense for their self-identity or self-image.

So, a feeling of connection means that people in the same social public or social group share the same values, traits, and beliefs. It comes from identifying with a community, because people think they have similar traits or features to other people in the same category. It affects people's emotions, which in turn affects their decision to join a sure social community or group & how they see themselves in connection to that public or group. It is generally accepted that a feeling of connection leads people to create a social link through a social the public or group. As a result, feeling like you belong makes people more likely to want to stay or keep their involvement in their social circle or neighbourhood. The idea of belonging has lately been put forward as a way to improve educational services by encouraging students to stay, improve their academic success, lower their failure rate, and so on.

3. METHODOLOGY

3.1. Participants

Individuals in this study were graduates of higher education institutions in Tanzania. The HEIs that were chosen are in Iringa, Arusha, Kilimanjaro, Morogoro, Dodoma, and Dar-es-Salaam. Alumni about 16 HEIs were able to take part in the study through an online poll. To get the needed sample size, the study got a list of graduates and their email addresses from certain higher education institutions. The study chose at least 40 graduates from each chosen HEI, taking into account the size of every HEI to make sure that the alumni were representative of all of them. In the end, 607 people took part in this study, which was the sample size. Fifteen higher education institutions were there; eleven were public and six were private. Higher education institutions offered a wide range of programs, both with and without degrees, in areas such as community strength, engineering along with mining, natural resources organization, computer science, law, instruction, political science, sociology, & business and management.

3.2. Procedures for Gathering Data:

An English version of the questionnaire was created. On a 6-point Likert scale, from "6-strongly agree" to "1-strongly disagree," respondents were asked to score each statement in measurement items. Since English is the language of instruction in Tanzanian universities, the choice of words seemed acceptable. Despite the fact that the study's measuring items have already been verified in other research, the survey instruments were pilot tested before data collection to ensure their reliability. The survey instruments were pilot tested with 111 participants, & the Cronbach alpha coefficient of each construct was 0.9, which is higher than the cutoff of 0.8. Therefore, the survey remained delivered to graduates via email once the dependability of the review gadgets was confirmed. In order to get enough or good responses from the research, we sent out questionnaires to certain alumni once we made sure they were willing to take part. In January 2022, information was gathered by means of an online survey. In addition, a solid response rate was ensured by regularly following up with remaining emails. There was a total of 651 surveys sent out; 93.3% of those returned legitimate and full questionnaires (607 in total). In order to create and verify the study's hypothesised model, structural equation modelling, or SEM, utilising AMOS 22 was finally used.

3.3. Units of Measurement:

Previous research in branding and academic branding provided the metrics that were used in this study. Cronbach alpha coefficients (α), Composite Reliability (CR) coefficients, and standardised factor loadings (λ) for all the scales that were used to test reliability are more than 0.8. To make assured the measure scale worked in the setting of higher education, however, revisions, especially phrasing, were done when needed. Researcher used a 6-point Likert scale, from 6 (strongly agree) to 2 (strongly disagree), to record all of the factors. University social group identity and university identification were assessed using the instruments. Additionally, a scale that was devised and verified was used to evaluate the sensation of belonging. Lastly, a scale was used to quantify the level of university brand advocacy. You can see outcomes of the reliability and validity tests that were conducted on the measure

4. EXAMINATION OF DATA AND FINDINGS

4.1. Personal Traits of the Participants:

This research included 607 participants who were graduates of 16 institutions within the higher learning industry in India. Figure 1 reveals that of the 607 responders, 401 were male (66.1%) and 207 were female (34.1%). Additionally, the relationship status of respondents reveals that 388 (63.10%) were married, while 220 (36.2%) were single. The age distribution of respondents indicates that 240 (39.5%) were aged 21–31, 308 (50.8%) were aged 32–41, 59 (9.7%) were aged 42–51, and 3 (0.4%) were aged 52–61.

Figure 1. Statistical Descriptions

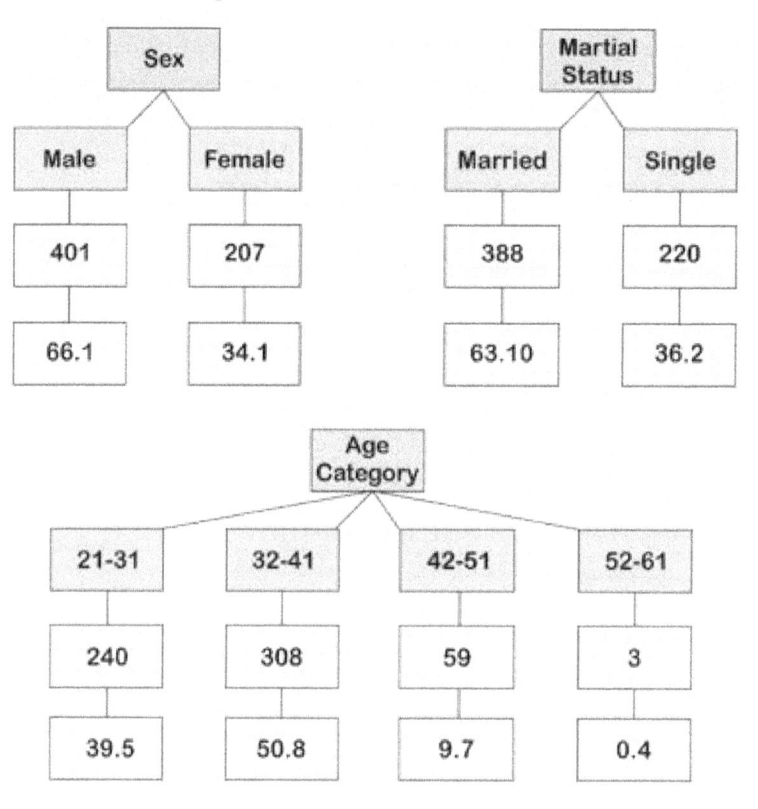

Sex		Martial Status	
Male	Female	Married	Single
401	207	388	220
66.1	34.1	63.10	36.2

Age Category			
21-31	32-41	42-51	52-61
240	308	59	3
39.5	50.8	9.7	0.4

4.2. Test for Common Technique Bias

The examine method used in the education made it likely that general method variation would be present. In particular, typical technique bias was likely to happen since all the measures were self-reported. As suggested through Podsakoff, Mackenzie, Lee, along with Podsakoff, Harman's single-factor method was used to find shared method variation in the data. The findings showed that a stable factor could only explain 7.4% of the whole 34.8% variation. Based on these results, general method error probably wasn't a big deal in this study.

4.3. Review of the Features of the Measurement Model

The research used confirmation factor analysis (CFA) through AMOS version 22 to evaluate the covariance construction of the dormant variables. The feature loadings for all variables exceed 0.6 and are both positive and significant, demonstrating that the items used effectively measure the latent variables and contribute to the estimation of their corresponding study constructs. The research assessed data normalcy using skewness and kurtosis metrics. The data in Figure 2 demonstrate that the skewness & kurtosis values fall below the threshold region of 1.97. The Cronbach Alpha Coefficient (α) was determined to exceed 0.8, signifying strong internal reliability, while the McDonald Construct dependability also above 0.8, suggesting robust construct dependability. Additional data demonstrate that convergent validity was satisfactory, as the average variance extracted (AVE) was higher of altogether specified variable overhead 0.6, and the Composite Reliability, or CR, Coefficient was 0.8. The findings indicate that the variables intended to assess a singular construction in the framework of measurement are consistent with one another. Consequently, the research constructs mostly exhibit robust psychometric assessment features.

When it came to discriminant validity, however, the methods suggested by Larcker and Fornell were followed. If you want your test to be discriminately valid, make sure that the square root of each variable's AVE is smaller than the value of the inter-construct correlation. Results from achieving discriminant validity are shown in Figure 2, which means that variables intended to assess a given concept are really unrelated. Put simply, the findings highlight how unique the research factors were.

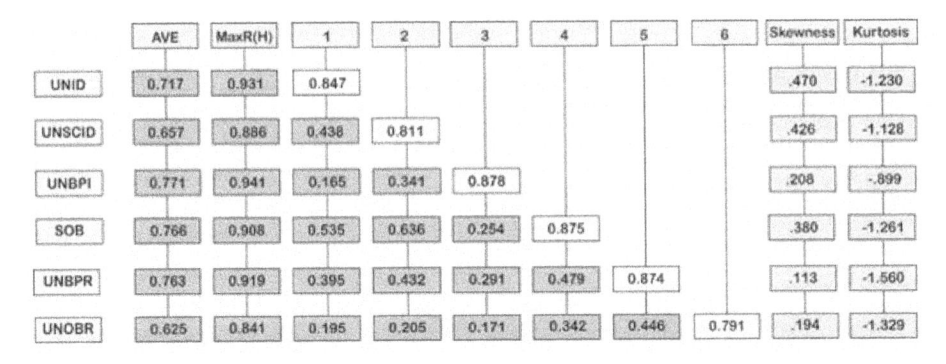

Figure 2. Fornell-Larcker Criteria Testing for Discriminant Validity

	AVE	MaxR(H)	1	2	3	4	5	6	Skewness	Kurtosis
UNID	0.717	0.931	0.847						.470	-1.230
UNSCID	0.657	0.886	0.438	0.811					.426	-1.128
UNBPI	0.771	0.941	0.165	0.341	0.878				.208	-.899
SOB	0.766	0.908	0.535	0.636	0.254	0.875			.380	-1.261
UNBPR	0.763	0.919	0.395	0.432	0.291	0.479	0.874		.113	-1.560
UNOBR	0.625	0.841	0.195	0.205	0.171	0.342	0.446	0.791	.194	-1.329

The following are some indications from the model fit data that the measurement model is a good fit: with $x^2 = 323.474$ (p < 0.002, df = 141); $x^2/df = 2.312$, which is just below the cutoff of < 4. The results of the other goodness of fit indices show that, while the recommended value is greater than 0.10, the Root Mean Square Error of an approximation (RMSEA) is less than 0.09, and the following values are above the recommended threshold: Comparative Fit Index (CFI), which = 0.932, Goodness of Fit Index (the GFI) = 0.954, Adjusted Goodness of Fit The index (AGFI) = 0.924, and Tucker-Lewis Coefficient (the TLI) = 0.973. Additionally, both the Parsimony Normed Fit Index (PNFI) and the Parsimony Comparative Fit Index (PCFI) are greater than the required threshold of 0.7, coming in at 0.646 and 0.655, respectively.

4.4. Testing of Assumptions and Assessment of Structural Model

The research took a look at how well the structural model fit before testing any hypothesis. The following model fit was achieved by the structural model analysis: $x^2 = 448.268$ (p < 0.001, /df = 2.838), CFI = 0.971, GFI = 0.938, AGFI = 0.911, TLI = 0.962, RMSEA = 0.056, PNFI = 0.718, PCFI = 0.731. In general, the results were satisfactory. Specifically, as seen in Figure 3, the predicted association between university identity & university social group identification is positive and statistically significant ($\beta = 0.397$; t > 1.97; p < 0.002). Moreover, a feeling of belonging is significantly and positively impacted by university identity ($\beta = 0.321$; t > 1.97; p < 0.002). Additionally, a strong positive correlation exists between belonging to a university social group and having a strong sense of self-identity ($\beta = 0.581$; t > 1.97; p < 0.002). University brand buying intent ($\beta = 0.274$; t > 1.97; p < 0.002), college optimistic brand referral ($\beta = 0.298$; t > 1.97; p < 0.002), along with university opposed a brand referral ($\beta = 0.590$; t > 1.97; p < 0.002) are all positively impacted by a intelligence of belonging, according to the following aspects of university brand evangelism.

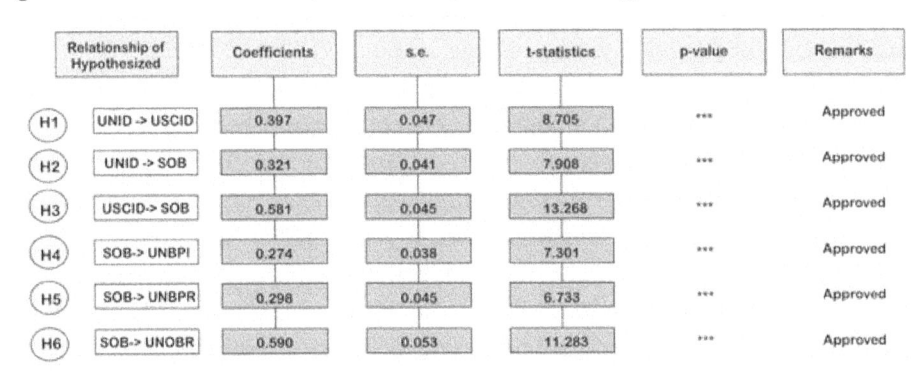

Figure 3. Critical Variables, T-Statistics, and Path Coefficient

Relationship of Hypothesized		Coefficients	s.e.	t-statistics	p-value	Remarks
H1	UNID -> USCID	0.397	0.047	8.705	***	Approved
H2	UNID -> SOB	0.321	0.041	7.908	***	Approved
H3	USCID -> SOB	0.581	0.045	13.268	***	Approved
H4	SOB -> UNBPI	0.274	0.038	7.301	***	Approved
H5	SOB -> UNBPR	0.298	0.045	6.733	***	Approved
H6	SOB -> UNOBR	0.590	0.053	11.283	***	Approved

5. DISCUSSION

In the setting of developing economies, this study is one of the first and few to look at how university identification along with university social group identity affect brand marketing. It turns out that alumni's connection with their alma mater and their social group play a big part in their desire to promote a brand. The results also show that a feeling of identity (i.e., "I am a part of this university") plays a part in how university identifying, and university social group identification affect public support for the university brand. So, having a good mental or emotional outlook towards HEIs can encourage graduates to go above and beyond as brand ambassadors for the university. This point is supported by important works like that show how the business image of higher education institutions affects all parties, such as workers, students, and graduates. This study shows that graduates who have a strong connection to higher education institutions feel like they belong, which leads to university brand promotion. Therefore, graduates who feel like they belong because they went to a certain university may strategy to buy HEIs' companies in the upcoming, give good reviews, and protect HEIs' names by giving bad reviews nearby participants' goods.

Based on the education's results, graduates feel a strong intelligence of community (i.e., "I am member of this university") when they think that their self-image or self-identity matches the HEI brand. This feeling of connection is what drives grads to do things outside of their normal duties, like building brands, giving money, and so on. Previous research, like that by Stephenson and Yerger, shows that alumni's connection with their alma mater can make them more likely to donate to their alma mater. Other areas of brand building study look into how university recognition affects brand-building behaviours like belonging to a university, wanting to promote the university, making ideas for change, and taking part in future happenings. Their results back up the present research that says scholars who have a stronger connection to their institution are likely to act in ways that help the university.

The study also showed that alumni's connection with their university's social group makes them more likely to want to promote the university's brand. Studies back up these results by showing that being a part of a university social group can affect people, employees as well as learners, in ways that aren't related to their job, like branding. Social identification theory says that people in an in-group show how unique they are by comparing themselves to people in an out-group. This means that people in an in-group would love for out-group members to think they are strange and treat them that way. Because of this, an increased degree of university social group connection can encourage graduates to build an intense feeling of community that regularly leads to brand marketing for the university. Alumni use brand marketing to try to get individuals outdoors their HEIs to apply by showing how their HEIs differentiate from others.

Another possible explanation for the study results is that alumni keep up their membership in the educational social community by regularly purchasing student publications or by becoming regular attendees of both social and educational activities put together by the universities. People who have graduated from higher education institutions can also take part in positive suggestions about those institutions in order to set their chosen HEIs apart and show how they see themselves as members of the university group. The behaviour of people in the same group trying to stand out from people in other groups, on the opposing hand, makes graduates feel like they belong, which makes them spread bad brand information about outgroup members as well as their homes schools. Using social identity theory as a guide, bad brand recommendation is when graduates try to show the educational market how great their own HEIs are. So, graduates can spread bad information about other HEIs in order to protect the reputations of the HEIs they went to and their participation in those HEIs. All of these data support the idea that social group is the main reason why people in HEIs do things that help their individual HEIs.

6. CONCLUSION & SUGGESTION

6.1. Conclusion

The point of this education was to look into how university social group identification along with university identification help people feel like they belong, which in turn leads to brand promotion. After getting data from a university in India, the study used quantitative research to test the proposed structure. The study results show that university social group identity and university identification have good effects on brand promotion through a sense of belongings. A strong feeling of belonging is a key factor in improving the connection between university social group identification, university identity, & brand promotion, as shown by the study. This shows that university social group identification along with university identifying are flattering more and more important for higher education institutions to build a good image. This study gives managers and brand managers at higher education institutions new ways to think about how university social group identity, university identification, and brand marketing through a sense of connection are connected.

6.2. Suggestion

According to the study's theory, the causes that can lead to university brand promotion have not been studied much. Within the context of the theory of social identity, the research suggests that alumni who develop personal and social identities to maintain their membership in HEI groups are more likely to want to engage in extra-role brand-building activities like university brand evangelism. Consequently, this education supports the idea that the theory of social identity is a good way to clarify why and how grads show improved support for their HEIs. Practically speaking, higher education institutions should make plans for their graduates to be able to take part in brand-building activities outside of their official roles, such as helping to build companies' names as co-creators of brand value. Higher education institutions should think about working together with alumni by building strong alumni groups and making sure that each participant of the organisation does their part in presenting the university as a co-creator of content value. Additionally, it is suggested that graduates be regularly asked to take part in HEI's academic and social events. Participants who regularly attend these events develop a sense of social connection and community, which can inspire former students to become brand ambassadors for the university. Managers of higher education institutions ought to concentrate on utilising social media to keep in touch with graduates. It is generally agreed that tactical instruments like websites have features that let graduates meet with current students and faculty.

REFERENCES

Al-Azzam, A. F., & Al-Mizeed, K. (2021). The effect of digital marketing on purchasing decisions: A case study in Jordan. *The Journal of Asian Finance. Economics and Business*, 8(5), 455–463.

Amani, D. (2022). The student Psychological Contract as a predictor of university brand evangelism in Tanzanian higher education. *International Journal of African Higher Education*, 9(2), 150–171. DOI: 10.6017/ijahe.v9i2.15379

Becerra, E. P., & Badrinarayanan, V. (2013). The influence of brand trust and brand identification on brand evangelism. *Journal of Product and Brand Management*, 22(5/6), 371–383. DOI: 10.1108/JPBM-09-2013-0394

Dwyer, B., Greenhalgh, G. P., & LeCrom, C. W. (2015). Exploring Fan Behavior: Developing a Scale to measure Sport eFANgelism. *Journal of Sport Management*, 29(6), 642–656. DOI: 10.1123/JSM.2014-0201

Franklin, S. (2013). *Biological relatives - IVF, stem cells and the future of kinship*. https://doi.org/DOI: 10.26530/OAPEN_469257

Goh, R. B. H. (2016). Christian capital: Singapore, evangelical flows and religious hubs. *Asian Studies Review*, 40(2), 250–267. DOI: 10.1080/10357823.2016.1156052

Hargitai, D. M., Grósz, A. S., & Sas, Z. (2023). Hallyu in the Heart of Europe: The rise of the Korean Wave in the digital space. *Management & Marketing*, 18(4), 537–555. DOI: 10.2478/mmcks-2023-0029

Ibrahim, B., Aljarah, A., Hazzam, J., Elrehail, H., & Qalati, S. A. (2023). Investigating the impact of social media marketing on intention to follow advice: The mediating role of active participation and benevolence trust. *FIIB Business Review*, 231971452211479. Advance online publication. DOI: 10.1177/23197145221147991

Kommineni, K. K., Madhu, G. C., Narayanamurthy, R., & Singh, G. (2022). IoT crypto security communication system. In *IoT Based Control Networks and Intelligent Systems: Proceedings of 3rd ICICNIS 2022* (pp. 27-39). Singapore: Springer Nature Singapore.

Narteh, B. (2018). Brand equity and financial performance. *Marketing Intelligence & Planning*, 36(3), 381–395. DOI: 10.1108/MIP-05-2017-0098

Ortiz, M. H., Reynolds, K. E., & Franke, G. R. (2013). Measuring Consumer devotion: Antecedents and consequences of passionate consumer behavior. *Journal of Marketing Theory and Practice*, 21(1), 7–30. DOI: 10.2753/MTP1069-6679210101

Selvan, R. S. (2020). Intersection Collision Avoidance in DSRC using VANET. *on Concurrency and Computation-Practice and Experience, 34*(13/e5856), 1532-0626.

Signes, Á. P., Miret-Pastor, L., Tsiouni, M., Siggia, D., & Galati, A. (2023). Determinants of consumers' response to eco-labelled seafoods: The interaction between altruism, awareness and information demand. *Journal of Cleaner Production*, 433, 139758. DOI: 10.1016/j.jclepro.2023.139758

Su, L., Wang, L., Law, R., Chen, X., & Fong, D. (2016). Influences of destination social responsibility on the relationship quality with residents and destination economic performance. *Journal of Travel & Tourism Marketing*, 34(4), 488–502. DOI: 10.1080/10548408.2016.1193101

Van Den Bercken, W. (1988). Ideology and atheism in the Soviet Union. In *De Gruyter eBooks*. https://doi.org/DOI: 10.1515/9783110857375

Chapter 14
AI-Based Customer Supporting and Preference System:
Digital Marketing for Food Delivery

Warshi Singh
CSJM University, India

Sidhanshu Rai
https://orcid.org/0009-0006-7269-9393
CSJM University, India

Arpana Katiyar
https://orcid.org/0009-0005-8161-7874
Chhatrapati Shahuji Maharaj University, India

Ruchi Katiyar
https://orcid.org/0009-0003-1723-7928
Harcourt Butler Technical University, Kanpur, India

Sanu Rajput
https://orcid.org/0009-0008-8657-0798
Harcourt Butler Technical University, Kanpur, India

ABSTRACT

The focus of this study is on the digital marketing strategies used by the food delivery business that make utilise ensembles applied machine learning. To provide suggestions based on artificial intelligence (AI), customer data is analysed, customer

DOI: 10.4018/979-8-3693-7773-4.ch014

preferences are determined, and customer behaviour is predicted. To provide a single forecast, the ensemble approach integrates the results of the closest neighbour, naïve Bayes, and decision tree algorithms. Perfect predictions were produced by the precision matrix plots of the closest neighbour and decision tree algorithms, with accuracy values of 0.000 error and 100.000%, respectively. The naïve Bayes method, on the other hand, demonstrated effective identification of the proper labels among every class with a high degree of accuracy, with a total precision matrix of 97.176% and a 0.029 error. A smaller amount than half of randomised data, along with the consumer knowledge data, may be used to incorporate the model into this process using the majority voting approach, which has a probability successful rate of more than 91%.

1. INTRODUCTION

The rise of new technology, business consolidation, and heightened pricing competitiveness are all contributing to the retail market's fast evolution (Buhalis et al., 2019). Retailers need to handle what follows trends and issues if they want to stay competitive. First and foremost, omnichannel marketing is crucial. Retailers need to embrace an omnichannel strategy that seamlessly integrates all of their customer touchpoints since consumers increasingly shop across several channels, including social networking applications, mobile devices, and online marketplaces (Buhalis et al., 2019b). The second thing to concentrate on should be customer personalisation. Retailers use analytics and data to provide individualised experiences for consumers by making special offers or customer suggestions. Improving the clientele's experience is crucial. With its ease and involvement, it has emerged as a crucial competitive element (Davenport et al., 2019). Consolidation of retail deliveries is a significant corporate development. Big companies are buying out smaller ones in the retail delivery industry, which is causing a shift in the competitive landscape. Venders are necessary to remain on the highest of these rapid shifts in the retail landscape (Dwivedi et al., 2019). Food delivery companies profit from the extra sales they receive from retail partnerships, while retail enterprises often depend on food distribution companies to type items accessible to a wider client base. Online meal delivery services have contributed to the substantial growth of the food delivery industry in recent years. It is anticipated that the global income over online food orders will reach US$467 billion through 2028, a roughly 61% increase from the US$297 billion number in 2022 (Dwivedi et al., 2021). Given all of its advantages, it's understandable that online meal ordering is growing in popularity. The food delivery industry has grown to many things, such as the widespread use of digital tools and on-demand services. Another sector hit hard by the COVID-19 epidemic is food delivery services. Many restaurants and customers have gone online to place orders in an attempt to avoid spreading the virus via personal contact (Dwivedi et al., 2022).

Food delivery companies have seen rapid growth, but they still have to overcome several obstacles to stay competitive, such as creating efficient digital advertising campaigns. Since firms in the food delivery industry must utilise tailored campaigns to attract prospective clients, digital advertising has grown in significance. To Keep firms competitive in market growth digital marketing strategies, need to be established. Digital advertising strategies need to be established as the market grows to keep firms competitive (Dwivedi, Ismagilova, et al., 2021). Because of the declining effectiveness of traditional advertising mediums like print, radio, and television, companies are increasingly forced to depend on online platforms to reach prospective clients. Among the many benefits of digital advertising is the ability to target prospective clients according to their location and interests and to track campaign effectiveness in real time. Retail businesses now count a lot on digital marketing to meet with and talk to customers (Huang & Rust, 2018). Conventional digital marketing includes using standard internet marketing methods like pay-per-click and SEO, as well as other methods like content marketing, social media marketing, email marketing, and flash ads. These strategies can help retail businesses improve their online profile and build relationships with customers. Most of the time, small datasets and set performance standards are used in traditional digital marketing to measure and improve efforts. This type of marketing is expensive, takes a lot of time, and needs a lot of assets to work. The use of artificial intelligence (AI) could be helpful here. Since artificial intelligence (AI) and machine learning (ML) technologies have become more common, online marketers are depending on them more and more to improve their marketing strategies. AI is an important part of this process because it helps businesses make better digital marketing plans. Depending on acquired information AI is capable of swift data examination & decision-making. In addition to efficiently reaching their target demographic, this helps advertisers save time and money. Ads and material can also be personalised to make them more successful and get more people to interact with them AI (Jiang & Wen, 2020).

The usage of artificial intelligence (also known as AI is on the rise, and it has several applications, one of which is digital marketing. In recent years, digital advertising has seen a rise in the use of artificial intelligence (AI). The help of this could make digital marketing and business methods for food service more effective. The app that serves food is growing its business around the world to the exponential development of mobile devices as well as online buying systems. AI & other new skills are being used by companies in this field to improve the customer experience and make processes run more smoothly. The market is likely to grow even faster as more people choose safe and simple ways to place their orders. The food service business is full of fierce competition. As more and more people buy meals online, food delivery services need to make the most of their methods to stay profitable and competitive. (Jiang & Wen, 2020) say that AI & other skills could help food delivery services improve results & make their operations more efficient. AI could be used to look at how people act, find trends, and come up with better ways to sell things. AI can also be used to handle many digital marketing tasks, such as targeting, content enhancement, and customer analysis. Machine learning (ML) can also be used to find fresh markets or groups of consumers and better understand what customers want and like. Machine learning is becoming increasingly vital for businesses that want to get the most out of their campaigns and make sure they make the most money (Min et al., 2019).

Implementing AI requires a certain level of tech know-how. Businesses that want to use AI in their digital marketing need to fully understand the methods and be familiar with the various computer languages and tools that are used to put them into action. For this, need to know about algorithms, data science, and statistics. It's also necessary to know how to use automation tools and merge processes and should have experience with both software engineering and app creation. A business additionally needs the money to allocate to creating and utilising AI solutions, especially hiring or keeping AI experts, especially for the endeavour (Nelson, 1970). On the other hand, this study not only gives a full picture of the problem but also suggests smart ways to solve it. Additionally, it might allow an analysis of the possible outcomes of different strategies for the settlement of the problem, which can help with the decision-making process.

This study suggests a new way to give customers ideas by mixing AI as well chance theory. This is because businesses need to be able to change and bounce back quickly in an extremely competitive marketplace. AI is used in this clever idea to find patterns in customer data and to come up with new, possibly useful solutions by looking at all the random options. Customers might have a more engaging and satisfying experience if the picking process is personalised in a way that goes above standard algorithms. Algorithms are used to break down client data into parts, which lets researchers look at the traits and tastes of specific customers. Then, random parts are introduced to the mix. This creates suggestions by mixing known factors with usual methods. Using both AI and chance theory, the final goal of this study is to make a better system for recommending products to people. To make users happier and keep customers coming back, the researchers want to make ideas that surprise and please customers.

The usage of AI in digital advertising in the food distribution industry is covered in this paper. It starts by giving a summary of the difficulties and present developments in this area. The benefits of utilising ensemble models to develop more successful digital advertising campaigns are therefore the main topic of discussion (Simon,

1991). After that, three strategies are looked at and their applicability to enhancing the success of digital marketing is explained. Lastly, an illustration of how the methods may be used in the food delivery industry is provided. It is believed that after reading this investigation, readers will have a better knowledge of how AI may be used with other technologies to provide more powerful digital marketing solutions.

2. PROCEDURES

This research approach uses a simulation method called association rule learning in conjunction with a mathematical model to find input-output links. The primary data comes from the specifications of a meal delivery service, and the client receives the outcomes of this AI-enabled study. To promote more learning, the system may also reverse user choices and input into the association rule. Figure. 1 provides a detailed description of the study framework.

Figure 1. Study Model Framework

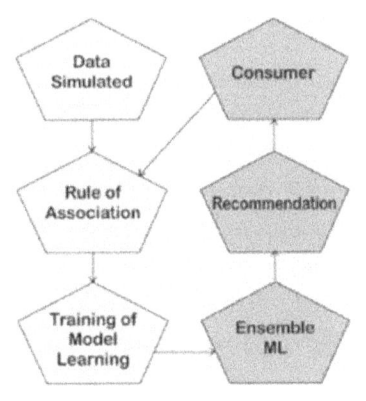

Simulated Data: Since it enables investigators to establish a ground fact to gauge perfect quality, preparing generated data is a vital first stage of the AI plan loop. Computer-generated sets that are specially made for the application to assist the AI system acquire the right traits & make the right guesses. Association Rule: It's important to describe the connections between the dataset's items once it's been made. This could be done with mining association rules as a way to find secret connections between things in datasets. This way of doing things let's look through and examine enormous quantities of data to find links that wouldn't have seen otherwise. The association rule method can help researchers find trends in data and make rules that make the connections between pieces of data clearer.

Scholars are required to use machine learning (ML) to teach their artificial intelligence models the way to find these ideas once they have made a rule of link for the dataset. The data is fed into a machine learning model so that it can acquire knowledge from the examples given to it. There are many data sets needed and a good idea of both data science and artificial intelligence to train machine learning. This way could help artificial intelligence get better at making decisions and guessing what will happen. Group ML: Researchers may choose to use group ML to render AI models more accurate. This method uses more than one model together to get better results than a single one could provide. A group of algorithms can help solve complicated problems and often lead to more accurate models. Researchers can use the results of mixed model training to figure out which models work better and then make those models even better to meet their needs. Advice: Once a group of models has been put together, it can be used to make ideas. By looking at the information and utilising rules of connection and ensemble machine learning, researchers may be able to tell a client what the best course of action or answer is. People who change current processes, add new goods and services, or give advice on how to best use the system are making ideas. The Client: Even if the suggestion tool helps, the customer still has to decide what the best mode of action is for them for each single case. There are times when the customer may choose not to follow the advice and instead take a different action. The AI system should back up the customer's choice with study and then be evaluated further about of cost, risk, and usefulness. Use of Simulation Data More Than Once: Once the client has made a choice, the whole cycle can be started overusing simulated data. This extra data could be used to build new models and set up new connections, which would make the computer's artificial intelligence even smarter. By doing the loop over and over, researchers can be sure that their artificially intelligent (also known as AI schemes remain always learning & changing according to the requirements of the client.

2.1. Ensemble ML

Because AI is such a wide-ranging subject, there are many ways to come across digital marketing plans for food delivery companies. Use these marketing strategies along with other strategies to get the best results out of them. This paper looks at all three of the more common methods: decision trees, closest friends, and naïve Bayes. Instead of just using one model, it talks about group methods that can be used to make digital marketing more effective by making more accurate predictions. Bagging, which takes the outputs of several algorithms and combines them into a single prediction, is the most common ensemble method. After every method has been tested on a different part of the training set, an extra technique called a meta-learner is used to combine the results. As seen, these methods can be used to look at information about customers, figure out what they like, and guess how they'll act by making ideas based on AI.

2.1.1. Decision Tree

The primary method uses an algorithm known as a decision tree to sort data into different categories by the things that make it unique. This method can be used to find out what clients want and to guess how they will act in the future. The questions are simple, and they split the data into groups based on rules that have already been set. Each node in the decision tree represents a different choice, and each of their parents represents the outcome of the choice. People who are more likely to return or buy certain kinds of food could be found this way. By looking for patterns in customer data, all algorithms are used to figure out the best way to run a marketing campaign. Decision tree procedures may be utilized to determine the kinds of material and platforms that will be most effective for a given campaign, along with the most significant target demographic. From a mathematics point of view, a decision tree is a list of steps that describe how to put data points into different groups. The following is the fundamental math of a decision tree:

$$f(x) = T(x) + U(x) \tag{1}$$

Where $U(x)$ is a collection of decision nodes that define the split criterion for the data, and $T(x)$ is a fatal node that holds the projected lesson label. To create decision trees, one may use the "Decision Tree" function included in the programming language. Fundamental parameters are a goal variable and a dataset; other factors include the splitting criteria, maximal tree depth, and kind of tree (regression or classification). Upon running this function, an object containing many tools for examining and modifying the tree is returned. A user may also see the structure of the tree using the object's "visualise" capability, which aids in their understanding of the decision-making process involved in predicting the value of the desired variable. The programming language has several functions for evaluating the decision tree's performance.

2.1.2. Naïve Bayes

The probability theory for sorting data into groups, the Naïve Bayes technique uses a disadvantage. Customers' likes and dislikes can be predicted using this program. Customers who have a greater inclined to order certain foods or from particular restaurants, for instance, may be identified using this information. Naïve Bayes methods are used to split customer information into many groups. These algorithms may not only figure out the best outlets and content to use, but they may also figure out the best audience for a promotion. The Bayes Theorem says that the chance of event A occurring when event B is present is equal to the chance of event B occurring when event A is present multiplied by the chance of event A occurring divided by the chance of event B occurring. This is what Naïve Bayes is based on. It's used to guess how likely an event is to happen based on a certain set of other events. The following are the mathematical concepts of naïve Bayes:

$$(PA \mid B) = \frac{P(B \mid A)P(A)}{P(B)} \qquad (2)$$

The factors P(A|B) and P(B|A) show how likely it is that event A will lead to event B, that event B will lead to event A, the chance of event A happening, and the event probability. This paper investigates the using naïve Bayes in languages used for programming. In particular, it examines the commonly employed approach of classifying and predicting datasets using functions. Giving a dataset and a set of classifiers that can be used to decide the labels of each data point is what it takes to divide the information through two or extra groups. This method can also be used to make forecasts based on new data opinions.

2.1.3. Closest Neighbours

The closest neighbour's procedure is a series of methods that are used for regression and non-parametric classification problems. It is also used to make predictions, particularly if the information is very erratic. Points of data that are close to each other are grouped in this way. These are called "neighbours." There must be a "distance" or "neighbourhood" between these two pieces of info for this process to work. According to the kind of data & the purpose, distance in several datasets can be restrained using a distance tool such as the Euclidean distance. On the other hand, distances in category datasets can be measured in a more standard way. The closest neighbour technique uses the "nearest neighbour" method to figure out how far apart two places are. This rule groups spots that are geographically near together based on how far apart they are thought to be. Use the nearest neighbours method, can find an individual data point of interest and find its k-closest neighbours. Based on the coefficient of regression of its neighbour and the names of the groups of the k-nearest points, the data item can then be put into a category. One example of data in a space of features is X. Let n be the number of neighbours that need to be considered in the account. If use the nearest neighbours method can find the data points $X_1, X_2,..., X_n$ that are closest to X in terms of traits. Next, the class label or regression value of X is found by taking the average of the k-nearest neighbours' class labels or reversion values. The following formula may be used to mathematically illustrate the closest neighbour principles:

$$Y = \frac{1}{n}(y_1 + y_2 + \ldots + y_n) \tag{3}$$

The writers of this article examine the nearest neighbour theory and its benefits for programming. A thorough tutorial is provided, which covers how to scale and normalise data, choose the appropriate distance measure, and use example codes and study findings to show how to use the closest neighbour method in programming. To help anyone interested in using the closest neighbour method in programming, the significance of every stage of the process is covered in depth.

2.2. Programming Procedure Ensemble ML

Multiple machine learning algorithms or approaches are combined in ensemble methods to increase the system's overall performance. With decision trees, naïve Bayes's & closest neighbours, the ensemble approach combines the output of each technique and analyses it to get a better result than each of the methods could produce on their own. To do this, the models are combined into a single, stronger model that has a greater ability to generalise than any of the separate models. Employing ensemble techniques has the benefit of generally reducing overfitting, increasing accuracy, and producing more healthy solutions to improved handle unknown information. Also, ensemble approaches may lower the amount of bias along with variation in the results of predictions, which makes them more accurate. The first code snippet shows a simple way to use ensemble ML.

Figure 2. Included are closest friends, decision trees, along with Naïve Bayes, as well as other machine learning methods

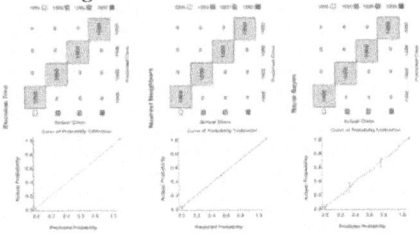

Ensemble machine learning methods are a good way to get high accuracy and flexibility. By putting together many data models, they make very accurate and reliable predictions. Ensemble methods can make more accurate predictions (with

a chance of more than 90%) because they can see tiny details in the information that separate models might miss. Also, ensemble methods can lower inaccurate information along with variation, making them useful for working with large, difficult datasets. As seen in Code Snippet 2, this research employs ensemble machine learning judgements with a probability higher than 90%.

Figure 3. A Group Machine Learning Model for Food Recognition

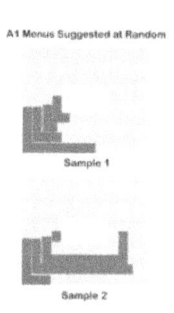

This research also recommends combining customer experience data with less than 50% of randomised generated data. By using a random theory, the results of these collective machine learning models may be utilised for reference. In any corporate plan, the random ratio suggestion, which spans from one to fifty per cent, helps to lessen consumer aggravation.

3. RESULTS

3.1. ML

The result of an accuracy and Model Learning curve may be used to determine how well a model generalises fresh, never-before-seen data. Typically, this was determined by contrasting how well the model performed using test and training sets of data. The ML curve demonstrated how the model's correctness rose when the training dataset was used, whilst the correctness curve indicated how well the model forecasted the right value of a particular production variable. The overall mistake the model produced when fitting the training set was the loss score.

The knowledge curve & the knowledge efficiency curve. Both plots showed that early learning continued to have poor accuracy and large loss scores. After around 700 data points, learning with no more than a 0.02 loss score was obtained, and even less after that. In addition to the accuracy number that was discovered after around 700 data points, the accuracy remained over 90% to the conclusion of the process of learning. According to this investigation, the decision tree technique had a lowermost loss score of 0.0476 ± 0.0069 and the highest accuracy of 99.24% ± 0.25%. At a low losing score of 0.0568 ± 0.0101 and an accuracy rate of 99.27% ± 0.33%, the closest neighbours technique demonstrated its high level of accuracy and effective model application. The naïve Bayes technique produced great results for the specified model, with an amazing reliability of 96.51% ± 0.71% and the lowest loss score of 0.0949 ± 0.0111.

The various accuracy ratings for the different machine learning algorithms that were used to generate predictions were visualised in the ML reliability matrix graphic. It displayed the degree of accuracy with which each algorithm had predicted the right labels given the dataset. It made it possible to rapidly determine the degree of accuracy of this machine learning model across various dataset segments and may have also assisted in identifying possible areas in need of development. Darker colours in the matrix denoted more accuracy. The colours in the matrix represented the model's relative accuracy in several categories. All things considered; the matrix plot offered a simple means of assessing the model's correctness about a variety of subjects. Usually, the machine learning accuracy was given as a percentage, with 100% accuracy denoting flawless data prediction by the model. Moreover, error served as a gauge for how far the model's forecasts deviated after the actual data. Usually, the error was given as a percentage, with a smaller error indicating higher accuracy and a zero error indicating perfect correctness.

The variance among two possibility supplies was measured using cross-entropy. It frequently served as a function of loss in machine learning to assess how well a model predicted an input dataset's output. When utilising any model to generate predictions, cross-entropy calculated represents the mean number of bits required to indicate the exact labels of samples taken from a particular supply. Greater classification accuracy was indicated by lower cross-entropy values, whilst lower accuracy was indicated by larger values.

A model's anticipated estimates of probability and the accompanying actual class labels are expressed graphically by a calibration curve. It was used to gauge a model's overall correctness; in contrast, a completely calibrated model would have shown a calibration curve with a completely diagonal line drawn on it. A model was typically regarded as working well and obtaining excellent accuracy when it achieved a benchmark number of 0.90 or above on the calibration curve. The standardization curve, represented with a precisely diagonal line in Figure 2, reveals that the model was operating properly and obtaining high precision, with the calibration curve's scale fitting greater than 0.10. With an associated defect of 0.00000 & mean crossover entropy of 0.0001010320, the decision tree technique produced a total precision matrix of 100.000%, according to the findings of the ML correctness matrix plot. Similar results were obtained using the closest neighbours approach, which had a mean cross-entropy of 0.0119720000, a 0.00000 error, and a total precision matrix of 100.000%. These outcomes showed that the model accurately anticipated the data. The naïve Bayes method then achieved a correctness matrix score of 97.176% overall. 0.0515655000 for the mean cross entropy and 0.02825 for the error. These findings indicated that the model can successfully recognise the excellent accuracy of the right labels in every class.

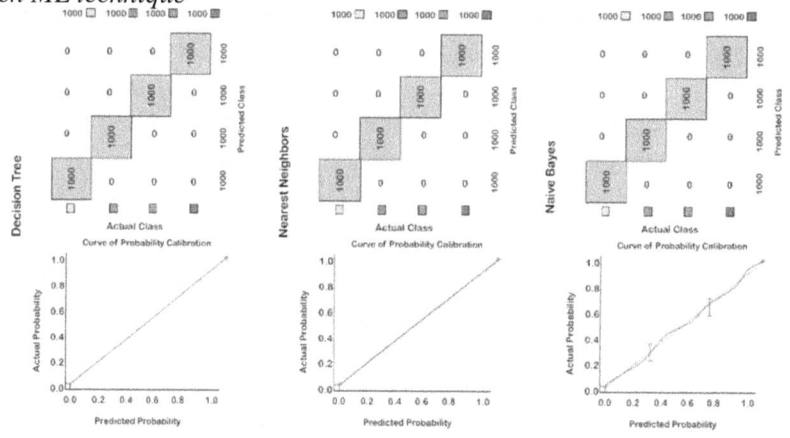

Figure 4. Plots of the probability calibration curves and the ML accuracy matrix for each ML technique

3.2. Validation of the Model

To create ML algorithms, validation of models was a crucial step that entailed evaluating and measuring a model's presentation on unobserved data. The objective was to ascertain if a model could successfully generalise its forecasts across datasets using statistical methods. This made it easier to find any possible biases or flaws in the model, that were then fixed. The process of validating a model usually included two basic parts. To assess the model's performance in hypothetical cases, it was first evaluated using a validation dataset. A dataset that was created at random and used to test a model with 100 menus is shown by Code Snippet 3. Based on consumer behaviour, randomisation may be repeated and a similar sequence might happen every time.

Figure 5. The trained dataset and the unknown random dataset were both modelled using identical parameters.

```
type=Range[xMin, xMax, {0.1}];
price=Range[yMin, yMax, {0.1}];
nMenu=100;
customerMenu=Table[If[i>0, {
            RandomChoice[Flatten[type, 1]],
            RandomChoice[Flatten[price, 1]]
            }, Nothing], {i, 1, nMenu}]
```

Second, an AI model's efficacy remained assessed on a sample set utilising a variety of measures, the most crucial of which were exactness, memory, accuracy, F-score, & area below the curve (AUC), to precisely gauge its predicted performance in "real-world" circumstances. The number of accurate forecasts out of all the predictions was measured by dividing the number of precise outcomes by the overall number of forecasts, and exactness was often stated as a percentage. A model was deemed to be producing accurate predictions if it produced a value greater than 85%. In a similar vein, recall and precision quantified the number of genuine positives and precise optimistic forecasts a model produced from all positive forecasts, correspondingly. In this case, results of more than 85% demonstrated that the model produced hopeful, accurate forecasts. Several 0.86 or above indicated reliable forecasts of both positive and negative outcomes. The F-score gave an average of accuracy and recall. Ultimately, the AUC evaluated the model's accuracy in classifying various lessons & was computed by graphing the true optimistic rate versus the false optimistic rate. An ideal model would have an AUC of 1.00, while values greater than 0.86 would typically indicate strong performance. Thus, overall precision, accuracy, remember, F-score and AUC values greater than 86% were critical markers of a model's efficacy. All things considered, model validation was necessary to guarantee that the ML models were reliable and suitable for implementation. Earlier the model was put into use in a real-world situation, any possible systematic mistakes, bias, or overfitting might have been addressed by thorough examination and improvement. Utilising the test set to verify the model was crucial. This helped fine-tune the model and provided insight into how effectively it might generalise fresh data. The results of the research showed that naïve Bayes was not always adequate for classification and that the closest neighbour models were the most effective for implementation. The results demonstrated that using a single machine-learning technique might lead to inadequate outcomes. As a result, this research suggests a way to make the ensemble machine learning model more efficient than 90% of the time for every machine learning technique. The merits and drawbacks of various machine learning models may be determined by researchers by comparing their efficacy, precision, recall, F-score, & AUC. This provides information that influences the choice of model for a certain application. Selecting the best machine learning model for the job requires an understanding of the costs and differences and similarities between the models. The quantitative performance metrics of the various machine learning techniques in the research demonstrate comparable quality to the used technique.

3.3. Technique of Random Suggestion

The use of AI-enabled the implementation of several tactics aimed at mitigating client irritation during menu item suggestions. Customers may "shuffle" through fresh options and sample a range of foods and cuisines via personalised recommendations based on their prior order history and preferences. Furthermore, a function was included to "refresh" the menu options periodically, offering patrons freshly selected suggestions. Additionally, ML models were used to examine consumer behaviour, which allowed for more accurate customisation of recommended menus. This research suggests combining customer experience data with fewer than fifty per cent of randomised data. Random theory recommendations might be made using ensemble machine-learning findings. For every given company plan, the recommended random ratio varied by one to 50% to minimise consumer irritation. In Figure. 3, the AI menu recommendations are randomly selected to a maximum of 50%. For every item on the menu, a different percentage was produced.

Figure 6. An AI menu example that incorporates consumer experience (light green) and randomly recommends four different kinds of food menus (red)

A1 Menus Suggested at Random

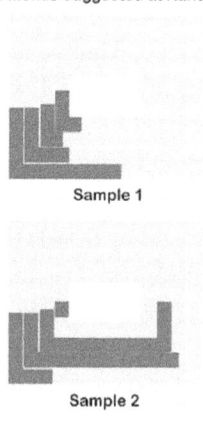

Sample 1

Sample 2

4. DISCUSSION

To outperform a single algorithm, many algorithms are combined in the ensemble machine learning approach. To provide a forecast that is more reliable than any of the individual models, it combines the predictions of many models. Ensemble approaches, as opposed to conventional single-algorithm ML implementations, enable the model better to represent the complexity of the issue by combining many algorithms into a single model. Predictive models' accuracy and resilience may be greatly increased by using ensemble machine learning models. Three ensemble machine learning models naïve Bayes, closest neighbours, and decision trees were examined in this work. The method of bagging was selected. High-performance predictive models may be produced using bagged ensemble models, particularly when working with big datasets and intricate problem spaces with plenty of characteristics. A subset of the data is chosen at random, separate models are trained on each subset, & the likelihood of overfitting is reduced by the use of bags.

An aggregate model may attain much more accuracy than just one baseline model by aggregating the findings of the different models. Impressively, the bagging ensemble models in this study outperformed the single baseline algorithm in terms of accuracy. This is significant since it improves the precision of forecasts made in the future. Furthermore, the bagging ensemble demonstrated better cross-dataset generalisation, indicating increased dependability when working with fresh data. Based on the findings, it is possible to improve prediction accuracy by using an ensemble of many machine learning models, since they have the potential to attain success rates over 90%. To further improve predictions, future studies might examine combinations of other ML models or other ensemble approaches like boosting. In this work, supervised learning techniques that have been effectively used as ensemble machine learning techniques include decision tree models, naïve Bayes, & closest neighbours. Using labelled training datasets, supervised training is a sort of machine learning that determines how to best predict future events from historical data. These kinds of learning relate inputs to intended outputs using algorithms, creating predictions along the way. Numerous ML algorithms, such as random forest, logistical regression, support vector machines, and linear regression, may be used with supervised learning techniques. While each algorithm uses a different method to classify designs in the information & forecast outcomes, supervised learning approaches may help all of them become more accurate and provide more trustworthy forecasts.

Because it offers the information required to create a prediction model that works, the training dataset for machine learning is crucial. Without a training sample with enough labels, it would be hard to make an ML system that is both effective and reliable. Using the training information, the algorithms are taught to find trends, tell the difference between things, and make predictions. By giving the algorithms relevant and well-marked past data, teach them the skills they need to make accurate guesses about the future. Precisely named datasets also make sure that the system works well by stopping bias and overfitting. For teaching, knowing about a customer's past is very important. Adding client background data to machine learning models might make them more accurate by giving them more information about how people have behaved in the past. Customer past data can help with segmentation by showing tastes and buying habits, which lets businesses make more focused offers. Using customer data, marketing can be adjusted to what customers want, which leads to more involvement and sales. Companies can better understand what customers want and make products and services that satisfy those needs by looking at past customers' purchases. By looking at customer past data with machine learning, businesses may be able to find patterns in customers' behaviour and respond quickly to problems or changes in customers' tastes. This could lead to more loyal customers and higher keeping prices.

This paper offers a popular vote method that uses ML models and has a success rate of over 90%. All of It with ML technology, digital marketers can influence what customers buy and make them more valuable. It could also decrease the cost of bad decisions by getting rid of fake wins and rejects. When less than half of the chosen data is mixed with customer information data, it may make customers less annoyed and offer possible benefits. Data may show places where the customer experience could be better, which would help customer service reps understand complicated customer behaviour and tailor services to their needs. This study talks about a new way to use AI to make random suggestions. To make better customer suggestions, think about a lot of different customers' likes and dislikes and how they act when for odd suggestions. For example, to make specific ideas, find trends in a person's buy history, reviews, and computer data. The randomisation may make customers happier by giving them ideas in real-time. It can also quickly spot trends, suggest interesting products, and offer special deals. Companies can employ randomisation to divide customers into groups and make personalised ideas to improve the customer experience. Better selection of consumer interests could lead to more sales and loyal customers. Randomisation could help marketing efforts by giving us useful information about how customers act so send them more relevant messages. Using this way could cut down on wasted resources and make the campaign run more smoothly. Randomization gives companies an edge over their rivals in the market. Businesses can stay strong and build customer trust by getting access to complex information that provides insight into what customers want and need. To win the store price war with AI technology, use predictive analytics. Predictive analytics helps stores guess what customers will want by looking at past data and changing their stock accordingly. This could help businesses better handle their goods by making sure that sales and restocking needs are fair. Machine learning might be able to spot patterns in the way customers buy things and suggest related items. This would help businesses focus their sales and make the most money possible.

While supervised ML is used, unsupervised learning offers an alternate approach. This approach's suitability for commercial applications relies on its pros and cons. Supervised learning excels at accurate predictions owing to labelled data. Training is easier and quicker than unsupervised learning, requiring fewer data points for trustworthy results. Unfortunately, labelled data is costly and difficult to collect simulating complicated interactions without background. Overfitting is possible with proper pre-processing for supervised models. Unsupervised learning does not request labelled data, avoiding the expense of getting labels. It can find hidden data patterns. Effective without further data. The downside, its computation-intensive and unreliable label-less results. Finally, evaluating efficacy is tough it lacks accuracy and error indicators to measure model efficacy. Guided learning requires. Lastly, monitored and Careful unsupervised learning has pros and cons. Picking one for a specific situation requires thought application. The usage of AI & ML in customer sentiment examination will be crucial for understanding customer behaviour, monitoring digital marketing campaigns, identifying success and failure, and addressing potential issues. In addition, sentiment research may be utilised to create personalised tactics for each client category, thereby enhancing campaign efficacy and ROI. Both organised and unstructured consumer data may be processed by algorithms that use artificial intelligence and machine learning to discover customer attitudes. Using AI and ML, businesses can find patterns in how customers behave and learn more about all of their products. Businesses can use AI and machine learning tools to look at purchaser explanations on social networks, web forums, & various other stages to find out what people think about an item or service as well as fix the problem. Tracking a customer's happiness over time can show changes in their mood and help with future decisions about how to connect and help them. Machine learning and artificial intelligence, businesses may now be able to get real-time information on how customers feel. AI and machine learning help businesses respond quickly to customer feedback and solve problems. As technology improves, AI and ML will be used more and more in customer opinion studies.

5. RESTRICTIONS

To use AI in food service, to have professional knowledge and experience. It is very important to be good at machine learning as well as natural language processing. AI should only be used to handle routine tasks; hard decisions or chores should be left to people. To make sure that data management processes are accurate and work well, they need to be optimised, integrated, tested, and maintained. Also, AI shouldn't be used to make decisions that depend on quality or regularity. Also, operations that are run by AI need to be constantly watched and managed to make sure that data is kept safe and private. Regulators and rules regarding data gathering and use must also be observed. Finally, AI models and findings must be transparent and explainable. Before being used, a variety of restrictions related to artificial intelligence and machine learning must be considered. First, there's the financial aspect. AI solutions are often costly in terms of software and hardware, which may prevent organisations or individuals with limited funds from adopting them. Second, for artificial intelligence algorithms to provide correct predictions, there must be an adequate amount of training data, which is sometimes expensive and challenging to collect. The third issue is data privacy and security; sufficient measures need to be taken to guarantee the safety of datasets & user data, then this is challenging since data privacy rules are intricate and there are no universally accepted standards. Furthermore, if the assumptions used while developing procedures are false or if the data utilised to teach the algorithms does not sufficiently represent the actual world, human bias may still find its way into AI solutions.

Furthermore, it may be challenging to understand the reasoning behind choices made or to draw conclusions from AI models as they are sometimes opaque and difficult to comprehend. Furthermore, it takes a lot of effort and specialised expertise to construct and train ML models, which makes it challenging to implement a solution rapidly. When given unknown data, machine learning models may potentially have poor generalisability and provide inaccurate findings. High-quality labelled datasets may be costly and difficult to get in certain areas because, in the end, the quantity and quality of the datasets may have a significant impact on model accuracy. Lastly, excessive complexity in machine learning models may lead to overfitting, which impairs generalisability by teaching them patterns from the training dataset which does not apply to new information.

6. CONCLUSION

It is possible to produce and optimise both short- & long-term sales in the food distribution industry by including an AI-driven collaborative consisting of three machine learning (ML) algorithms in numerical advertising campaigns. Companies within the food delivery industry have realised how they may improve their overall performance and efficiency by using ML algorithms using data-driven insights. Furthermore, there are certain operational advantages for the food delivery industry when using AI-driven ML technology in digital marketing tactics. Businesses may save time and effort and free up resources for additional tasks, such as growing their company, by automating operations like ad targeting, content personalisation, and campaign optimisation.

It has been shown that using supervised learning techniques such as decision trees, naïve Bayes, along adjoining neighbours' procedures to improve digital advertising tactics in the food distribution industry is a useful tool. These three methods work together to give a solid foundation for making data-driven decisions about things like how often to order, when to release new items, and what deals to offer. The results from the learnt models were more precise than those from traditional marketing methods. This shows that AI and ML can precisely forecast how customers will act and what they will like. By using AI-driven ML-overlooked knowledge technology, industries can easily get useful information from the huge amounts of customer data they collect. Just over half of randomised data paired with user experience data is utilised in the majority voting approach, which can participate in replicas with a degree of success of over 90% while minimising consumer dissatisfaction. AI's use in food delivery services is still very new, but it has already made a big difference in how well it works. Businesses can make smart, data-driven decisions because this technology gives them a lot of information about how customers act and what they like. Companies may be able to get an edge in their markets if they use machine learning techniques properly. AI, the food delivery service can better tailor its marketing efforts to meet the requirements and preferences of its customers. Businesses may be able to better service their customers by personalising their material and making predictions more accurate by using AI and ML tools. Food service businesses will make a lot of money as this technology continues to grow.

REFERENCES:

Buhalis, D., Harwood, T., Bogicevic, V., Viglia, G., Beldona, S., & Hofacker, C. (2019). Technological disruptions in services: Lessons from tourism and hospitality. *Journal of Service Management*, 30(4), 484–506. DOI: 10.1108/JOSM-12-2018-0398

Buhalis, D., Harwood, T., Bogicevic, V., Viglia, G., Beldona, S., & Hofacker, C. (2019b). Technological disruptions in services: Lessons from tourism and hospitality. *Journal of Service Management*, 30(4), 484–506. DOI: 10.1108/JOSM-12-2018-0398

Davenport, T., Guha, A., Grewal, D., & Bressgott, T. (2019). How artificial intelligence will change the future of marketing. *Journal of the Academy of Marketing Science*, 48(1), 24–42. DOI: 10.1007/s11747-019-00696-0

Dwivedi, Y. K., Hughes, L., Baabdullah, A. M., Ribeiro-Navarrete, S., Giannakis, M., Al-Debei, M. M., Dennehy, D., Metri, B., Buhalis, D., Cheung, C. M., Conboy, K., Doyle, R., Dubey, R., Dutot, V., Felix, R., Goyal, D., Gustafsson, A., Hinsch, C., Jebabli, I., & Wamba, S. F. (2022). Metaverse beyond the hype: Multidisciplinary perspectives on emerging challenges, opportunities, and agenda for research, practice and policy. *International Journal of Information Management*, 66, 102542. DOI: 10.1016/j.ijinfomgt.2022.102542

Dwivedi, Y. K., Hughes, L., Ismagilova, E., Aarts, G., Coombs, C., Crick, T., Duan, Y., Dwivedi, R., Edwards, J., Eirug, A., Galanos, V., Ilavarasan, P. V., Janssen, M., Jones, P., Kar, A. K., Kizgin, H., Kronemann, B., Lal, B., Lucini, B., & Williams, M. D. (2019). Artificial Intelligence (AI): Multidisciplinary perspectives on emerging challenges, opportunities, and agenda for research, practice and policy. *International Journal of Information Management*, 57, 101994. DOI: 10.1016/j.ijinfomgt.2019.08.002

Dwivedi, Y. K., Hughes, L., Ismagilova, E., Aarts, G., Coombs, C., Crick, T., Duan, Y., Dwivedi, R., Edwards, J., Eirug, A., Galanos, V., Ilavarasan, P. V., Janssen, M., Jones, P., Kar, A. K., Kizgin, H., Kronemann, B., Lal, B., Lucini, B., & Williams, M. D. (2021). Artificial Intelligence (AI): Multidisciplinary perspectives on emerging challenges, opportunities, and agenda for research, practice and policy. *International Journal of Information Management*, 57, 101994. DOI: 10.1016/j.ijinfomgt.2019.08.002

Dwivedi, Y. K., Ismagilova, E., Hughes, D. L., Carlson, J., Filieri, R., Jacobson, J., Jain, V., Karjaluoto, H., Kefi, H., Krishen, A. S., Kumar, V., Rahman, M. M., Raman, R., Rauschnabel, P. A., Rowley, J., Salo, J., Tran, G. A., & Wang, Y. (2021). Setting the future of digital and social media marketing research: Perspectives and research propositions. *International Journal of Information Management*, 59, 102168. DOI: 10.1016/j.ijinfomgt.2020.102168

Huang, M., & Rust, R. T. (2018). Artificial intelligence in service. *Journal of Service Research*, 21(2), 155–172. DOI: 10.1177/1094670517752459

Jiang, Y., & Wen, J. (2020). Effects of COVID-19 on hotel marketing and management: A perspective article. *International Journal of Contemporary Hospitality Management*, 32(8), 2563–2573. DOI: 10.1108/IJCHM-03-2020-0237

Kommineni, K. K., Madhu, G. C., Narayanamurthy, R., & Singh, G. (2022). IoT crypto security communication system. In *IoT Based Control Networks and Intelligent Systems:Proceedings of 3rd ICICNIS 2022* (pp. 27-39). Singapore: Springer Nature Singapore.

Majid, S., Zhang, X., Khaskheli, M. B., Hong, F., King, P. J. H., & Shamsi, I. H. (2023). Eco-efficiency, environmental and sustainable innovation in recycling energy and their effect on business performance: Evidence from European SMEs. *Sustainability (Basel)*, 15(12), 9465. DOI: 10.3390/su15129465

Min, S., Zacharia, Z. G., & Smith, C. D. (2019). Defining Supply Chain Management: In the past, present, and future. *Journal of Business Logistics*, 40(1), 44–55. DOI: 10.1111/jbl.12201

Nelson, P. (1970). Information and consumer behaviour. *Journal of Political Economy*, 78(2), 311–329. DOI: 10.1086/259630

Shalini, R., Mishra, L., Athulya, S., Chimankar, A. G., Kandavalli, S. R., Kumar, K., & Selvan, R. S. (2023, May). Tumor Infiltration of Microrobot using Magnetic torque and AI Technique. In *2023 2nd International Conference on Vision Towards Emerging Trends in Communication and Networking Technologies (ViTECoN)* (pp. 1-5). IEEE.

Simon, H. A. (1991). Bounded rationality and organizational learning. *Organization Science*, 2(1), 125–134. DOI: 10.1287/orsc.2.1.125

Chapter 15
AIML–Based Data Analytics to Cost Strategy in Simulating the Logistics Business

N. Sharfunisa
CMR University, India

Swarna Surekha
Annamacharya University, India

N. Pughazendi
CMR University, India

T. Veeranna
https://orcid.org/0000-0003-2248-4387
Sai Spurthi Institute of Technology, India

R. Pramodhini
Nitte Meenakshi Institute of Technology, India

R. Senthamil Selvan
Annamacharya Institute of Technology and Sciences, Tirupati, India

ABSTRACT

This study aims to determine if using ensemble machine learning (ML) with artificial intelligence (AI) can improve cost-cutting and profit-maximising tactics. This research aims to investigate how best practices for mitigating costs may be found through simulating business threshold cost information using ensemble machine learning driven by AI. To find patterns and correlations in cost information related to strategic choices, three ensemble machine-learning techniques are used as ML algorithms on the dataset, which contains 6561 possible tuples. This concept is innovative because it shows how simulated data might improve cost-cutting tactics for companies. By highlighting the perspective of machine learning applications for company proprietors and employees engaged in manufacturing and advertising, this

DOI: 10.4018/979-8-3693-7773-4.ch015

study adds to the body of knowledge already available on artificial intelligence and machine learning applications in business. The consequences of the study results are noteworthy for several businesses, such as retail, logistics, and transportation.

1. INTRODUCTION

Projections show that the global logistics delivery business will increase from 2022 to 2027, with an average annual growth rate of 8.5%. (Rashid et al. 2023) The faster shipping options are in high demand, and the use of contactless payment methods is on the rise, all thanks to the meteoric rise in online shopping. The expansion of e-commerce is a primary catalyst for the logistics delivery business. (Tseng et al., 2024) The rising prevalence of online shopping is amplifying the need for sophisticated logistical delivery services. The increasing demand for expedited shipping services is a significant trend in the logistical sector. (Illescas-Manzano et al., 2021) Customers are progressively seeking expedited delivery times, hence raising the need for express shipping services. Express delivery services often provide certain delivery timelines, which are crucial for enterprises requiring prompt product delivery to clients. A recent development that has surfaced in the aftermath of the COVID-19 epidemic is the growing use of contactless delivery. The rise of contactless delivery services may be attributed to the pandemic's heightened worries about the transmission of pathogens. Through contactless delivery services, clients may accept their items without ever having to interact with delivery workers. (Mantravadi, 2022) The anticipated revenue for the worldwide delivery logistics market is $622.69 billion by 2029. These reasons, together with the rising demand for logistical delivery services from both consumers and companies, are driving this expansion. To keep up with the competition in the fiercely competitive logistics delivery sector, the major firms are always innovating. (Malik et al., 2021) But for logistics carriers to be competitive, this increase also puts pressure on them to optimise their cost structures. The needs of contemporary companies need the use of conventional cost optimisation techniques like static pricing models and manual route planning. (Caeiro-Rodriguez et al., 2021) These approaches often lack speed, flexibility, and the ability to change with the rapidly evolving business. In the logistics industry, fresh and creative methods for cost optimisation are required.

Cost strategy optimisation may be achieved more effectively, adaptably, and efficiently using artificial intelligence ensemble machine learning, which has the potential to completely transform the business. The cost-optimization techniques utilised by logistic carriers are ineffective, rigid, and unable to change with the constantly evolving sector. Profitability is declining and expenses are rising as a result. Logistics is a data-intensive sector with route, customer, and fuel usage data. (Hemachandran et al., 2022) Traditional approaches for cost optimisation must account for complicated linkages and hidden patterns in data. Powered by AI ensemble ML can analyse data and uncover hidden patterns, making it useful for optimising cost strategies. This approach adapts to changing market circumstances, such as demand swings, fuel costs, and weather patterns. Continuous monitoring and real-time cost strategy adjustments using AI-powered ensemble ML help logistics carriers stay profitable and competitive in a changing industry. (Siddique & Chow, 2021) Logistics requires precise demand forecasts for the allocation of resources and cost optimisation. Machine learning and artificial intelligence in logistics might improve our lives. This cutting-edge technology will speed up delivery, minimise shipping costs, and provide more items at competitive pricing. AI and ML in logistics will boost efficiency, save costs, and boost customer satisfaction, making firms more lucrative. (Hasal et al., 2021) Artificial intelligence and machine learning are not only good for companies and customers. Integrating such technologies into logistics will also greatly affect the economy. It will boost other logistics-related companies and generate new specialised jobs. Machine learning (ML) and artificial intelligence (AI) in logistics lower transportation's carbon impact, making it eco-friendly. Single-system ML techniques, although easily implemented, often need help due to various disadvantages that restrict their efficiency and generalisability.

Hyperparameter feeling, underfitting, and overfitting are a few of these disadvantages. When a single machine intelligence model enhances overfit, it acts poorly on untried data cause it has enhanced excessive awareness of the oddities of the training set. On the other hand, underfitting occurs when a alone engine-education model is inadequate to adequately forecast the complications of the data. The choice of hyperparameters can intensely reduce the act of a distinct structure-education model, that is commonly susceptible to this issue. Multiple ML models are used in ensemble ML methods, that support a viable habit to overcome these restraints. Using ancient data, present patterns, and outside influences, AI-powered ensemble machine intelligence can exactly forecast changes standard. This allows logistic aircraft carriers to actively alter their movements, containing trained workers, fleet administration, as well as warehouse optimisation, to efficiently meet demand. Additionally, route slating and assigning resources are essential items of cost optimisation in management manufacturing. By analysing artery networks, and traffic patterns, in addition to customer districts, AI-compelled arrangement machine intelligence can decide the most effective routes to minimise fuel use, transmittal opportunities, and overall expenditures. To confirm that all the boats, attendants, and conveniences are being used effectively, AI algorithms can boost the classification network's support allocation.

Ultimately, AI-driven ensemble machine intelligence equips logistics carriers accompanying a healthy instrument for making experienced, data-principal choices. Artificial intelligence algorithms have the potential to upgrade procedural transmittal decision-making by way of the study of large amounts of data and the finding of unseen patterns. The management transmittal sector is difficult. Lost or ruined management, late delivery, overdone prices, contests, rules, & technology plague this trade. These impediments power hinder allied movements and competitiveness. Understanding these questions enables organisations to create experienced trade choices and flourish. The cost following helps firms evaluate worth. Understanding costs helps organisations price goods and duties, save money, and increase profits. Thus, monitoring electronics is important for cost administration and profit improvement in resourcefulness. Business payments must be traced for various reasons. It may help associations path their giving and reduce below. These dents incorporate expenditures that may be suffused by AI in various ways. Spending listening can be automatic by AI, saving up opportunities for different projects. This can guarantee exact and effective payment following can spot trends and abnormalities in expenditure, which may be used to pinpoint areas of excessive spending or possible issues. AI conceded the possibility specify pieces of advice for better spending, to a degree incisive loathe profligate giving or switching funds to more money-making uses.

Here are any particular instances by which AI power bridge breaks in guest expenditure. An internet dealer's ability to monitor a person engaged in private ownership of business it spends on advertising efforts. Artificial Intelligence (AI) has the potential to decide that works are ultimately favourable and imply ways to load profitable work better. A maker ability monitors the amount it has gone on raw materials. Artificial Intelligence (AI) has the potential to discover patterns in natural resource costs and specify advice for reconstructing supplier appraising. AI is fit automating control of product quality and stock administration. A dealer may monitor a person engaged in private ownership of a business it spends on stocks. Artificial intelligence (AI) has the potential to discover slow merchandise and provide plans for minimising the size of merchandise staying on the shelves. This research was compelled by one necessity for adaptation and elasticity in aggressive manufacturing. The after divisions concerning this work are organised as follows: Section 2 delineates the method for the machine intelligence treasure and operating system incident. Section 3 presents the findings in addition to the study concerning this search. The study's efficient associations and addition to the existing research are checked in Section 4, and the study's end is bestowed in Section 5.

2. METHODOLOGY

The research design was dictated by the needs of logistics delivery firms. Production and consumer cost data were taken into account to build a model that assigned several outcomes for decision-making. After identifying the key and value data using an association rule, the ML training procedure was initiated. The decision-making system's verification was intended to be at least 85% correct as a baseline, and the confidence in its usefulness was further bolstered by the addition of one additional machine-learning approach for iteration. Figure 1 presents a description of the study framework. Generating simulated information is an essential phase in the AI process, enabling investigators to establish ground truth for assessing model correctness by creating simulated datasets tailored to the particular application of the AI system. This guarantees that the AI method acquires the appropriate traits and generates the correct guess. Simulated news is an essential resource for AI research, reinforcing the accuracy, security, cost-influence, scalability, & privacy of AI structures. For the incident of AI arrangements, the synthetic data is frequently the only alternative, especially in cases when the authentic data is either troublesome, high-priced, or unavailable. When linked to accompanying physical data, fake data concede the possibility make AI plans more correct and effective.

Figure 1. Outline models

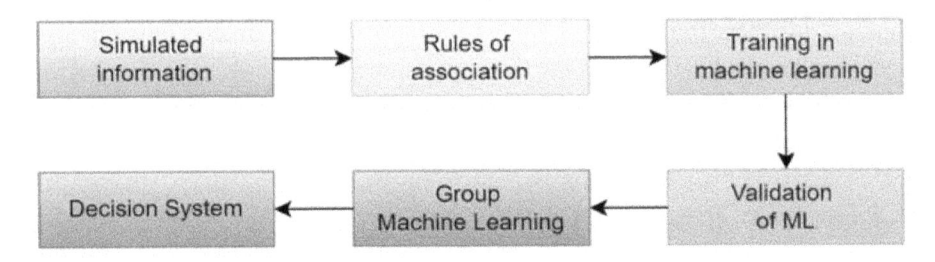

An active machine intelligence technique for recognizing interesting equivalences between variables in monstrous datasets is the union rule. It uses any interesting verification to find forceful rules stocked in databases. The rules that specify how or why certain objects are related to a range of other elements in a particular transaction are found using the association rule. Researchers must use machine learning training to educate their AI methods to identify these patterns after they have created a rule of association for a dataset. In machine learning (ML) training, data is fed into a framework so that it may learn from user-provided examples. The accuracy of the model increases with the amount of data utilised to train it. But using high-quality simulated information that accurately represents the real-world issue, the method is attempting to address is crucial. Machine learning validation is a crucial phase in the machine learning process that verifies the model's accuracy and its capacity to provide dependable predictions. Post-training of a model based on machine learning it is necessary to assess its precision using a distinct dataset that the system has not before seen. The estimations made by the model on the new information may be compared with the actual results to assess the model's accuracy. Ensembles ML is a methodology that amalgamates the forecasts of many ML methods to get a more accurate forecast. The idea insists that a diversified ensemble of orders is more inclined supply correct results than someone order. An ML means is immediately anticipated use in a decision order that engages machine intelligence models to form choices subsequently it has sustained preparation, confirmation, and revalidation. Usually, the decision whole accepts recommendations from the consumer and utilises the machine learning model to forecast or elect.

2.1 Method of Machine Learning

A synthesis of regression using logistics, decision trees, and closest neighbours may serve as an excellent approach for ensemble methods and enhancing the outcomes of machine learning classification problems. The decision tree is utilised to construct a classification method is regression using logistics, followed by the application of the closest neighbour's model to replicate the classification outcomes. By integrating these three methodologies, the biases or inaccuracies inherent in each model may be alleviated, enhancing their precision and dependability. Furthermore, some sophisticated machine learning approaches, like ensemble methods, may be utilised to amalgamate the outcomes to enhance the outcome.

2.1.1 Decision Tree

In AI, decision trees are a strong and well-liked method for resolving challenging issues. They provide a methodical approach to figuring out what to do in a certain scenario. Similar to flowcharts in structure, decision trees include branches that stand in for potential choices and results. Using predetermined criteria, the result tree looks for the most "correct" choice at each branch. Each division has a weight depending on the probability that a certain choice will result in the intended result. At the simplest level, decision trees are built utilising the scoring formula. This function receives inputs on the problem's present status and rates each potential course of action. It is recommended to pursue the course $h = w_1 X_1 + w_2 X_2 + + w_n X_n$ is an example of a standard scoring function. In this function, $X_1, X_2, \ldots,$ and X_n Re factors that describe the present state of the issue; w_1, w_2, ..., and w_n Re weights applied to the factors that reflect their comparative significance.

2.1.2 Regression using Logistics

One machine intelligence approach named logistic regression is used to resolve categorisation issues like predicting a client's purchase determined or investment return. It is a mathematical arrangement that delineates the link between the accumulation of independent determinants and reliant determinants. The determinants that is reliant are frequently a binary result, in the way that "yes" or "no," can be depicted as an expectation model. Logistic regression calculates the possibility of the helpless changeable established values of the liberated variables.

2.1.3 Closest Neighbours

An ML method called the closest neighbour is used to categorise objects or data points. A particular data point or article is distinguished to its tightest neighbours and established in the category at which point the adulthood of allure neighbours applies. The closest neighbour algorithm operates on the premise that comparable things are located nearby. This indicates that an object's class or label may be contingent on looking at allure tightest neighbours. Although the closest neighbour method is honest to use, its acting is reliant on the distance measure. The Manhattan distance and Euclidean distance are two together accepted verifications for distance used in the tightest neighbour system

2.2 Language for Programming

AI and ML engage Mathematica, an progressive programming speech. It offers a connection and functionalities for treasure development, rule creation, and data management. The use of AI and ML utilizing Mathematica allows the analysis of far-reaching datasets, understanding intricate connections, and the building of exact prediction models within minutes. Mathematica's functionalities are compelled by its refined representative computing library, permissive customers to work together with symbolic verbalizations for logic. This study made use of Wolfram Alpha's Mathematica Experimental Version 13.0.1, which was gossip MacBook Pro accompanying an M1 CPU and 8 GB whole memory.

2.3 Method

2.3.1 Trade-offs and Biases

The custom of fake information was examined in this place study. An artificial intelligence plan grants permission to learn in a sensible scene by utilizing simulated data, that presents several datasets from differing beginnings, containing simulations and real-realm synopsises. The AI system grants permission to gain patterns and correlations middle from two points of data beginnings with the aid of fake data. Furthermore, a simulation data can be used to determine the AI system's efficiency, which can help with future incidents and adaptations. Simulated data grant permission benefits AI research, but understanding the allure trade-destroy and biases is key. A bigger challenge is data likeness because simulated news cannot completely represent the complications of the real world. This can come into being-globe data models less generalisable. Simulated news conditions are crucial because incorrect or non-representative information power distorts models. Finally, the preparation data pile and condition impact model performance. Limited or partial preparation data may influence less healthy and generalizable models. Thus, when employing fake facts for AI research, these issues must be carefully thought out

.2.3.2 Prepare the information.

To meet the demands of an association, this study used the allure real key result cost news to produce enumerations. We were capable of producing datasets that are completely similar to actual globe data by way of this. The aim of machine intelligence searches out supply correct forecasts by constructing sensible models from fake data. Researchers may use imitation to study an arrangement's behaviour by constructing a model accompanying a building and rules that control it to produce different results. To create a fake dataset for machine intelligence, this study uses an approach to survey the potential use of killing beginning worth of cost. This news may embellish the accuracy of ML models & decrease the accompanying expenses. This study aims to decide if it is possible to judge or imitate information for machine intelligence projects utilizing the BTVC and to analyse the effects. In particular, it investigates how the preferred variables—like cost possibility—affect the effects and guide the administrative process of the adjustment between risk and cost. Lastly, it investigates the anticipated uses of the imitation of various hypothetic cost tuples established by BTVC.

3. RESULTS

3.1 ML Learning

An AI treasure's ability to gain recommendations over occasion is presented by a curve of knowledge in machine intelligence (ML). It displays the change in accuracy or misfortune score as a function of the preparation dataset's redundancies. The algorithm's prediction ability is gauged by its accuracy, and its fit to the data is shown by its loss score. An appropriate machine learning curve represents the inverse relationship between the number of repetitions and loss score. The precision and loss of metrics diminish as the procedure acquires more knowledge from the information. Figure 2 illustrates the learning curve with the precision of the knowledge curve. Both graphs indicate that early knowledge results in elevated loss slashes and decreased precision. On the other hand, knowledge with around 500 data points produced an accuracy close to 90% and a loss score of less than 1. When the loss scores dropped to less than 0.1, the system was successfully trained and produced outstanding outcomes.

Figure 2. Each ML method's accuracy and learnt curves are as follows: (a) The x-axis of the learning curve shows sample count and y-axis loss score, (b) The x-axis of the accuracy curve shows sample count and the y-axis accuracy score.

Decision Trees

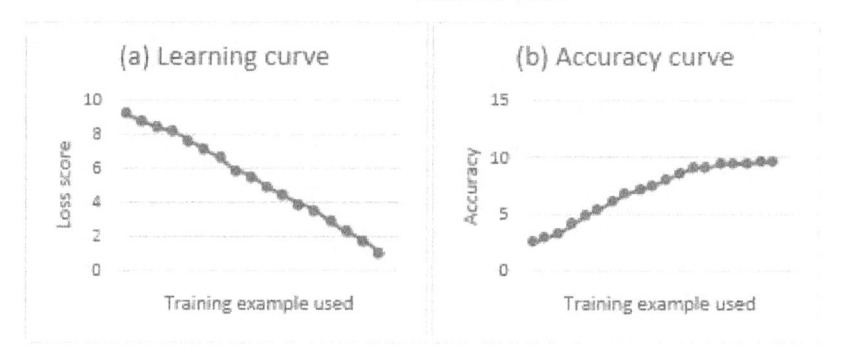

Regression using Logistics

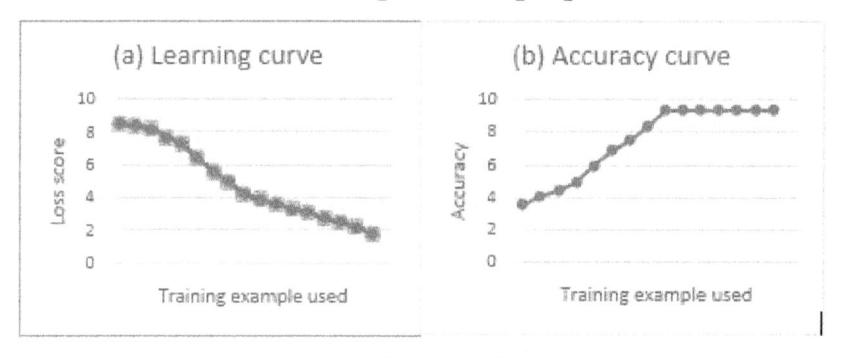

Nearest Neighbours

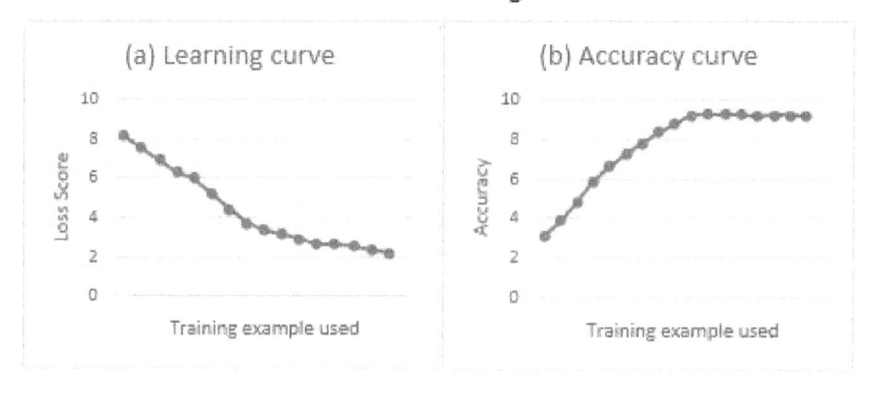

The machine learning training outcomes indicated that the decision tree methodology achieved a precision of 99.48% ± 0.20% as well as a minimal loss score of 1.0756 ± 0.0110. The deterioration using the logistics technique achieved the best precision of 99.90% ± 0.09%, with a minimum loss score of 0.0159 ± 0.0014. The closest neighbour's technique demonstrated remarkable accuracy, attaining 99.07% ± 0.35% with a minimal loss score of 0.0967 ± 0.0171, signifying effective model implementation and outstanding outcomes. The calibration curve allows one to compare observing the information points with their anticipated probabilities, indicating the dependability of a model's predicted probabilities. With the help of the confusion matrix, which offers a tabular summary of the organization algorithm's presentation, users may assess their model's recall and accuracy as well as determine which classes were incorrectly categorised. Figures 3 and 4 illustrate the confusion matrix & calibration curve, respectively, aligned with an ideal diagonal line, indicating that the method operates with exceptional precision. Matrix plots showing machine learning accuracy showed that three algorithms—regression of logistics, nearest neighbour, and decision trees—got 100% overall precision, having mean cross entropy of 0.00144, 0.00104, and 0.00978, respectively. The findings indicate that the system has successfully identified the proper labels for all classes.

Figure 3. For each ML training technique, the probability calibration curve displays real probabilities on the x-axis and anticipated probabilities on the y-axis.

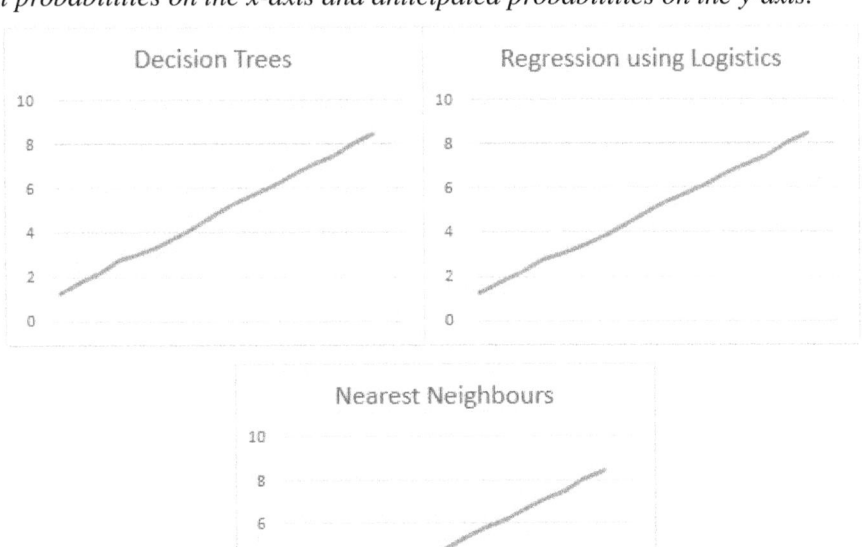

Figure 4. Each ML training method's accuracy matrix plot shows the actual class on the x-axis and the projected class on the y-axis.

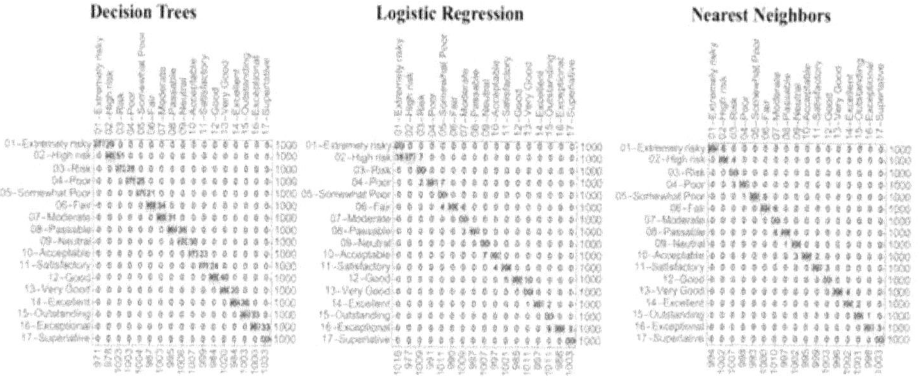

3.2 Validation of the Model

Model validity denotes the degree to which the calculated behaviour aligns with the solution. Model validation assesses the performance of a machine learning model on novel data, ascertaining the specificity, other metrics, accuracy, model precision, and sensitivity. This study employs cross-validation, a method that entails partitioning the innovative dataset into many smaller subsets for difficult and exercise the machine learning method. Cross-validation is crucial for assessing predictive methods since it mitigates overfitting by preventing train-test pollution. Recall, F-score, accuracy, AUC, & accuracy are frequently used metrics for assessing machine learning models. Metrics with values over 0.86 are essential markers of a system's efficacy. The confusion environment in Fig. 5 indicates that the models in this investigation had strong performance, with quantitative metrics above 0.96.

Figure 5. Each ML validation method's accuracy matrix plot shows the actual class on the x-axis and the predicted class on the y-axis.

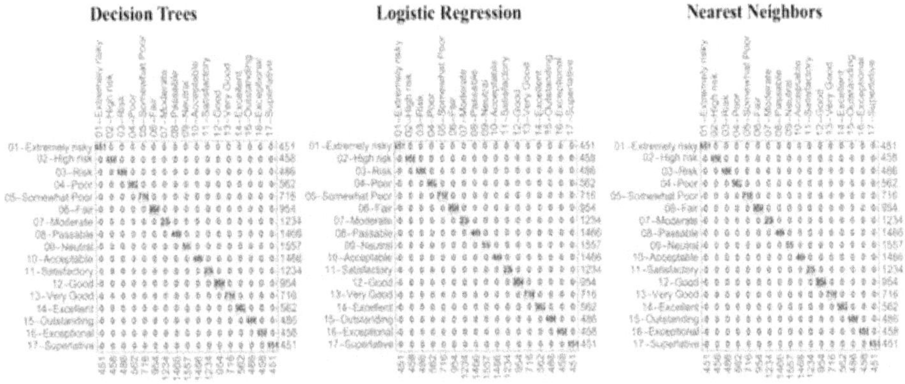

3.3 Ensemble Machine Learning

Combining many models using ensemble ML improves predictive model performance. An ensemble ML approach utilised in this work used three ML algorithms to achieve validation accuracies of 97 to 99%, indicating outstanding results. This research demonstrates that grouping is a better approach to summarising the three ML outputs than one. To examine numerous viewpoints, this technique selects the option with the greatest likelihood to be shared by two or more machine learning findings, with a possibility larger than 0.96. A null declaration is utilised if no ML outcome has a probability larger than 0.96. Figure 6 displays ML result probability greater than 0.96. To get a more accurate information assessment and increase cost-effectiveness, precision, and efficiency, businesses use AI to group ML findings. This method offers an extra degree of protection and confidence while lowering the possibility of mistakes and making judgements based on machine learning. Ensemble approaches are effective, attaining elevated accuracy and generalisation in machine learning. By integrating many data models, these approaches may provide very dependable and precise forecasts. Moreover, they may reduce volatility & bias in the information, thus making them appropriate for complicated datasets.

Figure 6. The probability of each ML approach is shown in the ML test results: (1) Decision tree is blue colour, (2) Green logistic regression, (3) Red closest neighbours, yellow probability above 0.95. The graph displays the tests utilised, rating class, and likelihood on the x, y, and z axes.

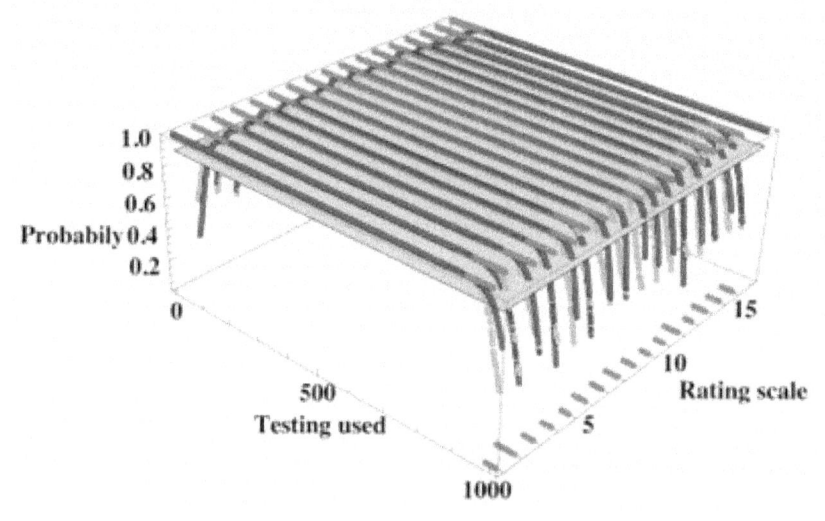

3.4 Identification of Costs

Machine learning categorisation enables enterprises to simplify cost management operations, therefore saving money and time. This technology uses predictive algorithms to identify cost-related trends and patterns, allowing firms to more effectively and correctly anticipate future expenditures and budgets. Machine learning categorisation concedes the possibility of ascertaining several cost types by checking previous payment styles, which may benefit firms pursuing to learn their spending behaviours to check unnecessary expenditures. Through the reasoning of ancient data, machine intelligence categorisation offers an inclusive amount of the company's payments and pinpoints potential opportunities for cost decline or embellished efficiency. This paper offers a mixture of the BTVC for machine intelligence categorization.

4. DISCUSSION

4.1 Contributions to Research

The purpose concerning this study searches to assess if utilizing machine intelligence and fake information to establish cost plans for the management service subdivision is doable. To pull off this goal, ensemble machine intelligence methods were used, and their effectiveness was proved for one dependability and validity of cost study methods. According to the study's verdicts, the suggested blueprint is feasible and may raise cost-incisive strategies used in management duty manufacturing. Additionally, the research sought to optimise management cost approaches by way of the use of AI-powered ensemble machine intelligence by evolving a decision-making system & active pursuing method for logistic transfer movements. The education results indicate that AI-compelled group machine intelligence has important promise for enhancing cost game plans in the management sector. The research checked three theories to idea this claim, highlighting the potential of AI to alter cost administration processes. The initial plan emphasised AI's ability to find out cost-reduction potential by way of data analysis, developing in upgraded profit borders. The second hypothesis emphasizes AI's competency to tell hidden expenses frequently missed by conventional cost-decline methods. The third theory emphasised AI's function in physical-time changeability to retail swings, furthering strategic adaptations.

This study's verdicts display that the AI-compelled group machine-education approach is more exact & offers superior cost estimates distinguished from individual wholes. These results have considerable meaning for the management help area, that may gain from utilizing this design to reinforce allure cost strategies. Researchers may receive a better understanding of AI's productiveness in cost optimisation and concrete the route for allure wider use in management by completely proving these beliefs. There are meaningful ramifications for this study. Logistics parties may boost worth, increase functional efficiency, and preserve a solid amount of services by utilizing AI-stimulated insights. This so leads to decreased transfer costs for clients, constituting a logistics transfer atmosphere that is to say both more competing and economical. The management subdivision be necessary to visualize increased adeptness, worth, & client satisfaction from now on as artificial intelligence (AI) evolves and plays a more meaningful part in cost procedure optimisation. These findings support important new facts on the potential of ensemble machine intelligence compelled by AI for cost strategy optimisation in the management area.

4.2 Group Machine Learning

ML double confirmation uses two confirmation sets for strength. Using a dataset that was not used for preparation or confirmation, the model is proven on a "settler of a dispute" dataset in the first validation set. Creating a "cross-confirmation" dataset by carelessly separating the preparation happens half admits for the second set of confirmation tests expected gossip the model. This procedure is more reliable than individual confirmation because it offers two liberated evaluations of scheme performance, lowering the chance of miscalculation. ML confirmation is urged for judging ML models, exceptionally those used result, to guarantee dependability and correct prophecies. Ensemble approaches humiliate fake still pictures taken with a camera by only judging better impacts than 95% of some form. However, double validation is not infallible because dishonest a still picture taken with a camera may happen if data is not thoughtful of type or models are not well measured.

By assessing AI-compelled cost means, this study fills a information vacuum. It too shows how fake data might correct management transfer cost designs. These findings support the understanding that AI can improve cost study. Additionally, ML classification can expect the cost of bearing a likely product or aid for the firm. The program estimates brand or aid costs utilizing variables like pricing points and production expenses. This data power helps the organisation set prices and stay competitive. Simulated facts reinforce the study of complex wholes by creating observations that project into the future while likewise examining archival occurrences to ascertain effects. This judgment grant permission has important ramifications for various areas and resourcefulness's. Moreover, it allows firms to comprehend the expenses that guide the preparation of machine intelligence models, facilitating more conversant judgements about the utilisation of machine intelligence against unoriginal approaches. Furthermore, it can enhance the accuracy of machine intelligence designs, making bureaucracy more careful.

4.3 Consequences

Logistics cost optimisation utilizing AEML has far-reaching proficient consequences. AEML enables management providers to minimise costs by optimising route preparation, pricing, & demand guessing, superior to increased effectiveness, lower money needed to run a business, and increased worth. Logistics companies can adopt changeful demand, fuel costs, and weather using palpable-opportunity information-compelled administrative facilitated by AEML. This adaptability optimises the system and expense administration. Logistics companies may again improve consumer knowledge as well as memory by optimising routes in addition to delivery schedules to give parts quicker, more dependable, and low. Logistics companies may provide cutthroat costing, retain profit borders, & engage new clients by utilizing AEML in the more complicated and cost-delicate management industry.

Companies may use the approach and conclusions of this research to undertake calculated risks that enhance earnings and reduce losses. By modelling several cost scenarios, firms may forecast the efficacy of machine learning along with its potential for achievement, therefore mitigating the danger of actual world expenditures failing to provide the anticipated outcomes. This simulation allows the organisation to evaluate the effect of the investment on profitability and returns, facilitating the identification of key areas for the use of AI or ML technology. Companies may also evaluate scenarios that replicate volatile market circumstances and modify their strategy to achieve their aims. AI and ML provide prospects for more productive and effective operations in addition to financial gains. Businesses may automate some jobs and procedures using machine learning and artificial intelligence to save costs and streamline operations. Additionally, by analysing client data and offering deeper insights into their choices, AI-driven analytics enables businesses to create goods and services that more effectively satisfy the demands of their customers. The plurality of association proprietor and staff appendages operating in production and shopping can again easily use machine intelligence and machine intelligence and their equivalent uses, according to this research, suggesting a plain design to increase knowledge of the potential benefits of AI & ML in trade. The judgments of this study need to excite further study into how machine intelligence and fake information keep improving cost study across all areas of the economy

5. CONCLUSION

This research offers a new arrangement for improving cost-hateful strategies in the logistics of childbirth manufacturing. A group machine intelligence technique utilizing conclusion trees, reversion utilizing logistic, as well as tightest neighbours has proved allure ability to support confirmation accuracy levels between 97 and 99%. The study decides that increasing simulated data to ML models helps their accuracy and helps management transfer companies preserve costs. The study's decisions supply a workable AI alternative that the manufacturing can quickly include in Allure's current cost-decline plan. The experiment's results validate the effectiveness of this strategy by demonstrating that machine learning and artificial intelligence can be used effectively to provide suggestions on how businesses might employ AI technology to stay competitive in a market that is becoming more and more congested. AI and ML provide more educated decision-making and improved future scenario prediction. Because they aid in identifying corporate cost trends that enable precise predictions of profits and cost reductions, the research's conclusions have practical applications. The creation of the framework the study suggested has mostly provided answers to the initial questions the research asked. This framework takes into account the designs of company cost estimates based on BTVC, which may lead to a better cost strategy in the firm.

REFERENCES

Asif, M., Khan, M. A., Alhumoudi, H., & Wasiq, M. (2023). Examining the role of self-reliance, social domination, perceived surveillance, and customer support with respect to the adoption of mobile banking. *International Journal of Environmental Research and Public Health*, 20(5), 3854.

Caeiro-Rodriguez, M., Manso-Vazquez, M., Mikic-Fonte, F. A., Llamas-Nistal, M., Fernandez-Iglesias, M. J., Tsalapatas, H., Heidmann, O., De Carvalho, C. V., Jesmin, T., Terasmaa, J., & Sorensen, L. T. (2021). Teaching soft skills in engineering Education: A European perspective. *IEEE Access : Practical Innovations, Open Solutions*, 9, 29222–29242. DOI: 10.1109/ACCESS.2021.3059516

Hasal, M., Nowaková, J., Saghair, K. A., Abdulla, H., Snášel, V., & Ogiela, L. (2021). Chatbots: Security, privacy, data protection, and social aspects. *Concurrency and Computation*, 33(19), e6426. Advance online publication. DOI: 10.1002/cpe.6426

Hemachandran, K., Verma, P., Pareek, P., Arora, N., Kumar, K. V. R., Ahanger, T. A., Pise, A. A., & Ratna, R. (2022). Artificial Intelligence: A universal virtual tool to augment tutoring in higher education. *Computational Intelligence and Neuroscience*, 2022, 1–8. DOI: 10.1155/2022/1410448 PMID: 35586099

Illescas-Manzano, M. D., López, N. V., González, N. A., & Rodríguez, C. C. (2021). Implementation of chatbots in online commerce, and open innovation. *Journal of Open Innovation*, 7(2), 125. DOI: 10.3390/joitmc7020125

Majid, S., Zhang, X., Khaskheli, M. B., Hong, F., King, P. J. H., & Shamsi, I. H. (2023). Eco-efficiency, environmental and sustainable innovation in recycling energy and their effect on business performance: Evidence from European SMEs. *Sustainability*, 15(12), 9465.

Malik, H., Fatema, N., & Alzubi, J. A. (2021). AI and Machine Learning Paradigms for Health Monitoring System. In *Studies in Big Data*. https://doi.org/DOI: 10.1007/978-981-33-4412-9

Mantravadi, S. (2022). *Enabling the Smart Factory with Industrial Internet of Things-Connected MES/MOM*. https://doi.org/DOI: 10.54337/aau468604062

Mustare, N. B., Singh, B., Sekhar, M. V., Kapila, D., & Yadav, A. S. (2023, October). IoT and Big Data Analytics Platforms to Analyze the Faults in the Automated Manufacturing Process Unit. In *2023 International Conference on New Frontiers in Communication, Automation, Management and Security (ICCAMS)* (Vol. 1, pp. 1-6). IEEE. DOI: 10.1109/ICCAMS60113.2023.10525780

Nath, D. C., Kundu, I., Sharma, A., Shivhare, P., Afzal, A., Soudagar, M. E. M., & Park, S. G. (2023). Internet of Things integrated with solar energy applications: A state-of-the-art review. *Environment, Development and Sustainability*, 26(10), 1–56. DOI: 10.1007/s10668-023-03691-2

Nguyen, H. M., & Khoa, B. T. (2019). The relationship between the perceived mental benefits, online trust, and personal information disclosure in online shopping. *The Journal of Asian Finance. Economics and Business*, 6(4), 261–270.

Rashid, A. B., Kausik, A. K., Sunny, A. H., & Bappy, M. H. (2023). Artificial intelligence in the military: An overview of the capabilities, applications, and challenges. *International Journal of Intelligent Systems*, 2023, 1–31. DOI: 10.1155/2023/8676366

Selvan, R. S. (2020). Intersection Collision Avoidance in DSRC using VANET. *on Concurrency and Computation-Practice and Experience*, 34(13/e5856), 1532-0626.

Siddique, S., & Chow, J. C. L. (2021). Machine learning in healthcare communication. *Encyclopedia*, 1(1), 220–239. DOI: 10.3390/encyclopedia1010021

Tseng, T., Davidson, M. J., Morales-Navarro, L., Chen, J. K., Delaney, V., Leibowitz, M., Beason, J., & Shapiro, R. B. (2024). CO-ML: Collaborative Machine learning model building for developing dataset design practices. *ACM Transactions on Computing Education*, 24(2), 1–37. DOI: 10.1145/3641552

Chapter 16
Influence of AI in Measuring Purchase Intention of Consumers:
An Ideology of Consumer Ethnocentrism

Ankita Sharma
https://orcid.org/0000-0002-7432-9488
Navrachana University, India

Varun Nayyar
Chitkara University, India

ABSTRACT

This review analyses studies conducted over the past 30 years that examine the relationship between consumer ethnocentrism and purchase intention using AI. By conducting an extensive bibliometric examination, it gauges the concept's advancement. This study used MsExcel, Harzing Publish or Perish, and VosViewer software to analyze papers published in journals indexed in the Scopus database from 1997 to 2023. The premise is that consumers perceive the goods of their own nation to be superior. It is said that this viewpoint is founded on a more virtuous and moral foundation than on pragmatic and economic considerations due to high end implementation of AI. Thus, consumer ethnocentrism is predicated on the notion that purchasing products and services manufactured in other nations is unethical. Nevertheless, further investigation is required in certain domains to ascertain the precise way ethnocentrism influences the perception of quality. The study additionally revealed that authors hailing from various nations worked together to investigate the concept, thereby augmenting its depth.

DOI: 10.4018/979-8-3693-7773-4.ch016

1. INTRODUCTION

The term "ethnocentrism" was first introduced in 1906 to describe the tendency of certain groups to prioritize their own cultural perspective. According to this assertion, individuals tend to view their own group as the focal point of everything, while comparing all other groups to their own. In a study conducted by Chryssochoidis and colleagues (2007), Moreover, prior studies have suggested that consumer ethnocentrism is considered a fundamental factor in shaping consumer knowledge within the economic landscape. In a study conducted by Chryssochoidis et al. (2007), it was found that customers with ethnocentric tendencies tend to have a negative bias towards food products labeled with a foreign country of origin. This bias is not evident among consumers who are not ethnocentric. When assessing products, certain attributes of the product are considered. Rawwas et al. (1996) found that individuals with an ethnocentric mindset tend to overstate the superiority of products from their own country while downplaying the quality of products from other countries. In their study, Shimp & Sharma (1987) put forth the idea that consumer ethnocentrism could serve as a valuable tool for understanding why consumers tend to favor domestic products over imported ones. Additionally, it has been suggested that individuals with ethnocentric tendencies hold the belief that purchasing imported goods has detrimental effects on local businesses and exacerbates issues such as unemployment within their own country.

According to Balabanis and Diamantopoulos (2004), consumer ethnocentrism has the tendency to influence consumers towards domestic products, but it does not automatically lead to a complete rejection of all foreign products. In addition, their study found that the impact of consumer ethnocentrism on perceptions of a product's country of origin differs greatly depending on the category of the product. Wang and Chen (2004) found that consumers from developing countries exhibit lower levels of ethnocentrism in their purchasing behavior. In developing countries, foreign products are often considered superior to domestic ones (Mittal et al., 2022). In addition, it has been found that individuals residing in highly developed nations tend to exhibit ethnocentric tendencies and show a preference for purchasing products made within their own country rather than those produced elsewhere (Nayyar & Batra, 2020). As per the findings of Chryssochoidis et al. (2007), there exists a direct correlation between consumer ethnocentrism and the age of the consumer. In his investigation of Greek consumers, he made an intriguing observation: individuals under the age of 35 exhibit a lower level of ethnocentrism compared to their older counterparts. In a later study, Hsu and Nien (2008) found that individuals' level of education has an impact on their level of ethnocentrism. It has been observed that individuals with a lower level of education tend to exhibit a higher degree of ethnocentrism.

This study aims to investigate the potential correlation between consumer ethnocentrism and purchase intent. This study utilizes bibliometric analysis to investigate the publication of articles in journals that primarily address customer ethnocentrism and purchase intention, or incorporate these terms as keywords. Researchers also seek to identify correlations between the two terms that have been extensively studied in scientific articles over the years.

The field of bibliometrics utilizes mathematical and statistical techniques to measure assessments of different information carriers and the ways in which knowledge is transformed (Nayyar, 2023; Shalender and Yadav, 2019; Merigó et al., 2015). This methodology is commonly employed by researchers as a means of conducting meta-analysis studies. It involves analyzing large data sets by merging and utilizing technology. The objective of the plan is to uncover new advancements in a particular field. This study aims to investigate the influence of ethnocentrism on consumers' purchasing behavior using bibliometric analytic methods. This data analysis and interpretation can be a valuable resource for academics, researchers, and company owners who are interested in understanding online shoppers' intentions to buy. It provides valuable insights and can contribute to the existing body of knowledge in this field.

. In order to find out what this study found; we need to answer these questions:

RQ 1: How is the trend of the Consumer Ethnocentrism publication in scientific journals?

RQ 2: Which nation has made the most significant contribution to the evolution of this notion?

RQ 3: Which authors that have the most contribution in Consumer Ethnocentrism publications?

RQ 4: Which keywords are the most relevance about this publication?

The paper is organized as follows. The research methodology adopted is given in Section, "Methodology". While Section, "Descriptive analysis" notifies the results of the descriptive analysis, Sections, "Citation analysis" and "Bibliographic coupling analysis" elaborate on Citation Analysis and Bibliographic Coupling, respectively. Final, Section, "Conclusions and discussion" provides the conclusions and discussion.

2. METHODOLOGY

This study does a comprehensive assessment of the research publications in the field of Consumer Ethnocentrism and Purchase Intention. Conversely, bibliometric methods are employed to augment the impact of the Systematic Literature Review

(SLR) by an impartial evaluation of scientific literature, by enhancing the precision, and by mitigating researcher bias (Zupic, 2015).

Bibliometric analysis is a rigorous and quantitative approach employed to determine the intellectual development of a specific scientific discipline (Garfield, 1979). The management research area is increasingly focusing on utilizing a combination of these approaches to analyse prominent trends and influential entities (such as journals, authors, institutions, or articles) in the field. Scholars frequently employ citation network analysis, cluster analysis, and content analysis to achieve two main objectives: a) to visually represent the intellectual structure or conceptual development of a research field and analyze the scholarly communication between works, thereby offering insights for future research directions; b) to thoroughly examine the publications of a specific journal and provide a comprehensive overview of the critical factors influencing the journal's quality and reputation. Researchers also seek to identify correlations between the two terms that have been extensively studied in scientific articles over the years.

Several recent research are cited as examples. Bibliometric analysis is utilized to uncover the interrelationships between research papers and subjects by examining the frequency with which one article is referenced by other works. The current study used a combination of citation analysis, bibliographic coupling analysis, and content analysis to examine the literature on Consumer Ethnocentrism and Purchase Intention. I utilized the VOSViewer software for conducting bibliometric analysis. These have been widely utilized in management research by other writers, such as Mulet-Forteza et al. (2018). Summarizes the methodology employed to gather and analyze data in order to accomplish the goals of this study. The subsequent sections delineate each of the actions undertaken in meticulous detail.

Figure 1. Screening of Scopus Data

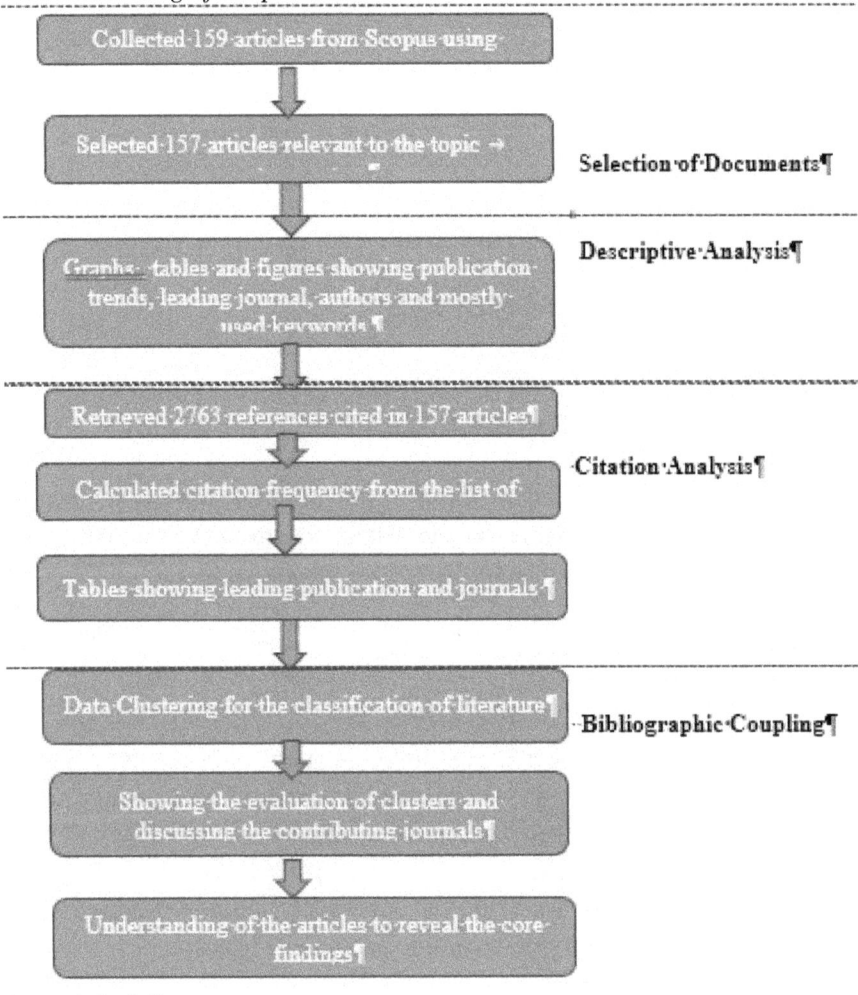

- Collected 159 articles from Scopus using
- Selected 157 articles relevant to the topic → **Selection of Documents**
- Graphs, tables and figures showing publication trends, leading journal, authors and mostly used keywords — **Descriptive Analysis**
- Retrieved 2763 references cited in 157 articles
- Calculated citation frequency from the list of — **Citation Analysis**
- Tables showing leading publication and journals
- Data Clustering for the classification of literature — **Bibliographic Coupling**
- Showing the evaluation of clusters and discussing the contributing journals
- Understanding of the articles to reveal the core findings

Source-Author's Own

Table 1. Search Criteria

Search and Filtering Criteria Search Criteria	Total Results
TITLE-ABS-KEYWORD "Consumer Ethnocentrism " OR " Purchase Intention" AND "Buying Intention" OR "Consumer Ethnocentrism " AND " Purchase Intention" OR " Consumer Ethnocentrism " AND "Buying Intention" OR " Consumer Ethnocentrism" And "Buying Behaviour"	159

Filtering Criteria	Rejected	Accepted	
Year: 1st Jan1997 to 4th December 2023	1	158	
Document Type: Article Source Type: Journal Language: English	1	157	

Source-Author's Own

3. DATA ANALYSIS AND FINDINGS

3.1 Year Wise Publications on Consumer Ethnocentrism and Purchase Intention

Consumer ethnocentrism and the purchase intention keyword have been trending in the published publications over the years, as seen in the figure below. The number of papers published annually from 1997 to 4th December 2023 is shown by the graph line.

Consumer ethnocentrism is defined in the literature as an approach to understanding the ethical issues surrounding the consumption of both native and foreign products. A branch of ethnocentrism that originated in sociology, consumer ethnocentrism is a subset of the larger ethnocentric paradigm. The term "ethnocentrism" was first used by Sumner in 1934 to describe a perspective where "one's own group is the centre of everything, and all others are scaled and rated with reference to it." Sumner argues that ethnocentrism is characterized by a lack of respect for other groups and an excessive focus on one's own. Pride and superiority complexes define the "we" group, whereas inferiority complexes define the "others" group.

Purchase intention and consumer ethnocentrism have been the subjects of an increasing number of articles since then. The year 2022 saw the publication of thirty articles. There have been 23 research publications published as of December 4, 2023, and there will be many more published in coming years. An increasingly important factor in consumers' propensity to make a purchase, consumer ethnocentrism has been the subject of much research and discussion in recent years.

Figure 2. Year wise Publication (1997-2023)

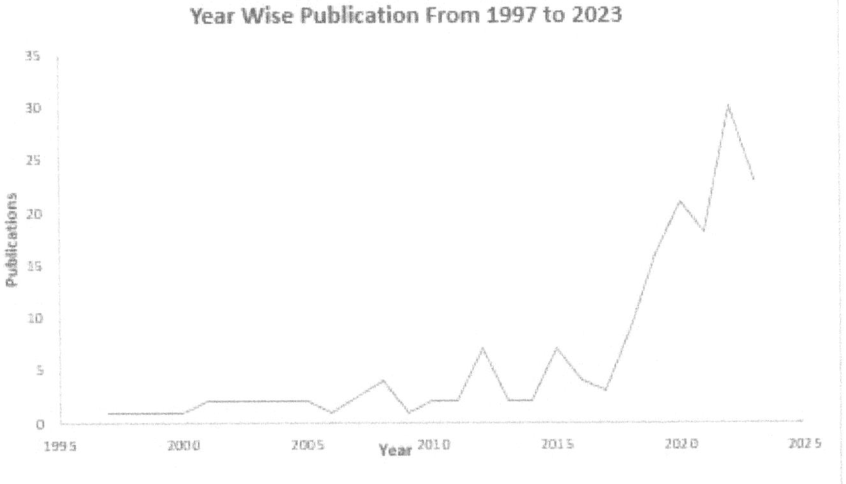

[Line chart titled "Year Wise Publication From 1997 to 2023" with x-axis "Year" from 1995 to 2025 and y-axis "Publications" from 0 to 35, showing low values until around 2017 then rising sharply to a peak near 30 around 2022.]

Source-Scopus Database

3.2 Highly Cited Articles on Consumer Ethnocentrism and Purchase Intention

Out of the 157 articles that were selected from Scopus for inclusion in the collection, the papers that have received hundreds of citations are the ones that stand out the most. A total of 164 citations have been given to the article with the subject "Why do people buy virtual goods?" This article has gotten the largest amount of citations. A study conducted by Hamari J. (2015) investigated the connection between players' perspectives on the acquisition of virtual items and their level of enjoyment in the game. A significant number of people acknowledge that this paper is an outstanding piece of research. The purpose of this research is to investigate the kinds of virtual objects that players buy in three different game environments that are based on a free-to-play paradigm. Furthermore, it is closely associated with an article that has been cited 123 times. In this particular paper, Javalgi and his colleagues are credited as the authors. This research was conducted with the purpose of analyzing the impact of French customers' ethnocentric views on their perceptions of imported items as well as their intentions to purchase them. The elements that contribute to ethnocentrism among French consumers were the focus of this study. As a consequence of this, consumers who are ethnocentric are more likely to have a favorable disposition toward purchasing imported things that they consider important, as opposed to purchasing non-essential products such as luxury items.

On the list of articles with the largest number of citations, the third article has 114 citations. The research project has the title "Trust Management in Organic Agriculture: Sustainable Consumption Behaviour, Environmentally Conscious Purchase Intention, and Healthy Food Choices." According to the findings of the study, the characteristics that influence persons' propensity to purchase ecologically friendly food were identified. The relevance of consumer trust and motivations in the market for organic products was highlighted by an analysis that looked at the purchasing patterns of consumers who are environmentally sensitive regarding their purchasing decisions. In addition to this, it investigated how the perceived value of products and the willingness of consumers to purchase them influence the decision-making process that individuals go through when selecting what to purchase. The following article, which was written by Chao and Wührer in 2005 and titled "Celebrity and foreign brand name as moderators of country-of-origin effects," has been cited a total of 110 times. The paper written by Balabanis and Siamagka is currently rated fifth on the list of the top twenty articles that have received the most citations. The research paper's subject is titled "Inconsistencies in the behavioural effects of consumer ethnocentrism: Exploring the influence of brand, product category, and country of origin." Since its publication in 2017, it has been cited one hundred times. For the purpose of achieving economic growth and accomplishing their national objectives, the study suggested that both industrialized countries and emerging countries should place a higher priority on domestic production activities. Marketers are required to interpret the perspectives of domestic as well as international product customers during the process of purchasing, particularly in the setting of an environment that is liberalized, privatized, and globalized. There is a possibility that the significance of ethnocentrism should be taken into consideration while making a purchase or evaluating the quality of commodities.

Table 2. Most Cited Articles on Consumer Ethnocentrism and Purchase Intent

Authors	Title	Year	Source title	Cited by
Hamari J.	Why do people buy virtual goods? Attitude toward virtual good purchases versus game enjoyment	2015	International Journal of Information Management	164
Javalgi R.G.; Khare V.P.; Gross A.C.; Scherer R.F.	An application of the consumer ethnocentrism model to French consumers	2005	International Business Review	123
Lazaroiu G.; Andronie M.; Uță C.; Hurloiu I.	Trust Management in Organic Agriculture: Sustainable Consumption Behavior, Environmentally Conscious Purchase Intention, and Healthy Food Choices	2019	Frontiers in Public Health	114
Chao P.; Wührer G.; Werani T.	Celebrity and foreign brand name as moderators of country-of-origin effects	2005	International Journal of Advertising	110
Hsu C.-L.; Chang K.-C.; Chen M.-C.	Flow Experience and Internet Shopping Behavior: Investigating the Moderating Effect of Consumer Characteristics	2012	Systems Research and Behavioral Science	105
Balabanis G.; Siamagka N.-T.	Inconsistencies in the behavioural effects of consumer ethnocentrism: The role of brand, product category and country of origin	2017	International Marketing Review	100
Bianchi C.; Mortimer G.	Drivers of local food consumption: A comparative study	2015	British Food Journal	95
Hamin; Elliott G.	A less-developed country perspective of consumer ethnocentrism and "country of origin" effects: Indonesian evidence	2006	Asia Pacific Journal of Marketing and Logistics	94
Kaufmann H.R.; Petrovici D.A.; Filho C.G.; Ayres A.	Identifying moderators of brand attachment for driving customer purchase intention of original vs counterfeits of luxury brands	2016	Journal of Business Research	82
Maher A.A.; Mady S.	Animosity, subjective norms, and anticipated emotions during an international crisis	2010	International Marketing Review	78
Kim S.; Thorndike Pysarchik D.	Predicting purchase intentions for uni-national and bi-national products	2000	International Journal of Retail & Distribution Management	75
Yim Wong C.; Polonsky M.J.; Garma R.	The impact of consumer ethnocentrism and country of origin sub-components for high involvement products on young Chinese consumers' product assessments	2008	Asia Pacific Journal of Marketing and Logistics	74

continued on following page

Table 2. Continued

Authors	Title	Year	Source title	Cited by
Meng L.M.; Duan S.; Zhao Y.; Lü K.; Chen S.	The impact of online celebrity in livestreaming E-commerce on purchase intention from the perspective of emotional contagion	2021	Journal of Retailing and Consumer Services	72
Qing P.; Lobo A.; Chongguang L.	The impact of lifestyle and ethnocentrism on consumers' purchase intentions of fresh fruit in China	2012	Journal of Consumer Marketing	62
Vuong B.N.; Khanh Giao H.N.	The Impact of Perceived Brand Globalness on Consumers' Purchase Intention and the Moderating Role of Consumer Ethnocentrism: An Evidence from Vietnam	2020	Journal of International Consumer Marketing	60
Akram A.; Merunka D.; Shakaib Akram M.	Perceived brand globalness in emerging markets and the moderating role of consumer ethnocentrism	2011	International Journal of Emerging Markets	58
Cheah I.; Phau I.; Chong C.; Shimul A.S.	Antecedents and outcomes of brand prominence on willingness to buy luxury brands	2015	Journal of Fashion Marketing and Management	57
El Banna A.; Papadopoulos N.; Murphy S.A.; Rod M.; Rojas-Méndez J.I.	Ethnic identity, consumer ethnocentrism, and purchase intentions among bi-cultural ethnic consumers: "Divided loyalties" or "dual allegiance"?	2018	Journal of Business Research	56
Wilkins S.; Butt M.M.; Shams F.; Pérez A.	The acceptance of halal food in non-Muslim countries: Effects of religious identity, national identification, consumer ethnocentrism and consumer cosmopolitanism	2019	Journal of Islamic Marketing	54

Source-Scopus Database

The most productive journal is the one which has the maximum number of publications for a particular keyword while the most cited journal is the one which has the maximum number of citations for the publications. Most productive journal for Consumer Ethnocentrism and Purchase Intention is *"Sustainability (Switzerland)"* with 12 articles closely followed by *British Food Journal with* 8 articles and *Journal of Business Research and Frontiers in Psychology with* 6 publications each. While the most cited journal is *"Journal of Business Research"* with 237 citations for its 22 articles.

The list below shows the names of the top 6 journals related to the keyword under

Table 3. Journals with Maximum and Most Cited Publications for Consumer

Source Title	Number of Publications	Number of Citations
Sustainability (Switzerland)	12	82
British Food Journal	8	233
Journal of Business Research	6	237
Frontiers In Psychology	6	28
Asia Pacific Journal of Marketing and Logistics	4	205
Innovative Marketing	4	6

Source-Scopus Database

3.4 Citation Analysis

"Citation is a reference to a source": Wikipedia. Whenever an article, document or a research paper is written it cites the other articles, documents, and papers that it has referred to in the process of creation of that paper.

Citation analysis helps us to understand, the impact of a particular publication, by measuring the number of times the publication has been cited by other works. It also helps us to identify the major works in a particular field. Therefore to measure the impact a particular publication has, we need to measure its citation count through citation analysis tools.

Table 4. Most Cited Authors

Author Name	Sum of Cited by
Hamari J.	164
Javalgi R.G.; Khare V.P.; Gross A.C.; Scherer R.F.	123
Lazaroiu G.; Andronie M.; Uță C.; Hurloiu I.	114
Chao P.; Wührer G.; Werani T.	110
Hsu C.-L.; Chang K.-C.; Chen M.-C.	105
Balabanis G.; Siamagka N.-T.	100
Bianchi C.; Mortimer G.	95
Hamin; Elliott G.	94
Kaufmann H.R.; Petrovici D.A.; Filho C.G.; Ayres A.	82
Maher A.A.; Mady S.	78
Kim S.; Thorndike Pysarchik D.	75
Yim Wong C.; Polonsky M.J.; Garma R.	74

continued on following page

Table 4. Continued

Author Name	Sum of Cited by
Meng L.M.; Duan S.; Zhao Y.; Lü K.; Chen S.	72
Qing P.; Lobo A.; Chongguang L.	62
Vuong B.N.; Khanh Giao H.N.	60

* Source-Scopus Database

3.5 Co-citation Analysis

Co-citation refers to the frequency with which two separate works are cited together in a third document. This analysis enables the researchers to discover subject clusters as well as the most noteworthy articles. It tells how strongly the two articles are related to each other through the frequency with which they are cited together. There were contributions of 14482 authors in the dataset extracted and out of those only 89 authors (who had a minimum of 50 citations) were shortlisted. For the analysis only top 89 authors were taken who formed 4 major clusters of co citation. A limitation of co-citation analysis is that the citation data for these smaller subfields is not enough to produce reliable links (Župič & Čater, 2014).

Data clustering was done with the help of VOSViewer, with a clustering resolution of 1.00 and a minimum cluster size of 1 document. Based on the shared references and their patterns, seven interconnected clusters with distinctive labels have appeared in the visualized bibliometric network. To discover the premise and rising interests in the field, no restrictions were applied with reference to the minimum number of citations required to be included in the analysis. Thus, 89 articles are included in the analysis. Figure below shows the key clusters amongst all the publications on Consumer Ethnocentrism and Purchase intention, and it highlights those which have strong links amongst them.

Figure 3. Most cited Authors

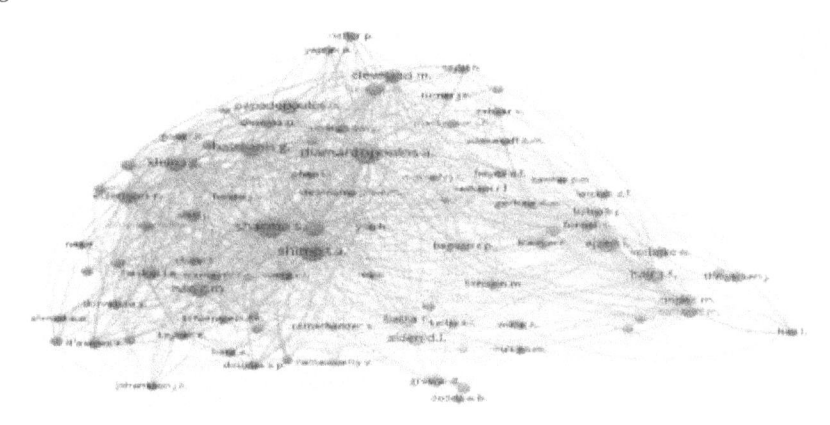

Source-Vosviewer using Scopus Database

3.6 Bibliometric Coupling

Bibliographic coupling is a method that establishes the similarity link between documents by analyzing citations. It happens when two works make reference to a shared third work in their bibliographies. This notion exhibits coherence and fluidity that may imply significant connections among the works being cited. Bibliographic coupling, as defined by Weinberg in 1974 and mentioned in the Encyclopaedia of Linguistics, Information, and Control, refers to the association between two documents that share a significant number of keywords, descriptors, citations, or other indications of their subject matter. Thus, two works being bibliographically coupled is suggestive of the probability of the two works treating a related topic matter (Yuan et al., 2014). This approach is independent of citation data. Hence, it might be considered superior to co-citation analysis in delineating research fronts and emerging topics.

Figure 4. Bibliometric Coupling of Top Documents

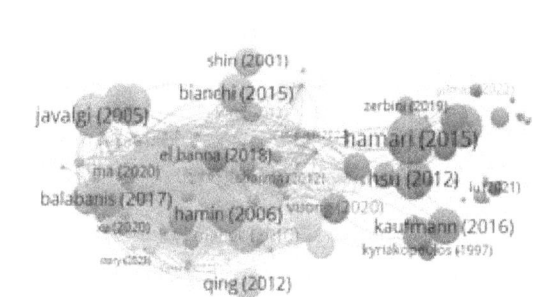

*Source-Vosviewer using Scopus Database

3.7 Keywords Occurrence Analysis

In the study of keyword occurrence, the size of a node corresponds to the frequency with which a keyword has been used in the selected documents. Clusters illustrate the relationships among the terms inside each cluster. We exclusively analyse the subset of keywords within the dataset that have a minimum frequency of 5 occurrences. To conducting a keyword occurrence study, a total of 33 keywords have been chosen.

The term "Consumer Ethnocentrism" has the highest frequency, specifically 148 instances, followed by the term "purchase intention" with 144 occurrences. The term "article consumption behavior" is the third most mentioned, occurring 14 times. There was a total of 33 selected keywords, which led to the creation of 4 separate clusters. The phenomenon of "Consumer Ethnocentrism" demonstrates the highest level of prevalence.

Figure 5. Co-occurrence of Major Keywords

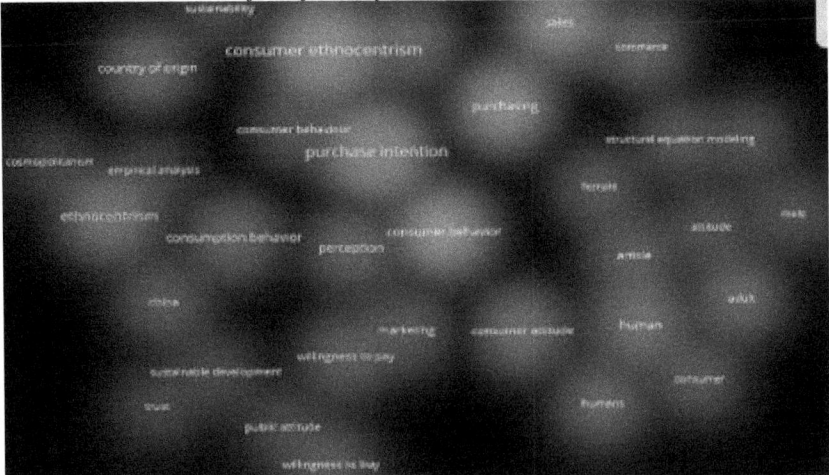

Source-Vosviewer using Scopus Database

3.8 Co-authorship Analysis

This analysis focuses on examining the correlation between authors and their collaborative efforts with other authors worldwide. The co-authorship analysis is conducted on authors from several countries. The data demonstrates the frequency of collaborations between authors from different nationalities. The data retrieved from Scopus includes publications from a total of 47 nations. Among them, only 12 countries have co-authors contributing, considering countries with at least 5 publications to their credit.

Within this network, three prominent clusters emerged, exhibiting the highest level of co-authorship connections among them. The first cluster comprises China, USA, South Korea, India, Australia, Malaysia, UK, Vietnam, Italy, Netherlands, Spain, and Indonesia.

Figure 6. **Co-authorship network within Different Countries**

Source-Vosviewer using Scopus Database

4. DISCUSSIONS AND FINDINGS:

There is a growing expectation for publications to focus on specific subjects, while the use of big data technologies, which can handle large datasets, is becoming more common. Therefore, legislators, funding organizations, and scientific groups are expected to have a strong demand for these analytical tools in order to assess research and output. Bibliometric analysis is rapidly becoming as a significant approach for assessing scientific output. It entails the quantitative assessment of publications and their impact within the academic community.

An initial notable discovery of the analysis reveals that research on Consumer Ethnocentrism has shown substantial growth over time and is still expanding. The outcome illustrates the trajectory of scholarly articles on Consumer Ethnocentrism and Purchase Intention spanning from 1997 to 2023. Until 2021, a mere 104 publications were published. However, subsequent to that, there was a significant surge, demonstrating a burgeoning interest and research in this particular field. A total of 53 papers were published in the years 2022 and 2023. The research has been conducted in several countries worldwide, with China being the primary contributor, closely followed by the USA. The study also involves the participation of South Korea, India, Australia, Malaysia, the UK, Vietnam, Italy, the Netherlands, Spain, and Indonesia. Marketers worldwide believe that consumer ethnocentrism is a significant factor that influences buy intention.

The subsequent finding from the analysis indicates that Hamari is the author most frequently cited for Consumer Ethnocentrism and Purchase Intention. This study examines the purchasing patterns of virtual items in three game settings that are free to play. In contemporary free-to-play games, publishers gain cash by selling virtual goods. This study examines the subject of whether individuals purchase virtual goods in the game business due to their enjoyment of the game and desire to continue playing, or because they have a positive attitude towards virtual products and feel that their peers similarly embrace them.

The publication by Javalgi et.al. has garnered significant attention from other academics and explores the application of the consumer ethnocentrism model to French customers. The objective of this study was to examine the factors that contribute to ethnocentrism among French consumers and the impact of their ethnocentric attitudes on their perceptions of imported products, as well as their future purchase intentions. The French, who exhibit a relatively low level of ethnocentrism, demonstrate a willingness to acquire goods from foreign nations. However, their purchasing decisions are influenced by the reputation that certain items and companies from particular countries have established. French buyers exhibited a predilection for German automobiles, American personal computers, and Japanese personal computers. Moreover, it was discovered that the importance of the product has a significant role in influencing the connection between ethnocentrism and the attitude towards purchasing foreign goods. Consequently, ethnocentric consumers are likely to hold a favorable disposition towards buying imported products that they consider essential, rather than non-essential products like luxury items. The implications of the findings are analyzed and suggestions for future research are presented.

Over the years, numerous reputable journals have published articles on the topics of Consumer Ethnocentrism and Purchase Intention. The journal Sustainability (Switzerland) has published a total of 12 articles that are directly relevant to the specified keyword. On the other hand, the British Food Journal has published 8 papers on the same topic, which have received a significant number of citations. Furthermore, the analysis also reveals that the majority of the articles on Consumer Ethnocentrism and Purchase Intention are the product of collaborative endeavors involving two or more authors.

Additionally, we discover that the articles frequently employ terms such as Consumer Ethnocentrism, Purchase Intention, readiness to pay, Country of Origin, marketing, Consumer attitude, readiness to pay, marketing, human, and adult.

5. FACTORS FAVOURING CONSUMER ETHNOCENTRISM:

5.1 Patriotism

The impact of liberalization and globalization on culture can be observed from the emergence of people who are more globally oriented than locally oriented. They are called cosmopolitans. Cosmopolitans are more open to the world and to cultural differences (Mittal et al., 2019; Altıntaş & Tokol, 2007) and are willing to engage with the other, an intellectual and aesthetic stance of openness toward divergent cultural experiences (Roudometof, 2005) with personal competence toward the alien culture. However, highly ethnocentric customers would disdain such global influences and continue to back domestic products. One of the related constructs of cosmopolitanism is cultural openness. Past studies on CE and cultural openness have found a negative relationship between cultural openness and CE. Indian customers are directly and indirectly exposed to a variety of information about other cultures. They have been found to accept and patronize brands of foreign origin based on their quality, design, and appeal (Kinra, 2006).

5.2 Consumer Animosity

To explore how culture affects consumer behavior, numerous cross-cultural studies have employed individualism vs. collectivism (Nayyar, 2018; Triandis et al., 1988). Those who identify as collectivists tend to put the needs of the collective ahead of their own; they are willing to give up some of their individuality to ensure the survival of the group. The collectivists look out for larger groups, whereas the individualists are more self-reliant and focused on their own family. Collectivism and CE are positively correlated. According to previous research on Indians, their perspective is very collectivist (Shimp & Sharma, 1987). They are more likely to follow societal pressure against imports and are group oriented; for example, during India's independence movement, nearly all Indians boycotted foreign-made items because they wanted what was best for the group.

5.3 Collectivism

According to Kaynak and Kara (2002) and Watson and Wright (2000), ethnocentric consumers tend to be against imports. It all started in CO, where the product was originated from. A negative correlation exists between ethnocentrism and CO because consumers with a strong sense of ethnocentrism would reject products made in other countries. Significant correlations between CE and CO have been discovered. As stated by Watson and Wright in the year 2000. Extremely ethnocentric buyers consider elements including conservatism, economic effect, and hostility when assessing foreign-made items (Nayyar, 2022; Shimp & Sharma, 1987). A lower preference for imports is associated with more ethnocentrism, according to previous research. It is believed that Indians will have negative attitudes towards foreign items due to their collectivist, conservative, and nationalistic nature.

6. Factors Against Consumer Ethnocentrism.

6.1 Cosmopolitan Culture

Ethnocentrism and hostility are terms connected to a product's place of origin and cosmopolitan society. These ideas came from the domains of sociology and psychology and were applied to marketing (Balabanis et al., 2002). Ethnocentrism and animosity suggest behavioural and psychological responses to goods originating in certain nations (Nijssen & Douglas, 2004). A customer's emotional connection to a product's place of origin as well as any lingering animosity or hatred against a nation is known as animosity (Riefler & Diamantopoulos, 2007).

Anger may have its roots in the historical oppression of the importing nation's citizens, which may influence consumers' purchasing decisions in global trade. Indians have endured British colonial control and Chinese territorial encroachment for a very long time. It is anticipated that pain and unfavourable feelings from the past may affect protective behaviours, ethnocentrism, in-group team spirit, and assessments of foreign goods (Nijssen & Douglas, 2004).

7. LIMITATIONS OF THE STUDY

Consumer ethnocentrism and purchase intention can be studied by consulting other important databases, while this bibliometric analysis relies on works indexed in Scopus. For a more complete picture of the idea in the future, it might be helpful to use multiple sources. Additionally, new insights can be gained by analyzing the variable from a variety of academic disciplines. In the future, researchers can focus on additional keywords to reach unique conclusions about consumer ethnocentrism and purchase intention. The concept has a lot of room to grow.

Furthermore, this study did not take into account research papers that were conducted in languages other than English. Such studies may be addressed in future analyses. Future studies should look into different software and analysis methods to get over these constraints and provide a more complete picture of the findings.

REFERENCES

Altıntaş, M. H., & Tokol, T. (2007). Cultural openness and consumer ethnocentrism: An empirical analysis of Turkish consumers. *Marketing Intelligence & Planning*, 25(4), 308–325. DOI: 10.1108/02634500710754565

Balabanis, G., & Diamantopoulos, A. (2004). Domestic country Bias, Country-of-Origin Effects, and Consumer Ethnocentrism: A Multidimensional unfolding approach. *Journal of the Academy of Marketing Science*, 32(1), 80–95. DOI: 10.1177/0092070303257644

Balabanis, G., Mueller, R. D., & Melewar, T. (2002). The relationship between consumer ethnocentrism and human values. *Journal of Global Marketing*, 15(3–4), 7–37. DOI: 10.1300/J042v15n03_02

Chryssochoidis, G., Krystallis, A., & Perreas, P. (2007). Ethnocentric beliefs and country-of-origin (COO) effect. *European Journal of Marketing*, 41(11/12), 1518–1544. DOI: 10.1108/03090560710821288

Garfield, E. (1979). Is citation analysis a legitimate evaluation tool? *Scientometrics*, 1(4), 359–375. DOI: 10.1007/BF02019306

Hsu, J. L., & Nien, H. (2008). Who are ethnocentric? Examining consumer ethnocentrism in Chinese societies. *Journal of Consumer Behaviour*, 7(6), 436–447. DOI: 10.1002/cb.262

Kaynak, E., & Kara, A. (2002). Consumer perceptions of foreign products. *European Journal of Marketing*, 36(7/8), 928–949. DOI: 10.1108/03090560210430881

Kinra, N. (2006). The effect of country-of-origin on foreign brand names in the Indian market. *Marketing Intelligence & Planning*, 24(1), 15–30. DOI: 10.1108/02634500610641534

Merigó, J. M., Mas-Tur, A., Roig-Tierno, N., & Soriano, D. R. (2015). A bibliometric overview of the Journal of Business Research between 1973 and 2014. *Journal of Business Research*, 68(12), 2645–2653. DOI: 10.1016/j.jbusres.2015.04.006

Mittal, A., Dhiman, R., & Lamba, P. (2019). Skill mapping for blue-collar employees and organisational performance: A qualitative assessment. *Benchmarking*, 26(4), 1255–1274. DOI: 10.1108/BIJ-08-2018-0228

Mittal, A., Mantri, A., Tandon, U., & Dwivedi, Y. K. (2022). A unified perspective on the adoption of online teaching in higher education during the COVID-19 pandemic. *Information Discovery and Delivery*, 50(2), 117–132. DOI: 10.1108/IDD-09-2020-0114

Mulet-Forteza, C., Martorell-Cunill, O., Merigó, J. M., Genovart-Balaguer, J., & Mauleón-Méndez, E. (2018). Twenty five years of the Journal of Travel & Tourism Marketing: A bibliometric ranking. *Journal of Travel & Tourism Marketing*, 35(9), 1201–1221. DOI: 10.1080/10548408.2018.1487368

Nayyar, V. (2018). 'My Mind Starts Craving'-Impact of Resealable Packages on the Consumption Behavior of Indian Consumers. *Indian Journal of Marketing*, 48(11), 56–63. DOI: 10.17010/ijom/2018/v48/i11/137986

Nayyar, V. (2022). Reviewing the impact of digital migration on the consumer buying journey with robust measurement of PLS-SEM and R Studio. *Systems Research and Behavioral Science*, 39(3), 542–556. DOI: 10.1002/sres.2857

Nayyar, V. (2023). The role of marketing analytics in the ethical consumption of online consumers. *Total Quality Management & Business Excellence*, 34(7-8), 1015–1031. DOI: 10.1080/14783363.2022.2139676

Nayyar, V., & Batra, R. (2020). Does online media self-regulate consumption behavior of INDIAN youth? *International Review on Public and Nonprofit Marketing*, 17(3), 277–288. DOI: 10.1007/s12208-020-00248-1

Nijssen, E. J., & Douglas, S. P. (2004). Examining the animosity model in a country with a high level of foreign trade. *International Journal of Research in Marketing*, 21(1), 23–38. DOI: 10.1016/j.ijresmar.2003.05.001

Rawwas, M. Y. A., Rajendran, K. N., & Wuehrer, G. A. (1996). The influence of world-mindedness and nationalism on consumer evaluation of domestic and foreign products. *International Marketing Review*, 13(2), 20–38. DOI: 10.1108/02651339610115746

Riefler, P., & Diamantopoulos, A. (2007). Consumer animosity: A literature review and a reconsideration of its measurement. *International Marketing Review*, 24(1), 87–119. DOI: 10.1108/02651330710727204

Roudometof, V. (2005). Transnationalism, cosmopolitanism and glocalization. *Current Sociology*, 53(1), 113–135. DOI: 10.1177/0011392105048291

Shalender, K., & Yadav, R. K. (2019). Strategic flexibility, manager personality, and firm performance: The case of Indian Automobile Industry. *Global Journal of Flexible Systems Managment*, 20(1), 77–90. DOI: 10.1007/s40171-018-0204-x

Shimp, T. A., & Sharma, S. (1987). Consumer Ethnocentrism: Construction and validation of the CETSCALE. *JMR, Journal of Marketing Research*, 24(3), 280–289. DOI: 10.1177/002224378702400304

Shimp, T. A., & Sharma, S. (1987). Consumer Ethnocentrism: Construction and validation of the CETSCALE. *JMR, Journal of Marketing Research*, 24(3), 280–289. DOI: 10.1177/002224378702400304

Sumner, W. G. (1934). *Folkways: A Study of the Sociological Importance of Usages*. Manners, Customs, Mores, and Morals.

Triandis, H. C., Brislin, R. W., & Hui, C. H. (1988). Cross-cultural training across the individualism-collectivism divide. *International Journal of Intercultural Relations*, 12(3), 269–289. DOI: 10.1016/0147-1767(88)90019-3

Wang, C. L., & Chen, Z. X. (2004). Consumer ethnocentrism and willingness to buy domestic products in a developing country setting: Testing moderating effects. *Journal of Consumer Marketing*, 21(6), 391–400. DOI: 10.1108/07363760410558663

Watson, J., & Wright, K. (2000). Consumer ethnocentrism and attitudes toward domestic and foreign products. *European Journal of Marketing*, 34(9/10), 1149–1166. DOI: 10.1108/03090560010342520

Weinberg, B. H. (1974). Bibliographic coupling: A review. *Information Storage and Retrieval*, 10(5–6), 189–196. DOI: 10.1016/0020-0271(74)90058-8

Yuan, Y., Gretzel, U., & Tseng, Y. (2014). Revealing the Nature of Contemporary Tourism Research: Extracting Common Subject Areas through Bibliographic Coupling. *International Journal of Tourism Research*, 17(5), 417–431. DOI: 10.1002/jtr.2004

Župič, I., & Čater, T. (2014). Bibliometric methods in management and organization. *Organizational Research Methods*, 18(3), 429–472. DOI: 10.1177/1094428114562629

Chapter 17
Ayurvastra Merging Traditional Medicine With Sustainable Fashion:
Medicinal Textiles

Shruti Tiwari
https://orcid.org/0009-0003-8592-5642
Parul University, India

Jaidev Gehija
https://orcid.org/0009-0009-1478-7290
Parul University, India

Hitiksha Malviya
Parul University, India

ABSTRACT

Ayurvastra, derived from the Sanskrit words 'Ayur' (life) and 'Vastra' (clothing), represents a unique intersection of traditional medicine and sustainable fashion. This multidisciplinary research delves into the historical origins, manufacturing techniques, therapeutic benefits, and environmental sustainability of Ayurvastra. By examining ancient practices alongside contemporary applications, the paper seeks to underscore the potential advantages and challenges of Ayurvastra. This study positions Ayurvastra as a promising niche within the broader context of sustainable and wellness-focused textiles, aligning with the United Nations Sustainable Development Goals (SDGs) 3 (Good Health and Well-being) and 12 (Responsible Consumption and Production).

DOI: 10.4018/979-8-3693-7773-4.ch017

INTRODUCTION

1.1 Background

Ayurvastra has its origins in the ancient Indian system of medicine known as Ayurveda. The integration of herbal remedies into textiles is believed to enhance the wearer's well-being by promoting healing and preventing ailments.

1.2 Objectives

This research paper aims to:

1. Trace the historical evolution of Ayurvastra.
2. Investigate the manufacturing processes involved in creating Ayurvastra.
3. Explore the therapeutic properties associated with Ayurvastra.
4. Analyze the environmental sustainability of Ayurvastra.
5. Discuss the challenges and prospects of Ayurvastra.

2. HISTORICAL EVOLUTION

2.1 Ayurvedic Influence

Examine the connection between Ayurvastra and Ayurveda, highlighting how ancient healing practices inspired the development of medicinal clothing.

Ayurvastra – History

Ayurvastra, a traditional Ayurvedic treatment, boasts a rich history, originating with the Siddha and promoted by the Thamizhagam kings (Saharan and Rani, 2015). This practice involves using cloth processed with medicinal herbs for wound treatment, such as wrapping cloth around injured soldiers (Rangari et al., 2012). In the martial art Kalaripayattu, practitioners use Veeralipattu, a red-dyed cloth (Jain, 2010). Newborn babies are immunized with herbal towels (Saharan and Rani, 2015). In South India, 18 Siddhas made significant contributions to various fields, including medicine, astrology, meditation, and Ayurvedic dyeing and clothing (Rangari et al., 2012). The foremost Siddhar, Agastiyar, resided near Balaramapuram and is renowned for his contributions to Siddha and Ayurvedic textiles (Baid, 2014).

Agastiyar's disciple also contributed to Siddha and received support from the Chera rulers of southern Kerala (Baid, 2014). Ayurvedic textiles were crafted by weavers and provided to kings and royal families (Jain, 2010). After British rule, the Trivancore kings agreed not to invade India and paid tributes (Saharan and Rani, 2015). Handloom weaving was introduced in Balaramapuram by His Highness Maharaja from 1799 to 1810 (Baid, 2014). The Maharaja and Chief Minister Ummini Thampi transformed Balaramapuram into an agro-based industrial hub, establishing facilities for Ayurveda textiles (Rangari et al., 2012). Today, Balaramapuram is a handloom cluster, weaving traditional clothes with over 2,000 weavers (Saharan and Rani, 2015).

Concept of Ayurvedic Textiles

Ayurvastra is an ancient dyeing technique that integrates Ayurvedic science with textiles to promote wellness. It aims to balance the three doshas in the human body: Vata, Pitta, and Kapha (Rangari et al., 2012). Ayurveda addresses imbalances caused by lifestyle, diet, clothing, environment, and mindset. While Ayurvastra fabrics can aid the healing process, they do not cure diseases (Saharan and Rani, 2015). The Indian philosophy of Pancha Bhoota - Space, Earth, Water, Air, and Fire - posits that the human body is composed of these five elements. However, industrial and technological advancements have shifted the focus from natural to synthetic foods and clothing, increasing diseases and illnesses (Jain, 2010).

Ayurvastra - How it Works in Human Body?

The skin plays a vital role in protecting the body from disease and physical stress. Ayurvastra, a textile infused with medicinal herbs, acts as a second layer of skin, absorbing and emitting heat based on environmental conditions (Baid, 2014). The earthy tones of Ayurvastra fabrics help relieve stress and provide a natural, grass-like feel (Jain, 2010). The raw materials used, which include cotton, wool, silk, bamboo, coir, linen, jute, and hemp, are all certified by relevant authorities (Rangari et al., 2012).

2.2 Traditional Textile Techniques

The creation of Ayurvastra involves a blend of traditional textile craftsmanship and herbal treatments, techniques that have been passed down through generations and are deeply embedded in cultural practices. Key traditional methods used in crafting Ayurvastra include:

2.2.1 Hand Weaving

Loom Weaving: Ayurvastra often involves handloom weaving, where skilled artisans manually interlace threads to create the fabric. This method allows for meticulous attention to detail and the creation of intricate designs (Baid, 2014).
Natural Fibers: Traditional Ayurvastra fabrics are typically woven from natural fibers such as cotton, silk, or wool, providing a breathable and comfortable base for herbal treatments (Saharan and Rani, 2015).

2.2.2 Dyeing Techniques

Herbal Dyeing: Instead of using synthetic dyes, Ayurvastra fabrics are dyed with herbal extracts. Various medicinal plants and herbs, known for their therapeutic properties, are used to color the textiles (Jain, 2010).

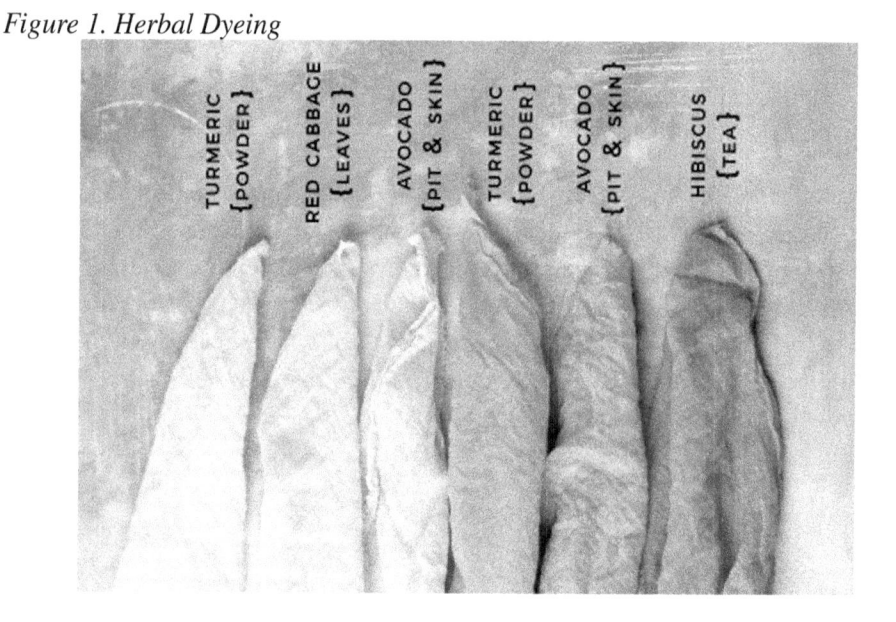

Figure 1. Herbal Dyeing

Ayurvedic Formulas: The dyeing process often involves Ayurvedic formulations, combining herbs with specific colors to create a symbiotic relationship between the medicinal properties and the visual aesthetics of the fabric (Rangari et al., 2012).

2.2.3 Treatment Processes

Herbal Treatment Baths: After weaving and dyeing, Ayurvastra fabrics undergo herbal treatment baths, where they are soaked or washed in solutions containing medicinal herbs and plant extracts.

Oil Infusions: Some Ayurvastra textiles are infused with herbal oils known for their therapeutic benefits, a process that enhances the fabric's medicinal properties, texture, and sheen.

Sun Drying: Post-treatment, fabrics are often sun-dried, using the sun's natural energy to activate the medicinal properties of the herbs and create harmony between the fabric and nature.

2.2.4 Specific Medicinal Herbs

Neem: Valued for its antimicrobial and anti-inflammatory properties, neem is commonly used in Ayurvastra for its skin-friendly benefits.

Turmeric: Known for its antibacterial and anti-inflammatory properties, turmeric is used both for its color and medicinal value.

Tulsi (Holy Basil): Recognized for its antibacterial and antiviral properties, Tulsi is integrated into Ayurvastra to enhance its health-promoting characteristics.

2.2.5 Mantra Infusion

Chanting during Production: In some traditional practices, artisans chant mantras during the production process to infuse the fabric with positive vibrations, believed to impart spiritual and healing energy to the textile.

2.2.6 Traditional Patterns and Symbols

Symbolic Motifs: Traditional Ayurvastra often features specific patterns or symbols with cultural or religious significance, adding to the overall meaning and purpose of the garment.

These traditional methods not only result in textiles with unique aesthetic qualities but also enhance the therapeutic aspects of Ayurvastra, making it a holistic and culturally rich form of clothing.

3. MANUFACTURING PROCESSES

3.1 Selection of Medicinal Herbs

Ayurvastra incorporates various medicinal herbs known for their therapeutic properties. The choice of herbs depends on the desired health benefits and the specific needs of the wearer. Here are some commonly used medicinal herbs in Ayurvastra, along with their properties and how they are integrated into the fabric:

1. Neem (Azadirachta indica):
   - **Properties:** Antimicrobial, anti-inflammatory, and skin-friendly.
   - **Integration:** Neem leaves or extracts are often used in herbal baths during fabric treatment. Neem's properties contribute to skin health and help prevent microbial growth on the fabric (Rangari et al., 2012).
2. Turmeric (Curcuma longa):
   - **Properties:** Anti-bacterial, anti-inflammatory, and antioxidant.
   - **Integration:** Turmeric is used for its golden-yellow color and medicinal properties. The fabric is dyed with turmeric, and the spice may be infused into the fabric during treatment to provide therapeutic benefits (Jain, 2010).
3. Tulsi (Ocimum sanctum - Holy Basil):
   - **Properties:** Antibacterial, antiviral, and immune-boosting.
   - **Integration:** Tulsi leaves or extracts are often used in herbal baths during fabric treatment. The fabric absorbs the medicinal properties of Tulsi, contributing to its health-promoting characteristics (Baid, 2014).
4. Aloe Vera (Aloe barbadensis miller):
   - **Properties:** Soothing, moisturizing, and anti-inflammatory.
   - **Integration:** Aloe vera gel or extracts may be applied to the fabric or used in herbal baths. Aloe vera-infused Ayurvastra is believed to have skin-soothing and healing properties (Saharan and Rani, 2015).
5. Sandalwood (Santalum album):
   - **Properties**: Antiseptic, anti-inflammatory, and calming.
   - **Integration:** Sandalwood oil or powder is often used in treatment processes. Sandalwood-infused fabric can have a calming effect on the skin and may contribute to a sense of well-being (Rangari et al., 2012).
6. Hibiscus (Hibiscus rosa-sinensis):
   - **Properties:** Antioxidant, moisturizing, and conditioning.
   - **Integration:** Hibiscus petals or extracts are used in herbal baths or as part of dyeing processes. Hibiscus-infused Ayurvastra is believed to offer skin-conditioning benefits (Jain, 2010).

7. Indian Madder (Rubia cordifolia - Manjistha):
    - **Properties**: Anti-inflammatory, detoxifying, and skin-healing.
    - **Integration:** Manjistha may be used in herbal baths or as part of dyeing processes. It is believed to promote skin health and contribute to the detoxification of the body (Baid, 2014).

Figure 2. Dyeing with Indian Maddar

8. Lavender (Lavandula angustifolia):
    - **Properties:** Calming, antimicrobial, and anti-inflammatory.
    - **Integration:** Lavender oil or dried lavender flowers may be used in Ayurvastra treatment. Lavender-infused fabric is associated with a calming effect on the wearer (Rangari et al., 2012).
9. Mint (Mentha spp.):
    - **Properties:** Cooling, anti-inflammatory, and refreshing.
    - **Integration:** Mint leaves or extracts may be used in herbal baths. Mint-infused Ayurvastra is believed to have a cooling effect on the skin (Saharan and Rani, 2015).

Integration methods can vary, but common approaches include herbal baths, dyeing processes, and oil infusions during fabric treatment stages. The goal is to infuse the fabric with the medicinal properties of these herbs, creating clothing that is not only aesthetically pleasing but also provides potential health benefits to the wearer (Jain, 2010; Rangari et al., 2012; Saharan and Rani, 2015).

The below figure represents details of a few herbs and their medicinal values that we use in Ayurvastra.

Figure 3. Herbs with their healing effects

Herbs	Shades	Medicinal Quality of fabric
Turmeric	Yellow	Anti-bacterial, anti-allergy, anti-septic and aromatic, anti-inflammatory properties. Controls Cholesterol, helps reducing the insulin resistance, thus controls diabetes, Boosts Immunity, anemia.
Indigo	Indigo Blue	Antiseptic, Anti-allergic and helps fight skin disease
Aloe Vera	Off White	Skin Infections, and burns, Control Diabetes, Boosts Immunity, Anemia
Tulsi	Green	Viral and bacterial infections, controls blood sugar levels, boosts immunity
Neem	Grey	Controls skin diseases, controls blood sugar levels
Sandalwood	Pink	Anti-septic, Anti-inflammatory, Cools the skin, curing skin itching, burns
Henna	Orange	Blood purifier, an anti-irritant, a deodorant, and an antiseptic. Because of this cooling property, henna used as a prophylactic against skin diseases like burns, bruises, and skin inflammations, including sores from leprosy
Mimosa Pudica	Green	controls blood sugar levels
Chirayata	Brown	Cures various skin diseases, anemia
Catechu	Brown	To treat Pimples, Control Diabetes

3.2 Treatment Techniques

Ayurvastra involves a variety of treatment methods to infuse textiles with medicinal properties, blending traditional knowledge with contemporary techniques to enhance the fabric's therapeutic benefits. Here are some common treatment methods used in Ayurvastra:

1. Herbal Dyeing:

Process: Fabrics undergo herbal dyeing, where medicinal herbs are used to naturally color the fabric. The fabric is immersed in a solution containing herbal extracts, allowing it to absorb both the color and medicinal properties of the herbs (Rangari et al., 2012; Baid, 2014).

2. Herbal Bath:

Process: The fabric is treated with herbal baths, soaking or washing in water infused with a blend of medicinal herbs. This process enables the fabric to absorb the therapeutic properties of the herbs, promoting skin health and overall well-being (Jain, 2010; Saharan and Rani, 2015).

3. Oil Infusions:

Process: Ayurvastra fabrics may undergo oil treatments, where they are infused with herbal oils known for their medicinal benefits. The fabric is soaked in or coated with these oils, imparting therapeutic properties and enhancing the fabric's texture and sheen (Baid, 2014).

4. Sun Drying:

Process: After herbal treatments, Ayurvastra fabrics are often sun-dried. Sun drying is believed to activate the medicinal properties of the herbs and contribute to the fabric's effectiveness in promoting health and well-being (Rangari et al., 2012).

5. Mantra Infusion:

Process: In some traditional practices, mantras are chanted during the production process. It is believed that the positive vibrations generated through chanting infuse the fabric with spiritual and healing energy, enhancing its therapeutic qualities (Saharan and Rani, 2015).

6. Herbal Steam Treatment:

Process: Fabrics may be exposed to herbal steam treatments, where steam infused with medicinal herbs is used to treat the textile. This method allows for the absorption of herbal properties without direct contact with water (Rangari et al., 2012).

7. Ayurvedic Formulas:

Process: Specific Ayurvedic formulations may be prepared and applied during various stages of fabric production. These formulations combine medicinal herbs in precise proportions to maximize therapeutic benefits (Jain, 2010).

8. Layered Application:

Process: Some Ayurvastra fabrics undergo layered applications of herbal treatments. Different herbs or formulations are applied in multiple stages, ensuring a thorough infusion of medicinal properties throughout the fabric (Saharan and Rani, 2015).

9. Customized Blends:

Process: Artisans may create customized blends of herbs and botanicals for treatment, tailoring Ayurvastra to address specific health concerns or preferences of the wearer (Baid, 2014).

10. Natural Fermentation:

Process: In certain traditional practices, fabrics are treated with herbal mixtures and allowed to undergo natural fermentation. This process is believed to enhance the efficacy of the herbal infusion (Rangari et al., 2012).

These treatment methods contribute to the unique characteristics of Ayurvastra, making it a holistic form of clothing that not only showcases cultural richness but also offers potential health benefits to the wearer. The combination of herbal elements and traditional textile techniques results in fabrics that are aesthetically pleasing and supportive of well-being (Jain, 2010; Rangari et al., 2012; Saharan and Rani, 2015).

4. THERAPEUTIC PROPERTIES

4.1 Health Benefits

Ayurvastra, or medicinal clothing infused with Ayurvedic herbs, offers various potential benefits that go beyond conventional apparel. While individual experiences may differ, here are some commonly cited advantages of Ayurvastra:

1. Skin Health:

Antimicrobial Properties: Ayurvastra fabrics infused with herbs like neem and turmeric have natural antimicrobial properties, helping to prevent skin infections and irritation (Jain, 2010).

Soothing Effects: Herbs such as aloe vera and lavender provide a soothing effect on the skin, making Ayurvastra suitable for those with sensitive or easily irritated skin (Saharan and Rani, 2015).

2. Therapeutic Effects:

Anti-Inflammatory Benefits: Ayurvastra garments infused with herbs like turmeric and Indian madder may offer anti-inflammatory benefits, potentially alleviating discomfort associated with inflammatory conditions (Baid, 2014).

Joint and Muscle Support: Some Ayurvastra fabrics are designed to support joint health, making them suitable for individuals dealing with arthritis or muscle stiffness (Rangari et al., 2012).

3. Stress Reduction:

sssssss Herbs like lavender and mint, known for their calming effects, are integrated into Ayurvastra. Wearing these fabrics may contribute to stress reduction and improved mental well-being (Saharan and Rani, 2015).

Figure 4. Herbal Dyeing

4. Holistic Well-Being:

Natural Healing: Ayurvastra is often seen as a holistic approach to well-being, with wearers attributing positive changes not just to their physical health but also to their overall sense of balance and harmony (Jain, 2010).

5. Environmental Sustainability:

Use of Natural Fibers: Ayurvastra often involves the use of natural and organic fibers like cotton and silk, promoting environmentally sustainable practices in the textile industry (Baid, 2014).
Herbal Dyeing: The herbal dyeing process used in Ayurvastra is considered eco-friendly compared to conventional synthetic dyeing methods (Rangari et al., 2012).

6. Customization and Personalization:

Tailored Herbal Blends: Ayurvastra can be customized based on individual preferences and health needs. Artisans may create specific herbal blends to address particular health concerns (Saharan and Rani, 2015).

7. Cultural and Spiritual Significance:

Symbolism and Rituals: Ayurvastra may be crafted with specific patterns or symbols that hold cultural or spiritual significance, adding a meaningful dimension to the clothing (Rangari et al., 2012).
Mantra Infusion: Some traditional practices involve chanting mantras during the production process, infusing positive energy into the fabric (Saharan and Rani, 2015).

Figure 5. Mindful Dressing

8. Increased Awareness of Well-Being:

   - Mindful Dressing: Wearing Ayurvastra encourages a more mindful approach to dress, with individuals recognizing that clothing can play a role in their well-being beyond aesthetics (Jain, 2010).

It's important to note that while Ayurvastra shows promise in promoting well-being, scientific research supporting specific health claims is still evolving. Individuals considering Ayurvastra for health purposes should consult with healthcare professionals, as personal experiences may vary. Additionally, the sustainable and eco-friendly aspects of Ayurvastra contribute to its appeal in an era where conscious consumerism is gaining prominence.

4.2 Case Studies

Present case studies or testimonials showcasing the impact of Ayurvastra on individuals' health and lifestyle.

Case Study 1: Enhancing Skin Health with Ayurvastra

Client Profile: Ms. Aanya, a 32-year-old professional with sensitive skin prone to allergies.

Background: Aanya struggled with skin irritation caused by synthetic fabrics. Seeking a natural solution, she incorporated Ayurvastra into her wardrobe.

Ayurvastra Intervention: Aanya chose Ayurvastra garments infused with neem and turmeric. She regularly wore these fabrics, especially during extended work hours.

Impact: After a few weeks, Aanya noticed a significant improvement in her skin health. The neem-infused fabric provided antimicrobial protection, reducing skin irritation and allergic reactions. The turmeric component contributed to a soothing effect, leaving her skin feeling refreshed.

Testimonial: "I never thought that clothing could make such a difference! Ayurvastra has transformed my daily experience. My skin feels healthier, and I no longer worry about allergic reactions. It's not just clothing; it's a holistic approach to well-being."

Figure 6. Enhancing Skin Health with Ayurvastra

Case Study 2: Stress Reduction and Well-Being

Client Profile: Mr. Raj, a 40-year-old executive dealing with high-stress levels.

Background: Raj experienced chronic stress, impacting both his physical and mental well-being. Seeking a natural remedy, he explored Ayurvastra.

Ayurvastra Intervention: Raj incorporated Ayurvastra garments infused with lavender and mint into his daily routine. He wore these fabrics during work hours and leisure activities.

Impact: The calming properties of lavender and mint had a noticeable effect on Raj's stress levels. He reported feeling more relaxed and focused throughout the day. The Ayurvastra became an integral part of his stress management strategy.

Testimonial: "I never imagined that clothing could influence my state of mind. Ayurvastra has been a game-changer for me. The calming effects are real, and now, I can navigate my high-pressure job with a sense of calm and clarity."

Case Study 3: Supporting Joint Health

Client Profile: Mrs. Sunita, a 50-year-old woman dealing with arthritis.

Background: Sunita sought alternatives to alleviate joint pain associated with arthritis. She explored Ayurvastra as a potential solution.

Ayurvastra Intervention: Sunita opted for Ayurvastra garments infused with herbs known for their anti-inflammatory properties, including turmeric and Indian madder.

Impact: Wearing Ayurvastra proved beneficial for Sunita's joint health. The anti-inflammatory properties of the infused herbs provided a soothing effect, reducing stiffness and discomfort in her joints.

Testimonial: "I can't express how much Ayurvastra has improved my daily life. Living with arthritis is challenging, but these garments have become my ally. The natural healing properties make a tangible difference, and I'm grateful for the relief they bring."

These case studies and testimonials illustrate the diverse ways in which Ayurvastra can positively impact individuals' health and lifestyle. From addressing skin sensitivities to promoting mental well-being and supporting joint health, Ayurvastra emerges as a holistic and personalized approach to clothing with tangible benefits.

5. ENVIRONMENTAL SUSTAINABILITY

5.1 Natural Fibers

Ayurvastra focuses on manufacturing 100 percent organic and chemical-free fabrics and attires. By doing this, Ayurvastra protects the planet's natural resources from the harmful toxic chemical wastes used in conventional agriculture and textile production. It also aims to revive the ancient Ayurvedic dyeing technology in its fabrics. The medicinal herbs used include turmeric, tulsi, neem, khus-khus (vetiver), sandalwood, and indigo. These herbs are blended with balancing herbs to create delicate colors that remain in the fibers (Jain, 2010; Saharan & Rani, 2015).

Figure 7. Natural Fibres

Ayurvastra dyeing is applied to natural fibers like cotton, silk, linen, wool, coir, hemp, nettle, and bamboo, making eco-friendly textiles. Each herb caters to different medicinal properties. For instance, tulsi helps fight allergies and toxins, while turmeric, known for its anti-inflammatory and antibacterial properties, protects against skin infections. To produce Ayurvastra fabrics, the cloth is immersed in a specially prepared Ayurvedic Kasayam containing more than 30 herbs (Rangari et al., 2012).

The herbal properties of these fabrics are released into the body, preventing various infections and diseases. Experiments on patients suffering from eczema, psoriasis, and rheumatism have shown progress (Baid, 2014).

5.2 Ayurvastra: The Doctor of the Future

"The doctor of the future will give no medicine but will interest his patients in the care of the human frame, in diet, and the cause and prevention of disease." This quote embodies the philosophy behind Ayurvastra, where two of the oldest sciences known to mankind come together. It's the amalgamation of Ayurveda—the science of increasing a person's longevity—and textile making.

From an early period, humans have used textiles in various forms like ropes, clothes, and more. To the layperson, textiles are generally synonymous with fabric. However, the unlikely yet remarkable combination of Ayurveda and textiles has resulted in Ayurvastra. This innovative concept of natural clothing involves infusing fabric yarns with plant extracts and herbs.

Developed under the auspices of The Handloom Weavers Development Society, a non-profit organization, Ayurvastra claims to help rid people of many diseases through the regular use of these specially treated clothes.

Figure 8. The Doctor of the Future

5.3 Dyeing Techniques

Evaluate the environmental impact of herbal dyeing methods compared to conventional dyeing processes.

The Ayurvastra dyeing process is a unique dyeing method. Which we have summarized in the below table -

Table 1. Comparison between Ayurvedic, Natural, & Synthetic Dyeing

Process	Ayurvedic Dyeing	Natural (Conventional) Dyeing	Synthetic Dyeing
Fabrics or Yarn	We use only natural fibre like Cotton, Silk, Linen, Jute, Bamboo, Wool and so on.	Apart from natural fibres, synthetic or petro chemical yarns are also used.	Synthetic or petro chemical yarns and all types of fabrics are used for dyeing.
Pre-processing of fabrics	**Desizing:** we used Natural surfactants like soap nut / araapu / leaves. **Scouring:** We use whey milk and natural alkaline's. **Bleaching:** Bleaching is done naturally using limestone, sunlight.	Many natural dyes use chemicals for pre-processing because cheap and easy work. Many natural units use washing soda, bleaching powder, chlorine, etc. for pre-processing.	Toxic synthetic chemicals and high viscosity wet agents. Caustic soda, paroxide / chlorine are used which cause heavy damage to the water bodies and the environment.
Dyeing	The dye extracts are directly taken from medicinal rich herbs. Some herbs itself will act as a mordant and dye.	Even through dye extracts are from natural sources but for fixing colors many toxic and heavy metals are used.	For making bright colors harmful chemical dyes like formaldehyde, Chrome, Copper, Dioxin are used for making colors.
Fixing	Natural herbs and natural mineral fixtures are used for finishing the fabrics.	Organic chemicals fixtures are used for finishing the fabrics.	Many type of fixtures are derived from a different chemical process which can create health problems.
Softening	Softener is made from natural oil, natural castor oil, aloe vera and natural emulsifying agents.	Eco-friendly chemical softener or synthetic softener is used.	Highly toxic chemical fixtures and softeners are used.
Gumming / Finishing	This is a special process made to give wellness to the fabrics with a unique finishing.	Chemical finishing process.	Chemical finishing process.

Herbal dyeing methods offer several environmental benefits compared to conventional dyeing processes. Ayurvastra uses natural dyes from medicinal herbs, which reduce the environmental footprint significantly. Sustainable practices within conventional dyeing are also evolving, with innovations in eco-friendly dye formulations, water recycling technologies, and adherence to strict environmental standards.

However, the shift towards herbal dyeing aligns better with broader sustainability goals within the textile industry (Jain, 2010; Saharan & Rani, 2015).

6. CHALLENGES AND FUTURE PROSPECTS

6.1 Challenges

Discuss challenges faced by Ayurvastra, such as market awareness, standardization of production processes, and scalability.

Ayurvastra, despite its potential benefits and unique approach to textile production, faces several challenges that affect its adoption, growth, and integration into mainstream markets. Some of the prominent challenges include:

1. **Limited Market Awareness:**
   - *Lack of Consumer Knowledge:* Many consumers are unfamiliar with Ayurvastra and its potential benefits. Limited awareness hinders its market penetration, as potential buyers may not understand the unique selling points of these medicinal textiles.
2. **Perception and Skepticism:**
   - *Perceived Efficacy:* Skepticism about the actual efficacy of Ayurvastra in delivering health benefits may be a barrier. Potential consumers may question whether herbal-infused textiles can genuinely contribute to well-being.
3. **Educational Barriers:**
   - *Complexity of Ayurvedic Principles:* The incorporation of Ayurvedic principles in Ayurvastra might be challenging for consumers to grasp. Bridging the gap between traditional Ayurveda and modern textile use requires effective educational strategies.
4. **Standardization of Production Processes:**
   - *Consistency in Herbal Infusions:* Achieving uniformity in herbal infusions across batches can be challenging. Standardization is crucial for ensuring that Ayurvastra consistently delivers the intended health benefits, and variations in production can impact the efficacy of the textiles.
5. **Quality Control:**
   - *Herb Sourcing and Quality:* The quality of Ayurvastra is heavily dependent on the sourcing and quality of medicinal herbs. Ensuring a consistent and high-quality supply of herbs is essential for maintaining the integrity of the product.
6. **Scalability:**

- *Limited Production Scale:* Many Ayurvastra producers operate on a smaller scale, which may limit their ability to meet the demands of larger markets. Scaling up production without compromising quality can be a significant challenge.

7. **Cost Considerations:**
   - *Production Costs:* Integrating herbal treatments into textiles may increase production costs. This could result in higher retail prices, making Ayurvastra less accessible to certain consumer segments.

8. **Consumer Preferences and Trends:**
   - *Fashion Trends:* Ayurvastra may need to adapt to changing fashion trends and consumer preferences without compromising its core principles. Balancing tradition with contemporary design is crucial for attracting a wider audience.

9. **Regulatory Compliance:**
   - *Certifications and Standards:* Meeting regulatory requirements for textile production, especially concerning herbal treatments, can be complex. Ensuring compliance with safety and quality standards is essential for gaining consumer trust.

10. **Cultural Sensitivity and Appropriation:**
    - *Respect for Traditions:* Ayurvastra involves the integration of traditional practices. Striking a balance between preserving cultural authenticity and adapting to a global market without cultural appropriation challenges is crucial.

11. **Globalization Challenges:**
    - *Adaptation to International Markets:* Adapting to diverse international markets while maintaining authenticity poses a challenge.

Addressing these challenges requires collaboration among producers, researchers, marketers, and regulatory bodies. Enhancing awareness, standardizing production, and adapting to market demands can contribute to the sustainable growth of Ayurvastra (Saharan & Rani, 2015; Jain, 2010).

6.2 Future Trends

Explore potential advancements and innovations in Ayurvastra, considering its integration with modern fashion trends and global sustainability goals.

Advancements and innovations in Ayurvastra can pave the way for its integration into modern fashion trends while aligning with global sustainability goals. Here are potential advancements in Ayurvastra:

1. **Smart Textiles and Technology Integration:**
    - *Incorporation of Sensors:* Integration of smart textile technologies, such as sensors, to monitor health metrics or environmental factors, creating a fusion of traditional Ayurvastra with modern health-tracking capabilities.
2. **Biodegradable Herbal Polymers:**
    - *Development of Biodegradable Fibers:* Innovation in creating biodegradable fibers infused with herbal properties, ensuring that Ayurvastra remains environmentally friendly and aligns with sustainability goals.
3. **Nanoencapsulation for Prolonged Efficacy:**
    - *Nanoencapsulation Technology:* Implementing nanoencapsulation to enhance the durability and prolonged efficacy of herbal treatments, ensuring that the therapeutic benefits are preserved over extended periods.
4. **3D Printing Techniques:**
    - *Customizable 3D Printing:* Utilizing 3D printing techniques to create customizable Ayurvastra designs tailored to individual preferences, providing a modern and personalized touch to traditional clothing.
5. **Blockchain for Transparency:**
    - *Supply Chain Traceability:* Implementing blockchain technology to enhance transparency in the supply chain, allowing consumers to trace the origin of herbs used in Ayurvastra, ensuring ethical and sustainable sourcing practices.
6. **Adaptive Fashion and Trend Integration:**
    - *Collaboration with Designers:* Partnering with fashion designers to create Ayurvastra collections that seamlessly integrate with contemporary fashion trends, appealing to a broader audience and breaking away from traditional perceptions.
7. **Aromatherapy Integration:**
    - *Aromatic Textiles:* Exploring ways to integrate aromatherapy into Ayurvastra, where herbal scents are embedded in the fabric, providing a sensory experience and additional therapeutic benefits.
8. **Microencapsulation for Fragrance Release:**
    - *Microencapsulation for Fragrance:* Implementing microencapsulation techniques to embed herbal fragrances that release upon contact with the skin, adding a new dimension to Ayurvastra as a sensory and wellness experience.
9. **Closed-Loop Water Recycling:**
    - *Water Recycling Systems:* Incorporating closed-loop water recycling systems in Ayurvastra production to minimize water usage, promot-

ing sustainability and reducing the environmental impact of dyeing processes.
10. **Educational Apps and Wearable Tech:**
    - *Interactive Educational Apps:* Developing interactive educational apps that provide information about Ayurvastra's benefits, history, and usage. Integrating wearable tech to enhance user engagement and understanding of the clothing's impact on well-being.
11. **Global Collaboration and Cultural Exchange:**
    - *Cultural Collaboration:* Encouraging global collaborations that respect and integrate diverse cultural influences, fostering a rich exchange of ideas and designs that enhance Ayurvastra's global appeal.
12. **ReCyclable packaging and Minimal Waste:**
    - *Eco-Friendly Packaging:* Implementing recyclable and minimal packaging for Ayurvastra products, aligning with sustainability goals and minimizing environmental impact.

These advancements can position Ayurvastra at the intersection of tradition, innovation, and sustainability, making it a choice for personal well-being and eco-conscious fashion on the global stage (Rangari et al., 2012; Jain, 2010).

7. DESIGN PROCESS

The design Process of Garment Range Development on the Theme - Ayurvastra

Ayurvastra, a concept rooted in Ayurveda, integrates the healing properties of natural fibers and herbs into textiles. The process of designing a garment range based on this theme involves a meticulous approach that combines traditional knowledge with contemporary fashion design.

Figure 9. (Part A) The design process of Garment Range Development on the Theme - Ayurvastra

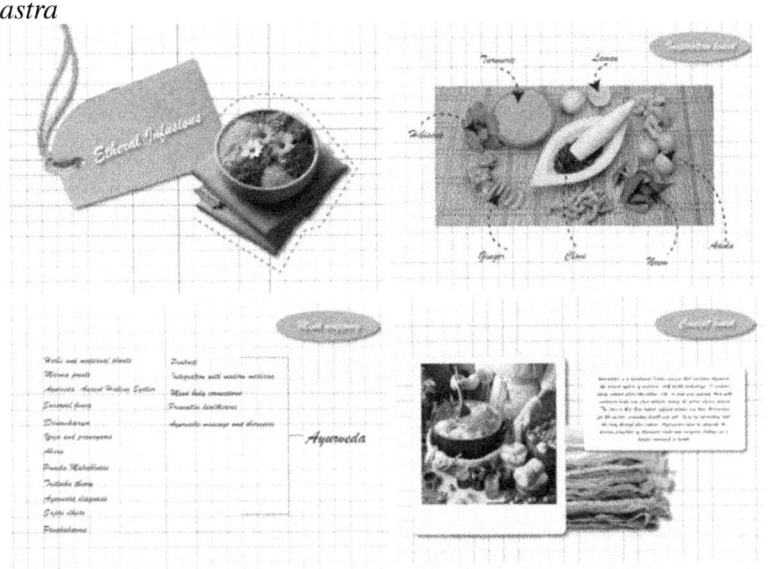

Figure 10. (Part B) **The design process of Garment Range Development on the Theme - Ayurvastra**

Figure 11. (Part C) The design process of Garment Range Development on the Theme - Ayurvastra

Design Development

By following steps, the design process for an Ayurvastra-themed garment range can effectively merge the ancient wisdom of Ayurveda with contemporary fashion design, creating garments that are not only stylish but also beneficial for health and well-being, dedicated to SDG Goals 3 and 12.

CONCLUSION

Ayurvastra is a unique clothing form that combines traditional medicine and sustainable fashion, offering a holistic approach to personal well-being and environmental consciousness. It integrates herbal dyeing methods, natural fibers, and eco-friendly production practices, aligning with global sustainability goals. Ayurvastra is a symbol of mindful dressing, where clothing becomes a conduit for cultural heritage, health enhancement, and environmental stewardship. However, overcoming challenges like market awareness and standardization requires collaboration between traditional artisans, technologists, fashion designers, and sustainability advocates. Ayurvastra encourages a reconsideration of our relationship with clothing, promoting balance, well-being, and a sustainable future.

REFERENCES

Baid, A. M. (2014). Method of dyeing textile article from medicinally rich herbs. Retrieved from http://www.patentgenius.com

. Fibre2Fashion. (n.d.). Ayurvastra: Herbal clothing for health and wellness.

. Indian Journals. (2015). Medicinal Plants - International Journal of Phytomedicines and Related Industries, 7(1),

Infosphere. (2021, March 5). Ayurvastra: The art of herbal textile and medicinal clothing. 15. Hindustan Times. (2020, March 17). Ayurvastra: Clothing that's good for your body, mind, and soul.

Jain, M. (2010). Ayurvedic textiles: A wonderful approach to handle health disorders. *Colourage*, 60(5), 45–52.

Kumar, A., & Sharma, A. (2021). Herbal textiles: Innovations and applications. In Kumar, A., & Sharma, A. (Eds.), *Advances in Sustainable Textile Processing* (pp. 105–120). Springer.

Narayan, S. (2017). Ayurvastra: Herbal clothing - A new technology to heal naturally. *International Journal of Advanced Research and Innovative Ideas in Education*, 3(4), 925–931.

Publishers, S. A. S. (2014)... *Journal of Applied Medical Sciences*, 3(2F), 925–931.

Rangari, N. T., Kalyankari, T. M., Mahajan, A. A., Lendhe, P. R., & Ruranik, P. K. (2012). Ayurvastra: Herbal couture technology in textile. *International Journal of Research in Ayurveda and Pharmacy*, 3(5), 733–736. DOI: 10.7897/2277-4343.03532

Red Yellow Exports. (n.d.).

. Saharan, M., & Rani, A. (2015). Ayurvastra: A miracle mediherbal cloth. Medicinal Plants - International Journal of Phytomedicines and Related Industries*, 7(1), 1.

Sharma, P. (2016). Ayurvastra: Textile innovation through herbal dyeing. *Journal of Medicinal Plants Studies*, 4(6), 33–37.

Singh, R., & Singh, S. (2021). Sustainable textile innovations: Ayurvastra and beyond. In Singh, R., & Singh, S. (Eds.), *Sustainable Innovations in Textile Processing* (pp. 90–102). Springer.

Singh, V. P., & Srivastava, N. (2022). Ayurvastra: A textile innovation for health benefits. *Environmental Science and Pollution Research International*, 29(12), 18818–18830. PMID: 34676482

. Springer. (n.d.). Innovations in textile processing and sustainability.

. Tajuniuyo, A. (2021). Ayurvastra textiles: Innovative healing through herbal dyeing.

The Hindu. (2019, June 3). The art of Ayurvastra.

The Hindu. (2019, June 3). The art of Ayurvastra.

Chapter 18
Emotional and Social Value Influence on Brand Trust and Customer Behavior on Organic Grocerant

Ashish Sharma
Lebanese French University, Iraq

Guna Sekhar Sajja
https://orcid.org/0000-0003-0327-2450
University of the Cumberlands, USA

Renu Vij
https://orcid.org/0000-0001-9202-8390
Chandigarh University, India

M. Clement Joe Anand
https://orcid.org/0000-0002-1959-7631
Mount Carmel College (Autonomous), India

Bharath Sampath
CMS B-School, Jain University (Deemed), India

ABSTRACT

The COVID-19 pandemic has led to an increase in the popularity of organic food and healthy living. The literature on food that is organic concentrates on the variables influencing consumer purchasing decisions. Both consistent consumption &

DOI: 10.4018/979-8-3693-7773-4.ch018

consumer contributions above and beyond buying customer involvement behaviour are necessary for an organic company to succeed. Examining potential motivators for member consumers to interact with organic grocery stores is the aim of this research. In order to investigate ways to promote consumer engagement behaviour, 281 Indian members of an organic grocery store were questioned for this research. This research suggested a "value acquisition–value co-creation" paradigm to investigate the connection among professed worth, make trust, & consumer assignation behaviour. It was created on worth co-creation theory with the literature on consumer assignation. The findings demonstrate how consumer engagement behaviour in organic grocery stores may be directly and successfully motivated by emotional and social values. However, via brand trust, customers' perceived values of quality and price will indirectly impact consumer engagement behaviour rather than having a direct impact. Moreover, enhancing the supposed worth of reaction, excellence, & cost helps fortify brand confidence in natural grocery stores. Research demonstrates the consumer engagement and organic grocery store success depend on brand trust. Research offers a fresh viewpoint on the connection between the benefits consumers get from eating organic food and value co-creation achieved via customer interaction practices.

1. INTRODUCTION

Since 2020, the COVID-19 pandemic continues to persist in altering people's dietary habits and consumption patterns (Angelakis et al., 2022). People desire a healthy diet, and the use of organic food has been rising in multiples, apart from health and environmental preservation. India's organic food market grew from 27.99 billion Rs in 2014 to 71.5 billion Rs in 2021, making India the fourth biggest organic foods market in the world and the largest in Asia (Benton & Stasch, 2024). People choose integrated food vendors who provide ready-to-eat foods, new supplies that should be ordered & distributed to their homelands, meals prepared on site, and nutritious foods that are healthy because of the hectic pace of contemporary living (Fonte, 2006). The combination between food retail & foodservice has given rise to an emerging phenomenon in the food industry known as the "grocerant." Organic grocers are establishments that provide organic living experiences, supply food that is organic services, and sell organic food (Gajdzik et al., 2023). Organic grocery stores satisfy the evolving requirements of customers for premium quality, simplicity, youthfulness, health, & home delivery as the current coronavirus pneumonia pandemic has swept the globe and resulted in the widespread usage of noncontact services (Gajdzik et al., 2023b).

Customer engagement behaviour is categorised into four areas: co-developing, influencing, enhancing, and mobilising behaviour. It combines the many ways that non-trading customer behaviour may impact businesses. In addition to purchasing goods or services, customers' non-transactional actions have a beneficial impact on the business. The marketing industry has researched consumer interaction behaviour in great detail, but less study is being done on the steadily declining organic grocery industry. In contrast to conventional eateries and supermarkets, organic grocers face challenges including exorbitant costs, a dearth of selection, disconnects between attitudes and purchases, a lack of consumer education, and mistrust among customers (Gajdzik et al., 2023c). The enhancement of company sales and marketing performance is contingent upon the efficient management of consumers' interaction with organic grocery stores. It enhances business success in addition to lowering customer attrition and switching behaviour. It also establishes and preserves enduring ties between customers and brands. Therefore, getting customers to contribute in ways other than just making a purchase is a difficult job for marketers (Herweyers, 2024).

Even if there is an attitude-purchase gap in the organic consumer market, some people are really still eager to make regular purchases and give to brands and businesses in addition to what they buy (Jeon & Yoo, 2021). Previous studies have demonstrated that brand supporters make great business partners as they participate more actively in social media, word-of-mouth marketing, and product development. For more authenticity and significance, this research concentrates on member consumers who have been eating food that is organic for a considerable amount of time. A strong relationship with the brand may be cultivated and ongoing organic consumption can be encouraged via membership. By paying a set sum up front, a member of a corporation might enter into a semi-contractual relationship. Members of organic grocery stores are eligible for exclusive discounts & improved value-added association benefits. Additionally, associate community organization provides members & businesses with a steady foundation for long-term co-creation of value, with frequent consumer involvement (Kanda et al., 2024). Studies have shown that patron impressions of restaurants' "value for money" take a favourable influence on referrals, word-of-mouth, & return business. Increased brand recognition leads to increased customer engagement with brands based on perceived value (Lewis et al., 2014). Member clients will provide more value to the company since they may be valued more than non-member customers. consumer involvement is thus a need for value co-creation, and member consumer perceived value drives client engagement behaviour. Engaging consumers may inspire value co-creation, provide ideas for bettering current offerings, draw in prospective new clients, and support long-term growth (Sakr, 2023).

In reaction to the COVID-19 "new normal" and intense market competition, an increasing amount of companies remain using digital commercial models, innovative trade alterations, & product association groups to vigorously engage through consumers & create long-term worth. Co-creation of value arises from interactions between businesses and consumers. Businesses may better grasp value co-creation and build enduring connections with their customers by observing consumer interaction behaviour (Yu et al., 2022). "Transaction relationship-engagement" has evolved into the central component of brand-customer management. Nonetheless, the solitary route of "enterprises create value by goods and services, and consumers benefit through consuming" continues to be the foundation of research on organic consumption. Numerous studies have linked the behavioural goals of restaurant brands to a variety of perceived value aspects (Yu, Han, et al., 2022). Seldom has the history of India's rapidly expanding organic food industry and organic grocery store industry been examined. There is still much to learn about the value co-creation hypothesis of consumer engagement behaviour in the setting of organic grocery stores. By beginning with certain perceived values such as emotional, social, quality, & pricing values this research may more effectively investigate the types of values that customers bring to organic grocery stores.

Since it is hard to learn about the qualities of organic food by touching & eating it, trust is a critical component influencing consumption. Customers' desire to visit a restaurant might be influenced by their level of confidence in the business, particularly during the COVID-19 epidemic. Point-of-sale data improves customer trust, which closes the intent-behaviour divide amongst consumers of organic groceries. Prior research on customers' confidence in buying organic products has often concentrated on the organic item itself, including nutritional qualities, ecologically friendly production methods, and product certification requirements. The brands of organic food service providers, however, have received less attention from researchers, and the social and emotional drivers of brand trust antecedents have not been as well examined. Perceived value will have an additional impact on consumers' behaviour and psychological condition. The study reiterates the fundamental idea that "value, not product, is what customers consume" and poses an additional two research questions:

RQ1: How do customers' engagement behaviours to support the brand become motivated by the perceived value they get from organic grocery stores?

RQ2: How does consumer perception of value and involvement in organic grocery stores relate to brand trust?

This research goes beyond previous studies on consumer purchase patterns to investigate how different aspects of the perceived value of organic groceries affect customer involvement and brand trust (Zopounidis et al., 2022). This approach is what researcher refer to as value co-creation and acquisition. The study's subjects are members of organic grocery stores, and its findings advance both brand strategy and consumer value theory in the natural food service sector.

2. TECHNIQUES

2.1. Measures and Questionnaire:

Self-reports from the questionnaire survey were used in this study's empirical investigation. Two doctorate students in advertising with study abroad experiences created the original questionnaire in English and translated it into Indian. The professor of marketing took one last look. Two components make to the design of the questionnaire. This section contains the fundamental data. The inconstant amount used in the model is examined in the second section. Only member consumers who previously needed a semi-contractual connection with an organic grocery company are eligible to see the findings. The respondents have firsthand knowledge of the ongoing use of organic groceries. The study's findings do not address the position of non-purchasers. A suitability sample consisting of 34 participant consumers & 5 PhD students studying advertising were pretested to identify any issues related to procedure, comprehension, or clarity. It has resulted in a few small adjustments.

Every measurement was modified for the organic grocery store environment and based on earlier research. The four aspects of perceived value found in Sweeney and Soutar's study are referred to as the perceived value scale. The firm-specific trust scale serves as the foundation for the measuring of brand trust. Four sub-dimensions of customer engagement behaviour are generated from the created scale. Every item was assessed using a Likert scale with six points.

2.2. Information Gathering

China's Sichuan Province provided the statistics. The samples came from one of M's 14-year-old clients, who is renowned throughout the region for being an organic grocery store. Distribution of the questionnaire took place offline as well as online 1. A total of 281 respondents all M brand members who have regularly eaten organic food were surveyed in order to gather data.

Of these, the majority of respondents (n = 183, 65%) remained female; the popular (n = 218, 77.6%) were among the ages of 31 & 51; and the majority (n = 232, 82.6%) held a bachelor's degree or higher. Of these clients, 33.10 percent (96 members) pre-deposited less than 6,000 rupees, 38.10 percent (110 members) between 6,000 and 21,50 percent (65 members) between 20,000 and 51 thousand rupees, & 4.4% (13 members) beyond 51 thousand rupees. This research does not take purchase intention into account since the poll's objects all belong to member consumers & the pre-deposit quantity ranges from 5,000 and 50,000 rupees.

2.3. Data Interpretation:

Structural equation modelling (SEM), a two-step method, was used for data analysis. First, the validity and dependability of the scale were examined using confirmatory factor analysis (CFA). Second, the mediating effect and the study hypothesis were tested using SEM.

3. RESULTS:

3.1. Validity and Dependability

Before examining the link between variables, each possible variable must undergo a reliability test. To evaluate each item's dependability, factor loadings are compared to the suggested cutoff of 0.7, and the brand trust factor is eliminated from the study. Each item's final factor loading is more than 0.8, showing sufficient internal dependability. All of the variables' composite reliability (CR) ratings and Cronbach's alpha were more than 0.9, suggesting that the scale had adequate internal consistency. Using average variance extracted (AVE), the scale's convergent validity was examined. The nine variables' AVEs, which met the 0.6 minimum requirement, varied between 0.62 to 0.822, demonstrating excellent convergent validity.

The extent to which the constructs vary is referred to as the discriminatory reliability of the scale. A comparison between the variables' correlation coefficient and the squared root of AVE is used as the test technique. An appropriate level of discriminant validity for the variable is shown when the former is smaller than the latter. Figure 1 shows a correlation coefficient as high as 0.760, although the lowest possible AVE square root values is 0.782, which is higher.

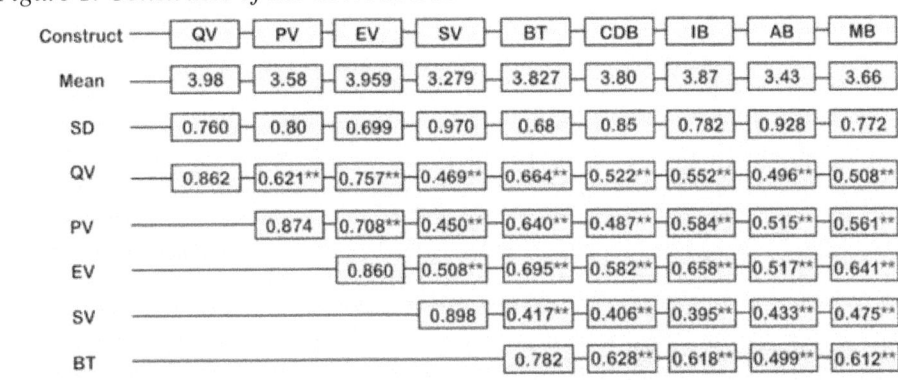

Figure 1. Constructs of the Correlations

Construct	QV	PV	EV	SV	BT	CDB	IB	AB	MB
Mean	3.98	3.58	3.959	3.279	3.827	3.80	3.87	3.43	3.66
SD	0.760	0.80	0.699	0.970	0.68	0.85	0.782	0.928	0.772
QV	0.862	0.621**	0.757**	0.469**	0.664**	0.522**	0.552**	0.496**	0.508**
PV		0.874	0.708**	0.450**	0.640**	0.487**	0.584**	0.515**	0.561**
EV			0.860	0.508**	0.695**	0.582**	0.658**	0.517**	0.641**
SV				0.898	0.417**	0.406**	0.395**	0.433**	0.475**
BT					0.782	0.628**	0.618**	0.499**	0.612**
CDB						0.907	0.737**	0.662**	0.697**
IB							0.872	0.760**	0.732**
AB								0.890	0.683**
MB									0.850

3.2. Model for Structural Equations

Following Figure 2, a model of structural equations was created. It uses the SEM of the greatest probability estimate to test the suggested hypothesis. As expected, the model of structural equations had a good fitting index (CMIN/DF = 2.18 ^ 4, the CFI = 0.904 > 0.10, an IFI = 0.905 > 0.10, the TLI = 0.905 > 0.10, the NFI = 0.892 > 0.9, the RMR = 0.0450 < 0.06 the RMSEA = 0.079 < 0.09).

Figure 2. Model of Research

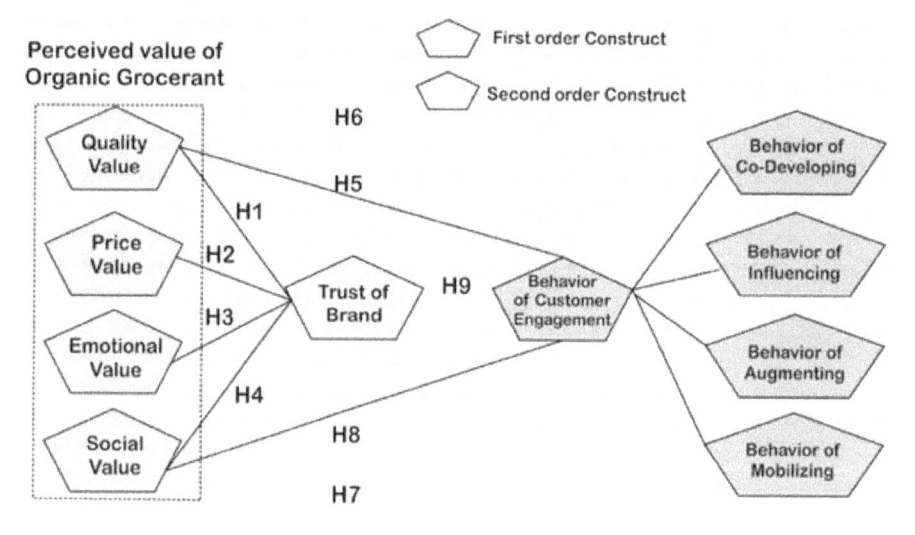

3.3. Examining the Hypotheses

Figure 3 shows the outcomes of the structural equation model. To keep things simple, we use solid lines to denote the figures' important routes and dotted lines to denote their inconsequential pathways.

Figure 3. Findings from the study model's route analysis. **P < 0.02, *P < 0.06, and ***P <0.002.

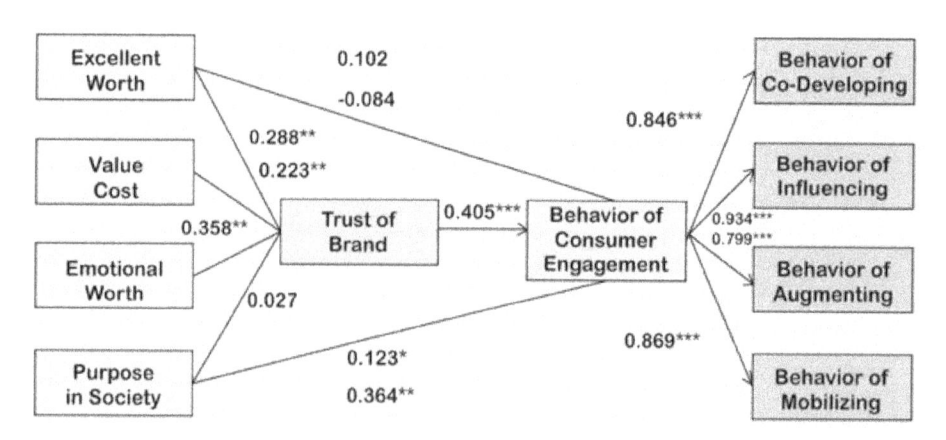

By way of a whole, the route coefficients and potential outcomes are summarised in Figure 4. The results of the hypothesis test show that brand trust is positively correlated with customer perceived organic grocery worth ($\beta = 0.287$, P = 0.003 < 0.01), emotional worth ($\beta = 0.357$, P = 0.002 < 0.01), and cost value ($\beta = 0.222$, P = 0.005 < 0.01), lending support to hypotheses H1, H2, and H3. Researcher discovered that among these factors, organic grocery shoppers' confidence in brands is most affected by emotional value. Nevertheless, there is no evidence to support H4 since social value has no effect on consumer confidence in brands (t = 0.482).

Figure 4. Findings from Testing Hypotheses

Hypothesis	Paths of Structure	Non Standarized Coefficient b	SE	Standarized Coefficient β	t value	P	Results
H1	QV-BT	0.276	0.092	0.288**	3.015	0.004	Supported
H2	PV-ST	0.198	0.072	0.223**	2.796	0.006	Supported
H3	EV-BT	0.339	0.12	0.358**	3.083	0.003	Supported
H4	SV-BT	0.019	0.038	0.027	0.483	0.64	Not Supported
H5	QV-CEB	-0.087	0.2	-0.084	-0.864	0.389	Not Supported
H6	PV-CEB	0.098	0.077	0.102	1.274	0.204	Not Supported
H7	EV-CEB	0.369	0.125	0.364**	2.975	0.004	Supported
H8	SV-CEV	0.10	0.040	0.123	2.282	0.024	Supported
H9	BT-CEB	0.435	0.102	0.405**	4.302	***	Supported

Collaborative development, product enhancement, persuading, and mobilisation are all examples of customer engagement behaviour, which is a second-order construct. All four categories of behaviour were adequately explained by the scales (see Figure 3). Researchers discovered that both emotional worth ($\beta = 0.363$, p = 0.003 < 0.01) & social worth ($\beta = 0.122$, p = 0.023 < 0.05) significantly affect consumer engagement behaviour, lending support to H7 and H8 in relation to the influence of perceived value on this behaviour. Nevertheless, client engagement behaviour is not substantially impacted by either value for money (t = −0.863) or cost value (t = 1.273), thereby nullifying H5 and H6. H9 is supported because, as expected, consumer engagement behaviour is highly affected by brand trust ($\beta = 0.404$, p < 0.001).

3.4. Evaluations of Mediation

Researchers suggest that there could be a mediating effect, even if both the cost and the value of organic groceries do not directly alter consumer engagement behaviour from the current route. As a result, we dig deeper into the data to find out how four consumers' perceptions of value and engagement behaviour relate to brand trust. To build and intermissions of confidence for facilitating effects, Preacher & Hayes suggested the boot strapping approach using 5,000 examples.

The significant indirect effect of excellence worth ($\beta = 0.118$; $p = 0.002 < 0.01$) along with cost worth ($\beta = 0.085$; $p = 0.008 < 0.01$) on consumer assignation behaviour through brand trust. As stated by Shrout and Bolger (2002), there is no zero between the upper along with smaller assurance intermissions of bias modified & percentile throughout the 95% confidence interval. Brand trust completely mediates the relationship between value for money (bias-modified CI = −0.285 to 0.099, comprised 0) & cost worth as neither of these variables directly affects customer engagement behaviour when brand trust is controlled. There is a subsidiary result via trust in the brand ($\beta = 0.145$; $p = 0.003 < 0.01$) that partly mediated the result of consumer emotional value as perceived on consumer assignation behaviour, in relation to expressive worth, which has a stronger immediate impact ($\beta = 0.365$; $p = 0.005 < 0.01$) on consumer appointment behaviour. No mediation impact of brand trust was found but social value directly affects consumer engagement behaviour ($\beta = 0.095$; $p = 0.024 < 0.05$).

4. DISCUSSION

The factors that drive the construction of consumer engagement behaviours towards organic groceries are explored in this research, which is founded on worth formation theory & the professed worth viewpoint. Consumer behaviour, such as purchase and repurchase behaviour, has been the primary focus of prior study on organic groceries and organic food. Members whose diets consist mostly on organic foods have been the subject of very few research efforts. Researcher are curious as to whether the perceived worth of organic groceries among member customers would influence their company's trust and consumer behaviour. Organic grocery store quality, pricing, emotional, & social values all have a role in how customers trust and connect with the brand, according to the research.

To start, social value has little effect on consumers' faith in brands; nevertheless, price, emotional value, and quality all do. This indicates that consumers will have more faith in organic grocery shops if they have a positive experience with the brand on all front's quality, price, and emotion. These results are consistent with those of

Sankaran and Chakraborty. Above everything else, emotional worth is more important than monetary value or even quality. In settings like restaurants, hotels, and shopping malls, previous studies have also shown that customers' emotions play a significant role in explaining their behavioural intentions. One possible explanation for the lack of impact of social values on brand trust is that the study's respondents have become members of the organic grocery store consumer group. They are no longer enticed by the social benefits of eating organic food. This finding lends credence to earlier research that indicated customers' perceptions of organic food's social worth had no impact on their trust.

The second point is that consumers' involvement behaviour is strongly impacted by their emotional and social values. Consumers' perceptions of value have a favourable effect on their propensity to interact. Emotional & social values can be more subjective and experience-based than monetary and quality values, which seem to be more concrete and practical. Perceptions of intangible worth are crucial for encouraging non-transactional behaviour, while perceptions of physical value encourage trust and buy behaviour. According to social identity theory, customers' perceptions of the brand's worth might motivate them to develop a stronger emotional connection to it. Organic grocery shoppers have an innate emotional and social identity based on their shared values of health and sustainability. Customers' involvement behaviour is therefore only impacted by their emotional and social values.

Organic grocery shopping is all about making people happy and satisfied, as emotional value has a direct impact on consumer engagement behaviour. Customers are more likely to have a favourable impression of the brand or business after a satisfying encounter and the fulfilment of anticipated advantages. Consumers are more likely to have a good impression of the brand or business after having a pleasant encounter and enjoying the expected advantages. The foundation of customer and brand value co-creation, according to existing research, is emotional value. Consumers' sense of self-worth and the degree to which they are accepted by their social circle are factors that contribute to a product's social value. Research has shown that customers' pursuit of social values significantly influences electronic word-of-mouth, referrals, and advocacy, reflecting their self-efficacy, self-image drive, along with social identity. More proof that social value affects consumer engagement behaviour is provided by these results.

The research concludes by confirming that brand trust is a mediator between perceived value and consumer involvement. In particular, customer engagement behaviour is impacted by the degree to which customers believe that organic grocery store items and food are consistently of outstanding value and quality for money. The most probable reason for this is because organic grocery store members have high standards for their own health and wellness, and they automatically assume that these stores would deliver better food and better service. At the same time, consumers can rest easy knowing that organic products are reliable, which lowers transaction costs by decreasing ambiguity and risk in the customer experience. Furthermore, the study's findings highlight the significance of trust in consumer engagement behaviour, particularly on the fact that consumers' trust in a brand might inspire them to take an advantageous action.

5. POSSIBLE OUTCOMES AND CONSTRAINTS

5.1. Possible Theoretical Consequences

This study makes a substantial contribution to the research on food service with marketing by studying the connection between consumers' perceptions of the value of organic groceries and their engagement behaviours, which in turn motivate consumers to become marketers for organic groceries. The food hospitality and service businesses tend to ignore consumer interaction despite the extensive study on the topic. Perception of value literature along with co-creation theory are utilised in a broader sense in the field of hospitality via the application of pricing, excellence, expressive, & communal aspects of consumer worth perception as drivers of consumer behaviour. This work primarily adds to the body of knowledge by providing theoretical underpinnings and empirical proof. The first important finding is a new paradigm for the acquisition-creation value framework for organic consumer behaviour. As a result of the value they get from the company, consumers will participate in behaviours that generate even more value and advantages for the business.

Second, researchers augmented what is already known about organic grocery store literature's coverage of perceived value and consumer interaction. Quality, pricing, emotional, and social aspects of organic grocery store perceived value were used to examine the effect on consumer engagement behaviour. This sets it apart from other research on the perceived value of organic grocery store products. Furthermore, this research adds to our knowledge of what motivates customers to interact by highlighting the significance of social and emotional value. Third, our understanding of confidence in brands in relation to organic grocery purchasing has been expanded by this research. According to this research, the effect of perceived worth on trust varies between nations, with Indian consumers being the most affected. Customers are more likely to interact when they trust the brand, which is influenced by quality and price value. Additionally, it is stressed that trust is essential for both organic consumption and consumer involvement. Finally, prospective purchasers whose statements and deeds have historically been contradictory are not the target audience here; rather, the research focusses on regular organic grocery store members. Membership, with its implied semi-contractual connection, boosted the organic market even more. Furthermore, it shows that in order to increase organic consumption in the long run, it is necessary to target the most valuable customers.

5.2. Implications for Reality

Before anything else, this research teaches organic grocery store managers and marketers' new tricks for keeping customers engaged. A great approach to engage consumers is to concentrate on advertising and leadership methods that provide them with greater value and help them trust the company. Building trust in a brand is an ongoing activity. When making decisions on organic product selection, service pricing, and activity planning, managers must keep the customer's value in mind. At the same time, managers need to identify several value kinds for personalised marketing and divide their clients into distinct segments. Additionally, there are other approaches of establishing and maintaining consumer confidence in a brand that promotes well-being and security. With the use of traceability technologies, transparent and secure supply chains, and fully accessible kitchens, grocery stores can ensure that their customers are eating nutritious, worry-free food. Supermarkets also have a responsibility to ensure that their customers get good value for their money. Customers will do better for the brand because they believe in it, and that faith is based on the brand's quality and cost value.

Third, with the implementation of cause-related marketing and entertainment events, organic grocery stores may provide customers with a delightful shopping experience. Organic dining, high-quality organic food, engaging organic information sharing, and rich organic experiential activities (like baking) are all ways in which grocery stores may elevate their customers' emotional experiences. When it comes to the factors that affect engagement behaviour, social significance is second after emotional worth. Organic grocers should attain customer awareness by regularly delivering superior organic products and services while establishing a reliable brand image. In addition to making a positive impression, these will motivate customers to share the brand with their friends and family and provide constructive criticism.

Lastly, this study offers solutions for customer membership management that firms might use.

Both the buying and interaction behaviours of member consumers contribute to the brand in a direct and indirect way. Businesses are able to have more meaningful conversations with their members via brand communities and social media, which in turn allows them to produce smarter, more personalised products in response to member input. Consumers' reliance on social media for research, brand communication, opinion sharing, and recommendation purposes paves the way for C2B value generation. Organic grocerants may capitalise on membership as a business strategy to expand their reach in China and beyond.

6. CONCLUSION AND DIRECTIONS FOR THE FUTURE

Although there are several limits and need for further expansion, this research does have some theoretical and practical importance. To begin, there is room for expansion and subdivision within the study objective of this work. As a jumping off point for future research comparing member consumers of one grocery brand to average organic consumers or possibly expanding to other nations, our study primarily focusses on these individuals. The second limitation is that additional factors that may have affected customer involvement were not included in this research. Potential future moderators include things like value consciousness, social support, and brand loyalty. Lastly, this research has not yet analysed the ways in which perceived value affects brand confidence and participation behaviour or refined the estimated worth for natural grocerants to the good or customer service, since information concerning organic grocers is difficult to collect. Hence, future studies must use this as a springboard to investigate uncharted territory.

REFERENCES

Angelakis, G., Lemonakis, C., Galariotis, E., & Zopounidis, C. (2022). Current trends on food tourism approaches through a conceptual framework of food tourism management. *International Journal of Knowledge Management in Tourism and Hospitality*, 2(4), 331. DOI: 10.1504/IJKMTH.2022.124089

Benton, R.Jr, & Stasch, S. F. (2024). The U.S. government's program of welfare for the Wealthy. *Journal of Macromarketing*, 44(2), 250–257. Advance online publication. DOI: 10.1177/02761467231225129

Fonte, M. (2006). Slow Food's Presidia: What do Small Producers do with Big Retailers? *Research in Rural Sociology and Development*, 12, 203–240. DOI: 10.1016/S1057-1922(06)12009-0

Gajdzik, B., Jaciow, M., & Wolny, R. (2023). Types of E-Consumers and their Implications for Sustainable Consumption—A study of the behavior of Polish E-Consumers in the second decade of the 21st century. *Sustainability (Basel)*, 15(16), 12647. DOI: 10.3390/su151612647

Gajdzik, B., Jaciow, M., & Wolny, R. (2023b). Types of E-Consumers and their Implications for Sustainable Consumption—A study of the behavior of Polish E-Consumers in the second decade of the 21st century. *Sustainability (Basel)*, 15(16), 12647. DOI: 10.3390/su151612647

Gajdzik, B., Jaciow, M., & Wolny, R. (2023c). Types of E-Consumers and their Implications for Sustainable Consumption—A study of the behavior of Polish E-Consumers in the second decade of the 21st century. *Sustainability (Basel)*, 15(16), 12647. DOI: 10.3390/su151612647

Herweyers, L. (2024). *Designing long-term reuse : uncovering motivators and barriers to sustained use of reusable alternatives to single-use products.* https://doi.org/DOI: 10.63028/10067/2043990151162165141

Jeon, H. M., & Yoo, S. R. (2021). The relationship between brand experience and consumer-based brand equity in grocerants. *Service Business*, 15(2), 369–389. DOI: 10.1007/s11628-021-00439-8

Kanda, W., Klofsten, M., Bienkowska, D., Henry, M., & Hjelm, O. (2024). Challenges of circular new ventures: An empirical analysis of 70 cases. *Journal of Cleaner Production*, 442, 141103. DOI: 10.1016/j.jclepro.2024.141103

Kommineni, K. K., Madhu, G. C., Narayanamurthy, R., & Singh, G. (2022). IoT crypto security communication system. In *IoT Based Control Networks and Intelligent Systems:Proceedings of 3rd ICICNIS 2022* (pp. 27-39). Singapore: Springer Nature Singapore.

Kshirsagar, P. R., Reddy, D. H., Dhingra, M., Dhabliya, D., & Gupta, A. (2022, December). A Review on Comparative study of 4G, 5G and 6G Networks. In *2022 5th International Conference on Contemporary Computing and Informatics (IC3I)* (pp. 1830-1833). IEEE.

Lewis, G., Crispin, S., Bonney, L., Woods, M., Fei, J., Ayala, S., & Miles, M. (2014). Branding as innovation within agribusiness value chains. *Journal of Research in Marketing and Entrepreneurship*, 16(2), 146–162. DOI: 10.1108/JRME-03-2014-0005

Sakr, S. S. (2023). Banana Peel Utilization: Practice and Perspective, Highlights from Lebanon. *International Journal of Clinical Studies and Medical Case Reports*, 34(4). Advance online publication. DOI: 10.46998/IJCMCR.2023.34.000842

SenthamilSelvan, R. (2017). Analysis Of EDFC And ADFC Algorithms For Secure Communication In VANET. *JARDCS, 9*(18), 1171-1187.

Yu, W., Han, X., & Cui, F. (2022). Increase consumers' willingness to pay a premium for organic food in restaurants: Explore the role of comparative advertising. *Frontiers in Psychology*, 13, 982311. Advance online publication. DOI: 10.3389/fpsyg.2022.982311 PMID: 35992425

Yu, W., He, M., Han, X., & Zhou, J. (2022). Value acquisition, value co-creation: The impact of perceived organic grocerant value on customer engagement behavior through brand trust. *Frontiers in Psychology*, 13, 990545. Advance online publication. DOI: 10.3389/fpsyg.2022.990545 PMID: 36275242

Zopounidis, C., Galariotis, E., Lemonakis, C., & Angelakis, G. (2022). Current trends on food tourism approaches through a conceptual framework of food tourism management. *International Journal of Knowledge Management in Tourism and Hospitality*, 1(1), 1. DOI: 10.1504/IJKMTH.2022.10044988

Chapter 19
Consumption Approach R&D Strategies in Brand Value in Fortune Companies

Dharani Haribabu
Easwari Engineering College, India

Marisha Ani Das
Easwari Engineering College, India

K. Santha Kumari
BS&H Narasaraopeta Engineering College, India

R. Senthamil Selvan
Annamacharya Institute of Technology and Sciences, India

N. B. Mahesh Kumar
https://orcid.org/0000-0002-9272-3032
Hindusthan Institute of Technology, Tamil Nadu, India

ABSTRACT

Consumption has also grown at the same pace as increases in technology in the global globe, which is experiencing fast technological development. It is possible for information to go to another side of the globe in an instant, and it is also possible for consumer items to be transported to the opposite end of the earth only a short while later. Within the context of the global environment, where quick consumption is attained, producers are likewise engaged in a fierce competitive situation. In the

DOI: 10.4018/979-8-3693-7773-4.ch019

Copyright © 2025, IGI Global. Copying or distributing in print or electronic forms without written permission of IGI Global is prohibited.

context of marketing, this circumstance has evolved into a strategy with the purpose of ensuring that customers ultimately become a society that consumes brands. In order to create novel technology-based items, businesses have been concentrating their efforts on research and development initiatives in order to adapt to this consumption style. In order to establish a connection between research and development as production of innovation & trademark as consuming data, the link between research and development spending and brand value will be investigated.

1. INTRODUCTION

Within the twenty-first century, the process of globalisation has reached its conclusion, and technological advancement is occurring at a fast pace (Anderson et al., 2004). Additionally, consumption is continuing to rise at a fast rate. The growth of technology has resulted in the transformation of consuming patterns into consumer items or services that are based on technology (Balasubramanian, 1994). It has been turned into an object that can be manufactured rapidly, transmitted to the user, delivered, and eaten immediately from the moment it is supplied (Barney, 1995). The production of technology-based consumer things or services become starting point of opposition since it has resulted in increased investments in research and development, which in turn has led to the growth of original products or services (Carney, 2005) (Carney, 2005b). Furthermore, within the marketing strategy, these advances define all of the qualities of the items that are associated with the brand identity.

Because of this, the brand has been able to contact the customer in a more expedient manner and has evolved into interaction instrument that provide the customer the ability to enter the unconscious mind. Due to this circumstance, customers are now able to consume brands as if they were products (Dwivedi et al., 2019b) (Karnani, 2007). To summarise, innovative goods, which are the result of research and development operations, have evolved into a brand that is consumed by its target audience. The objective of this study is to analyse the extent to which R&D and brand related to one another (Luo & Bhattacharya, 2006) (Luo & Bhattacharya, 2006b). To emphasise that new services or goods are supplied to consumers as an production of research and development actions along with the input of the brand, this has been the intention of this statement (Morsing, 2006) (Prahalad & Hart, 2010). In order to provide an explanation for the beneficial influence that research and development has on a brand, it is aimed to relate the brand values of firms with their R&D operations (Stefan & Paul, 2008).

2. RESEARCH AND DEVELOPMENT, FRESH CONCEPTS & BRANDING

The ideas of R and D & Fresh concepts remain conflated and remain sometimes hard to differentiate. To differentiate these notions and categorise the collected data for the formation of an pointer, altogether terminology & ideas pertaining to Fresh concepts are elucidated in Oslo Guide. This document defines Fresh concepts as follows: Fresh concept refers to the creation of a novel or substantially enhanced product (goods or services), process, marketing strategy, or organisational approach inside corporate operations, workplace structure, or external interactions. Innovation doings are characterised as: Fresh concepts actions include all technical, technical, organisational, economic & marketable measures aimed at facilitating the execution of innovations. invention activities include research and development that is not explicitly tied to the creation of a particular invention.

The fundamental criteria for an innovation, as delineated in the Oslo Manual, stipulate that the good or service, procedure, advertising technique, or else organisational system must be novel to the firm. These ideas may have been either originally produced inside the firm or adopted from other organisations. According to Maslow, individuals typically want to fulfil their biological, security, public, regard, and fulfilment of individual requirements in that order. Maslow's hierarchy of requirements serves as a foundational framework for the formulation of marketing strategy. Companies create new items (services or goods) that fulfil consumer wants or provide changes to their current offerings. Consequently, organisations are striving to enhance their commercial success. In this fundamental scenario, it is evident that enterprises must concentrate the good development on innovative activities to consistently address and fulfil consumer requirements.

Innovation is directly connected to research and development (R&D). In the process of developing a new product or concept via research and development (R&D), a methodical and scientific investigation is carried out using both fundamental & applied scientific activities. As a consequence of this research, new knowledge and concepts have been brought to light. These outputs serve as the foundation for the development of new goods, the creation of innovations in the existing product, as well as innovations in marketing, manufacturing, and organisational practices. The activities that are associated with innovation & must be carried out jointly are, in a nutshell, the process of commercialisation of the successes that have been gained as a consequence of research and development.

Companies have been concentrating their efforts on raising the demands that they place on the requirements of customers, and customers have begun to diversify their desired outcomes by reacting at the same rate. As a result of waiting for various features to be added to the items that they use in order to satisfy the requirements of individuals, the requirements have evolved into a diverse spectrum of expectations. These factors have prompted manufacturers to broaden the range of their goods and come up with innovative characteristics that will pique the attention of consumers. In addition to this, it has instructed the manufacturers to present their goods as brands and to develop a view of their brand in order to establish a devotion to their products.

It is clear that labelling has been utilised ever since ancient times, as seen by the traces that have been left behind by the employment of the brand. Numerous handprints that were thought to have been made about the year 15000 BC were discovered in the Cave Walls of Lascaux, which are located in the south area of France. Up to the present day, several definitions have been formulated, and various methods have been taken with regard to the brand. The following is the definition of the business-oriented brand that was provided by the AMA, in 1959. Phrase "brand" refers to the title, period, symbol, sign, or project is used to identify and differentiate the goods or services of a company or collection of sellers from those of their rivals. The following is the definition of a consumer-oriented brand: "The brand is the promises given by businesses about the features that the consumer purchases and satisfies the consumer."

3. RELATED WORKS

The link between research and development (R&D) and brand is handled in a variety of different ways in the academic publications that were read. Both a Table 1 & a synopsis of the scholarly papers that were looked at can be found below.

Table 1. Summary Table for Literature Review

Year/Author	Titles	Outcomes
Lee.J.Y.(2014)	The Impact of Advertising and Research and Development on Firm Performance and Brand Equity as They Relate to Customer-Centric Structures	Advertising and research and development budgets have an effect on brand quality and value that is proportional to how much attention they get from consumers.
Sharma P.et al (2017)	The Mediating Role of Product Innovation in the Relationship Between Research and Development Spending, Brand Equity, and Marketing Outcomes.	When compared to small and medium-sized enterprises (SMEs) and retail organisations, the marketing returns on investment (ROI) for highly valued brands may be both positive and negative.
Ho Y.K. Et al (2006)	An Analysis of Manufacturing and Nonmanufacturing Firms Regarding the Impact of Research and Development and Advertising on Firm Value.	Companies in the manufacturing sector are shown to benefit more from research and development and advertising in terms of one-year stock performance compared to non-manufacturing enterprises.

continued on following page

Table 1. Continued

Year/Author	Titles	Outcomes
Peterson R.A. and Jeong J. (2011)	Investigating how advertising and research and development budgets affect the value of corporate brands and the bottom line of individual firms.	The company's brand value and financial success are favourably impacted by advertising and research and development spending.
Akyuz A.M. and Berberoglu M. (2017)	Business Market Values as a Function of Advertising Spending and the Moderating Role of Research and Development Expenses	Spending on advertising and research and development raises a company's market worth by 20%.

Investing in research and development, according to the findings of a number of studies, will lead to increased marketing efficiency, financial gain, financial development, & transmit. Based on the information of initial public offering (IPO) firms over the time frame of 2006-2012, the emphasis on customer orientation is used to determine the impact of advertising and research and development expenditure on the reputation of the business as well as the activity efficiency of the company.

Because of his efforts, the author emphasises the fact that in need for a business to enhance the value of its brand as well as the perceived quality of its brand, as well as the amount of money it spends on advertising and research and development, the focus should be on the consumer. The amount of this contribution demonstrates that advertising and research and development efforts are closely tied to the level of consumer orientation, despite the fact that it is not denying its product consciousness or its involvement to the value of brand. On the other hand, the organisational structure of the corporation provides an explanation for the substantial nature of this influence. Different research was conducted by Sharma, Davick, and Pillai, in which they explored the role that innovation plays in the influence that spending on research and development and brand value have on marketing success.

In order to investigate a panel of data for a food brand with a rating of 1.357, the writers used regression & pro bit analysis. It is clear that worldwide corporations place a higher priority on research and development expenditures than small and medium-sized enterprises (SMEs) and merchants do in order to expand their innovation & market share. A strong brand's values are indicative of the fact that they have the potential to negatively impact product modernization & accomplishment of new-fangled items. Each of the writers investigated influence that R and D outlays along with brand worth have on marketplace portion in their own unique way. They contrasted the effects of small and medium-sized enterprises (SMEs) with those of multinational firms and retail companies.

Research and development outlays consume a significant optimistic influence on the overall marketplace portion of global firms in comparison to small and medium-sized enterprises (SMEs) and retail companies. On the other hand, the value of brands has a negative impression on the marketing share of global corporations in comparison to SMEs and retail organisations.

Consequently, the authors have provided compelling evidence that research and development consume a good influence on fresh concepts. However, they have also showed that globally trademarked and valued patented firms may consume either positive or negative effects on small and medium-sized enterprises (SMEs) and retail organisations when it comes to the R and D-based innovation in products approach. Ho, Keh & Omg conducted a different study in which they investigated the value of research and development & marketing outlays made by producers and non-producers over the course of 1 yr and 3 yrs, using the data set that had produced over a 41yrs spanning from 1963 to 2002. The research and development investments made by manufacturing companies were shown to have a favourable impact on the yearly stock performance of such companies, however the same scenario was not seen for companies that were not manufacturing companies.

Though, they too discover indications of a nonlinear link among research and development & marketing and business worth. This finding, in their view, constitutes a caveat of the current investigation. In addition, they propose that the scope of the study should be broadened in order to investigate the ways in which the connection between research and development and advertising on US companies would have an effect on the worth of the company, as well as on other industries and nations. "The" The purpose of this study is to conduct an empirical analysis under four different data situations by offering a framework that establishes a connection between the company's brand value and its spending on research and development.

The information procedure, kind of brand, the monetary presentation criteria, & the postponement construction are the components that make up this component. The information that was gathered from 126 businesses that were active between the years 1992 and 2008 was used. As an outcome of the evaluation of variance, it was shown that expenditures on advertising and research and development have a positive impact on the brand value, and that the brand value has a positive impact on the financial performance of the company. This study investigates the moderating influence that research and development expenditures have on connection among the marketing expenses of businesses & market standards.

As a means of gathering information, the analysis of panel data technique was used to the expenditures of 47 businesses that were operating over the years 2008-2012. The findings of the analyses showed that spending on advertising and research and development contributed to a 21% rise in the overall market value of firms. According to the findings of the research, it is also noted that the marketing expenditures of companies that have high R&D expenditures are relatively low, but the advertising expenses of companies that have poor R&D expenses are high.

Because of this, branded items that have considerable investment on research and development need less advertising.

4. INFORMATION AND APPROACH:

This study has generated data sets by utilising data of several indicators based on firms in order to investigate the link between research and development activities & brand value. These data sets have been developed in order to explore the relationship. The yearly report includes a listing of the top 501 firms with the greatest revenue, which includes the corporations that are included on the Fortune 501 list.

The information that pertains to these businesses that are featured on the Fortune 501 is associated with values of brands, patent counts, and research and development expenditures. The yearly brand principles of the 29 firms that are included on the Fortune 501 list, together with their sales, R&D expenses, & patent facts, will be used in panel data analysis that will be carried out. As a result of the fact that our research investigates the impact of the value of brands on indications that are associated with research and development activities, researcher have chosen to make brand worth the dependent inconstant, while R&D indicators are the independent variable quantity. Both independent and dependent variable quantity are broken down into their respective descriptions in Table 2 according to Figure 1.

Table 2. The Variable Description in Table

Variables	Variable Name	Variable	Description
	Brand Value	BV	Companies Brand Value (Milton Dollar)
Independent Variables	Revenue	Revenue	Total sales revenue for the year (in millions of dollars)
	No. of Patents	Patents	All patents filed with the US Patent and Trademark Workplace
	R and D Expenses	RD	Company Research and Development Spending (Millions of Dollars) Each Year

Figure 1. The Variables Description

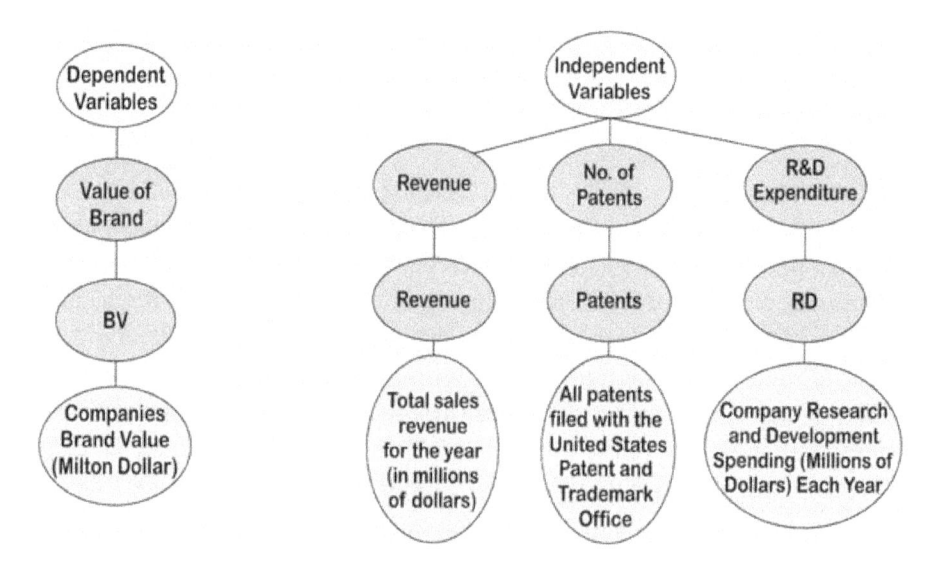

These variables are used to define the following model.

$$BV_{it} = \beta_0 + \beta_1 (revenue)_{it} + \beta_2 (patent)_{it} + \beta_3 (RD)_{it} + \varepsilon_{it} \qquad (1)$$

Within the context of this model, $\beta_1, \beta_2, \beta_3$ the error term is denoted by the self-governing variable constants, i each unit, t time sequence, and constant worth via use of estimate information that was acquired via the examination of the framework, the hypotheses that follow will be investigated:

A correlation exists between the value of a company's brand and the amount of money it spends on research and development among the businesses that are included in the Fortune 501.

There exists a correlation among the brand value of Fortune 501 firms and their sales, as stated in Hypothesis 2. There is a link among the number of trademarks held by Fortune 501 firms and the value of their brand's reputation.

5. RESULTS

In order to assess whether or not our model conforms to a fixed-effects or random effects model, the Hausman test was used throughout the analysis. It will use the model with random effects to explain a model if there's a connection between the error term and the independent factors. The idea of a null hypothesis was accepted.

This is the case if one exists. The acceptance of the other theory is contingent upon the absence of any correlation between the error term and the independent variables. There are the findings of the Hausman test shown in Table 3 and Figure 2.

After doing the test, it was determined that the likelihood score is not significant since the value of 11,98% is more than 7%. It may be concluded that the null hypothesis is accepted, and the outcomes of the random-effects framework will be taken into consideration.

Table 3. Table of Hausman Test

	Model of Fixed Effect	Model of Random Effects	Var (Diff.)	Prob.
Revenue	0.035071	0.043044	0.000020	0.0680
Patent	-1.017486	-0.628416	0.698819	0.06417
RD	5.819282	5.400863	0.043003	0.0437
Chi-Sq. Statistic		5.835180		
Chi-Sq. d.f.		4		
Prob>Chi-Sq		0.1198		

Figure 2. Hausman Test

	Revenue	Patent	RD	Chi-Sq. Statistic	Chi-Sq. d.f.	Prob> Chi-Sq.
Model of Fixed Effect	0.035071	-1.017486	5.819282			
Model of Random Effect	0.043044	-0.628416	5.400863	5.835180	4	0.1198
Var (Diff)	0.000020	0.698819	0.043003			
Prob.	0.0680	0.6417	0.0437			

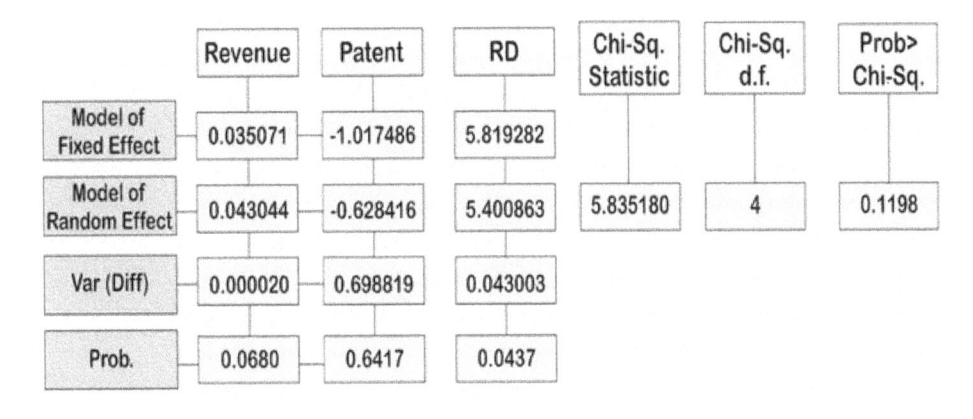

Table 4 and Figure 3 contains the findings of the study of regression with random effects. The value of the probability is lower than 0.06 if the F test outcome is taken into consideration, which indicates that our model is of statistical significance. The square root of the R-squared statistic is 0.485. Within the framework of our model, independent variables are capable of explaining 48.5% of the variables that are dependent. In order to provide an explanation for the value of the brand dependent variable, the model should include more factors, as shown by the low degree of explanatory level.

Table 4. Table for Test Findings

Model		
Variables	**Model of Fixed Effects**	**Model of Random Effects**
Revenue	0.035071 (0.0075)	0.043044 (0.0006)
Patent	-1.017486 (0.5197)	-0.628415 (0.6388)
RD	5.819282 (0.0001)	5.400863 (0.0001)
Constant	-678.4898 (0.7890)	-708.4485 (0.8575)
F	41.27332	56.03733
Prob>F	0.0001	0.0001
R-Sqr	0.894525	0.492836
Adjusted R-squared	0.872852	0.484041

Figure 3. Findings of Test

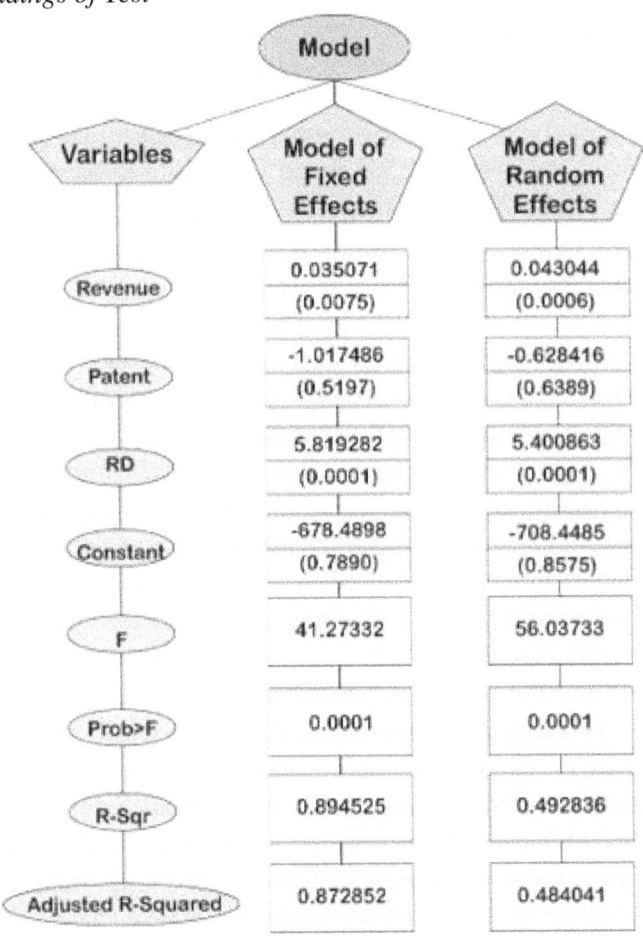

Variables	Model of Fixed Effects	Model of Random Effects
Revenue	0.035071 (0.0075)	0.043044 (0.0006)
Patent	-1.017486 (0.5197)	-0.628416 (0.6389)
RD	5.819282 (0.0001)	5.400863 (0.0001)
Constant	-678.4898 (0.7890)	-708.4485 (0.8575)
F	41.27332	56.03733
Prob>F	0.0001	0.0001
R-Sqr	0.894525	0.492836
Adjusted R-Squared	0.872852	0.484041

As a consequence of the findings of the T test, it has been determined that the variables pertaining to research and development and revenue have a substantial impact on the brand value, with the significance level being less than 0.06. Despite the fact that there's a positive correlation among them, the impact of the revenue variable on the worth of the brand is rather minor. As a consequence of this, the H1 and H2 are going to be accepted meanwhile the R and D spending & sales have a large and optimistic influence on the brand value. Due to the fact that the copyright variable is more than 0.06, we are able to assert that there is no impact on the value of the franchise. As a result of the fact that the patent variable does not have a substantial & positive effect on the worth of a brand the H3 must be denied.

6. CONCLUSION

This study is investigating the link among the brand value of select firms that are included on the list of the Fortune 501 most valuable corporations and the research and development activities that such companies engage in. On the international market, businesses that have a strong brand value tend to have higher levels of revenue income. On the list of businesses that have the most income, the brand ethics associated with these concerns are somewhat increased. Many businesses remain exerting a great deal of effort in order to enhance their competition in the international market and, as a result, to introduce new goods in order to enhance their economic performance. So, they put a large amount of money into research and development. Product innovation and patents gained as a result of the investment are among the most important variables for determining whether or not this investment was successful. Research and development expenditures, income, and brand value all have a positive association with one another. On the other hand, there was no correlation between the quantity of patents and the value of the brand.

As a result of research and development operations, the no. of patents remained thought to be a productivity, and it was anticipated that there would be a connection between brand value, R and D expenses. The parameters that placed restrictions on our investigation was the number of patents held by corporations. Because of the large number of patents which were only registered with the United States Patent and Trademark Office (USTPO), this was the result.

As an additional point of interest, the total amount of copyrights for altogether firms has not been achieved, & the total number of remarks has reduced. For the purpose of our research, which was modelled using revenue, R and D spending, & patent variables, degree of explanation was determined to be 48.5%. This is a level that is intermediate, and it even has a low rate of explanation. Due to the reality that the brand is not tangible, while the results of research and development operations remain physical, and the earnings has a big influence on the calculation of the brand value and possessing increases revenue as well as brand worth in comparison to the decreased R and D level of firms, this is the reason why this is the case. There is a 48.5% overlap between our model and the layer that provides explanations.

Because of this, we are able to assert that the worth of the brand is connected to the amount of money spent on research and development. There is a general consensus that the analyses that are conducted on the foundation of the firms and that are classified according to the industries will provide outcomes that have a greater degree of explanation. This research, for instance, may be broadened by categorising high-tech sectors that have significant R and D power, such as the internet, pharmaceutical, automotive & biotechnology, as well as sector with decreased R and D strength, including as power, food, finance, retail and fashion. This classification would allow for a more comprehensive analysis of the industry.

In research projects that are quite similar to this one, the influence of research and development to the economic development, financial presentation & marketing actions of businesses is being explored. Increasing the value of the brand and establishing a positive impression of the brand among customers are the primary goals of marketing operations. With the help of this study, it is possible to assert that research and development, which is the primary movement in which advanced goods are generated as output, makes a contribution to the body of literature by creating a link among innovative products and brand, which is the fundamental input in activities involving consumption. In the research study, a model was constructed to describe this circumstance. This model may be enhanced by utilising more data connected to research and development. The results of the study indicate that efforts related to research and development have the potential to influence one's financial performance, marketing activities, and brand value. In the process of formulating investment plans, it is emphasised that businesses should take into consideration the effect that investments in research and development have on the value of their brand.

REFERENCES:

Anderson, E. W., Fornell, C., & Mazvancheryl, S. K. (2004). Customer satisfaction and shareholder value. *Journal of Marketing*, 68(4), 172–185. DOI: 10.1509/jmkg.68.4.172.42723

Balasubramanian, S. K. (1994). Beyond advertising and publicity: Hybrid messages and public policy issues. *Journal of Advertising*, 23(4), 29–46. DOI: 10.1080/00913367.1943.10673457

Barney, J. B. (1995). Looking inside for competitive advantage. *The Academy of Management Perspectives*, 9(4), 49–61. DOI: 10.5465/ame.1995.9512032192

Carney, M. (2005). Corporate Governance and competitive advantage in Family-Controlled firms. *Entrepreneurship Theory and Practice*, 29(3), 249–265. DOI: 10.1111/j.1540-6520.2005.00081.x

Carney, M. (2005b). Corporate Governance and competitive advantage in Family-Controlled firms. *Entrepreneurship Theory and Practice*, 29(3), 249–265. DOI: 10.1111/j.1540-6520.2005.00081.x

Dwivedi, Y. K., Hughes, L., Ismagilova, E., Aarts, G., Coombs, C., Crick, T., Duan, Y., Dwivedi, R., Edwards, J., Eirug, A., Galanos, V., Ilavarasan, P. V., Janssen, M., Jones, P., Kar, A. K., Kizgin, H., Kronemann, B., Lal, B., Lucini, B., & Williams, M. D. (2019b). Artificial Intelligence (AI): Multidisciplinary perspectives on emerging challenges, opportunities, and agenda for research, practice and policy. *International Journal of Information Management*, 57, 101994. DOI: 10.1016/j.ijinfomgt.2019.08.002

Karnani, A. (2007). The mirage of marketing to the bottom of the pyramid: How the private sector can help alleviate poverty. *California Management Review*, 49(4), 90–111. DOI: 10.2307/41166407

Kolli, S., Ranjani, M., Kavitha, P., Daniel, D. A. P., & Chandramauli, A. (2023, January). Prediction of water quality parameters by IoT and machine learning. In *2023 International Conference on Computer Communication and Informatics (ICCCI)* (pp. 1-5). IEEE. DOI: 10.1109/ICCCI56745.2023.10128475

Kshirsagar, P. R., Reddy, D. H., Dhingra, M., Dhabliya, D., & Gupta, A. (2022, December). A Review on Comparative study of 4G, 5G and 6G Networks. In *2022 5th International Conference on Contemporary Computing and Informatics (IC3I)* (pp. 1830-1833). IEEE.

Luo, X., & Bhattacharya, C. (2006). Corporate social responsibility, customer satisfaction, and market value. *Journal of Marketing*, 70(4), 1–18. DOI: 10.1509/jmkg.70.4.001

Luo, X., & Bhattacharya, C. (2006b). Corporate social responsibility, customer satisfaction, and market value. *Journal of Marketing*, 70(4), 1–18. DOI: 10.1509/jmkg.70.4.001

Morsing, M. (2006). Corporate social responsibility as strategic auto-communication: On the role of external stakeholders for member identification. *Business Ethics (Oxford, England)*, 15(2), 171–182. DOI: 10.1111/j.1467-8608.2006.00440.x

Prahalad, C. K., & Hart, S. L. (2010). The fortune at the bottom of the pyramid. *Revista Eletrônica De Estratégia & Negócios*, 1(2), 1. DOI: 10.19177/reen.v1e220081-23

Ramgopal, N. C., Gantela, P., Rajagopal, R., & Thankam, T., & SenthamilSelvan, R. (2022, December). Automatic Liver Cancer Detection in Abdominal Liver Images Using Soft Optimization Techniques. In *2022 International Conference on Knowledge Engineering and Communication Systems (ICKES)* (pp. 1-5). IEEE.

Stefan, A., & Paul, L. (2008). Does it pay to be green? A systematic overview. *The Academy of Management Perspectives*, 22(4), 45–62. DOI: 10.5465/amp.2008.35590353

Chapter 20
Influential Social Media Marketing by Integrating the Strategic Implementation

Rajiv Mishra
Galgotias University, India

Sweta Saurabh
I Business Institute, India

Sachi Dwivedi
I Business Institute, India

Vikas Singh
https://orcid.org/0000-0002-1258-8863
Galgotias University, India

ABSTRACT

This study explains the strategic application of influencer marketing in the business to business (B2B) context and reveals the challenges that B2B organisations face in influencer marketing. It does this by drawing on theories related to employee advocacy, customer reference marketing, and organisational endorsement. A total of twenty-two senior management marketing experts from various industries were interviewed in-depth by the researchers. An examination of these stories reveals that business-to-business marketers promote the term "influential marketing," setting it apart from the more common term "influencer marketing" used by marketers targeting consumers directly. Credibility, knowledge, professionalism, and the sharing of

DOI: 10.4018/979-8-3693-7773-4.ch020

industry secrets are at the heart of business-to-business (B2B) persuasive marketing.

1. INTRODUCTION

The influence of informal Internet-mediated communication known as electronic word-of-mouth (eWOM) on customers' behaviours is growing (Van Eyssen, 2024), which has ramifications for the marketing strategies used by firms. A distinct subset of electronic word-of-mouth marketing, influencer marketing has recently arisen (Dong et al., 2024). Organisations and businesses engage in influencer marketing when they form partnerships with certain social media (SM) influencers to produce or/and promote sponsored content. This strategy aims to reach both the influencers' and the brands' respective audiences (Shelbert & Narayan, 2024). The majority of its value, however, lies in the estimated fifteen per cent of business-to-consumer firms that use influencer marketing initiatives (Brown et al., 2024), which, according to reports, may provide a return on investment (ROI) that is ten times greater than that of more conventional digital marketing strategies.

Although there has been much speculation among B2B academics that influencer marketing would be the "next big thing," very little study has looked at the breadth of influencer marketing specifically within the B2B sector (Pereira et al., 2024). While some academics touch on the idea of business-to-business (B2B) influencer marketing, thorough studies on the subject have been sluggish to materialise (Long et al., 2024). Using online channels has been crucial during the COVID-19 epidemic, and research acknowledges that SM may change the dynamics between various organisations (Singh, G, 2022). Research on influential advertising in the B2B context is scarce, in spite of the growing interest in studying how businesses (B2B) can use influencer marketing to build mutually beneficial relationships (Aslan et al., 2024; Hoffmann & Strauß, 2024). This is despite the fact that influencers are vital in connecting different organisations within business relationships.

This research fills a need in the literature by conducting one of the first empirical investigations of business-to-business (B2B) influencer marketing (Spanjol et al., 2024). The focus is on the characteristics, methods, and techniques that influencers utilise to attract a larger audience on social media. Our work makes a significant addition to the B2B SM literature in four aspects, all because this research area is still in its early phases (Sagala & Őri, 2024). To begin, provide a framework for thinking about business-to-business (B2B) influencer marketing and how it differs from business-to-consumer (B2C) marketing. The second one pinpoints the characteristics of influential people that are critical for building relationships in the business-to-business sector (Deutz et al., 2024). As for the third piece, it delves into the mechanics of business-to-business (B2B) influencer marketing, namely the typical tactical and strategic methods. Lastly, highlight the difficulties of business-to-business influencer marketing strategies (Arkadan et al., 2024), which may be useful for marketers as they create and implement influencer marketing campaigns.

Based on an analysis of twenty-two interviews with top marketers from various industries, this study distinguishes between business-to-business and business-to-consumer influencer marketing (Saridakis et al., 2024), and advertising, especially about influencer qualities like authority, audience size, and content kind. Broadly speaking, business-to-business (B2B) influencer marketing aims to build trusted connections and meaningful interaction with a variety of stakeholders by using endorsement and experience-based content created by prominent actors, both inside and external to the company (Islam et al., 2024). Further obstacles that B2B firms have when attempting to implement influencer marketing strategies include conservatism, an absence of relevant practical expertise, and an inadequate level of strategic integration with such strategies (Sundar, K. S. 2019). Understand the concept of influencer marketing as a fresh method of building and sustaining connections, and speculate about how modern business-to-business relationship marketing utilises influencers to promote employee advocacy, client referrals, brand awareness advertising and the support of organisations. To wrap up, provides valuable insights for managers on the crucial factors to consider when using influencer marketing for business-to-business companies. Future study directions are also proposed.

2. METHODOLOGY

A qualitative technique was used to investigate the recently developed phenomena of B2B influencer marketing, and in-depth semi-structured interviews were conducted at 2 firms worldwide. With research on B2B influencer marketing still in its early stages, the researchers take an experimental approach. The study aims to shed light on influencer marketing, how it is used in businesses, and how the corporate world now perceives it.

2.1 Data Collection and Conducting Samples

Managers having experience with influencer marketing at the highest levels of strategy decision-making were the major criteria for the researcher's selection in this understudied field. Chief marketing officers, chief innovation officers, chief executives, managing directors, and head of digital marketing and innovation are among the informants. Experience in influencer marketing in managerial positions, either present or past, was a critical criterion for selection. To find and contact several well-known B2B companies, the research team deliberately adopted a theoretical sampling strategy, depending on personal contacts and networks.

The central phenomenon can be better understood by interviewing B2B professionals, senior communication and marketing professionals, and company leaders who have extensive knowledge of influencer marketing strategy. These are some additional sampling criteria. 25 different companies provide various products and services, including advertising, marketing, finance, and insurance, as well as arts and crafts, office supplies, and electronics. To "reach beyond the superficial layers of their experience to generate informative, novel accounts of the phenomenon of interest," the purpose of the 39–73-minute interviews was to gain a genuine, in-depth knowledge of the respondents' inner and outer lives. The identities of the companies and key informants have been concealed to safeguard the financial interests of each group.

2.2 Analysing Data, Ensuring Authenticity and Reliability

The interviews are structured into four main parts. The first part consists of general questions meant to establish rapport and make the informant feel comfortable. These questions may include enquiries about their marketing and communications background, the industry in which they work, and their specific role within the organisation. Section 2 of the interview asks participants to describe the characteristics of B2B influencers and provide their thoughts on the efficacy of influencer marketing and related organisational strategies. Section 3 delves into the importance of influencer marketing in the business-to-business sector. The last round of the interviews asks participants to provide their thoughts on the most important problems and obstacles they've encountered while using influencer marketing. When more investigation is no longer yielding fresh information or when it seems that all pertinent insights have been explored, the interview process ends. To provide the highest level of interpretative and descriptive validity, interviews were immediately transcribed and examined, enabling the interviewer to make note of any extra observations that arose during the interview. By going through this procedure, the interviewer may address any unmentioned insights in the subsequent session.

One researcher collected the data, but two researchers worked together to analyse it to make sure it was consistent. Using template analysis, the interviews were examined in the NVivo software tool. To achieve investigator triangulation guarantee, construct validity and allow evaluation of the replies from diverse viewpoints, two researchers coded and evaluated the interviews separately after they were completed. This ensured inter-coder consistency. Coders reached the target score of 0.96 for the inter-rater reliability coefficient, and strong intercoder reliability was shown in 99% of situations where they agreed. This validates the classifications. The study team discussed and ultimately overcame the little conflicts via teamwork. The validity of the analyses was further enhanced by our practice of verifying and re-verifying emerging themes and interpretations. The two researchers monitored the emerging interpretations through the analytic period to ensure evaluative validity with many coders and to examine inter-coder consistency. When different people came to different conclusions, tried to achieve an agreement.

3. RESULTS

This section delineates the findings about the increasing significance of B2B influencer marketing and the distinctions seen by our respondents in comparison to the B2C scenario. The dimensions of business-to-business influencer marketing are also covered, along with the processes involved. These are illustrated by highlighting the tactical (such as content types and communication focus) and strategic (such as prior, new, and collaborative relationships) uses of influencer marketing. Finally, addresses the difficulties faced by B2B companies that engage in influencer marketing.

3.1 Growing Significance of 'Influential' Marketing

The findings indicate that influencer marketing is a relatively new concept for B2B companies, with all responding organisations using it to some extent: In the new position Influencer marketing is essential due to the increasingly diverse audience; hence, the influencer strategy inside the company has gained significance, focussing on the spheres of influence. Influencers are key objectives for the marketing approach and the platforms used to interact with the intended audiences, according to businesses who use influencer marketing to reach new customers and expand their networks beyond traditional marketing techniques. Moreover, utilising them and their connections is crucial for fostering collaborations. The informants concur that influencer marketing not only extends outreach to new audiences but also sustains current relationships. Consequently, respondents see the significance of influencer marketing for both acquisition and relationship-building, prompting companies to aggressively use influencer marketing for transactional and relational objectives, as indicated.

Businesses quickly see the benefits of influencer marketing when it comes to reaching out to people they have never met before, even if they may be a source of sales income. So, it's clear that influencer marketing isn't just a communication tool that works in an existing network; it's a technique to "reach out beyond" the crowd. The influencers' vast networks help to explain why this is the best approach to reach the audiences that these people have worked so hard to cultivate. According to the sources, influencers may connect faraway networks, which, when backed by organisations, can lead to the development of new connections between previously unrelated groups: Word of mouth and influencer marketing play a significant role in the creative B2B sector. When one establishes ties with influencers, they may provide valuable information, and ultimately, the success of the business depends on these connections. Sales are no longer the primary focus, and procedures shift to focus on encounters. A lot of people in marketing and sales at companies still don't get it; they're stuck in the past when it comes to relationships. According to respondents, the new relationships made via powerful partners have the potential to become organisational endorsers, which might lead to even more connections being made.

The importance of influencer marketing and the validity of its principles were echoed by all interviewees when discussing the growing importance of B2B marketing. Still, most people who took the survey either don't like or feel uncomfortable using the term "influencer marketing." Because of its use by business-to-consumer enterprises and unfavourable depictions in the media, the term may have taken on a pejorative meaning. In the consumer world, the term "influencer" might evoke unfavourable feelings. Referencing it in boardrooms will elicit disapproving expressions and associations with 'Kim Kardashian'. The language may provide challenges; nonetheless, the underlying idea is robust and significant. Interestingly, this is one of the social metrics are very keen to examine: the engagement of powerful individuals with social content. The negativity surrounding "influencer marketing" stems from certain business-to-consumer social media influencers that put too much emphasis on the entertainment value of their material and have become too monetised. This motive contradicts the principles of B2B marketing, which prioritise specialised knowledge and professionalism. The respondents' reluctance around the term influence marketing prompts them to employ the phrase "influential users," referring to those who wield considerable influence inside B2B groups. This also correlates effectively with some respondents.

Organisations that now use the phrase influential marketing instead of influencer marketing: Influential users in B2B contexts vary in several aspects from influencers in B2C settings. The researcher's reply underscores that it is commitment, the influence and regard of prominent figures as experts inside a highly insular group that holds significant authority. This pertains to B2B inside a limited echo chamber, as opposed to a prominent influencer; yet, if any of them were to send me anything, I would recognise its value. B2C influencer marketing primarily emphasises the influencer's public profile, including physical attractiveness, level of renown, and follower count, with their expertise in a certain domain such as fashion or gaming.

On the other side, business-to-business (B2B) influencer marketing focusses on the second part: influential people in the business world who have strong views, a lot of information about the rise of the self-proclaimed expert, and a lot of power in their own right. Since influencer marketing mimics consumer thought, it presents substantial dangers. Therefore, exclusively call B2B influencer marketing influencing marketing throughout this research. The term includes internal as well as external users who are influential since research suggests that influencing marketing may involve workers and others, as discussed below.

3.2 Influential Marketing Dimensions

Consistent with industry literature indicating its recent expansion, shows that influencer marketing is becoming more important to our respondent organisations. To promote their products in the consumer market, several firms use semi-professional influencers who already have a following. Influencers in business-to-business (B2B) settings are different from those in business-to-consumer (B2C) literature in that they often do not function as amateur social media (SM) content providers but rather have powerful positions within the sector. Consequently, categorise potential influential users into two separate categories: internal influentials, including well-connected employees, and external influentials, consisting of outside entities possessing influence and a voice in the domain. Next, discuss how influential marketing may be used in a relational context, what kind of content should concentrate on certain subjects, and what characteristics B2B influentials should possess.

3.2.1 Important Characteristics

3.2.1.1 Attributes of influential people and professionalism. Companies sought out B2B influentials based on their professionalism and other market-relevant qualities. In both business-to-business and business-to-consumer influencer marketing, one of the biggest challenges is finding external agents with the right qualities. Intriguingly, almost all 25 organisations that participated in this survey spoke about how they may improve their internal influence marketing by recognising and rewarding workers for being thought leaders in their industries and promoting them as organisational ambassadors. The researchers established technology days and created round tables to let staff are feeling they're a part of the adventure while tackling anything new, whether it an invention, uncharted area, or anything else. The researchers have been thinking about how they can help these employees' become influencers. Companies like this get their workers involved and even urge them to make a splash in the social media world. Though this may also be a part of business-to-consumer marketing in theory, our B2B responders have made it a strategic priority to address a problem that has not been addressed in the existing literature.

Examples of externally influenced marketing include case studies and news articles. This definition applies equally to business-to-business and consumer-to-business interactions; in both contexts, the goal is to identify users who will make meaningful contributions to the community of stakeholders in the focal brand through the sharing of valuable content. Don't call it public relations. Respected elders who have used our services before and had a good time are now representing our brand and promoting it. So, instead of being paid content makers, influentials are seen as knowledgeable people who freely share what they learnt. Some examples of external influences are current customers, members of the trade press, or prominent figures in the sector. Unlike influencers, business-to-consumer (B2C) influencers are chosen for their reach within a target demographic rather than their sector expertise; they often generate professional or semi-professional social media content.

3.2.1.2 Grab hold of it. When opposed to business-to-consumer influencer marketing, business-to-business influencer marketing focuses on reaching a more particular sector. Employees have a lot of sway over customers and other stakeholders, and those with clout within an organisation have an incentive to paint a favourable picture of their boss. Some businesses go above and beyond to hire influential users in addition to cultivating relationships with important network collaborators like consumers and job seekers. One example is when a company recruits someone with a reputation in the field for something like product success, speaking at events, having a blog, or even appearing on podcasts. This strategy has been proven to be effective, according to Interview 18. In contrast to the current literature on influencer marketing in the business-to-consumer sector, the focus in B2B influential marketing is on internal influences. Because many B2B industries are quite specialised, having important inside contacts is invaluable. This confirms what has been found in the literature on the importance of staff in business-to-business social media management.

However, many external influentials in business-to-business businesses are portrayed as micro-influencers, who help organisations connect with new audiences outside their current consumer base. B2B is more about micro-influencers, according to respondents, who include CEOs, specialists, and prominent professionals in their fields who are seen as corporate buddies or partners. Someone whose B2B audience is in the thousands, but interested in them nevertheless. An example of an influencer is an analyst company; like other influentials in our industry, they play a key role, but not in the same way. On the other hand, many influentials in the business-to-business sector have fewer networks than their consumer-facing colleagues. Most powerful people, nevertheless, have a small circle of acquaintances in the business world, including colleagues, partners, and peers, and their fan base is similarly limited.

Working with prominent people who are already familiar with the firm is a common way to start a business-to-business relationship with influentials. Instead of reaching out to influential who are new to the brand, B2B firms prefer to work with people they already know and trust to create genuine, industry-specific, and trustworthy social media content. This is in contrast to business-to-consumer interactions, where it is not essential to emphasise past or current ties. Although B2B influential users have modest audiences, their importance is in reaching certain sectors and encouraging excellent involvement from community members: The selection of influentials in B2B is driven by an emphasis on network quality rather than quantity.

Employees who are well-known and respected in their industry are more likely to represent their B2B company positively. Members of the community with a track record of involvement with the focus organisation and a degree of respect for their knowledge and experience are prime candidates for the role of external influence. Even yet, external influentials who have a small network might still make a lot of money because of the impact they have on the community.

3.2.2 Favourite Marketing Content

Informers prioritise the quality of B2B material above quantity. Influentials may engage audiences via diverse content and communication methods. B2B influencer marketing prioritises quality over quantity in content as contrasted to influencer marketing.

3.2.2.1 Content Types. B2B influential marketing, like B2C, focuses the content based on endorsement and on experience. Influential individuals develop experience-based material to share their firsthand experience working with the business. Customers often contribute experience-based information via social media platforms for customer reference marketing. Positive reviews provide valuable anecdotal feedback from delighted consumers who recommend your business, which is crucial since it directly impacts income. The material focuses on pleasant shared experiences between two parties, with stakeholders acting as endorsers to assist the main organisation reach a broader audience. It might be interpreted as a recommendation for your services. In contrast, endorsement-based material is provided by community leaders who possess specialist expertise about the company. The distinctive features of the brand may be shown via endorsement-based content that is created by internal as well as external influencers. Different types of endorsement-based material exist outside social media posts: take responsibility for obtaining references from clients and influencers. They provide references to potential clients to demonstrate credibility and trustworthiness throughout the sales process. Influentials are not only references but also qualified business partners. Collaborative marketing enables the focal brand to reach more audiences and the influential to develop their brand on social media. It involves considering the organization's brand's perception, trustworthiness, and power over customers. A two-way street between the target brand and the B2B influencer might lead to the two parties becoming strategic allies or even friends.

3.2.2.2 Communication Focus. Influential marketing material focuses on creating trust and reputation, rather than hard selling. Trust is crucial in the modern world. Some organisations emphasise brand in their marketing content, while others focus on trust and reputation. The aims are to provide professional information and connect with the audience. The goal is to establish credibility and become top-of-mind among powerful individuals, prompting them to recommend our organisation and individual when asked whom to collaborate with. Influential content and interaction may build credibility among audiences, reducing consumer uncertainty and risk perception towards the focus brand.

The targeted networks of B2B influencers allow them to project credibility, knowledge, and authority via their content. Authenticity is key to building trust and advocacy programs. While there is no one solution for B2B, it is easier than it seems due to the modest size of client groupings (verticals). For authenticity, provide great material backed by a relevant network of influentials.

External influencers can promote brand-created content, leading to meaningful engagement and trusting relationships. The business strategy involves using hashtags and direct messages to retweet or reshare useful content, sometimes for recognition. Content produced by prominent figures who are more forthcoming with personal information tends to be more interesting to viewers since it reveals not just their technical skills but also their human side. Self-disclosure also enhances brand love and perception. Influencers who are more open about themselves are regarded as more real, leading to better audience engagement.

Influential B2B marketing requires authenticity, knowledge, and credibility. Influentials create material that conveys the qualities created between the main brand and them to a larger audience. Influentials in B2B marketing might function as a brand's corporate buddy by sharing favourable information via experience or endorsements. This content production strategy aims to create and distribute useful material to a targeted audience.

3.2.3 Influential marketing relationships

Influential marketing is a strategic relations method that aims to build and retain connections, leading to brand results. This section explores B2B impactful marketing's relational characteristics by studying current, new, and collaborative partnerships.

3.2.3.1 Known Relationships. Online methods are widely used by B2B organisations to create client connections and reputations, such as via endorsements. Effective marketing strategies begin with leveraging existing connections and identifying important influencers inside company networks, according to a study. When planning influential marketing, B2B firms take time to analyse their networks and identify essential people. Organisations may create relationships with powerful individuals and exhibit their expertise via successful initiatives. Understanding the grasp and networks of significant individuals is crucial for successful B2B marketing use.

PowerPoint presentation, the researchers suggest changing the term 'influencer marketing' to 'relationship' or 'BD' to emphasise its behavioural importance. Organisations commonly use existing connections to communicate and interact with customers, suppliers, and other stakeholders. Influential marketing serves as a tool for company expansion and acquisition, creating new chances for businesses.

3.2.3.2 New and Existing Collaborations. The respondents saw B2B influential marketing as a constant activity of building collaborative connections with internal and external influencers and network players. Organisations using influential marketing prioritise engaging influencers and business partners as a key strategic aim. The main organisation aims to attract new customers and strengthen current relationships by using influential' endorsements and audience involvement. A prominent industry figure endorses the white paper. Thus, B2B organisations anticipate influentials to generate engaging content and mediate audience engagement. Through this ongoing partnership, both sides gain influence and must invest in content production, engagement, and endorsement.

Section 3.2.1.2 highlights the importance of external influencers in increasing brand recognition among new customers for the focus firm. Influentials aid the focus brand in establishing new relationships with possible business partners, such as consumers, suppliers, and community stakeholders. Initially, these linkages may be weak relationships. Continuous partnership with influentials promotes brand awareness, pleasant customer experiences, and increased trust among new audiences. Influential marketing effectively supports us and our clients, boosting their experience. Instead of relying on gut instinct, it's more of a deliberate process rather than a mere influence. Interview 4. Developing strong business collaborations and a planned marketing approach may take time and several exposures.

Influential endorsements may enhance current connections and attract new consumers and networks, especially when the target groups of the focus organisation and the influential coincide. Influencers are individuals and interact with in many areas. To exploit online connections via influential marketing, organisations establish teams dedicated to communicating with and engaging influentials. As part of the business development strategy, identify influencers, such as government policymakers or thought leaders in payment and open banking. Identified individuals are followed on Twitter and LinkedIn Establishing a link with internal or external influencers might facilitate content development by the influential.

To conclude, B2B businesses must carefully study, choose, and engage with linked influential to strategically deploy influential marketing. Use experience-based material and/or endorsers to promote good and trustworthy brand representation on social media. Influencers may link brands with their following, increasing brand reach and visibility in their market. Collaborating with a brand enables B2B influencers to showcase their industry knowledge and effect, promoting personal branding on an SM platform. Influential marketing creates mutual benefit between B2B businesses and influentials.

3.3 Challenges of Powerful Marketing

Given the novelty and limited research on influence marketing in B2B, businesses face problems and limitations in implementing it. A common challenge in B2B businesses is the thinking towards relationship management. Identify instances of resistance to influence marketing owing to unfamiliarity with the issue outside the marketing department. Many B2B organisations have been sluggish to adopt persuasive marketing, despite its potential future importance. Influencer marketing is not presently a priority for the financial sector, but it may be in the future. However, the industry has yet to fully embrace its potential.

While influence marketing is valued in B2B, the data indicates that firms have not completely adopted it. In B2B, complicated buying cycles make it less probable that marketing influences purchase choices, unlike in B2C. Organisations have difficulties in finding industry experts owing to the intricacy of the subject matter, despite their efforts to use consumer references marketing and organisational endorsements via influential marketing. Companies have a hard time capitalising on connections because their employees lack the necessary expertise. Implementing persuasive marketing necessities resources as well as strategic preparation, but B2B firms' awareness of its effectiveness is still developing. Using individuals to tell the brand narrative is key to social media since it is about connecting with people rather than just the brand. Influencer marketing in B2C businesses is an established business strategy that includes cash or product payments for brand endorsement material. In contrast, B2B engagement efforts, such as customer referring, staff advocacy, and endorsement, are often unpaid, making it challenging to determine content deployment, timing, and quantity.

Implementing persuasive marketing needs resources and strategic preparation, staff should be reputable persons who can promote the primary brand. However, the prevailing assumption that workers remain hinders powerful marketing. As a result, ended up parting ways with them.

To avoid falling behind, businesses must have the correct personnel and strategy for digital marketing. To comprehend and use the strategy, individuals must be repositioned inside the company.

Awareness of its effectiveness is still developing. Part of this is using individuals to convey the brand narrative since social media is about connecting with people, not just brands. Influencer marketing in B2C businesses is an established business strategy that includes cash or product payments for brand endorsement material. In contrast, B2B engagement efforts, such as customer referring, staff advocacy, and endorsement, are often unpaid, making it challenging to determine content deployment, timing, and quantity.

Implementing influencing marketing may have a good influence, but it faces problems in resource allocation, strategy, selection, and implementation, in connection with other marketing methods. Influential marketing requires rigorous planning, strategic implementation, and continuous monitoring to support overall marketing objectives.

This study delves into the workings of influential marketing, a relatively new phenomena, in the business-to-business sector. The results of our interviews point to the increasing significance of influential marketing research, which is still in its early stages in B2B literature. Use a theories-in-use approach that focusses on organisational endorsement, consumer reference marketing, and staff advocacy to get a deeper understanding of how organisations are strategically adopting influence marketing. Using the knowledge of both internal (workers) and external (experts outside the business) influentials, companies build connections, both with current customers and with potential new ones. The study's findings highlight the ways in which B2B firms may manage their workers' SM activity and teach them to generate good impact material, even if researchers do identify certain unique traits of SM users. In addition to classifying both internal and external consumers into broad groups, our research sheds light on what makes an influential person successful and details the strategies and tactics used to put influence marketing into action. Interviewees prefer the phrase "influential marketing" over "influencer marketing" due to negative connotations in B2C. Our analysis found that B2B influencer marketing is similar to consumer influencer marketing, but with several key differences. B2B influencer marketing usually targets specialist sectors. Unlike B2C influencer marketing, B2B influencers are local and work with smaller audiences. Engaging in influencer marketing may either fortify pre-existing company connections or create new ones via the influentials' network, allowing the main brand to reach a wider audience. This research provides a deeper understanding of the relational part of effective business-to-business marketing. Workers in any given industry are vital linkages between the company and its current and potential customers. On the other hand, the B2C social media marketing literature noticeably fails to address the correlation between increased employee engagement with influencer marketing and SM-mediated employee advocacy.

Since influential marketing has received so little attention in the literature until now, they provide a theoretical framework for understanding its application to the business-to-business (B2B) sectors. Through three channels—1) staff campaigning, 2) organisational approval, and 3) consumer reference marketing—our conceptualisation reveals that influentials from both within and outside the company contribute to influential marketing. In particular, influentials facilitate communication with both current and potential audiences by producing endorsement-and experience-based material and encouraging participation. As advocated by influentials, the concept of influential marketing is that it aims to build lifetime value via interconnected interactions in an expanding customer-base.

Influential marketing is becoming an integral part of the material that develops and maintains relationships in the business-to-business sector. The activity ties between organisations allow for the extension of relationships between prominent individuals and the organisations' prospective customers and partners via employee participation, organisational endorsement, and customer referrals. In addition, the influentials promote the main company on social media via broadcasting experience-based content and creating authentic branded content, also called endorsement-based content. For instance, this might refer to reposting company information or initiating online conversations with other artists and SM audiences. A variety of connections may be formed along this route, which in turn influence the relationships inside the network. Relationships like this may build over time via endorsements, referrals, and content production, but for the best results, it's important for personal and corporate voices to work together. Consequently, business-to-business (B2B) firms must establish methods for the strategic and tactical administration of impactful marketing campaigns.

The participants in business-to-business (B2B) networks form dyadic relationships of varying strengths. Interactions between actors may be thought of as a network connection pattern; weak links are often linked to information benefits, while strong relationships are more indicative of trust and commitment. Strategically using influential marketing allows one to build strong connections with internal as well as external influentials, along with other network partners. A variety of methods and strategies, including content kinds and communication foci, as well as existing, new, or collaborative partnerships, may be used to achieve this goal. Organisations can benefit from internal influentials' strong relationships with committed and trustworthy partners, as well as those with external influentials, in order to expand their business networks. On the other hand, external influentials can help strengthen existing strong relationships and connect with weaker ones within the focal brand's network.

Influential marketing, however, helps both the focus organisation and influentials gain from working together, which in turn strengthens their relationship over time.

This study leads us to create an integrated framework (see Fig. 1) that illustrates the strategic approach of persuasive marketing in the business-to-business (B2B) space. By executing impactful marketing strategies, the primary brand may attract new consumers, therefore expanding its present networks, while simultaneously preserving existing connections inside its speciality sector. The active involvement of influential individuals, including workers and specialists, in the target businesses' influential marketing plan fosters increased trust and commitment, attributable to the characteristics and reach of these influentials. By using these ties, the B2B business may connect and work with both internal and external influencers. As a result, trust and dedication are the two most important factors for influential cooperation to succeed. Collaborating with genuine, well-informed, and prominent community members is an option for B2B firms' employees and/or industry specialists inside their business networks. Mediators, influencers create and post various forms of social media material pertaining to a central brand, interact with their followers (the point of contact), and aid in the expansion of the central brand's online visibility and professional network. Relationships with clients, partners, and suppliers may be fortified by such actions. Furthermore, powerful advertising may be used as a tool for company growth and partnerships, among other collaborative interactions. Such strategic results strengthen the main brand's assets, enabling them to efficiently deploy various resources and establish connections and alliances among stakeholders to back their impactful marketing campaign. Meanwhile, the influentials' personal branding and online impact are both boosted by the brand-influencer relationship.

Figure 1. Integrated Framework

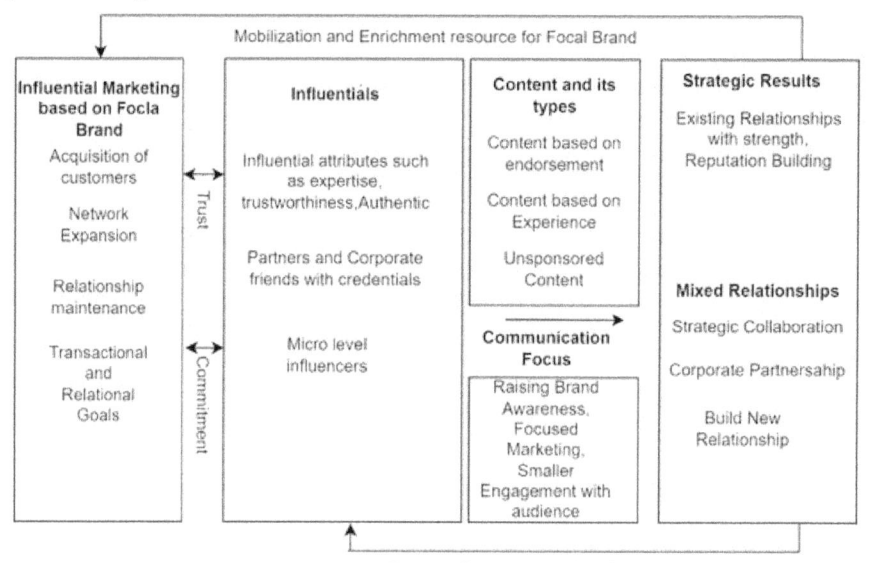

4. CONCLUSION

This study's takeaway is that business-to-business (B2B) companies should work towards achieving their marketing objectives by coordinating their effective marketing tactics with other marketing efforts and aspects of their company culture. Incorporating influential marketing into a marketing strategy requires a B2B organisation to strategically organise and allocate resources. This can require a significant financial investment as well as the provision of human capital as well as employee engagement education. Additional costs result from the need of coordinating across many areas, including marketing, human resources, and operations. Influential marketing is relational, so you'll need to put in some time and effort now to see a return in the future. Building and sustaining corporate friendships with powerful individuals also demands a substantial time commitment, which is inherent to B2B relationships. The importance of both internal and external influentials is the subject of this third recommendation. External influentials have a choice between reaching more people and having less say over what they post, while internal influentials may have to choose between a lower level of persuasiveness and less coordinating work.

There should be cooperation between internal and external influentials, rather than competition between the two.

Instead of making a black-and-white decision, business-to-business companies may interact with their workers via advocacy programs while collaborating with other industry experts who can vouch for and reference the company. By combining the two methods, we can expand our online business networks to their full potential. In addition, business-to-business (B2B) influential marketing sometimes involves a partnership in which the B2B company permits its influentials to share unique company news, which serves the influencers' self-interest in building their own brands on social media. A long-term partnership between the company and the influencer may be achieved via this type of mutual support.

REFERENCES

Arkadan, F., Macdonald, E. K., & Wilson, H. N. (2024). Customer experience orientation: Conceptual model, propositions, and research directions. *Journal of the Academy of Marketing Science.* Advance online publication. DOI: 10.1007/s11747-024-01031-y

Aslan, A., Öztürk, M., & Eryeşil, K. (2024). Mapping and Current Trends in Sustainable Communication: A Bibliometric View. *Erciyes İletişim Dergisi*, 11(2), 539–562. DOI: 10.17680/erciyesiletisim.1445304

Brown, J. A., Hughes, A., Bhutta, M. F., Trautrims, A., & Trueba, M. L. (2024). Synergistic state governance of labour standards in global value chains: Forced labour in the Malaysia–Nepal–UK medical gloves supply chain. *Competition & Change*, 28(5), 581–603. Advance online publication. DOI: 10.1177/10245294241272190

Deutz, P., Vermeulen, W. J., Baumgartner, R. J., Ramos, T. B., & Raggi, A. (2024). Circular Economy realities. In Routledge eBooks. https://doi.org/DOI: 10.4324/9781003295631

Dong, Y., He, X., & Blut, M. (2024). How and when does digitalization influence export performance? A meta-analysis of its consequences and contingencies. *International Marketing Review.* Advance online publication. DOI: 10.1108/IMR-02-2024-0044

Hoffmann, C. P., & Strauß, N. (2024). Effective financial communication. https://doi.org/DOI: 10.4324/9781003271826

Islam, T., Miron, A., Nandy, M., Choudrie, J., Liu, X., & Li, Y. (2024). Transforming Digital Marketing with Generative AI. *Computers*, 13(7), 168. DOI: 10.3390/computers13070168

Long, N. T., Tho, B. D., Linh, D. H., & Tuan, B. D. (2024). Evaluating Brand Awareness of Tea Brand with the Case of Moc Suong Oolong Tea Brand Vietnam. *Journal of Social and Political Sciences*, 7(3). Advance online publication. DOI: 10.31014/aior.1991.07.03.502

Pereira, V., Jayawardena, N. S., Sindhwani, R., Behl, A., & Laker, B. (2024). Using firm-level intellectual capital to achieve strategic sustainability: Examination of phenomenon of business failure in terms of the critical events. *Journal of Intellectual Capital.* Advance online publication. DOI: 10.1108/JIC-03-2024-0074

Sagala, G. H., & Őri, D. (2024). Toward SMEs digital transformation success: A systematic literature review. *Information Systems and e-Business Management*. Advance online publication. DOI: 10.1007/s10257-024-00682-2

Saridakis, G., Khan, Z., Knight, G., Idris, B., Mitra, J., & Khan, H. (2024). A Look into the Future: The Impact of Metaverse on Traditional Theories and Thinking in International Business. *MIR. Management International Review*, 64(4), 597–632. DOI: 10.1007/s11575-024-00550-8

Shelbert, V., & Narayan, A. (2024). Discussion paper. In IWA Publishing eBooks. https://doi.org/DOI: 10.2166/9781789064964

Singh, G., Appadurai, J. P., Perumal, V., Kavita, K., Ch Anil Kumar, T., Prasad, D. V. S. S. S. V., Azhagu Jaisudhan Pazhani, A., & Umamaheswari, K. (2022). Machine Learning-Based Modelling and Predictive Maintenance of Turning Operation under Cooling/Lubrication for Manufacturing Systems. *Advances in Materials Science and Engineering*, 2022(1), 9289320. DOI: 10.1155/2022/9289320

Spanjol, J., Noble, C. H., Baer, M., Bogers, M. L. M., Bohlmann, J., Bouncken, R. B., Bstieler, L., De Luca, L. M., Garcia, R., Gemser, G., Grewal, D., Hoegl, M., Kuester, S., Kumar, M., Lee, R., Mahr, D., Nakata, C., Ordanini, A., Rindfleisch, A., & Wetzels, M. (2024). Fueling innovation management research: Future directions and five forward-looking paths. *Journal of Product Innovation Management*, 41(5), 893–948. Advance online publication. DOI: 10.1111/jpim.12754

Sundar, K. S. (Ed.). (2019). *Globalization, Labour Market Institutions, Processes and Policies in India*. Palgrave Macmillan. DOI: 10.1007/978-981-13-7111-0

Van Eyssen, T. (2024). *Sourcing, analysing, and Visualising stories: Multidisciplinary programme development in data journalism*. https://doi.org/DOI: 10.26686/wgtn.27115939

Compilation of References

Aaker, D. A. (2021). *Building Strong Brands*. Free Press.

Abd Rashid, M. H., & Ahmad, F. S. (2014). The role of recovery satisfaction on the relationship between service recovery and brand evangelism: A conceptual framework. *International Journal of Innovation, Management and Technology*, 5(5), 401. DOI: 10.7763/IJIMT.2014.V5.548

Abddulhai, I. N., Husin, M. H., Baharudin, A. S., & Abdullah, N. A. (2022). Determinants of Facebook adoption and its impact on service-based small and medium enterprise performance in Northwestern Nigeria. *Journal of Systems and Information Technology*, 24(3).

Abdul Ghan, N., Hamid Ibrahim, S., Targio Hashem, A., & Ahmedc, E. (2019). Social media big data analytics: A survey. *Computers in Human Behavior*, 101, 417–428. DOI: 10.1016/j.chb.2018.08.039

Abidin, C. (2016). Visibility labor: Engaging with influencers' fashion brands and #OOTD advertorial campaigns on Instagram. *Media International Australia, Incorporating Culture & Policy*, 161(1), 86–100. DOI: 10.1177/1329878X16665177

Abkenar, S. B., Kashani, M. H., Mahdipour, E., & Jameii, S. M. (2021). Big data analytics meets social media: A systematic review of techniques, open issues, and future directions. *Telematics and Informatics*, 57, 101517. DOI: 10.1016/j.tele.2020.101517 PMID: 34887614

Acceleration Partners. (n.d.). Convergence of influencer and affiliate marketing. Retrieved September 3, 2024, from https://www.accelerationpartners.com/resources/convergence-influencer-affiliate-marketing/

Acikgoz, F., & Burnaz, S. (2021). The influence of "influencer marketing" on YouTube influencers. *International Journal of Internet Marketing and Advertising*, 15(2), 201. DOI: 10.1504/IJIMA.2021.114331

Agnihotri, D., Chaturvedi, P., Kulshreshtha, K., & Tripathi, V. (2023). Investigating the impact of authenticity of social media influencers on followers' purchase behavior: Mediating analysis of parasocial interaction on Instagram. *Asia Pacific Journal of Marketing and Logistics*, 35(10), 2377–2394. DOI: 10.1108/APJML-07-2022-0598

Agnihotri, R., Dingus, R., & Krush, M. (2020). Social media use in B2B sales and its impact on competitive intelligence. In *Proceedings of the 53rd Hawaii International Conference on System Sciences*, 367-376. DOI: 10.24251/HICSS.2020.345

Ainin, S., Parveen, F., Moghavvemi, S., Jaafar, N. I., & Mohd Shuib, N. L. (2015). Factors influencing the use of Social Media by SMEs and its Performance outcomes. *Industrial Management & Data Systems*, 115(3), 570–588. DOI: 10.1108/IMDS-07-2014-0205

Ajzen, I. (1991). The theory of planned behavior. *Organizational Behavior and Human Decision Processes*, 50(2), 179–211. DOI: 10.1016/0749-5978(91)90020-T

Akdim, K., Casaló, L. V., & Flavián, C. (2022). The role of utilitarian and hedonic aspects in the continuance intention to use social mobile apps. *Journal of Retailing and Consumer Services*, 66, 102888. DOI: 10.1016/j.jretconser.2021.102888

Aktan, M., Anjam, M., Zaman, U., Khwaja, M. G., & Akram, U. (2023). Missing link in 'new-normal' for higher education: Nexus between online experiential marketing, perceived-harm, social distancing concern and university brand evangelism in China. *Journal of Marketing for Higher Education*, •••, 1–26. DOI: 10.1080/08841241.2023.2253743

Alam, F., Tao, M., Lahuerta-Otero, E., & Feifei, Z. (2022). Let's buy with social commerce platforms through social media influencers: An Indian consumer perspective. *Frontiers in Psychology*, 13, 853168. DOI: 10.3389/fpsyg.2022.853168 PMID: 35496238

Al-Azzam, A. F., & Al-Mizeed, K. (2021). The effect of digital marketing on purchasing decisions: A case study in Jordan. *The Journal of Asian Finance. Economics and Business*, 8(5), 455–463.

Albahri, A. S., Alnoor, A., Zaidan, A. A., Albahri, O. S., Hameed, H., Zaidan, B. B., Peh, S. S., Zain, A. B., Siraj, S. B., Masnan, A. H. B., & Yass, A. A. (2021). Hybrid artificial neural network and structural equation modelling techniques: A survey. *Complex & Intelligent Systems*, 8(2), 1781–1801. DOI: 10.1007/s40747-021-00503-w PMID: 34777975

Albert, N., & Merunka, D. (2013). The role of brand love in consumer-brand relationships. *Journal of Consumer Marketing*, 30(3), 258–266. DOI: 10.1108/07363761311328928

Algaba, A., Ardia, D., Bluteau, K., Borms, S., & Boudt, K. (2020). ECONOMETRICS MEETS SENTIMENT: AN OVERVIEW OF METHODOLOGY AND APPLICATIONS. *Journal of Economic Surveys*, 34(3), 512–547. DOI: 10.1111/joes.12370

Alharthey, B. K. (2024). Influencing smartphone choices: The interplay of social media marketing and brand image on purchase intentions. *British Journal of Management and Marketing Studies*, 7(1), 19–34. DOI: 10.52589/BJMMS-5R9ZO4ZW

Alkadrie, S. A. (2024). Exploring the impact of digital marketing strategies on consumer purchase behavior in the e-commerce sector. *The Journal of Academic Science*, 1(4), 273–282. DOI: 10.1002/some_journal_reference

Alkateeb, M. A., & Abdalla, R. A. (2021). Social Media Adoption and its Impact on SMEs Performance A Case Study of Palestine. *Estudios de Economía Aplicada*, 39(7). Advance online publication. DOI: 10.25115/eea.v39i7.4872

Allen, L. (2022). The Rise of the Micro-Influencer as a new Form of Marketing in Neoliberal Times. *Critical Reflections: A Student Journal on Contemporary Sociological Issues*, 1 (1), 208-220.

AlSharji, A., Ahmad, S. Z., & Bakar, A. R. A. (2018). Understanding Social Media Adoption in SMEs Empirical Evidence from the United Arab Emirates. *Journal of Entrepreneurship in Emerging Economies*, 10(2), 302–328. DOI: 10.1108/JEEE-08-2017-0058

Altıntaş, M. H., & Tokol, T. (2007). Cultural openness and consumer ethnocentrism: An empirical analysis of Turkish consumers. *Marketing Intelligence & Planning*, 25(4), 308–325. DOI: 10.1108/02634500710754565

Alvarez-Monzoncillo, J. M. (2023). *The dynamics of influencer marketing: A multidisciplinary approach*. Taylor & Francis.

Amani, D. (2022). Demystifying factors fueling university brand evangelism in the higher education sector in Tanzania: A social identity perspective. *Cogent Education*, 9(1), 2110187. DOI: 10.1080/2331186X.2022.2110187

Amani, D. (2022). The student Psychological Contract as a predictor of university brand evangelism in Tanzanian higher education. *International Journal of African Higher Education*, 9(2), 150–171. DOI: 10.6017/ijahe.v9i2.15379

Anderson, E. W., Fornell, C., & Mazvancheryl, S. K. (2004). Customer satisfaction and shareholder value. *Journal of Marketing*, 68(4), 172–185. DOI: 10.1509/jmkg.68.4.172.42723

Angelakis, G., Lemonakis, C., Galariotis, E., & Zopounidis, C. (2022). Current trends on food tourism approaches through a conceptual framework of food tourism management. *International Journal of Knowledge Management in Tourism and Hospitality*, 2(4), 331. DOI: 10.1504/IJKMTH.2022.124089

Anggarini, L. (2018).. . *Understanding Brand Evangelism and the Dimensions Involved in a Consumer Becoming Brand Evangelist*, 2(1), 63–84.

Anggraini, L. (2018). Understanding brand evangelism and the dimensions involved in a consumer becoming brand evangelist. *Sriwijaya International Journal of Dynamic Economics and Business*, 63-84.

Anggraini, L. (2018). Understanding brand evangelism and the dimensions involved in a consumer becoming brand evangelist. *Sriwijaya International Journal of Dynamic Economics and Business*, 63-84. https://doi.org/DOI: 10.1234/some_doi

Ang, L. (2011). Community relationship management and social media. *Journal of Database Marketing & Customer Strategy Management*, 18(1), 31–38. DOI: 10.1057/dbm.2011.3

Antoniou, G., Grobelnik, M., Simperl, E., Parsia, B., Plexousakis, D., De Leenheer, P., & Pan, J. Z. (Eds.). (2011). The Semantic Web: Research and Applications: *8th Extended Semantic Web Conference, ESWC 2011,* Heraklion, Crete, Greece, May 29–June 2, 2011. *Proceedings, Part II* (Vol. 6644). Springer.

Ao, L., Bansal, R., Pruthi, N., & Khaskheli, M. B. (2023). Impact of social media influencers on customer engagement and purchase intention: A meta-analysis. *Sustainability (Basel)*, 15(3), 2744. DOI: 10.3390/su15032744

Arkadan, F., Macdonald, E. K., & Wilson, H. N. (2024). Customer experience orientation: Conceptual model, propositions, and research directions. *Journal of the Academy of Marketing Science*. Advance online publication. DOI: 10.1007/s11747-024-01031-y

Arnesson, J. (2023). Influencers as ideological intermediaries: Promotional politics and authenticity labour in influencer collaborations. *Media Culture & Society*, 45(3), 528–544. DOI: 10.1177/01634437221117505

Arora, A., Bansal, S., Kandpal, C., Aswani, R., & Dwivedi, Y. (2019). Measuring social media influencer index- insights from Facebook, Twitter and Instagram. *Journal of Retailing and Consumer Services*, 49, 86–101. DOI: 10.1016/j.jretconser.2019.03.012

Arriagada, A., & Bishop, S. (2021). Between commerciality and authenticity: The imaginary of social media influencers in the platform economy. *Communication, Culture & Critique*, 14(4), 568–586. DOI: 10.1093/ccc/tcab050

Asad, A. I., Popesko, B., & Godman, B. (2024). Unravelling the internal drivers of pharmaceutical company performance in Europe: A DEMATEL analysis. *Equilibrium Quarterly Journal of Economics and Economic Policy*, 19(2), 661–702. DOI: 10.24136/eq.2896

Ashley, C., & Tuten, T. (2015). Creative strategies in social media marketing: An exploratory study of branded social content and consumer engagement. *Psychology and Marketing*, 32(1), 15–27. DOI: 10.1002/mar.20761

Asif, M., Khan, M. A., Alhumoudi, H., & Wasiq, M. (2023). Examining the role of self-reliance, social domination, perceived surveillance, and customer support with respect to the adoption of mobile banking. *International Journal of Environmental Research and Public Health*, 20(5), 3854.

Asim, M., & Arif, M. (2023). Internet of Things adoption and use in academic libraries: A review and directions for future research. *Journal of Information Science*, •••, 01655515231188338. DOI: 10.1177/01655515231188338

Aslan, A., Öztürk, M., & Eryeşil, K. (2024). Mapping and Current Trends in Sustainable Communication: A Bibliometric View. *Erciyes İletişim Dergisi*, 11(2), 539–562. DOI: 10.17680/erciyesiletisim.1445304

Atkins, J. (2023). The Perils of Advocacy. *arXiv preprint arXiv:2306.09492*.

Attri, R., & Bhagwat, J. (2022). Influencer marketing in data-driven world. *Management Dynamics*, 22(2), 8.

Audrezet, A., de Kerviler, G., & Moulard, J. G. (2020). Authenticity under threat: When social media influencers need to go beyond self-presentation. *Journal of Business Research*, 117, 557–569. DOI: 10.1016/j.jbusres.2018.07.008

Au-Yong-Oliveira, M., Cardoso, A. S., Goncalves, M., Tavares, A., & Branco, F. (2019). Strain effect-a case study about the power of nano-influencers. *2019 14th Iberian Conference on Information Systems and Technologies (CISTI)*, 1–5.

Badenes-Rocha, A., Bigne, E., & Ruiz, C. (2021). Impact of cause-related marketing on consumer advocacy and cause participation: A causal model based on self-reports and eye-tracking measures. *Psychology and Marketing*, mar.21590. Advance online publication. DOI: 10.1002/mar.21590

Baid, A. M. (2014). Method of dyeing textile article from medicinally rich herbs. Retrieved from http://www.patentgenius.com

Bakker, D. (2018). Conceptualizing influencer marketing. Journal of emerging trends in marketing and management, 1(1), 79-87.

Bakker, D. (2018). Conceptualising influencer marketing. *Journal of Emerging Trends in Marketing and Management*, 1(1), 79–87.

Balaban, D. C., & Szambolics, J. (2022). A proposed model of self-perceived authenticity of social media influencers. *Media and Communication*, 10(1), 235–246. DOI: 10.17645/mac.v10i1.4765

Balaban, D., & Mustatea, M. (2019). Users' perspective on the credibility of social media influencers in Romania and Germany. *Romanian Journal of Communication and Public Relations*, 21(1), 31–46. DOI: 10.21018/rjcpr.2019.1.269

Balabanis, G., & Diamantopoulos, A. (2004). Domestic country Bias, Country-of-Origin Effects, and Consumer Ethnocentrism: A Multidimensional unfolding approach. *Journal of the Academy of Marketing Science*, 32(1), 80–95. DOI: 10.1177/0092070303257644

Balabanis, G., Mueller, R. D., & Melewar, T. (2002). The relationship between consumer ethnocentrism and human values. *Journal of Global Marketing*, 15(3–4), 7–37. DOI: 10.1300/J042v15n03_02

Balasubramanian, S. K. (1994). Beyond advertising and publicity: Hybrid messages and public policy issues. *Journal of Advertising*, 23(4), 29–46. DOI: 10.1080/00913367.1943.10673457

Bandara, A., & Wong, W. W. (2024). Examine the factors influencing the firm performance of local travel companies in Malaysia. *Quantum Journal of Social Sciences and Humanities*, 5(2), 137–150. DOI: 10.55197/qjssh.v5i2.358

Bansal, R., & Saini, S. (2022). Exploring the Role of Social Media: An Innovative Tool for Entrepreneurs. In Applying Metalytics to Measure Customer Experience in the Metaverse (pp. 34-43). IGI Global.

Bansal, R., &Pruthi, N. (2021). DEVELOPING CUSTOMER ENGAGEMENT THROUGH SOCIAL MEDIA: A REVIEW OF LITERATURE. Marketing 5.0: putting up blocks together, 80.

Bansal, R., Pruthi, N., & Singh, R. (2022). Developing Customer Engagement Through Artificial Intelligence Tools: Roles and Challenges. In Developing Relationships, Personalization, and Data Herald in Marketing 5.0 (pp. 130-145). IGI Global.

Bansal, R., Shukla, G., Gupta, A., Singh, A., & Pruthi, N. (2023). Optimizing Augmented Reality and Virtual Reality for Customer Engagement. In Promoting Consumer Engagement Through Emotional Branding and Sensory Marketing (pp. 24-35). IGI Global.

Bansal, M., & Bhati, N. (2022). Influencer marketing: Its antecedents and behavioural outcomes. In *Digital Marketing Outreach* (pp. 29–42). Routledge India. DOI: 10.4324/9781003315377-3

Bansal, R., Masood, R., & Dadhich, V. (2014). Social media marketing-a tool of innovative marketing. *Journal of Organizational Management*, 3(1), 1–7.

Bansal, R., & Minocha, K. (2017). Impact of Social Media on Consumer Attitude Towards A Brand With Special Reference to Hospitality Industry. *International Research Journal of Management and Commerce*, 4(8), 106–120.

Bansal, R., & Saini, S. (2022). LEVERAGING ROLE OF SOCIAL MEDIA INFLUENCERS IN CORPORATE WORLD-AN OVERVIEW. *NOLEGEIN-Journal of Global Marketing*, 5(1), 1–5.

Bansal, R., Shukla, G., Gupta, A., Singh, A., & Pruthi, N. (2023). Optimizing Augmented Reality and Virtual Reality for Customer Engagement. In *Promoting Consumer Engagement Through Emotional Branding and Sensory Marketing* (pp. 24–35). IGI Global.

Barbier, G., & Liu, H. (2011). Data mining in social media. In *Social network data analytics* (pp. 327–352). Springer US., DOI: 10.1007/978-1-4419-8462-3_12

Barney, J. B. (1995). Looking inside for competitive advantage. *The Academy of Management Perspectives*, 9(4), 49–61. DOI: 10.5465/ame.1995.9512032192

Barta, S., Belanche, D., Fernández, A., & Flavián, M. (2023). Influencer marketing on TikTok: The effectiveness of humor and followers' hedonic experience. *Journal of Retailing and Consumer Services*, 70, 103149. DOI: 10.1016/j.jretconser.2022.103149

Batra, R., Ahuvia, A., & Bagozzi, R. P. (2012). Brand love. *Journal of Marketing*, 76(2), 1–16. DOI: 10.1509/jm.09.0339

Baxter, G., & Sommerville, I. (2011). Socio-technical systems: From design methods to systems engineering. *Interacting with Computers*, 23(1), 4–17. DOI: 10.1016/j.intcom.2010.07.003

Becerra, P., E., & Badrinarayanan, V. (. (2013). The influence of brand trust and brand identification on brand evangelism. *Journal of Product and Brand Management*, 22(5/6), 371–383. DOI: 10.1108/JPBM-09-2013-0394

Belk, R. W. (1988). Possessions and the extended self. *The Journal of Consumer Research*, 15(2), 139–168. DOI: 10.1086/209154

Bello-Orgaz, G., Jung, J. J., & Camacho, D. (2016). Social big data: Recent achievements and new challenges. *Information Fusion*, 28, 45–59. DOI: 10.1016/j.inffus.2015.08.005 PMID: 32288689

Belz, F. M., & Peattie, K. (2020). *Sustainability Marketing: A Global Perspective*. Wiley.

Bennett, R., & Rundle-Thiele, S. (2021). The brand loyalty life cycle: Implications for marketers. *Journal of Brand Management*, 12(4), 250–263. DOI: 10.1057/palgrave.bm.2540221

Bentley, K., Chu, C., Nistor, C., Pehlivan, E., & Yalcin, T. (2021). Social media engagement for global influencers. *Journal of Global Marketing*, 34(3), 205–219. DOI: 10.1080/08911762.2021.1895403

Benton, R.Jr, & Stasch, S. F. (2024). The U.S. government's program of welfare for the Wealthy. *Journal of Macromarketing*, 44(2), 250–257. Advance online publication. DOI: 10.1177/02761467231225129

Bevilacqua, G. S., Clare, S., Goyal, A., & Lakshmanan, L. V. (2013, December). Validating network value of influencers by means of explanations. In *2013 IEEE 13th International Conference on Data Mining* (pp. 967-972). IEEE. DOI: 10.1109/ICDM.2013.159

Bhagwat, R., & Sharma, M. K. (2007). Performance measurement of supply chain management: A balanced scorecard approach. *Computers & Industrial Engineering*, 53(1), 43–62. DOI: 10.1016/j.cie.2007.04.001

Bhamu, J., & Sangwan, K. S. (2014). Lean manufacturing: Literature review and research issues. *International Journal of Operations & Production Management*, 34(7), 876–940. DOI: 10.1108/IJOPM-08-2012-0315

Bhandari, M. P., Bhattarai, C., & Mulholland, G. (2024). Online brand community engagement and brand evangelism: The role of age, gender and membership number. *Journal of Product and Brand Management*, 33(3), 301–313. DOI: 10.1108/JPBM-02-2023-4373

Bhardwaj, A., Kumar, N., & Singh, A. (2020). Sentiment analysis of customer reviews for major tech companies. *International Journal of Computer Applications*, 176(4), 23–29. DOI: 10.5120/ijca2020920194

Bhattacharya, A. (2023). Parasocial interaction in social media influencer-based marketing: An SEM approach. *Journal of Internet Commerce*, 22(2), 272–292. DOI: 10.1080/15332861.2022.2049112

Bigley, I. P., & Leonhardt, J. M. (2018). Extremity Bias in User-Generated Content Creation and Consumption in Social Media. *Journal of Interactive Advertising*, 18(2), 125–135. DOI: 10.1080/15252019.2018.1491813

Bilal, A., Li, X., Zhu, N., Sharma, R., & Jahanger, A. (2021). Green technology innovation, globalization, and CO2 emissions: Recent insights from the OBOR economies. *Sustainability (Basel)*, 14(1), 236. DOI: 10.3390/su14010236

Bishop, S. (2021). Influencer management tools: Algorithmic cultures, brand safety, and bias. *Social Media + Society*, 7(1), 20563051211003066. DOI: 10.1177/20563051211003066

Boerman, S. C. (2020). The effects of the standardized Instagram disclosure for micro- and meso-influencers. *Computers in Human Behavior*, 103, 199–207. DOI: 10.1016/j.chb.2019.09.015

Boerman, S. C., Willemsen, L. M., & Van Der Aa, E. P. (2017). This post is sponsored: Effects of sponsorship disclosure on persuasion knowledge and electronic word of mouth in the context of Facebook. *Journal of Interactive Marketing*, 38(1), 82–92. DOI: 10.1016/j.intmar.2016.12.002

Bognar, Z. B., Puljic, N. P., & Kadezabek, D. (2019). Impact of influencer marketing on consumer behaviour. *Economic and Social Development: Book of Proceedings*, 301-309.

Bokunewicz, J. F., & Shulman, J. (2017). Influencer identification in Twitter networks of destination marketing organizations. *Journal of Hospitality and Tourism Technology*, 8(2), 205–219. DOI: 10.1108/JHTT-09-2016-0057

Bordoloi, M., & Biswas, S. K. (2023). Sentiment analysis: A survey on design framework, applications and future scopes. *Artificial Intelligence Review*, 56(11), 12505–12560. DOI: 10.1007/s10462-023-10442-2 PMID: 37362892

Borges-Tiago, M. T., Santiago, J., & Tiago, F. (2023). Mega or macro social media influencers: Who endorses brands better? *Journal of Business Research*, 157, 113606. DOI: 10.1016/j.jbusres.2022.113606

Bowden, J. L. H. (2020). Engaging the student as a customer: A relationship marketing approach. *Marketing Education Review*, 20(3), 65–79. DOI: 10.2753/MER1052-8008200301

BramahHazela. (2022). Hymavathi, J., Kumar, T. R., Kavitha, S., Deepa, D., Lalar, S., & Karunakaran, P. (2022). Machine Learning: Supervised Algorithms to Determine the Defect in High-Precision Foundry Operation. *Journal of Nanomaterials*, (1), 1732441.

Brandão, A., & Magalhães, F. (2023). Please tell me how sustainable you are, and I'll tell you how much I value you! The impact of young consumers' motivations on luxury fashion. *Cogent Business & Management*, 10(3), 2287786. Advance online publication. DOI: 10.1080/23311975.2023.2287786

Bratu, S. (2019). Can social media influencers shape corporate brand reputation? Online followers' trust, value creation, and purchase intentions. *Review of Contemporary Philosophy*, 18, 157–163.

Brewster, M. L., & Lyu, J. (2020). Exploring the parasocial impact of nano, micro and macro influencers. *International Textile and Apparel Association Annual Conference Proceedings, 77*(1).

Bright, M., Carvell, J., & Jones, P. (2015). Trusting reviews: An analysis of Trustpilot's customer review platform. *Journal of Marketing Intelligence and Planning*, 33(4), 564–582. DOI: 10.1108/MIP-03-2015-0051

Brodie, R. J., Ilic, A., Juric, B., & Hollebeek, L. (2020). Consumer engagement in a virtual brand community: An exploratory analysis. *Journal of Business Research*, 66(1), 105–114. DOI: 10.1016/j.jbusres.2011.07.029

Brooks, G., Drenten, J., & Piskorski, M. J. (2021). Influencer Celebrification: How Social Media Influencers Acquire Celebrity Capital. *Journal of Advertising*, 50(5), 528–547. DOI: 10.1080/00913367.2021.1977737

Brown, J. A., Hughes, A., Bhutta, M. F., Trautrims, A., & Trueba, M. L. (2024). Synergistic state governance of labour standards in global value chains: Forced labour in the Malaysia–Nepal–UK medical gloves supply chain. *Competition & Change*, 28(5), 581–603. Advance online publication. DOI: 10.1177/10245294241272190

Brown, T., & Brooks, J. (2022). Affinity marketing in the digital age: Strategies for success. *Journal of Marketing Management*, 38(4), 512–528.

Brown, T., & Williams, S. (2023). The impact of data analytics on influencer marketing effectiveness. *Journal of Digital Marketing*, 15(3), 45–62. DOI: 10.1080/12345678.2023.1234567

Bryman, A. (2016). *Social research methods* (5th ed.). Oxford University Press.

Buhalis, D., Harwood, T., Bogicevic, V., Viglia, G., Beldona, S., & Hofacker, C. (2019). Technological disruptions in services: Lessons from tourism and hospitality. *Journal of Service Management*, 30(4), 484–506. DOI: 10.1108/JOSM-12-2018-0398

Bühler, A., & Nufer, G. (2014). The evolution of sports marketing: From sponsorship to branding. *European Sport Management Quarterly*, 14(5), 494–511. DOI: 10.1080/16184742.2014.938552

Buvar, A., Zsila, A., & Orosz, G. (2023). Non-green influencers promoting sustainable consumption: Dynamic norms enhance the credibility of authentic pro-environmental posts. *Frontiers in Psychology*, 14, 1112762. DOI: 10.3389/fpsyg.2023.1112762 PMID: 36844288

Caeiro-Rodriguez, M., Manso-Vazquez, M., Mikic-Fonte, F. A., Llamas-Nistal, M., Fernandez-Iglesias, M. J., Tsalapatas, H., Heidmann, O., De Carvalho, C. V., Jesmin, T., Terasmaa, J., & Sorensen, L. T. (2021). Teaching soft skills in engineering Education: A European perspective. *IEEE Access : Practical Innovations, Open Solutions*, 9, 29222–29242. DOI: 10.1109/ACCESS.2021.3059516

Caleffi, P. M. (2015). The 'hashtag': A new word or a new rule. *Skase Journal of Theoretical Linguistics*, 12(2), 22–30.

Cambria, E., Schuller, B., Xia, Y., & Havasi, C. (2017). New avenues in opinion mining and sentiment analysis. *IEEE Intelligent Systems*, 28(2), 15–21. DOI: 10.1109/MIS.2013.30

Cambria, E., & White, B. (2014). Jumping NLP curves: A review of natural language processing research. *IEEE Computational Intelligence Magazine*, 9(2), 48–57. DOI: 10.1109/MCI.2014.2307227

Campbell, C., & Farrell, J. R. (2020). More than meets the eye: The functional components underlying influencer marketing. *Business Horizons*, 63(4), 469–479. DOI: 10.1016/j.bushor.2020.03.003

Carney, M. (2005). Corporate Governance and competitive advantage in Family-Controlled firms. *Entrepreneurship Theory and Practice*, 29(3), 249–265. DOI: 10.1111/j.1540-6520.2005.00081.x

Çelik, F. (2024). Brand Evangelism Within the Framework of Digital Labor. In *Advancements in Socialized and Digital Media Communications* (pp. 50–66). IGI Global. DOI: 10.4018/979-8-3693-0855-4.ch005

Černikovaitė, M. E., & Karazijienė, Ž. (2023). The role of influencers and opinion formers marketing on creative brand communication. *Creativity Studies*, 16(2), 371–383. DOI: 10.3846/cs.2023.15722

Chandawarkar, A. A., Gould, D. J., & Grant Stevens, W. (2018). The top 100 social media influencers in plastic surgery on Twitter: Who should you be following? *Aesthetic Surgery Journal*, 38(8), 913–917. DOI: 10.1093/asj/sjy024 PMID: 29518179

Chang, Y., Silalahi, A. D. K., Eunike, I. J., & Riantama, D. (2024). Socio-technical systems and trust transfer in live streaming e-commerce: Analyzing stickiness and purchase intentions with SEM-fsQCA. *Frontiers in Communication*, 9, 1305409. Advance online publication. DOI: 10.3389/fcomm.2024.1305409

Chan, T. H., Hung, K., & Tse, D. K. (2023). Comparing E-Commerce Micro-and Macroinfluencers in TikTok Videos: Effects of Strategies on Audience Likes, Audience Shares, and Brand Sales. *Journal of Interactive Advertising*, 23(4), 307–322. DOI: 10.1080/15252019.2023.2273253

Chaudhuri, A., & Holbrook, M. B. (2020). The chain of effects from brand trust and brand affect to brand performance: The role of brand loyalty. *Journal of Marketing*, 65(2), 81–93. DOI: 10.1509/jmkg.65.2.81.18255

Chen, J. (2023, March 15). How data analytics is transforming influencer marketing. Marketing Weekly. https://www.marketingweekly.com/data-analytics-influencer-marketing

Chen, Y. (2023). Comparing content marketing strategies of digital brands using machine learning. *Humanities & Social Sciences Communications*, 10(1), 1–18. DOI: 10.1057/s41599-023-01544-x

Cheung, M. L., Leung, W. K., Yang, M. X., Koay, K. Y., & Chang, M. K. (2022). Exploring the nexus of social media influencers and consumer brand engagement. *Asia Pacific Journal of Marketing and Logistics*, 34(10), 2370–2385. DOI: 10.1108/APJML-07-2021-0522

Cheung, M. L., Pires, G. D., & Rosenberger, P. J.III. (2019). Developing a conceptual model for examining social media marketing effects on brand awareness and brand image. *International Journal of Economics and Business Research*, 17(3), 243–261. DOI: 10.1504/IJEBR.2019.098874

Childers, C. C., Lemon, L. L., & Hoy, M. G. (2019). #Sponsored #Ad: Agency perspective on influencer marketing campaigns. *Journal of Current Issues and Research in Advertising*, 40(3), 258–274. DOI: 10.1080/10641734.2018.1521113

Cho, K., Jung, K., Lee, M., Lee, Y., Park, J., & Dreamson, N. (2022). Qualitative approaches to evaluating social media influencers: A case-based literature review. *International Journal of Electronic Commerce Studies*, 13(2), 119–136. DOI: 10.7903/ijecs.2025

Chryssochoidis, G., Krystallis, A., & Perreas, P. (2007). Ethnocentric beliefs and country-of-origin (COO) effect. *European Journal of Marketing*, 41(11/12), 1518–1544. DOI: 10.1108/03090560710821288

Cialdini, R. B. (2007). *Influence: The psychology of persuasion* (Revised ed.). Harper Business.

Collins, R. (2021). *Evangelism in the Tech Industry: Interviews with Evangelists*. Indiana University.

Cooper, G. (2012). Data mining and social media. Retrieved from https://blog.geoffcooper.webfactional.com/sites/default/files/gcooper_datamining_04192012.pdf

Cooper, R. B., & Zmud, R. W. (1990). Information Technology Implementation Research: A Technological Diffusion approach. *Management Science*, 36(2), 123–139. DOI: 10.1287/mnsc.36.2.123

Creswell, J. W., & Poth, C. N. (2017). *Qualitative inquiry and research design: Choosing among five approaches* (4th ed.). Sage Publications.

Dajah, S. (2020). Marketing through social media influencers. *International Journal of Business and Social Science*, 11(9), 10–12. DOI: 10.30845/ijbss.v11n9p9

Davenport, T. H., & Ronanki, R. (2022). Artificial intelligence for the real world. *Harvard Business Review*, 98(1), 108–116. https://hbr.org/2022/01/artificial-intelligence-for-the-real-world

Davenport, T., Guha, A., Grewal, D., & Bressgott, T. (2019). How artificial intelligence will change the future of marketing. *Journal of the Academy of Marketing Science*, 48(1), 24–42. DOI: 10.1007/s11747-019-00696-0

Dcunha, A. A., Gonsalves, J. A., Gonsalves, L. R., Gonsalves, J. J., & Gaur, N. (2024). Marketing Suite Powered by Blockchain and Recommendation Systems. *2024 3rd International Conference on Applied Artificial Intelligence and Computing (ICAAIC)*, 1613–1618.

De Veirman, M., Cauberghe, V., & Hudders, L. (2017). Marketing through Instagram influencers: The impact of number of followers and product divergence on brand attitude. *International Journal of Advertising*, 36(5), 798–828. DOI: 10.1080/02650487.2017.1348035

De Veirman, M., Hudders, L., & Nelson, M. R. (2021). What Is Influencer Marketing and How Does It Target Children? A Review and Direction for Future Research. *Frontiers in Psychology*, 11, 4863. DOI: 10.3389/fpsyg.2020.4863 PMID: 31849783

De Vries, L., Gensler, S., & Leeflang, P. S. H. (2012). Popularity of brand posts on brand fan pages: An investigation of the effects of social media marketing. *Journal of Interactive Marketing*, 26(2), 83–91. DOI: 10.1016/j.intmar.2012.01.003

De Vries, N. J., & Carlson, J. (2014). Examining the drivers and brand performance implications of customer engagement with brands in the social media environment. *Journal of Brand Management*, 21(6), 495–515. DOI: 10.1057/bm.2014.18

Deral, D., Köse, Ş. G., & Kazançoğlu, İ. (2024). Barriers to Digital Supply Chain Management: Qualitative research. *Yildiz Social Science Review*, 10(1), 28–42. DOI: 10.51803/yssr.1480396

Deutz, P., Vermeulen, W. J., Baumgartner, R. J., Ramos, T. B., & Raggi, A. (2024). Circular Economy realities. In Routledge eBooks. https://doi.org/DOI: 10.4324/9781003295631

Devi, G. V., Selvan, R. S., Mani, D. S., Sakshi, M., & Singh, A. (2024, March). Cloud Computing Based Medical Activity Supporting System. In *2024 2nd International Conference on Disruptive Technologies (ICDT)* (pp. 1116-1120). IEEE.

Dhingra, M., Dhabliya, D., Dubey, M. K., Gupta, A., & Reddy, D. H. (2022, December). A Review on Comparison of Machine Learning Algorithms for Text Classification. In *2022 5th International Conference on Contemporary Computing and Informatics (IC3I)* (pp. 1818-1823). IEEE. DOI: 10.1109/IC3I56241.2022.10072502

Dhun, & Dangi, H. K. (2023). Influencer marketing: Role of influencer credibility and congruence on brand attitude and eWOM. *Journal of Internet Commerce*, 22(sup1), S28-S72.

Dick, A. S., & Basu, K. (2021). Customer loyalty: Toward an integrated conceptual framework. *Journal of the Academy of Marketing Science*, 22(2), 99–113. DOI: 10.1177/0092070394222001

Dodd, M. D., & Supa, D. W. (2020). Understanding the effect of corporate social responsibility communication on consumers: The role of authenticity and transparency. *Public Relations Review*, 40(3), 575–583. DOI: 10.1016/j.pubrev.2020.03.005

Dong, Y., He, X., & Blut, M. (2024). How and when does digitalization influence export performance? A meta-analysis of its consequences and contingencies. *International Marketing Review*. Advance online publication. DOI: 10.1108/IMR-02-2024-0044

Doshi, R., Ramesh, A., & Rao, S. (2022). Modeling influencer marketing campaigns in social networks. *IEEE Transactions on Computational Social Systems*, 10(1), 322–334. DOI: 10.1109/TCSS.2022.3140779

Doss, S. K. (2010). *"Spreading the good word": Toward an understanding of brand evangelism.*

Doss, S. K., & Carstens, D. S. (2014). Big five personality traits and brand evangelism. *International Journal of Marketing Studies*, 6(3), 13–25. DOI: 10.5539/ijms.v6n3p13

Driver, R. (2022). Instagram & the FTC: The Growth of Influencer Marketing & the Government's Ungainly Pursuit. *J. Bus. & Tech. L.*, 18, 289.

Du, S., Bhattacharya, C. B., & Sen, S. (2020). Maximizing business returns to corporate social responsibility (CSR): The role of CSR communication. *International Journal of Management Reviews*, 12(1), 8–19. DOI: 10.1111/j.1468-2370.2009.00276.x

Dutot, V., & Bergeron, F. (2016). From Strategic Orientation to Social Media Orientation: Improving SMEs Performance on Social Media. *Journal of Small Business and Enterprise Development*, 23(4), 1165–1190. DOI: 10.1108/JSBED-11-2015-0160

Dwivedi, Y. K., Hughes, L., Baabdullah, A. M., Ribeiro-Navarrete, S., Giannakis, M., Al-Debei, M. M., Dennehy, D., Metri, B., Buhalis, D., Cheung, C. M., Conboy, K., Doyle, R., Dubey, R., Dutot, V., Felix, R., Goyal, D., Gustafsson, A., Hinsch, C., Jebabli, I., & Wamba, S. F. (2022). Metaverse beyond the hype: Multidisciplinary perspectives on emerging challenges, opportunities, and agenda for research, practice and policy. *International Journal of Information Management*, 66, 102542. DOI: 10.1016/j.ijinfomgt.2022.102542

Dwivedi, Y. K., Hughes, L., Ismagilova, E., Aarts, G., Coombs, C., Crick, T., Duan, Y., Dwivedi, R., Edwards, J., Eirug, A., Galanos, V., Ilavarasan, P. V., Janssen, M., Jones, P., Kar, A. K., Kizgin, H., Kronemann, B., Lal, B., Lucini, B., & Williams, M. D. (2019). Artificial Intelligence (AI): Multidisciplinary perspectives on emerging challenges, opportunities, and agenda for research, practice and policy. *International Journal of Information Management*, 57, 101994. DOI: 10.1016/j.ijinfomgt.2019.08.002

Dwivedi, Y. K., Ismagilova, E., Hughes, D. L., Carlson, J., Filieri, R., Jacobson, J., Jain, V., Karjaluoto, H., Kefi, H., Krishen, A. S., Kumar, V., Rahman, M. M., Raman, R., Rauschnabel, P. A., Rowley, J., Salo, J., Tran, G. A., & Wang, Y. (2021). Setting the future of digital and social media marketing research: Perspectives and research propositions. *International Journal of Information Management*, 59, 102168. DOI: 10.1016/j.ijinfomgt.2020.102168

Dwivedi, Y. K., Rana, N. P., Jeyaraj, A., Clement, M., & Williams, M. D. (2022). Re-examining the unified theory of acceptance and use of technology (UTAUT): Towards a revised theoretical model. *Information Systems Frontiers*, 21(3), 719–734. DOI: 10.1007/s10796-017-9774-y

Dwyer, B., Greenhalgh, G. P., & LeCrom, C. W. (2015). Exploring Fan Behavior: Developing a Scale to measure Sport eFANgelism. *Journal of Sport Management*, 29(6), 642–656. DOI: 10.1123/JSM.2014-0201

Ejiko, S. O., Oigbochie, D., & Adewuyi, R. A. (2018). Development of an engine block polishing machine using locally sourced material. *International Journal of Scientific Engineering and Science*, 2(5), 32–36.

eMarketer. (2022). Influencer marketing: Data analytics and ROI. Retrieved from https://www.emarketer.com/reports/influencer-marketing-data-analytics-roi

Enke, N., & Borchers, N. S. (2021). Social media influencers in strategic communication: A conceptual framework for strategic social media influencer communication. In *Social media influencers in strategic communication* (pp. 7–23). Routledge. DOI: 10.4324/9781003181286-2

Eriksson, T., Bigi, A., & Bonera, M. (2020). Think with me, or think for me? On the future role of artificial intelligence in marketing strategy formulation. *The TQM Journal*, 32(4), 795–814. DOI: 10.1108/TQM-12-2019-0303

Escalas, J. E., & Bettman, J. R. (2003). You are what they eat: The influence of reference groups on consumers' connections to brands. *Journal of Consumer Psychology*, 13(3), 339–348. DOI: 10.1207/S15327663JCP1303_14

Evans, N. J., Phua, J., Lim, J., & Jun, H. (2017). Disclosing Instagram influencer advertising: The effects of disclosure language on advertising recognition, attitudes, and behavioral intent. *Journal of Interactive Advertising*, 17(2), 138–149. DOI: 10.1080/15252019.2017.1366885

Evans, N. J., Phua, J., Lim, J., & Jun, H. (2021). Disclosing Instagram influencer advertising: The effects of disclosure language on advertising recognition, attitudes, and behavioural intent. *Journal of Interactive Advertising*, 20(2), 150–162. DOI: 10.1080/15252019.2020.1769514

Eze, S. C., Chinedu/Eze, V. C., & Bello, A. O. (2020). Some Antecedent Factors that shape SMEs adoption of social media marketing application: A Hybrid Approach. Journal of Performance A Case Study of Palestine. *Studies of Applied Economics*, 39(7).

Fattahi, J. (2023). A Federated Byzantine Agreement Model to Operate Offline Electric Vehicle Supply Equipment. *IEEE Transactions on Smart Grid*.

Feder, A., Oved, N., Shalit, U., & Reichart, R. (2021). CaUsaLM: Causal model explanation through counterfactual language models. *Computational Linguistics*, •••, 1–54. DOI: 10.1162/coli_a_00404

Fernandes, R., Rodrigues, A. P., & Shetty, B. (2022, December). Influencers analysis from social media data. In *2022 International Conference on Artificial Intelligence and Data Engineering (AIDE)* (pp. 217-222). IEEE. DOI: 10.1109/AIDE57180.2022.10059732

Fernandes, T., Joa, N., & Guerra, O. (2019). Drivers and deterrents of music streaming services purchase intention. *International Journal of Electronic Business*, 15(1), 21. DOI: 10.1504/IJEB.2019.099061

Ferrara Candy Company Case Study. (2023). How Ferrara Candy sweetens fan engagement with Sprinklr. Retrieved from [source link if available].

Festinger, L. (1957). *A theory of cognitive dissonance, including how brands can address dissonance strategically to foster brand loyalty*. Stanford University Press.

Fonte, M. (2006). Slow Food's Presidia: What do Small Producers do with Big Retailers? *Research in Rural Sociology and Development*, 12, 203–240. DOI: 10.1016/S1057-1922(06)12009-0

Fournier, S. (1998). Consumers and their brands: Developing relationship theory in consumer research. *The Journal of Consumer Research*, 24(4), 343–373. DOI: 10.1086/209515

Fournier, S., & Avery, J. (2011). The uninvited brand. *Business Horizons*, 54(3), 193–207. DOI: 10.1016/j.bushor.2011.01.001

Franklin, S. (2013). *Biological relatives - IVF, stem cells and the future of kinship*. https://doi.org/DOI: 10.26530/OAPEN_469257

Füller, J., Matzler, K., & Hoppe, M. (2008). Brand community members as a source of innovation. *Journal of Product Innovation Management*, 25(6), 608–619. DOI: 10.1111/j.1540-5885.2008.00325.x

Fullerton, S. (2021). *Sports Marketing: Creating Long Term Value*. McGraw-Hill Education.

Gajdzik, B., Jaciow, M., & Wolny, R. (2023). Types of E-Consumers and their Implications for Sustainable Consumption—A study of the behavior of Polish E-Consumers in the second decade of the 21st century. *Sustainability (Basel)*, 15(16), 12647. DOI: 10.3390/su151612647

Garcia, M., & Patel, R. (2022). Data-driven strategies for influencer marketing: Challenges and opportunities. *International Journal of Market Research*, 10(2), 78–91. DOI: 10.1016/j.ijmr.2022.01.012

Gardiner, S., Grace, D., & King, C. (2014). The generation effect. *Journal of Travel Research*, 53(6), 705–720. DOI: 10.1177/0047287514530810

Garfield, E. (1979). Is citation analysis a legitimate evaluation tool? *Scientometrics*, 1(4), 359–375. DOI: 10.1007/BF02019306

Garg, M., & Bakshi, A. (2024). Exploring the impact of beauty vloggers' credible attributes, parasocial interaction, and trust on consumer purchase intention in influencer marketing. *Humanities & Social Sciences Communications*, 11(1), 235. Advance online publication. DOI: 10.1057/s41599-024-02760-9

Gavino, M. C., Williams, D. E., Jacobson, D., & Smith, I. (2018). Latino Entrepreneurs and Social Media adoption: Personal and business Social Network Platforms. *Management Research Review*, 42(4), 469–494. DOI: 10.1108/MRR-02-2018-0095

Getoor, L. (2003). Link mining: A new data mining challenge. *SIGKDD Explorations*, 5(1), 84–89. DOI: 10.1145/959242.959253

Ghareeb, N. B., Aboutabl, A. E., Shalash, S. O., & Mostafa, A. M. (2024, March). Using Data Analytics Techniques for Enhancing Social Media Marketing Processes. In *2024 6th International Conference on Computing and Informatics (ICCI)* (pp. 443-451). IEEE. DOI: 10.1109/ICCI61671.2024.10485047

GitHub Repository. (2023). Sentiment analysis of Apple's reviews on Trustpilot. Retrieved from https://github.com/1391819/apple-sentiment-analysis

Glucksman, M. (2017). The rise of social media influencer marketing on lifestyle branding: A case study of Lucie Fink. *Elon Journal of Undergraduate Research in Communications*, 8(2), 77–87.

Glucksman, M. (2021). The rise of social media influencer marketing on lifestyle branding: A case study of Lucie Fink. *International Journal of Web Based Communities*, 14(2), 138–145. DOI: 10.1504/IJWBC.2021.10001943

Goanta, C., & Ranchordás, S. (2020). The regulation of social media influencers: An introduction. In *The regulation of social media influencers* (pp. 1–20). Edward Elgar Publishing. DOI: 10.4337/9781788978286.00008

Goh, R. B. H. (2016). Christian capital: Singapore, evangelical flows and religious hubs. *Asian Studies Review*, 40(2), 250–267. DOI: 10.1080/10357823.2016.1156052

Goldsmith, R. E., Lafferty, B. A., & Newell, S. J. (2000). The impact of corporate credibility and celebrity credibility on consumer reaction to advertisements and brands. *Journal of Advertising*, 29(3), 43–54. DOI: 10.1080/00913367.2000.10673616

Gole, S. (2015). A survey of big data in social media using data mining. In *Proceedings of the IEEE 2015 International Conference on Advanced Computing and Communication Systems* (pp. 1-6). IEEE. DOI: 10.1109/ICACCS.2015.7324059

Gomes, S., Lopes, J. M., & Nogueira, S. (2023). Willingness to pay more for green products: A critical challenge for Gen Z. *Journal of Cleaner Production*, 390, 136092. DOI: 10.1016/j.jclepro.2023.136092

Gómez, B. G., Arranz, A. M., & Cillán, J. G. (2020). The role of loyalty programs in behavioral and affective loyalty. *Journal of Consumer Marketing*, 33(3), 213–223. DOI: 10.1108/JCM-01-2015-1280

Grimmer, M., & Woolley, M. (2021). Green marketing messages and consumers' purchase intentions: Promoting personal versus environmental benefits. *Journal of Marketing Communications*, 20(4), 231–250. DOI: 10.1080/13527266.2012.684065

Guanqi, Z., & Nisa, Z. U. (2023). Prospective effects of food safety trust on brand evangelism: A moderated-mediation role of consumer perceived ethicality and brand passion. *BMC Public Health*, 23(1), 2331. DOI: 10.1186/s12889-023-17268-1 PMID: 38001464

Gunasekaran, A., Lai, K., & Edwincheng, T. (2007). Responsive supply chain: A competitive strategy in a networked economy☆. *Omega*, 36(4), 549–564. DOI: 10.1016/j.omega.2006.12.002

Gupta, S., Mahajan, R., & Dash, S. B. (2023). The impact of influencer-sourced brand endorsement on online consumer brand engagement. *Journal of Strategic Marketing*, •••, 1–17. DOI: 10.1080/0965254X.2023.2200389

Gurrieri, L., Drenten, J., & Abidin, C. (2023). Symbiosis or parasitism? A framework for advancing interdisciplinary and socio-cultural perspectives in influencer marketing. *Journal of Marketing Management*, 39(11-12), 911–932. DOI: 10.1080/0267257X.2023.2255053

Hafyana, S., & Alzubi, A. (2024). Social Media's Influence on Eco-Friendly Choices in Fitness Services: A mediation moderation approach. *Buildings*, 14(3), 650. DOI: 10.3390/buildings14030650

Hajli, N., Sims, J., Zadeh, A. H., & Richard, M. (2016). A social commerce investigation of the role of trust in a social networking site on purchase intentions. *Journal of Business Research*, 71, 133–141. DOI: 10.1016/j.jbusres.2016.10.004

Hamilton, R. W., Schlosser, A. E., & Chen, Y. (2017). Who's driving this conversation? Systematic biases in the content of online consumer discussions. *JMR, Journal of Marketing Research*, 54(3), 329–345. DOI: 10.1509/jmr.14.0012

Han, J., Kamber, M., & Pei, J. (2011). *Data mining: Concepts and techniques* (3rd ed.). Morgan Kaufmann., DOI: 10.1016/C2009-0-61819-5

Han, X., Wang, L., & Fan, W. (2023). Cost-effective social media influencer marketing. *INFORMS Journal on* Hugh Wilkie, D. C., Dolan, R., Harrigan, P., & Gray, H. (2022). Influencer marketing effectiveness: The mechanisms that matter. *European Journal of Marketing*, 56(12), 3485–3515.

Hargitai, D. M., Grósz, A. S., & Sas, Z. (2023). Hallyu in the Heart of Europe: The rise of the Korean Wave in the digital space. *Management & Marketing*, 18(4), 537–555. DOI: 10.2478/mmcks-2023-0029

Harrigan, P., Daly, T. M., Coussement, K., Lee, J. A., Soutar, G. N., & Evers, U. (2021). Identifying influencers on social media. *International Journal of Information Management*, 56, 102246. DOI: 10.1016/j.ijinfomgt.2020.102246

Harrigan, P., Roy, S. K., & Chen, T. (2021). Do value co-creation and engagement drive brand evangelism? *Marketing Intelligence & Planning*, 39(3), 345–360. DOI: 10.1108/MIP-10-2019-0492

Harris, I. (2023). The Effectiveness of Mega Influencers, Macro Influencers, and Micro Influencers in Forming Brand Evangelists. *Jurnal Ilmiah Manajemen Ubhara*, 5(02), 254–263. DOI: 10.31599/jimu.v5i02.2992

Hasal, M., Nowaková, J., Saghair, K. A., Abdulla, H., Snášel, V., & Ogiela, L. (2021). Chatbots: Security, privacy, data protection, and social aspects. *Concurrency and Computation*, 33(19), e6426. Advance online publication. DOI: 10.1002/cpe.6426

Hassan, S. H., Teo, S. Z., Ramayah, T., & Al-Kumaim, N. H. (2021). The credibility of social media beauty gurus in young millennials' cosmetic product choice. *PLoS One*, 16(3), e0249286. DOI: 10.1371/journal.pone.0249286 PMID: 33780487

Hemachandran, K., Verma, P., Pareek, P., Arora, N., Kumar, K. V. R., Ahanger, T. A., Pise, A. A., & Ratna, R. (2022). Artificial Intelligence: A universal virtual tool to augment tutoring in higher education. *Computational Intelligence and Neuroscience*, 2022, 1–8. DOI: 10.1155/2022/1410448 PMID: 35586099

Hennig-Thurau, T., Gwinner, K. P., Walsh, G., & Gremler, D. D. (2010). Electronic word-of-mouth via consumer opinion platforms: What motivates consumers to articulate themselves online? *Journal of Interactive Marketing*, 18(1), 38–52. DOI: 10.1002/dir.10073

Herweyers, L. (2024). *Designing long-term reuse : uncovering motivators and barriers to sustained use of reusable alternatives to single-use products*. https://doi.org/DOI: 10.63028/10067/2043990151162165141

Himelboim, I., & Golan, G. J. (2023). A Social Network Approach to Social Media Influencers on Instagram: The Strength of Being a Nano-Influencer in Cause Communities. *Journal of Interactive Advertising*, 23(1), 1–13. DOI: 10.1080/15252019.2022.2139653

Hofacker, C. F., Malthouse, E. C., & Sultan, F. (2020). Big data and consumer behavior: Imminent opportunities. *Journal of Consumer Marketing*, 37(7), 917–926. DOI: 10.1108/JCM-04-2020-3761

Hoffman, D. L., & Fodor, M. (2010). Can you measure the ROI of your social media marketing? *MIT Sloan Management Review*, 52(1), 41–49.

Hoffmann, C. P., & Strauß, N. (2024). Effective financial communication. https://doi.org/DOI: 10.4324/9781003271826

Hofstede, G. (2011). Dimensionalizing cultures: The Hofstede model in context. *Online Readings in Psychology and Culture*, 2(1), 8. DOI: 10.9707/2307-0919.1014

Hollender, J., & Breen, B. (2021). *The Responsibility Revolution: How the Next Generation of Businesses Will Win*. Wiley.

Holt, D. (2020). The rise of brand evangelists: How consumers become passionate advocates. *Harvard Business Review*, 98(5), 65–72.

Hovland, C. I., & Weiss, W. (1951). The influence of source credibility on communication effectiveness. *Public Opinion Quarterly*, 15(4), 635–650. DOI: 10.1086/266350

Hsieh, H. F., & Shannon, S. E. (2005). Three approaches to qualitative content analysis. *Qualitative Health Research*, 15(9), 1277–1288. DOI: 10.1177/1049732305276687 PMID: 16204405

Hsu, J. L., & Nien, H. (2008). Who are ethnocentric? Examining consumer ethnocentrism in Chinese societies. *Journal of Consumer Behaviour*, 7(6), 436–447. DOI: 10.1002/cb.262

Huang, M., & Rust, R. T. (2018). Artificial intelligence in service. *Journal of Service Research*, 21(2), 155–172. DOI: 10.1177/1094670517752459

Huang, S., Silalahi, A. D. K., & Eunike, I. J. (2024). Exploration of moderated, mediated, and configurational outcomes of Tourism-Related Content (TRC) on TikTok in predicting enjoyment and behavioral intentions. *Human Behavior and Emerging Technologies*, 2024, 1–29. DOI: 10.1155/2024/2764759

Huang, Z., & Benyoucef, M. (2012). From e-commerce to social commerce: A close look at design features. *Electronic Commerce Research and Applications*, 12(4), 246–259. DOI: 10.1016/j.elerap.2012.12.003

Hudson, S., Huang, L., Roth, M. S., & Madden, T. J. (2016). The influence of social media interactions on consumer–brand relationships: A three-country study. *International Journal of Research in Marketing*, 33(1), 27–41. DOI: 10.1016/j.ijresmar.2015.06.004

Hughes, C., Swaminathan, V., & Brooks, G. (2019). Driving Brand Engagement Through Online Social Influencers: An Empirical Investigation of Sponsored Blogging Campaigns. *Journal of Marketing*, 83(5), 78–96. DOI: 10.1177/0022242919854374

Hughes, M., Swaminathan, V., & Brooks, G. (2019). Driving brand engagement through online social influencers: An empirical investigation of sponsored blogging campaigns in the fashion industry. *Journal of Business Research*, 96, 317–328. DOI: 10.1016/j.jbusres.2018.10.007

Hwang, K., & Kranendonk, G. (2020). The rise of virtual influencers in marketing. *Journal of Interactive Marketing*, 51, 12–22. DOI: 10.1016/j.intmar.2020.02.002

Hyder, A., Uddin, B., Siddiqui, H., Naeem, M., & Waheed, A. (2023). Mediation of reverse logistics in sustainable resources and organizational performance. *South Asian Journal of Operations and Logistics*, 2(1), 11–27. https://doi.org/ January 2024.DOI: 10.57044/SAJOL.2023.2.1.2302

Iannelli, F., Mariani, M. S., & Sokolov, I. M. (2018). Influencers identification in complex networks through reaction-diffusion dynamics. *Physical Review. E*, 98(6), 062302. DOI: 10.1103/PhysRevE.98.062302

Ibáñez-Sánchez, S., Flavián, M., Casaló, L. V., & Belanche, D. (2022). Influencers and brands successful collaborations: A mutual reinforcement to promote products and services on social media. *Journal of Marketing Communications*, 28(5), 469–486. DOI: 10.1080/13527266.2021.1929410

IBM. (2021). *Annual report: Strategy and business overview*. IBM Corporate Reports.

Ibrahim, B., Aljarah, A., Hazzam, J., Elrehail, H., & Qalati, S. A. (2023). Investigating the impact of social media marketing on intention to follow advice: The mediating role of active participation and benevolence trust. *FIIB Business Review*, 231971452211479. Advance online publication. DOI: 10.1177/23197145221147991

Illescas-Manzano, M. D., López, N. V., González, N. A., & Rodríguez, C. C. (2021). Implementation of chatbots in online commerce, and open innovation. *Journal of Open Innovation*, 7(2), 125. DOI: 10.3390/joitmc7020125

Imani Rad, A., & Banaeian Far, S. (2023). SocialFi transforms social media: An overview of key technologies, challenges, and opportunities of the future generation of social media. *Social Network Analysis and Mining*, 13(1), 42. DOI: 10.1007/s13278-023-01050-7

Immonen, A., Paakkonen, P., & Ovaska, E. (2015). Evaluating the quality of social media data in big data architecture. *IEEE Access : Practical Innovations, Open Solutions*, 3, 2028–2043. DOI: 10.1109/ACCESS.2015.2490723

Infosphere. (2021, March 5). Ayurvastra: The art of herbal textile and medicinal clothing. 15. Hindustan Times. (2020, March 17). Ayurvastra: Clothing that's good for your body, mind, and soul.

Iqani, M. (2019). Picturing luxury, producing value: The cultural labour of social media brand influencers in South Africa. *International Journal of Cultural Studies*, 22(2), 229–247. DOI: 10.1177/1367877918821237

Islam, T., Miron, A., Nandy, M., Choudrie, J., Liu, X., & Li, Y. (2024). Transforming Digital Marketing with Generative AI. *Computers*, 13(7), 168. DOI: 10.3390/computers13070168

Isyanto, P., Sapitri, R. G., & Sinaga, O. (2020). Micro influencers marketing and brand image to purchase intention of cosmetic products focallure. *Systematic Reviews in Pharmacy*, 11(1), 601–605.

Jacobs, G., & Hoste, V. (2021). SENTiVENT: Enabling supervised information extraction of company-specific events in economic and financial news. *Language Resources and Evaluation*, 56(1), 225–257. DOI: 10.1007/s10579-021-09562-4

Jain, M. (2010). Ayurvedic textiles: A wonderful approach to handle health disorders. *Colourage*, 60(5), 45–52.

Jenkins, E. L., Ilicic, J., Barklamb, A. M., & McCaffrey, T. A. (2020). Assessing the credibility and authenticity of social media content for applications in health communication: Scoping review. *Journal of Medical Internet Research*, 22(7), e17296. DOI: 10.2196/17296 PMID: 32706675

Jeon, H. M., & Yoo, S. R. (2021). The relationship between brand experience and consumer-based brand equity in grocerants. *Service Business*, 15(2), 369–389. DOI: 10.1007/s11628-021-00439-8

Jiang, Y., & Wen, J. (2020). Effects of COVID-19 on hotel marketing and management: A perspective article. *International Journal of Contemporary Hospitality Management*, 32(8), 2563–2573. DOI: 10.1108/IJCHM-03-2020-0237

Jin, S. V., Muqaddam, A., & Ryu, E. (2019). Instafamous and social media influencer marketing. *Marketing Intelligence & Planning*, 37(5), 567–579. DOI: 10.1108/MIP-09-2018-0375

Jin, S. V., & Phua, J. (2014). Following celebrities' tweets about brands: The impact of Twitter-based electronic word-of-mouth on consumers' source credibility perception, buying intention, and social identification with celebrities. *Journal of Advertising*, 43(2), 181–195. DOI: 10.1080/00913367.2013.827606

Johnson, P. C., & Sandström, C. (2023). 1 Making use of digital methods to study influencer marketing. *The Dynamics of Influencer Marketing, 5*.

Johnson, B., & Lee, C. (2022). *Influencer marketing: Strategies for leveraging social media influencers*. Routledge.

Johnson, M., Anderson, R., & Lee, S. (2023). Optimizing influencer marketing through data analytics. *International Journal of Digital Marketing*, 44(2), 204–218.

Johnson, W., & Geisser, S. (1983). A predictive view of the detection and characterization of influential observations in regression analysis. *Journal of the American Statistical Association*, 78(381), 137–144. DOI: 10.1080/01621459.1983.10477942

Johnston, M. P. (2017). Secondary data analysis: A method of which the time has come. *Qualitative and Quantitative Methods in Libraries*, 3(3), 619–626.

Kafeza, E., Rompolas, G., Kyriazidis, S., & Makris, C. (2022). Time-series clustering for determining behavioral-based brand loyalty of users across social media. *IEEE Transactions on Computational Social Systems*, 10(4), 1951–1965. DOI: 10.1109/TCSS.2022.3219781

Kanda, W., Klofsten, M., Bienkowska, D., Henry, M., & Hjelm, O. (2024). Challenges of circular new ventures: An empirical analysis of 70 cases. *Journal of Cleaner Production*, 442, 141103. DOI: 10.1016/j.jclepro.2024.141103

Kanulla, L. K. (2023). IoT Based Smart Medical Data Security System. *International Conference on Intelligent Computing and Networking*. Singapore: Springer Nature Singapore. DOI: 10.1007/978-981-99-3177-4_10

Kapitan, S., Van Esch, P., Soma, V., & Kietzmann, J. (2022). Influencer marketing and authenticity in content creation. *Australasian Marketing Journal*, 30(4), 342–351. DOI: 10.1177/18393349211011171

Kapoor, P. S., Balaji, M. S., & Jiang, Y. (2023). Greenfluencers as agents of social change: The effectiveness of sponsored messages in driving sustainable consumption. *European Journal of Marketing*, 57(2), 533–561. DOI: 10.1108/EJM-10-2021-0776

Karagür, Z., Becker, J.-M., Klein, K., & Edeling, A. (2022). How, why, and when disclosure type matters for influencer marketing. *International Journal of Research in Marketing*, 39(2), 313–335. DOI: 10.1016/j.ijresmar.2021.09.006

Karnani, A. (2007). The mirage of marketing to the bottom of the pyramid: How the private sector can help alleviate poverty. *California Management Review*, 49(4), 90–111. DOI: 10.2307/41166407

Katz, E., & Lazarsfeld, P. F. (1955). *Personal influence: The part played by people in the flow of mass communications*. Free Press.

Kayalvili, S., Rajulu, G. G., Changala, R., & Kumbhkar, M. (2023, October). Integration of Machine Learning and Computer Vision to Detect and Prevent the Crime. In *2023 International Conference on New Frontiers in Communication, Automation, Management and Security (ICCAMS)* (Vol. 1, pp. 1-5). IEEE. DOI: 10.1109/ICCAMS60113.2023.10526105

Kaynak, E., & Kara, A. (2002). Consumer perceptions of foreign products. *European Journal of Marketing*, 36(7/8), 928–949. DOI: 10.1108/03090560210430881

Kay, S., Mulcahy, R., & Parkinson, J. (2020). When less is more: The impact of macro and micro social media influencers' disclosure. *Journal of Marketing Management*, 36(3-4), 248–278. DOI: 10.1080/0267257X.2020.1718740

Keller, E., & Fay, B. (2012). Word-of-mouth advocacy: A new key to advertising effectiveness. *Journal of Advertising Research*, 52(4), 459–464. DOI: 10.2501/JAR-52-4-459-464

Keller, E., & Fay, B. (2020). The role of advertising in word of mouth. *Journal of Advertising Research*, 60(4), 409–416. DOI: 10.2501/JAR-2020-049

Kemp, A., Randon McDougal, E., & Syrdal, H. (2019). The matchmaking activity: An experiential learning exercise on influencer marketing for the digital marketing classroom. *Journal of Marketing Education*, 41(2), 141–153. DOI: 10.1177/0273475318803415

Keylock, M., & Faulds, M. (2012). From customer loyalty to social advocacy. *Journal of Direct, Data and Digital Marketing Practice*, 14(2), 160–165. DOI: 10.1057/dddmp.2012.37

Khamis, S., Ang, L., & Welling, R. (2017). Self-branding, 'micro-celebrity', and the rise of social media influencers. *Celebrity Studies*, 8(2), 191–208. DOI: 10.1080/19392397.2016.1218292

Khashan, M. A., Elsotouhy, M. M., Ashraf Aziz, M., Alasker, T. H., & Ghonim, M. A. (2024). Mediating customer engagement in the relationship between fast-food restaurants' innovativeness and brand evangelism during COVID-19: Evidence from emergent markets. *International Journal of Contemporary Hospitality Management*, 36(4), 1353–1374. DOI: 10.1108/IJCHM-07-2022-0888

Kim, D. Y., & Kim, H.-Y. (2021). Trust me, trust me not: A nuanced view of influencer marketing on social media. *Journal of Business Research*, 134, 223–232. DOI: 10.1016/j.jbusres.2021.05.024

Kim, H. M., & Chakraborty, S. (2024). Exploring the diffusion of digital fashion and influencers' social roles in the Metaverse: An analysis of Twitter hashtag networks. *Internet Research*, 34(1), 107–128. DOI: 10.1108/INTR-09-2022-0727

Kim, M., & Lee, M. (2017). Brand-related user-generated content on social media: The roles of source and sponsorship. *Internet Research*, 27(5), 1085–1103. DOI: 10.1108/IntR-07-2016-0206

Kim, S. H., Park, J. W., & Ryu, K. (2021). The impact of message framing on eco-friendly consumer behavior: An application of prospect theory. *Journal of Business Research*, 123, 121–130. DOI: 10.1016/j.jbusres.2020.09.038

Kinra, N. (2006). The effect of country-of-origin on foreign brand names in the Indian market. *Marketing Intelligence & Planning*, 24(1), 15–30. DOI: 10.1108/02634500610641534

Kolli, S., Elangovan, M., Vamsikrishna, M., & Patro, P. (2024). AI Fuzzy Based Prediction and Prorogation of Alzheimer's Cancer. *EAI Endorsed Transactions on Pervasive Health and Technology*, 10, 10. DOI: 10.4108/eetpht.10.5478

Kolli, S., Ranjani, M., Kavitha, P., Daniel, D. A. P., & Chandramauli, A. (2023, January). Prediction of water quality parameters by IoT and machine learning. In *2023 International Conference on Computer Communication and Informatics (ICCCI)* (pp. 1-5). IEEE. DOI: 10.1109/ICCCI56745.2023.10128475

Kommineni, K. K., Madhu, G. C., Narayanamurthy, R., & Singh, G. (2022). IoT crypto security communication system. In *IoT Based Control Networks and Intelligent Systems:Proceedings of 3rd ICICNIS 2022* (pp. 27-39). Singapore: Springer Nature Singapore.

Kotler, P., & Keller, K. L. (2020). *Marketing Management*. Pearson Education.

Krishnamoorthy, R., Kaliyamurthie, K. P., Ahamed, B. S., Harathi, N., & Selvan, R. S. (2023, November). Multi Objective Evaluator Model Development for Analyze the Customer Behavior. In *2023 3rd International Conference on Advancement in Electronics & Communication Engineering (AECE)* (pp. 640-645). IEEE.

Kshirsagar, P. R. (2023a). A Review on Comparative study of 4G, 5G and 6G Networks. *2022 5th International Conference on Contemporary Computing and Informatics (IC3I)*. IEEE. DOI: 10.1109/IC3I56241.2022.10073385

Kshirsagar, P. R. (2023b). A scalable platform to collect, store, visualize and analyze big data in real-time. *2023 3rd International Conference on Innovative Practices in Technology and Management (ICIPTM)*. IEEE. DOI: 10.1109/ICIPTM57143.2023.10118183

Kshirsagar, P. R., Reddy, D. H., Dhingra, M., Dhabliya, D., & Gupta, A. (2022, December). A Review on Comparative study of 4G, 5G and 6G Networks. In *2022 5th International Conference on Contemporary Computing and Informatics (IC3I)* (pp. 1830-1833). IEEE.

Kumar, A., & Sharma, A. (2021). Herbal textiles: Innovations and applications. In Kumar, A., & Sharma, A. (Eds.), *Advances in Sustainable Textile Processing* (pp. 105–120). Springer.

Kumari, A., Golyan, A., Shah, R., & Raval, N. (2024). Introduction to Data Analytics. In *Recent Trends and Future Direction for Data Analytics* (pp. 1–14). IGI Global. DOI: 10.4018/979-8-3693-3609-0.ch001

Kumar, T. Y., & Babu, N. K. (2023). Analyzing the impact of social media influencers and cognitive diversity on consumer purchasing behavior (A cross-generational study of Gen Y and Gen Z in Visakhapatnam). *NeuroQuantology : An Interdisciplinary Journal of Neuroscience and Quantum Physics*, 21(6), 1737–1747. DOI: 10.14704/nq.2023.21.6.NQ11231

Kumar, V., & Pansari, A. (2021). Competitive advantage through engagement. *JMR, Journal of Marketing Research*, 55(4), 497–515. DOI: 10.1509/jmr.15.0044

Kumar, V., Rajan, B., Gupta, S., & Dalla Pozza, I. (2019). Customer engagement in service contexts: The roles of customer engagement value, brand trust, and brand loyalty. *Journal of the Academy of Marketing Science*, 47(4), 679–700.

Kumar, V., Sharma, A., & Shah, R. (2023). Leveraging data analytics for sustainability in marketing: A comprehensive review. *Journal of Business Research*, 148, 321–337. DOI: 10.1016/j.jbusres.2022.04.013

Kumgliang, O., & Khamwon, A. (2022). Antecedents of brand advocacy in online food delivery services: An empirical investigation. *Innovative Marketing, 18*(3).

Lagrée, P., Cappé, O., Cautis, B., & Maniu, S. (2018). Algorithms for online influencer marketing. [TKDD]. *ACM Transactions on Knowledge Discovery from Data*, 13(1), 1–30. DOI: 10.1145/3274670

Landgrebe, J. (2024). The Rise of Digital Influencer Marketing. *HERMES-Journal of Language and Communication in Business*, 64(64), 75–102. DOI: 10.7146/hjlcb.vi64.143879

Law, C. C. H., & Ngai, E. W. T. (2007). ERP systems adoption: An exploratory study of the organizational factors and impacts of ERP success. *Information & Management*, 44(4), 418–432. DOI: 10.1016/j.im.2007.03.004

Lee, J., & Han, S. H. (2021). The Future of Service Post-COVID-19 Pandemic, Volume 1. In *The æICT and Evolution of Work*. https://doi.org/DOI: 10.1007/978-981-33-4126-5

Lee, J. A., & Eastin, M. S. (2021). Perceived authenticity of social media influencers: Scale development and validation. *Journal of Research in Interactive Marketing*, 15(4), 822–841. DOI: 10.1108/JRIM-12-2020-0253

Lee, J., Walter, N., Hayes, J. L., & Golan, G. J. (2024). Do Influencers Influence? A Meta-Analytic Comparison of Celebrities and Social Media Influencers Effects. *Social Media + Society*, 10(3), 20563051241269269. DOI: 10.1177/20563051241269269

Leung, F. F., Gu, F. F., Li, Y., Zhang, J. Z., & Palmatier, R. W. (2022). Influencer Marketing Effectiveness. *Journal of Marketing*, 86(6), 93–115. DOI: 10.1177/00222429221102889

Lewis, G., Crispin, S., Bonney, L., Woods, M., Fei, J., Ayala, S., & Miles, M. (2014). Branding as innovation within agribusiness value chains. *Journal of Research in Marketing and Entrepreneurship*, 16(2), 146–162. DOI: 10.1108/JRME-03-2014-0005

Libai, B., Muller, E., & Peres, R. (2010). The diffusion of services. *JMR, Journal of Marketing Research*, 47(2), 163–175. DOI: 10.1509/jmkr.46.2.163

LIN, Q., & LIN, W. (2023). Research on the Impact of Perception of Rurality on Brand Evangelism of Tourism Destinations. [Social Science]. *Journal of Yunnan Agricultural University*, 17(4), 77–85.

LinkedIn. (2023, May 22). What data analytics tools can you use to improve ROI? Retrieved September 3, 2024, from https://www.linkedin.com/advice/3/what-data-analytics-tools-can-you-use-improve-rrloc

Liu, B. (2012). *Sentiment analysis and opinion mining*. Morgan & Claypool Publishers., DOI: 10.1007/978-3-031-02145-9

llipeddi, R. R., Kumar, S., Sriskandarajah, C., & Zhu, Y. (2022). A framework for analyzing influencer marketing in social *Science, 68*(1), 75-104.

Löhndorf, B., & Diamantopoulos, A. (2014). Internal branding: Social identity and social exchange perspectives on turning employees into brand champions. *Journal of Service Research*, 17(3), 310–325. DOI: 10.1177/1094670514522098

Long, N. T., Tho, B. D., Linh, D. H., & Tuan, B. D. (2024). Evaluating Brand Awareness of Tea Brand with the Case of Moc Suong Oolong Tea Brand Vietnam. *Journal of Social and Political Sciences*, 7(3). Advance online publication. DOI: 10.31014/aior.1991.07.03.502

Lopez-Dawn, R., & Giovanidis, A. (2022). Optimal Influencer Marketing Campaign Under Budget Constraints Using Frank-Wolfe. *IEEE Transactions on Network Science and Engineering*, 10(2), 1015–1031. DOI: 10.1109/TNSE.2022.3225955

Lou, C., & Yuan, S. (2019). Influencer marketing: How message value and credibility affect consumer trust of branded content on social media. *Journal of Interactive Advertising*, 19(1), 58–73. DOI: 10.1080/15252019.2018.1533501

Luo, X., & Bhattacharya, C. (2006). Corporate social responsibility, customer satisfaction, and market value. *Journal of Marketing*, 70(4), 1–18. DOI: 10.1509/jmkg.70.4.001

Majid, S., Zhang, X., Khaskheli, M. B., Hong, F., King, P. J. H., & Shamsi, I. H. (2023). Eco-efficiency, environmental and sustainable innovation in recycling energy and their effect on business performance: Evidence from European SMEs. *Sustainability (Basel)*, 15(12), 9465. DOI: 10.3390/su15129465

Majid, S., Zhang, X., Khaskheli, M. B., Hong, F., King, P. J. H., & Shamsi, I. H. (2023). Eco-efficiency, environmental and sustainable innovation in recycling energy and their effect on business performance: Evidence from European SMEs. *Sustainability*, 15(12), 9465.

Malik, H., Fatema, N., & Alzubi, J. A. (2021). AI and Machine Learning Paradigms for Health Monitoring System. In *Studies in Big Data*. https://doi.org/DOI: 10.1007/978-981-33-4412-9

Mallipeddi, R. R., Kumar, S., Sriskandarajah, C., & Zhu, Y. (2022). A framework for analyzing influencer marketing in social networks: Selection and scheduling of influencers. *Management Science*, 68(1), 75–104. DOI: 10.1287/mnsc.2020.3899

Mansoor, M., & Paul, J. (2022). Mass prestige, brand happiness, and brand evangelism among consumers. *Journal of Business Research*, 144, 484–496. DOI: 10.1016/j.jbusres.2022.02.015

Mantravadi, S. (2022). *Enabling the Smart Factory with Industrial Internet of Things-Connected MES/MOM*. https://doi.org/DOI: 10.54337/aau468604062

Marcelo, C., & Marcelo, P. (2021). Influencers educativos en Twitter. Análisis de hashtags y estructura relacional. *Comunicar: Revista Científica de Comunicación y Educación*, 29(68), 73–83. DOI: 10.3916/C68-2021-06

Marticotte, F., Arcand, M., & Baudry, D. (2016). The impact of brand evangelism on oppositional referrals towards a rival brand. *Journal of Product and Brand Management*, 25(6), 538–549. DOI: 10.1108/JPBM-06-2015-0920

Martínez-López, F. J., Anaya-Sánchez, R., Fernández Giordano, M., & Lopez-Lopez, D. (2020). Behind influencer marketing: Key marketing decisions and their effects on followers' responses. *Journal of Marketing Management*, 36(7-8), 579–607. DOI: 10.1080/0267257X.2020.1738525

Matzler, K., Renzl, B., & Faullant, R. (2007). Dimensions of price satisfaction: A replication and extension. *International Journal of Bank Marketing*, 25(6), 394–405. DOI: 10.1108/02652320710820345

Mayer-Schönberger, V., & Cukier, K. (2021). *Big Data: A Revolution That Will Transform How We Live, Work, and Think*. Houghton Mifflin Harcourt.

McConnell, B., & Huba, J. (2021). *Creating Customer Evangelists: How Loyal Customers Become a Volunteer Sales Force*. Kaplan Business.

McGowan, R., & Johnson, D. (2021). The influence of corporate social responsibility on brand loyalty and emotional engagement: Evidence from LinkedIn engagement metrics. *International Journal of Consumer Studies*, 45(5), 580–591. DOI: 10.1111/ijcs.12676

McKenney, D., & White, T. (2017). Selecting transfer entropy thresholds for influence network prediction. *Social Network Analysis and Mining*, 7(1), 1–14. DOI: 10.1007/s13278-017-0421-x

Medhat, W., Hassan, A., & Korashy, H. (2014). Sentiment analysis algorithms and applications: A survey. *Ain Shams Engineering Journal*, 5(4), 1093–1113. DOI: 10.1016/j.asej.2014.04.011

Mediakix. (2019). *State of influencer marketing: 2019 survey*. Mediakix.

Mehran, M. M., Kashmiri, T., & Pasha, A. T. (2020). Effects of brand trust, brand identification and quality of service on brand evangelism: A study of restaurants in Multan. *Journal of Arable Crops and Marketing*, 2(2), 35–46. DOI: 10.33687/jacm.002.02.3191

Merigó, J. M., Mas-Tur, A., Roig-Tierno, N., & Soriano, D. R. (2015). A bibliometric overview of the Journal of Business Research between 1973 and 2014. *Journal of Business Research*, 68(12), 2645–2653. DOI: 10.1016/j.jbusres.2015.04.006

Ming, J. (2023, October). Data Advocacy for Visibility of Home Care Workers. In *Companion Publication of the 2023 Conference on Computer Supported Cooperative Work and Social Computing* (pp. 444-447). DOI: 10.1145/3584931.3608922

Min, S., Zacharia, Z. G., & Smith, C. D. (2019). Defining Supply Chain Management: In the past, present, and future. *Journal of Business Logistics*, 40(1), 44–55. DOI: 10.1111/jbl.12201

Mishra, M., Kesharwani, A., & Gautam, D. R. V. (2021). Examining the relationship between consumer brand relationships and brand evangelism. *Australian Journal of Business and Management Research*, 6(1), 84–95. DOI: 10.52283/NSWRCA.AJBMR.20210601A07

Mittal, A., Dhiman, R., & Lamba, P. (2019). Skill mapping for blue-collar employees and organisational performance: A qualitative assessment. *Benchmarking*, 26(4), 1255–1274. DOI: 10.1108/BIJ-08-2018-0228

Mittal, A., Mantri, A., Tandon, U., & Dwivedi, Y. K. (2022). A unified perspective on the adoption of online teaching in higher education during the COVID-19 pandemic. *Information Discovery and Delivery*, 50(2), 117–132. DOI: 10.1108/IDD-09-2020-0114

Mohawesh, R., Xu, S., Tran, S. N., Ollington, R., Springer, M., Jararweh, Y., & Maqsood, S. (2021). Fake Reviews Detection: A survey. *IEEE Access : Practical Innovations, Open Solutions*, 9, 65771–65802. DOI: 10.1109/ACCESS.2021.3075573

Molinillo, S., Aguilar-Illescas, R., Anaya-Sánchez, R., & Liébana-Cabanillas, F. (2021). Social commerce website design, perceived value and loyalty behavior intentions: The moderating roles of gender, age and frequency of use. *Journal of Retailing and Consumer Services*, 63, 102404. DOI: 10.1016/j.jretconser.2020.102404

Morsing, M. (2006). Corporate social responsibility as strategic auto-communication: On the role of external stakeholders for member identification. *Business Ethics (Oxford, England)*, 15(2), 171–182. DOI: 10.1111/j.1467-8608.2006.00440.x

Mulet-Forteza, C., Martorell-Cunill, O., Merigó, J. M., Genovart-Balaguer, J., & Mauleón-Méndez, E. (2018). Twenty five years of the Journal of Travel & Tourism Marketing: A bibliometric ranking. *Journal of Travel & Tourism Marketing*, 35(9), 1201–1221. DOI: 10.1080/10548408.2018.1487368

Muniz, A. M.Jr, & O'Guinn, T. C. (2001). Brand community. *The Journal of Consumer Research*, 27(4), 412–432. DOI: 10.1086/319618

Muntinga, D. G., Moorman, M., & Smit, E. G. (2011). Introducing COBRAs: Exploring motivations for brand-related social media use. *International Journal of Advertising*, 30(1), 13–46. DOI: 10.2501/IJA-30-1-013-046

Mustare, N. B., Singh, B., Sekhar, M. V., Kapila, D., & Yadav, A. S. (2023, October). IoT and Big Data Analytics Platforms to Analyze the Faults in the Automated Manufacturing Process Unit. In *2023 International Conference on New Frontiers in Communication, Automation, Management and Security (ICCAMS)* (Vol. 1, pp. 1-6). IEEE. DOI: 10.1109/ICCAMS60113.2023.10525780

Nandagiri, V., & Philip, L. (2018). Impact of influencers from Instagram and YouTube on their followers. *International Journal of Multidisciplinary Research and Modern Education*, 4(1), 61–65.

Narassiguin, A., & Sargent, S. (2019). Data Science for Influencer Marketing: feature processing and quantitative analysis. *arXiv preprint arXiv:1906.05911*.

Narayan, S. (2017). Ayurvastra: Herbal clothing - A new technology to heal naturally. *International Journal of Advanced Research and Innovative Ideas in Education*, 3(4), 925–931.

Narteh, B. (2018). Brand equity and financial performance. *Marketing Intelligence & Planning*, 36(3), 381–395. DOI: 10.1108/MIP-05-2017-0098

Nassif, A. B., Azzeh, M., Banitaan, S., & Neagu, D. (2016). Guest editorial: Special issue on predictive analytics using machine learning. *Neural Computing & Applications*, 27(8), 2153–2155. DOI: 10.1007/s00521-016-2327-3

Nath, D. C., Kundu, I., Sharma, A., Shivhare, P., Afzal, A., Soudagar, M. E. M., & Park, S. G. (2023). Internet of Things integrated with solar energy applications: A state-of-the-art review. *Environment, Development and Sustainability*, 26(10), 1–56. DOI: 10.1007/s10668-023-03691-2

Nayyar, V. (2018). 'My Mind Starts Craving'-Impact of Resealable Packages on the Consumption Behavior of Indian Consumers. *Indian Journal of Marketing*, 48(11), 56–63. DOI: 10.17010/ijom/2018/v48/i11/137986

Nayyar, V. (2022). Reviewing the impact of digital migration on the consumer buying journey with robust measurement of PLS-SEM and R Studio. *Systems Research and Behavioral Science*, 39(3), 542–556. DOI: 10.1002/sres.2857

Nayyar, V. (2023). The role of marketing analytics in the ethical consumption of online consumers. *Total Quality Management & Business Excellence*, 34(7-8), 1015–1031. DOI: 10.1080/14783363.2022.2139676

Nayyar, V., & Batra, R. (2020). Does online media self-regulate consumption behavior of INDIAN youth? *International Review on Public and Nonprofit Marketing*, 17(3), 277–288. DOI: 10.1007/s12208-020-00248-1

Nelson, P. (1970). Information and consumer behaviour. *Journal of Political Economy*, 78(2), 311–329. DOI: 10.1086/259630

Nguyen, H. M., & Khoa, B. T. (2019). The relationship between the perceived mental benefits, online trust, and personal information disclosure in online shopping. *The Journal of Asian Finance. Economics and Business*, 6(4), 261–270.

Nguyen, P.-H., Nguyen, D. N., & Nguyen, L. A. T. (2023). Quantitative insights into green purchase intentions: The interplay of health consciousness, altruism, and sustainability. *Cogent Business & Management*, 10(3), 2253616. DOI: 10.1080/23311975.2023.2253616

Nielsen. (2021). Global responsibility report: Consumers seek companies that care about environmental impact. https://www.nielsen.com/us/en/insights/report/2021/global-responsibility-report

Nielsen. (2023). The state of influencer marketing: Trends and insights. Retrieved from https://www.nielsen.com/reports/influencer-marketing-trends-2023

Nijssen, E. J., & Douglas, S. P. (2004). Examining the animosity model in a country with a high level of foreign trade. *International Journal of Research in Marketing*, 21(1), 23–38. DOI: 10.1016/j.ijresmar.2003.05.001

Ningrum, A. M., Rofiaty, R., & Moko, W. (2024). The Influence of Social Media Marketing and Corporate Image on Customer Loyalty is Mediated by Customer Satisfaction (Study of 5 Star Hotel Customers in Malang City). *Journal of Economics Finance and Management Studies*, 07(01). Advance online publication. DOI: 10.47191/jefms/v7-i1-16

Nobi, B., Kim, K. M., & Lee, S. (2021). The aftermath of a brand transgression: The role of brand forgiveness and brand evangelism. *Journal of Asia Business Studies*, 16(6), 1030–1040. DOI: 10.1108/JABS-05-2021-0204

NURFARIDA, I. N., Endi SARWOKO, & Mohammed ARIEF. (2021). The Impact of Social Media Adoption on Customer Orientation and SME Performance: An Empirical Study in Indonesia. Journal of Asian Finance, Economics and Business, 8(6).

Nurhayati, N., Furkan, L. M., & Rinuastuti, B. H. (2024). The Effect of Brand Salience and Brand Perception on Brand Evangelism of Gili Trawangan Lombok Tourism with Brand Happiness as a Mediating Variable. *International Journal of Multicultural and Multireligious Understanding*, 11(8), 702–720.

Ofori, K. S., Anyigba, H., Adeola, O., Junwu, C., Osakwe, C. N., & David-West, O. (2021). Understanding post-adoption behaviour in the context of ride-hailing apps: The role of customer perceived value. *Information Technology & People*, 35(5), 1540–1562. DOI: 10.1108/ITP-06-2019-0285

Okonkwo, I., & Namkoisse, E. (2023). The Role of Influencer Marketing in Building Authentic Brand Relationships Online. *Journal of Digital Marketing and Communication*, 3(2), 81–90. DOI: 10.53623/jdmc.v3i2.350

Oliveira, M., Barbosa, R., & Sousa, A. (2020). The Use of Influencers in Social Media Marketing. In Rocha, Á., Reis, J. L., Peter, M. K., & Bogdanović, Z. (Eds.), *Marketing and Smart Technologies* (Vol. 167, pp. 112–124). Springer Singapore., DOI: 10.1007/978-981-15-1564-4_12

Oliver, R. L. (2020). *Satisfaction: A Behavioral Perspective on the Consumer*. Routledge.

Ortiz, M. H., Reynolds, K. E., & Franke, G. R. (2013). Measuring Consumer devotion: Antecedents and consequences of passionate consumer behavior. *Journal of Marketing Theory and Practice*, 21(1), 7–30. DOI: 10.2753/MTP1069-6679210101

Osmanova, I., Ozerden, S., Dalal, B., & Ibrahim, B. (2023). Examining the relationship between brand symbolism and brand evangelism through consumer brand identification: Evidence from Starbucks coffee brand. *Sustainability (Basel)*, 15(2), 1684. DOI: 10.3390/su15021684

Ottman, J. A. (2021). *The New Rules of Green Marketing: Strategies, Tools, and Inspiration for Sustainable Branding*. Greenleaf Publishing.

Oyewobi, L. O., Adedayo, O. F., Olorunyomi, S. O., & Jimoh, R. (2021). Social Media Adoption and Business Performance: The Mediating Role of Organizational Learning Capacity. *Journal of Facilities Management*, 19(4), 413–436. DOI: 10.1108/JFM-12-2020-0099

Oztamur, D., & Karakadilar, I. S. (2014). Exploring the Role of Social Media for SMEs: As a New Marketing Strategy Tool for the Firm Performance Perspective. *Procedia: Social and Behavioral Sciences*, 150, 511–520. DOI: 10.1016/j.sbspro.2014.09.067

Ozuem, W., & Willis, M. (2022). Influencer marketing. In *Digital marketing strategies for value co-creation: Models and approaches for online brand communities* (pp. 209–242). Springer International Publishing. DOI: 10.1007/978-3-030-94444-5_10

Painoli, A. K., Bansal, R., Singh, R., & Kukreti, A. (2021). Impact of Digital Marketing on the Buying Behavior of Youth With Special Reference to Uttarakhand State. In Big Data Analytics for Improved Accuracy, Efficiency, and Decision Making in Digital Marketing (pp. 162-182). IGI Global. DOI: 10.4018/978-1-7998-7231-3.ch012

Palakshappa, N., Bulmer, S., & Dodds, S. (2024). Co-creating sustainability: Transformative power of the brand. *Journal of Marketing Management*, 40(9–10), 820–850. DOI: 10.1080/0267257X.2024.2380261

Pangarkar, A., & Rathee, S. (2023). The role of conspicuity: Impact of social influencers on purchase decisions of luxury consumers. *International Journal of Advertising*, 42(7), 1150–1177. DOI: 10.1080/02650487.2022.2084265

Parguel, B., Benoît-Moreau, F., & Larceneux, F. (2021). How sustainability ratings might deter 'greenwashing': A closer look at ethical corporate communication. *Journal of Business Ethics*, 102(1), 15–28. DOI: 10.1007/s10551-011-0901-2

Paschen, J., Wilson, M., & Ferreira, J. J. (2020). The future of AI-powered marketing and sales: A review and research agenda. *Journal of Business Research*, 116, 274–287. DOI: 10.1016/j.jbusres.2020.05.042

Patterson, A., & Khare, A. (2021). Glossier's beauty influencer marketing: How to harness the power of micro-influencers. *Journal of Digital & Social Media Marketing*, 8(2), 134–143.

Peattie, K. (2021). *Green Marketing*. Sage Publications.

Pedalino, F., & Camerini, A.-L. (2022). Instagram use and body dissatisfaction: The mediating role of upward social comparison with peers and influencers among young females. *International Journal of Environmental Research and Public Health*, 19(3), 1543. DOI: 10.3390/ijerph19031543 PMID: 35162562

Pentina, I., & Koh, A. C. (2012). Exploring Social Media Marketing Strategies in SMEs. *International Journal of Internet Marketing and Advertising*, 7(4), 292–310. DOI: 10.1504/IJIMA.2012.051613

Pereira, V., Jayawardena, N. S., Sindhwani, R., Behl, A., & Laker, B. (2024). Using firm-level intellectual capital to achieve strategic sustainability: Examination of phenomenon of business failure in terms of the critical events. *Journal of Intellectual Capital*. Advance online publication. DOI: 10.1108/JIC-03-2024-0074

Perez Breton Borbn, D. A. (2024). *Examining The Impact Of Different Types Of Social Media Influencers On Attitudes, Trust & Purchase Intent: Travel User Generated Content*.

Pitt, L. F., Campbell, C., Berthon, P. R., & Laranjeiro, R. (2018). GoPro or go home: Exploring the roles of word-of-mouth and user-generated content in encouraging brand advocacy. *Journal of Strategic Marketing*, 26(4), 316–331. DOI: 10.1080/0965254X.2017.1384036

Polonsky, M. J., & Jevons, C. (2020). Understanding issues in social and ethical marketing. *Journal of Business Ethics*, 27(1-2), 71–79. DOI: 10.1023/A:1006442818505

Pornsrimate, K., & Khamwon, A. (2021). How to convert Millennial consumers to brand evangelists through social media micro-influencers. *Innovative Marketing*, 17(2).

Pourazad, N., Stocchi, L., & Narsey, S. (2023). A comparison of social media influencers' KPI patterns across platforms: Exploring differences in followers and engagement on Facebook, Instagram, YouTube, TikTok, and Twitter. *Journal of Advertising Research*, 63(2), 139–159. DOI: 10.2501/JAR-2023-008

Poureisa, A., Aziz, Y. A., & Ng, S. (2024). Swipe to Sustain: Exploring consumer behaviors in organic food purchasing via Instagram social commerce. *Sustainability (Basel)*, 16(6), 2338. DOI: 10.3390/su16062338

Pöyry, E., Pelkonen, M., Naumanen, E., & Laaksonen, S.-M. (2021). A call for authenticity: Audience responses to social media influencer endorsements in strategic communication. In *Social media influencers in strategic communication* (pp. 103–118).

Pradhan, B., Kishore, K., & Gokhale, N. (2023). Social media influencers and consumer engagement: A review and future research agenda. *International Journal of Consumer Studies*, 47(6), 2106–2130. DOI: 10.1111/ijcs.12901

Prahalad, C. K., & Hart, S. L. (2010). The fortune at the bottom of the pyramid. *Revista Eletrônica De Estratégia & Negócios*, 1(2), 1. DOI: 10.19177/reen.v1e220081-23

Prelipcean, M., Acatrinei, C., Gradinescu, I., & Canda, A. (2023). The Impact of Blockchain Technology on Marketing through Social Media. *Journal of Emerging Trends in Marketing and Management*, 1(1), 46–54.

Publishers, S. A. S. (2014).. . *Journal of Applied Medical Sciences*, 3(2F), 925–931.

Purohit, S., & Arora, R. (2024). Engagement: The Dynamic Evolution of Influencer Marketing in the Digital. *Advances in Data Analytics for Influencer Marketing: An Interdisciplinary Approach*, 29.

Purohit, S., Hollebeek, L. D., Das, M., & Sigurdsson, V. (2023). The effect of customers' brand experience on brand evangelism: The case of luxury hotels. *Tourism Management Perspectives*, 46, 101092. DOI: 10.1016/j.tmp.2023.101092

Qalati, S. A., Li, W., Ahmed, N., Mirani, M. A., & Khan, A. (2020). Examining the Factors Affecting SME Performance: The Mediating Role of Social Media Adoption. Sutainability, 13(1).

Rachmad, Y. E. (2024). *The future of influencer marketing: Evolution of consumer behavior in the digital world*. PT. Sonpedia Publishing Indonesia.

Rahman, K. T., Bansal, R., & Pruthi, N. (2023). Consumer Adoption of Technologies: A Mindset-Oriented Approach. In Contemporary Studies of Risks in Emerging Technology, Part B (pp. 243-255). Emerald Publishing Limited. DOI: 10.1108/978-1-80455-566-820231013

Rahman, K. T. (2022). Influencer Marketing and Behavioral Outcomes: How Types of Influencers Affect Consumer Mimicry? *SEISENSE Business Review*, 2(1), 43–54. DOI: 10.33215/sbr.v2i1.792

Rajendiran, A., & Dorai, S. (2020). Friendship to kinship: Evaluating the role of consumer brand engagement to promote brand evangelism. In *Handbook of Research on the Impact of Fandom in Society and Consumerism* (pp. 171–192). IGI Global. DOI: 10.4018/978-1-7998-1048-3.ch009

Rajput, A., Suryavanshi, K., Thapa, S. B., Gahlot, P., & Gandhi, A. (2024). The Impact of Social Media Influencers on Ecoconscious Consumers. *2024 ASU International Conference in Emerging Technologies for Sustainability and Intelligent Systems (ICETSIS)*, 1–6. DOI: 10.1109/ICETSIS61505.2024.10459444

Ramgopal, N. C., Gantela, P., Rajagopal, R., & Thankam, T., & SenthamilSelvan, R. (2022, December). Automatic Liver Cancer Detection in Abdominal Liver Images Using Soft Optimization Techniques. In *2022 International Conference on Knowledge Engineering and Communication Systems (ICKES)* (pp. 1-5). IEEE.

Rangari, N. T., Kalyankari, T. M., Mahajan, A. A., Lendhe, P. R., & Ruranik, P. K. (2012). Ayurvastra: Herbal couture technology in textile. *International Journal of Research in Ayurveda and Pharmacy*, 3(5), 733–736. DOI: 10.7897/2277-4343.03532

Rapaccini, M., Adrodegari, F., Pezzotta, G., & Saccani, N. (2024). Overcoming the knowledge gaps in early-stage servitization journey: A guide for small and medium enterprises. *IET Collaborative Intelligent Manufacturing*, 6(3), e12106. Advance online publication. DOI: 10.1049/cim2.12106

Rashid, A. B., Kausik, A. K., Sunny, A. H., & Bappy, M. H. (2023). Artificial intelligence in the military: An overview of the capabilities, applications, and challenges. *International Journal of Intelligent Systems*, 2023, 1–31. DOI: 10.1155/2023/8676366

Rausch, A., Abele, S., Deutscher, V., Greiff, S., Kis, V., Messenger, S., Shackleton, J., Tramonte, L., Ward, M., & Winther, E. (2024). Designing an International Large-Scale Assessment of Professional Competencies and Employability Skills: Emerging Avenues and Challenges of OECD's PISA-VET. *Vocations and Learning*, 17(3), 393–432. Advance online publication. DOI: 10.1007/s12186-024-09347-0

Rawwas, M. Y. A., Rajendran, K. N., & Wuehrer, G. A. (1996). The influence of worldmindedness and nationalism on consumer evaluation of domestic and foreign products. *International Marketing Review*, 13(2), 20–38. DOI: 10.1108/02651339610115746

Red Yellow Exports. (n.d.).

Reddy, A. B., Mahesh, K. M., Prabha, M., & Selvan, R. S. (2023, October). Design and implementation of A Bio-Inspired Robot Arm: Machine learning, Robot vision. In *2023 International Conference on New Frontiers in Communication, Automation, Management and Security (ICCAMS)* (Vol. 1, pp. 1-5). IEEE.

Report, H. A. (2021). *Sentiment analysis and social listening for brand campaigns.* Retrieved from. [source link if available]

Riefler, P., & Diamantopoulos, A. (2007). Consumer animosity: A literature review and a reconsideration of its measurement. *International Marketing Review*, 24(1), 87–119. DOI: 10.1108/02651330710727204

Riivits-Arkonsuo, I., Kaljund, K., & Leppiman, A. (2014). Consumer journey from first experience to brand evangelism. *Research in Economics and Business: Central and Eastern Europe*, 6(1), 5–28.

Riivits-Arkonsuo, I., Kaljund, K., & Leppiman, A. (2014). Consumer journey from first experience to brand evangelism. *Research in economics and business: Central and eastern. Europe*, 6(1), 5–28.

Riorini, S. V., & Widayati, C. C. (2016). Brand relationship and its effect towards brand evangelism to banking service. *International Research Journal of Business Studies*, 8(1), 33–45. Advance online publication. DOI: 10.21632/irjbs.8.1.33-45

Rocamora, A. (2022). The datafication and quantification of fashion: The case of fashion influencers. *Fashion Theory*, 26(7), 1109–1133. DOI: 10.1080/1362704X.2022.2048527

Rohde, A. (2020). How to use nano influencers to grow your brand. *Business News Daily.* https://www.businessnewsdaily.com

Romero-Rodriguez, L. M., & Castillo-Abdul, B. (2023). Toward state-of-the-art on social marketing research in user-generated content (UGC) and influencers. *Journal of Management Development*, 42(6), 425–435. DOI: 10.1108/JMD-11-2022-0285

Roudometof, V. (2005). Transnationalism, cosmopolitanism and glocalization. *Current Sociology*, 53(1), 113–135. DOI: 10.1177/0011392105048291

Rungruangjit, W., Chankoson, T., & Charoenpornpanichkul, K. (2023). Understanding Different Types of Followers' Engagement and the Transformation of Millennial Followers into Cosmetic Brand Evangelists. *Behavioral Sciences (Basel, Switzerland)*, 13(3), 270. DOI: 10.3390/bs13030270 PMID: 36975295

Rungruangjit, W., & Charoenpornpanichkul, K. (2022). Building stronger brand evangelism for sustainable marketing through micro-influencer-generated content on Instagram in the fashion industry. *Sustainability (Basel)*, 14(23), 15770. DOI: 10.3390/su142315770

Rust, R. T., & Huang, M. H. (2021). The service revolution and the transformation of marketing science. *Marketing Science*, 40(3), 527–528. DOI: 10.1287/mksc.2021.1312

Safeer, A. A., & Le, T. T. (2023). Transforming customers into evangelists: Influence of online brand experience on relationship quality and brand evangelism in the banking industry. *Asia Pacific Journal of Marketing and Logistics*, 35(12), 2947–2964. DOI: 10.1108/APJML-12-2022-1018

Sagala, G. H., & Őri, D. (2024). Toward SMEs digital transformation success: A systematic literature review. *Information Systems and e-Business Management*. Advance online publication. DOI: 10.1007/s10257-024-00682-2

Sahu, S., Chandra, G., & Dwivedi, S. K. (2019, November). E-Governance Initiatives and Challenges in the State of Uttar Pradesh. In *2019 International Conference on Cutting-edge Technologies in Engineering (ICon-CuTE)* (pp. 108-112). IEEE. DOI: 10.1109/ICon-CuTE47290.2019.8991499

Saini, S., & Bansal, R. (2023). Geo-Marketing: A New Tool for Marketers. In Enhancing Customer Engagement Through Location-Based Marketing (pp. 102-112). IGI Global. DOI: 10.4018/978-1-6684-8177-6.ch008

Saini, S., Ngah, A. H., Sahai, S., & Bansal, R. (2024). When AI Meets Influence: Exploring the Integration of ChatGPT and Influencer Marketing. In *Leveraging ChatGPT and Artificial Intelligence for Effective Customer Engagement* (pp. 272-284). IGI Global.

Sakr, S. S. (2023). Banana Peel Utilization: Practice and Perspective, Highlights from Lebanon. *International Journal of Clinical Studies and Medical Case Reports*, 34(4). Advance online publication. DOI: 10.46998/IJCMCR.2023.34.000842

Saldanha, N., Mulye, R., & Japutra, A. (2024). How do consumers interact with social media influencers in extraordinary times? *Journal of Research in Interactive Marketing*, 18(3), 333–348. DOI: 10.1108/JRIM-02-2023-0062

Sammis, K., Lincoln, C., & Pomponi, S. (2016). *Influencer marketing for brands: What YouTube and Instagram can teach you about the future of digital advertising*. Palgrave Macmillan.

Sandi, H. A., & Atmaja, F. T. (2024). The impact of information content and entertainment content on customer engagement and customer loyalty: A study on Scarlett's customer base. *Journal of Entrepreneur & Business*, 5(1), 69–78. DOI: 10.24123/jeb.v5i1.6115

Sanjari Nader, B., Yarahmadi, F., & Baluchi, H. (2020). The Impact of Social Network Based Brand Communities on Brand Evangelism through Strengthening Brand Trust. *Consumer Behavior Studies Journal*, 7(2), 24–47.

Santiago, J. K., & Castelo, I. M. (2020). Digital influencers: An exploratory study of influencer marketing campaign process on instagram. [OJAKM]. *Online Journal of Applied Knowledge Management*, 8(2), 31–52. DOI: 10.36965/OJAKM.2020.8(2)31-52

Saridakis, G., Khan, Z., Knight, G., Idris, B., Mitra, J., & Khan, H. (2024). A Look into the Future: The Impact of Metaverse on Traditional Theories and Thinking in International Business. *MIR. Management International Review*, 64(4), 597–632. DOI: 10.1007/s11575-024-00550-8

Saritas, O., Bakhtin, P., Kuzminov, I., & Khabirova, E. (2021). Big data augmented business trend identification: The case of mobile commerce. *Scientometrics*, 126(2), 1553–1579. DOI: 10.1007/s11192-020-03807-9 PMID: 33424052

Sashittal, H. C., Jassawalla, A. R., & Sachdeva, R. (2023). The influence of COVID-19 pandemic on consumer–brand relationships: Evidence of brand evangelism behaviors. *Journal of Brand Management*, 30(3), 245–260. DOI: 10.1057/s41262-022-00301-w

Schau, H. J., Muñiz, A. M.Jr, & Arnould, E. J. (2009). How brand community practices create value. *Journal of Marketing*, 73(5), 30–51. DOI: 10.1509/jmkg.73.5.30

Schivinski, B., & Dabrowski, D. (2016). The impact of brand communication on brand equity through Facebook. *Journal of Research in Interactive Marketing*, 10(1), 31–53. DOI: 10.1108/JRIM-02-2014-0007

Schlaile, M. P., Mueller, M., Schramm, M., & Pyka, A. (2017). Evolutionary Economics, responsible innovation and demand: Making a case for the role of consumers. *Philosophy of Management*, 17(1), 7–39. DOI: 10.1007/s40926-017-0054-1

Scholz, J. (2021). How consumers consume social media influence. *Journal of Advertising*, 50(5), 510–527. DOI: 10.1080/00913367.2021.1980472

Schorn, A., Vinzenz, F., & Wirth, W. (2022). Promoting sustainability on Instagram: How sponsorship disclosures and benefit appeals affect the credibility of sinnfluencers. *Young Consumers*, 23(3), 345–361. DOI: 10.1108/YC-07-2021-1355

Schouten, A. P., Janssen, L., & Verspaget, M. (2020). Celebrity vs. influencer endorsements in advertising: The role of identification, credibility, and product-endorser fit. *International Journal of Advertising*, 39(2), 258–281. DOI: 10.1080/02650487.2019.1634898

Schouten, A. P., Janssen, L., & Verspaget, M. (2022). Celebrity vs. influencer endorsements in advertising: The role of identification, credibility, and Product-Endorser fit. *International Journal of Advertising*, 41(3), 414–438. DOI: 10.1080/02650487.2020.1815201

Schouten, J. W., & McAlexander, J. H. (1995). Subcultures of consumption: An ethnography of the new bikers. *The Journal of Consumer Research*, 22(1), 43–61. DOI: 10.1086/209434

Schwemmer, C., & Ziewiecki, S. (2018). Social Media Sellout: The Increasing Role of Product Promotion on YouTube. *Social Media + Society*, 4(3), 205630511878672. DOI: 10.1177/2056305118786720

Sebastián-Morillas, A., Martín-Soladana, I., & Clemente-Mediavilla, J. (2020). Importancia de los 'insights' en el proceso estratégico y creativo de las campañas publicitarias. *Estudios sobre el Mensaje Periodístico*, 26(1), 339–348. DOI: 10.5209/esmp.66570

Sedda, P., & Husson, O. (2023). Social Media Influencers: A New Hybrid Professionalism in the Age of Platform Capitalism? In *Professionalism and Social Change: Processes of Differentiation Within, Between and Beyond Professions* (pp. 281–304). Springer International Publishing. DOI: 10.1007/978-3-031-31278-6_13

Selvan, R. S. (2020). Intersection Collision Avoidance in DSRC using VANET. *on Concurrency and Computation-Practice and Experience, 34*(13/e5856), 1532-0626.

SenthamilSelvan, R. (2017). Analysis Of EDFC And ADFC Algorithms For Secure Communication In VANET. *JARDCS, 9*(18), 1171-1187.

SenthamilSelvan, R., Wahidabanu, R. S. D., & Karthik, B. (2022). Intersection collision avoidance in dedicated short-range communication using vehicle ad hoc network. *Concurrency and Computation*, 34(13), e5856.

Shaari, H., & Ahmad, I. S. (2016). Brand evangelism among online brand community members. *International Review of Management and Business Research*, 5(1), 80–88.

Shalender, K., & Yadav, R. K. (2019). Strategic flexibility, manager personality, and firm performance: The case of Indian Automobile Industry. *Global Journal of Flexible Systems Managment*, 20(1), 77–90. DOI: 10.1007/s40171-018-0204-x

Shalini, R., Mishra, L., Athulya, S., Chimankar, A. G., Kandavalli, S. R., Kumar, K., & Selvan, R. S. (2023, May). Tumor Infiltration of Microrobot using Magnetic torque and AI Technique. In *2023 2nd International Conference on Vision Towards Emerging Trends in Communication and Networking Technologies (ViTECoN)* (pp. 1-5). IEEE.

Shang, Y., & Li, F. S. (2024). How does ritualistic service increase brand evangelism through E2C interaction quality and memory? The moderating role of social phobia. *International Journal of Hospitality Management*, 116, 103624. DOI: 10.1016/j.ijhm.2023.103624

Sharada, K. A., Swathi, R., Reddy, A. B., Selvan, R. S., & Sivaranjani, L. (2023, October). A New Model for Predicting Pandemic Impact on Worldwide Academic Rankings. In *2023 International Conference on New Frontiers in Communication, Automation, Management and Security (ICCAMS)* (Vol. 1, pp. 1-4). IEEE.

Sharma, B. K., Bhatt, V. K., & Arora, L. (2021). Influencer marketing—An instrument to proliferation of the digital occurrence. *International Journal of Enterprise Network Management*, 12(4), 340. DOI: 10.1504/IJENM.2021.119662

Sharma, P. (2016). Ayurvastra: Textile innovation through herbal dyeing. *Journal of Medicinal Plants Studies*, 4(6), 33–37.

Sharma, P. (2023). Destination evangelism and engagement: Investigation from social media-based travel community. *Electronic Commerce Research and Applications*, 57, 101228. DOI: 10.1016/j.elerap.2022.101228

Sharma, P., & Khandeparkar, K. (2024). Exploring the nexus between influencers and brand evangelism. *Asia Pacific Journal of Marketing and Logistics*. Advance online publication. DOI: 10.1108/APJML-06-2023-0581

Sha, W., & Basri, M. (2018). Social Media and Corporate Communication Antecedents of SME Sustainability Performance A Conceptual Framework for SMEs of Arab World. *Journal of Economic and Administrative Sciences*, 35(3).

Shelbert, V., & Narayan, A. (2024). Discussion paper. In IWA Publishing eBooks. https://doi.org/DOI: 10.2166/9781789064964

Shimp, T. A., & Sharma, S. (1987). Consumer Ethnocentrism: Construction and validation of the CETSCALE. *JMR, Journal of Marketing Research*, 24(3), 280–289. DOI: 10.1177/002224378702400304

Shravanthi, C. (2023, March 10). How AI and big data analytics are changing influencer marketing. LinkedIn. https://www.linkedin.com/pulse/how-ai-big-data-analytics-changing-influencer-marketing-shravanthi-c-kfhpc/

Siakas, K., Georgiadou, E., Rahanu, H., Siakas, E., Meggoudis, N., & Siakas, D. (2024). Overcoming obstacles in Global Requirements Elicitation: A Multicultural perspective. *Journal of Software Engineering Research and Development*, 12(1). Advance online publication. DOI: 10.5753/jserd.2024.2552

Siddharth, L., Blessing, L., & Luo, J. (2022). Natural language processing in-and-for design research. *Design Science*, 8, e21. Advance online publication. DOI: 10.1017/dsj.2022.16

Siddique, S., & Chow, J. C. L. (2021). Machine learning in healthcare communication. *Encyclopedia*, 1(1), 220–239. DOI: 10.3390/encyclopedia1010021

Signes, Á. P., Miret-Pastor, L., Tsiouni, M., Siggia, D., & Galati, A. (2023). Determinants of consumers' response to eco-labelled seafoods: The interaction between altruism, awareness and information demand. *Journal of Cleaner Production*, 433, 139758. DOI: 10.1016/j.jclepro.2023.139758

Simon, H. A. (1991). Bounded rationality and organizational learning. *Organization Science*, 2(1), 125–134. DOI: 10.1287/orsc.2.1.125

Singh, N. (2024). Consumers' Choice Behavior Towards Sustainable Fashion Based on Social Media Influence. In *Driving Green Marketing in Fashion and Retail* (pp. 1–25). IGI Global.

Singh, B., Bhagyalakshmi, K., & Shukla, A. (2023, October). Big Data Analytics–Future Trend. In *2023 International Conference on New Frontiers in Communication, Automation, Management and Security (ICCAMS)* (Vol. 1, pp. 1-3). IEEE.

Singh, G., Appadurai, J. P., Perumal, V., Kavita, K., Ch Anil Kumar, T., Prasad, D. V. S. S. S. V., Azhagu Jaisudhan Pazhani, A., & Umamaheswari, K. (2022). Machine Learning-Based Modelling and Predictive Maintenance of Turning Operation under Cooling/Lubrication for Manufacturing Systems. *Advances in Materials Science and Engineering*, 2022(1), 9289320. DOI: 10.1155/2022/9289320

Singh, R., & Singh, S. (2021). Sustainable textile innovations: Ayurvastra and beyond. In Singh, R., & Singh, S. (Eds.), *Sustainable Innovations in Textile Processing* (pp. 90–102). Springer.

Singh, V. P., & Srivastava, N. (2022). Ayurvastra: A textile innovation for health benefits. *Environmental Science and Pollution Research International*, 29(12), 18818–18830. PMID: 34676482

Sivakumar, S.Scada energy management system under the distributed decimal of service attack using verification techniques by IIoT. *2023 International Conference on Artificial Intelligence and Knowledge Discovery in Concurrent Engineering (ICECONF)*. IEEE. DOI: 10.1109/ICECONF57129.2023.10083924

Smith, A. (2021). *Digital marketing and analytics: How to use data-driven insights for better campaigns*. Springer.

Smith, B. G., Hallows, D., Vail, M., Burnett, A., & Porter, C. (2021). Social media conversion: Lessons from faith-based social media influencers for public relations. *Journal of Public Relations Research*, 33(4), 231–249. DOI: 10.1080/1062726X.2021.2011728

Smith, P. R., & Zook, Z. (2021). *Marketing communications: Integrating offline and online with social media*. Kogan Page Publishers.

Spanjol, J., Noble, C. H., Baer, M., Bogers, M. L. M., Bohlmann, J., Bouncken, R. B., Bstieler, L., De Luca, L. M., Garcia, R., Gemser, G., Grewal, D., Hoegl, M., Kuester, S., Kumar, M., Lee, R., Mahr, D., Nakata, C., Ordanini, A., Rindfleisch, A., & Wetzels, M. (2024). Fueling innovation management research: Future directions and five forward-looking paths. *Journal of Product Innovation Management*, 41(5), 893–948. Advance online publication. DOI: 10.1111/jpim.12754

Sprout Social. (2024, July 18). Influencer analytics tools: How to measure success. Retrieved September 3, 2024, from https://sproutsocial.com/insights/influencer-analytics-tools/

Srinivasa, K. G. GM, S., Srinivasa, K. G., & GM, S. (2018). Introduction to Data Analytics. *Network Data Analytics: A Hands-On Approach for Application Development*, 3-28.

Srivastava, S., Anshu, Bansal, R., Soni, G., & Tyagi, A. K. (2022, December). Blockchain Enabled Internet of Things: Current Scenario and Open Challenges for Future. In International Conference on Innovations in Bio-Inspired Computing and Applications (pp. 640-648). Cham: Springer Nature Switzerland.

Stefan, A., & Paul, L. (2008). Does it pay to be green? A systematic overview. *The Academy of Management Perspectives*, 22(4), 45–62. DOI: 10.5465/amp.2008.35590353

Steils, N., Martin, A., & Toti, J. F. (2022). Managing the transparency paradox of social-media influencer disclosures: How to improve authenticity and engagement when disclosing influencer–sponsor relationships. *Journal of Advertising Research*, 62(2), 148–166. DOI: 10.2501/JAR-2022-008

Stoldt, R., Wellman, M., Ekdale, B., & Tully, M. (2019). Professionalizing and Profiting: The Rise of Intermediaries in the Social Media Influencer Industry. *Social Media + Society*, 5(1), 205630511983258. DOI: 10.1177/2056305119832587

Sudha, M., & Sheena, K. (2017). Impact of influencers in consumer decision process: The fashion industry. *SCMS Journal of Indian Management*, 14(3), 14–30.

Su, L., Wang, L., Law, R., Chen, X., & Fong, D. (2016). Influences of destination social responsibility on the relationship quality with residents and destination economic performance. *Journal of Travel & Tourism Marketing*, 34(4), 488–502. DOI: 10.1080/10548408.2016.1193101

Sumner, W. G. (1934). *Folkways: A Study of the Sociological Importance of Usages*. Manners, Customs, Mores, and Morals.

Sundar, K. S. (Ed.). (2019). *Globalization, Labour Market Institutions, Processes and Policies in India*. Palgrave Macmillan. DOI: 10.1007/978-981-13-7111-0

Sundermann, G., & Raabe, T. (2019). Strategic communication through social media influencers: Current state of research and desiderata. *International Journal of Strategic Communication*, 13(4), 278–300. DOI: 10.1080/1553118X.2019.1618306

Sutrisno, B., & Ariesta, Y. (2019). Beyond the use of code mixing by social media influencers in instagram. *Advances in Language and Literary Studies*, 10(6), 143–151. DOI: 10.7575/aiac.alls.v.10n.6p.143

Syrdal, H. A., Myers, S., Sen, S., Woodroof, P. J., & McDowell, W. C. (2023). Influencer marketing and the growth of affiliates: The effects of language features on engagement behaviour. *Journal of Business Research*, 163, 113875. DOI: 10.1016/j.jbusres.2023.113875

Tafesse, W., & Wood, B. P. (2021). Followers' engagement with instagram influencers: The role of influencers' content and engagement strategy. *Journal of Retailing and Consumer Services*, 58, 102303. DOI: 10.1016/j.jretconser.2020.102303

Tafheem, N., El-Gohary, H., & Sobh, R. (2022). Social media user-influencer congruity: An analysis of social media platforms parasocial relationships. [IJCRMM]. *International Journal of Customer Relationship Marketing and Management*, 13(1), 1–26. DOI: 10.4018/IJCRMM.289213

Tajfel, H., & Turner, J. C. (1986). The social identity theory of intergroup behavior. In Worchel, S., & Austin, W. G. (Eds.), *Psychology of intergroup relations* (pp. 7–24). Nelson-Hall.

Tang, B., Han, S., Yiu, M. L., Ding, R., & Zhang, D. (2017, May). Extracting top-k insights from multi-dimensional data. In *Proceedings of the 2017 ACM international conference on management of data* (pp. 1509-1524). DOI: 10.1145/3035918.3035922

Tanwar, A. S., Chaudhry, H., & Srivastava, M. K. (2022). Trends in influencer marketing: A review and bibliometric analysis. *Journal of Interactive Advertising*, 22(1), 1–27. DOI: 10.1080/15252019.2021.2007822

Teoh, C. W., Khor, K. C., & Wider, W. (2022). Factors influencing consumers' purchase intention towards green home appliances. *Frontiers in Psychology*, 13, 927327. Advance online publication. DOI: 10.3389/fpsyg.2022.927327 PMID: 35846659

The Hindu. (2019, June 3). The art of Ayurvastra.

Thomson, M., MacInnis, D. J., & Park, C. W. (2005). The ties that bind: Measuring the strength of consumers'' emotional attachments to brands. *Journal of Consumer Psychology*, 15(1), 77–91. DOI: 10.1207/s15327663jcp1501_10

Tiwari, P. (2024). Unleashing brand evangelism: The role of HEXACO personality traits and self-efficacy in the smartphone user community. *SN Business & Economics*, 4(3), 32. DOI: 10.1007/s43546-024-00630-9

Triandis, H. C., Brislin, R. W., & Hui, C. H. (1988). Cross-cultural training across the individualism-collectivism divide. *International Journal of Intercultural Relations*, 12(3), 269–289. DOI: 10.1016/0147-1767(88)90019-3

Tripathi, P., & Kapoor, S. (2024). Impact of Consumers' Sustainability Consciousness on Consumers' Evangelism. In *Resilient Businesses for Sustainability* (Vol. 34, pp. 97–112). Emerald Publishing Limited. DOI: 10.1108/S1877-63612024000034B009

Tseng, T., Davidson, M. J., Morales-Navarro, L., Chen, J. K., Delaney, V., Leibowitz, M., Beason, J., & Shapiro, R. B. (2024). CO-ML: Collaborative Machine learning model building for developing dataset design practices. *ACM Transactions on Computing Education*, 24(2), 1–37. DOI: 10.1145/3641552

Tuten, T. L., & Solomon, M. R. (2017). *Social media marketing* (3rd ed.). Sage Publications.

Vaidya, R., & Karnawat, T. (2023). Conceptualizing influencer marketing: A literature review on the strategic use of social media influencers. *International Journal of Management, Public Policy and Research*, 2(SpecialIssue), 81–86.

Van Den Bercken, W. (1988). Ideology and atheism in the Soviet Union. In *De Gruyter eBooks*. https://doi.org/DOI: 10.1515/9783110857375

Van Doorn, J., Lemon, K. N., Mittal, V., Nass, S., Pick, D., Pirner, P., & Verhoef, P. C. (2020). Customer engagement behavior: Theoretical foundations and research directions. *Journal of Service Research*, 13(3), 253–266. DOI: 10.1177/1094670510375599

Van Eyssen, T. (2024). *Sourcing, analysing, and Visualising stories: Multidisciplinary programme development in data journalism*. https://doi.org/DOI: 10.26686/wgtn.27115939

Vangelov, N. (2019). Efficient communication through influencer marketing. *Styles of Communication*, 11(1), 72–80.

Vanninen, H., Mero, J., & Kantamaa, E. (2023). Social media influencers as mediators of commercial messages. *Journal of Internet Commerce, 22*(sup1), S4-S27.

Vassio, L., Garetto, M., Leonardi, E., & Chiasserini, C. F. (2022). Mining and modelling temporal dynamics of followers' engagement on online social networks. *Social Network Analysis and Mining*, 12(1), 96. DOI: 10.1007/s13278-022-00928-2 PMID: 35937770

Vidani, J., & Das, S. G. (2021). A review on evolution of social media influencer marketing: Reflection on consumer behaviour and consumer's decision-making process. *Turkish Online Journal of Qualitative Inquiry*, 12(9), 1–15. DOI: 10.17569/tojqi.979362

Wallace, E., Buil, I., & de Chernatony, L. (2020). Consumer engagement with self-expressive brands: Brand love and WOM outcomes. *Journal of Product and Brand Management*, 29(4), 407–421. DOI: 10.1108/JPBM-09-2018-2026

Wang, C. L., & Chen, Z. X. (2004). Consumer ethnocentrism and willingness to buy domestic products in a developing country setting: Testing moderating effects. *Journal of Consumer Marketing*, 21(6), 391–400. DOI: 10.1108/07363760410558663

Wang, E. S.-T., & Weng, Y.-J. (2024). Influence of social media influencer authenticity on their followers' perceptions of credibility and their positive word-of-mouth. *Asia Pacific Journal of Marketing and Logistics*, 36(2), 356–373. DOI: 10.1108/APJML-02-2023-0115

Wang, F., & Scheinbaum, A. C. (2021). Communicating sustainability: How different message frames influence consumers' perceptions and behavioral intentions. *Journal of Advertising*, 50(2), 190–204. DOI: 10.1080/00913367.2021.1882998

Wang, J., Yang, Y., Liu, Q., Fang, Z., Sun, S., & Xu, Y. (2022). An empirical study of user engagement in influencer marketing on Weibo and WeChat. *IEEE Transactions on Computational Social Systems*, 10(6), 3228–3240. DOI: 10.1109/TCSS.2022.3204177

Wan, Y., Liu, Y., Chen, Z., Chen, C., Li, X., Hu, F., & Packianather, M. (2024). Making knowledge graphs work for smart manufacturing: Research topics, applications and prospects. *Journal of Manufacturing Systems*, 76, 103–132. DOI: 10.1016/j.jmsy.2024.07.009

Watson, J., & Wright, K. (2000). Consumer ethnocentrism and attitudes toward domestic and foreign products. *European Journal of Marketing*, 34(9/10), 1149–1166. DOI: 10.1108/03090560010342520

Wedel, M., & Kannan, P. K. (2020). Marketing analytics for data-rich environments. *Journal of Marketing*, 84(1), 97–121. DOI: 10.1177/0022242919882077

Weinberg, B. H. (1974). Bibliographic coupling: A review. *Information Storage and Retrieval*, 10(5–6), 189–196. DOI: 10.1016/0020-0271(74)90058-8

Wei, X., Chen, H., Ramirez, A., Jeon, Y., & Sun, Y. (2022). Influencers as endorsers and followers as consumers: Exploring the role of parasocial relationship, congruence, and followers' identifications on consumer–brand engagement. *Journal of Interactive Advertising*, 22(3), 269–288. DOI: 10.1080/15252019.2022.2116963

Wellman, M. L., Stoldt, R., Tully, M., & Ekdale, B. (2020). Ethics of Authenticity: Social Media Influencers and the Production of Sponsored Content. *Journal of Medical Ethics*, 35(2), 68–82. DOI: 10.1080/23736992.2020.1736078

Wentzell, K., Walker, H. R., Hughes, A. S., & Vessey, J. A. (2021). Engaging social media influencers to recruit hard-to-reach populations. *Nursing Research*, 70(6), 455–461. DOI: 10.1097/NNR.0000000000000544 PMID: 34334700

Wibawa, R. C., Pratiwi, C. P., & Larasati, H. (2021). The role of nano influencers through Instagram as an effective digital marketing strategy. *Conference Towards ASEAN Chairmanship 2023 (TAC 23 2021)*, 233–238.

Widodo, M., & Ginting, A. M. (2024). Factors Influencing and Their Impact On Brand Evangelism. *Enrichment: Journal of Management*, 13(6), 3773–3781.

Wielki, J. (2020). Analysis of the role of digital influencers and their impact on the functioning of the contemporary on-line promotional system and its sustainable development. *Sustainability (Basel)*, 12(17), 7138. DOI: 10.3390/su12177138

Williams, E. (2024, January 10). Navigating the challenges of data and influencer marketing convergence. Forbes. https://www.forbes.com/navigating-challenges-data-influencer-marketing

Wongkitrungrueng, A., & Assarut, N. (2018). The role of live streaming in building consumer trust and engagement with social commerce sellers. *Journal of Business Research*, 117, 543–556. DOI: 10.1016/j.jbusres.2018.08.032

Woolley, S. C. (2022). Digital propaganda: The power of influencers. *Journal of Democracy*, 33(3), 115–129. DOI: 10.1353/jod.2022.0027

Xiao, Y., Zhu, Y., He, W., & Huang, M. (2023). Influence prediction model for marketing campaigns on e-commerce platforms. *Expert Systems with Applications*, 211, 118575. DOI: 10.1016/j.eswa.2022.118575

Yan, M., Kwok, A. P. K., Chan, A. H. S., Zhuang, Y. S., Wen, K., & Zhang, K. C. (2023). An empirical investigation of the impact of influencer live-streaming ads in e-commerce platforms on consumers' buying impulse. *Internet Research*, 33(4), 1633–1663. DOI: 10.1108/INTR-11-2020-0625

Yan, Y., Qian, Y., Sharif, H., & Tipper, D. (2012). A survey on Smart Grid Communication Infrastructures: Motivations, requirements and challenges. *IEEE Communications Surveys and Tutorials*, 15(1), 5–20. DOI: 10.1109/SURV.2012.021312.00034

Ye, G., Hudders, L., De Jans, S., & De Veirman, M. (2021). The value of influencer marketing for business: A bibliometric analysis and managerial implications. *Journal of Advertising*, 50(2), 160–178. DOI: 10.1080/00913367.2020.1857888

Yesiloglu, S., & Costello, J. (2020). *Influencer marketing: Building brand communities and engagement.* Routledge. DOI: 10.4324/9780429322501

Yildirim, S. (2021). Do green women influencers spur sustainable consumption patterns? Descriptive evidences from social media influencers. *Ecofeminism and Climate Change*, 2(4), 198–210. DOI: 10.1108/EFCC-02-2021-0003

Yoon, S. J., & Kim, H. H. (2020). Data analytics and artificial intelligence in influencer marketing: A systematic literature review. *Sustainability*, 12(8), 3150. DOI: 10.3390/su12083150

Yuan, Y., Gretzel, U., & Tseng, Y. (2014). Revealing the Nature of Contemporary Tourism Research: Extracting Common Subject Areas through Bibliographic Coupling. *International Journal of Tourism Research*, 17(5), 417–431. DOI: 10.1002/jtr.2004

Yu, W., Han, X., & Cui, F. (2022). Increase consumers' willingness to pay a premium for organic food in restaurants: Explore the role of comparative advertising. *Frontiers in Psychology*, 13, 982311. Advance online publication. DOI: 10.3389/fpsyg.2022.982311 PMID: 35992425

Yu, W., He, M., Han, X., & Zhou, J. (2022). Value acquisition, value co-creation: The impact of perceived organic grocerant value on customer engagement behavior through brand trust. *Frontiers in Psychology*, 13, 990545. Advance online publication. DOI: 10.3389/fpsyg.2022.990545 PMID: 36275242

Zhang, Y., & Chen, X. (2020). Explainable recommendation: a survey and new perspectives. *Foundations and Trends® in Information Retrieval, 14*(1), 1–101. https://doi.org/DOI: 10.1561/1500000066

Zhang, K. Z., Benyoucef, M., & Zhao, S. J. (2020). The influence of social commerce on consumer behavior: An empirical study. *Electronic Commerce Research and Applications*, 39, 100906. DOI: 10.1016/j.elerap.2019.100906

Zhang, X., & Choi, J. (2022). The importance of social influencer-generated contents for user cognition and emotional attachment: An information relevance perspective. *Sustainability (Basel)*, 14(11), 6676. DOI: 10.3390/su14116676

Zhang, Y., & Choi, H. (2023). Brand anthropomorphism and consumer brand evangelism on social networking sites: Prevention focus as a moderator. *Social Behavior and Personality*, 51(12), 12726E–12738E. DOI: 10.2224/12726

Zikra, F. K., Widodo, A., Silvianita, A., & Rubiyanti, N. (2024). The Impact of Multidimensional Innovation on Brand Evangelism: Empirical Evidence from Starbucks. *International Journal of Scientific Multidisciplinary Research*, 2(5), 453–466. DOI: 10.55927/ijsmr.v2i5.9137

Zniva, R., Weitzl, W. J., & Lindmoser, C. (2023). Be constantly different! How to manage influencer authenticity. *Electronic Commerce Research*, 23(3), 1485–1514. DOI: 10.1007/s10660-022-09653-6

Župič, I., & Čater, T. (2014). Bibliometric methods in management and organization. *Organizational Research Methods*, 18(3), 429–472. DOI: 10.1177/1094428114562629

About the Contributors

Fazla Rabby is an accomplished academic and professional with a diverse background in education, management, and marketing. Holding a Ph.D. from the University of Southern Queensland, their education includes degrees and diplomas in management, leadership, and information systems from Central Queensland University and the University of Madras. As a Teaching Academic at Macquarie University and Lecturer at Canterbury Institute of Management, Dr. Rabby designs and delivers educational activities, assesses student progress, and contributes to curriculum development. Their role as Academic Director at Stanford Institute of Management and Technology highlights their leadership in stakeholder relationships, business strategies, and HR management. Previously, Dr. Rabby excelled in sales and marketing roles, including Director of Australian Sales and Marketing and Managing Director of Sales Solutions Australia. A prolific researcher and presenter, they focus on blockchain, digital marketing, AI, service marketing and consumer behavior, with upcoming projects on industry innovation and AI in education.

Rohit Bansal is working as a Faculty in Department of Management Studies in Vaish College of Engineering, Rohtak. He obtained Ph.D. in Management from Maharshi Dayanand University, Rohtak. With a rich experience of 17 years, he has achieved growth through robust and proactive academic initiatives. He has authored & edited 45 books with renowned national & international publishers including Springer Nature, IGI Global, Scrivener-Wiley Publishing, De Gruyter, Central West Publishing etc. In addition to, Dr. Rohit has published 160 research papers and chapters in journals of repute including Scopus indexed as well as edited books. His research work is published in leading publishers like Springer, MDPI, HIndawi, IGI Global, Cell Press, De Gruyter, Elseveir, Inderscience, Wiley etc. He has also presented papers in 55 conferences and seminars including IIM Indore, IIM Ranchi, IIM Jammu and IIM Kozhikode. His area of interest includes marketing management, organizational behavior, services marketing, customer engagement, digital marketing, influencer marketing, human resource management, emerging technologies, e-learning and sustainable development. He is Managing Editor of International Journal of 360° Management Review. He has served as member of technical committee in many international conferences. He has acted as Session Chair and speaker in many international conferences. He has been awarded many times for contribution to academics and research.

Aziza Chakir is a Senior Lecturer, Keynote Speaker and currently serve as a HDR professor in the university Hassan II. Her research interests include in the area of Computer Engineering, Information Systems, Digital culture, Consumer Behavior, Software Engineering, Knowledge Transfer Technology, IT Governance, Cloud Computing, Suitable Development (Green IT..), Machine Learning, Big Data, Data mining... She is currently working on many projects such as "Green computing" Her disciplines include Architectural Engineering Information Technology, Politics Information Systems (Business Informatics) and Artificial Intelligence Distributed Computing. Her skills and expertise fall into the fields of Risk Management, Business Intelligence, IT Governance, Corporate Governance, Information Technology, Cloud Computing, and E-Government. She has authored & edited many books with renowned national & international publishers including IGI Global USA, Lambert Academic Publishing, Springer, etc. In addition, she has published research papers in national and international journals indexed by Scopus. She has also reviewed many international journals indexed by Scopus., "Ecological frameworks"

Ajay Jain is working as assistant professor in SCMKVM, Indore and National Coordinator-India, Research Foundation of India. He is research head ABVP (Malwa Prant) Indore, MP. Besides, he is an editorial board member of IJIERM and AJEEE. He has published a few books with renowned publishers. Moreover, he has many publications to his credit in ugc care and scopus indexed journals. He has been awarded many times for contribution to academic and research. His area of interest includes Digital Marketing, Consumer Behavior, Information Technology, Communication and Marketing/Finance skills.

***

M. Clement Joe Anand is working as an Assistant Professor in the Department of Mathematics, Mount Carmel College (Autonomous), Bengaluru, Karnataka. He has 12 years of teaching and research experience and received an honorary award from the University of Mexico, USA by the Board of Neutrosophic Science International Association. A total of 50 research articles were published indexed in Scopus and SCI databases. He has two Indian patents. He has completed a short-term course at the Indian Institute of Technology, Madras. He has received a doctoral degree from the University of Madras, Chennai. He is a reviewer of Scopus, SCI-indexed journals: 1. International Journal of Applied and Computational Mathematics (Scopus) 2. International Journal of Fuzzy Systems (Scopus, SCI) 3.Journal of Mathematics and Computer Science (Scopus, SCIE) 4.Iraqi Journal of Computer Science and Mathematics (Scopus) 5.Journal of Applied Mathematics and Informatics (Scopus) 6.Journal of Computer Science (Scopus, SCI) 7.IEEE Conferences (Scopus) He has received a grant from the Science and Engineering Research Board (SERB)-DST, Government of India.

Zev Asch is a distinguished marketing executive and successful entrepreneur with over 30 years of experience across various industries, including IT, Retail, and medical device manufacturing. Mr. Asch served as a Graduate Marketing Professor and Director of Innovation and entrepreneurship at Touro University in New York City. He is also a distinguished marketing, leadership, and entrepreneurship professor at Amity Education Group's Long Island campus.

Amrish Kumar Choubey is working as an Associate Professor, with Amity International Business School, Amity University, Noida. He is a pure academician and has more than 18 years of teaching experience. He has an extensive background in General Management, Information Technology Management, Cloud Computing, Software development and implementation. He has participated in several National and International Conferences and presented several research Papers. He has also guided several research projects of students of different courses.

Yashu Garg is a currently Ph.D. candidate at Mittal School of Business (MHRD NIRF India Rank 34; ACBSP USA, Accredited), Lovely Professional University, Phagwara, Punjab (India). She completed her Bachelor of Commerce and Master of Commerce in Marketing. Her interests lie in various aspects of marketing including Social Media Marketing, Product Marketing, Digital Marketing, Content Marketing, Influencer Marketing, and more. Her aim is to share valuable insights about marketing in academic circles and use my knowledge to help businesses and brands succeed in the real world.

Krishan Gopal is currently working as Associate Professor at Mittal School of Business (MHRD NIRF India Rank 34; ACBSP USA, Accredited), Lovely Professional University, Phagwara, Punjab (India). He has received his Ph.D degree from Lovely Professional University Punjab in the year 2020. His area of interest in teaching and research includes Business Research Methods, Strategic Management and Consumer Behaviour. Dr. Krishan Gopal has published more than 12 research papers in refereed national and international journals, 17 book chapters and cases, edited one book, attended various national and international seminars and acted as a resource person in different faculty development programs. He has written 4 chapters of "Tourism and Hospitality Marketing" available on "e-PG-Pathshala"- a Project of UGC (MHRD).

Preeti Jain is an accomplished academic and researcher with a Ph.D. in Commerce from CT University, and qualifications including UGC NET and an MBA from Lovely Professional University. she excels in communication, office automation, and data visualization tools. With a rich teaching background and numerous publications and patents, she has presented and published research on integrated marketing, sustainable development, and AI in finance. Dr. Jain has coordinated cultural events and academic programs at esteemed institutions and actively participates in workshops and FDPs on research methodology and innovation management.

Rishikaysh Kaakandikar boasts an exceptional academic journey, spanning over 12 years of dedicated teaching and a year of valuable industrial experience, and currently holds the esteemed position of Associate Professor at SaiBalaji Education Society's SaiBalaji International Institute of Management Sciences in Pune. His scholarly contributions shine brightly, encompassing a remarkable portfolio of over 40 research papers in prestigious journals. A sought-after intellectual resource, He has contributed substantially to academia through guest lectures, seminars, workshops, and conferences at esteemed institutions across India. His insights have enriched the academic community and stimulated engaging discussions on various facets of his field. He is a prominent finance columnist for leading newspapers in Maharashtra, including Sakal, Lokmat, Punyannagari, and Prabhat.

Harendra Kumar is working as an Associate Professor at Amity International Business School, Amity University, Noida, UP, India. He is an academician and has more than 20 years of teaching and research experience. He has an extensive background in Economics and International Business. He has participated in and presented several research Papers at National and International Conferences. He has also conducted national and international seminars and conferences. He has authored many research papers in indexed journals. He has also guided several research projects and Ph.D. students.

Anchal Luthra is an AIBS, Amity University, Noida Assistant Professor. She has done Ph.D., MBA in HR, M.Phils., & M.Ed. She has 12 rich years of experience in industry, research, and academia. Her specialization areas are Human Resource Management, Data analytics, and Research Methodology. She has Presented her research work at various national and international conferences and won 2 best paper awards along with best Teacher Award and Excellence in research award. She has published research papers in Scopus and ABDC-listed journals, successfully delivered two industry consultation projects in the area of HR, and is also engaged in academic consultation.

Varun Nayyar is a result-oriented, proactive, and dedicated working professional with 17+ years of end-to-end achievement driven experience in the field of education, research and industry. Currently working as Program Head (Chitkara University, Centre for Distance and Online Education). Previously, he has managed multiple responsibilities, such as convener placements and convener admissions, in the MBA department while teaching. In addition, he has been invited by numerous colleges and industries for guest lectures on the topics of research, marketing, stress management, motivation, and others. His academic proficiency in research tools like SPSS, AMOS, R, PLS-SEM, VOSVIEWER, BIBLIOSHINY and NVIVO has fetched 15 research papers and articles in leading international journals like SCI, Scopus, and (ABDC: A, B, and C) categories.

Dheeraj Nim is a seasoned educator and industry veteran boasting over 16 years of immersive training experience for students and academics alike, coupled with an additional 6 years in the corporate sphere. With a rich background encompassing Business Analytics, Marketing Analytics, and Data Analysis, Dr. Nim is passionate about the latest advancements and trends shaping research and analysis. Currently serving as Professor and Dean Student Welfare at Oriental University, Indore,. Beyond academia, Dr. Nim's commitment to excellence shines through his extensive certification portfolio in Data Analytics from esteemed institutions like the University of Virginia, University of Michigan, and IITs, among others. His academic contributions are equally impressive, with six book chapters, 30 research publications, and five awarded Ph.D. scholars under his mentorship. Noteworthy are his publications in renowned journals, including Scopus Indexed, Web of Science, and ABDC Journals. His dedication to academic excellence extends to his role as a reviewer for numerous Scopus and Web of Science indexed journals. Notably, he has chaired technical sessions in prestigious international conferences.

Supriya Tiwari Pathak is President – Institution Innovation Council Innovation Ambassador – Ministry of Education Director Foreign Affairs, Witty Gossip Association Key Note coordinator to Lead India for foreign collaborations and business networking. Auditor - Quality Certification –London, Adjudicator- World Book of Records, London, Thought Leader, Visionary for Women, Certified Life Coach, Businesswoman, Humanitarian, knowledge Seeker and Compelling Speaker,

Dr. Supriya Tiwari Pathak multifaceted leadership with compassion & humility in different group of companies. Awards & Accolades: DrSupriya Pathak has been awarded Ph.D (Managment) Degree in the Convocation ceremony 2019 in the honorable presence of Dr. Varun kapur (IPS), ADG, Indore by Oriental University, Indore. Recognized and lauded for her work across Asia and Africa Continent, Dr. Supriya Pathak has been awarded as an Exceptional National Excellence Award, organized by Alma group of companies, London (UK) held in Indore, Madhya Pradesh, India. She achieved with feeling of proud and has been honored among prominent "Guest speakers and Guest of honors" around the world in International Digital summit by Witty Gossip Association –She was highly Delighted to Represent South Asian Chamber of Commerce and Industries (SACCI) being Director Foreign Affairs along with World Book of Records,UK at Awareness Programme of World Intellectual Property Organization in the gracious presence Mr.Mougamadou Abidine(Head, PCT Switzerland) and Mr.Chen Yinghua (Technical cooperation officer, WIPO),South Korea.

Guna Sekhar Sajja works as an SAP consultant in the retail industry and is a Research scholar at the University of the Cumberland's, USA. He has more than 8 years of work experience as an SAP consultant and covered in these areas as a Supply chain management expert (Manufacturing, Medical, Agriculture, and Retail Sector). His educational qualifications include a Ph.D. in Information Technology, complemented by Master's and Bachelor's degrees in Information Systems security and Mechanical Engineering. He published many research papers in reputed national and international journals & conference papers, and book chapters. He worked as a reviewer for Springer, Elsevier, InderScience, Web of Science, Hindawi (Wiley), PeerJ and Taylor & Francis Journals. He has a track record of publications that underscores my commitment to research and innovation, particularly in AI, Machine Learning, and their applications within supply chain management. An enterprising, dynamic go-getter with solid presentation, relationship-building, analytical & problem-solving skills, ensuring optimal utilization of resources, processes, and technology.

Ridhima Sharma is an Assistant Professor of Management at Vivekananda Institute of Professional Studies-Technical Campus. With a teaching and research experience of 12 years, she has contributed several articles to the journals of national & international repute and have presented papers in national and international conferences apart from authoring books. Her research interest includes Customer Relationship Management & sustainable consumer behavior. She is currently pursuing Post Doc from Amity University, Dubai.

Veeranna Thotakura is working as an Associate Professor & HOD in the Department of Computer Science and Engineering(AI&ML) and AI&DS, Sai Spurthi Institute of Technology, has about 19 years of teaching experience. He received his B.Tech degree in Computer Science and Engineering with distinction and M.Tech. degree in Computer Science and Engineering with distinction from JNTU University, Hyderabad. He received Ph.D degree in Computer Science and Engineering from JNTU University, Kakinada, Andhra Pradesh. He has published 10 research papers (SCI & Scopus) in refereed international journals and 3 research papers in the proceedings of various international conferences. His areas of research include Data Mining, Information Security, Artificial Intelligence and Machine Learning.

Shruti Tiwari is the founder, owner, and freelance designer of Shatakshi's design studio as well as an academician in the field of design. Presently serving as Sr. Development officer of Centre for Multidisciplinary and Interdisciplinary Education & NEP Cell, Professor in Design, PhD Coordinator at Parul University. Graduate & Postgraduate with merit from DAVV, Indore, Design course from IPW (International Polytechnic for Women, New Delhi) and PhD in the field of Textiles. Pursuing her career as a freelance designer for almost 25 years, she handled many design projects, some of them such – "Theme Pavillion of Buyer Seller meet – 2009", conducting a Fashion Show for "Mrignaynee Emporium", Costumes for a Halloween Party for NewYork Clients – 2010, bagged Best Presentation Award in a show organized by GrahShobha in 2009.. As an Academician for 20 years, she has been a Jury member of NIFT (National Institute of Fashion), Bhopal, SOFT (School of Fashion Technology), Pune, 2010 – 2016, and panelist of NCERT under (MHRD – Ministry of Human Recourses and Development) for Fashion & Textile vocational courses since 2009. She Member of the Board of studies of SNDT University Mumbai (2012 – 2017), M.S University, Vadodara – 2016, Maharaja Mansingh Tomar University, Bhopal - 2018, Avantika University, MIT Ujjain – 2023 – 24. She has been a recipient of the Academic Review and Research Excellence Award 2023 at Parul University She has authored a book – "Maheshwari: Legacy of a Queen", presented & published 35 research papers in national & international conferences, received the best research paper award, and got an opportunity to get an article published in the International magazine "Business Images of Fashion" – 2007 in Heritage Section. Except being a Designer & Academician she has a love for Trekking and had done trekking of ROHTANG PASS (13,000ft) of Himachal Pradesh, in 1996 while pursuing her Post Graduation.

Renu Vij is a seasoned educator with a robust 16-year career in teaching at the master's level Strategic HR courses. She has made significant contributions to academic research, authoring over 15 research papers published in Scopus-indexed journals and contributing chapters to Scopus-indexed books. Her expertise extends beyond academia, as she is a certified trainer in HR analytics and an accomplished workplace psychologist. Additionally, she holds certification from AON, further solidifying her credentials in the field. Her work reflects a deep commitment to advancing knowledge in her areas of specialization, making her a respected figure in both academic and professional circles.

Index

Symbols

6561 possible tuples 309

A

AI 15, 67, 120, 142, 148, 162, 163, 165, 170, 171, 202, 233, 253, 287, 289, 290, 291, 292, 293, 299, 300, 302, 303, 304, 305, 306, 307, 309, 311, 312, 313, 314, 315, 316, 317, 321, 323, 324, 325, 327, 329, 408, 428
altruistic values 237, 243, 247, 249
Alumni Impact 269
Artificial Intelligence 14, 15, 16, 39, 75, 95, 120, 125, 145, 148, 163, 170, 216, 234, 287, 289, 292, 303, 304, 306, 307, 309, 310, 311, 312, 316, 323, 325, 327, 328, 408
Authenticity 1, 5, 7, 8, 10, 12, 13, 22, 25, 26, 27, 28, 29, 37, 44, 46, 50, 53, 57, 58, 59, 61, 63, 71, 73, 77, 78, 79, 81, 82, 85, 86, 90, 91, 92, 94, 95, 96, 100, 104, 107, 109, 110, 114, 115, 116, 117, 119, 121, 122, 123, 124, 126, 127, 128, 131, 141, 142, 144, 146, 147, 148, 149, 150, 191, 192, 195, 256, 258, 264, 265, 370, 381, 414, 420
Ayurvastra 351, 352, 353, 354, 355, 356, 357, 358, 359, 360, 361, 362, 363, 364, 365, 366, 367, 368, 369, 370, 371, 372, 375, 376, 377, 378
Ayurveda 352, 353, 367, 369, 372, 375, 377

B

behaviour 64, 68, 112, 134, 137, 138, 149, 179, 187, 216, 220, 226, 227, 232, 238, 239, 240, 241, 248, 249, 253, 255, 257, 258, 259, 265, 266, 271, 274, 282, 288, 298, 300, 302, 303, 307, 316, 320, 333, 336, 348, 380, 381, 382, 383, 387, 388, 389, 390, 391, 392
BERT 219, 220, 222, 226, 230
Bibliometric Analysis 68, 149, 331, 332, 344, 347
brand 3, 4, 5, 6, 7, 8, 9, 11, 12, 13, 14, 16, 17, 19, 20, 21, 22, 23, 24, 25, 26, 27, 28, 29, 30, 31, 32, 33, 34, 35, 36, 37, 39, 40, 43, 44, 45, 46, 47, 48, 49, 50, 51, 52, 53, 54, 55, 56, 57, 58, 59, 60, 61, 63, 64, 65, 66, 67, 68, 69, 71, 72, 73, 74, 75, 76, 77, 78, 79, 80, 81, 82, 83, 85, 86, 87, 90, 91, 92, 93, 94, 95, 97, 98, 100, 101, 103, 104, 106, 107, 108, 109, 110, 111, 112, 113, 114, 115, 116, 117, 118, 119, 120, 121, 122, 123, 124, 125, 126, 127, 128, 129, 130, 133, 134, 135, 136, 138, 139, 140, 141, 142, 143, 144, 145, 146, 147, 148, 149, 151, 152, 153, 154, 155, 156, 157, 158, 159, 160, 162, 163, 164, 165, 166, 167, 168, 169, 170, 171, 172, 173, 174, 175, 176, 177, 178, 179, 180, 182, 183, 185, 186, 187, 188, 189, 190, 191, 192, 193, 194, 195, 196, 197, 198, 199, 220, 221, 222, 223, 227, 228, 229, 230, 231, 232, 233, 238, 239, 240, 241, 242, 243, 247, 248, 249, 250, 251, 255, 256, 257, 258, 259, 263, 264, 266, 267, 269, 270, 271, 272, 273, 274, 277, 280, 281, 282, 283, 284, 324, 336, 337, 338, 348, 379, 380, 381, 382, 383, 384, 387, 388, 389, 390, 391, 392, 393, 394, 395, 396, 398, 399, 400, 401, 402, 404, 405, 406, 407, 413, 418, 419, 420, 421, 422, 423, 424, 425, 428
Brand Affinity 151, 152, 153, 154, 155, 156, 157, 158, 159, 162, 164, 165, 166, 167, 168, 169, 171, 172, 179, 180
Brand Evangelism 19, 20, 21, 22, 23, 24, 26, 27, 29, 30, 31, 32, 33, 34, 35, 36, 37, 39, 40, 43, 44, 45, 46, 47, 48, 50, 51, 52, 53, 54, 55, 56, 57, 58, 59, 60, 61, 63, 64, 65, 66, 67, 68, 71, 72, 74, 77, 78, 79, 81, 82, 85, 86, 90, 92, 94, 95, 100, 103, 104, 111, 112, 114, 116, 117, 118, 119, 121, 122, 123, 124, 125,

127, 128, 129, 130, 133, 134, 143, 144, 148, 151, 153, 185, 186, 187, 188, 189, 193, 195, 197, 198, 199, 255, 256, 258, 259, 263, 264, 269, 270, 271, 273, 280, 283, 284

Brand Trust 22, 23, 24, 37, 40, 63, 95, 97, 112, 124, 154, 188, 198, 199, 284, 379, 380, 382, 383, 384, 387, 388, 389, 394

Brand Value 239, 283, 389, 395, 396, 399, 400, 401, 402, 405, 406, 407

Business-to-business 162, 411, 412, 413, 414, 415, 417, 418, 419, 423, 424, 425, 426, 427

C

consumer engagement 16, 40, 50, 71, 73, 74, 75, 76, 77, 78, 79, 81, 82, 85, 86, 90, 91, 92, 93, 94, 95, 98, 100, 111, 136, 137, 148, 152, 158, 181, 238, 239, 240, 241, 243, 248, 252, 266, 380, 382, 387, 388, 389, 390

Consumer engagement behaviour 238, 240, 241, 248, 266, 380, 382, 387, 388, 389, 390

Consumer Ethnocentrism 329, 330, 331, 332, 333, 334, 335, 336, 337, 338, 340, 342, 344, 345, 346, 347, 348, 350

Consumer Experience 185, 186, 189

Consumer Influencer 257, 264, 265, 413, 417, 418, 423

Consumer interaction 43, 158, 266, 381, 382, 390

Consumer Loyalty 20, 73, 74, 76, 91, 93, 241

Consumption 23, 52, 68, 74, 112, 124, 126, 131, 137, 156, 189, 193, 238, 239, 240, 241, 248, 250, 251, 259, 334, 336, 337, 342, 349, 351, 379, 380, 381, 382, 390, 391, 393, 395, 396, 407

Convergence 1, 2, 3, 5, 7, 9, 11, 13, 14, 15, 16, 244

Credibility 5, 6, 15, 20, 21, 25, 26, 28, 29, 33, 34, 37, 44, 46, 53, 56, 57, 58, 59, 61, 65, 66, 68, 72, 73, 77, 90, 91, 92, 93, 94, 97, 98, 103, 105, 114, 115, 117, 120, 121, 123, 124, 125, 126,

127, 129, 131, 136, 138, 141, 145, 152, 158, 159, 173, 183, 192, 240, 258, 266, 411, 419, 420

Customer Satisfaction 21, 35, 161, 201, 203, 204, 205, 211, 212, 213, 232, 268, 311, 408, 409

D

Data Analytics 1, 2, 3, 4, 5, 7, 8, 9, 10, 11, 12, 13, 14, 15, 16, 41, 71, 72, 74, 75, 77, 78, 79, 81, 82, 85, 86, 90, 91, 92, 94, 97, 100, 129, 133, 134, 135, 139, 140, 142, 145, 146, 149, 181, 253, 309, 327

Desired self-identity 237, 241, 247, 248

Digital Engagement 1, 3, 7, 9, 17

Digital Marketing 2, 3, 9, 13, 14, 15, 16, 41, 44, 46, 63, 67, 97, 106, 128, 131, 140, 144, 146, 221, 230, 284, 287, 289, 290, 291, 292, 303, 304, 412, 413, 423, 428

E

Emotional Connection 22, 27, 43, 47, 51, 56, 59, 61, 93, 112, 113, 157, 166, 167, 168, 169, 180, 195, 231, 347, 389

Engagement Metrics 5, 12, 106, 133, 135, 136, 137, 151, 152, 153, 154, 156, 157, 158, 159, 163, 164, 165, 166, 167, 168, 169, 172, 176, 179, 180, 183

environmental sustainability 238, 250, 351, 352, 362, 366

ERP Systems 202, 203, 204, 208, 209, 210, 211, 212, 213, 216

evangelism 19, 20, 21, 22, 23, 24, 25, 26, 27, 29, 30, 31, 32, 33, 34, 35, 36, 37, 39, 40, 41, 43, 44, 45, 46, 47, 48, 50, 51, 52, 53, 54, 55, 56, 57, 58, 59, 60, 61, 63, 64, 65, 66, 67, 68, 71, 72, 74, 77, 78, 79, 81, 82, 85, 86, 90, 92, 94, 95, 100, 103, 104, 111, 112, 114, 116, 117, 118, 119, 121, 122, 123, 124, 125, 127, 128, 129, 130, 133, 134, 143, 144, 148, 151, 153, 185, 186, 187, 188, 189, 193, 195, 197, 198, 199,

255, 256, 258, 259, 263, 264, 269, 270, 271, 273, 280, 283, 284
experience 7, 23, 26, 28, 32, 40, 45, 46, 56, 67, 114, 136, 159, 170, 171, 185, 186, 187, 188, 189, 190, 191, 192, 193, 194, 195, 196, 198, 199, 201, 205, 206, 211, 213, 227, 239, 250, 267, 274, 285, 288, 289, 290, 296, 300, 302, 303, 305, 328, 337, 364, 371, 388, 389, 390, 391, 393, 413, 414, 419, 420, 421, 422, 424, 428

F

Food Delivery 146, 287, 288, 289, 290, 291, 292, 304, 305

G

green 96, 98, 105, 124, 127, 130, 131, 186, 197, 237, 238, 239, 240, 241, 243, 247, 248, 249, 250, 251, 252, 253, 409
green business 250

H

herbal textiles 377

I

Influencer Marketing 1, 2, 3, 5, 7, 8, 9, 10, 11, 13, 14, 15, 16, 19, 20, 22, 23, 24, 26, 27, 29, 31, 33, 35, 36, 37, 39, 40, 43, 44, 45, 46, 47, 48, 49, 50, 53, 58, 59, 60, 61, 62, 63, 64, 65, 66, 67, 68, 69, 71, 72, 73, 79, 86, 90, 92, 95, 96, 97, 103, 104, 105, 106, 107, 108, 109, 114, 115, 116, 117, 118, 119, 120, 121, 122, 123, 124, 125, 126, 127, 128, 129, 130, 133, 134, 135, 136, 137, 138, 139, 140, 141, 142, 143, 144, 145, 146, 147, 148, 149, 152, 183, 256, 267, 411, 412, 413, 414, 415, 416, 417, 418, 419, 421, 422, 423, 424
Influencers marketing 126
Influential Marketing 411, 416, 417, 418, 419, 420, 421, 422, 423, 424, 425, 426, 427
Information Quality 201, 204, 205, 208, 209, 212, 213
Instagram 7, 14, 15, 23, 25, 26, 27, 28, 31, 35, 46, 48, 49, 52, 54, 58, 63, 64, 67, 69, 96, 103, 104, 105, 106, 107, 108, 109, 111, 113, 118, 123, 125, 126, 127, 128, 129, 130, 131, 134, 148, 161, 166, 168, 172, 175, 220, 222, 223, 230, 255, 256, 258, 259, 260, 268

L

logistics 123, 130, 131, 145, 199, 253, 307, 309, 310, 311, 312, 313, 314, 315, 319, 323, 324, 325, 337, 339

M

Machine Learning 1, 2, 137, 139, 142, 143, 145, 147, 153, 161, 178, 234, 252, 253, 267, 287, 289, 290, 292, 295, 296, 297, 299, 300, 301, 302, 303, 304, 305, 309, 310, 311, 313, 314, 317, 319, 320, 321, 322, 324, 325, 327, 328, 408, 429
marketing 1, 2, 3, 5, 6, 7, 8, 9, 10, 11, 13, 14, 15, 16, 19, 20, 21, 22, 23, 24, 26, 27, 29, 31, 33, 35, 36, 37, 39, 40, 41, 43, 44, 45, 46, 47, 48, 49, 50, 53, 54, 56, 58, 59, 60, 61, 62, 63, 64, 65, 66, 67, 68, 69, 71, 72, 73, 74, 75, 76, 78, 79, 86, 90, 92, 95, 96, 97, 98, 99, 100, 103, 104, 105, 106, 107, 108, 109, 110, 112, 114, 115, 116, 117, 118, 119, 120, 121, 122, 123, 124, 125, 126, 127, 128, 129, 130, 131, 133, 134, 135, 136, 137, 138, 139, 140, 141, 142, 143, 144, 145, 146, 147, 148, 149, 152, 153, 156, 157, 161, 170, 172, 173, 174, 176, 181, 182, 183, 185, 186, 188, 189, 195, 197, 198, 199, 220, 221, 222, 226, 227, 230, 232, 239, 240, 250, 251, 252, 256, 257, 258, 259, 264, 267, 268, 271, 281, 282, 283, 284, 285, 287, 288,

493

289, 290, 291, 292, 293, 302, 303, 304, 305, 306, 307, 337, 338, 339, 345, 346, 348, 349, 350, 381, 383, 390, 391, 394, 396, 397, 398, 399, 400, 407, 408, 409, 411, 412, 413, 414, 415, 416, 417, 418, 419, 420, 421, 422, 423, 424, 425, 426, 427, 428

Marketing Campaigns 5, 7, 14, 16, 21, 29, 49, 74, 78, 100, 109, 110, 133, 134, 136, 137, 141, 145, 149, 256, 303, 413, 424

medicinal clothing 352, 360, 377

ML 289, 290, 292, 295, 296, 297, 298, 299, 300, 301, 302, 303, 304, 305, 309, 311, 313, 314, 315, 316, 317, 321, 324, 325, 328

N

NLP 153, 179, 182, 220, 222

O

Organic grocery store 380, 382, 383, 388, 389, 390, 391

P

Perceived value 52, 237, 240, 241, 248, 249, 253, 268, 336, 381, 382, 383, 387, 389, 390, 392

perception 43, 45, 48, 59, 66, 75, 77, 101, 143, 157, 164, 171, 172, 179, 187, 192, 193, 195, 198, 231, 240, 241, 247, 248, 249, 329, 369, 382, 390, 420

PLS-SEM 238, 244, 248, 255, 256, 261, 262

Positive Effect 92, 256, 405

Purchase Intention 16, 126, 152, 181, 197, 252, 253, 267, 329, 331, 332, 333, 334, 335, 336, 337, 338, 340, 342, 344, 345, 347, 384

Q

Qualitative Research 43, 114, 191, 195, 196, 215

Quality of Service 198, 212, 213

R

Regression Analysis 84, 146, 201, 262

S

Secondary Data 46, 66, 114, 135, 163

Sentiment Analysis 61, 139, 151, 152, 153, 159, 160, 162, 163, 164, 165, 166, 167, 168, 169, 170, 171, 172, 176, 177, 178, 179, 180, 181, 182, 183, 219, 220, 221, 222, 226, 229, 234

Social community Identification 24, 274

Social Media 2, 5, 6, 7, 11, 12, 14, 15, 16, 20, 21, 24, 25, 26, 30, 31, 35, 36, 37, 39, 40, 41, 43, 44, 45, 46, 48, 49, 50, 51, 54, 55, 56, 57, 58, 59, 60, 63, 65, 66, 67, 68, 75, 93, 95, 96, 97, 98, 100, 103, 104, 105, 106, 108, 109, 110, 113, 114, 116, 122, 123, 124, 125, 126, 127, 128, 129, 130, 131, 134, 135, 137, 139, 140, 141, 142, 143, 144, 145, 146, 147, 148, 149, 152, 153, 154, 160, 161, 162, 163, 166, 167, 168, 169, 170, 171, 172, 180, 181, 182, 183, 188, 197, 221, 229, 230, 256, 257, 258, 259, 260, 265, 266, 267, 268, 283, 284, 289, 307, 381, 391, 411, 412, 416, 417, 418, 419, 422, 423, 424, 425, 427

social media influencers 15, 16, 40, 43, 44, 48, 56, 63, 66, 95, 104, 105, 108, 123, 124, 125, 126, 127, 128, 129, 130, 131, 137, 141, 145, 147, 148, 149, 181, 197, 257, 259, 265, 266, 416

Social network 23, 40, 48, 126, 138, 147, 149, 156, 181, 195, 199, 256, 270

Strategic Integration 413

sustainable fashion 49, 117, 130, 351, 375

sustainable marketing 72, 73, 74, 75, 76, 78, 103, 114, 119, 120, 121, 148, 256

T

traditional medicine 351, 375

transportation 238, 239, 240, 310, 311

Trust 7, 8, 10, 12, 15, 20, 21, 22, 23, 24,

25, 26, 27, 29, 31, 32, 34, 37, 40, 43, 44, 45, 46, 49, 51, 53, 56, 57, 59, 61, 63, 66, 72, 73, 77, 90, 91, 92, 93, 94, 95, 97, 100, 101, 104, 105, 109, 111, 112, 113, 114, 115, 116, 117, 118, 119, 120, 121, 122, 124, 126, 127, 128, 136, 139, 151, 152, 154, 155, 157, 158, 159, 162, 174, 175, 178, 183, 188, 192, 197, 198, 199, 220, 227, 228, 239, 240, 256, 257, 267, 268, 284, 302, 328, 336, 337, 370, 379, 380, 382, 383, 384, 387, 388, 389, 390, 391, 394, 419, 420, 421, 424, 425

U

University Brand 24, 39, 197, 269, 270, 272, 273, 277, 280, 281, 283, 284

University Identity 269, 272, 273, 274, 280, 283

V

Value Co-Creation 47, 50, 65, 67, 380, 381, 382, 389, 394

VosViewer 329, 332, 340

Y

YouTube 7, 25, 27, 29, 30, 31, 46, 48, 49, 50, 58, 59, 67, 103, 104, 105, 106, 107, 108, 113, 123, 127, 128, 129, 135, 136, 173, 174, 175, 194